THE BOOK OF BOXING

EDITED BY W.C. HEINZ AND NATHAN WARD

KINGSTON, NEW YORK   NEW YORK, NEW YORK

For information about permission to reproduce sections of this book, please write to:
Permissions
Total/SPORTS ILLUSTRATED
100 Enterprise Drive
Kingston, New York 12401

A conscientious attempt has been made to contact proprietors of the rights in every item
used in the book. If through inadvertence the publisher has failed to identify any holder of
rights, forgiveness is requested and corrected information will be entered in future printings.

Library of Congress Catalog Card Number: 99-63231
ISBN 1-892129-13-2

THE BOOK OF BOXING was prepared by
Bishop Books, Inc.
611 Broadway
New York, New York 10012

Printed in the United States of America
1 3 5 7 9 10 8 6 4 2

COVER PHOTO: Ernie Durando (right) and Paddy Young. Photograph from Brown Brothers.

ACKNOWLEDGMENTS

"Melted Sugar" by Jesse Abramson. Copyright 1952. Reprinted by permission of *The New York Times*.

"He Swung and He Missed" from "Neon Wilderness" by Nelson Algren. Copyright 1947 by Nelson Algren. Used by permission of Doubleday, a division of Random House, Inc.

"Michelangelo's Masterpiece" by Dave Anderson. Copyright by *The New York Times* April 8, 1987. Reprinted by permission of *The New York Times*.

"The Orthodox Champion" by Heywood Broun. Reprinted by permission of the estate of Heywood Broun.

"Twenty-five Bucks" by James T. Farrell from *The Short Stories of James T. Farrell*. Copyright 1932. Reprinted by permission of the author's estate.

"The Joe Louis I Remember" by Jimmy Cannon. Copyrighted *Sport* magazine. Reprinted with permission.

"Title Battle in Typhoon" by Nat Fleischer. Copyright 1954. Reprinted by permission of *The Ring* magazine.

"Pity the Poor Giant" by Paul Gallico. From *Farewell to Sport*. Copyright 1937, 1938, 1964, 1966, by Paul Gallico. Reprinted by permission of Harold Ober Associates Incorporated.

"All the Way to the Grave" by Frank Graham. Reprinted by permission of the author's son.

"The Day of the Fight" by W.C. Heinz. Reprinted by permission of the author.

"Stop the Fight!" by Norman Katkov. Copyright 1952. Reprinted by permission of the author's agents, Harold Matson Co.

"Lawdy, Lawdy, He's Great" by Mark Kram. Reprinted by permission of *Sports Illustrated*.

"The Great Almost White Hope" by Mark Kriegel. Reprinted by permission of the author.

"Two Visits with Sam Langford" by Al Laney. Copyright 1954, *New York Herald Tribune*. Reprinted by permission of *The New York Times*.

"Epigrams" reprinted by permission of the publishers and the Loeb Classical Library, from *Greek Anthology* (in five volumes) translated by W.R. Paton: Cambridge, Mass.: Harvard University Press, 1912-1918.

"Death" by Norman Mailer. Copyright © 1963 by Norman Mailer, first printed in *The Presidential Papers*, reprinted with the permission of The Wylie Agency, Inc.

"How it Feels to be Champ" by Rocky Marciano, used by permission of the Estate of Rocky Marciano, c/o Michael Gilbert.

Selection from "The Everlasting Mercy" by John Masefield by permission of The Society of Authors as the literary representative of the Estate of John Masefield.

"Dempsey–Firpo" by Frank G. Menke originally appeared in *The Sporting News* January 27, 1944.

"News of a Champion" by W.O. McGeehan. Copyright 1927, 1955. Reprinted by permission of *The New York Times*.

"The Sour Taste in Jack Bodell's Pop" by Hugh McIlvanney, reprinted by permisssion of Mainstream Publishing Co. Ltd.

"Siki and Civilization" by Westbrook Pegler from *The Chicago Tribune* December 18, 1925. Reprinted by permission of *The Chicago Tribune*.

Selection from *Shadow Box* by George Plimpton reprinted by the permission of Russell & Volkening, Inc., as agents for the author. Copyright © 1977 by George Plimpton.

"Eight Minutes of Fury" by Pat Putnam, April 22, 1985. Reprinted by permission of *Sports Illustrated*.

"Kid Dynamite Blows Up" by David Remnick. Copyright 1998. Reprinted by permission of the author.

"The Great Benny Leonard" by Budd Schulberg. Reprinted by permission of the author.

Selection from *Cashel Byron's Profession* by George Bernard Shaw, reprinted by permission of The Society of Authors, on behalf of the Bernard Shaw Estate.

"The Nose" by Red Smith from *The Red Smith Reader*. Reprinted by permission of *The New York Times*.

Selection from *The Thebaid* reprinted by permission of the publishers and the Loeb Classical Library from *Status: Thebaid, Volume I and II*, Translated by J.H. Mosley: Cambridge, Mass.: Harvard University Press, 1928.

"End of the Line for Leo" by Emmett Watson by permission of the *Seattle Post-Intelligencer*.

CONTENTS

PREFACE

Thirty-eight years have passed since the first coming of this book entered the arena of anthologies, and while much has changed one thing has not. That is the resolve of the editors and publisher to present, for at least the life of the covers that preserve it, the best journalism, literature and art of the most fundamental form of competition and completely expressive of the arts, as it has survived for some 3,000 years.

While previously we cited the first fight on the steps of the Church of the Holy Sepulcher in Jerusalem, know that in Rome, more recently and not far from the Coliseum their Chamber of Deputies bypassed parliamentary procedure for a fistic free-for-all. Over here baseball players are still dropping their bats and gloves, hockey players their armament as, frustrated by the conventions of their callings, they go at one another with their bare fists.

Still regretting this instinct in man, one must celebrate that boxing, affording recognition and release, still continues even in times that are not in its favor, as truth has a way of doing. From voluminous studies, economists and sociologists derive that these are the best of times and the worst of times. They find that as the rich get richer the poor get poorer, as boxing, always a barometer, could have told them.

It also could have told them that the Latinos are the new force in this country, pushing out of the barrios and at the doors of the fight gyms and fight clubs even as the Irish and then the Jews and Italians and blacks before them. One of them, Oscar De La Hoya, revealed herein by Mark Kriegel, may well be the best pound-for-pound and punch-for-punch practitioner of this time.

Meanwhile champions and their challengers are being rewarded with purses of $20,000,000 or more while contestants on undercards are making less than the ring announcer, and those struggling on the limited small club circuit are often holding other jobs.

In spite of this, and due to the same television that has all but severed boxing's roots, worldwide audiences from Africa to Australia, Alaska to Antarctica have come to know Muhammad Ali and the endeavor he has publicized better than any fighter before him. Certainly he has made more fans of boxing than anyone else in the history of the sport. The best athlete, and many would hold the best fighter to hold the heavyweight title, he was a rhymer, politician and religious advocate who also derided and often embarrassed his opponents and the United States government, and in the Ali Shuffle introduced a move purists found as appropriate as a clog step in the middle of "Swan Lake."

Unfortunately, like so many before him, he stayed too long at the dance. Now, suffering mentally and physically, he may yet end up as an example by the boxing-should-be-banned boys who would take the gloves off an Ali, a Sugar Ray Robinson or a Willie Pep, telling them to play baseball instead. One wonders if they would take the violin out of the hands of a Jascha Heifets while telling him to play piano. A man has the right to do what he does, especially if he does it superbly, and it is not against the law.

Again we have been fortunate that the right writers were around and about with the right fighters and the right fights. Thus we have Mark Kram at what was one of the greatest heavyweight fights, the ineptly titled "Thrilla in Manila" and George Plimpton was there for—will it never stop?—the "Rumble in the Jungle" in Zaire. Pat Putnam covered the classic go between Marvin Hagler and Tommy Hearns, and David Remnick was present when Mike Tyson, once regarded by many as the best heavyweight prospect of all time, made his mandibular attack on the auricular appendages of Evander Holyfield, losing not only the fight but his license as well.

Leonard Gardner recounts the first milling between Roberto Duran and Sugar Ray Leonard, easily the best of their three meetings, in the second of which the latter made the former throw up his heralded "Fists of Stone" in frustration and cop out in the eighth round. Budd Schulberg knew and witnessed the ethnic impact of the great Benny Leonard, Jack Murphy was a hometown observer of Archie Moore, Edgar Lee Masters knew Bob Fitzsimmons, and James R. Fair Harry Greb.

"There are two honest managers in boxing," Damon Runyon once wrote. "Jack Hurley is one, and I can't remember the name of the other."

Hurley, who passed away in 1972 but still lives here in the Emmett Watson entry, comes to mind again as television continues to exact its toll. It wasn't long after it began attracting viewers to bars and neighbors' homes that Hurley saw the future and unloaded his one-two.

"Television cheapens everything it puts its hands on," he said. "It would even cheapen The Second Coming."

Now it seems that its major boxing promoters and TV producers are determined to prove Jack right. With fireworks, raucous music and an announcer whose "Let's get ready to rrrrrumbllle!" reveals an insensitivity to the art that not only insults our best boxers but also those of us who appreciate them, they seem bent on bringing Joe Liebling's "Sweet Science" down to the level of a demolition derby or professional wrestling, both of which he also introduces.

It has been reported that he is a former model from Philadelphia, which previously used to apologize for its southpaws. How he makes the heart yearn now for Harry Balogh, the Mr. Malaprop of the old Madison Square Garden. If only once again, as the fighters return to their corners to face each other for the start of the first round, we could hear him intone with the grammatical precision of a Groton headmaster: "And may the better participant emerge victorious!"

Someone has said that one man's anthology is another man's doorstep, and Nathan Ward, being forty-eight years younger than his associate and possessor of a locker in New York City's storied Gleason's Gym, did the heavy lifting as well as the screening for the previously unpreserved pieces deserving of inclusion. Peter Ehrmann found the superb story by Hugh McIlvanney, Britain's boast, and for help beyond that we are beholden to editor Nigel Collins, and the people at The Ring magazine for answering our queries, and to John Mosedale, who started a chain reaction. He led us to Carlo Rotella, Professor of English at the University of Massachusetts, whose scholarly research uncovered, in the newer translation of Homer's The Iliad, appearing here, the similarities between a well-known heavyweight of our time and Epeus, the Greek champion of some time between 1200 and 850 B.C.

Unless a writer has his own printing press he is indebted to his publisher, and that goes for anthologists too. That means that John Thorn and his team at Total Sports Publishing get this one's thanks and, it is hoped, the reader's.

Dorset, VT.   W.C. Heinz
1999

TO THOSE WHO DID THE FIGHTING
THIS BOOK IS DEDICATED

MELTED SUGAR

This newspaper story describes the most bizarre championship fight of our time, and it is typical of the work of the best all-around, or pound-for-pound, sports reporter of his time. It was written under almost insufferable conditions and in sixty-five minutes for the late editions of the June 26, 1952, *New York Herald Tribune*.

JESSE ABRAMSON

In a weird and sensational finish to a duel of champions fought in brutal heat that registered 104 degrees under the Yankee Stadium lights on the hottest June 25 in New York history, Sugar Ray Robinson collapsed on his stool in the corner and could not come out for the fourteenth round when he had an unbeatable lead over Joey Maxim and a third world championship virtually in his grasp.

Sugar Ray could not beat that furnace heat and the fifteen and a half pounds he gave away to the light heavyweight champion. All he had to do was last the limit. But the brilliant middleweight champion, who had made all the fight for thirteen rounds, outpunching and outboxing the plodding, dull defender, exhausted himself by carrying all the fighting load on this roasting, burning night.

Maxim, who did nothing to deserve this Christmas gift in June except to stand up in that furnace, retained his 175-pound crown in his second defense of it and balked Sugar Ray's gallant attempt to become the third triple champion of the Queensberry era.

It was a knockout in the fourteenth round for Maxim—the fourteenth round because the bell rang for that round while all his seconds and Dr. Alexander Schiff were still working over the worn-out lighter man. It was the first knockout, such as it was, ever scored against the great Robinson in 137 professional fights of which he had lost only two previously.

Robinson wasn't the only victim of the stove-box which the Yankee Stadium was last night. For the first time in the history of championship fights, a referee was knocked out, too. Ruby Goldstein, the referee, began to show distress in the tenth round from his burdensome task of chasing around the ring and repeatedly breaking the fighters out of clinches by force. He took a restorative from the doctor while he pranced around the ring.

But at the end of the tenth round referee Goldstein, on the verge of collapse, was helped from the torture chamber under those 38,500 watts of photo-flood lamps. Ray Miller replaced him in the eleventh round, the first substitute referee that ever was in a title bout.

All Sugar Ray needed was a relief pitcher, too.

It was a heartbreaking blow to the hopes of the thirty-one-year-old New Yorker, so long acclaimed the best and most resourceful fighter of his day. But he had to go fifteen rounds this night, and he failed to pace himself properly, or failed in the end to handle the weight of the bigger man. Maxim did little in this fight except to catch it, but his strength and wrestling and mauling in the interminable clinches and his digs to the body, though they carried little power or authority, helped to weaken the gallant challenger.

Robinson, an authentic middleweight, who, of course, is still the middleweight champion of the world, weighed 157½ pounds to Maxim's 173. Those were the weights for their second weighing yesterday. On Monday when rain forced a two-day postponement, Robinson had weighed 160 to Maxim's 174¾.

A crowd of 47,983, every one of them soaked in his own perspiration, paid more than $400,000 at the gate. These gate receipts, plus the approximate $100,000 received for theater TV, created a new receipts record for a light heavy-weight championship bout. Twenty-six years ago in Ebbets Field, Paul Berlenbach and Jack Delaney drew $461,789.

This score card showed Robinson in front, 10 rounds to 3, when the bout ended abruptly. In the confusion and tumult that ensued, it was not possible to get the officials' score cards, except that Artie Aidala, one of the judges, recalled that he scored Robinson in front, 9 rounds to 3, with one even.

So Robinson was home free with his third world championship if he could only stand on his feet.

A sign that he was going to be in trouble standing on his feet came as early as the eleventh round. Though he smote Maxim a tremendous right on the head that shook up the champion just before the bell, Robinson dragged himself to his corner.

But Robinson won that round and he also won the twelfth, staggering Maxim with a smashing hook in an exchange, but taking some hooks to the body in close. Robinson was now more palpably tired going to his corner. He flopped wearily onto his stool. His seconds gave him smelling salts or some restorative.

The signs of approaching disaster became ominously clear in the thirteenth round. Robinson came out of his corner slowly. He tried to move around as he had been moving around. Earlier he had been dancing on springy feet, the lightfooted dazzling Robinson. Now his legs were leaden. He backed away, he clinched. Maxim forced his head through the ropes. Maxim raked his head with a hook. It wasn't any harder than the weak blows he had been landing, but Ray staggered back.

Robinson had been fighting on grit and guts for some rounds, it was now all too evident. Maxim hadn't been able to hit him at all from long range for the first ten rounds. Now Maxim, still plodding, but still strong, was hitting Ray. He hit him with a hook. Robinson turned in desperation and swung a long right that missed.

He missed with another full right-hand swing in mid-ring, missed so completely that he fell flat on his face—the only time either had been on the floor in this fight.

That fall, not from a punch, drained Robinson's last ounce of strength. When he got up they exchanged hard rights, and Maxim followed with a one-two that sent Robinson reeling crazily along

the ropes on the northern side of the ring—not so much from the blows, but from his own unutter-able weariness. The bell rang.

His seconds, Harry Wiley and Peewee Beal, rushed from the corner and had to lift and carry Robinson to his stool. Dr. Alexander Schiff, commission physician, went to the corner. It was clear that Robinson, completely exhausted from his brilliant fight, had gone as far as a human could in that torture chamber.

When the bell rang for the fourteenth round Maxim rushed to center ring, as he saw that Robinson wasn't coming out. It was the most lively bit of action Maxim had shown all through the fight. He had lasted, Robinson hadn't. He was still the champion.

It was some minutes before Robinson recovered sufficiently to leave the ring, but in the dressing room, where Mayor Impellitteri, his good friend, was the only one admitted besides Robinson's own retinue, there were signs that Robinson was suffering from the exhausting task. He was heard to say, "God willed it," as he went under the shower, the Mayor holding on to him.

One stresses this fact again and again, because Robinson did all the fighting for so many rounds. They say a mule can't beat a race horse, but in this instance a plodding mule did beat the race horse, because the race horse collapsed before the finish.

I scored the first seven rounds for Robinson. Round after round he was the ring master we have known. No one expected he would be so dominant for so long. He was the master of versatility, the virtuoso. He played on Maxim as though he were a violin. He played up and down his body with left leads, he stormed into volleys and barrages and fusillades. He hit and got away clean, or he erupted into two-fisted body attacks in close when he wasn't tying Maxim up in the repeated clinches.

They clinched again and again, and often Ruby Goldstein had to pry them apart as though he were a can-opener. Robinson was tactically the master. He did what he wanted with Maxim, and he wasn't going to let Maxim do anything in close where Maxim, the defensive fighter, is at his best. At long range, Maxim didn't hit Robinson a solid blow until the fight was half over.

If Maxim intended to wear Robinson out by letting him do all the fighting and moving, it was an infernally clever and diabolical plan. In the inferno of last night it worked.

Robinson forced most of the fighting, except when he tactically backed up to lure Maxim in or took a breather for an instant. It was so easy the way he handled Maxim, the Maxim who had fought heavyweights without getting hurt, that Robinson, as it turned out, was lured into his self-destruction.

Round after round Maxim plodded along, hardly threw a punch that counted. He was the negative, defensive fighter he always has been throughout his boxing life. But he did get many chances to clinch, and these clinches were to be Robinson's doom.

Robinson's speed of foot and speed of hand flashed in the night like heat lightning. There's no need to detail all the blows Robinson hit Maxim. Sugar Ray was the more forceful and powerful hitter, though he was hitting a guy who prides himself that he has taken the best punches of heavyweights for years. Maxim was jolted and shaken by the punches, but never in danger of going down. They all added up to an unbeatable lead by the time Maxim won the eighth by a shade with his infighting as Robinson coasted a bit. There were boos from the crowd, chiefly because Maxim was doing so poorly. Robinson came back to win the ninth, landing a couple of direct hits with powerful hooks on the jaw that stung Joey. Maxim showed bruises under both eyes.

By the tenth, Goldstein became the center of attention as he showed signs of distress and had to quit the ring. Maxim won the round, getting a hook and a right to the jaw, though Robbie flared back with a hook that rocked Maxim's head. Then came the mounting tension as Robinson began to tire, and the stunning denouement in his corner at the end of the thirteenth.

[FICTION]

HE SWUNG AND HE MISSED

Rocco was a pro. It came out not only in the fight, but in the way he squared his wife.

NELSON ALGREN

It was Miss Donahue of Public School 24 who finally urged Rocco, in his fifteenth year, out of eighth grade and into the world. She had watched him fighting, at recess times, from his sixth year on. The kindergarten had had no recesses or it would have been from his fifth year. She had nurtured him personally through four trying semesters and so it was with something like enthusiasm that she wrote in his autograph book, the afternoon of graduation day, "Trusting that Rocco will make good."

Ultimately, Rocco did. In his own way. He stepped from the schoolroom into the ring back of the Happy Hour Bar in a catchweight bout with an eight-dollar purse, winner take all. Rocco took it.

Uncle Mike Adler, local promoter, called the boy Young Rocco after that one and the name stuck. He fought through the middleweights and into the light-heavies, while his purses increased to as much as sixty dollars and expenses. In his nineteenth year he stopped growing, his purses stopped growing, and he married a girl called Lili.

He didn't win every one after that, somehow, and by the time he was twenty-two he was losing as often as he won. He fought on. It was all he could do. He never took a dive; he never had a setup or a soft touch. He stayed away from whisky; he never gambled; he went to bed early before every bout and he loved his wife. He fought in a hundred corners of the city, under a half dozen managers, and he fought every man he was asked to, at any hour. He substituted for better men on as little as two hours' notice. He never ran out on a fight and he was never put down for a ten count. He took beatings from the best in the business. But he never stayed down for ten.

He fought a comer from the Coast one night and took the worst beating of his career. But he was on his feet at the end. With a jaw broken in three places.

After that one he was hospitalized for three months and Lili went to work in a factory. She wasn't a strong girl and he didn't like it that she had to work. He fought again before his jaw was ready, and lost.

Yet even when he lost, the crowds liked him. They heckled him when he was introduced as Young Rocco, because he looked like thirty-four before he was twenty-six. Most of his hair had gone during his layoff, and scar tissue over the eyes made him look less and less like a young anything. Friends came, friends left, money came in, was lost, was saved; he got the break on an occasional decision, and was occasionally robbed of a duke he'd earned. All things changed but his weight, which was 174, and his wife, who was Lili. And his record of never having been put down for ten. That stood, like his name. Which was forever Young Rocco.

That stuck to him like nothing else in the world but Lili.

At the end, which came when he was twenty-nine, all he had left was his record and his girl. Being twenty-nine, one of that pair had to go. He went six weeks without earning a dime before he came to that realization. When he found her wearing a pair of his old tennis shoes about the house, to save the heels of her only decent pair of shoes, he made up his mind.

Maybe Young Rocco wasn't the smartest pug in

town, but he wasn't the punchiest either. Just because there was a dent in his face and a bigger one in his wallet, it didn't follow that his brain was dented. It wasn't. He knew what the score was. And he loved his girl.

He came into Uncle Mike's office looking for a fight and Mike was good enough not to ask what kind he wanted. He had a twenty-year-old named Solly Classki that he was bringing along under the billing of Kid Class. There was money back of the boy, no chances were to be taken. If Rocco was ready to dive, he had the fight. Uncle Mike put no pressure on Rocco. There were two light-heavies out in the gym ready to jump at the chance to dive for Solly Classki. All Rocco had to say was okay. His word was good enough for Uncle Mike. Rocco said it. And left the gym with the biggest purse of his career, and the first he'd gotten in advance, in his pocket; four twenties and two tens.

He gave Lili every dime of that money, and when he handed it over, he knew he was only doing the right thing for her. He had earned the right to sell out and he had sold. The ring owed him more than a C-note, he reflected soundly, and added loudly, for Lili's benefit, "I'll stop the bum dead in his tracks."

They were both happy that night. Rocco had never been happier since Graduation Day.

He had a headache all the way to the City Garden that night, but it lessened a little in the shadowed dressing room under the stands. The moment he saw the lights of the ring, as he came down the littered aisle alone, the ache sharpened once more.

Slouched unhappily in his corner for the windup, he watched the lights overhead swaying a little, and closed his eyes. When he opened them, a slow dust was rising toward the lights. He saw it sweep suddenly, swift and sidewise, high over the ropes and out across the dark and watchful rows. Below him someone pushed the warning buzzer.

He looked through Kid Class as they touched gloves, and glared sullenly over the boy's head while Ryan, the ref, hurried through the stuff about a clean break in the clinches. He felt the robe being taken from his shoulders, and suddenly, in that one brief moment before the bell, felt more tired than he ever had in a ring before. He went out in a half-crouch and someone called out, "Cut him down, Solly."

He backed to make the boy lead, and then came

in long enough to flick his left twice into the teeth and skitter away. The bleachers whooped, sensing blood. He'd give them their money's worth for a couple of rounds, anyhow. No use making it look too bad.

In the middle of the second round he began sensing that the boy was telegraphing his right by pulling his left shoulder, and stepped in to trap it. The boy's left came back bloody and Rocco knew he'd been hit by the way the bleachers began again. It didn't occur to him that it was time to dive; he didn't even remember. Instead, he saw the boy telegraphing the right once more and the left protecting the heart slipping loosely down toward the navel, the telltale left shoulder hunching—only it wasn't down, it wasn't a right. It wasn't to the heart. The boy's left snapped like a hurled rock between his eyes and he groped blindly for the other's arms, digging his chin sharply into the shoulder, hating the six-bit bunch out there for thinking he could be hurt so soon. He shoved the boy off, flashed his left twice into the teeth, burned him skillfully against the middle rope, and heeled him sharply as they broke. Then he skittered easily away. And the bell.

Down front, Mike Adler's eyes followed Rocco back to his corner.

Rocco came out for the third, fighting straight up, watching Solly's gloves coming languidly out of the other corner, dangling loosely a moment in the glare, and a flatiron smashed in under his heart so that he remembered, with sagging surprise, that he'd already been paid off. He caught his breath while following the indifferent gloves, thinking vaguely of Lili in oversize tennis shoes. The gloves drifted backward and dangled loosely with little to do but catch light idly four feet away. The right broke again beneath his heart and he grunted in spite of himself; the boy's close-cropped head followed in, cockily, no higher than Rocco's chin but coming neckless straight down to the shoulders. And the gloves were gone again. The boy was faster than he looked. And the pain in his head settled down to a steady beating between the eyes.

The great strength of a fighting man is his pride. That was Young Rocco's strength in the rounds that followed. The boy called Kid Class couldn't keep him down. He was down in the fourth, twice in the fifth, and again in the seventh. In that round he stood with his back against the ropes, standing the boy off with his left in the sec-

onds before the bell. He had the trick of looking impassive when he was hurt, and his face at the bell looked as impassive as a catcher's mitt.

Between that round and the eighth Uncle Mike climbed into the ring beside Young Rocco. He said nothing. Just stood there looking down. He thought Rocco might have forgotten. He'd had four chances to stay down and he hadn't taken one. Rocco looked up. "I'm clear as a bell," he told Uncle Mike. He hadn't forgotten a thing.

Uncle Mike climbed back into his seat, resigned to anything that might happen. He understood better than Young Rocco. Rocco couldn't stay down until his knees would fail to bring him up. Uncle Mike sighed. He decided he liked Young Rocco. Somehow, he didn't feel as sorry for him as he had in the gym.

"I hope he makes it," he found himself hoping. The crowd felt differently. They had seen the lean and scarred Italian drop his man here twenty times before, the way he was trying to keep from being dropped himself now. They felt it was his turn. They were standing up in the rows to see it. The dust came briefly between. A tired moth struggled lamely upward toward the lights. And the bell.

Ryan came over between rounds, hooked Rocco's head back with a crooked forefinger on the chin, after Rocco's Negro handler had stopped the bleeding with collodion, and muttered something about the thing going too far. Rocco spat.

"Awright, Solly, drop it on him," someone called across the ropes.

It sounded, somehow, like money to Rocco. It sounded like somebody was being shortchanged out there.

But Solly stayed away, hands low, until the eighth was half gone. Then he was wide with a right, held and butted as they broke; Rocco felt the blood and got rid of some of it on the boy's left breast. He trapped the boy's left, rapping the kidneys fast before grabbing the arms again, and pressed his nose firmly into, the hollow of the other's throat to arrest its bleeding. Felt the blood trickling into the hollow there as into a tiny cup. Rocco put his feet together and a glove on both of Kid Class's shoulders, to shove him sullenly away. And must have looked strong doing it, for he heard the crowd murmur a little. He was in Solly's corner at the bell and moved back to his own corner with his head held high, to control the bleeding. When his handler stopped it again, he knew, at last, that his own pride was double-crossing him. And felt glad for that much. Let them worry out there in the rows. He'd been shortchanged since Graduation Day; let them be on the short end tonight. He had the hundred—he'd get a job in a garage and forget every one of them.

It wasn't until the tenth and final round that Rocco realized he wanted to kayo the boy—because it wasn't until then that he realized he could. Why not do the thing up the right way? He felt his tiredness fall from him like an old cloak at the notion. This was his fight, his round. He'd end like he'd started, as a fighting man.

And saw Solly Kid Class shuffling his shoulders forward uneasily. The boy would be a full-sized heavy in another six months. He bulled him into the ropes and felt the boy fade sidewise. Rocco caught him off balance with his left, hook-fashion, into the short ribs. The boy chopped back with his left uncertainly, as though he might have jammed the knuckles, and held. In a half-rolling clinch along the ropes, he saw Solly's mouthpiece projecting, slipping halfway in and halfway out, and then swallowed in again with a single tortured twist of the lips. He got an arm loose and banged the boy back of the ear with an overhand right that must have looked funny because the crowd laughed a little. Solly smeared his glove across his nose, came halfway in and changed his mind, left himself wide and was almost steady until Rocco feinted him into a knot and brought the right looping from the floor with even his toes behind it.

Solly stepped in to let it breeze past, and hooked his right hard to the button. Then the left. Rocco's mouthpiece went spinning in an arc into the lights. Then the right.

Rocco spun halfway around and stood looking sheepishly out at the rows. Kid Class saw only his man's back; Rocco was out on his feet. He walked slowly along the ropes, tapping them idly with his glove and smiling vacantly down at the newspapermen, who smiled back. Solly looked at Ryan. Ryan nodded toward Rocco. Kid Class came up fast behind his man and threw the left under the armpit flush onto the point of the chin, Rocco went forward on the ropes and hung there, his chin catching the second strand, and hung on and on, like a man decapitated.

He came to in the locker room under the stands, watching the steam swimming about the pipes directly overhead. Uncle Mike was somewhere near, telling him he had done fine, and then he was alone. They were all gone then, all the six-bit hecklers and the iron-throated boys, in the sixty-cent seats. He rose heavily and dressed slowly, feeling a long relief that he'd come to the end. He'd done it the hard way, but he'd done it. Let them all go.

He was fixing his tie, taking more time with it than it required, when she knocked. He called to her to come in. She had never seen him fight, but he knew she must have listened on the radio or she wouldn't be down now.

She tested the adhesive over his right eye timidly, fearing to hurt him with her touch, but wanting to be sure it wasn't loose.

"I'm okay," he assured her easily. "We'll celebrate a little 'n' forget the whole business." It wasn't until he kissed her that her eyes avoided him; it wasn't till then that he saw she was trying not to cry. He patted her shoulder.

"There's nothin' wrong, Lil!—a couple days' rest 'n' I'll be in the pink again."

Then saw it wasn't that after all.

"You told me you'd win," the girl told him. "I got eight to one and put the whole damn bank roll on you. I wanted to surprise you, 'n' now we ain't got a cryin' dime."

Rocco didn't blow up. He just felt a little sick. Sicker than he had ever felt in his life. He walked away from the girl and sat on the rubbing table, studying the floor. She had sense enough not to bother him until he'd realized what the score was. Then he looked up, studying her from foot to head. His eyes didn't rest on her face: they went back to her feet. To the scarred toes of the only decent shoes; and a shadow passed over his heart. "You got good odds, honey," he told her thoughtfully. "You done just right. We made 'em sweat all night for their money." Then he looked up and grinned. A wide, white grin.

That was all she needed to know it was okay after all. She went to him so he could tell her how okay it really was.

That was like Young Rocco, from Graduation Day. He always did it the hard way; but he did it.

Miss Donahue would have been proud.

MICHELANGELO'S MASTERPIECE

The New York Times' Pulitzer Prize–winning sports columnist, while covering Sugar Ray Leonard's 1987 upset of middleweight champion Marvin Hagler, left us more than an account of the fight. By setting the scene and then stepping aside he contributed a self portrait by Angelo Dundee, one of the all-time great trainers of fighters.

DAVE ANDERSON

His name is Angelo Dundee, but it should be Michelangelo now. He's the trainer who sculpted a boxing masterpiece—Sugar Ray Leonard's tactical triumph over both Marvelous Marvin Hagler and Father Time after a virtual five-year leave of absence.

"Box, box, move and glide," Dundee kept telling him in the corner. "Don't trade shots with this guy. That's a no-no."

Like a good student, Leonard not only listened, he accepted what Dundee told him, then went out and did it to earn the middleweight title with a split decision. Some boxing people are trying to compare what Leonard did Monday night with what Muhammad Ali once did under Dundee's guidance against Sonny Liston and later against George Foreman, but Dundee doesn't see it that way.

"This guy," Dundee was saying yesterday of Leonard, "is a completely different cat."

One difference is that Leonard accepted Dundee's advice while Ali tended to resist it.

"With Muhammad, I'd go around the mulberry bush," Dundee said. "Make him think he's the innovator. When he beat Liston for the title, I wanted him to surround Liston's jab. Liston could knock you dead with a jab. After awhile Muhammad thought it was his idea. When he won the title the second time, from Foreman, the rope-a-dope just happened. I was yelling for him to get off the ropes. The rope-a-dope wasn't planned." But on Monday night at Caesars Palace, virtually everything that Leonard did had been choreographed by Dundee at their training camp in Hilton Head,

S.C. "Angelo probably had as much to do and maybe more to do with Ray winning than anybody," Leonard's attorney, Mike Trainer, said. "By the time Angelo got there Feb. 28th, Ray was ready for Angelo's input. Angelo told him, 'You've got your body, you're in great shape, now let me show you what we have to do to beat this guy.' They'd talk before the workout about what to concentrate on, then they'd watch the tape of the workout, then they'd watch tapes of Hagler's fights."

Hagler hadn't lost in 11 years, but Dundee knew that Roberto Duran and Juan Roldan had confused him.

"Hagler's a hopper and a two-stepper," Dundee said. "When Hagler throws a double jab, he slides to the right, so Ray would slide to his right and he wouldn't be there for Hagler to hit. Duran had done that, Roldan had done that until he got tagged. Another thing I kept telling Ray, 'When this guy leans on you, slide out right, slide out left.' Ray's so smooth, he could do it. And he's willing to accept instructions. You could never tell Muhammad what to do. You can tell Ray what to do." Over his four decades of working with fighters, Dundee has managed six left-handed boxers.

"I had Andy Arel, who gave Willie Pep fits," Dundee said. "I had Irish Bobby Lloyd, Arthur King, Sonny Boy West, pretty good southpaws. But Hagler's not the usual southpaw. Sometimes he's a rightpaw and you got to watch for that. You usually never go right with a southpaw, but with Hagler you can go right and nail him with a right hand. Hagler's a sucker for a right-hand counter.

Hagler hadn't lost for 11 years but there's always somebody out there who can lick you."

Three years ago, when Leonard told Dundee that he was retiring again after having stopped Kevin Howard, the trainer said, "Amen." But when Leonard decided to defy the boxing commandment that "they never come back," Dundee agreed.

"Ray told me that he had to do it, he had to fight Hagler and I said 'Amen' to that, too," Dundee said. "It wasn't five years, it was two and a half years. He's been training for this fight for one solid year. For six months, he worked three days a week, which was just enough. When he was in Miami a few months ago, I put him in with three southpaws and he outspeeded those guys."

Around that time, Dundee was in Trevor Berbick's corner the night Mike Tyson won the World Boxing Council heavyweight title with a savage second-round knockout.

"I told Trevor some of the same things I told Ray, that it was all angles, that you got to keep yourself at an angle against Tyson just like Ray had to do with Hagler. If you keep him straight in front of you, you're licked. If you stand there, adios. I thought I'd convinced Trevor, but coming down the aisle some dummy must've yelled, 'You're as strong as that kid.' Trevor must've listened to him instead of to me. Trevor didn't do anything I told him. You don't fight strength with strength." On my scorecard, Monday night's fight was a draw. I gave Leonard the first four rounds, Hagler the next six and Leonard the last two. In points, that's 114–114. But on the judges' cards, the fight turned on Leonard's winning the sixth, the 10th and the 11th.

"Another thing we knew about Hagler, he flattens out in the middle rounds," Dundee said. "He likes to dictate the early rounds, then he flattens out, then he comes on. Our idea was to make sure to win the early rounds, then steal a couple in the middle. And when Ray had to, he even pushed Hagler back a few times. Ray's strong."

In the ninth round, Leonard wobbled twice but escaped each time in a flurry of punches. In the 10th, Hagler not only let the moment get away, on the judges' cards he let the round get away. And it was clear that Hagler had let the first four rounds get away. But over 15 rounds, perhaps Hagler would have been able to produce a knockout.

"No way," Dundee said. "Great fighters suck it up."

Great trainers do too, but boxing's Michelangelo wasn't about to take any bows for his masterpiece.

"I'm not star quality," Angelo Dundee said. "The fighter's the star."

All those Michelangelo statues in museums are stars too, but he's still the sculptor.

THE KID'S LAST FIGHT

This was a barroom and vaudeville favorite.

ANONYMOUS

Us two was pals, the Kid and me:
'Twould cut no ice if some gayzee,
As tough as hell jumped either one,
We'd both light in and hand him some.

"He'd rather fight than eat," they said,
"He's got the punch, he'll knock 'em dead."
There's only one I hadn't met,
That guy they called "The Yorkshire Pet."

Both of a size, the Kid and me,
We tipped the scales at thirty-three;
And when we'd spar 'twas give and take,
I wouldn't slug for any stake.

One day we worked out at the gym,
Some swell guy hangin' round called "Slim,"
Watched us and got stuck on the Kid,
Then signed him up, that's what he did.

This guy called "Slim" he owned a string
Of lightweights, welters, everything;
He took the Kid out on the road,
And where they went none of us knowed.

I guessed the Kid had changed his name,
And fightin' the best ones in the game.
I used to dream of him at night,
No letters came—he couldn't write.

In just about two months or three
I signed up with Bucktooth McGee.
He got me matched with Denver Brown,
I finished him in half a round.

Next month I fought with Brooklyn Mike,
As tough a boy who hit the pike;
Then Frisco Jim and Battlin' Ben,
And knocked them all inside of ten.

I took 'em all and won each bout,
None of them birds could put me out;
The sportin' writers watched me slug.
Then all the papers run my mug.

He'd cleaned 'em all around in France,
No one in England stood a chance;
And I was champ in U.S.A.,
And knocked 'em cuckoo every day.

Now all McGee and me could think
Was how we'd like to cross the drink,
And knock this bucko for a row,
And grab a wagonload of dough.

At last Mac got me matched all right,
Five thousand smackers for the fight;
Then me and him packed up our grip,
And went to grab that championship.

I done some trainin' and the night
Set for the battle sure was right;
The crowd was wild, for this here bout
Was set to last till one was out.

The mob went crazy when the Pet
Came in, I'd never seen him yet;
And then I climbed up through the ropes,
All full of fight and full of hopes.

The crowd give me an awful yell
('Twas even money at the bell),
They stamped their feet and shook the place; The
Pet turned 'round, I saw his face!

My guts went sick, that's what they did,
For Holy Gee, it was the Kid—
We just had time for one good shake,
We meant it, too, it wasn't fake.

Whang! went the bell, the fight was on,
I clinched until the round was gone,
A-beggin' that he'd let me take
The fall for him—he wouldn't fake.

Hell, no, the Kid was on the square,
And said we had to fight it fair,
The crowd had bet their dough on us
We had to fight (the honest cuss).

The referee was yellin' "break,"
The crowd was sore and howlin' "fake."
They'd paid their dough to see a scrap.
And so far we'd not hit a tap.

The second round we both begin.
I caught a fast one on my chin;
And stood like I was in a doze,
Until I got one on the nose.

I started landin' body blows,
He hooked another on my nose,
That riled my fightin' blood like hell,
And we were sluggin' at the bell.

The next round started, from the go
The millin' we did wasn't slow,
I landed hard on him, and then,
He took the count right up to ten.

He took the limit on one knee,
A chance to get his wind and see;
At ten he jumped up like a flash
And on my jaw he hung a smash.

I'm fightin', too, there, toe to toe,
And hittin' harder, blow for blow,
I damn soon knowed he couldn't stay,
He rolled his eyes—you know the way.

The way he staggered made me sick,
I stalled, McGee yelled, "Cop him quick!"
The crowd was wise and yellin' "fake,"
They'd seen the chance I wouldn't take.

The mob kept tellin' me to land,
And callin' things, I couldn't stand;
I stepped in close and smashed his chin,
The Kid fell hard; he was all in.

I carried him into his chair,
And tried to bring him to for fair,
I rubbed his wrists, done everything,
A doctor climbed into the ring.

And I was scared as I could be,
The Kid was starin' and couldn't see;
The doctor turned and shook his head,
I looked again—the Kid was dead!

EPIGRAMS

Arthur (Bugs) Baer, into whose hopper of humor vaudeville, radio, night-club and literary comics dipped for over fifty years, was born in Philadelphia in 1886. Starting as a sports cartoonist, he worked on newspapers there and in Washington, where he turned to writing. He joined the New York *Evening World* in 1915 and four years later went to work for Hearst. Present at the Dempsey–Gibbons fight, he described Shelby, Montana, as "so tough that the canaries sing bass."

BUGS BAER

[After Jack Dempsey knocked out Fred Fulton in 18⅗ seconds on July 27, 1918]—Fulton would do better selling advertising space on the soles of his shoes.

[After Jack Dempsey knocked out Georges Carpentier in the fourth round on July 2, 1921]—The joint was a sellout, and Carpentier had the last seat in the house.

[After Jack Dempsey, knocked out of the ring in the first round, knocked out Luis Firpo in the second round on September 14, 1923]—If the fight had been held on a barge Firpo would be champion because Dempsey would have drowned.

[After Gene Tunney outboxed Jack Dempsey for the second time, on September 22, 1927]—If there had been a gate in the ring, Dempsey would be champion again.

[After Joe Louis knocked out James J. Braddock in the eighth round on June 22, 1937]—The old champion was as game as a butcher's chopping block.

[Before Rocky Marciano knocked out Don Cockell in the ninth round on May 16, 1955]—Cockell's manager is complaining about the size of the ring and demanding one that measures 20 feet. What difference does it make? His man isn't that tall.

BILLY MISKE'S LAST CHRISTMAS

George Barton wrote sports for Minneapolis newspapers for fifty-three years and covered every heavyweight title fight from Jack Johnson–Jim Jeffries through Floyd Patterson–Ingemar Johansson. He also won a six-round decision over Terry McGovern, sparred exhibitions with Joe Gans, Battling Nelson and Frankie Neil, refereed more than 12,000 bouts and is the source of the Billy Miske story. Since Barton first wrote it for the Minneapolis *Tribune* the story has appeared in hundreds of newspapers and has been rewritten or reprinted in seven magazines. This is from Barton's autobiography, *My Lifetime in Sports.*

GEORGE A. BARTON

This is the story of Billy Miske, the most courageous fighter I have known in more than half a century of association with professional boxing. Miske came to the end of the fistic trail early in 1923. Although he had not reached his twenty-ninth birthday, Billy was mortally ill with Bright's disease; his days were numbered and he knew it.

Billy Miske's entire ring career, however, marked him as a boxer with a great fighting heart. When he became a victim of Bright's disease in 1916 his family doctor told him he had five years to live, provided he quit boxing and took care of himself. Miske shrugged off the advice. Knowing that his number was up, he participated in seventy fights in the next six years, meeting the leading light heavyweights and heavyweights. Included were three bouts with Jack Dempsey, three with Tommy Gibbons, three with Jack Dillon, three with Bill Brennan and two with Harry Greb.

At one time Billy was matched with Gibbons for a ten-round fight to be staged at Nicollet Park in Minneapolis on June 19, 1919. A week before the bout, Billy became ill and was ordered to bed by his doctor. An assortment of boils added to his misery in the humid ninety-degree heat.

Four days before the fight Jack Reddy, the St. Paul boxing promoter who was Billy's manager, informed Mike Collins, who was then promoting boxing matches in Minneapolis, that it would be impossible for Miske to go through with the match. Collins, faced with this dilemma, called me and asked if I would go with him to Miske's home in St. Paul.

"Any chance of your fighting on Friday night?"

an anxious Collins asked Miske. "We've already got $18,000 in advance sales in the till and the gate is a cinch to hit $30,000. The Minneapolis baseball team is coming home Saturday for a three-week stand and a postponement of that long will kill interest in the fight. It means a big pay day for all of us if you fight Gibbons Friday night. Try to make it, will you, Billy?"

Miske, still in bed and running a temperature, told Collins, "I'll get up tomorrow. If I can walk around the block without falling down, I'll fight Gibbons for you Friday night."

True to his promise, Miske was on hand for the battle. Weak as he was, Billy waged a furious fight for ten rounds and Gibbons was extended to the limit in gaining the decision. As referee of the match, I can vouch for the fury of Miske's fighting.

Due to his health, Billy retired from boxing in the spring of 1920 and entered the automobile business. Within five months he lost $55,000 and needed additional money to carry on. He accepted a guarantee of $25,000 to meet champion Jack Dempsey in a title fight at Benton Harbor, Michigan, on Labor Day.

This match was their third meeting. Miske had lost a ten-round decision to Dempsey after a terrific battle in St. Paul on May 3, 1918. In their second fight, a six-round bout in Philadelphia on November 28 of the same year, Jack had gained a newspaper decision.

Physically ailing, Miske merely went through the motions of training for this third fight with Dempsey and Jack knocked him out in the third round. It was the only knockout suffered by Miske in 150 bouts. After paying Reddy his manager's percentage, Billy had about $18,000 left. Intimate friends, his wife and his manager, all knowing that the automobile business was doomed to failure, begged Billy to go through bankruptcy and save the Dempsey purse for a nest egg.

"Not me," Billy said, proudly. "Nobody is going to point a finger at Billy Miske and say he ever beat them out of even a dime. I'm going to pay off even if I go broke again."

He put $15,000 into the business and eventually was wiped out with a loss of $70,000. Flat broke, Miske returned to the ring in 1921 and participated in twenty-four more fights before his death. He won thirteen by knockouts, ten were no-decision and he was held to one draw.

Miske's illness finally forced him to retire again after he knocked out Harry Foley in one round in Omaha on January 12, 1923. Unable to fight, and too ill to work, Billy stayed home most of the time with his wife, Marie, and their three children. Late November came, with Christmas in the offing. Months of idleness had depleted the Miske bank roll. He needed money badly. That was his predicament as he entered the office of Jack Reddy.

"Jack," Miske said, "get me a fight."

"You must be kidding," replied Reddy. "You're in no condition to fight."

"Get me a fight anyway," Miske said.

"But Billy," answered the manager, "do you want me ruled out of boxing for tossing a sick man into the ring?"

"Look, Jack," pleaded Miske, "here's how it is. I'm flat broke and I haven't done anything for eleven months. I know I haven't long to go, and I want to give Marie and the children one more happy Christmas before I check out. I won't be around for another. Please get me one more pay day. I want to make Christmas this year something Marie and the children will always remember me for."

"This may hurt your feelings, Bill," Reddy said, "but you know as well as I do that if you were to fight in your present condition, you might be killed. You might die right in the ring."

"Sure," answered Miske. "I know better than you do but I'm a fighter and I'd rather die in the ring than sitting home in a rocking chair."

Reddy continued to protest. He offered to do anything he could to help Billy financially. He pleaded with Miske to abandon the idea; he didn't want his pal's death on his conscience.

"Here's what I'll do," Reddy said, finally. "You go to the gym and start working out. If you get into any reasonable kind of shape, we'll talk about getting you a match."

"You know I can't do that," replied Miske. "It's impossible for me to train, but I've got to have one more fight for my family's sake. Please get it for me."

As there was no talking Miske out of his scheme, Reddy reluctantly said he'd look around. After pondering over the matter for several days, Jack engineered a match between Miske and Bill Brennan at Omaha. Billy had decisioned Brennan in three previous fights, all closely contested, and there had been enough excitement created to warrant a fourth meeting.

Bill Brennan was a tough hombre who had fought the best and had been knocked out only once—by Jack Dempsey in the twelfth round of a championship fight at New York in 1920. Brennan led on points in that fight up until the moment the Manassa Mauler flattened him.

I received a tip regarding Miske being matched with Brennan and I immediately called Reddy. I gave him a verbal lashing over the telephone for being willing to risk Miske's life to make a few bucks for himself. I also threatened to expose Billy's condition and promised to blast Reddy for being a party to such an affair.

"Hold everything," said Reddy, when I paused for breath. "Don't write anything until I bring Billy to your office. We'll be there shortly to explain everything."

When they arrived, Miske told me his story and begged me not to reveal it. I was a close friend of both Miske and Reddy; with reluctance I finally agreed to keep Billy's condition secret although, like Reddy, I feared that Miske might die in the ring.

All of these preliminaries took place about a week before Thanksgiving Day with the fight set for December 7. Miske, of course, wasn't able to train. When inquisitive newspapermen and boxing fans asked Reddy why Billy wasn't working out in the Rose Room gym in St. Paul, Jack explained he had a gym rigged up at his Lake Johanna home and Miske intended to do all his training there.

This was all ballyhoo. Billy remained at home, conserving his strength. He didn't go to

Omaha until two days before the fight. State athletic commissions weren't as strict with medical examinations as they now are; probably the doctor gave Miske only a cursory examination. I wouldn't know.

What I do know is that Billy knocked out a well-conditioned Brennan in four rounds and picked up a purse of approximately $2,400. Reddy waived his manager's share so Miske kept the entire sum.

Billy spent Christmas Day at home with Marie and their three children—Billy, Jr., aged six, Douglas, four, and Donna, eighteen months—gathered around him. He was just about the happiest man in the world although he knew it would be his last Christmas. Although actually in agony from pain, Billy told Marie he felt fine. He romped with the children and laughed and kidded with relatives.

Early on the morning of December 26, Reddy received a telephone call from Miske. "Come and get me to a hospital, Jack," groaned Billy. "I can't stand the pain any longer. I know I'm dying."

Reddy and Mrs. Miske rushed the courageous fighter to St. Mary's Hospital in Minneapolis. Billy Miske died there six days later early on New Year's Day, 1924.

Mrs. Miske (now Mrs. Alfred Peterson of St. Paul) remained a widow for seventeen years, working to support the three children. Her eldest son, Billy, Jr., boxed professionally for several years before going to work for a St. Paul meat-packing plant. The second son, Douglas, named after Douglas Fairbanks who was an ardent admirer of Billy, Sr., was an Air Force pilot in the South Pacific in World War II. He returned to service early in the Korean War and was killed in a training-plane crash. The daughter, Donna, received her bachelor's degree in education and a master's degree in recreation from the University of Minnesota. Until her marriage in 1954, she was playgrounds director in St. Louis Park, a suburb of Minneapolis.

Maybe someone can name a gamer boxer than Billy Miske. I can't.

[FACT]

THE PRIZE FIGHT

On December 4, 1919, the author of *The Old Wives' Tale* saw Georges Carpentier box Joe Beckett at Holborn Stadium, London, and was deeply interested.

ARNOLD BENNETT

During the last stage of the dinner the host came round to you and said, in that politely casual tone of a man who knows more than you do, but who would not like the fact to appear: "Got your ticket safe? Might be as well to keep an eye on it till you're inside." You then divined that you were about to enter another world, a world where the eruptive potentialities of the social organization may show themselves more disconcertingly than in yours. And the inflections of your reply tried to prove that you were an accustomed citizen of that other world. Later, the host said: "I brought a knuckle duster with me." He presented the steely instrument for inspection. "You can do some useful work with that on your fingers," he said, and added fatalistically: "But, of course, it wouldn't be any good if half a dozen of 'em set on you at once." In answer to the naïve query, "How do you get there?" he said: "Oh! That'll be all right. I've got fifteen taxis at the door." Fifteen taxis at the door! It indeed is another world, and one which the taxi driver comprehends and approves. Could anybody get fifteen taxis at any door for an excursion to the Albert Hall for a League of Nations meeting, or to Lowndes Square to hear Robert Nichols recite at Mrs. Kinfoot's? Nobody could.

The crowds began long before the Stadium was reached. The street was narrow and dark, and in an empty space scores of huge policemen were watching the eruptive potentialities. You clutched your ticket, for, after all, it bore the figures £10 10s. Still, there was no difficulty about entering. You noticed the thick solidity of the barriers paneled with barbed wire, but they opened quickly for you, and the strong attendants had none of the geographical indecision which characterizes nonchalant program girls in figleaf white aprons over short black frocks. As you squeezed into the central enclosure of the auditorium, close to the ring (a squared circle), where one of the preliminary bouts was in progress, the final attendant said quickly: "Sit down here until the end of the round, sir." Ferocious homicidal yells from behind reinforced him: "Sit down! Sit down!" You sat down quickly—anywhere. The attendant crouched on his haunches. (This was not Tristan, of which ten or twenty bars don't in the least matter. This was pugilism, the most holy and impassioning sacrament of its world.) A few seconds more and you were in your seat, one of four or five thousand. You realized that the affair had been wonderfully organized and rehearsed.

In came Mr. Cochran, the mysterious organizer, escorting the Prince of Wales, the Prince holding a cigar just in the manner of his grandfather, and Mr. Cochran looking rather like one of the Antonines. Mr. Cochran gazed around at the vast advertisements of his own theaters, and at the cinema operators precariously suspended over balconies. Mr. Cochran had thoughtfully provided loops of rope for them to rest their feet in. Mr. Cochran had forgotten nothing. It was his hour. He deserved it. It pains me as a professional observer that I cannot recall whether the Prince and Mr. Cochran wore smoking jackets or swallowtails. Opinion was divided as to the sartorial proprieties. Some star actors and some millionaires wore smoking jackets; some star actors and some millionaires wore swallowtails. The millionaires were richly represented. There they were, dotted about, the genial wizards who have removed Arlington Street from the map, who are said to have the Government in their pockets, and who assert with calm conviction that "Lloyd George can't put it over them." Women were certainly too few; some had sought to atone for the paucity by emulating the attire of the gladiators in the ring. They made futile spots of sex on ten guineas' worth of plush in an environment where Aphrodite had no status whatever.

The raised ring was already well illuminated, but soon many lamps that had been unlit fizzed into activity, and dazzling torrents of bluish light rained down a treble-X radiance on the battleground. The cinema men prepared themselves. The last of the preliminary bouts finished. An M.C. climbed into the ring and besought the audience to stop smoking, so that the champions about to dispute the mastery of a continent might breathe more easily. The celebrated Mr. B.J. Angle, whose word was to be law to the champions, climbed into the ring and delivered a short homily. Mr. B.J. Angle was evidently a man who knew his own mind, and who also knew his world. Some persons were pained because he wore a gray suit and brown boots at ten p.m., in the presence of the Prince, and they did not hesitate to express their narrow-mindedness. A little box, covered with advertisement, was deposited in the center of the ring. It contained the gloves. The sublime moment approached. You had a unique sensation; you admitted to yourself that it was well worth ten guineas, and also that the subject of the reconstruction of Europe lacked actuality.

Beckett and train appeared first, and the train was so numerous as to be bewildering. For a moment you thought that both boxers and both trains must be in the ring. You understood better the immense costliness of a really great fight, and the complexity of the machinery which is necessary to perfect it. You perceived that though eight thousand pounds was to be divided between the combatants, neither would be overpaid when he had reckoned his time and discharged his expenses. When Carpentier and train appeared, the ring was like a market place. One figure, Carpentier, stood out astonishingly from all the rest. All the rest had the faces and the carriage of bruisers. Nobody could have taken Carpentier for a boxer. He might have been a barrister, a poet, a musician, a Foreign Office attaché, a Fellow of All Souls; but not a boxer. He had an air of intellectual or artistic distinction. And long contact with the very physical world of pugilism had not apparently affected his features in the slightest degree. In the previous six years he had matured, but not coarsened. He seemed excessively out of place in the ring. You could not comprehend what on earth he was doing there. Surely he must have lost his way! Beckett, a magnificent form, but with a countenance from which you would not infer much power of ratiocination, gazed long at Carpentier from under his forehead, whereas Carpentier scarcely glanced at Beckett. At one moment Beckett appeared to you like a dumb victim trying to penetrate the secrets of a higher and inscrutable power; at another moment you were persuaded that grim Beckett was merely contemplating his poor destined intellectual victim with the most admirable British detachment. At one moment you felt that Carpentier must inevitably be crushed; at another moment you were convinced that if Carpentier was not too many for Beckett, then the course of civilization had been very misleading.

I know nothing about boxing; my opinion on boxing would be worth about as much as Beckett's on Scriabin. But I had seen Carpentier, in 1913, when he was a boy, knock out Bombardier Wells at the National Sporting Club in less than two minutes, and the performance was so brilliant, so easy, so natural, that I could not believe that anybody else would ever knock out Carpentier. Now, however, I was overborne by the weight of expert prophecy. All the experts were certain that Beckett must win. Some of them murmured something perfunctory about the million-to-one chance of an early knockout by Carpentier, but none of them had in reality any fear of such a chance. I surrendered, and privily told myself what a simpleton I had been to imagine for a single instant that Carpentier would not be smashed. (I forgot the peculiar accents in which Lord Fisher said to me in 1915, that *his* life then was "nothing but one damned expert after another.") Further, the experts killed Carpentier

immediately they saw him. They said he was not in condition; they liked not the color of his skin; they said he had gone right off; they said he was a dead man. And I submissively persuaded myself that this was so.

The ritualistic prologue to the encounter seemed to take a very long time. But it served excellently its purpose of heightening the excitement of expectation. When the bell at length rang, and Beckett and Carpentier approached each other lonely in the ring, beneath a million candle power of radiance, and the whole barbaric Stadium was stilled, and hearts knocked remindingly under waistcoats—in that moment, even those who had paid twenty-five guineas for a ten-guinea seat must have felt that they had got a bargain.

There had been some grand fighting before the big event, particularly between Eddie Feathers and Gus Platts, and experts had said: "This will be the best fighting of the evening. You'll see. A championship match is never any good." The devoted experts were wrong again. In five seconds the championship fighting stood plainly in a class apart, thanks solely to Carpentier. Carpentier caught Beckett on the nose at once. Beckett positively had to rub his nose, an act which made strong men around me shudder. Beckett was utterly outclassed. He never had a chance.... The Stadium beheld him lying stunned on his face. And the sight of Beckett prone, and Carpentier standing by him listening to the counting of allotted seconds, was the incredible miraculous consummation of all the months of training, all the organization, all the advertising, all the expenditure, all the frenzy. Aphrodite, breaking loose in the shape of a pretty girl *bien Maquillée*, rushed to the ring. Men raised her in their arms, she raised her face; and Carpentier bent over the ropes and kissed her, passionately amid the ecstasies of joy and disillusion that raged around them. That kiss seemed to be the bright flower of the affair. It summed up everything. Two minutes earlier Beckett in his majestic strength had been the idol of a kingdom. Now Beckett was a sack of potatoes, and Carpentier in might and glory was publicly kissing the chosen girl within a yard of the Prince of Wales.

We left the Stadium immediately, though the program of boxing was by no means concluded, and in Red Lion Square found our taxi driver, whose claim to distinction was that his grandfather had been a friend of Mr. George R. Sims.

All the streets of the vicinity were full of people

abroad for the event. They were all aware of the result, for at the very doors of the Stadium, on our emerging, a newspaper boy had offered us the news in print. They all stood or moved in attitudes of amaze, watching with rapt faces the long lines of departing motors. You perceived that the English race was profoundly interested and moved, and that nothing less than winning the greatest war could have interested and moved it more profoundly. This emotion was no product of a press campaign, but the press campaign was a correct symptom of it. It was as genuine as British fundamental decency.

Not Beckett alone had been stunned. The experts were stunned. Their prime quality of being ever cheery had gone from them. They could scarcely speak; there was naught to say; there was no ground for any argument. They were bowed with grief. Fate had heavily smitten them. One of them murmured: "I consider it's a disgrace to Great Britain." Another: "It's the champion of Great Britain that's been beaten. ... This—after Mlle. Lenglen!" Where to go in these circumstances of woe? Obviously to the Eccentric Club. We went, and were solaced and steadied with an aged Courvoisier brandy. Sipping the incomparable liquid, and listening to the exact reconstitution of the battle by the experts, I reflected, all solitary in my own head, upon what, with such magnificent and quiet hospitality, I had been taken to see. Was the show worthy of the talents and the time lavished on its preparation and accomplishment, worthy of the tradition, of the prowess, of the fostering newspapers, of Mr. Cochran? It was. Was it a moral show? It was—as moral as an Inter-University Rugger match. Was it an aesthetic show? It was. Did it uplift? It did. Did it degrade? It did not. Was it offensive? No. Ought the noble art to continue? It ought. I had been deeply interested.

[REPORTING]

A VISIT WITH JOHN L. SULLIVAN

Six weeks before he knocked out Jake Kilrain in Richburg, Miss., in the seventy-fifth round, John L. Sullivan was interviewed by Nellie Bly (Mrs. Elizabeth Cochrane Seaman). She asked the good questions, and this excellent piece of reporting occupied the first three columns on page 13 of *The World* (of New York) on Sunday, May 26, 1889.

NELLIE BLY

If John L. Sullivan isn't able to whip any pugilist in the world I would like to see the man who is. I went to Belfast, N.Y., to see him last week and I was surprised. Why? Well, I will tell you.

I have often thought that the sparring instinct is inborn—in everything—except women and flowers, of course. I have seen funny little spring roosters, without one feather's sprout to crow about, fight like real men. And then the boys! Isn't it funny how proud they are of their muscle, and how quiet the boy is who hasn't any? Almost as soon as a boy learns to walk he learns to jump into position of defense and double up his fists.

We reached Belfast about 7:30 o'clock in the morning and were the only passengers for that place. Mr. William Muldoon's house, where Mr. Sullivan is training, is in the prettiest part of the town and only a short distance from the hotel. Fearing that Mr. Sullivan would go out for a walk and that I would miss him, I went immediately to the Muldoon cottage.

One would never imagine from the surroundings that a prize fighter was being trained there. The house is a very pretty little two-story building, surrounded by the smoothest and greenest of green lawns, which helps to intensify the spotless whiteness of the cottage. A wide veranda surrounds the three sides of the cottage, and the easy chairs and hammocks give it a most enticing look of comfort. Large maple trees shade the house from the glare of the sun.

I rang the bell, and when a colored man came in answer I sent my letter of introduction to Mr. Muldoon. A handsome young man, whose broad shoulders were neatly fitted with a gray corduroy coat, came into the room, holding a light gray cap in his hand. His face was youthful, his eyes blue, his expression pleasing, his smile brought two dimples to punctuate his rosy cheeks, his bearing was easy and most graceful, and this was the champion wrestler and athlete, William Muldoon.

"We have just returned from our two-mile walk," he said, when I told him I had come to see Mr. Sullivan, "and Mr. Sullivan is just being rubbed down. If you will excuse me one moment I will tell him."

In a few moments Mr. Muldoon returned, followed by a man whom I would never have taken for the great and only Sullivan. He was a tall man, with enormous shoulders, and wore dark trousers, a light cheviot coat and vest and slippers. In his hand he held a light cloth cap. He paused almost as he entered the room in a half-bashful way, and twisted his cap in a very boyish but not ungraceful manner.

"Miss Bly, Mr. Sullivan," said Mr. Muldoon, and I looked into the great fighter's dark, bright eyes as he bent his broad shoulders before me.

"Mr. Sullivan, I would like to shake hands with you," I said, and he took my hand with a firm, hearty grasp, and with a hand that felt small and soft. Mr. Muldoon excused himself, and I was left to interview the great John L.

"I came here to learn all about you, Mr. Sulli-van, so will you please begin by telling me at what time you get up in the morning," I said.

"Well, I get up about 6 o'clock and get rubbed down," he began, in a matter-of-fact way. "Then Muldoon and I walk and run a mile or a mile and a half away and then back. Just as soon as we get in I am given a showerbath, and after being thoroughly rubbed down again I put on an entire fresh outfit."

"What kind of clothing do you wear for your walk? Heavy?" I asked.

"Yes, I wear a heavy sweater and a suit of heavy corduroy buttoned tightly. I also wear gloves. After my walk I put on a fresh sweater, so that I won't take cold."

"What's a sweater?" I asked.

"I'll show you," he said, with a smile, and, excusing himself, he went out. In a moment he returned with a garment in his hand. It was a very heavy knit garment, with long sleeves and a standing collar. It was all in one piece and, I imagine, weighed several pounds. "Well, what do you wear a sweater for, and why do you take such violent walks?" I asked, my curiosity being satisfied as to the strange "sweater."

"I wear a sweater to make me warm, and I walk to reduce my fat and to harden my muscles. Last Friday I lost six pounds and last Saturday I lost six and a half pounds. When I came here I weighed 237 pounds, and now I weigh 218. Before I leave here I will weigh only 195 pounds."

"Do you take a cold showerbath when your walk is finished?"

"No, never, I don't believe in cold water. It chills the blood. I always have my showerbath of a medium temperature."

"How are you rubbed down, then, as you term it?"

"I have two men give me a brisk rubbing with their hands. Then they rub me down with a mixture of ammonia, camphor and alcohol."

"What do you eat?"

"I eat nothing fattening. I have oatmeal for breakfast and meat and bread for dinner, and cold meat and stale bread for supper. I eat no sweets nor potatoes. I used to smoke all the day, but since I came here I haven't seen a cigar. Occasionally Mr. Muldoon gives me a glass of ale, but it doesn't average one a day."

"Then training is not very pleasant work?"

"It's the worst thing going. A fellow would

rather fight twelve dozen times than train once, but it's got to be done," and he leaned back in the easy chair with an air of weariness. "After breakfast I rest awhile," he continued, "and then putting on our heaviest clothes again we start out at 10:30 for our twelve-mile run and walk, which we do in two hours. We generally go across the fields to Mr. Muldoon's farm because it is all uphill work and makes us warm. When we get back I am rubbed down again and at one we have dinner. In the afternoon we wrestle, punch a bag, throw football, swing Indian clubs and dumbbells, practice the chest movement and such things until suppertime. It's all right to be here when the sun is out, but after dark it's the dreariest place I ever struck. I wouldn't live here if they gave me the whole country."

The 'Champion Rest,' the name by which Mr. Muldoon's home is known, is surrounded by two graveyards, a church, the priest's home and a little cottage occupied by two old maids.

"I couldn't sleep after 5 o'clock this morning on account of Mr. Muldoon's cow. It kept up a hymn all the morning and the birds joined in the chorus. It's no use to try to sleep here after daybreak. The noise would knock out anything."

"Do you like prize fighting?" I asked Mr. Sullivan, after he had laid his complaint about the "singing cow" before Mrs. Muldoon.

"I don't," he replied. "Of course I did once, or rather I was fond of traveling about and the excitement of the crowds, but this is my last fight."

"Why?"

"Well, I am tired and I want to settle down. I am getting old," and he leaned back wearily.

"What is your age?"

"I was born the 15th of October, 1858. I began prize fighting when I was only nineteen years old. How did I start? Well, I had a match with a prize man who had never been downed, and I was the winner. This got me lots of notice, so I went through the country giving exhibitions. I have made plenty of money in my day, but I have been a fool and today I have nothing. It came easy and went easy. I have provided well for my father and mother, and they are in comfortable circumstances."

"What will you do if you stop fighting?"

"If I win this fight I will travel for a year giving sparring exhibitions, and then I will settle down. I have always wanted to run a hotel in New York, and if I am successful I think I shall spend the rest of my life as a hotel proprietor."

"How much money have you made during your career as a prize fighter?"

"I have made $500,000 or $600,000 in boxing. I made $125,000 from September 26, 1883, to May 26, 1884, when I traveled through the country offering $1,000 to anyone I couldn't knock out in four rounds, which takes twelve minutes."

"How do you dress when you go in a prize ring?"

"I wear knee breeches, stockings and shoes, and no shirt."

"Why no shirt?"

"Because a man perspires so freely that if he wears a shirt he is liable to chill, and a chill is always fatal in a prize ring. I took a chill when I fought with Mitchell, but it didn't last long."

"What kind of shoes do you wear?"

"Regular spike shoes. They have three big spikes to prevent slipping."

"How will you fight Kilrain, with or without gloves?"

"I will fight Kilrain according to the London prize-ring rules. That's without gloves and allows wrestling and throwing a man down. We get a rest every thirty seconds. Under the Marquis of Queensberry rules we wear gloves, anything under eleven ounces. They give us three minutes to a round under the Queensberry, and when the three minutes are up you have to rest whether you could whip your man the next instant or not."

"Your hands look very soft and small for a fighter."

"Do they?" and he held one out to me for inspection. "My friends tell me they look like hams," and he laughed. "I wear number nine gloves."

I examined his hand, he watching me with an amused expression. It looks a small hand to bear the record of so many "knockout" blows. The fingers were straight and shapely. The closely trimmed nails were a lovely oval and pink. The only apparent difference was the great thickness through.

"Feel my arm," he said, with a bright smile, as he doubled it up. I tried to feel the muscle, but it was like a rock. With both my hands I tried to span it, but I couldn't. Meanwhile the great fellow sat there watching me with a most boyish expression of amusement.

"By the time I am ready to fight there won't be any fat on my hands or face. They will be as hard as a bone. Do I harden them? Certainly. If I didn't I would have pieces knocked off of me. I have a mixture of rock salt and white wine and vinegar and several other ingredients which I wash my hands and face with."

"Do you hit a man on the face and neck and anywhere you can?" I asked.

"Certainly, any place above the belt that I get a chance," and he smiled.

"Don't you hate to hit a man so?"

"I don't think about it," still smiling.

"When you see that you have hurt him don't you feel sorry?"

"I never feel sorry until the fight is over."

"How do you feel when you get hit very hard?"

The dark, bright eyes glanced at me lazily and the deep, deep voice said with feeling: "I only want a chance to hit back."

"Did you ever see a man killed in the ring?"

"No, I never did, and I only knew of one fellow who died in the ring, and that was Walker, who died at Philadelphia from neglect after the fight was over."

Although I had my breakfast before reaching Mr. Muldoon's cottage I accepted his proposal to break bread with him and his guests. At a nearer view the dining room did not lose any of its prettiness and the daintiness of everything—the artistic surroundings, the noiseless and efficient colored waiter, the open windows on both sides, giving pretty views of green lawns and shady trees; the canary birds swelling their yellow throats occasionally with sweet little thrills, the green parrot climbing up its brass cage and talking about "crackers," the white table linen and beautiful dishes, down to the large bunch of fragrant lilacs and another of beautifully shaped and colored wild flowers, separated by a slipper filled with velvety pansies—was all entirely foreign to any idea I had ever conceived of prize fighters and their surroundings.

Yes, and they were all perfectly at ease and happy. At one end of the table sat Mrs. Muldoon and facing her was Mr. Muldoon. Next to Mrs. Muldoon sat my companion, then came myself, and next Mr. Sullivan. On the opposite side were the assistant trainers, Mr. Barnitt, a well-bred,

scholarly-looking man, and Mr. Cleary, a smooth-faced, mischievous man who doesn't look much past boyhood. Mr. Sullivan's brother, who is anxious to knock out somebody, sat opposite Mr. Sullivan. And the wild flowers which graced the table were gathered by these great, strong men while taking their morning walk through the country.

About a mile from Champion Rest, his town home, is Mr. Muldoon's beautiful farm of seventy acres, which is well stocked with fine cattle. In the rear of Champion Rest are the barn and the training quarters. On the first floor are three stalls, fitted out after the latest improved method, where Mr. Muldoon keeps his favorite horses. Everthing is as clean and pleasant as in a dwelling house.

In the next room, suspended from the ceiling, is a Rugby football, which Mr. Sullivan pounds regularly every day in a manner which foretells hard times for Kilrain's head. The big football with which they play ball daily is also kept here. It is enormous and so heavy that when Mr. Muldoon dropped it into my arms I almost toppled over. Upstairs the floor is covered with a white wrestling pad, where the two champions wrestle every afternoon. In one corner is a collection of dumbbells, from medium weight to the heaviest, and several sizes of Indian clubs. Fastened to one side of the wall is a chest expander, which also comes in for daily use.

Downstairs is Champion Muldoon's den. Everything about it, as about the barn, is of a hardwood finish. There is no plaster nor paper anywhere. In one corner of the den is a glass case, where hang a fur-lined overcoat and several other garments. Along the top of the case is suspended a gold-headed cane. In the center of the room is a writing table, with everything ready for use. Along one side of the hall is a rattan lounge, at the foot of which is spread a yellow fur rug. The floor is neatly carpeted, and several rocking chairs prove that the den is for comfort.

The walls are covered with photographs of well-known people and among them several of Modjeska, with whom Mr. Muldoon at one time traveled. There are also a number of photographs of Mr. Muldoon in positions assumed in posing as Greek statues. On a corner table are albums filled with photographs of prominent athletes, and scrapbooks containing hundreds of notices of Champion Muldoon's athletic conquests. Then there are a number of well-bound standard works and the photographs of Mr. Muldoon's favorite authors—Bryant, Longfellow and, I believe, Shakespeare.

"I don't make any money by this," said Mr. Muldoon, in speaking about turning his home into training quarters, "but I was anxious to see Mr. Sullivan do justice to himself in this coming fight. It was a case of a fallen giant, so I thought to get him away from all bad influences and to get him in good trim. This is the healthiest place in the country and one of the most difficult to reach—two desirable things. On the way here we had a special car, but there were more people in our car than in any other. When we go to New Orleans we will keep our car locked and none but Mr. Sullivan's backers and representatives of the press will be admitted. Mr. Sullivan is the most obedient man I ever saw. He hasn't asked for a drink or a smoke since he came here and takes what I allow him without a murmur. It is a pleasure to train him."

"Does Mr. Sullivan never get angry?" I asked.

"If you would hear him and Mr. Barnitt sometimes, you would think they were going to eat one another," said Mrs. Muldoon.

"When he does get angry he runs over the fields until his good humor returns," said Mr. Barnitt, while Mr. Muldoon said that Mr. Sullivan was as docile as a lamb. They all spoke in praise of his strong will power and his childlike obedience.

"You are the first woman who ever interviewed me," said Mr. Sullivan in the afternoon, "and I have given you more than I ever gave any reporter in my life. They generally manufacture things and credit them to me, although some are mighty good fellows."

"When reporters act all right we will give them all they want," said Mr. Muldoon. "The other day a fresh reporter came here, and he thought because he was going to interview prize fighters he would have to be tough, so he said, 'Where's old Sullivan? That queered him. We wouldn't give him a line."

"Yes, he came up to me first and said, 'Where's old Sullivan?' " said Mr. Sullivan. "And I told him, 'In the barn.' And he soon got put out of there for his toughness."

At suppertime Mr. Cleary had a great story to tell about his Irish bird trap. He had caught one robin, which Mrs. Muldoon released, and another had left his tail behind him. Then Mr. Barnitt and Mr. Sullivan's brother told how they had put some bird feathers in the cage to cheat the bird trapper.

And then the carriage came to take us to the train, and after I bade them all goodby I shook hands with John L. Sullivan and wished him success in the coming fight, and I believe he will have it, too, don't you?

FROM: LAVENGRO

George Borrow spent seven years on *Lavengro,* a now classic autobiographical blend of fact and fiction (and prejudice) that first appeared in 1851. His father, Captain Thomas Borrow of the West Norfolk Militia, had once fought Big Ben Bryan (or Brain), and Borrow himself took boxing lessons from John Thurtell, who ran a roadhouse at Ipswich that was a rendezvous of the Fancy.

GEORGE BORROW

How for everything there is a time and a season, and then how does the glory of a thing pass from it, even like the flower of the grass. This is a truism, but it is one of those which are continually forcing themselves upon the mind. Many years have not passed over my head, yet, during those which I can call to remembrance, how many things have I seen flourish, pass away, and become forgotten, except by myself, who, in spite of all my endeavors, never can forget anything. I have known the time when a pugilistic encounter between two noted champions was almost considered in the light of a national affair; when tens of thousands of individuals, high and low, meditated and brooded upon it, the first thing in the morning and the last at night, until the great event was decided. But the time is past, and many people will say, thank God that it is; all I have to say is, that the French still live on the other side of the water, and are still casting their eyes hitherward—and that in the days of pugilism it was no vain boast to say that one Englishman was a match for two of t'other race; at present it would be a vain boast to say so, for these are not the days of pugilism.

But those to which the course of my narrative has carried me were the days of pugilism; it was then at its height, and consequently near its decline, for corruption had crept into the ring; and how many things, states and sects among the rest, owe their decline to this cause! But what a bold and vigorous aspect pugilism wore at that time! And the great battle was just then coming off: the day had been decided upon, and the spot—a convenient distance from the old town; and to the town were now flocking the bruisers of England, men of tremendous renown. Let no one sneer at the bruisers of England—what were the gladiators of Rome, or the bullfighters of Spain, in its palmiest days, compared to England's bruisers? Pity that ever corruption should have crept in amongst them—but of that I wish not to talk; let us still hope that a spark of the old religion of which they were priests, still lingers in the breasts of Englishmen. There they come, the bruisers, from far London, or from wherever else they might chance to be at the time, to the great rendezvous in the old city; some came one way, some another; some of tiptop reputation came with peers in their chariots, for glory and fame are such fair things that even peers are proud to have those invested therewith by their side; others came in their own gigs, driving their own bits of blood, and I heard one say: "I have driven through at a heat the whole hundred and eleven miles, and only stopped to bait twice." Oh, the blood-horses of old England! but they too have had their day—for everything beneath the sun there is a season and a time. But the greater number come just as they can contrive; on the tops of coaches, for example; and amongst these there are fellows with dark sallow faces, and sharp shining eyes; and it is these that have planted rottenness in the core of pugilism, for they are Jews, and, true to their kind, have only base lucre in view.

It was fierce old Cobbett, I think, who first said that the Jews first introduced bad faith amongst pugilists. He did not always speak the truth, but at any rate he spoke it when he made that observation. Strange people the Jews—endowed with every gift but one, and that the highest, genius divine—genius which can alone make of men demigods, and elevate them above earth and what is earthly and groveling; without which a clever nation—and who more clever than the Jews?—may have Rambams in plenty, but never a Fielding nor a Shakespeare. A Rothschild and a Mendoza, yes—but never a Kean nor a Belcher.

So the bruisers of England are come to be present at the grand fight speedily coming off; there they are met in the precincts of the old town, near the field of the chapel, planted with tender saplings at the restoration of sporting Charles, which are now become venerable elms, as high as many a steeple; there they are met at a fitting rendezvous, where a retired coachman, with one leg, keeps an hotel and a bowling green. I think I now see them upon the bowling green, the men of renown, amidst hundreds of people with no renown at all, who gaze upon them with timid wonder. Fame, after all, is a glorious thing, though it last only for a day. There's Cribb, the champion of England, and perhaps the best man in England; there he is, with his huge massive figure, and face wonderfully like that of a lion. There is Belcher, the younger, not the mighty one, who is gone to his place, but the Teucer Belcher, the most scientific pugilist that ever entered the ring, only wanting strength to be, I won't say what. He appears to walk before me now, as he did that evening, with his white hat, white greatcoat, thin genteel figure, springy step, and keen, determined eyes. Crosses him, what a contrast! grim, savage Shelton, who has a civil word for nobody, and a hard blow for anybody—hard! one blow, given with the proper play of his athletic arm, will unsense a giant. Yonder individual, who strolls about with his hands behind him, supporting his brown coat lappets, undersized, and who looks anything but what he is, is the king of the lightweights, so called—Randall! the terrible Randall, who has Irish blood in his veins; not the better for that, nor the worse; and not far from him is his last antagonist, Ned Turner, who, though beaten by him, still thinks himself as good a man, in which he is, perhaps, right, for it was a near thing; and "a better shentleman," in which he is quite right, for he is a Welshman. But how shall I name them all? They were there by the dozens, and all tremendous in their way. There was Bulldog Hudson, and fearless Scroggins, who beat the conqueror of Sam the Jew.

There was Black Richmond—no, he was not there, but I knew him well; he was the most dangerous of blacks, even with a broken thigh. There was Purcell, who could never conquer till all seemed over with him. There was—what! shall I name thee last? ay, why not? I believe that thou art the last of all that strong family still above the sod, where mayst thou long continue—true species of English stuff, Tom of Bedford—sharp as winter, kind as spring.

Hail to thee, Tom of Bedford, or by whatever name it may please thee to be called, spring or winter. Hail to thee, six-foot Englishman of brown eye, worthy to have carried a six-foot bow at Flodden, where England's yeomen triumphed over Scotland's king, his clans and chivalry. Hail to thee, last of England's bruisers, after all the many victories which thou hast achieved—true English victories, unbought by yellow gold; need I recount them? nay, nay! they are already well known to fame—sufficient to say that Bristol's Bull and Ireland's Champion were vanquished by thee, and one mightier still, gold itself, thou didst overcome; for gold itself strove in vain to deaden the power of thy arm; and thus thou didst proceed till men left off challenging thee, the unvanquishable, the incorruptible. 'Tis a treat to see thee, Tom of Bedford, in thy "public" in Holborn way, whither thou hast retired with thy well-earned bays. 'Tis Friday night, and nine by Holborn clock. There sits the yeoman at the end of his long room, surrounded by his friends: glasses are filled, and a song is the cry, and a song is sung well suited to the place; it finds an echo in every heart—fists are clenched, arms are waved and the portraits of the mighty fighting men of yore, Broughton, and Slack, and Ben, which adorn the walls, appear to smile grim approbation, whilst many a manly voice joins in the bold chorus:

Here's a health to old honest John Bull,
When he's gone we shan't find such another,
And with hearts and with glasses brim full,
We will drink to old England, his mother.

But the fight! with respect to the fight, what shall I say? Little can be said about it—it was soon over. Some said that the brave from town, who was reputed the best of the two, and whose form was a perfect model of athletic beauty, allowed himself, for lucre vile, to be vanquished by the massive champion with the flattened nose. One thing is certain, that the former was suddenly seen to sink to the earth before a blow of by no means extraordinary power. Time, time! was called, but there he lay upon the ground apparently senseless, and from thence he did not lift his head till several seconds after the umpires had declared his adversary victor.

There were shouts—indeed, there's never a lack of shouts to celebrate a victory, however acquired; but there was also much grinding of teeth, especially amongst the fighting men from town. "Tom has sold us," said they, "sold us to the yokels; who would have thought it?" Then there was fresh grinding of teeth, and scowling brows were turned to the heavens. But what is this? is it possible, does the heaven scowl too? Why, only a quarter of an hour ago—but what may not happen in a quarter of an hour? For many weeks the weather has been of the most glorious description; the eventful day, too, had dawned gloriously, and so it had continued till some two hours after noon. The fight was then over and about that time I looked up. What a glorious sky of deep blue, and what a big fierce sun swimming high above in amidst of that blue! Not a cloud—there had not been one for weeks—not a cloud to be seen, only in the far west, just on the horizon, something like the extremity of a black wing. That was only a quarter of an hour ago, and now the whole northern side of the heaven is occupied by a huge black cloud, and the sun is only occasionally seen amidst masses of driving vapor. What a change! But another fight is at hand, and the pugilists are clearing the outer ring. How their huge whips come crashing upon the heads of the yokels! Blood flows—more blood than in the fight. Those blows are given with right good will; those are not sham blows, whether of whip or fist. It is with fist that grim Shelton strikes down the big yokel. He is always dangerous, grim Shelton, but now particularly so, for he has lost ten pounds betted on the brave who sold himself to the yokels. But the outer ring is cleared, and now the second fight commences. It is between two champions of less renown than the others, but is perhaps not the worse on that account. A tall thin boy is fighting in the ring with a man somewhat under the middle size, with a frame of adamant. That's a gallant boy! He's a yokel, but he comes from Brummagem, he does credit to his extraction; but his adversary has a frame of adamant. In what a strange light they fight, but who can wonder, on looking at that frightful cloud usurping now one half of heaven, and at the sun struggling with sulphurous vapor. The face of the boy, which is turned towards me, looks horrible in that light; but he is a brave boy, he strikes his foe on the forehead, and the report of the blow is like the sound of a hammer against a rock. But there is a rush and a roar overhead, a wild commotion, the tempest is beginning to break loose; there's wind and dust, a crash, rain and hail! Is it possible to fight amidst such a commotion? Yes! the fight goes on; again the boy strikes the man full on the brow; but it is of no use striking that man, his frame is of adamant. "Boy, thy strength is beginning to give way, thou art becoming confused." The man now goes to work amidst rain and hail. "Boy, thou wilt not hold out ten minutes longer against rain, hail, and the blows of such an antagonist."

And now the storm was at its height; the black thundercloud had broken into many, which assumed the wildest shapes and the strangest colors, some of them unspeakably glorious; the rain poured in a deluge, and more than one water spout was seen at no great distance. An immense rabble is hurrying in one direction; a multitude of men of all ranks, peers and yokels, prize fighters and Jews, and the last came to plunder, and are now plundering amidst that wild confusion of hail and rain, men and horses, carts and carriages. But all hurry in one direction, through mud and mire. There's a town only three miles distant, which is soon reached and soon filled; it will not contain one third of that mighty rabble. But there's another town farther on—the good old city is farther on, only twelve miles; what's that!

Who'll stay here? Onward to the old town!

SULLIVAN–MITCHELL

Arthur Brisbane covered the John L. Sullivan–Charley Mitchell fight for the *New York Tribune*. He was twenty-four years old, it was his most important assignment up to that time and, in spite of the fact that Sullivan had befriended him, it marked the start of his disdain for professional pugilism. Like the other thirty-nine spectators, the gladiators and their handlers, Brisbane was rain-soaked and chilled. After eluding the gendarmes he had to rush back to Paris where he wrote this story and filed it by cable. While he was composing, however, the Blizzard of 1888 was burying the northeast coast of the United States, and on the day after the fight, March 11, it was impossible to distribute newspapers in New York. It was not, however, until Brisbane had become William Randolph Hearst's strong right hand, or Mary Ann, that he summed up his attitude toward the ring in his classic criticism of two contestants: "A gorilla could lick them both."

ARTHUR BRISBANE

PARIS, MARCH 10, 1888—The Sullivan–Mitchell fight at Chantilly today was an even gloomier and more depressing fiasco than the battle between Kilrain and Smith a few months ago on an island in the Seine. It took scarcely twenty minutes of sharp fighting to show that six years of a brutal, dissipated life had sapped the once astonishing power of the American champion. He could not close with his wiry English antagonist, and the effort to force the fighting cost him all the strength which his fatuous admirers counted on for the critical rounds at the finish.

Then the rain came, drenching the pugilists and turning the turf of the prize ring into a mass of slippery mud. Mitchell held out doggedly in the wet, but Sullivan was seized with chills, and after thirty-nine rounds—most of them dragging and ineffectual—the contest ended in a draw. The American pugilist cried with mortification at his ignominious failure to make good the threats he had been hurling so lavishly at Mitchell. Mitchell's friends were equally chagrined at their champion's inability to fight out a decided victory. The credit, at any rate, remained with the London man and it was agreed on all hands—Sullivan's backers not excepted—that the Boston prize fighter had met with a stinging reverse, as crushing to his hopes of international championship as an actual defeat.

The battle was fought on the country place of Baron Alphonse Rothschild, at Apremont, near the Chantilly station. The backers of both men had spent yesterday wrangling at Amiens over the details of the match, unable to agree on a place to pitch the ring. The lookout dispatched from London early in the week had arranged for a battleground nearer at hand, but at the last moment the spot was found unsuitable. The Sullivan party thereupon charged Mitchell was trying to wriggle out of the fight, and much acrimonious discussion followed. Finally, Mitchell's backers agreed to leave the choice of a ring to the American contingent, and "Johnny" Gideon of *The London Sportsman*, who had once hunted up a battleground for Sayers, with two other of *The Sportsman's* representatives, started out late last night at Sullivan's request, to pitch a ring and make all ready for today's contest.

Gideon and his two assistants traveled as far toward Paris as Creil, and early this morning found a quiet spot on the Rothschild grounds, just behind the Baron's stable, the white villa showing through the trees in the distance. Forty people in all were in the secret and saw the fight, the scouting party sending word back at once, and the warring factions at Amiens arriving after a few hours' delay. The French police were on the alert all along the line, short files being drawn up at the different stations which the pugilists and their friends had to pass. Some officers were hanging around even at Creil, but they made no sign as the English and Americans got out of the railway carriages, and shortly afterward straggled by twos and threes over toward the woods at the back of the Baron's country seat.

The last man was on hand, finally, at 11 a.m. The ring was up and the seconds and backers were dividing into two hostile camps. The ropes were drawn about a little plat of turf under the trees. The ground was good and the weather fair enough, except for a threat of rain to the north.

Some well-known English sporting men were in the groups at each end of the ring. "Jake" Kilrain, the Baltimore pugilist, who fought the draw with "Jem" Smith, and Baldock, of the Pelican Club, were Mitchell's seconds. "Jack" Ashton and Macdonald were seconds for Sullivan. A London stockbroker, named Angle, was referee. "Jack" Bennett was Sullivan's umpire, and "Charlie" Rowell, the long-distance pedestrian, did a similar office for Mitchell. "Pony" Moore, Mitchell's father-in-law, and "Chippy" Norton, the well-known London bookmaker, and holder of the stakes in the coming match, stood in a group to one side with Carew Young, Sir Michael Sandys, Lord Wemyss and a few other aristocrats who figure as patrons of the London ring. On the American side were Dominick McCaffrey, "Charley" Dougherty and a few newspaper men.

Mitchell had been talking a good deal all the morning, and his face was flushed with excitement. He had trained hard, and his face was a trifle thin. Still, his spirits were good, and he said he was confident of holding his own. Sullivan had not pushed himself so hard in training, and his face and muscles showed it. He was as arrogant and contemptuous as ever, and boastfully pulled out a £500 note as he entered the ring and, flourishing it aloft, called for Mitchell to cover it. His manager, Phillips, also opened a roll of bills and offered odds of £1,000 to £300 on the Boston pugilist. No takers could be found, however. The English partisans had all their money up at long odds, and as the battle drew near they looked more and more despondently across at the big, self-confident bully who had never yet met his match in the prize ring.

Sullivan, stripped to the waist, stepped out from his corner of the inclosure about half-past twelve. He looked ruddy and burly enough, but as the crucial rounds soon showed, his staying powers had already vanished under the double bombardment of French champagne and American whiskey. Mitchell followed him into the ring four minutes later. The two men were old antagonists and personal enemies, and they glared at each other fiercely. Mitchell made the first movement toward

shaking hands, the two men touched palms weakly, the referee called time, and the first round in the fight began. The time taken by the watchers was 12:30 p.m.

The first round opened savagely, Sullivan, as usual, forcing the fighting and making one or two powerful rushes. The American landed his first blow, a heavy left-handed, just to the left of Mitchell's jaw. The Londoner was dazed, but soon got in a light return on Sullivan's chest. Then he sparred cautiously about the ring, warding off successfully two or three of his pursuer's leads. Finally Sullivan got angry and rushed in close. His left hand fell in short, Mitchell dodging, but his big right fist crashed against the unlucky Englishman's head, and the wiry Londoner fell in a heap over toward the ropes in his corner.

The American contingent was jubilant, and odds ran up as high as £1,000 to £100 on the big Bostonian. Sullivan was a trifle winded, but it looked as if the Briton could not stand up before many more rushes like that just ended.

After half a minute or so Mitchell was up again, sponged off and in the ring. Sullivan soon followed. This time Mitchell fought shy, retreating from one part of the ring to the other. Sullivan's fierce rush was too much for him, however, and the two were closed. The first blow caught the Londoner on the chest, and Mitchell staggered as if he had been hit by a pile driver. He made a feeble effort to parry, and then to run away, but another blow on the head from Sullivan's deadly right hand laid him flat on the turf near the middle of the ring. His seconds lifted him over to the corner, where a little sponging brought him to in a minute.

The pace was too fast for the Englishman, but it was also beginning to tell on the greatest of short-distance "sluggers." Sullivan was red in the face, and the cool defensive strategy of his antagonist ruffled the big bully's temper. Still everything looked rose-hued to the little party at his back, which was now frantically waving the Stars and Stripes and the green flag of Ireland in anticipatory triumph. "Pony" Moore had a scowl on his face, and the Union Jack and the Royal ensign over Mitchell's quarters drooped disconsolably in the heavy air that threatened a coming storm.

Mitchell had profited by his experience so far, and from the beginning of the third round fought a waiting battle. He ran all over the ring, Sullivan bounding after him and getting in an occasional ineffective blow. The American champion at last made a desperate rush, broke down the Englishman's defenses and sent him sprawling to the ground with a right-hand blow in the face. Sullivan seemed to have hurt his hand a little in this last rush, and Mitchell, though badly battered, was far from being "knocked out." Sullivan was pushing himself hard, and seemed to feel the strain.

In the fourth round Mitchell squirmed and dodged for several minutes before Sullivan could close with him. When he did reach the Englishman his blows fell lightly, and though Mitchell went down in the last rush, he fell more in the tussle than under any one blow. In the fifth and sixth rounds he took to the tactics that Smith had found so successful in his fight with Kilrain. Sullivan charged again and again, but every time the Londoner got away. Once when he was cornered he dropped to the ground on one hand and one knee—a foul by the London ring rules. Sullivan had come near striking him as he dropped, and the referee cautioned both men about making or causing a foul stroke.

In the next three rounds Sullivan kept up his ineffectual chase after the fleet-footed Englishman. Mitchell got off without any damage to speak of, and even planted his fist two or three times on Sullivan's face.

In the tenth round rain began to fall, and the shower soon turned into a steady pour. Sullivan was chilled to the bone and began to shake with ague. He kept pluckily on, however, pounding through the mud after his opponent, falling shorter and shorter on each rush. His backers kept up their courage, but looked for nothing better than a draw! Mitchell's backers hoped now that their man might outlast the American and win the championship and the £500.

The rounds from the tenth to the thirty-second dragged stupidly. Sullivan, who was beginning to shiver all over, could do nothing. Neither could Mitchell, though he tried with all his might. The terrible punishment of the first four rounds had nearly crippled him. The thirty-second round lasted twenty-seven minutes. The thirty-fifth round was fought through fifteen minutes. Both men were weak and could no longer hit out from the shoulder.

After half an hour's fighting in the last round, Baldock, Mitchell's second, broke into the ring and cried out that the men had had enough. "Make it a draw," he urged. The fight had now lasted three hours and ten minutes. The principals readily agreed to stop, and shook hands, though the champion was soon after looking with rage and chagrin, and his backers folded up their flags, the most heartsore set of sportsmen that has ever traveled 3,000 miles to see a great international fight.

Mitchell was badly trussed. There was a big lump on his jaw, his left eye was bunged up, and his body was a good deal battered. Sullivan was sick and worn out, but not much hurt. Both parties started for this city on the evening train.

The stakes, £500 a side, will be doubled, of course. But it looks as if Sullivan's career was nearly over.

His fight today will be a sad blow, at least, to his "hippodroming" box-office receipts.

THE FIRST BOXING RULES

Jack Broughton (1704–1789) was the third recognized heavyweight champion of the prize ring and the first great ring scientist. He stood five feet, ten and a half inches, weighed 196 pounds and, a one-time yeoman of the guard of George II, was intelligent and educated. In 1742, while still champion, he erected an amphitheater at Tottenham Court Road in London, and he is called the Father of Boxing because, the following year, he drew up and published the first boxing rules.

JACK BROUGHTON

For the better regulation of the Amphitheater approved of by the gentleman, and agreed to by the Pugilists:

I. That a square of a yard be chalked in the middle of the stage; and every fresh set-to after a fall, or being parted from the rails, each second is to bring his man to the side of the square, and place him opposite to the other, and till they are fairly set to at the lines, it shall not be lawful for one to strike the other.

2. That, in order to prevent any disputes, the time a man lies after a fall, if the second does not bring his man to the side of the square within the space of half a minute, he shall be deemed a beaten man.

3. That in every main battle, no person whatever shall be upon the stage except the principals and their seconds; the same rule to be observed in by-battles, except that in the latter, Mr. Broughton is allowed to be upon the stage to keep decorum, and to assist gentlemen in getting to their places, provided always he does not interfere in the battle; and whoever pretends to infringe these rules to be turned immediately out of the house. Everybody is to quit the stage as soon as the champions are stripped, before set-to.

4. That no champion be deemed beaten unless he fails coming up to the line, in the limited time; or, that his own second declares him beaten. No second is to be allowed to ask his man's adversary any questions, or advise him to give out.

5. That in by-battles, the winning man to have two-thirds of the money given, shall be publicly divided upon the stage notwithstanding any private agreements to the contrary.

6. That to prevent disputes in every main battle, the principals shall, on coming on the stage, choose from among the gentlemen present, two umpires, who shall absolutely decide all disputes that may arise about the battle; and if the two umpires cannot agree, the said umpires to choose a third, who is to determine it.

7. That no person is to hit his adversary when he is down, or seize him by the hair, the breeches, or any part below the waist; a man on his knees to be reckoned down.

THE ORTHODOX CHAMPION

The guardians of our literature have refused to recognize Heywood Broun as a great essayist because he had one obvious weakness—he wrote for newspapers.

In this column Broun presented his interpretation of Benny Leonard's successful defense of his lightweight title against Rocky Kansas on February 10, 1922. The fight went fifteen rounds, but later Patsy Haley, the veteran fighter and referee, announced that never had he seen a short right hand as perfectly executed as that with which Leonard dropped Kansas in the eleventh round.

HEYWOOD BROUN

The entire orthodox world owes a debt to Benny Leonard. In all the other arts, philosophies, religions and whatnots conservatism seems to be crumbling before the attacks of the radicals. A stylist may generally be identified today by his bloody nose. Even in Leonard's profession of pugilism the correct method has often been discredited of late.

It may be remembered that George Bernard Shaw announced before "the battle of the century" that Carpentier ought to be a fifty-to-one favorite in the betting. It was the technique of the Frenchman which blinded Shaw to the truth. Every man in the world must be in some respect a stand-patter. The scope of heresy in Shaw stops short of the prize ring. His radicalism is not sufficiently far-reaching to crawl through the ropes. When Carpentier knocked out Beckett with one perfectly delivered punch he also jarred Shaw. He knocked him loose from some of his cynical contempt for the conventions. Mr. Shaw might continue to be in revolt against the wellmade play, but he surrendered his heart wholly to the properly executed punch.

But Carpentier, the stylist, fell before Dempsey, the mauler, in spite of the support of the intellectuals. It seemed once again that all the rules were wrong. Benny Leonard remains the white hope of the orthodox. In lightweight circles, at any rate, old-fashioned proprieties are still effective. No performer in any art has ever been more correct, than Leonard. He follows closely all the best traditions of the past. His left-hand jab could stand without revision in any textbook. The manner in which he feints, ducks, sidesteps and hooks is unimpeachable. The crouch contributed by some of the modernists is not in the repertoire of Leonard. He stands up straight like a gentleman and a champion and is always ready to hit with either hand.

His fight with Rocky Kansas at Madison Square Garden was advertised as being for the lightweight championship of the world. As a matter of fact much more than that was at stake. Spiritually, Saint-Saëns, Brander Matthews, Henry Arthur Jones, Kenyon Cox, and Henry Cabot Lodge were in Benny Leonard's corner. His defeat would, by implication, have given support to dissonance, dadaism, creative evolution and bolshevism. Rocky Kansas does nothing according to rule. His fighting style is as formless as the prose of Gertrude Stein. One finds a delightfully impromptu quality in Rocky's boxing. Most of the blows which he tries are experimental. There is no particular target. Like the young poet who shot an arrow into the air, Rocky Kansas tosses off a right-hand swing every once and so often and hopes that it will land on somebody's jaw.

But with the opening gong Rocky Kansas tore into Leonard. He was gauche and inaccurate but terribly persistent. The champion jabbed him repeatedly with a straight left which has always been considered the proper thing to do under the circumstances. Somehow or other it did not work. Leonard might as well have been trying to stand off a rhinoceros with a feather duster. Kansas kept crowding him. In the first clinch Benny's hair was rumpled and a moment later his nose began to bleed. The incident was a shock to us. It gave us pause and inspired a sneaking suspicion that perhaps there was something the matter with Tennyson after all. Here were two young men in the ring and one was quite correct in everything he did and the other was all wrong. And the wrong one was winning. All the enthusiastic Rocky Kansas partisans in the gallery began to split infinitives to show their contempt for Benny Leonard and all other stylists. Macaulay turned over twice in his grave when Kansas began to lead with his right hand.

But traditions are not to be despised. Form may be just as tough in fiber as rebellion. Not all the steadfastness of the world belongs to heretics.

Even though his hair was mussed and his nose bleeding, Benny continued faithful to the established order. At last his chance came. The young child of nature who was challenging for the championship dropped his guard and Leonard hooked a powerful and entirely orthodox blow to the conventional point of the jaw. Down went Rocky Kansas. His past life flashed before him during the nine seconds in which he remained on the floor and he wished that he had been more faithful as a child in heeding the advice of his boxing teacher. After all, the old masters did know something. There is still a kick in style, and tradition carries a nasty wallop.

[FACT]

THE PORTABLE A.C.

Before this country's leading promoters formed their vicious alliance with the razor-blade tycoons and beer barons, the small fight club was the foundation of boxing. The following tribute by the veteran Chicago sports columnist is from his book *Win, Lose, or Draw* and celebrates a truly talented small-club promoter.

WARREN BROWN

When I took up residence in Chicago, late in 1923, the questionable sport of prize fighting was being conducted on a scale peculiar to that area. It was not too hard for me to adjust myself to the surroundings. After all, I had served my time years before, keeping up with the oddities of the four-round game as practiced in California before the game became legalized there.

Chicago's loosely run game would have to move very dizzily to surpass my beloved four-rounders. They were served in San Francisco and Oakland on a regular weekly show basis. Real headliners by any boxing standards would participate occasionally, as was the case when Willie

Ritchie, the former lightweight champion, essaying a comeback, was cast as an opponent for Benny Leonard, then the champion of all the world, and so skilled there was a constant argument whether he or Joe Gans had been the greatest of all the lightweights in history.

Benny was not geared for the four-round game. Ritchie, having emerged from it, was able to fit his comeback to its requirements. One night, in the Civic Auditorium, Leonard was somewhat embarrassed when Ritchie hit him a harder punch on the nose than anyone had ever done before. It surprised Benny, but it did not surprise me.

In the four-round game I had learned to expect

almost anything. That schooling prepared me for Chicago's boxing, which was of the bootleg variety and presented under something called an injunction, in the days before the solons decided to legalize it.

Nowhere else in the country have I ever witnessed more remarkable exploits of the prize ring than those that Chicagoans patronized when James C. Mullen was promoter and matchmaker, and his club was known to the trade as the Portable A.C.

The reason for that name was valid. Sometimes the shows took place at Aurora. Sometimes they took place at East Chicago. At irregular intervals Mullen would attempt to put over a fast one and come right into a Chicago arena. Usually there were difficulties that only the most resourceful promoter could surmount.

Mullen, for all his promotional eccentricities, was a splendid matchmaker. He might have prospered greatly and found himself ranked with Tex Rickard were it not for one strange turn of his nature. He fancied his ability to find promising fighters and build them into great drawing cards. This he did many times. Then he could hardly wait until he was able to find someone to knock his star crowd-gatherer over. Most promoters other than Mullen have been very careful to protect their drawing cards in and out of all matchmaking clinches.

Mullen was not able to produce any such memorable attractions as Ah Wing, Tanglefoot McGovern, and Cockey O'Brien of my younger days in San Francisco, but with what he had, Mullen did all right. He was a law unto himself. Perhaps that is why he was able to stage some notable events upon which any legalized commission would have frowned quickly.

There were in Chicago's Loop a couple of characters belonging to the set I was pleased to term the Rover Boys of Randolph Street. Each had a leg disability causing him to limp. They became involved in an argument one evening in Henrici's Restaurant, and were about to start swinging when Mullen suggested that they hold their fire. He could use them. He did, too, and after sufficient exploitation the pair appeared in the ring at Aurora as an added attraction to one of Mullen's shows. On that night Randolph Street was as quiet as the main street in Fork-in-the-Road, Utah. Everybody was at Aurora.

Playing baseball (it was alleged) for the White Sox was a character out of Texas, Art Shires, who styled himself "The Great." He thought well of himself as a fighter. First thing he knew he was given a match on one of Mullen's East Chicago cards. When his opponent went out on schedule, Shires became a great attraction.

His major showing in the ring was against George Trafton. Trafton had been a famous Notre Dame center and was later even more famous as a player with the Chicago Bears. The fight between these two created as much excitement among Mullen's clientele as any event he ever staged. It went to East Chicago. It was an awful fight to behold, but it did provoke an incident that indicated the occupational hazards of broadcasting from the ringside.

The broadcaster, Pat Flanagan, a famous figure on Chicago's air lanes, had established his reputation on baseball and football. He was taking this epoch-making fight in stride and showering the air with hysterical words and phrases as Shires and Trafton lumbered about the ring, each wondering what to do next, or whether to skip the whole thing.

Right behind the broadcaster sat one of Trafton's teammates on the Bears. He had come to the show properly fortified with emotional outpourings. In the very thick of the furious battle in the ring, he detected something the broadcaster said that he thought reflected on the fighting character of his pal Trafton. Being a man of action, he reached over and popped the broadcaster right on the nose. This caused a sudden flow of expression that set new heights for airways ring reporting. In the confusion that followed, the fight came to an end, with the sneak-punch victimized broadcaster utterly unable to let his clients know who had won.

Not that this was unusual for radio broadcasting in the twenties. I once sat directly behind Graham McNamee while he was describing the Gene Tunney-Tom Heeney fight. That contest, which marked Tunney's farewell, came to an end under somewhat unusual circumstances.

The champion had steadily cut Heeney down to size, and at the very end of a round deposited the Australian on the floor. Punches were flying from Tunney's fists so fast that McNamee was several wallops behind in his description.

I don't know whether Graham noticed that Heeney was on the floor, or that his seconds had rushed across the ring to carry him to his corner as the bell rang. I know he paid no attention to their frantic efforts to get him up and out for the next round.

For Graham, the instant the bell sounded, plunged into a dramatic reading of the commercial, which was due then in behalf of the tire company that had sponsored the broadcast.

The commercial was timed for a minute's reading. Graham finished just on the dot as the bell for the next round rang. It rang for everybody but Heeney, who couldn't hear it. The fight was over. That much McNamee gathered from a quick survey, but what had caused the sudden ending seemed as dark a mystery to him as it must have been to his listeners.

Under any other circumstances he might have explained, after a quick brushing up on the facts. But it was customary in those days to get at that windup commercial as soon as the fight ended. That's what Graham did, and presently he was on his way out of the arena. He was content to let his clients find out what they wanted to know by reading the papers. Or perhaps he suspected that they had been just as bored with Heeney as he was.

The listening audience of the broadcast of the Shires-Trafton fight was hardly comparable to that of the Tunney-Heeney, but soon after that Mullen came up with another fight project that promised to be national in its scope.

Shires, the White Sox "fighting" first baseman, had been getting so much attention that friends of the Cubs, hated rivals of the White Sox, began to resent it. They looked around for a Cub who might have ring aspirations. In no time at all they found one. At least, Mullen found one for them. One day he announced that "Hack" Wilson, the home-run hitter of the Cubs, would be the next opponent for Shires. That was all the notice this event needed. From then on Mullen had to worry about finding an arena large enough to seat the crowd that wanted in on this battle.

The papers played it up with might and main. There is no telling what might have happened if the event had ever gone through. Even if it did not revolutionize boxing, as it threatened to do, it offered numerous other possibilities. So many, in fact, that Kenesaw M. Landis summoned Wilson and Shires into his presence. He told them how much he appreciated their willingness to prove their athletic versatility, but that he would be sore as hell if he ever heard another word from either of

them about fighting each other in a public prize ring as long as they were identified with baseball.

In my private list of the great fights that never took place the Shires-Wilson affair is near the top. It belongs on the same card with the main event of Jack Dempsey in his prime versus Joe Louis in his.

Right behind them is the one that Mullen arranged at East Chicago, outdoors, involving Mickey Walker and Billy Wells, an English warrior who was being handled in this country by Charley Harvey. Harvey was one of the last of the honorable old-line managers and affected a curling, very black mustache.

Walker was a great drawing card, and Wells was a likely enough opponent, so that the arena was sold out many days in advance of the date of the fight. On the day it was scheduled, rain fell, and Mullen ordered a postponement.

Next day he was called by Harvey, who wanted to know if the promoter had any idea where Wells was. Mullen had not. Nor did anyone else. The English fighter simply disappeared. It was several months afterward before he was heard from again. By that time he had crossed the Atlantic. But never a word of why he had walked out on an engagement that figured to return him more money than any in which he participated before or since.

Walker was a performer in several of Mullen's extravaganzas after boxing had become legalized in Illinois. In one of them he was given the decision by referee Benny Yanger over Tiger Flowers, a verdict that made Mickey world's champion. This distinction he held with honor for a long time thereafter.

In its own quiet way, this bout created as much furor as the "long count" episode in Tunney's fight with Dempsey at Soldier Field. There was so much adverse comment over the decision, Yanger was hailed before the Commission to explain.

He told an interesting story. He quoted the rules under which boxing was conducted in Illinois, particularly that part treating of "flicking or hitting with an open glove," a practice at which Flowers was adept. The rule, Yanger went on to say, stated that it was at the discretion of the referee to disqualify the offender *or* award the decision to his opponent.

"With all those people there, I thought there might be trouble if I disqualified Flowers," Yanger explained. So he took the other alternative, and gave the decision to Walker at the end of the fight.

"Oh," said the august Commission, in effect. Which was all right, except for the fact that the law did *not* offer any alternative. What it said was that the referee at his discretion could disqualify the offender *and* award the decision to his opponent. In other words, the referee, if he were to call into effect that rule, had to do so as soon as he was convinced there was an offense. He was not justified in waiting until the fight was over. But the Commission didn't read the rules too carefully, either.

Well, we had situations like that when Chicago's boxing was very young.

Yet another of Walker's Chicago appearances under Mullen's direction was in a bout with Mike McTigue. The latter was the light-heavyweight whom the incredible Battling Siki, the Singular Senegalese, had the temerity to fight in Dublin on St. Patrick's Day, with the world's championship at stake.

McTigue was something much less than a champion on the night he met Walker. Perhaps Mullen realized that, for in his advertising material he announced that every fight on the card would end in a knockout. It did, too, with Walker draping the unconscious McTigue across the ropes with a punch or two. All of Mullen's clients were back to their normal haunts before ten o'clock from a complete fight show that did not begin until eight-thirty. There should be more of those.

The advent of legalized boxing in Illinois found Mullen putting on the first show, a lightweight contest between Sammy Mandell and Rocky Kansas. Kansas was the lightweight champion going in, but Mandell, a clever sort, outspeeded him and emerged with the title. It was a popular decision.

No other two citizens of Illinois did more to make possible legalized boxing than Ed Hughes, then a member of the Senate, and Michael Igoe, then of the House. They were both regular patrons of the fine arts on display at the Portable A.C.

Once boxing was legalized, it was interesting to observe the demands of the solons for complimentary tickets as their just due for having fostered the sport. But it isn't as interesting as a notation in the memory book of Sol Katz, who was Mullen's head box-office man in the Portable A.C. days and who followed him into the presentation of Illinois' first legalized contest.

His first two purchasers of tickets were Hughes and Igoe, who had put the bill across. Neither had ever acquired the habit of mooching complimentary tickets. Neither cared to start, now that boxing—it was piously hoped—was going on a scale in Illinois that might rival New York.

FROM: TALE OF JAMES CARABINE

There have been a few trainers like Brian Oswald Donn Byrne's Shadrach Kennedy. In 1925, when Charley Phil Rosenberg signed to fight for the bantamweight title, he weighed 155 pounds. Ray Arcel worked him down to 118. "He hated me," Arcel said. "He used to scream at me: 'You copper!' But he made the weight and went fifteen tough rounds with Eddie Cannonball Martin and won the championship of the world."

DONN BYRNE

If you were to meet him on the roads about Destiny Bay, or in Dublin, whither he goes as body servant sometimes to my Aunt Jenepher, with his black clothes, with his erect carriage, with his suspicion of side whiskers, you might take Carabine for a minister of some faith dissenting from the Church of Ireland, by law established. There is something so honest, so clear about his gray eyes. Indeed, you might avoid him, fearing he would pluck you by the sleeve and ask you that most intimate and embarrassing of all questions: Have you found Salvation?

Of course, if you notice his broken nose, his heavy hands, you might say: This man has been a prize fighter in his youth, but there—a Christian missionary might receive these stigmata telling the gentle tale of Bethlehem and Calvary to some emphatic, lusty pagan. We who know the race course and the ring, recognize his craft from the hunched left shoulder, the eye that moves while the head does not. We who know his name recognize him as James Carabine, former champion, the last of the giants of the London prize ring, the conqueror of Simon Kennedy, and Diamond, the Black Man; McCoy, the Glasgow Plasterer, and that most terrible of fighters who was called the Bristol Lamb.

I know the modern glovemongers—they are rather a sordid lot. They are not the thugs and monsters the Society of Friends would have us believe—indeed, one wishes often they were, watching a fumbling match of men stalling through a ten-round bout. Nor are they the romantics certain journalists would have us think. Good journeymen athletes with a knack of their hands. . . . The prize ring bred better, braver men, the men of the bare knuckles and the finish fights—Tom Cribb, who fought and conquered the Negro Molyneux; Tom Sayers, who drew with Heenan, the Benicia Boy, in a battle thought the most terrific of the ring; that Gully, whom the Game Chicken conquered, whose aspiration it was in early life to be champion of England, owner of the Derby winner, and member of Parliament, and who achieved all three; Sir Daniel Donelly, our great Irish Champion, who was knighted by the Prince Regent after his defeat of the gigantic Captain Cooper at the Curragh of Kildare; Bendigo, who gave his name to a great race horse, and to an Australian city; that Gentleman Jackson, winner over Mendoza, who was friend to Byron, and to our own overrated and greatly loved Tom Moore; the Tipton Slasher, that terrific hitter, who succumbed to great Sayers. Great men these, lion-hearted, proud of their craft—and the last of these was Carabine.

James Carabine is somewhat over sixty years of age. His tale of years he doesn't know exactly, for he can neither read nor write. When he wants to date a matter, he will say it occurred in the spring of the year of So-and-so's Derby, and such a horse's Grand National, or the year that Sullivan beat Paddy Ryan for the championship of America. He has a prodigious memory, and a gift for selecting the outstanding features of comparatives such as we literates, with our science of filing by numbers, can hardly conceive. There is none who knows the mood of the sea better than Carabine, or the approaching changes of the weather. He knows the name of each bird and flower and small animal in our land, and such strength of mind has Nature given him, such innate kindliness, such broad fearless wisdom, that I have come to think very little of the teaching of books....

"...I came into New York with a cloud in my heart, Mister Kerry," said Carabine, "and what I saw there didn't lift it any. From all I had heard tell of New York, it was a golden city, rich as Jerusalem, and the Irish reigned there. At every corner I expected to see the Irish dancing and fiddling, and jingling the money in their pockets the people had given them just for being Irish, and maybe doing an hour's work now and then, just for the looks of the thing. It is a great city, young and strong, and like everything that is young and strong, cruel, and cruelest of all upon the Irish. The hunger of Famine Days is nothing to the hunger of the unlucky Irish...."

"The place where you meet the Irish in America, Mister Kerry," said James Carabine, "is in public drinking houses, but they're not like our public drinking houses at all. At home here, when the sun goes down, you can go into a place that is quiet and orderly, order your pot of beer, smoke your pipe, and talk about the weather and the crops, and play a game of five hundred up. But over there you've got to stand against a bar and drink quick and drink often, or they don't want your custom at all. In the latter end I got very tired of it, Mister Kerry, for I'm not by temperament a drinking man. It was drink, drink, drink, and never a word of getting a fight for me. So that I decided I'd drop the whole thing and get back to Ulster. The old ring had nearly gone in America; the glove men, the tip-and-run fellows were coming along and talking about scientific fighting. People are always for listening to a new thing. So I said: 'I'll go back to the old country where the old things are in honor.'..."

"All this time I was trying in New York to get a fight according to prize ring rules. The gloves are grand for exercise, but they're not the real measure of a fighting man. Besides, with the gloves there's too much trickery. You can hit harder with the gloves than your bare hands, for there's protection for the hands in gloves. In the prize ring, you've got to think more of your wrestling than hitting. The hitting is more to prevent a man getting into position for a back heel or a cross-buttock or a flying mare. I don't like these three-minute rounds where a crooked timekeeper can shorten or lengthen the

round, Mister Kerry, with his watch in his hand. And these draws, and winning on points—they aren't good. In my day you went into the ring and you came out either beaten or conqueror. And there was no talk about fouling. And the minute's rest between rounds gave an unlucky fellow a chance to come to. A man may be the better man, and have no luck, and that's not a right thing, Mister Kerry.

"I came at a time, Mister Kerry, when the prize ring was setting in glory. The men weren't maybe the equals of Tom Figg, or Sayers, or the Negro Molyneux, though it's hard to say. But they fought like champions. The time when Gentleman Jackson won from Mendoza by holding his hair and hitting him with the other hand, and when a man got his opponent's head in chancery and hammered his face, that time was gone. We fought each other's strength, not infirmities. When I was fighting Simon Kennedy, and slipped on a patch of wet grass, and threw out my hand for the ropes, Simon could have hit me, but he stepped back. And when I twisted my right wrist in a fall against Tom Hill of Bradford, and couldn't use my right hand for hitting, Tom would only use his left, too. And they weren't all just bruisers, Mister Kerry; Simon Kennedy was a schoolmaster, and Deaf Wallace was a maker of fine jewelry, and Dan Lane afterward became a great preacher in Sydney.

"They promised me a fight in New York as soon as they could get a man. They said it would be hard on account of it being against the law, but: 'We'll find a man for you,' they said....

"At last Mills brought this fellow along he was fixing to fight me. 'Meet Blanco Johnson,' he said, 'the champion of Canada.' And there before me was a fellow you would and you wouldn't have taken for a fighter. He was tall and broad in the shoulder, Mister Kerry, but very light below for a prize-ring man. You would think that the very weight of his shoulders would be too heavy for his legs and that he would have little power when it came to wrestling. I'd have great respect for that fellow in a glove fight, but in the London ring I wasn't worried at all. He had beautiful long muscles, and a small head that would be hard to get the range of, and when he walked he had the nice springy step of a fighter. But there's the funny thing, Mister Kerry, he was the handsomest fellow I ever laid my eyes on. He was fair and he had a face that was symmetrical in each degree, but for one. His hair was wavy like a woman's. The only thing wrong about him, Mister Kerry, was that his eyes were too small and a wee bit too close together. But dress that fellow up, and put him on at a smoking concert, and you'd never take him for a fighter. 'Beauty' Johnson was his nickname, and there was never a truer one.

"Well, the match was made, Mister Kerry, for a purse of two thousand five hundred dollars, which was great money, and three hundred pounds a side, London Prize Rules, at a place to be decided later, for this was to put the police off. We signed our names to the articles, I making my mark, and he writing like a schoolmaster. He was a nonpareil.

"Well, Mister Kerry, you'd think I'd done this fellow the honor of the world in fighting him. It was 'Mr. Carabine' here and 'Mr. Carabine' there, and 'What is your opinion of this, Mr. Carabine?' . . .

"The fight was called in New Jersey, across the river from New York, in a clearing in the woods. It was six o'clock of a June morning, and the birds were singing to raise your heart. I never saw a bonnier day. The ring was pitched on fine springy turf and there was a big crowd from New York, Tammany men, gamblers, fellows of society who liked to be known as sportsmen, a big crowd of Irish fellows. . . . The Johnson and I met in the middle of the ring and the referee talked, and Mister Kerry, I've never seen a man in better shape. He shone. He was fit to fight for the world. And his legs that I thought were weak were only light, like a deer's. There was no 'Mr. Carabine' now. He only was curt and ugly. And when I held out my hand he looked at it.

" 'What's that for?' he said.

" 'To shake hands,' I said.

" 'To hell with that!' said he, and walked to his corner.

"I felt hurt at that, Mister Kerry. The men I had fought with before hadn't been like that. It was: May the best man win! I tell you there was a queer feel in the air that morning, for all the birds were singing.

"Time was called and we met, Mister Kerry. And he began sparring like a glove lightweight instead of a prize-ring man. One instant he was in front, in the next breaking ground to the right or left, dancing in and out like a ballet master. I had a trick, as most boxers have tricks, of feinting with the left before leading it, and someone must have told this fellow of it, for as my shoulder moved he

let fly with his left hand, and Mister Kerry, it was like a slingshot or a golf ball going through the air. He got me fair. And before I could answer he was away dancing. Four times he did it in a row. Once I crowded him in a corner, and began to hit, but he rolled to the punch, and when the crowd began to roar, thinking I was doing for him, I wasn't hurting him at all. And when he got out of the corner he began with the left again. He had great tricks, this fellow. When it looked as if I'd corner him, he'd bend like an acrobat and catch me by the ankles. There was nothing in the rules against or for that. So I'd look down at him and wonder what I'd do. And then he'd straighten up and let go with the right. When I'd set myself, as a heavy man will, to let go with a knockdown punch, he'd drop his hands and walk away laughing, so that I felt like a fool. And then I'd do what a fool will do, rush him furiously to be a mark for his left hand. When I'd get close to throw him, he'd go limp and loose and fall with me of his own accord. Take his minute's rest and come up grinning.

"There's no use telling you about that fight, Mister Kerry; there was only one man in it and that wasn't me. First I could hear the crowd roar for me and then be silent, and then begin to roar for the other man. That is always cruel hearing, Mister Kerry. In the fourth round I couldn't see, so that Nick had to open my eyes with a knife to give me a glimpse of the fellow at all. This man fought a great heady fight. He never let up on my eyes, so that in a little while I didn't know that it was day, only for the singing of the birds. They had to lead me to my corner, and once I hung on by hands to the rope to avoid going down. I had a hope he'd close, so that I could take the strength out of him wrestling, but he was too clever.

"And then in my corner I heard the towel go through the air.

" 'Are you throwing up, Nick?' I asked.

" 'I'm sorry, Shamus,' said he, 'but I can't see a fellow countryman killed.'

"So that was the end of that fight.

"There is no person in the world so friendless as the conquered fighting man. He is like a star that shot across the sky and is lost. The people who were cheering him a month before turn and say: 'Sure, he was no damned good!' The cheering and the handshaking are all for the other fellow, while you are in your corner by yourself, and your trainer and your seconds, even they feel uncomfortable, and wish they were with the other man. The crowd that has been waiting for you before the fight now passes you by as if you were a convict. There is no person in the crowd that doesn't feel he is a better man than you.

"I went across to New York and to a Turkish bath, to steam the sores out of myself, and to get my face patched up, and my eyes painted. . . .

"Well, now, Mister Kerry, I'll tell you a difficult thing. I took to the drink. . . . I was there one night drinking, and a voice came through the place that made me drop the glass from my hands and turn cold. . . . I looked up and it was true. There was your Uncle Valentine before me. . . .

" 'This fellow calling himself champion of Ireland, it's hard,' said he.

" 'It is, Mister Valentine,' I agreed. 'None feels it more than I?'

" 'Did he beat you fair?' asked your Uncle Valentine.

" 'He did,' said I. 'He was too quick for me. His left hand was like a rocket in my face.'

" 'Would you take him on again?' said your Uncle Valentine.

" 'I would,' said I. 'But I don't know if it would be any different. He's too clever for me, and besides, the heart is out of me.'

" 'There was never an attack yet that there wasn't a defense for,' said your Uncle Valentine. 'As to the heart being out of you, you've no right to say that. If it were your own small fight, for a purse of money or a woman, then you could feel any way you liked about it, but this is to keep it from being said that the Irish Belt passed to a cheap bully from overseas.'

" 'Mister Valentine,' I told him, 'get me that match and I'll fight till I die.'

" 'That's better,' said your Uncle Valentine. . . .

"So I said: 'Mister Valentine, when do I start training?'

" 'Come down to Castle Gardens tomorrow,' he said, 'and meet your trainer. He'll tell you.' But who the trainer was I couldn't get out of him.

"I went down with him, and off the Irish boat there comes an old fellow in a beaver hat, and with a gray shawl around his shoulder, and, Living God! Mister Kerry, it would raise the hair on your scalp, for who was it but Shadrach Kennedy, the Irish fighter who had won the championship of Europe at the age of twenty in the camp of Waterloo. I'd often heard of him, and how he was greater than

Daniel Donelly himself. He had killed Gaffer Casey at the Curragh of Kildare, and after that had never fought, but the country people said he had sold his soul to the devil for knowledge of boxing. And looking into his eye you might believe that thing. His body was a man's of near ninety, but his eye was a man's of twenty-five. There was no stroke in the game unknown to him.

" 'So you're the young man that lost the championship of Ireland, and have taken me from my deathbed.'

" 'I'm sorry, Mister Kennedy,' said I.

" 'You'll be sorrier before I'm through with you,' he promised, and he looked me over. 'You've got a fighter's frame. Was it cowardice?' he sneered.

" 'He was too quick for me, Mister Kennedy.'

" 'Before I'm through with you, you'll beat a hare in full Right.' . . .

"We had our camp near Stamford in the state of Connecticut which is a seaport town, but not on the sea, on a sort of lake as it were, Mister Kerry, a great healthy place. Your Uncle Valentine chose the boxers and wrestlers. There was a big Pole who couldn't speak English but was a nice fellow, and an American fellow from the Far West, and the boxers were Paddy Moynihan, the Irish-American boxer, and John Rhys, and Cornstalk Bill Ryan, who was looking for a fight. They were the best to be found and if there were better, I'd have had them. They'd all seen men trained in their day, but they themselves had never seen the like of the cruelty of Shadrach Kennedy. Mister Kerry, if I were a poor sinner and he a devil, he couldn't have been worse. He'd sit there with his shawl over his shoulders and his snuffbox in his hand and while I boxed and wrestled, his tongue would cut me like a whip. He would drive out, with me behind the buggy, as they called it, and make me run until I'd nearly drop. It was no trotting. It was swing your legs. And he'd get the Pole to pitch a football at my stomach and ribs until I could have taken the kick of a mule there. Then he had another trick, which was getting the boys to chuck a bag of sand in the air, and for me to catch it on my jaw and neck. Mister Kerry, at times I could have cried with rage, and killed the old man, and your Uncle Valentine wouldn't stay in the room, he was so sorry for me. But this wasn't the worst, Mister Kerry. One day he had my arms tied to my sides with three twists of rope, and made Paddy Moynihan put on riding gloves with welts.

" 'Now cut the face off him,' he told Paddy.

" 'I'll hit no man that can't put his hands up.'

"Well, Mister Kerry, you'll hardly believe it, but Shadrach Kennedy laid on to Paddy with a driving whip until the big fighting man was nearly crying. In the end he made Paddy go for me. It was cruel. But after a few days of it, I noticed I could sway and duck and draw away my head in a manner I hadn't thought possible. But it was hard.

" 'Mister Kennedy,' I protested, 'I'm sure you were never trained as hard as this.'

" 'I was not,' he said, 'for two reasons. The one was there was never as good a trainer as myself when I was a boxer. Now, ax me the second,' he said, 'and I'll give you a good answer.'

" 'Well,' said I, 'Mister Kennedy, what is the second?'

" 'I was never,' said he, 'such a traitorous cowardly third-rate tinker's pup as to lose the championship, and to have to go after it again. Is there anything else you'd like to hear?'

" 'No, sir,' said I. For I'd heard enough.

"He was clever, Mister Kerry, He'd have none of the old slip the left and cross-counter. He'd make you catch your man's left on your right wrist and counter with the left straight to the face. A dandy blow. He'd teach you to hit, in a long fight, at the point where a man's left shoulder and arm joins. After a while his left hand is useless. He'd teach you to weave inside a guard instead of breaking it down, and to punish your man with short punches to the body. He taught me to catch my man's left arm, and twisting around pull him over my shoulder in the 'flying mare.' A terrible throw.

"He was good, Mister Kerry. He never pushed me past my strength for all his cruelty. He kept me fresh as new butter. Twice a day he'd work at my hands, fingering the muscles and bones until they were like hard rubber balls with steel inside them....

"He let up on the training one day, and sent me out for a walk. And that evening he called me into his room. 'I've one more thing to tell you,' he went on, 'don't watch your man's eyes, or his feet, or his hands. Watch the point of his jaw, and when he drops that into his shoulder, jump in and punish.'

"Your Uncle Valentine came in and laid his hand on my shoulder. 'We sail over to the Oyster Bay, Jim,' he told me.

"Then I knew I had to fight on the morrow....

"Your Uncle Valentine would not let me out or see anything until the next morning. There was the early note of winter in it, and the trees brown and the black crows in the fields. We left the farmhouse where we were staying after breakfast, and your uncle huddled me up in one of his great frieze coats with a white muffler about my neck.

" 'I have a present here,' he told me, 'for you from the gypsy folk of Destiny Bay.' And out of his pocket he pulls a green scarf of silk so delicate you could pull it through a ring. And on it in gold thread was the Irish harp. 'You'll wear it on your way back, Jim.'

" 'Please God!' said I.

"The ring was pitched on the shore of the bay, fine springy turf, with the sound of the little waves in your ears. And if there were plenty of people at the New Jersey fight there was a multitude here. You wouldn't have thought it was against the law at all. There were folk of quality, acquaintances of your Uncle Valentine, and the scum of the Bowery, horsemen, gamblers, and Irish. There was a sea of faces around the ring, and on the rim of this crowd were carriages of all sorts with people standing on them. I noticed maybe a dozen of our sort, North of Ireland fellows, very quiet men would knock the head off your shoulders for twopence and I saw your Uncle Valentine had taken no chance against the ring being rushed in case of my winning. I was in the ring first and Johnson made me wait a while for him. Your Uncle Valentine was talking to Paddy Moynihan about the trotting horse, and I, I'm not ashamed to admit it, Mister Kerry, I was saying a bit prayer. All around the ring the gamblers were shouting: 'I'll lay fives against the Irishman. Here, I'll lay sixes. Six to one against.' One fellow shouted: 'I'll take tens,' said he. No sooner were the words out of his mouth than a big man with a sealskin waistcoat pulls a roll of bills out of his pocket and passes it up. 'A hundred thousand to win ten thousand dollars on Johnson,' he agreed. The man who offered the bet looked green. There was big money at that ringside.

"Your Uncle Valentine heard the other man coming through the crowd, and had my coat and muffler off, and pulled the sweater over my head. For an instant I stood stripped.

"Then I saw my man was in the ring.

"I went forward to hear the referee go over the rules—his name was Kilrain, a fine fellow and a good fighter in his day!—and there I met Johnson, who had a smile on his face, but it left as I looked at him. He had plaster on his hands.

" 'Do you object to this, Carabine?' the referee asked.

" 'I object to nothing, Mister Kilrain, not even brass knuckles.'

"As we turned to our corners I held out my hand to Johnson, for a prize ring is no place for private spite, and a championship fight is above personal feeling. He looked at my hand without taking it, and turned away. There was a lot of laughing at the ringside, but there was a good deal of hissing. I went back to my corner, and 'Good luck, Jim!' whispered your Uncle Valentine and whipped my coat off, and time was called.

"Mister Kerry, there's nothing in the world as lonely as a man in the ring when his seconds get out of it, and he's left there with the man he's to fight, and the referee like the blinded woman that's the dispenser of justice on the outside of the law courts. Every one who has fought knows the dropping of the heart. The Southern Irish fellow will cross himself and the Jewish fighter touch a praying shawl. I gave a good pull to the ropes to loosen up and walked out to meet my man.

"I don't know what there was about me, Mister Kerry, but I could see Johnson change his mind as he came forward. He closed up, in a way. We fiddled for a few minutes, breaking ground, moving here and there. Around the ring you could have heard a pin fall, as the saying is, with the silence that was in it. Then Johnson jumped at me with his left hand. I didn't try to stop, but pulled my head away, as Shadrach Kennedy had instructed me, and each time he missed. He looked back and looked puzzled. And when he was thinking I rushed him myself, and letting go with the left caught him with a swash in the ribs that made the wind go through his teeth whistling, and bringing it up caught him on the side of the head and sent him staggering across the ring. I followed him, Mister Kerry, but he covered up on the corner, so I had to clout him a couple of right-handers at the back of the neck to straighten him up. He slipped under my guard and got away. We sparred and I noticed his chin going down and I jumped in and hit. It spread him on his back in the middle of the ring, and the first round was over.

"I never heard such a minute's commotion as there was at the ringside then. The crowd was roaring. It stopped as time was called for the second round. One minute it was shouting and the next it was silent as night. I noticed the marks of my blows on Johnson, the red knuckle marks against the white skin. He had taken it too easy, Mister Kerry. It never does to take a man too easy, even though you've beaten him easily the first shot. He was thinking; he was thinking hard. He feinted at my head and went in for a swing at the ribs, but I got him with right and left as he came in. He was clever, Mister Kerry; he slid behind me to hold and got a full Nelson on. But the Pole had taught me how to beat that. I dropped forward on my knees and threw him over my head. He was quick, so his hands saved him. We were both up on our feet and at it hammer and tongs. He hit hard. He shook me on the neck and jaw. But I got home with an uppercut that finished the round.

"Mister Kerry, in spite of everything, Shadrach Kennedy's instructions nearly did me. He had told me to watch my man's chin and I watched nothing else. In the first fight I had lost to him with my little trick of feinting with my left before leading. The man that beats another to the punch is the man that wins. My feint was a personal trick, but the dropping of the chin to the shoulder is universal. Everyone will protect himself before he attacks. I was doing so well beating him to the punch that I paid no attention to anything else. Once he tried a hard left on me, and dropping my head I caught his knuckles on my skull, and that must have hurt his hand, for he switched with his right hand forward quickly.

" 'For God's sake, look out!' shouted your Uncle Valentine.

"I had only time to set the muscles of my stomach, no time to drop my hands even, before his left with all his body pivoting behind it socked me in the midriff. It was like the blow of a sledge hammer, or a bullet. And the crack of it could be heard all over the ring, so that the people swayed forward, and a big groan came out of them. If I hadn't been in time myself for it, it would have been an end of that fight, and maybe of any other fight. And if I hadn't been in condition, I could never have weathered it. Mister Kilrain, the referee, looked at me, and his face was white as a sheet.

"And then some Irish fellow from the ringside shouts: 'Sure, he's laughing at you, Johnson!'

"Well, I wasn't laughing at him, Mister Kerry. My face was just twisted with the grin of pain. Pain does either of two things to you. It makes you senseless or it drives you mad. It drove me crazy and I went for Johnson, hitting him with everything I had, jolt and chop; hooking him, and backhandling him on the return, as we were allowed to do in the prize ring. It must have been like hailstones hitting him, until he went down and lay quiet. The ringside was in a roar, men trying to hedge their bets, taking any money offered on Johnson, where before there wasn't a penny to be taken from his supporters except by the ignorant Irish and your Uncle Valentine. Your Uncle Valentine was the only calm person there. His face was pale and he was whistling 'The Boyne Water,' and he dropped on his knee and began to rub my stomach. Before the minute was up, I was all right. 'I'm fine, Mister Valentine,' I said. 'It's nearly over, Jim,' said he, 'but just keep your eye open.'

"It didn't need any advice from anyone to make me pay attention, for the pivot blow was a master tradesman's punch. I went after Johnson in the next round, giving him the straight left and bringing over the right occasionally. All he did was to try and push me off with the left hand. And then after two minutes of fighting he drew his last trick. He swung his right, high, overhand to my jaw. He brought it from his right heel and as quick as lightning, a punch nobody but a fool or a great boxer uses. If it had caught me on the temple, I'd have been dropped like a felled ox. If it had caught me on the jaw, I'd have been through. I took it on the neck and as it was my knees gave and my hands dropped, and a cloud came before my eyes. And I could hear the roar of the ringside, and the cry: 'Carabine's gone!' But the fog cleared away. I hadn't time to fall, and there was Johnson in front of me, looking more dazed than myself. He couldn't understand I wasn't down. I waded in and began to punch at him. And when I wrestled with him I knew I was strong again. He gave a look over his shoulder at his corner, and threw his shoulders up, and then I knew I was only beating a beaten man.

"He was game, Mister Kerry. There was no black spot on him. He was a better man losing than he ever was winning. I could feel the vitality pouring out of him with every punch I landed. Once he slipped from weakness and fell, and I helped him to his feet. He said: 'Thanks, Jim,' and he put out his right hand and I took it. It was as fine an apology as was ever made.

"The ringside was bawling, Mister Kerry, a mad roar. The men of the North, I noticed, had brass knuckle-dusters on, and worse than that in their pockets, for they weren't going to see the ropes cut and me done out of my fight. I worked Johnson over to his corner, and held him up, he was so weak, and I called to his second: 'Can't you throw in the sponge? Can't you see your man's done? What's the use of punishing any further?' But his seconds were surly and dumb.

"I called to the referee: 'Mister Kilrain,' I said, 'this man's finished. Can't you stop the fight to save him?'

" 'It's a championship fight,' said the referee, 'and I've got to give him every chance of keeping his title, if it's only the chance of an earthquake. You've got to knock him out of time,' said Mister Kilrain.

"I appealed to the fellow himself. 'If I land you a light one,' said I, 'will you go down and stay down? There's no disgrace to losing a fight like this. You've given a lot and taken a lot. Will you do that?' said I

"He shook his head, meaning he wouldn't. . . .

"There was nothing for it, Mister Kerry, but to finish him, so I pushed him off, and bit my heels into the ground for a stance. He knew the end was coming and he tried to get his hands up, but his arms were tired and numb. I let him have it with both hands, and stood back. And he thumped forward on his face. Then I turned and walked to my corner."

FROM: LETTERS AND JOURNAL

In England in the first quarter of the nineteenth century, pugilism and poetry reached their peaks, and although a youthful street fighter and lifelong fistic fan named John Keats had a head start on him, Byron was the foremost contributor to both the arts. He not only frequented the fights but backed fighters and took a lengthy course in sparring from Gentleman John Jackson.

LORD BYRON, GEORGE GORDON

September 12, 1813—One of Matthew's passions was "the Fancy"; and he sparred uncommonly well. But he always got beaten in rows, or combats with the bare fist. In swimming, too, he swam well; but with *effort* and *labor*, and *too* high out of the water; so that Scrope Davies and myself, of whom he was therein somewhat emulous, always told him that he would be drowned if ever he came to a difficult pass in the water. He was so; but surely Scrope and myself would have been most heartily glad that

"the Dean had lived, And our prediction proved a lie."

His head was uncommonly handsome, very like what *Pope's* was in his youth.

His voice, and laugh, and features, are strongly resembled by his brother Henry's, if Henry be *he* of *King's College.* His passion for boxing was so great, that he actually wanted me to match him with Dogherty (whom I had backed and made the match for against Tom Belcher), and I saw them spar together at my own lodgings with gloves on. As he was bent upon it, I would have backed Dogherty to please him, but the match went off. It was of course to have been a private fight, in a private room.

November 24, 1813—Just returned from dinner with Jackson (the Emperor of Pugilism) and another of the select, at Crib's the champion's. I drank more than I like, and have brought away some three bottles of very fair claret—for I have no headache. We had Tom ___ up after dinner; very facetious, though somewhat prolix. He don't like his situation—wants to fight again—pray Pollux (or Castor, if he was the *miller*) he may! Tom has been a sailor—a coal heaver—and some other genteel profession, before he took to the cestus. Tom has been in action at sea, and is now only three-and-thirty. A great man! has a wife and a mistress, and conversations well—bating some sad omissions and misapplications of the aspirate. Tom is an old friend of mine; I have seen some of his best battles in my nonage. He is now a publican, and, I fear, a sinner—for Mrs. ___ is on alimony, and ___'s daughter lives with the champion. This ___ told me; Tom, having an opinion of my morals, passed her off as a legal spouse. Talking of her, he said, "she was the truest of women"—from which I immediately inferred she could *not* be his wife, and so it turned out.

March 20, 1814—Sparred with Jackson again yesterday morning, and shall tomorrow. I feel all the better for it, in spirits, though my arms and shoulders are very stiff from it. Mem. to attend the pugilistic dinner:—Marquess Huntley is in the chair.

April 9, 1814—I am but just returned to town, from which you may infer that I have been out of it; and I have been boxing, for exercise, with Jackson for this last month daily. I have also been drinking, and, on one occasion, with three other friends at the Cocoa Tree, from six till four, yea, unto five in the matin.

April 26, 1814—I can't for the head of me, add a line worth scribbling; my "vein" is quite gone, and my present occupations are of the gymnastic order—boxing and fencing—and my principal conversation is with my macaw and Bayle.

June 19, 1814—My mornings are late, and passed in fencing and boxing, and a variety of most unpoetical exercises, very wholesome, &c., but would be very disagreeable to my friends, whom I am obliged to exclude during their operation.

[PORTRAIT]

THE JOE LOUIS I REMEMBER

Joe Louis was Jimmy Cannon's favorite fighter. Jimmy Cannon was Joe Louis' favorite writer. The following is as fine a tribute as has ever been paid to any fighter by any writer.

JIMMY CANNON

The truths of our youth often become falsehoods in our middle years. It is the fee we pay for being alive. We tolerate leniently the rotting of the flesh and the defeat of beauty, but it is harder to accept the decay of ideals. So I am grateful I am still able to admire Joe Louis for what he was. We were young together and he has survived in my estimation. It is because he was a symbol and a force for good, and because he is a decent man.

We have a tendency in this country to praise athletes beyond their worth. It is natural because we are essentially a lighthearted people and this is an age of turbulence. It is a tribute to us that we were able to appreciate Louis. He is a simple man with little education, but the truths he uttered gave him a special radiance. Perhaps his observations were ungrammatical. But often they seemed profoundly witty because they were told with a candor that was unblemished by cleverness. I've never known him to seek the sanctuary of a lie. And I was there from the beginning.

He was an historic heavyweight champion. The others were John L. Sullivan and Jack Dempsey.

They were before my time. But I know Joe Louis improved the fight racket with his presence. He ducked no one and he bragged less than any champion I've known. He is a good-humored man who had pride in what he was. The night that Rocky Marciano knocked him out, people who didn't know him wept in Madison Square Garden. Their grief was not restricted by color.

On his fortieth birthday Louis refereed a wrestling match in Decatur, Illinois. Stooging for these comedians of sport demeans a man who was the greatest fighter I've ever covered as a sports writer. I telephoned him long distance to wish him a happy birthday. I expected him to be cranky. Wrestling is a slum, and in this squalid bazaar Louis was selling his tarnished splendor for a night's pay.

"Have you," I asked, "any regrets?"

"No," Louis said. "I had a wonderful time. I still can make as much as I want to make."

I expected him to claim the second fight with Max Schmeling as the finest night of his life or, maybe, the night he beat Jimmy Braddock out of the heavyweight championship. He chose neither. It was, he insisted, the Max Baer fight. "I felt better that night," he explained. "I felt like I could fight for two, three days."

"What was your worst fight?"

"Arturo Godoy," he answered. "I guess I try too hard with him. I was stale. I couldn't do nothing."

So there he is, now nearing forty-one, on the road, performing in the clumsy tableaus of the wrestlers. It is sad, of course, but there is little joy in the fight racket. Maybe Louis is fortunate. At least he doesn't have to bleed for the money he picks up working with the clowns. Maybe I'm being too dramatic about it but I wish he could find another way to exhibit himself. Of course, Dempsey did it and so did a lot of other great fighters. The hours are short and the pay is good. But Louis doesn't belong in a ring to incite laughter. Neither does any other fighter who suffered publicly to make the toughest dollar an athlete earns. We find it hard to forgive the likes of Louis for submitting to these indignities. We want to remember them as they were, and who was greater than Louis? Let me tell you how I found him to be. He is still my friend and I don't think he really has changed. Of course the years took the skills with them. They made his body a burden. But he never became bitter and nasty, the way some champions do. The history of his fights is in the guides. The matchless record is public knowledge. So this will be a personal recollection of Louis. It is not complete and there will be much that is missing. But none of it is in the files or the books. It is out of my mind and my heart.

The first time I saw Louis fight he humiliated Primo Carnera. The knockout didn't impress me as much as the first left hook that tore Carnera's slack mouth. It was a small punch but it ripped Carnera's high-curved upper lip and his mouth seemed to be crawling up the sides of his face in an agonized grin. The eyes in the big head rolled in terrible wonder, marveling at the force of the blow. Ask me the way Louis punched and I'll tell you about Carnera's mouth breaking into that idiot's smile.

After the Baer fight, Louis' hands were bruised. Baer was sick with despair. Afterward, Jack Dempsey, who worked his corner, said that Baer had been bragging in the dressing room about what he would do to Louis. But a man shouted it was time for the main event to go on and Baer began to pant.

"I can't go on," said Baer, according to Dempsey.

Dempsey regarded him with loathing and amazement.

"I can't breathe," Baer insisted.

"I conned him into the ring," Dempsey remembers. "After the first round, Max came back to the corner and said he couldn't breathe. I told him I'd kill him with the water bottle if he didn't go back out there and get knocked out."

It wasn't Baer, removing his mouthpiece and waving goodbye to the crowd as he sat on his legs, that I remember. It wasn't Louis' handquick ferocity. It was the look on Louis' face when Baer hit him after the bell. Louis' hands were down and he took the punch and a grimace of contempt puckered his fare. It degraded Baer, that brief glance. It told what Baer was and what Louis was and never was the difference so clear. The referee didn't have to count.

Instead of an opponent, Paolino Uzcudun seemed more of a confederate. No one gave him a chance. People wondered how long he would last.

Paolino wasn't clever and he couldn't punch much. But he fought with the vanity of the pug who is a fighter in his heart. He stooped over and hunched forward, his face concealed behind the stockade his crossed arms made. The corner had told Louis to be careful. They were afraid he would break his hands on Uzcudun's head. So Louis jabbed, carefully, precisely, lightly. He was patient and cautious. It happened in the fourth round. Paolino looked up and his head came out of the cage of his arms. One punch did it. It was a right hand and Paolino was down. Gold teeth sprinkled on the dirty canvas, the way tiny charms might fall off a woman's broken bracelet.

Paolino, began to push himself up. His back was to Louis. But he was in another country, lost and hurt through. The boxing journalists forgot they were reporters. They stood up and shouted to referee Arthur Donovan.

"Stop it!" they yelled. "Stop it!"

And Donovan stopped it.

The sports editor of the old *American*, the late Eddie Frayne, called me into his office. I had a choice of assignments. Did I want to go West with the Yankees or stay in New York to cover the Schmeling-Louis fight? There was a kid with the Yankees who was making his first road trip. I decided I would rather travel with Joe DiMaggio.

"Schmeling's all washed up," I told Frayne. "It won't be much of a fight."

We were in Detroit. I went to Tony Lazzeri's room. We sat around the radio. Clem McCarthy broadcast the fight. I remember him shouting above the tumult of the crowd.

"He's down!" came McCarthy's hoarse, excited voice.

"I told you," I said.

But it was Louis who was down, and he would be knocked out that night. In the city of Detroit people lit red flares and a parade of automobiles rolled through the downtown streets to celebrate the knockout of a home-town kid. I never understood that.

Let the others tell you how stately Jimmy Braddock was in defeat. Go to the library if you would know how Louis won the heavyweight championship of the world. But what belongs to me was what Louis said after it was over. It is not important now but it impressed a sports writer who was still young enough to be moved by a champion.

I had to shove my way into Louis' dressing room. The special cops on the door barred my way. There was a pushing crowd behind me. They threw me into the room, past the cops who fell and were walked upon. There was a radio announcer clinging to Joe, holding a microphone in his face. I collided with Louis and he grabbed me to hold me up.

"This is Jimmy Cannon," he said, "the assistant heavyweight champion of the world!"

I remember that.

I believe Louis was the greatest fighter who ever lived the night he took Max Schmeling apart. But I'm concerned with the soft evening I spent with him the night before the fight. I had gone to Pompton Lakes after I had written my piece. We had dinner together and sat on the porch of the old farmhouse he lived in.

"You make a pick?" he asked.

"Yes," I said.

"Knockout?" Louis asked.

"Six rounds," I said.

"No," Louis said. "One." He held up a big finger. "It go one," he said.

That's all it went.

I was in the Army when Louis was matched with Lou Nova. I came to New York on a pass and went up to the Polo Grounds early. I was sitting in my seat when John Roxborough, who was one of his managers, came down to the working-press section.

"Joe wants to see you," he said.

I went back to the dressing room. It was a half hour before the fight. But Joe was asleep, burbling little snores. The crowd sounds awakened him and he sat up. We talked about the Army and about people we knew.

"Time to go, Chappie," one of his handlers said, taking up Joe's robe.

"I got to go to work," Louis said.

As long as I've been on the sports beat, I've never seen a cooler guy.

There are those who are small-hearted and forever afraid, and they shall always fail in every crisis of their lives. But more unfortunate than these are the ones with sufficient courage who betray themselves intentionally by relying solely on caution. When a fighter discards recklessness as though it were a vice he had conquered, it is possible he will survive, but with such a gesture frequently he also abandons his dignity. It was not cowardice that I saw in Jersey Joe Walcott the first time he fought Louis and knocked him down. It is the penalty the mediocre man must pay when he tries to counterfeit greatness. I made Walcott the winner over Louis, eight rounds to seven. But Louis, although knocked down twice, was still the champion because Walcott refused to reject his concocted meekness and replace it with even an imitation of boldness.

The great champion felt disgraced after that night. He ducked into seclusion and no one could see him. It became a big story because he hadn't told his version of the fight. I made a telephone call to a friend of Louis'. I told him I wanted to see Joe, alone. The champion called me back himself.

"You want me?" asked the thick, soft voice that had awakened me.

"Yeah," I said.

"Come up the apartment then," Louis said.

"Where are you?" I asked.

He gave me the address of an apartment house in upper Manhattan. He told me not to mention his name to the elevator boy but to come directly to the flat which was rented in a friend's name. He had been there a week and hadn't been out. He opened the door himself. He wore pajamas and a black-and-white striped cotton bathrobe. The left eye was still pinched by a discolored mound of flesh. His face was bloated. The knuckles of his right hand were swollen.

"What happened to you?" I asked after we had chatted about inconsequential happenings.

"I made the fight tough for myself," Louis said. "He didn't make it tough for me. He did so many wrong things. I saw every opening. But I couldn't go get him. It was a lousy fight. I saw him when he made the mistakes. It's like a guy running. You can't make a sprint near the end. Your legs feel you can go but you feel bad in the pit of your stomach."

"Sounds like you're getting old," I said.

"Diet and drying out," said Louis, who had weighed 211 pounds for the fight. "I wanted to weigh 12," he continued, omitting the 200 as most fighters do. "I should have weighed 14. I weighed 15, and sometime the day before the fight I killed myself taking off the four pounds. But that ain't no excuse. It was a real lousy fight."

"Why did you dry out?" I asked.

"I don't know," he said. "I guess I figured it was a good weight."

He pointed to a thicket of roses standing in a white vase on the table in the room. "If I water those flowers every day," he said, "and then I don't put no water on them, if I don't keep them alive—the flowers got to die. That's me. The day before the fight I had four lamb chops. No juice. Nothing else. No water all day. I eat no more—not even water—until two o'clock the day I fight. You got to have strength to go to a guy. I was weak."

"When did you know you weren't right?"

"In the dressing room," Joe said. "I was warming up in there for fifteen minutes. I knew I didn't have the strength in the dressing room."

"The punch that knocked you down in the first was a sucker punch," I told him.

"You can see it coming when you're weak," he said, "but you're late getting up there. I saw every right hand, but it hit me anyway. One thing I'm happy to know. . . ."

"What's that?" I asked.

"I made it tough for myself," he said. "He didn't."

Had he been persecuted into panic by the knowledge that he was losing the title? I told him I thought he had lost the fight and didn't deserve the decision.

"On my little daughter" he said earnestly, "I never thought at any time I lost the fight. I chased his tail all the rest of the night. You knock a man down, you're supposed to go at a man. He knocked me down and then . . . run . . . run . . . run."

"Suppose they had given him the decision?"

"If they had given it to him," he said, "I wouldn't have cared about it. What I mean is it would have been all right with me. What the decision says—you got to go by it. I wouldn't have mentioned it."

"But you were so sore," I reminded him. "You tried to leave the ring before the decision came down."

"I was mad because I was so silly," he said. "Getting hit by them sucker punches. Seeing them coming—and getting hit. This is no excuse—what I told you—it was a lousy fight. Everybody say something. Everyone give a reason why you do this. No one knows what's in your mind, but you do. I can tell you how I feel but you don't *know* how I feel. I know I had no excuse for a lousy fight."

Not once during the three hours I spent with him did Louis call Walcott by his name.

I found out afterward that the people who live off Louis had tried to discourage him from giving me an exclusive interview.

"You'll make a lot of enemies if you give this to Cannon," one of them said.

"Cannon's my friend," he said, "if I win or I lose."

The second time he knocked Walcott out and announced he would fight no more. The night after the fight I had dinner with him in the dining room of the Hotel Theresa in Harlem. There were a lot of people standing on the sidewalk when we came out. With us was his wife, Marva, and Leonard Reed, a vaudeville actor, who was his closest friend. The people didn't nag him for autographs but followed him quietly as he walked through the Saturday night crowd to the Alhambra Theater, which is across the street from the Theresa. The usher took us to the loge, off to the side, and from this angle the figures on the screen were thin and very tall. The fight movies started as we sat down. The audience was amused by Walcott's skipping and shoulder-shrugging and they reacted as though they were watching a comedy. They shrieked with laughter as Walcott made his preposterous and solemnly funny gestures. Louis didn't talk to me until the ninth round when he reached Walcott with a solid jab. He nudged me with his elbow. "Got him now," he said.

The audience stood up and shouted when Louis knocked him out, as though the finish was unexpected and had surprised them. We went out through a side door, unnoticed by the majority of the crowd, and strolled back to the hotel.

"It was dreadful," Mrs. Louis said.

"I thought it was terrific," Reed said.

"It might have been the other way," Mrs. Louis said.

"It's all over now," Reed said.

"I hope so," Mrs. Louis said. "But you know how it is … like an opera singer with a new role— But I hope not."

"Did you enjoy the picture?" I asked Louis.

"It had a real nice ending," Joe said.

We went up to the two-room hotel suite after the movies and Louis took off the dark glasses. His left cheek was puffed. The flesh around his eyes was scraped and bruised. He believed he was finished with fighting forever. I asked him about his financial condition.

"I won't ask anybody for nothing," he said.

"Suppose," Reed asked, "you could get a soft fight for, say, half a million clams?"

"If they put half a million in my hand—I got half a million," he replied. "But this way— retired—I can make a hundred thousand a year the rest of my life. The championship is an annuity like."

There was a night in Philadelphia when he drifted through a four-round exhibition with Arturo Godoy. The dressing room was humid but Louis lay under a woolen blanket on a rubbing table, kidding Ike Williams, who was then the lightweight champion. They were talking about golf.

"If Ike keeps his head down, he's a real good 85 shooter," Louis said.

"That's not me," Williams protested. "My score's 72."

"How about a match for a thousand?" said Blinky Palermo, who managed Williams.

"I don't want to take his money," Louis said. "It would be pitiful. They put people in jail for taking money that way. Seventy-two—he better buy shoes for his caddie. The caddie would wear out his shoes kicking the ball for a 72."

"Do you like these exhibitions?" I asked.

"Sure," Louis said. "There's a lot of difference between fights and exhibitions. Exhibitions. Big gloves. Don't have to fight hard. Expenses ain't much."

That night 7,285 people paid to see him.

They put Louis in with Joe Chesul, a main-event fighter from the obscure clubs of New Jersey, on the exhibition tour. There was a referee to do the counting if there was a knockdown. The seconds acted as though these were genuine contests. But it was show business, not the fight racket.

The cast was the same when I went down into the basement of the Newark Armory. There were cops on the door and inside were the vague hangers-on you know you met before but can't remember where. There was always a guy carried strictly for laughs. This was George Nicholson, who used to be a sparring partner for Louis. There was Manny Seamon, who still trained Joe. There was Marshall Miles, who did the business for him. I had visited Louis in so many bleak rooms like this in so many towns. But the excitement was gone and so was the strain. There was no guessing. Nothing was at stake. It was just another pay night.

Into the place came a guy with a fighter's face. "You remember me, Joe?" the guy asked.

"How are you?" Louis stalled.

"Steve Hamas," the guy said.

This was Steve Hamas, who once licked Max Schmeling, who, until Marciano did it, was the only man ever to knock Louis out. Their conversation was limited to fighters they both knew. After a while, Louis got up and went out to earn his touch.

"Whatever became of Ezzard Charles?" a guy yelled.

This was before Louis fought Charles, and I wonder now what caused the guy to say that. The people there, about 5,000 of them, grumbled when Louis' weight was announced as 228½.

I realized what the years had done to Louis

when a kid like Chesul made him miss and lunge. The grace was gone and so was the quickness of hand. I was positive that night that Louis would never try to fight again.

I was a war correspondent in Korea when Louis was beaten by Ezzard Charles. There had been no mail for us since we made the landing at Inchon. The last radio I had heard had mumbled with static. On the sports page of the last copy of *Stars and Stripes* I had was a photograph of Louis, placid and immense, staring drowsily at Charles. There was no talk about the fight in Korea. But I thought about it one night when I couldn't sleep in a cottage on the road to Seoul. One of the guys was snoring with a whimpering moan. There was the smell of feet and the sound of men turning stiffly in their blankets. I went out onto the porch with a shelter-half wrapped around me to shield my cigarette in the blackout of the command post.

Much of my life had been spent writing about Louis or hanging around his training camps. My youth was gone with his and middle age was upon the both of us. I felt especially old among the very young Marines. That photograph of Louis had aged me. My thigh bones ached from climbing hills. There was a knot on my hip from sleeping on the ground. I was weary with a deep tiredness that never diminished and only seemed to increase. Shaving with cold water had chapped my face. I had worn the same clothes for six days. I was the only sports writer there and I found no companions who cared to argue fights.

I knew Louis couldn't win. But I still had faith in him. At dawn I sat down at a typewriter and filed a sports piece. I wrote that Louis would knock out Charles in six rounds. I was homesick and tired of combat and feeling my age. I wanted to be there when they fought. It seemed to be wrong to be against Louis when I was so far away. So I picked him. It didn't surprise me when I was told that Charles had trimmed him. But it depressed me.

Of course, Louis won his fight with Cesar Brion in Chicago. I told him I thought he should quit. But the liars said he still had a couple of more good fights in him. He was thirty-six, but older than Methuselah in the fight racket. One observation he made clarified it all.

"My right hand don't leave me no more," Louis said. "I got to think to throw it now. When you're young, you see an opening and throw punches you can't even remember throwing."

It was said quietly. Louis wasn't being dramatic about it. But here was a guy giving me his own obituary as a fighter.

I went to Pompton Lakes where Louis worked to get ready for Lee Savold. He was obstinate in a courteous way when I asked him about his condition. I told him that he should have taken Brion out because he had a lot of shots at him.

"I ain't lost my punch," he said stubbornly.

"You nailed Brion," I said.

"Not so good," he said sadly, "not so good."

"How's training this time?"

"Very nice," he said. "Very nice. But it's tough to do what you want to do. When you start in boxing, you want to throw a punch but you can't do it. You have to force yourself."

We walked out of the gymnasium and into the glade where the ring was pitched. There was a pig-tailed young woman waiting for him with a clump of photographers. She wore boxing gloves, white trunks and a white T shirt. On the T shirt were the figures of two women boxers. Above them, in blocked blue letters, was the legend, "Female Joe Louis."

"I got seventeen knockouts in twenty-two fights," Female Joe Louis said. "I fight boys and everything. I'm a champion, too."

I asked Female Joe Louis where she boxed.

"Mexico City," Female Joe replied. "I'm fighting a girl there for the championship very soon."

"What's her name?" I asked.

"It's in the contract," Female Joe Louis said. "It's an odd name. I don't remember it. I like to fight men. The harder I pop them, the better I like it."

"You scare me," Joe Louis said to Female Joe Louis.

They knew what he meant even after they had beaten him. It embarrassed Rocky Marciano a little when he knocked out Louis.

"They didn't like me," he said, "because of what I done to Joe."

Small remembrances return to me as I write this piece. Now it is the dressing room after the first Walcott fight. Louis sat on a rubbing table. He got the decision but he looked like the loser.

"How is your cold?" was the first thing he said to me.

I had been laid up for a couple of days. It impressed me that a guy, bleary and angry, could be that considerate of a friend in such a spot.

I was in Chicago for a football game. Louis telephoned me and said he had a surprise for me. Would I, he asked, come to a night club on the South Side? He wouldn't tell me what would happen. I went and there were people standing in line outside. There was an immense photograph of Louis in the lobby. There was a sticker pasted across the chest. The legend on it read "In Person." He did a comedy act with a straight man. It was very bad and Louis broke up and laughed away the punch lines. The people liked it. Afterward, Louis came to my table and I asked him why he did it.

"Some friends got the joint," he said. "I give them a hand. But don't print that. Just say I'm having some fun."

There were stories in the newspapers that Louis was broke. I met him at Mike Jacobs' offices which were then in the Brill Building on Broadway. I asked him if it were true he had been trimmed.

"No," he said. "I'll let you see my books."

He paused. "I made some investments with friends," he said. "They turned out bad. Look at the books but don't put that in."

There was a hot day at Yankee Stadium when the Red Sox were playing the Yankees. I came upon Louis, who was sitting behind third base.

"You know Ted Williams?" he asked.

I said I did.

"A good hitter," Louis said.

"Would you like to meet him?"

"Yeah," he said.

I took Louis back to the Boston dressing room. Williams was in his underwear, standing before his locker. They looked at one another and Louis spoke first. He didn't wait to be introduced.

"My," he said, "you skinny."

Frankie Harmon, whose father, Paddy, built the Chicago Stadium, promoted an exhibition match between Louis and Billy Conn when both were finished with fighting. Louis dropped by Harmon's office before the fight and asked him:

"What percentage Billy getting?"

Harmon told him.

"Take five per cent of my end," Joe said. "Put it on Billy's."

He never told Conn that.

Gee Walker, who played the outfield for the Tigers, was the ballplayer Joe admired most. He talked about him continually and explained what a thrill it was to see Walker play. I said the records showed Walker wasn't the best. I told Louis to prove he was.

"You know a man's the best," Louis said, "he's the best. You don't have to prove it."

There was a season when Louis toured with a softball team and played first base.

"What did you hit?" I asked him.

"Round .200," he said.

We talked awhile about other matters. Louis returned to the topic of softball. "You don't have to put my average in the paper?" he asked.

"I do," I said.

He thought about it a while. "You're a bad hitter," he said, "I guess you're a bad hitter."

There was a time when the late Paul Small, a theatrical agent, arranged a profitable movie deal for Louis. The managers sat at a table and discussed terms. They finally reached an agreement.

"This all right with you?" Small said to Louis.

"Can my softball team be in the picture?" Louis asked.

And that was the only question he asked.

The rest is in the book, but what he was isn't there. There was conceit in him but he controlled it. There was a lot of pride in him, too, but it never took charge of him. He was shy and he hid in silence when there were strangers around, but he was easygoing and good company if you were a friend. I admired him but I tried to see him clearly. At the end, when he needed help, I was sympathetic but I knew he was a goner and I said so. He never complained about it and it never spoiled our relationship. He was a great champion and I'm glad he was a champion in my time. He was mean at his work but he was able to leave it in the ring. The cruelty was there, all right. The poverty of his boyhood formed him as it does all fighters. But he was never resentful and he always did the best he could. His best was wonderful.

The night Marciano knocked him out, a guy said it was pretty sad to see him go that way.

"I've knocked out lots of guys," Louis said.

He was a fighter. Many a guy makes a good living fighting for money and many become champions. They can show you licenses to prove they're fighters, and there isn't any way I can dispute them. But Louis was a boy's dream of a fighter. There was joy and innocence in his skills and this gave him what the others lacked. There have been others but I'm sure of Louis.

Joe Louis was a fighter. It is the finest compliment I can give him.

So I'll stop right here.

[FACT]

THE MARQUIS OF QUEENSBERRY RULES

The most important single piece of boxing writing ever done was turned out in London in 1865 by John Graham Chambers, a member of the Amateur Athletic Club, who is often confused with Arthur Chambers, who, in 1872, won the lightweight championship of America. Chambers drew up twelve rules to govern the conduct of matches, prescribing gloves, three-minute rounds and the ten-count, and barring wrestling and hugging. When Chambers found a sponsor in John Sholto Douglas, the eighth Marquis of Queensberry, who gained lasting fame merely by lending his name, it was the beginning of the end of bare-knuckle fighting.

The Queensberry Rules supplanted the Revised London Prize Ring Rules, which had grown out of the first boxing rules drawn up by Jack Broughton in 1743. They were applied in full for the first time in a tournament in London in 1872, and in a championship fight when Jim Corbett knocked out John L. Sullivan in twenty-one rounds in New Orleans on September 7, 1892.

JOHN GRAHAM CHAMBERS

RULE 1—To be a fair stand-up boxing match in a twenty-four-foot ring, or as near that size as practicable.

RULE 2—No wrestling or hugging allowed.

RULE 3—The rounds to be of three minutes' duration, and one minute's time between rounds.

RULE 4—If either man fall through weakness or otherwise, he must get up unassisted, ten seconds to be allowed him to do so, the other man meanwhile to return to his corner, and when the fallen man is on his legs the round is to be resumed, and continued until the three minutes have expired. If one man fails to come to the scratch in the ten seconds allowed, it shall be in the power of the referee to give his award in favor of the other man.

RULE 5—A man hanging on the ropes in a helpless state, with his toes off the ground, shall be considered down.

RULE 6—No seconds or any other persons to be allowed in the ring during the rounds.

RULE 7—Should the contest be stopped by any unavoidable interference, the referee to name the time and place as soon as possible for finishing the contest; so that the match must be won and lost, unless the backers of both men agree to draw the stakes.

RULE 8—The gloves to be fair-sized boxing gloves of the best quality and new.

RULE 9—Should a glove burst, or come off, it must be replaced to the referee's satisfaction.

RULE 10—A man on one knee is considered down, and if struck is entitled to the stakes.

RULE 11—No shoes or boots with springs allowed.

RULE 12—The contest in all other respects to be governed by revised rules of the London Prize Ring.

[REPORTING]

SULLIVAN–FLOOD

This was barge fighting. On May 16, 1881, John L. Sullivan fought John Flood at dockside on the Hudson River at Yonkers, New York. Nine months and four fights later he was to knock out Paddy Ryan in nine rounds in front of a hotel in Mississippi City, Mississippi, for the heavyweight title.

DONALD BARR CHIDSEY

Nobody could say that John L., his eye on the championship, picked easy ones. John Flood, the Bull's Head Terror, was the biggest and toughest member of the toughest and one of the biggest gangs in New York, that which controlled the neighborhood of the Bull's Head horse market in Twenty-fourth Street. He was redheaded and huge, a good inch taller than John L., at least ten pounds heavier. Called the best rough-and-tumble fighter in the country, conceded at least to be the best in New York, he had no use for fancy things like boxing gloves. Anybody who fought him fought with bare fists. Which was all right with John L. Sullivan. Flood had never failed to knock his man out of time.

The purse was to be one thousand dollars—seven hundred and fifty dollars to the winner, two hundred and fifty dollars to the loser. Somebody else must have made that arrangement, for John L. Sullivan, with his superb confidence, tried as often as possible to have his fights on a winner-take-all basis.

As such things went, the fight was kept tolerably secret. Everybody knew it was going to be held—the night of May 16—but very few knew, up until the last minute, where. Betting was two and three to one in favor of Flood.

The Strong Boy had his picture taken. This is mentionable because the picture is the most familiar one, the one that was used on cigarette cards, among other things, all over the country, the one generations of youngsters gazed at in awe. It's a beauty, too. It shows John L. in profile, fists raised, leaning slightly forward on his left leg as though ready to attack. Staring at this picture, you can feel a slim shiver of fright; for the young Sullivan, John L. in his prime, must have been a terrible thing to see. He is wearing white tight trunks, black shoes, black stockings, a plain black belt. Above the belt he is naked; and the muscles, not bunched, not protrusive, are bland, sleek, flat. He is clean-shaven, and the hair of his head is shorn close. This was before he developed a taste for evening clothes, diamond studs, candles on the table, wine. Here he is a fighter pure and simple, a lowbrow, a tough, touchy, and a very strong mick from a back street, with an unmatchable talent for using his fists.

At dusk on the sixteenth Boston visitors began drifting into the back room of a certain East Twenty-fourth Street saloon. They were sold tickets for a "chowder party" at ten dollars apiece and told to go to the foot of *East* Forty-Third Street. This was esteemed by the Bull's Head gang a very funny joke, for the barge upon which it had been secretly agreed the fight should be held was moored at the foot of *West* Forty-Third Street. The local crowd wanted to have things its own way.

John L. himself, of course, was directed to the right place. He arrived at eight o'clock, and with him were two followers and nobody else—Billy Madden and Joe Goss. There were about three hundred of the Bull's Head crowd, grinning. There were a few others, members of neither party, among them Al Smith, who was going to referee (not Alfred Emanuel Smith, later governor of New York and a Presidential nominee), and Paddy Ryan, the champion.

John L. had been warned that if he won the Bull's Head crowd, thugs all, and armed, might get nasty. He shrugged. Nervousness was a thing he never knew.

A tug came out of the night and was tied to the barge, and they started up the river. Knowing that the police in both states were looking for them, they showed no light. They stood in little groups, whispering, watching, except that John L. and Madden and Goss remained below.

There was a bar, and it did a lot of business.

They crossed the river, still heading upstream, and somewhere in the hushed shadows of the Palisades they stopped long enough to pitch a ring. It was a very small ring, but large enough. Neither John Flood nor John L. Sullivan was the kind of man to do much running away in a fight.

The tug started up again. After a while the barge bumped softly against a dock in Yonkers. There was nobody around. With very few preliminaries the fight was started.

They did not use bare fists after all but pulled on skintight gloves, which were easier on the hands, though no whit easier on the other fellow's face.

Kerosene lamps were lit at the last moment.

It must have been a great fight. Neither man gave an inch, save when forced backward by the weight of attack. There was nothing scientific about it; it was sheer slugging.

In the middle of it another tug came alongside. The Boston crowd had chartered this and pursued the barge. Now they wanted to come aboard. They were warned to stay away, and knives and pistols were shown. Greatly outnumbered, the Boston crowd backed into midstream, where they waited for the rest of the fight, hearing the shouts that came across the water, "Come on John!" "Kill him, John!" never knowing, agonizingly wondering, which John was meant.

There were eight rounds, all ending in honest falls or knockdowns. There was no stalling. There was a total of sixteen minutes of fight. After that Flood couldn't come to the scratch. John L. stood panting, fists up, feet spread, the red light of lamps shining on his chest and arms, while wavelets slap-slapped the sides of the barge and every man's breath was held. It was not the first time that he had seen his opponent stretched senseless at his feet, nor was it to be by any means the last; yet I think it was one of the happiest. After a while he lowered his arms, looked around. He caught sight of Paddy Ryan, the champion, and he grinned.

"Ready for yours, Paddy?"

The champion grinned back and shook his head.

It had happened so suddenly, so swiftly, so dramatically too, that if the Bull's Head gang truly had contemplated violence in the event of their leader being beaten, they forgot it. John L. himself helped to pick up the unconscious Flood, and he himself started to pass the hat for the benefit of the loser, contributing a ten-dollar bill. He was always gracious to men he had whipped.

Then the other tug came alongside again, and the Boston men tumbled aboard the barge, nobody trying to stop them. They never got back the money they had paid for "chowder party" tickets, but now they didn't care, having won their bets.

John Flood was taken home and put to bed, where he remained for several days and where John L. visited him. Later he was given a benefit, John L. donating his services free.

John L. and Goss and Madden were carried boisterously down to the St. James Hotel at Broadway and Twenty-sixth Street, where the lobby floor was made up of big black and white marble squares and where there were giddy prism chandeliers and life-sized gilt statues. He ate, it is certain, no less than twelve filets á la Chateaubriand, the house specialty, afterward, with the grand manner which was coming naturally to him even in these unaccustomed surroundings, calling in the chef, Mr. Baptiste, to congratulate him. He drank, it is almost equally certain, his first champagne.

[REPORTING]

DEMPSEY–CARPENTIER

When Jack Dempsey (188) knocked out Georges Carpentier (172) in four rounds at Boyle's Thirty Acres in Jersey City, New Jersey, on July 2, 1921, it was not much of a fight, but it was a great promotion. The 80,000 persons who paid $1,789,238 to sit in formed the first of the million-dollar gates, and thus *The New York Times* showed journalistic ingenuity in borrowing Irvin S. Cobb from the *Saturday Evening Post* to write its color story.

In his description of the second round Cobb, no boxing expert, hurt Dempsey more than Carpentier ever did. One of the "mute, inglorious, preliminary scrappers" of whom Cobb wrote was Gene Tunney, who knocked out Soldier Jones in the seventh round and five years later beat Dempsey for the heavyweight title.

IRVIN S. COBB

Through a hundred entrances the multitude flows in steadily, smoothly, without jamming or confusion. The trickling streams run down the aisles and are absorbed by capillary attraction in the seats. If it takes all sorts of people to make up the world then all the world must be here already. That modest hero of the cinema, Tom Mix, known among friends as the Shrinking Violet of Death Valley, starts a furore by his appearance at 12:15, just as the first of the preliminary bouts is getting under way. His dress proclaims that he recently has suffered a personal bereavement. He is in mourning. He wears a sea-green sport suit, a purple handkerchief, a pair of solidgold-filled glasses and a cowboy hat the size of a six-furlong track. Actress ladies in make-up and also some few in citizens' clothes jostle against society leaders and those who follow in their wake.

The arts, the sciences, the drama, commerce, politics, the bench, the bar, the great newly risen bootlegging industry—all these have sent their pink, their pick and their perfection to grace this great occasion. A calling over of the names of the occupants of the more highly priced reservations would sound like reading the first hundred pages of Who's Ballyhooed in America. Far away and high up behind them, their figures cutting the skyline of the mighty wooden bowl, are perched the pedestrian classes. They are on the outer edge of events if not actually in it.

Conspicuous at the front, where the lumbermade cliffs of the structure shoal off into broad flats, is that type which is commonest of all alongside a fight ring. He is here in numbers amounting to a host. There must be thousands of him present. He is the soft-fleshed, hard-faced person who keeps his own pelt safe from bruises, but whose eyes glisten and whose hackles lift at the prospect of seeing somebody else whipped to a soufflé. He is the one who, when his favorite pug is being hammered to a sanguinary Spanish omelet, calls out: "That's all right, kid, he can't hurt you." I see him countlessly repeated. For the anonymous youths who in the overtures are achieving a still greater namelessness by being put violently to sleep he has a listless eye. But wait until the big doings start. Then will his gills pant up and down as his vicarious lusting for blood and brute violence is satisfied.

Bout after bout is staged, is fought out, is finished. Few know who the fighters are and nobody particularly cares. Who is interested in flea-biting contests when he came to see a combat between young bull elephants? Joe Humphries, the human Cave of the Winds, bulks as a greater figure of interest as he vouches for the proper identities of these mute, inglorious, preliminary scrappers than do the scrappers themselves.

It's one o'clock now. Where an hour ago there were wide vacant stretches of unoccupied seating space, now all is covered with piebald masses—the white of straw hats, the black of men's coats, with here and there bright patches of cola-like peonies blossoming in a hanging garden, to denote the presence of many women in gay summer garb. The inflowing tides of humanity have inundated and swallowed up the desert. Still there has been no congestion, no traffic jams. However the fight may turn out the handling of the crowd has been competent. Tex Rickard is the world's greatest showman.

The hour of one has arrived. Harry Stevens, the official caterer, can't figure within ten thousand of what the full attendance will be and so prepares to slice another ham. One thing is sure—today Boyle's Thirty Acres has given to Tex Rickard a richer harvest than any like area of this world's surface ever yielded.

At this moment—one-sixteen—atmospheric troubles impend. A drizzle has begun to fall. It is a trickle as yet but threatens to develop into an authentic downpour. The air has grown sodden and soggy with moisture, thickened to the saturation point. It is as though one breathed into a wet sponge. I figure this sort of thing, continuing or growing worse, will slow up the two chief clouters when their turn comes.

Governor Edwards of New Jersey comes at one-thirty: the first good solid knockdown in the ring at one-thirty-six. Both are heartily approved with loud thunders of applause. Not everyone can be the anti-dry sport-loving governor of a great commonwealth, but a veritable nobody can win popular approval on a day like this by shoving his jaw in front of a winged fist. There are short cuts to fame though painful.

The shower has suspended, but the atmosphere is still as soppy as a wet shirt. This certainly is a stylish affair. I have just taken note of the fact that the corps of referees all wear white silk blouses and white trousers like tennis players and that the little fat boy who holds up big printed cards with numerals on them to show the number of the next round is done up in spotless white linen like an antiseptically bandaged thumb. The humidity with which the air is freighted is beginning now to be oppressive. Even the exertion of shoving a pencil across paper brings out the perspiration and the two ambitious novices up in the ring are so wet and so slick with their own sweat that they make you think of a pair of fresh-caught fish flapping about in a new sort of square net.

It's three o'clock. Prompt on the appointed hour, for once in the history of championship goes, the men are brought forth on time. Carpentier comes first, slim, boyish, a trifle pale and drawn-looking, to my way of thinking. He looks more like a college athlete than a professional bruiser. A brass band plays the "Marseillaise," ninety-odd thousand men and women stand to greet him—or maybe the better to see him—and he gets a tremendous heartening ovation. Dempsey follows within two minutes. A mighty roar salutes him, too, as he climbs into the ring and seats himself within the arc of a huge floral horseshoe; but so near as may be judged by the applause for him, an American born, it is not so sincere or spontaneous as the applause which has been visited upon the Frenchman.

He grins—but it is a scowling, forbidding grin—while photographers flock into the ring to focus their boxes first on one and then on the other. Dempsey sitting there makes me think of a smoke-stained Japanese war idol; Carpentier, by contrast, suggests an Olympian runner carved out of fine-grained white ivory. Partisans howl their approval of the champion. He refuses to acknowledge these. One figures that he has suddenly grown sulky because his reception was no greater than it was.

A little crowd of ring officials surrounds Dempsey. There is some dispute seemingly over the tapes in which his knobby brown hands are wrapped. Carpentier, except for one solicitous fellow countryman, is left quite alone in his corner.

Dempsey keeps his eyes fixed on his fists. Carpentier studies him closely across the eighteen feet which separate them. The Gaul is losing his nervous air. He is living proof to give the lie to the old fable that all Frenchmen are excitable.

Overhead airplanes are breezing, and their droning notes come down to be smitten and flung up again on the crest of the vast upheaval of sound rising from the earth. A tiresome detail of utterly useless announcements is ended at last.

As the fighters are introduced, Dempsey makes a begrudged bow, but Carpentier, standing up, is given such an ovation as never before an alien fighter received on American soil. It is more plain by this test who is the sentimental favorite. The bettors may favor Jack; the populace likes Georges.

Without handshaking they spring together; Carpentier lands the first blow. Dempsey, plainly enraged, is fast; Carpentier is faster still. But his blows seem to be wild, misplaced, while Dempsey, in the clinches into which they promptly fall, plans punishing licks with swift, short-armed strokes. The first half minute tells me the story. The Frenchman is going to be licked, I think, and that without loss of time. A tremendous roar goes up as Dempsey brings the first blood with a glancing lick on the side of his opponent's nose; it increases as the Frenchman is shoved half through the ropes, The first round is Dempsey's all the way. He has flung Carpentier aside with thrusts of his shoulders. He has shoved him about almost at will.

But midway of the second round Carpentier shows a flash of the wonderful speed for which he is known. With the speed he couples an unsuspected power. He is not fighting the defensive runaway-and-come-again fight that was expected of him. He stands toe to toe with Dempsey and trades 'em. He shakes Dempsey with a volley of terrific right-handed clouts which fall with such speed you do not see them. You only see that they have landed and that Dempsey is bordering on the state technically known as groggy.

It is a wonderful recovery for the Frenchman. His admirers shriek to him to put Dempsey out. To my mind the second round is his by a good margin. Given more weight I am sure now that he would win. Yet I still feel sure Dempsey's superiority in gross tonnage and his greater aptitude at infighting will wear the lesser man down and make him lose.

The third round is Dempsey's from bell to bell. He makes pulp of one of Carpentier's smooth cheeks. He pounds him on the silken skin over his heart. He makes a xylophone of the challenger's short ribs. The Frenchman circles and swoops, but

the drubbing he gets makes him uncertain in his swings. Most of his blows go astray. They fly over Dempsey's hunched shoulders—they spend themselves in the air.

In the fourth round, after one minute and sixteen seconds of hard fighting—fighting which on Carpentier's part is defensive—comes the foreordained and predestined finishment. I see a quick flashing of naked bodies writhing in and out, joining and separating. I hear the flop, flap, flop of leather bruising human flesh. Carpentier is almost spent—that much is plain to everyone. A great spasmodic sound—part gasp of anticipation, part groan of dismay, part outcry of exultation—rises from a hundred thousand throats. Carpentier totters out of a clinch; his face is all spotted with small red clots. He lunges into the air, then slips away, retreating before Dempsey's onslaught, trying to recover by footwork. Dempsey walks into him almost deliberately, like a man aiming to finish a hard job of work in workman-like shape. His right arm crooks up and is like a scimitar. His right fist falls on the Frenchman's exposed swollen jaw; falls again in the same place even as Carpentier is sliding down alongside the ropes. Now the Frenchman is lying on his side.

Dempsey knows the contract is finished—or as good as finished. Almost nonchalantly he waits with his legs spraddled and his elbows akimbo, hearkening to the referee's counting. At the toll of eight Carpentier is struggling to his knees, beaten, but with the instinct of a gallant fighting man, refusing to acknowledge it. At nine he is up on the legs which almost refuse to support him. On his twisted face is the look of a sleepwalker.

It is the rule of the ring that not even a somnambulist may be spared the finishing stroke. Thumbs down means the killing blow, and the thumbs are all down now for the stranger.

For the hundredth part of a second—one of those flashes of time in which an event is photographed upon the memory to stay there forever, as though printed in indelible colors—I see the Frenchman staggering, slipping, sliding forward to his fate. His face is toward me and I am aware that on his face is no vestige of conscious intent. Then the image of him is blotted out by the intervening bulk of the winner. Dempsey's right arm swings upward with the flailing emphasis of an oak cudgel and the muffled fist at the end of it lands again on its favorite target—the Frenchman's jaw.

The thud of its landing can be heard above the hysterical shrieking of the host. The Frenchman seems to shrink in for a good six inches. It is as though that crushing impact had telescoped him. He folds up into a pitiable meager compass and goes down heavily and again lies on the floor, upon his right side, his face half covered by his arms as though even in the stupor following that deadly collision between his face and Dempsey's fist, he would protect his vulnerable parts. From where I sit writing this I can see one of his eyes and his mouth. The eye is blinking weakly, the mouth is gaping, and the lips work as though he chewed a most bitter mouthful. I do not think he is entirely unconscious; he is only utterly helpless. His legs kick out like the legs of a cramped swimmer. Once he lifts himself halfway to his haunches. But the effort is his last. He has flattened down again and still the referee has only progressed in his fateful sum of simple addition as far as "six."

My gaze shifts to Dempsey. He has moved over into Carpentier's corner and stands there, his arms extended on the ropes in a posture of resting. He has no doubt of the outcome. He scarcely shifts his position while the count goes on. I have never seen a prize fighter in the moment of triumph behave so. But his expression proves that he is merely waiting. His lips lift in a snarl until all his teeth show. Whether this be a token of contempt for the hostile majority in the crowd or merely his way of expressing to himself his satisfaction is not for me to say.

The picture lingers in my mind after the act itself is ended. Behind Dempsey is a dun background of gray clouds, swollen and gross with unspilt rain. The snowy white horizontals of the padded guard ropes cut across him at knee and hip and shoulder line; otherwise his figure stands out clear, a relaxed, knobby figure, with tons of unexpended energy still held in reserve within it. The referee is close at hand, tolling off the inexorable tally of the count—"seven, eight, nine"—but scarcely is one cognizant of the referee's presence, of his arithmetic either. I see only that gnarled form lolling against the ropes and, eight feet away, the slighter, crumpled shape of the beaten Frenchman, with its kicking legs and its sobbing mouth, from which a little stream of blood runs down upon the lolled chin.

In a hush which instantaneously descends and as instantaneously is ended, the referee swings his arm down like a semaphore and chants out "ten."

The rest is a muddle and mass of confusion—Dempsey stooping over Carpentier as though wishful to lift him to his feet; then Dempsey encircled by a dozen policemen who for some reason feel called upon to sourround him; two weeping French helpers dragging Carpentier to his corner and propping him upon a stool. Carpentier's long, slim legs dangling as they lift him, and his feet slithering in futile fashion upon the resined canvas; Dempsey swinging his arms aloft in tardy token of appreciation for the whoops and cheers which flow toward him; all sorts of folks crowding into the ring; Dempsey marching out, convoyed by an entourage of his admirers; Carpentier, deadly pale, and most bewildered-looking with a forlorn, mechanical smile plastered on his face, shaking hands with somebody or other; and then the ring is empty of all save Humphries the orator, who announces a concluding bout between Billy Miske and Jack Renault.

As I settle back now to watch with languid interest this anticlimax, three things stand out in my memory as the high points of the big fight, so far as I personally am concerned.

The first is that Carpentier never had a chance. In the one round which properly belonged to him he fought himself out. He trusted to his strength when his refuge should have been in his speed.

The second is that vision of him, doubled up on his side, like a frightened, hurt boy, and yet striving to heave himself up and take added punishment from a foe against whom he had no shadow of hope.

The third—and most outstanding—will be my recollection of that look on Dempsey's towering front when realization came to him that a majority of the tremendous audience were partisans of the foreigner.

THE SECOND LOUIS – SCHMELING FIGHT

On the night of June 22, 1938, when Max Schmeling entered the ring for the second time against Joe Louis, he was, by choice, a representative of the super race and thus an extension of Adolf Hitler. Louis was, by birth, a member of a race Hitler, if successful, would have enslaved or liquidated. Thus this meeting had a political importance never before or since associated with a prize fight, and Louis had his greatest night.

BOB CONSIDINE

Listen to this, buddy, for it comes from a guy whose palms are still wet, whose throat is still dry, and whose jaw is still agape from the utter shock of watching Joe Louis knock out Max Schmeling.

It was a shocking thing, that knockout—short, sharp, merciless, complete. Louis was like this:

He was a big lean copper spring, tightened and retightened through weeks of training until he was one pregnant package of coiled venom.

Schmeling hit that spring. He hit it with a whistling right-hand punch in the first minute of the fight—and the spring, tormented with tension, suddenly burst with one brazen spang of activity. Hard brown arms, propelling two unerring fists, blurred beneath the hot white candelabra of the ring lights. And Schmeling was in the path of them, a man caught and mangled in the whirring claws of a mad and feverish machine.

The mob, biggest and most prosperous ever to see a fight in a ball yard, knew that here was the end before the thing had really started. It knew, so it stood up and howled one long shriek. People who had paid as much as one hundred dollars for their chairs didn't use them—except perhaps to stand on, the better to let the sight burn forever in their memories.

There were four steps to Schmeling's knockout. A few seconds after he landed his only punch of the fight, Louis caught him with a lethal little left hook that drove him into the ropes so that his right arm was hooked over the top strand, like a drunk hanging to a fence. Louis swarmed over him and hit him with everything he had—until Referee Donovan pushed him away and counted one.

Schmeling staggered away from the ropes, dazed and sick. He looked drunkenly toward his corner, and before he had turned his head back Louis was on him again, first with a left and then that awe-provoking right that made a crunching sound when it hit the German's jaw. Max fell down, hurt and giddy, for a count of three.

He clawed his way up as if the night air were as thick as black water, and Louis—his nostrils like the mouth of a double-barreled shotgun—took a quiet bead and let him have both barrels.

Max fell almost lightly, bereft of his senses, his fingers touching the canvas like a comical stewbum doing his morning exercises, knees bent and tongue lolling in his head.

He got up long enough to be knocked down again, this time with his dark unshaven face pushed in the sharp gravel of the resin.

Louis jumped away lightly, a bright and pleased look in his eyes, and as he did the white towel of surrender which Louis' handlers had refused to use two years ago tonight came sailing into the ring in a soggy mess. It was thrown by Max Machon, oblivious to the fact that fights cannot end this way in New York.

The referee snatched it off the floor and flung it backwards. It hit the ropes and hung there, limp as Schmeling. Donovan counted up to five over Max, sensed the futility of it all, and stopped the fight.

The big crowd began to rustle restlessly toward the exits, many only now accepting Louis as champion of the world. There were no eyes for Schmeling, sprawled on his stool in his corner.

He got up eventually, his dirty-gray-and-black

robe over his shoulders, and wormed through the happy little crowd that hovered around Louis. And he put his arm around the Negro and smiled. They both smiled and could afford to—for Louis had made around $200,000 a minute and Schmeling $100,000 a minute.

But once he crawled down in the belly of the big stadium, Schmeling realized the implications of his defeat. He, who won the title on a partly phony foul, and beat Louis two years ago with the aid of a crushing punch after the bell had sounded, now said Louis had fouled him. That would read better in Germany, whence earlier in the day had come a cable from Hitler, calling on him to win.

It was a low sneaking trick, but a rather typical last word from Schmeling.

[FACT]

SULLIVAN VS. CORBETT

This was the first heavyweight title fight with gloves (5-ounce) and under the Marquis of Queensberry Rules. Sullivan was 33 and weighed 212. Corbett was 26 and weighed 178. The purse was $25,000, plus a $20,000 stake, and Sullivan got nothing but a beating and the chance to make a speech in which he said he was glad that the title was remaining in America.

The New York Times report describes eleven punches landed by Sullivan. Corbett, as he had in the ring, ignores these in this story, but it remains the most lucid account any fighter has left of his crowning experience.

JAMES J. CORBETT

I started in to do some light training in the Southern Athletic Club and all the time thousands of people were in and out watching me. There were also large audiences at the other club watching Sullivan, and after seeing both of us, the bettors decided that instead of three to one on Sullivan the odds should go up to four to one. This increase was due, I think, to our difference in weights.

If I had ever relied much on others' opinions I wouldn't have had much confidence or strength left for the fight. Even my old friend from California, Tom Williams, who had backed me heavily in the Choinyski fight, and had also seen me fight my sixty-one rounds with Peter Jackson, blew into New Orleans and bet, so someone was kind enough to tell me, five thousand dollars on Sullivan. Not because I was hurt at all but simply because I liked Williams, I wrote him a letter the day before the fight. In it I said: "Tom, I under-

stand you are betting on Sullivan. I'm not mad, but I wish you would switch your bet and put it on me. I'm in splendid condition. You saw me fight Choinyski and Jackson. You know I can go the distance; and no man who has lived the life that Sullivan has lived can beat me in a finish fight."

A few years later when I was going abroad, I happened to run into Tom Williams on the steamer. We were talking over old times and got down to this fight. "Do you remember the letter you wrote me," he said, "before your fight with Sullivan, telling me to bet on you?"

"Yes," I replied, and somehow managed not to grin.

"Well," continued Williams, "after I received your letter I went out and bet a thousand more on Sullivan!"

I had also written to my father and figured he would receive the letter a day or two before the fight—which he did. I told him in what good condition I was, and prophesied that by taking my time and being careful I would win the fight between the twentieth and the twenty-fifth round; and my dear old dad wore that letter out after the fight, just as he did the telegram after the Kilrain battle.

The excitement in New Orleans was intense from the start, as this was the first heavyweight championship fight ever arranged to be fought under the protection of the police. All other fights up to this time had been under London prize-ring rules and with bare knuckles, and, being against the law, had been pulled off in private.

Just before we left New York for New Orleans, I had told Brady to see how much money he could dig up to bet on me. He took all the money his wife had and what he could skirmish up himself, and it amounted to three thousand dollars. All I had in the world on the day of the fight was nine hundred dollars—we had used up so much for training expenses; but that morning I gave it to Brady and said, "You take this nine hundred and the three thousand you have, and go down and put it on me."

"Jim," he said, "I'll bet my three thousand, but you had better keep your money. If we should lose the fight, that's all we'd have, and we'll have to ride the brakes out of town."

So after thinking it over, I took his advice and kept my nine hundred, Brady going downtown to bet the three thousand—four to one.

In a couple of hours he came back, all excitement, and exclaimed: "They're betting five to one on Sullivan!"

"That's great!" I replied. "Did you put the money up?"

"No," he answered, looking a little sheepish. Then he added, "Don't you think, Jim, we'd better keep it in case you get licked?"

I got angry at this.

"You fool!" I blurted out. "You were willing to take four to one, but now when it's five to one you get cold feet. Sullivan and I are just the same as when it was three to one: we haven't changed any."

Then, pushing him out of the door, I gave him this parting message: "Don't you come back here unless that three thousand is on!"

I had noticed that the strain was beginning to tell on my trainers, and even Delaney. With all his coolness, he was trying to hum little songs to himself to make me feel he was happy and wasn't thinking about the fight at all. And others were whistling too loud and too often. All their actions, I could see, were so unnatural and unlike them. They were all doing it for the effect on me, and, if I do say it myself, I think I was the only one in the whole crowd that really felt normal.

To lead up to the climax, the club had arranged bouts between famous fighters to be fought on successive nights before the heavyweight battle—Monday night, George Dixon fought Jack Skelly for the featherweight championship of the world; on Tuesday, the wonderful lightweight, Jack McAuliffe, defended his lightweight title against Billy Meyers of Streator, Illinois; on Wednesday night, John L. Sullivan was to defend his title.

McAuliffe gave Meyers an awful beating on Tuesday night, and it suddenly occurred to me that it would be a grand idea to have the last meal before I fought Sullivan with poor Billy Meyers. This did not strike me as ominous, for I was never superstitious—in fact, often defied and flew in the face of superstition purposely. This annoyed my companions considerably sometimes, so now when I suggested that I go out with the loser, Billy Meyers, there was a terrible uproar. "Why, he's a 'Jonah!'" they said.

They begged and pleaded with me, but I insisted on going and dragged them all out there with me!

Meyers came down into the dining room and met us. I knew him very well and liked him very much. He had a big black eye and a cracked lip, and I started to "kid" him about these marks of his battle. "You may look worse than I do when Sullivan gets through with you tonight," he retorted.

"No, Billy," I replied. "Sullivan won't have to hit me as many times as McAuliffe did you, to lick me. If it's done, it will be done with one punch!"

So we talked and joked with each other, and finally, about nine o'clock, we started for the Olympic Club.

Now the following incident comes back to me as I write these words, thirty-three years afterwards.

As I was starting to put on a light summer suit, with a straw hat and a little bamboo cane to match, Delaney exclaimed, "You're not going to the fight that way, are you?"

"Certainly, Mr. Delaney," I replied, examining myself in the mirror, as if I thought I looked grand.

It was too much for him. He wanted me to go to the arena like the usual short-haired, big-sweatered type of pug with a scowl that would scare people, and here I looked like a dude that a good man could break in two. For a moment, he couldn't say anything; simply looked his disgust.

"What difference does it make how I'm dressed going up?" I continued, as I gave a little extra twist to my tie. "I don't expect to fight in these clothes."

The streets of the city were black with people, and as our carriage was working through, all I could hear from every side was the murmur: "Sullivan," "Sullivan," "Sullivan!" Not once did I hear the name of "Corbett"; it was all Sullivan in the air.

We reached the club and I stepped out. As I walked in at the door, right ahead of me hurried my old friend, Mose Guntz, from San Francisco, the one who gave Jack Dempsey a thousand dollars to second Choinyski. After that incident we had become great friends, and have been such ever since.

He turned around at my hail and started to speak cheerfully, but when he saw my getup, he looked kind of embarrassed and strange, and, although he didn't say anything about my trimmings, I knew what effect they had on him, also that it wouldn't be but a couple of minutes before someone would tell Sullivan that Corbett came to the club with a cane in his hand and a straw hat on, like a dude! I could picture the look on Sullivan's face when he heard this news.

When I reached my dressing room, one of the club managers came in and announced, "Sullivan wants to toss up for the corners."

"Let him take any corner he likes," I answered as I started to get ready. "He's going in the ring first anyway."

Word immediately came back that I was to go in the ring first. However, the question was settled by Brady's going down to Sullivan's dressing room and tossing a coin.

Now the only reason for my insisting that Sullivan enter ahead of me was the wonderful ovation I knew Sullivan would receive. Just then I felt quite calm, and I didn't want anything to excite me in any way, and it was possible his great reception might. But Brady had won the toss and finally it was announced that Sullivan was in the ring.

My seconds and I started down the aisle. The seats were banked circus fashion and only a few of the audience could see us, but I could see the ring

and Sullivan was not in it. The managers had lied to me. So I stopped.

Now Sullivan thought I was in the ring, because I had started and enough time had elapsed for me to get there. As I stopped and turned back I met Sullivan, for the first time since I had boxed with him in San Francisco at my benefit. I looked him in the eye and said, "You're the champion and I'm the short end. You're going in that ring first, if we stand here all night!"

This enraged Sullivan, who was always aggressive in manner anyway. He gave a roar like a wounded lion, strode down the aisle and bounded into the ring. Never before or since have I heard an ovation equal to that given him as he came through the ropes.

I said a little prayer to myself: "I hope to God I am as cool in the ring as I am now," and then, as the cheers subsided, skipped into the ring, receiving the usual reception that any fellow would get from an audience, which meant about as much as, "Well, anyway he showed up!"

When I entered the ring I noticed that the floor was of turf instead of boards, on which I had always trained and fought. My shoes were of the solid sort used nowadays and I wondered how my feet would hold on turf. As soon as I entered the ring I started dancing around, and found that my feet would hold pretty well—in fact, much better than I had expected—so I was considerably relieved.

There was a reason, you see, for these jumping-jack antics that night, but I wish someone would tell me why present-day fighters do the same thing. They have been training on boards, and are fighting on boards, and using the same shoes and everything, so there is no reason for the practice unless to cover up nervousness. But it has been followed generally by fighters ever since that night. It is funny how customs and habits go down from generation to generation.

Meanwhile, Sullivan sat in his corner trying to catch my eye, his clenched fists on his knees, elbows out, and his head thrust forward in an ugly fashion. He had a wicked eye.

Now, as I had always done before, I was trying to convince him that he was the last person or thing in the world I was thinking about. I was bowing to people I didn't even see, smiling at entire strangers, waving my hand and talking to my seconds, laughing all the time.

Finally the referee, whose name was John Duffy, called us up to the center of the ring for our final instructions. We walked up, Sullivan with his arms still folded, looking right at my eyes—not in them, for I never met his stare—and rising and falling on his toes without a pause. I waited for the referee, my gaze on him, and you could have heard a pin drop in the place. You wouldn't think 10,000 people could be so quiet. At last the referee got down to "hitting in clinches."

"When I tell you to break," he told us, "I want you to drop your arms."

Immediately I grasped the referee by the shoulder—mind you, all for the effect on Sullivan—and sneered, "That's very well for you to say, 'Drop your arms when I say break!' But suppose this fellow"—even then I didn't look at Sullivan, just jerked my thumb at him—"takes a punch at me when I drop my arms?"

"If he does that, he'll lose the fight; and you'll lose, too, if you try it," Duffy answered.

"Then what about clinching like this?" I asked, and took hold of the referee and put my elbow up under his chin, pushing his head back, and repeated, "What if he does this?"

"That's a foul, of course," he answered. "The one that does it will be cautioned once. If he tries it a second time, he loses the fight."

"All right," I said, as gruffly as I could, "that's all I wanted to know."

Then, for the first time since entering the ring, I looked Sullivan square in the eye and very aggressively, too. He stopped his rising and falling on his toes and stood staring at me as if he were petrified, so surprised was he at this sudden change in my attitude, and I saw at once it had the effect I intended: I had him guessing!

In a very cocksure manner I jerked the towel from my shoulders, turned my back on him and ripped out, "Let her go!"

This piece of business had its effect not only on Sullivan, but also on the audience, for they cheered me louder then than they had when I entered the ring. They must have come to the conclusion, "Why, this fellow thinks he can whip Sullivan. We'll see a fight!"

"Time" was called, and the first round was on.

Now, I knew that the most dangerous thing I could do was to let Sullivan work me into a corner when I was a little tired or dazed, so I made up my mind that I would let him do this while I was still fresh. Then I could find out what he intended doing when he got me there. In a fight, you know, when a man has you where he wants you, he is going to deliver the best goods he has.

From the beginning of the round Sullivan was aggressive—wanted to eat me up right away. He came straight for me and I backed and backed, finally into a corner. While I was there I observed him setting himself for a right-hand swing, first slapping himself on the thigh with his left hand—sort of a trick to balance himself for a terrific swing with his right. But before he let the blow go, just at the right instant, I sidestepped out of the corner and was back in the middle of the ring again, Sullivan hot after me.

I allowed him to back me into all four corners, and he thought he was engineering all this, that it was his own work that he was cornering me. But I had learned what I wanted to know—just where to put my head to escape his blow if he should get me cornered and perhaps dazed. He had shown his hand to me.

In the second round he was still backing me around the ring. I hadn't even struck at him yet, and the audience on my right hissed me for running away and began to call me "Sprinter." Now I could see at a glance that Sullivan was not quite near enough to hit me, so suddenly I turned my side to him, waved both hands to the audience and called out, "Wait a while! You'll see a fight."

That made an awful "sucker" out of Sullivan, as the gallery birds say, and it was quite unexpected. And since he didn't know that I knew he couldn't reach me when I pulled this stunt, he was the more chagrined. So he dashed right at me, angry as a bull, but immediately I was away again. At the end of the round I went to my corner and said to Brady and Delaney, "Why, I can whip this fellow slugging!"

At this there was a panic in my corner, all of them starting to whine and pleading with me.

"You said you were going to take your time," they said. "What are you going to take any chances for?"

"All right," I replied, to comfort them, "but I'll take one good punch at him this round, anyway."

So far Sullivan hadn't reached me with anything but glancing blows, and it was my intention, when the third round started, to hit him my first punch, and I felt that it *must* be a good one! If my first punch didn't hurt him, he was going to lose all respect for my hitting ability.

So, with my mind thoroughly made up, I allowed him to back me once more into a corner. But although this time I didn't intend to slip out, by my actions I indicated that I was going to, just as I had before. As we stood there, fiddling, he crowding almost on top of me, I glanced, as I had always done before, first to the left, then to the right, as if looking for some way to get out of this corner. He following my eye and thinking I wanted to make a getaway, determined that he wouldn't let me out this time!

For once he failed to slap himself on the thigh with his left hand, but he had his right hand all ready for the swing as he was gradually crawling up on me. Then, just as he finally set himself to let go a vicious right I beat him to it and loosed a left-hand for his face with all the power I had behind it. His head went back and I followed it with a couple of other punches and slugged him back over the ring and into his corner. When the round was over his nose was broken.

At once there was pandemonium in the audience! All over the house, men stood on their chairs, coats off, swinging them in the air. You could have heard the cheers clear to the Mississippi River!

But the uproar only made Sullivan the more determined. He came out of his corner in the fourth like a roaring lion, with an uglier scowl than ever, and bleeding considerably at the nose. I felt sure now that I would beat him, so made up my mind, though it would take a little longer, I would play safe.

From that time on I started doing things the audience were seeing for the first time, judging from the way they talked about the fight afterwards. I would work a left-hand on the nose, then a hook into the stomach, a hook up on the jaw again—a great variety of blows, in fact, using all the time such quick side-stepping and footwork that the audience seemed to be delighted and a little bewildered, as was also Mr. Sullivan. That is, bewildered, for I don't think he was delighted.

In the twelfth round we clinched, and with the referee's order, "Break away," I dropped my arms, when Sullivan let go a terrific right-hand swing from which I just barely got away; as it was it just grazed the top of my head. Some in the audience began to shout "Foul!" but I smiled and shook my head, to tell him, "I don't want it that way."

So the next eight rounds continued much in the fashion of toreador and the bull, Sullivan making his mad rushes and flailing away with his arms, rarely landing on me, but as determined as ever. Meanwhile I was using all the tricks in my boxing repertoire, which was an entirely new one for that day and an assortment that impressed the audience. Then I noticed that he was beginning to puff and was slowing down a little.

When we came up for the twenty-first round it looked as if the fight would last ten or fifteen rounds longer. Right away I went up to him, feinted with my left and hit him with a lefthand hook alongside the jaw pretty hard, and I saw his eyes roll. Quicker than it takes to tell it, I saw that I had then the same chance that I had had in the fight with Peter Jackson, but had failed to take— the same chance that was Firpo's when Dempsey stood helpless before him, and which he also failed to take.

This time I did not let it slip. Summoning all the reserve force I had left I let my guns go, right and left, with all the dynamite Nature had given me, and Sullivan stood dazed and rocking. So I set myself for an instant, put just a little more in a right and hit alongside the jaw. And he fell helpless on the ground, on his stomach, and rolled over on his back! The referee, his seconds, and mine picked him up and put him in his corner; and the audience went wild.

As Sullivan struck the floor, the few people who were for me jumped up and yelled, but the mass of that vast audience were still as death; just clenched their hands, hoping their champion would rise. When the last count ended and it was over beyond doubt, then came an uproar like Niagara tumbling over the cliffs, followed by the greatest shower you ever saw, of hats, coats, canes, belts, flowers from buttonholes, everything, falling on me and my seconds and all over the floor of the ring. I have often thought what a business I could have started down in Baxter Street with such an assorted stock!

So the roar of the crowd went on. I should have felt proud and dazed, but the only thing I could think of, right after the knockout, was Sullivan lying there on the floor. I was actually disgusted with the crowd, and it left a lasting impression on me. It struck me as sad to see all those thousands who had given him such a wonderful ovation when he entered the ring turning it to me now that he was down and out.

In justice to the man who had reigned so long as champion of the world, I think it is only fair to say that I was not fighting the Sullivan I had seen and admired in San Francisco at the Paddy Ryan bout, then twenty-six and in the pink of condition; but a man who had not been careful of his habits and who had enjoyed too much the good fellowship and popularity the championship brings.

I got him when he was slipping; and that goes for all the champions down the line.

[FACT]

CORBETT–FITZSIMMONS

Robert Prometheus Fitzsimmons was born in Cornwall, England, and reared in New Zealand, although he is usually referred to as an Australian. He won the middleweight title from the Nonpareil Jack Dempsey in 1890, the heavyweight championship from Jim Corbett at Carson City, Nevada, in 1897, and in 1903, at the age of forty-one, took the light-heavyweight crown from George Gardner. He finally retired in 1914 at the age of fifty-two, and died three years later of pneumonia.

In the Corbett fight Fitzsimmons introduced the champion to the left hook to the body, and Bob Davis, hearing two San Francisco doctors talking about it, introduced the "solar plexus punch" to the lexicon of boxing.

ROBERT H. DAVIS

In preparing Fitzsimmons for his fight with Corbett, Dan Hickey, Ernest Roeber, and Jack Stelzner had laid out a careful course of boxing and wrestling with plenty of road running and lots of sleep. Our cuisine was in the hands of a Chinaman, whose idea of high-class cooking was a platter of pork chops with every meal.

About the first of March Bob's wife, with her two sons, Robert and Martin, accompanied by a maid, came to the camp and took entire charge of his diet, much of which she prepared with her own hands. He had an obsession for calf's foot jelly, which he consumed by the pound. Half a chicken, two vegetables, and a rice or custard pudding was an average meal for him. For breakfast he ran to eggs, toast and coffee, ham and eggs, bacon and eggs, and lamb chops. I was a close second at the table.

He was always overweighted with clothing, believing that a continuous mild warmth was preferable to one single chill. He slept under thin blankets and never moved until he rolled out in the morning.

His road work was the most systematic part of his program. Ten, twelve or fifteen miles a day were nothing for him. Roeber, who weighed close to two hundred pounds, did not care much about those jogging exercises, but Hickey and Stelzner followed him valiantly....

The most interesting episode that occurred on the highway was when Corbett and his retinue came over into the bailiwick of Fitzsimmons. The two men met about a mile from the Fitzsimmons camp.

Fitz sighted the Corbett party coming down the penitentiary road, which leads to the state prison and also to the Cook ranch. Billy Delaney, Charley White, Jim Jeffries, and a boxer named McCarthy were with Corbett. The late Bill Naughton, sporting editor of the San Francisco *Examiner,* ambled along in the rear in a two-wheeled cart, waiting to see what he could see. I always thought that Bill negotiated that little meeting by inducing Corbett to go out of his own jurisdiction into the enemy's country.

Fitzsimmons was accompanied by Dan Hickey

and the great Dane, Yarum. When the two groups drew together Bob and Hickey walked up and shook hands with Delaney, Charley White, Jeffries, and McCarthy. The next man in the procession was Corbett. Fitz strode forward and offered his palm. Corbett made a gesture as though to accept and then suddenly changed his mind.

"I'll shake hands with you over there," he said, waving his arm in the direction of the nearly completed arena visible across the fields.

Fitz seemed quite embarrassed and flushed.

"I'll shake after I've licked you," continued Corbett, as though to add a period to his statement.

"Then we'll never shake!" replied Fitz.

"You don't think you can lick me?" asked Corbett.

Fitz released a guttural laugh.

"What am I up 'ere training for?"

"I'll see you next Wednesday over there, and you had better bring your dog," retorted Corbett.

"I don't need the dog. You needn't wait until Wednesday," bristled the Australian, preparing to shed a light coat he was wearing. "I can lick you right 'ere and now!"

Bill Delaney took immediate charge of the situation, mumbling something about the absurdity of two gentlemen acting up on the public highway, thus averting what might have been an utterly profitless affair without motion pictures or gate receipts.

I knew nothing about this meeting until Hickey came running into my quarters, breathless and full of glee.

"Fitz just licked Corbett!"

"What do you mean?"

"Exactly what I say! They met on the road above the prison and had some words."

He then described the meeting in full.

"Thought you said he licked him?"

Dan Hickey is a first-class Irish gentleman and believes in banshees, leprechauns and fairies.

"That's the idea," he said hurriedly. "The minute Bob started to take off his coat Corbett knew that Bob wasn't afraid of him. From that moment defeat set on Corbett's shoulders. He will go into the ring a whipped man. He hasn't got a chance! Delaney, Jeffries and Charley White know he is licked, and so far as I'm concerned, the fight's won."

The fire and conviction with which Dan Hickey emitted this observation quite convinced me that

there was nothing left except the referee counting "Ten!" over the prostrate Californian. It had quite the opposite effect on Fitz. For several days he brooded over the fact that Corbett had refused what Bob had intended to be a cordial salutation. By nature Fitzsimmons was a more or less sentimental, even-tempered man, slow to anger and swift to forgiveness. Rancor, hatred and enmity had no part in his composition. I have heard him repeatedly say that he never fought a fight in his life but that he always felt sorry when he saw his adversary fall.

In the meeting with the original Jack Dempsey at New Orleans, when the Nonpareil was staggering around that dirt arena helpless and facing defeat, Fitzsimmons begged him to quit.

"The champion never quits," retorted Dempsey, puffing a crimson spray from his bloody lips. "You've got to knock me out."

Fitzsimmons considered it an act of mercy to drop this incomparable man and terminate his agony. Dempsey fell face forward with his shattered mouth in the mud.

"To my dying day," said Fitzsimmons, describing this fight, "I will see Dempsey lying there with the little red bubbles busting as 'e breathed heavily into the red earth. I picked 'im up and helped carry 'im to his corner. I never lifted a braver man to 'is feet." ...

March 17, 1897—One of those perfect mountain mornings, the atmosphere like crystal, not a cloud in the deep-blue sky. Mrs. Fitzsimmons cooked Bob's breakfast: half a chicken, two slices of toast, one cup of coffee, and a compote of stewed fruit. Bob did a little shadow boxing in the gymnasium and was subjected by Hickey to a thorough rubdown, after which he was wrapped in blankets and remained quiet until eleven o'clock, when we left for the arena in which had gathered about seven thousand customers.

Just before departing we weighed Bob, stripped, on a steelyard, than which there is no more accurate weighing device in the world. He tipped the scale at exactly one hundred and fifty-six and a half pounds.

"I'm still a middleweight. Now let's see wot 'appens," was his only observation.

The dressing room had been built in under the reserved seats and was extremely cold. Fitzsimmons disrobed and was reblanketed so completely that nothing was visible except a lock of his light hair, his eyes, and his nostrils. He remained perfectly quiet and said very little.

Dan Steward, the promoter of the fight, came in and asked one question: "Are you all right?"

"Never better," replied Fitz. . . .

George Siler, the referee, called the principals to the center of the ring and delivered the customary preliminary instructions, after which both men returned to their corners.

The gong sounded. Corbett stepped out of his corner and walked toward Fitzsimmons with his hand extended. Fitz, still smarting under the indignity that had occurred on the highway, declined the hand of his foe. No one at the ringside, not even his wife, had an inkling of Bob's intention. Corbett flushed as Fitzsimmons had flushed a few days before on the open road; but there is a vast difference between embarrassment in the presence of a baker's dozen and before ten thousand fight fans.

For an instant a profound stillness settled over the arena. Both men, in the pink of condition, stood like a pair of stone images, Corbett with his high guard, buoyant in posture, apparently poised on the balls of his feet; Fitzsimmons with his left foot far in advance of his right, apparently standing flat, his massive battering rams swinging from his shoulders.

Action! Lead! Block! Counter! Cross in and out! Blow for blow! Caution! Craft! Each coaxed the other to lead, to come forward, to start a right or a left.

The lithe Californian moved like a shadow. At times the Australian appeared to be like the bronze blacksmith who used to strike the chimes on *The New York Herald* clock, moving only at the hips, waiting to release a sledge hammer at his adversary. A cautious pair.

The gong sounded at the end of the first round. I climbed up behind Fitz and showered him with queries, which he answered by nodding or shaking his head.

Second round. Third round. Fourth round. All pretty much alike. Numerous blows were struck, none of particular consequence. It was plain that Corbett was the better boxer.

At the end of the fourth round, as Fitzsimmons took his seat, he blurted into my right ear: "Ask any questions you want. I'll talk to you. I'm not winded. 'E can't knock me out. I haven't felt a single punch. If 'e will only lead."

Well, from that moment until the end of the fight Fitz and I carried on a running conversation after each round, discussing his condition, his hopes, and his irritation at delay. He chafed at Corbett's activity. He seemed to have one idea, one desire: to get close enough to plant that invincible left.

The morning of the fight S. S. Chamberlain, managing editor of the *New York Journal*, sent me this telegram: PLEASE WIRE YOUR GUESS AS TO RESULT. S.S. CHAMBERLAIN.

Having had no experience with the prize ring, I handed the telegram to Fitz. After a moment of reflection he said, "Tell him I'll win in seven rounds."

"Which hand?"

"Left hand."

"Chin or body?"

"I'll 'it 'im somewhere in the body. It ain't so easy to 'it 'is chin."

I went to my typewriter, thought the matter over for a while, and decided that the seven rounds idea was a bad lay. Being mildly superstitious and believing in the number seven, I decided finally to double Fitzsimmons' guess; to take seven for each of us and let him have his own way with the left hand. I wired: MY GUESS IS FOURTEEN ROUNDS. LEFT-HAND BODY BLOW. FITZSIMMONS WINS. R.H. DAVIS.

The whole transaction was the wild guess of an untutored individual posing as an expert. It was passed around the office and met with wild guffaws. Furthermore, it was chalked on the bulletin board in front of the *Journal* office, where it remained for about half an hour, and was finally erased.

Due to the high, dry atmosphere of the mountains, four thousand feet above sea level, a crack had developed in Fitzsimmons' thick lower lip and widened by Hickey in training bouts. It would not heal. During the fourth and fifth rounds Corbett reached this tender spot with repeated left jabs. At the beginning of the sixth round it began to bleed. A thin stream of blood ran down to Bob's chin, where it began to smear.

Corbett mistook this red badge for something important and stepped in with considerable vigor. He planted a left on Bob's cheekbone. Bob slipped it off with a slight turn to the right. Both men then mixed it and as Bob came out of the clinch he slipped. Corbett was setting himself for a right wallop, but Fitzsimmons, slightly off his balance, seized Corbett around the legs and slid down his body to the floor.

Not a blow was struck during that entire performance. It was merely a question of one man off his balance reaching the floor through a little play of tactical dexterity. The moment his right knee touched he let go of Corbett and Siler began to count. Corbett stepped back with an air of confidence. At the count of nine Fitzsimmons, whose mouth and chin were pretty well covered with blood, got up, backed away, and set himself. Corbett showed no inclination to mix it the rest of that round. He must have known that it was no blow of his that floored his opponent.

There was so little concern in the Fitzsimmons corner between the sixth and seventh rounds that we joked about the prophecy.

"Here comes the seventh, Bob," I said. "What are you going to do?"

"I can't get at 'im. 'E's fast. Wait."

One swipe of a sponge cleared the blood from the lip and chin, upon which there was not the slightest abrasion.

It is a curious commentary upon reportorial accuracy that the eighth, ninth and tenth rounds as described in the American newspapers prove that the human equation plays an important role when even the manly art is under discussion. A review of the files of twenty metropolitan journals will convince the reader that after all the hand is quicker than the eye. There were blows described, shifts analyzed, blocks, feints, etc., carefully pointed out, but somehow or other they seemed to have escaped the cinematograph.

Both men were singularly cautious from the very beginning, and to my unpracticed eye it seemed either man's fight up to the beginning of the thirteenth round, during the latter half of which Fitzsimmons began to land his blows on Corbett's face. During the mix-up Fitzsimmons shot a short right across his own left guard. One of Corbett's gold teeth fell out, smote the canvas and ricocheted among the boxholders.

In this round Bob circled Jim four or five times, seeking a chance to plant his left. On one occasion, when Fitzsimmons stopped with his back to the north, he made a gesture as though to shade his eyes from the blazing sun that was riding a blue sky in the southern quarter.

"Keep out of the sun, Bob," shouted Mrs.

Fitzsimmons, waving her hand at her husband. That was the only audible remark uttered by Mrs. Fitzsimmons during the entire fight. She spoke casually to Senator John Ingalls and myself four or five times, generally in monosyllables and always with commendable reserve.

Just before the close of the thirteenth round Fitzsimmons worked close to Corbett and began to plant body blows. The San Franciscan for the first time seemed to be in actual distress, whereas Fitzsimmons was gaining confidence and moving with pantherlike alacrity. When the round ended both men were in the middle of the ring. Fitz took his corner with one bound.

Before I had an opportunity to ask him a question, he placed his left glove against his right cheek, leaned down close to the post where I was standing and said deliberately, "'Ave you got any money on you?"

"Eighty dollars in gold."

"Bet it all on the next round. I am going to knock 'im out."

I jumped down, turned to Fred Bushnell, official photographer for both camps, handed him my own eighty dollars and imparted the thrilling information with instructions to put it all up as fast as he could and in as many directions. There was so much interest centering on the ring at that moment that the little transaction between Bushnell and myself attracted no attention. It was easy for him to place it at odds of two, three, and five to one.

The gong! Fourteenth round. Corbett led and was blocked. He followed with a left at Fitzsimmons' head. Fitzsimmons swung on Corbett's neck and Jim gave ground. Bob stabbed him with a left and a right. Corbett became wild and missed with both hands.

The most accurate description of this fourteenth round came from the lips of Fitzsimmons in the form of dictation. I quote it herewith as follows:

"When the opportunity came in the beginning of the fourteenth round Corbett was fighting a little wild, and made a swing which I sidestepped. In a flash I saw a clean opening on his stomach and came in with the left-hand shift on his wind, and then, without changing position of my feet, shot the same hand against his jaw, thus giving him the identical finish which I administered to Sharkey in San

Francisco. I was sure I had done the trick, and although he made a hard struggle to get back on his feet, he was counted out by the referee and lost the championship."

Mr. James W. Coffroth, at that time a young man and a very efficient typist and stenographer, now a boxing and racing promoter of international fame, volunteered to take my dictation after the fight. When I reached the fourteenth round Fitzsimmons insisted upon describing it in his own words, as above.

Threescore and ten correspondents of the ringside have packed that round with the description of the one great punch: *the left shift to the pit of the stomach.* Corbett appeared to be standing still, but such was the speed and violence of the blow that Fitzsimmons' left arm seemed to disappear into Corbett's midst almost to the elbow.

A groan came from Jim's open mouth. He strained as though stricken with lockjaw, the whole upper body retching in apparent effort to reassemble the bodily functions and start to live again.

The late Dr. John W. Girdner, upon reading the dispatches describing the blow, announced that Corbett had been struck in the "solar plexus." This was the birthday of a new blow felt 'round the world.

As soon as Siler counted Corbett out and tapped Fitzsimmons as victor, pandemonium broke loose at the ringside. Instantly the squared circle was filled with seconds, backers, trainers, advisers, officers of the law, and souvenir seekers. Fitzsimmons stepped back to his corner, leaned down over the ropes and kissed his wife thrice full upon the mouth, leaving a little group of red stains upon her trembling lips.

Senator John Ingalls of Kansas, stunned to silence, rose from his seat, inserted his right hand between the folds of his frock coat and surveyed the battleground in the manner of Daniel Webster confronting the Senate just before his reply to Hayne. Above the melee rose the voice of William A. Brady inveighing against something the nature of which nobody could quite understand. Corbett was assisted to his feet, dazed and helpless. All powers of resistance had left him. Presently, however, he recovered with great effort and demanded the privilege of confronting his conqueror.

The confusion was so great that in order to prevent myself from being separated from Fitzsimmons I grabbed a towel hanging on the ropes and tied my right arm to Bob's left, requesting Jack Stelzner to make a double knot as a guarantee of permanency. He made a good job of it and almost stopped the circulation of my blood.

This Siamese twin of press and pugilism was surrounded by twenty people, most of whom had no right in the ring. Suddenly the group separated and Corbett appeared on Fitzsimmons' right.

"You've got to fight me again!" he shouted. "I'm entitled to another chance!"

Fitzsimmons then offered his hand, which Corbett accepted without for one second stemming his clamor for a return match.

"I am through with the ring," said Fitz.

"If you don't fight me," said Jim, "I'll lick you every time I meet you in the street!"

Fitzsimmons replied very earnestly, "If you ever lay a hand on me outside the prize ring, I'll kill you."

HOW TO TRAIN FOR A FIGHT

Professor Mike Donovan (1847–1918) was the third of the middleweight champions, and the first to earn wide acclaim. In thirty-four fights, five of them bare-knuckle, he lost only twice, both times on fouls. He fought at between 145 and 150 pounds, knocked out men who outweighed him by forty-five pounds and twice held his own with John L. Sullivan, who had forty pounds on him.

In 1884 Donovan beat Walter Watson (180 pounds) for a purse and the position of boxing instructor at the New York Athletic Club. Four years later, at the age of forty-one, he came out of retirement to box a six-round draw with Jack Dempsey, "The Nonpareil," then middleweight champion. His son, Arthur Donovan, was for many years instructor at the N.Y.A.C. and refereed more heavyweight title fights—fourteen—than any other man. The Professor's views on training, written in 1893, are included here as those of the most respected teacher and trainer of his time and as a record of the methods of that time.

PROFESSOR MICHAEL J. DONOVAN

Methods must differ according to the habits and constitutions of the men to be trained.

The man who inclines to make flesh must work harder, wear heavier clothes, and undergo a more restricted diet than a man whose habit is the opposite.

Before beginning real work, say about three days, every man should take mild doses of physic to act on the bowels, liver and kidneys, to get the whole system purged from impurities and ready for sustained active work.

The best clothes to work in are fine lamb's wool underclothes; they absorb the perspiration and tend to keep the body free from irritation. The outer garments, sweaters, coats and pants, should fit comfortably, and must be varied according to the season of the year and the amount of flesh to be taken off.

When at work, seven o'clock is a good hour to rise; the trainer should give his man an alcohol bath, followed by vigorous hand-rubbing, to get the blood in good circulation.

Dress leisurely, but before beginning exercise take the yolk of an egg in a glass of sherry, with a cracker or slice of toast. Should you find that the sherry makes you feverish, take, instead, a small glass of cold water with the egg.

Walk, at an easy pace, a mile to a mile and a half, frequently expanding the chest by breathing through the nose to fill your lungs with the pure morning air; this will increase their capacity and give you a good appetite for breakfast. Nothing can equal fresh and pure air as an appetizer.

For breakfast, eat "H-O" oatmeal with milk, broiled lamb chops, one or two poached eggs, with moderately stale bread or toast with a little butter, according to fancy; drink tea, not too strong, with a small amount of sugar. The meat can be varied by eating a broiled steak instead of the chops. After breakfast dress to suit the conditions of the weather; walk briskly, between six and seven miles, genuine heel and toe (this style develops the muscles of the legs more thoroughly than the ordinary easygoing gait). Should this style of walking fail to promote perspiration rapidly enough, vary it by an occasional run of fifty to one hundred yards.

When you return to your quarters strip in a room free from drafts; let two men rub you gently with soft Turkish towels until dry, then with coarser towels, to quicken the circulation and harden the skin.

Take a sponge bath of half a gallon of water and two gills of alcohol, followed by massage rubbing of the body and limbs; this loosens and rests the muscles, which is especially needed in the legs.

The following incident will show the benefit of massage properly administered: Some two weeks before my fight with Dempsey I injured my left shoulder so that my left arm was almost useless. Of course I was greatly worried. Mr. Edward Rauscher, massage rubber of the New York Athletic Club, undertook to cure me. He massaged my shoulder, vigorously rubbing it with Anti-Stiff liniment. After each treatment I noticed an improvement, and thanks to Mr. Rauscher's efforts, in a week I had entirely recovered.

After your bath make a complete change of clothing from head to foot, and you will be ready for dinner. This meal should consist of roast beef, cooked to your taste, or roast mutton, always well done; but little salt should be used at the table; no pepper; a moderate quantity of mashed or baked potatoes without seasoning; spinach is palatable and aids digestion; eat it as often as you choose for dinner, with very little salt, as salt creates thirst; drink a bottle of Bass's ale, if it does not make you feel heavy and disinclined to work. If you desire to increase your weight, drink Guinness' stout instead of Bass's ale. Should either have a bad effect, drink tea; carbonic and lime water are good to quench thirst and relieve the stomach of surplus gases; rice pudding with currants is a good dessert.

After dinner take one hour's rest.

The afternoon's work can be varied by exercise in the gymnasium or a walk of three to four miles. But the ball should be punched for twenty minutes every afternoon, and you should also spar with your trainer. At the close of the day's exercise let your attendants rub you down, and put on a change of flannels.

For supper, eat cold roast beef, lamb or mutton, or broiled chops or steak, according to fancy, with bread; if you like currant bread and applesauce without sugar and well strained, or baked apples, either can be taken with a cup of tea.

Spend the time between the supper hour and bedtime in strolling gently, reading, or genial conversation.

The man who trains honestly as directed should be ready for bed not later than ten o'clock, as he needs ten hours' sleep and rest. Wholesome rest after a hard day's work makes a man fresh the morrow.

Choose your training quarters in a mountainous or hilly part of the country, where you can be sure of pure air and be free from dust.

It is a good plan to train at a long distance from centers of business and pleasure, where you can be fairly safe from the intrusion and interruption of the curious.

Select for your trainer a man thoroughly informed in his business, one who has been through the mill himself; he should have qualities that will make him a genial companion.

A good boxer is an indispensable qualification. The prize fighter who would select a trainer unable to box is like a gentleman engaging a secretary who cannot write.

The trainer should have two efficient assistants to do the rubbing and principal part of the walking in company with the man in training.

The trainer will have enough to do if he boxes with his man and oversees his daily work.

In sparring with you every day, your trainer should take the place of your expected opponent, imitate his style of fighting, and if he has any peculiar blows practice them constantly, your work being to guard or evade these blows; practice side-stepping and ducking rather than hard hitting, as the latter cannot be done without the risk of injuring your hands. The prize fighter cannot give too much care to his hands. To harden and strengthen them a wash of strong beef brine can be used morning and night, or they can be rubbed with a mixture of fine varnish and one third of alcohol twice a day. Your hands may not look very nice if rubbed with the varnish mixture, but appearances should not count for much in preparing for a fight, for, should your hands give way in the ring, there would not be much chance of your defeating a man inferior to yourself.

Should the skin of your face chap or crack by being exposed to the weather, use a mixture of one third each of glycerine, alcohol and Florida water whenever it becomes sore.

The amount of work and kind of diet must depend upon whether you wish to reduce or retain your weight. In this regard you must depend upon the advice of an experienced trainer, for men in training often become irritable and unreasonable and ask for food that is injurious. Above all things, let common sense rule in your training.

If stale or tired from overwork, rest a day, or even two, to recover your vigor and appetite.

Avoid pastry; it causes indigestion. Many a good man has lost a fight through carelessly eating unwholesome food. The greatest danger is during the week preceding the fight. Tobacco should never be used; smoking parches the throat and weakens the whole nervous system.

In taking walking exercise, take the country "as the crow flies," over hill and dale, and always choose the grass in preference to hard, dusty roads, as it gives better work for your legs. For running, pick out a level stretch of country.

In this way you can get a pleasant change of scene impossible on a beaten road.

Choose your quarters in a place where you can have a small gymnasium fitted up. The most important thing is the punching ball; practicing with it quickens the eyes, develops the hitting muscles, and makes a man a two-handed hitter. The distance from the ceiling to the loop on the ball should be three feet. The center of the ball should swing just below the level of the eyes. Punch it as much as possible alternately with the left and right; this style of hitting is good practice for two-handed infighting, and two hands are always better than one.

By frequently using the bare knuckles on the ball, it will harden the hands, and give you a greater variety of blows.

I regard the punching ball as the most valuable mechanical assistant to a fighter in training. Sixteen years ago I brought it into use; I was then training in Troy to fight William C. McClellan. I began by using an old-fashioned round rubber football with a canvas cover, for arm exercise, in a room, bouncing it alternately with the right and left hand from the floor to the ceiling, when the idea came to me of swinging it from the ceiling. In company with my old friend and, at the time, adviser, Jimmy Killoran, of Troy, I swung it from the ceiling, and found it gave me invaluable exercise. I used to punch it for hours. It made me a two-handed hitter. My first attempt to make this rig was crude, as I had a ten-and-a-half-foot ceiling to swing it from. I soon found that a lower ceiling was a great improvement as it gave me much quicker work.

I took the ball to California with me, where it created equal surprise and admiration among both pugilists and amateur boxers, foremost among whom I may name dear old Joe Winrow, my trainer, who also trained Tom Hyer for his fight with Yankee Sullivan, Pat Coyle (the assistant trainer), Billy Jordan and Billy Riley, and the two leading amateur boxers of the Pacific Coast, Charley Bennett and J. B. Lewis.

For variety in exercise the skipping rope can be used moderately; in doing so, use the legs as when boxing, stepping forward and backward with the left foot in front, or side-stepping to the left or right. Lawn tennis is an exciting game, and gives splendid exercise for the legs, and improves the wind. It is good training for the eyes, and will make a pleasant change in the afternoon exercises, the movements of the legs being very similar to those required in boxing.

These exercises will give you the sort of practice you want in your actual work. If tired, but not sleepy, just before going to bed take a small glass of Bass's ale, as it tends to produce sound sleep.

If you are unwell, do not trust to the prescriptions of your trainer, but immediately seek the advice of a first-class physician.

Six weeks of honest training should make a thoroughly sound man fit to fight for his life; no other should enter the prize ring.

JERSEY JOE WALCOTT—ROCKY MARCIANO

The first radio broadcast of a fight emanated from Boyle's Thirty Acres in Jersey City, New Jersey, on July 2, 1921, when Jack Dempsey defended his heavyweight title against Georges Carpentier, and the announcer was Major Andrew White. Don Dunphy, the all-time best of the radio blow-by-blow announcers, reported the weekly Friday-night fights and major championship matches from June 18, 1941, through June 24, 1960. During that period he covered more than 800 fights, and this is a sample of what more than 20,000,000 listeners heard when, on September 23, 1952, Jersey Joe Walcott defended the heavyweight championship against Rocky Marciano in Philadelphia in the best heavyweight title fight since Jack Dempsey vs. Luis Angel Firpo twenty-nine years before.

DON DUNPHY

ROUND ONE

Thank you, Harry Curran. Good evening, everyone. They get out there [several words missing due to sound failure] wide with a left hand. They go into a clinch. Marciano tries a left to the body. It's short. And referee Charlie Daggert goes over and gets them apart. Marciano, missing a left hand, goes into a clinch. And the big apple is on the line down here at the Municipal Stadium in Philadelphia. They're still on the inside. Walcott is slow with a right hand to the chin. Now they're at long range. Walcott misses with a right over the head; it grazed the hair. In close, Walcott chops a right to the head, brings it to the body. Marciano tries to tie him up on the inside. Most of the milling is in close. At long range Walcott lands with a jab, puts a right on the face, misses a right, crosses a right, chops away with two more rights to the head, bangs both hands to the body, crosses a right to the jaw. Marciano mainly trying to tie him up for a moment, moves his way into a clinch. And Walcott is throwing heavily here in round one. Marciano rips a long right hand to the body, crosses a right to the jaw. Marciano is hurt, with a left and a right to the head by Walcott as they clinch over in Marciano's corner. Two minutes to go. And Marciano is down by a left hook on the chin. He takes a two-count and he's up. Marciano was down by a left hook. Walcott on top of him again with another left hook, rips a right to the head, misses a left jab. Marciano goes in and holds on for a moment and Walcott was within a few seconds of victory. Walcott misses a left hand over the head, and there they are in a clinch again. Now they're at long range. Walcott takes a light right and a long right hand to the head thrown by Marciano. In close. Half the round is gone. Marciano gets away from a right, smashes a right to the jaw and hurts Walcott. And Walcott may have let him get away. Now they're at long range again. Marciano has recovered from the early battering. He takes a solid left hook on the jaw by Walcott, a right high on the head, and Walcott is in trying for a quick knockout if he possibly can. At long range, Marciano makes Walcott miss, drives a left and a right to the jaw and takes a right chop high on the head by the champion, Jersey Joe Walcott. One minute to go in round one now. Walcott crosses a right hand to the jaw. Marciano, as you know, was down for about a two-count. Now they're at long range again. Walcott, working his way in, takes a solid right hand to the jaw, a light right hand to the body by Marciano. Now they're in close again and the referee is getting them apart. At long range, Walcott comes back with a left to the head, moves in close, and Marciano ties him up on the inside. It's been a rocky round for the challenger so far. He takes a solid left hook to the jaw and throws his own right hand to the head as Walcott comes in on him. They're in close again. Now at long range. Marciano misses a left over the head, takes a right chop a couple of times to the body by Walcott. In a clinch. Out of it again. Parted by referee Charlie Daggert. Walcott misses a right over the head, misses a left, and Marciano has gone into a crouching style and on the inside chops a short right to the jaw. A right to the head and a right and a left to the jaw by Marciano.

After Walcott had scored first, Marciano comes back with solid thumps to the head. Marciano digs a left hand to the body. They're in a clinch just above us now. Walcott backs away to the center of the ring and now they tie each other up on the inside and this round is almost over. [Sound of bell] There's the bell.

ROUND THIRTEEN

All right, Harry. Marciano has been in trouble—in trouble the last couple of rounds—but he gets out there quickly and moves in on Walcott, who paws out with a left hand to the body. It's short. Marciano is short with a left jab aimed at the head. Marciano digs a left hand to the pit of the stomach of Walcott, Walcott backing away now. Here's Marciano moving in on him again, Walcott feinting the left hand, going into a shuffle, Marciano bulling his way in close. Walcott's ageless legs keep taking him back out of trouble whenever he gets into it. Marciano bulling his way in close. Walcott is back to the ropes. Takes a right to the jaw. Walcott is staggered and helpless on the ropes, with a right to the jaw. Walcott is down on his stomach and they're counting over him. It may be a knockout. I don't think Walcott can get up. It's going to be a knockout for Marciano. Rocky Marciano by a knockout. A straight right-hand punch to the jaw. And Walcott rolls over. He is still out cold. It is a knockout, and we have a new heavyweight champion of the world. It is Rocky Marciano, still undefeated, from Brockton, Massachusetts.

[FACT]

JEM BELCHER

Pierce Egan (177?-1849) was the first to make a career of sports writing, and boxing's first historian. In 1812 he put out the first paperbound installment of *Boxiana*, a monthly publication covering boxing, or milling as it was called in Regency England. Between 1813 and 1828 he brought out five bound volumes containing biographical sketches of the fighters, round-by-round descriptions of their key fights and ringside sidelights such as the fluctuations in the price, the weather or the temper of the crowd. He was a stakeholder, a song writer, a novelist and an inspiration to Charles Dickens. Corinthian Tom and Jerry Hawthorne, from his 1821 best seller, *Life in London,* gave their names to the toddy.

PIERCE EGAN

FROM BRISTOL
(one of the most heroic champions of England)
Descending from the mighty Slack, of pugilistic celebrity, and grandson of that renowned boxer. The family of the Belchers have long been distinguished for their prowess—and the three brothers, Jem, Tom, and Ned, in their various trials of skill, have, in no degree, *sullied* the *milling* fame of their ancestor. In tracing the valorous deeds of Belcher, candour alone dictates us to observe that, in finding scarcely any thing to condemn, we are almost overwhelmed with circumstances to applaud. To him modem boxing is principally indebted for that extensive patronage and support which it has experienced from the *higher flights* of the Fancy! Upon Jem's first appearance as a pugilist he was considered a perfect phenomenon in the gymnastic art—a mere boy, scarcely twenty years of age, putting all the celebrated heroes of the *Old School* at defiance their scientific efforts, when placed in competition with his peculiar mode of fighting,

79

were not only completely baffled, but rendered unavailing. Belcher had a prepossessing appearance, genteel, and remarkably placid in his behavior. There was nothing about his person that indicated superior bodily strength; yet, when stripped, his form was muscular and elegant. The *science* that he was master of appeared exclusively his own—and his antagonists were not aware of the singular advantages that it gave him over those who studied and fought upon the accustomed principles of pugilism; it was completely intuitive; practice had rendered its effects powerful, and in confusing his antagonists he gained considerable time to improve this native advantage with promptitude and decision. The quickness of his *hits* were unparalleled; they were severely *felt*, but scarcely *seen;* and in springing backwards and forwards, his celerity was truly astonishing—and, in this particular respect, it might be justly said that Jem was without an equal! Belcher's style was original; the amateur was struck with its excellence; his antagonist terrified from the gaiety and decision it produced; and the fighting men, in general, were confounded with his *sang froid* and intrepidity. It appears that Belcher made his appearance under the auspices of *Bill Warr,* and it is but justice to observe that the talents of so *finished* a pupil reflected great credit upon that experienced veteran in the gymnastic art.

In his social hours, Jem was good-natured in the extreme, and modest and unassuming to a degree almost bordering upon bashfulness. In the character of a publican, no man entertained a better sense of propriety and decorum than Belcher did; and the stranger, in casually mixing with the *Fancy* in his house, to behold *Nature* in her *primest* moments of recreation, never felt any danger of being affronted, from the attentive conduct of the landlord. Good order reigned predominant, and frequently very animated criticisms have taken place concerning the merits of the *stage,* and the various talents of most of the first-rate performers, who *sported* their *figures* upon the boards, have given rise to considerable discussion, in which the high and dignified legislator has been heard to *argufy the topic* in the most earnest manner, to convince his *plebeian* opponent (whose situation in life was, perhaps, not more elevated than that of a *coal-porter* or a *costermonger*) of the superior abilities of some

particular actor, whose *action* has proved more *convincing* in a few minutes than all the words contained in *Johnson's* folio dictionary could effect; and, in turn, those *composites* of the state have been listening with the most minute attention to the flowing harangue of some *dusty cove, blowing a cloud* over his porter, and lavish with his *slum* on the beauties possessed by some *distinguished* pugilist, whose talents for *serving it out* were elegant and *striking.* And also where *flash* has been *pattered* in all that native purity of style and richness of eloquence that would have startled a *high toby gloque* and put a *jigger screw* upon the alert to find so many *down;* and, even among the heterogeneous crowd have been found admirers of *Hermes,* who have retired well persuaded that all *were not barren!*

"Yet more; the diff'rence is as great between
The optics seeing, as the object seen.
All manners take a tincture from our own,
Or come discolour'd, through our passions shown,
Or Fancy's beam enlarges, multiplies,
Contracts, inverts, and gives ten thousand dyes."

Belcher's *bottom,* judgment, and activity, have never been surpassed—in his battle with *Paddington Jones,* a pugilist extremely well versed in the *science,* and of good *bottom,* who had also distinguished himself in several fights, and was considered by the amateurs a man that might be depended upon, and one that was not *easily* disposed of, was compelled, in a short conflict, to yield to Belcher. *Jack Bartholomew* (a thoroughbred and sound pugilist) was defeated by Jem; when the latter performed such prodigies of valour that he astonished the most scientific professors. *Gamble,* who had *milled* all the *primest coves* in the kingdom for some years, *lost,* in a few minutes, all his *consequence,* from the dexterity of Belcher. In his various fights with *Burke,* either prepared or taken *unawares,* he *hit* away, and gave that most inordinate *glutton* several hearty meals, with all the ease and facility of an experienced caterer. *Fearby* (the *young Ruffian*), who had distinguished himself so manfully in several excellent matches, and who had obtained the appellation of a first-rate pugilist, both for science and bottom, from the best judges among the amateurs, yet, when in competition with Belcher, his abilities were so reduced as to appear more like that of a third- or fourth-rate boxer, and was *punished* most dreadfully by Jem, while Belcher scarcely appeared touched: such, most undoubtedly, was the superiority of Belcher's talents in all the above battles.

It was warmly, if not perhaps ill-naturedly expressed, by one of the most scientific pugilists in the whole circle of boxers, in giving his opinion respecting the battle between the *Game Chicken* and Belcher, *"That had Jem been in possession of four eyes, he was never able to beat Pearce."* Here it was, for the first time in his life, that his judgment proved defective as a pugilist; and, in acting from the envious impulse of the moment, Jem Belcher only portrayed the infirmities of human nature, and the want of stability in man. His character was established, and never did any pugilist's fame stand upon a more elevated and stronger basis; he had retired into private life, respected by his friends, and supported and admired by the *Fancy* in general, who were no strangers to his integrity and private worth— there he should have remained, where his days might have glided happily along, without regret, and his life, in all probability, been lengthened from the placid scene—but his rest was unhappily disturbed, and poor Jem, like the greatest part of mankind, had not *fortitude* enough to rise superior to the baleful attacks of

"…malicious Envie rode
Upon a ravenous wolf, and still did chaw
Between his cank'red teeth a venomous toad,
that all the poyson run about his jaw
But inwardly he chawed his own maw,
At neighbour's wealth, that made him ever sad,
For death it was, when any good he saw,
And wept, that cause of weeping none HE had!"

In constitution Belcher had materially declined, independent of the loss of an eye, and the serious effects which his frame sustained upon that afflicting accident had endangered the safety of his life. Upwards of two years had elapsed in retirement, when Belcher came forward to meet an opponent more formidable than any one he had hitherto met with, and who possessed, in a superior degree, every requisite to constitute a first-rate pugilist, and who, likewise, had improved under his tuition, and might be said *a chicken of his own rearing!* Belcher, unfortunately,

could not be persuaded of the difficulties he would have to encounter from the loss of an eye, and that the *chance* of success was against him, *till it was too late!* and then the error was too glaring to be retrieved. But how did he fight? How he *did fight* will be long remembered by those who witnessed the *grievous,* yet truly honourable combat; a combat in which more unaffected courage was never seen, and where humanity was more conspicuously displayed and gratefully applauded. Animosity appeared to have no resting-place, and it was proud honour, only, struggling for victory. Belcher fought in his accustomed style, and planted his favourite *hits* with his usual adroitness; but he lost his distance, and became an easy victim to his own incredulity. In the course of the fight, as Jem afterwards acknowledged, his sight became so defective, from the *hits* which he received over his good eye (the peculiar object of his antagonist's aim), that the blows he gave his adversary were merely accidental, his aim was lost in confusion, and certainty was out of the question. Belcher, with the most undaunted heroism, endeavoured to make up the deficiency of sight by a display of *bottom* and gaiety, astonishing and unequalled. The skill upon both sides claimed universal respect: yet, notwithstanding the spectators perceived a deficiency in Belcher's fighting in several parts, from his not being able to guard off the attacks as heretofore, and the severe *punishment* which his head and face had sustained in the combat; his afflicting situation made a deep impression, not only upon his friends, but the company in general, and the involuntary tear was seen silently stealing down the iron cheek of many present, for the loss of departing greatness in their favourite hero. Jem's spirits never forsook him; and, in surrendering his laurels, honour consoled him, that he had transferred them *unsullied;* and appeared only affected, by declaring, "that his sorrow was more occasioned from the recollection of the severe loss of a particular friend, who, in fact, had sported everything which he possessed upon his head, and also one of his most staunch backers and supporters through life, than as to any particular consideration respecting himself." Notwithstanding the excellence evinced by the *Chicken* in science, wind, strength, and bottom, and, by no means, feeling the slightest wish to detract from the merits of so respected and deservedly distinguished a pugilist—yet, if we may be allowed the supposition, that had the above contest taken place when Jem Belcher possessed his eye-sight in full perfection, we hesitate not in observing, that its termination might have been very *doubtful!*

Respecting Belcher's two battles with *Cribb,* when the circumstances of the case are duly appreciated; when it is recollected that his spirits must have been somewhat damped in descending from his elevated eminence, to rank only with men of minor talents, who, when in the plenitude of his health and strength, dared not to have thus presumed; but Jem was down, and *down with him,* as is too generally the case with the unfortunate, and his powers well known to be on the decay, previous to his *set-to* with the *Chicken,* and which were by no means improved from that circumstance; yet still his heroism and *science* shone resplendent, and he left his opponents at a vast distance.

In the first fight with Cribb, as may be traced, Jem's superiority was evidently manifest. The former was severely *punished,* and not until Belcher had received a most violent *hit* over his good eye, and sprained his right hand did *Cribb* appear to have much *chance.* In the seventeenth round, the odds were two to *one* on Belcher, and in the eighteenth, five to *one* when *Cribb* was so much beaten, that considerable doubts were entertained whether he would be able to come again; and even at the conclusion of the battle, *Cribb* was in a very exhausted state. The amateurs were delighted with the uncommon skill Belcher displayed upon this occasion, and were completely astonished at his gaiety and vigour; and, till he had lost his *distance,* from his confused sight, victory appeared to hover round him.

In the last battle that ever Belcher fought, his bottom was good in the extreme, and he by no means proved an easy conquest to *Cribb.* Since the loss of his eye, it was the positive wish of his best friends that he would fight no more; but he was not to be deterred, unfortunately neglected good advice, and seemed not aware of the decline of his physical powers. In his last *set-to* the disadvantages he had to contend against were great indeed: his antagonist had made a rapid improvement in the science, was in full vigour, and a glutton that was not to be *satisfied*

in a common way; yet still Jem portrayed that the *science* was left in him, but the *strength* had departed; his hands had become enfeebled, and could not execute their accustomed task, and were so dreadfully lacerated for several of the last rounds, that the flesh had separated from the nails. *Death* was almost as agreeable to his feelings as to utter those unwelcome sounds to the courageous mind, as acknowledgment of *defeat.* Never was it given with more reluctance, and his friends positively forced it from him, after a contest of forty minutes!

Belcher's display with *Tom* (better known by the name of *Paddington*) *Jones,* convinced the amateurs of his peculiar *science, spirit,* and *bottom:* and after a desperate conflict, in which considerable judgment was shown upon both sides, Belcher was declared the conqueror. He soon rose rapidly into fame, and was matched against the most distinguished pugilists.

The *sporting world* were now all upon the alert, with a match which had long excited considerable attention, between *Jack Bartholomew,* a pugilist of high repute, and Jem Belcher. The former was a great favourite among the *Fancy,* and had attained the age of thirty-seven; while the latter had not reached his *twentieth year.* The battle was for 300 guineas, and fought upon a stage, on Finchley Common, on Thursday, May 15, 1800.

About half-past one the combatants appeared, and the *set-to* immediately commenced: —sparring was out of the question, and ferocity the leading feature; but Belcher showed himself off in such good style, and convinced the spectators that the advantage was upon his side, that the odds were now laid upon him. *Bartholomew,* not in the least dismayed, went in boldly, and gave Belcher a *leveller.* The friends of *Bartholomew* were weak enough, upon this circumstance, to send a pigeon to London with the intelligence, making up their minds that the battle was a *dead thing* in their favour; but they soon had to repent of their temerity, for in the fourth round Belcher with great agility threw *Bartholomew* upon his head, the shock of which was so violent as nearly to deprive him of his senses, and materially to affect his eye-sight. *Bartholomew,* still *prime,* fought in good style, and contested the battle with great firmness, and dealt out some most tremendous blows, until the close of the seventeenth round, wherein he received a desperate hit in the stomach from Belcher, that made him vomit great quantities of blood, when he acknowledged he had had *enough*. The battle, for the time it continued, twenty minutes, was very desperate; and considered as obstinate a contest as had been for some years. *Bartholomew* entertained the idea that there was a *chance* left, and ventured a second trial; but he became an easy conquest, and in considerable less time.

Gamble, having been successful in eighteen battles, and his knowledge of the *science* being undisputed, it now became the wish of the amateurs that he should enter the lists with Jem Belcher, who had given such early proofs of excellence, and that it should be decided, whether the honour of the *Championship* was to remain with England or Ireland. Accordingly, a match was agreed upon for one hundred guineas, to be decided in the hollow, near the gibbet of that extraordinary character, *Jerry Abbershaw*, upon Wimbledon-common, on Monday, December 22, 1800. It would be impossible to describe the roads to Wimbledon; the numerous vehicles of all descriptions, and the pedestrians who were flocking to witness this combat. It seemed as if all the inhabitants of London were upon the alert; and the swells of the Fancy were unusually prominent besides the heroes of the pugilistic art, as *Mr. Jackson, Bill Gibbons, Brown, Back, Paddington Jones, &c.*

Belcher entered the ring about twelve o'clock, accompanied by his second, *Joe Ward*, and *Bill Gibbons* as his bottle-holder; and *Tom Tring* as an assistant. *Mendoza* was the second to *Gamble*; his bottle-holder *Coady*, and *Crabbe* as deputy. Messrs. *Cullington, Mountain*, and *Lee*, were the umpires. *Cullington*, the publican, held the stakes.

Notwithstanding *Gamble* had beat *James* the Cheshire man, a pugilist that had been successful in seventeen pitched battles, and whose *bottom* was said to be superior to any man in the kingdom; yet still the bets from the first making of the match were *seven* to five in favour of Belcher; and *Bill Warr*, before the combatants stripped, offered *twenty-five* guineas to twenty. However, on stripping, *Gamble* appeared much the heaviest man, and his friends and countrymen sported *three* to two upon him; but that was

by no means the general opinion. A few minutes before one o'clock the fight commenced:—

FIRST ROUND. —The set-to was good, and *Gamble* put in the first hit, which was neatly warded off by Belcher, and who, with a celerity unequalled, planted in return three severe blows in different parts of Gamble's face: they soon closed, and Belcher, being well aware of the superiority of his opponent's strength, dropped. The *paddies*, in their eagerness to support their countryman, offered five to four.

Second. —Belcher, full of spirit, advanced towards Gamble, who retreated. Jem made a feint with his right hand, and with his left struck Gamble so dreadfully over his right eye, as not only to close it immediately, but knocked him down with uncommon violence. Two to one on Belcher.

Third. —Gamble began to retreat, but put in several severe blows on the body of his antagonist. Belcher, by a sharp hit, made the *claret* fly copiously from his opponent; but Gamble, notwithstanding, threw Belcher with considerable violence, and fell upon him cross-ways. The odds rose to four to one upon Jem.

Fourth. —Belcher, full of coolness and recollection, showed himself possessed of excellent science. His blows were well directed and severely felt, particularly one in the neck, which brought Gamble down. Twenty to one Belcher was the winner.

Fifth and last round. —Gamble received two such blows that struck him all of a heap—one on the stomach, that nearly deprived him of breath; and the other on the kidneys, which instantly swelled as big as a twopenny loaf. Gamble, completely exhausted, gave in.

It is reported that not less than *twenty thousand pounds* were sported upon this occasion. The Irish were completely *dished*, and full of murmurings at *Gamble's* conduct, who was beaten in five rounds, and in the short space of *nine minutes* and *three quarters!* Gamble fought very badly; and from his former experience much was expected: but he appeared frightened of his opponent's activity. Belcher laughed at him throughout the fight, and treated his knowledge of the art with the most sovereign contempt. Belcher was carried upon the shoulders of friends round the ring, in triumph, after the battle was over.

The following conversation immediately afterwards took place between *Mendoza* and Belcher. A match had been in agitation for some time past between the above celebrated pugilists, for a considerable sum; and, to prevent any injury arising to *Mendoza*, in his capacity as a publican, or the possibility of an interruption to the contest, it was agreed that it should be decided in Scotland; but the match was off, and Jem felt rather displeased at the circumstance:

Belcher. *Dan Mendoza!*

Mendoza. Well, what do you want?

Belcher. I say, these were the shoes I bought to give you a thrashing in Scotland.

Mendoza. Well, the time may come.

Belcher. I wish you'd do it now.

The parties becoming rather irritated with each other, an immediate *set-to* was nearly the consequence; but their friends stepped in, and prevented it.

Belcher, witnessing a battle between *Elias*, a *Jew*, and one *Jones*, which took place upon Wimbledon-common, on Monday, July, 13, 1801, a man of the name of *Burke*, a butcher, who had behaved himself improperly in the outer ring, and who had been *milled* out of it twice by some of the professed pugilists, called out for Belcher, the Champion. Upon Jem's mildly asking him what he wanted, the latter received a blow in return for his civility. A dreadful *set-to* instantly commenced-in which *Burke* displayed so much *bottom* and strength, although intoxicated, that the spectators scarcely knew what to think about the termination of the contest. An opinion also prevailed, that had not Belcher possessed a thorough knowledge of the *science*, there was a great probability of his falling a sacrifice to this outrageous *knight of the cleaver.*

Burke having showed so much *game* under such evident disadvantages, *Lord Camelford* was induced to back him, for a second combat in a more *regular* manner, for one hundred pounds. He was accordingly put out to *nurse*; a *teacher* appointed to initiate him into the mysteries of the *science*; and it was reported of *Burke* that he was a *promising child*—took his food regularly, minded what his master said to him and, for the short time that *he* had taken to *study*, great improvement was visible. *Burke* ultimately turned out one of the most *troublesome* customers, and the hardest to be disposed of, that ever entered the lists with Belcher.

After some time having elapsed, occasioned by the interruption of magistrates, a stage was erected at Hurley-bottom, a few miles distant from Maidenhead, on November 25, 1801. *Joe Ward* and a *Bristol lad* filled the usual offices for Belcher—and *Harry Lee* attended as *Burke's* second, and *Rhodes* as his bottle-holder. The odds were nearly two to one, on *setting-to*, upon Belcher.

FIRST ROUND. —Burke did not give much signs of *improvement* from his tuition—several blows were exchanged, Burke gave Belcher a terrible blow under his right eye that made him reel. They closed, and fell.

Second, third, and fourth. —Blows were the leading features in these rounds. *Science* was not displayed by either of the combatants.

Fifth. —Burke had his nose laid open, by a severe *hit* from Belcher, and *floored*. —Ten to one Jem—no takers.

Sixth. —Shyness was prominent; but Belcher put in a blow upon Burke's forehead; the blood now issued copiously from all parts of his head, that his second found it a difficult task to keep him clean.

Seventh, eighth and ninth. —The former two were of little consequence; but in the latter Belcher was thrown with considerable violence.

Thirteenth. —*Milling* was the signal, and this round displayed a fine specimen of their talents for *hammering*. The best round in the fight.

Sixteenth. —Burke completely *done up*—yet too much pride to confess he was beat; and his second declared that the fight was over.

Since the days of *Johnson* and *Ben*, it was the opinion of the amateurs, so desperate a battle had not taken place. Twenty-five minutes of hard fighting. *Burke* was heavier than Belcher, and greatly superior in point of stature; Jem appeared little the worse for the conflict, declaring that he had scarcely felt a blow in the fight: and, in the gaiety of the moment, challenged *Mendoza* to fight in less than a month for three hundred against two hundred guineas: but *Dan* was not to be had, and observed, he had done with pugilism.

Warrants were now issued for the apprehension of Belcher, *Burke,* and their seconds, *Harry Lee* and *Joe Ward,* "for unlawfully assembling, and publicly fighting, at Hurley, in Berkshire." But this proved to be nothing more than a *reprimand* when brought into Court, on their promising not to break the peace again.

Burke was not yet *satisfied;* and another trial of skill was granted, Captain *Fletcher* backing him; and *Fletcher Reid,* Esq., on the part of Belcher, for fourteen hundred and fifty guineas aside, which were made good. The combatants appeared upon the stage, which was erected in a bye-place, at a village called Grewelthorpe, about nineteen miles from Middleham, in Yorkshire. A dispute taking place about *Burke's* second, Belcher offered to fight him a few rounds for *love;* but as *Burke* would neither fight for *love* nor *money,* the consequence was, that the *Fancy* were got into a complete *string!* Jem received fifty pounds for his trouble from Mr. *Reid,* who also allowed him five pounds for travelling expenses.

Burke now endeavoured to justify himself through the medium of the *Oracle* newspaper, in a long letter to the editor: but it was looked upon as *gammon!*

At Camberwell fair, these heroes met for the first time after the *bubble* in Yorkshire. *Burke* was rather *lushy,* and entertained the *swells* round him, how he would *serve it out* to Jem if he was present. Belcher was nearer than he imagined, and overheard this *bouncing* of *Burke,* and invited him to another taste; which the latter readily accepted, and on the bowling-green, at the Golden-Lion, they *set-to. Burke* commenced so furiously, that he attacked Belcher before he was undressed; but Jem, on being prepared for the fray, put in his blows so hard and fast, that *Burke* had one of his front teeth knocked out, and a prime *leveller* into the bargain. Belcher was somewhat indisposed, and *Burke,* now coming a little more to his *recollection*—their friends interfered—and they mutually agreed to postpone the fight till the next day. They met according to appointment (August 20, 1802); and in a field behind St. George's Chapel, near Tyburn turnpike, a most extensive ring was prepared, and though the circumstance was so sudden, and kept very private, yet the spectators were immense. Mr. *Fletcher Reid* and Mr. *Cook* being the only two of the principal amateurs present. A purse of thirty guineas was subscribed for the winner, and five for the loser. *Joe Ward* seconded Belcher, and *Bill Gibbons* was his bottle-holder; *Burke* had *Owen* for a second, and *Yokel,* a Jew, as bottle-holder. *Burke* expressed a wish that three quarters of a minute might be allowed instead of half, which was resisted.

FIRST ROUND. —Burke was determined to avail himself of his uncommon strength, and ran in upon Belcher, and endeavoured to throw him, but failed in the attempt. Belcher, taking advantage of his mistake, soon had him down by his dexterity, Several blows exchanged, but no *corks* were drawn.

Second. —Burke still upon the same suit, but received a *throttler* for his attempt, that made the *claret* fly. They closed, and Burke found himself upon the *ground.*

Third. —Burke, full of spirit, ran in and put home a fierce blow on the right cheek-bone with his left hand; and another between the shoulder and breast, which was of no effect. They closed, and Burke was down.

Fourth. —Burke, still *prime,* rushed upon his opponent, but missing his blow, fell. Some murmurs, and calling out "Burke's at his old tricks"; but he soon showed the charge was false.

Fifth. —Burke, with the most determined resolution, ran in and caught Belcher by the hams, doubled him up, and gave him a cross-buttock. The spectators were in fear that Belcher's neck was broken, as Jem pitched upon his head with great violence. "Foul, foul!" was shouted; but Belcher rose with uncommon gaiety, and said, "No, no—never mind!"

Sixth. —The best round that had been fought. As usual, Burke ran in full of spirit, and severe blows were exchanged. Belcher put in several severe hits on the head, neck, and throat. They closed, and considerable skill was manifested on both sides in wrestling; but they both fell without any advantage.

Seventh. —Burke on the decline; his strength was leaving him, but his spirit was good. Closed, and Burke thrown.

Eighth. —Burke wished now to convince the spectators that he was not destitute of *science,* and fought upon the defensive; but Belcher smiled at the attempt, gave him several severe blows, and ultimately had Burke upon the floor.

Ninth. —Twenty to one on Jem, who was as sprightly as if he had not been fighting—laughing and talking to his antagonist, but not forgetting to put in severe hits. Burke down again.

Tenth. —Burke, full of *pluck*, set-to with great spirit, and close fighting ensued. Belcher, losing no time, cut Burke under the left eye; under the right; and another blow so dreadful in its effects between the throat and chin, as to hoist Burke off his feet, and he came down head foremost. Belcher also fell from the force with which he gave it. Both on the floor, when Burke squirted some blood out of his mouth over Belcher: Jem threatened that in the next round he should have it for such conduct—but Burke declared it was accidental.

Eleventh. —Burke's face was now one mass of blood, and he was completely beaten. But still he stood up; few blows were exchanged—they closed, and Burke was thrown; when Jem, very honourably, fell upon his hands, with an intent not to hurt Burke any more by falling on him, which practice is not unusual, and consistent with fair fighting.

Twelfth. —Burke's weakness was now too evident to be disguised; his second could scarcely get him from the floor.

Thirteenth. —Burke came again, but Belcher did as he pleased with him; closed and threw Burke. The latter now was convinced there was no *chance*, and wished to give it in; but his seconds persuaded him to proceed.

Fourteenth. —Burke was *game*, but it was useless and only rendered his situation worse; he was knocked about like a feather, and not the least shadow of success remained for him. Belcher closed, and Burke was thrown upon his chest, he could not come in time, and gave it in.

Thus was this *desperate customer* disposed of at last. His face was so disfigured, that scarcely any traces of a human being were left; while, on the contrary, Belcher was without any visible marks of the contest, excepting a bruise upon his cheek. Belcher's rapidity of action in this battle claimed universal attention and astonishment—and his judgment was equally sure and good. *Burke* was too strong for him, and he never closed but when necessity compelled him. Belcher walked round the field several times after the fight, displaying feats of agility.

The *sporting men* were not satisfied of Jem's superiority; and the whole of the immense bets depending upon the Yorkshire contest were decided by the above battle.

Notwithstanding *Burke* suffered so severely from the effects of this battle, his recovery and strength surprised every one—for in three days after, at a pugilistic dinner, given by Mr. *Fletcher Reid*, at the One Tun public-house, St. James's Market, Burke dined there—shook hands with Belcher, and acknowledged Jem the best man: a match was made for one hundred yards for the best runner, to be decided immediately. *Burke*, to the astonishment of all present, beat *Jack Ward* (son to the veteran) by five yards.

Belcher, soon after the above battle, was taken into custody for not keeping his promise to keep the peace, and bound over for £200, and two sureties in £100 each.

Jack Fearby, better known by the appellation of the Young Ruffian, who had acquired great fame as a pugilist, was now matched with Belcher for one hundred guineas. The contest was to have been decided at Newmarket; but the magistrates interfering, they travelled out of the country, and halted at a spot of ground about half a mile beyond Linton, and fifteen from Newmarket, and made a ring. The combatants then agreed that the winner should have ninety guineas, and the loser ten. On Tuesday, April 12, 1803, at a quarter past nine, the *set-to* commenced.

FIRST ROUND. —Great anxiety prevailed for the first blow—sparring took place for some seconds, when Fearby put in a blow at Belcher's head, which Jem parried, and returned two blows right and left; no mischief done: they closed, and Belcher fell underneath. Offers to take two to one—that Fearby would win—Betters shy.

Second. —Fearby received a severe blow on the mouth, the blood from which issued most copiously; and Jem followed it up by a desperate right-handed hit upon the Ruffian's side, that brought him down. Three to one Belcher was the conqueror.

Third. —Much science displayed on both sides—blows reciprocally given and stopped—when Belcher fighting half-armed, and following up his adversary close, the Ruffian fell.

Fourth. —A good rally, and several severe blows exchanged. They closed, Belcher fell upon his knee, and in that situation received a blow from Fearby. "Foul! foul!" was the cry, and Belcher wished the point to be decided, but had no desire to take advantage of the circumstance. A constable, followed by a clergyman, now made their appearance; but the clamour was so great that the *exhortations* of the reverend divine could not be heard, and the

Fifth round commenced. —Fearby seemed rather shy of his opponent; his eye now appeared black, and he vomited a great deal of blood—Belcher smiled and beckoned the *Ruffian* to come forward. Fearby made a blow, but it was too slow, and which Belcher avoided by bobbing his head aside; and Jem, in aiming to put in a desperate blow on Fearby's ribs, fell. The Ruffian appeared distressed.

Sixth. —The best round in the fight— Belcher quite gay, but Fearby on the decline. The Ruffian, irritated, made several blows at his antagonist, but they were all thrown away. Belcher taunted him, and with the most apparent ease put in a severe hit upon the stomach; and, in closing, Fearby received a violent cross-buttock.

Seventh. —*Milling* on both sides. Ten to one on Belcher.

Eighth. —Fearby rallied with a good spirit, and made a hit at Belcher, which he parried with great neatness: and, in return, cut the Ruffian's lips severely. Fearby, still *game*, gave Jem a sharp touch, but did not fetch the *claret*. Odds reduced to five to one.

Ninth. —Belcher, full of gaiety, and without ceremony, put in a desperate hit over his adversary's right eye, and with all the coolness imaginable, put himself in a defensive posture, and sarcastically asked, "How do you like that, Johnny?" This was too much for Fearby, who was not quite so placid as to pass it over without some notice, and immediately endeavoured to answer the question by a severe blow, but overreached himself in so doing, and fell upon the ground, Belcher smiled, and pointed at him very ironically.

Eleventh. —Belcher now tried to put an end to the fight, by following Fearby round the ring, and putting in several blows which the Ruffian tried to parry off, but not sufficiently. Belcher, at length, put in a *leveller*, when Fearby's friends made him decline the contest.

The amateurs were much disappointed in this battle, in not witnessing that excellent display of the science so much expected. *Fearby* had no *chance* whatever, and appeared like a different man—his former excellence seemed *frightened* away. It was over in twenty minutes.

The above extraordinary pugilist was bom at his father's house, in *St. James's Church-yard*, Bristol, on the 15th of April, 1781. Jem lived some years with a butcher of that place, but was never apprenticed to the trade; and, when quite a boy, he signalised himself for his pugilistic prowess, and at Lansdown Fair his feats soon rendered him conspicuous. He was about five feet eleven inches and a half in height. On his coming to London, *Bill Ward* invited Belcher to his house, and a private sparring-match (with the gloves on) took place in *Ward's* dining-room, when the veteran was astonished at Jem's superior knowledge of the art, that he exclaimed, in falling over a table from one of Belcher's *touches*—"By G-d! Jem, I am perfectly satisfied that you can beat any man in the kingdom." In conversation with *Ward*, after dinner, Belcher observed, *"I could have done better, Sir, but I was afraid I might hit you too hard, and you should be affronted."* —"Come along, my boy," replied the Veteran, "we'll have no gloves on now, and you shall do your best; I am not, nor ever was afraid of a blow!" The *set-to* instantly commenced, when the guest (out of pure friendship) *levelled* his host several times. Ward wanted no further *convincing* proofs of his talents. They sat down, and spent the remainder of the evening very harmoniously, and *Ward* immediately offered to back Jem against any man in the country.

After the unfortunate circumstance of losing his eye, on July 24, 1803, in playing at Racquets, in company with Mr. *Stuart*, in St. Martin's Street—Jem declined in health; his spirits were not so good as heretofore; and, at times, he felt much depressed from this afflicting loss. Soon after the above accident, he took the *Jolly Brewer*, in Wardour-street, Soho, which house was well attended. In losing the battle with the *Chicken* (which, we are credibly informed, was principally occasioned by a quarrel between *Pearce* and a brother of Jem's since dead), his brave heart was almost bursting with grief. The loss of his eye now preyed upon him so much that his temper became very irritable; and so confident of success was Belcher, in his last contest with *Cribb*, that, after betting all his money, he sported his gold watch, worth thirty pounds. After this fight he began to droop, and fretted considerably. His confinement in Horsemongerlane for twenty-eight days, also having to pay a considerable sum for breaking the peace by that battle; added to a cold he caught in the above prison, hastened his death. It was, however, an expressed opinion, that he died more from a family complaint, than from the blows he had received as a pugilist. His circumstances at one time after his defeats were much injured, and he was considerably reduced. The *Fancy* ought not to have let such a man as Jem Belcher (at any period of his life) suffer loss from his pugilistic efforts; —for more honour, integrity, and affection never resided in the human heart. In his latter moments he displayed much sense, penitence, and resignation, and endeavored to atone for those errors which he had committed, with all the firmness and piety of a good Christian. He suffered a great deal from expectoration, having an ulcer upon his liver. A short period previous to his death, he made his will.

On Tuesday, July 30, 1811, died, at the sign of the Coach and Horses, Frith-street, Soho (of which he was the landlord), the renowned James Belcher, in the 31st year of his age; and on Sunday, August 4, he was buried in Mary-le-bone ground. The concourse of people eager to witness the last of their once-distinguished Champion was immense. His funeral was of the most respectable, kind:

THE HEARSE
Preceded by a Man carrying a Plume of Feathers.

In the First mourning Coach,
Mrs. Belcher (his Widow), Mrs. Philpot, Tom Belcher, &c.
Second Ditto,
Mr. Harmer (his Nephew), Mrs. Harmer, Messrs. Gregson, Richmond, Bitton, &c.
In the Third,
Mr. Summer (an Attorney), Mr. Shabner, Mr. Hawkins, &c.
And in a Glass Coach following,
Bill Wood, Powers, and several Amateur Friends.

As they moved along in solemn procession, the numbers of people were so great in joining it, that, upon their arrival at the church-yard, which was nearly filled, the mourners could scarcely reach the grave. *Wood* and *Jack Powers* staid to pay the last respects to their departed friend, and dropped a tear to his memory. A more general sympathy was never witnessed among spectators (principally sporting persons), in shedding a profusion of tears; as did most of his pugilistic brethren, at the loss of so great a hero!

In visiting the ground where his remains are deposited, we should think BOXIANA wanting in respect, if not incomplete, were we to omit the words upon his tombstone:

In Memory of
JAMES Belcher
Late of St. Anne's Parish, Soho,
who died
The 30th of July, 1811,
Aged 30
Universally regretted by all who knew him.

With patience to the last he did submit,
And murmur'd not at what the Lord thought fit,
He with a Christian courage did resign
His soul to God at his appointed time!

THE IRON CITY EXPRESS

Harry Greb, the fast-living and wild-fighting "Pittsburgh Windmill" or "Iron City Express", was a natural middleweight who not only held that title but over 192 fights—many of them while he had only one seeing eye—met some of the best light-heavyweights of his time. He was the only man to beat Gene Tunney, giving him a savage beating. He died at age 32, following an eye operation, on October 22, 1926, two months after losing his title by decision to Tiger Flowers.

JAMES R. FAIR

Two hours before be would be taxi-ing down to Old Madison Square Garden to fight Tommy Gibbons on a March evening in 1922, Harry Greb lay on his back across the bed in his Pennsylvania Hotel room. He was blind in one eye, a secret shared only by a few trusted friends, was outweighed by seven and a half pounds (Greb 163½, Gibbons 171), and was on the short end of 2-to-1 betting. The room was crowded with pugs past their prime and the atmosphere chunky with small talk.

Downstairs in the lobby, Pittsburgh gamblers, who had come over to back Greb, were heaving chairs at the New York coterie who refused to cover on the betting odds. A friend phoned Greb, who rushed down in fighting trunks and dressing gown. By then the lobby was a shambles, Pittsburgh vs. New York, with some of the boys slinging furniture from the mezzanine. Greb jumped up on a reading table, and with a few choice epithets brought about peace and contentment. An hour later, he was in the ring with the man who had come to New York with 23 consecutive knockouts to his credit and two years later went 15 rounds with Dempsey.

It was New York's first view of the principals, and it watched amazed while at intervals both parties spat out teeth in a fight featured by rough tactics, at which Greb was the aggressor and the more adept. He won 12 of the 15 rounds and got the decision.

That was the Greb who for nine years had broken all accepted training rules, who in an early professional fight in 1913 was knocked out by Joe Chip but came on to engage in more than 250 bouts and to win two titles before he died in 1926—the Greb who in his early ring days clutched the ropes with unsteady hands and told those within hearing to come back to his dressing room where he would refund every cent they had lost when the same Gibbons had beaten him in their first fight. It was the Greb whom New York newspapers were later to call the Pittsburgh Windmill, the Iron City Express, the Ring Marvel, the Inexhaustible, and yet it was not Greb at the height of his pugilistic brilliance.

Before he ever fought in New York, and when he was little more than an oversized welterweight, he won with such monotonous regularity that when he spotted Gunboat Smith thirty pounds in weight and knocked him out, out-of-town newspapers carried only a squib. Two years earlier when Dempsey got up off the floor to do the same thing, it established him as the foremost heavyweight contender.

Greb beat other heavyweights who had given Dempsey trouble before and after he won the title from Willard in 1919. In 1917, he beat Willy Meehan, who the following year out-fumbled Dempsey.

He fought big Bill Brennan six no-decision bouts—Brennan, who, after Dempsey became champion, cut him to ribbons for eleven rounds only to go down, and out, in the twelfth under the latter's rally.

In retrospect and by comparison, Greb belonged to the day of Ketchel, for, like him, he fought as often as he could get a fight and gave opponents up to fifty pounds in weight and knocked their ears off.

But, unlike Ketchel, he was not a puncher; he was a charging, unorthodox clubber who was coming faster in the last round than in the first. The idea that he would ever lose a fight was the only one that could amaze him.

Outside the ring, he believed life was meant for enjoyment. He thought fighting was so much necessary nonsense—like getting drunk—and that fighters were never bargains at any price. He used his influence to get bouts for stablemates, but he refused to take the boys seriously.

One day, he was talking to Harry Keck, the Pittsburgh sports editor, about a former stablemate—a junior lightweight named Cuddy de Marco. Greb said, "I saw Cuddy the other day, and you know, he's got a busted konk and looks just like a prize-fighter!"

When a title was not involved, Greb was never sure how many rounds the articles called for and he didn't care.

On his way to California to fight Ted Moore in an over-the-weight match (Greb was middleweight champion of the world), he stopped off in New Orleans to fight Tony Marullo, one of the toughest boys in the ring. He was met at the train by sportswriters, who, dropping him at his hotel, suggested they would see him at the gym that afternoon when he limbered up before the fight. But Greb said he wasn't going to limber up, that he had fought a guy the night before, and that he was very limber, indeed. After some persuasion, however, he agreed to work out, and on his way to the gym, unconcernedly inquired if any of the sports writers knew how many rounds the fight was scheduled for. That night, for 15 rounds, he lambasted Marullo from here to there and back again and left town on the midnight train. A few nights later, he repeated against Mr. Moore in California.

After the Gibbons fight, Greb came back to New York to fight Tunney. He was not much for pre-battle statements, but he allowed that he would lift the American light-heavyweight crown from Tunney and punch him full of holes in the process.

For this fight, in May, 1922, Greb came in at 162½ against 174½ for Tunney. Greb's frame was beginning to creak under the strain of nine years of ring warfare, he was 28 years old, and the sight in his good eye was failing. An even worse handicap

was the threat of newspapers and the Boxing Commission that he would be thrown out of the ring if he roughed Tunney as he had Gibbons a few months before.

Tunney, on the other hand, was young and strong and coming along. He had seen Greb fight and he thought he had what it took to bring him down—patience, and a right jolt to the heart. It was good logic, but he never got a chance to use it against the wily Greb, who in the first round rushed him to close quarters and made him hit low repeatedly by pulling himself up at the waist and taking in foul territory punches that otherwise would have landed in fair. It was Greb strategy to make Tunney look bad and it worked. The referee told Tunney to keep his punches up.

After that, it was a typical Greb fight. In close, he mauled, slapped, heeled, hit on the break-aways and used his knees. When Tunney began to work out a defense, Greb called on more tricks and brought into play an artistic left thumb to Tunney's eye.

In the end, he gave Tunney over to his handlers, a bleeding, helpless bulk, and loped off with his title. That night, he rented a night club orchestra and danced until the musicians fell asleep.

Greb got his blind eye in a fight with Kid Norfolk in Pittsburgh. Before the bout he had learned that Norfolk was blind in one eye. Greb said that if the going got too tough he could stop him by giving him the thumb in the other eye. He did, after the Kid dropped him in the third round. But the Kid gave it right back to him. Next day Greb complained that he saw a red ball of fire in front of the thumbed eye and that it wouldn't go away. A friend took him to a specialist, who said the retina was detached and advised him to quit fighting. Greb swore his friend to secrecy on the eye, and kept on fighting.

Unlike Baer and Carnera and other present-day fighters, Greb never allowed himself to be subdivided; he owned himself, his optimistic faith in managers never getting beyond the stage of permitting them to carry his baggage.

He was ready to go into the ring on short notice, though a great deal of his training consisted in leafing a list of phone numbers.

He was tossed out of the ring on at least one occasion for "not trying." Arm-weary from punching Captain Bob Roper, he sought to kill time by trying to sink his teeth into the lobe of the Captain's ear. The City (Pittsburgh) Boxing Commission called this "horseplay" and handed Greb a suspension.

Back in Pittsburgh, Greb's home town, five out of six fight fans would tell you Greb was a trifler. But they put their money on his nose every time he crawled through the ropes. When he fought in New York, they came in "Greb Specials" to back their boy.

Such a crowd followed Greb to New York the night he defended his light-heavyweight title against Tommy Loughran, whose Philadelphia admirers came in "Loughran Specials" and were rash enough to establish him a heavy favorite. The two contingents met at the Pennsylvania station and when Greb climbed into the ring he was the prohibitive favorite.

His work wasn't up to standard in the first three rounds, which he lost, but he found himself in the fourth, and from there on, it was Greb at his best. In the clinches, he used his head as a battering ram, and held with one hand as he hit with the other; and on the breaks he used his shoulders and elbows. He won 10 of the 15 rounds in a manner that left no doubt even in the minds of the Philadelphians.

Greb lost his title back to Tunney in a return fight, but the decision was so unpopular that William Muldoon, then chairman of the New York State Boxing Commission, denounced it as a "steal." They fought three times after that and, if memory serves me, Greb came out of the last one with two cracked ribs. He thought Tunney "carried" him through the final rounds, because Tommy Gibbons, who had just gone 15 rounds with Dempsey and whom Tunney wanted to fight, was looking on. Later, admitting Tunney's superiority, Greb said:

"That guy is getting too big and tough and he's hitting too hard; it's time for somebody else to fight him for a change. He's a good boy and he'll beat Dempsey if they ever fight."

Greb was middleweight champion of the world in his last two Tunney fights, having won the title from Johnny Wilson, a murderous southpaw puncher, in a roughhouse scuffle in 1923.

The crowds that followed Greb to the gymnasium to watch him work were usually disappointed. He'd play a game of handball, box a round or so, punch the light bag for rhythm, and call it a day. He was wont to walk up to a Sharkey or a Baer and say:

"You big bum, why don't you do your fighting in the ring?"

Greb had little traffic with New York sports writers; he wasn't interested in their opinions, and after a fight, scarcely read their stories. But he read everything that Harry Keck, Chester Smith and Harvey Boyle, back home in Pittsburgh, had to say about him, though it was not always pleasant.

Greb seldom planned a fight in advance; he depended on speed, withering and relentless. But he had a very definite plan for his fight with Mickey Walker, and that was to make Walker carry the fight to him, staking his lone chance of victory on his own ability to absorb a dreadful beating in the early rounds, and to come from behind after Walker had spent himself.

Everything favored Walker, who was welterweight champion of the world. He was young and growing and a terrific hitter; he would enter the ring close to the middleweight poundage and as strong as a bull.

Greb, on the other hand, was 32 years old, was rapidly losing the sight in his one good eye and had to get down from 175 pounds. To do it, he lived on synthetic orange juice, which he bought at Broadway holes-in-the-wall, ate just enough food to keep alive, and had to sweat out in steam rooms every day. On the afternoon of the fight, he had to run twice around the Central Park Reservoir to get rid of surplus weight.

On the card with him were Jimmy Slattery vs. Dave Shade, the former making his debut in the big time. Slattery was knocked out in the third round and left the ring to weep in Greb's dressing room while the latter awaited the gong that would send him into the hardest fight of his career.

Greb entered the ring first, wan and frail, followed by Walker, looking hard and optimistic. Greb drew boos from a predominantly Walker crowd. The weights were:

Greb, 159; Walker, 152.

For four rounds on that July night in 1925, Greb absorbed one of the worst beatings any man has ever been called on to take. There were shouts of "Stop it!" To the spectators it looked like the end of the trail for Greb; to Greb, it was what the blueprints had called for in the early rounds.

But now the blueprints called for reverse action. Coming out for the fifth round, he ducked under Walker's lead and held. He looked over Walker's shoulder and smiled—a smile that said, "Now I'm going to work on him"—and he began firing leather. Greb outslugged, outroughed, and made Walker break ground, as he had said he would, in a fight which, before it ended, saw the referee twice knocked down when he tried to separate the principals. Greb dazzled Walker with his speed, twirled him around until he was dizzy, then stepped back and bit him while he spun. Walker went down to his finger-tips in a later round and was so completely baffled that he stood crying and talking to Greb in the center of the ring. In the fifteenth, it seemed that Greb could have knocked him out if he had chosen, but Walker, though in a state of collapse, finished on his feet. Greb, helping him to his corner, patted him on the back, and said, "You're all right, Mickey!"

Joe Humphreys held Greb's hand aloft and said: "Winner, and still Champion!"

Greb shuffled back to his dressing room, took the still sobbing Slattery under his arm, and an hour later was dancing at the Silver Slipper. Between dances, he sought to console the broken-hearted Slattery, but the latter just sat at the table and cried.

Greb was only a shell of his former self when six months later, in February, 1926, he peeled down to the middleweight poundage and lost his title to Tiger Flowers.

A few months later, be was punching the small bag at Philadelphia Jack O'Brien's gym in preparation for a return match with Flowers when Jack Dempsey sauntered in. Dempsey was coming out of retirement to defend his heavyweight championship against Tunney.

"Hello, Harry," he said, extending his hand.

Greb said, "Hello, Jack," and touched his gloved hand to Dempsey's while he kept up a rat-a-tat-tat on the bag with the other.

Dempsey looked on for a moment, told Greb he looked good, then said:

"How about training me for Tunney?"

"What'll you pay me?" asked Greb.

"Eight thousand," said Dempsey.

"Not enough," said Greb. "Make it ten."

"Can't do it," said Dempsey.

"Nothing doing," said Greb, still punching the bag. "I want to fight you myself, anyhow!"

"Forget it," said Dempsey, leaving. "Nobody'd pay to see a fight like that."

Whereat Greb smiled, obviously remembering how, in a training-camp workout, he moved in on Dempsey, leaned a shower of righthand leads against his chin, then moved out before the Champ, punching out of a weave, could get his range. For two days he had the great Tiger Jack floundering awkwardly about the ring, trying vainly, like Mickey Walker, to reach with a solid punch the human windmill that swept about him. It was what Dempsey needed to put him in shape, but Manager Jack Kearns immediately dismissed Greb for being too aggressive.

This would be in 1920 when Dempsey was getting ready for his fight with Billy Miske in Benton Harbor. A year or so later, Greb accepted terms from Charley Murray, the Buffalo promoter, for a fight with Dempsey. But again Manager Kearns interfered, saying, "No, thanks. We don't want Greb."

Greb bet his entire purse on himself when he met Flowers in a return match. The fight was rough, and more than once Flowers complained to the referee that Greb was gouging his eyes out with his thumb. But Greb failed to regain his title, though the referee voted for him and the majority of the spectators booed the decision.

It broke Greb's heart and for the first time following a fight be broke down and cried. It was not because he had failed to win back his title, but because he felt be had been robbed of a justly earned decision.

He never fought again, and four months later, he died following a minor operation in Atlantic City.

But back home in Pittsburgh, his admirers will remember him as a man with a hurrah and a cheer in his heart—a man who thrilled them when he was in there shooting. His intimates, like Harry Keck, will remember him for what he was both inside and outside those ropes.

TWENTY-FIVE BUCKS

The fight crowd is the most unreasoning, unjust, vicious, and vindictive of the audiences of sport.

JAMES T. FARRELL

Fifteen years is a hell of a long time to live in grease. Fifteen years is a hell of a long time to keep getting your jaw socked. Fifteen years is a hell of a long time for a broken-down, never-was of a palooka named Kid Tucker. Fifteen years stretched back through a reeking line of stale fight clubs, of jeers and clammy dressing rooms, and lousy gyms, and cheap canhouses, of ratty saloons with sawdust floors—OH, MEET ME TONIGHT IN THE MOON-LIGHT—of flophouses whose corridors were fouled with musty lavatory odors, of training camps, gyps, speakeasies—IT'S A LONG, LONG TRAIL A-WINDING INTO THE LAND OF MY DREAMS—of mouldy dumps and joints, of crooks, pikers, louses, lice, and war. ... Fifteen years stretched back all the way through these things to a boxcar, with *Armour's Meats* printed on its sides in white lettering, moving out of Lima, Ohio, and across sweet Ohio landscapes on a morning when the world was young with spring, and grass, and the hopeful if idiotic dreams of a good-natured adolescent yokel.

It was all over with Kid Tucker and there had never been any shouting—only boos. His fare had been punched into hash: cauliflower ears, a flattened nose, a scar above his right eye. His greenish eyes were shifty with the fleeting nervous cowardice of the sacked and broken man. He was flabby. The muscles in his legs were shot. There was a scar on one leg, the medal he had received for carrying a badly wounded farm boy from Iowa through a wheat field near Soissons on a day when the sun was mad over a mad world, the earth nauseous from the stink of corpses, and the wheat fields slashed

with ripping machine-gun bullets. Kid Tucker was through. Toss him aside. Another boloney drowned in grease and defeat.

Sol Levison matched him with K.O. Dane for a six-round preliminary bout at Sol's West Side Arcade Boxing Club. Sol always wore a derby and a race-track vest. He made money out of a mouldy dump of a boxing club. He made money out of a string of ham scrappers. He made money out of everything he touched. Dane was one of Sol's stable, fresh from Minnesota. Sol was nursing him along on pushovers, building up a reputation so that Dane could get a match with a first-rater for a good purse. It did not matter that the big-time boy would slaughter him in a round. He was being prepared for it just as cattle were fed for the Chicago stockyards. Tucker was another setup for Dane. And the Kid needed the twenty-five dollars Sol guaranteed him for the bout. He took the match. He earned his living by taking smashes on the jaw. But Sol told him that this time he would have to fight. No taking a dive in this fight.

"Lissen, now, that ring ain't no swimming pool. See! No divin'! It ain't gonna be nothin' like bed or a park bench. It's a prize ring, and you're in there to fight. So don't act like you ain't never seen a bed for a month. Yuh gotta fight this time ... or no dough. See!"

Kid Tucker had heard that before.

He reported on time at the West Side Arcade Boxing Club, a rambling building in a shambling district. He dressed for the bout, putting on a pair of faded trunks. With his hands taped, and a dirty bathrobe thrown over his shoulders, he sat on a slivery bench, waiting, watching a cockroach scurry up and down the wall. Two seconds sat on tilted chairs, one sleeping with his mug opened like a fly trap, the other reading a juicy rape story from *The Chicago Questioner*. Tucker sat. He didn't have many thoughts any more. He never became nervous before a fight. He had caught every kind of a punch already. He sat and watched the cockroach on the peeling green wall, with its many spots of broken plaster. It crawled up toward a window, turned back, scrambled sidewise, about-faced, turned downwards, and cut across the floor to lose itself in the shadows of a corner.

Kid Tucker wished that the scrap was over. He might manage to catch this kid off balance, and put him away. But then, he mightn't get any more fights from Levison, because this Dane was one of Sol's comers. Sol wanted him to put up a fight, because he was sure he couldn't take Dane. Anyway, he wished that the fight was over, and he was sitting in a speakeasy with a shot before him. He did not think much any more. Fools think. One day he had been a young ox, puking with excitement in a dressing room, awaiting the gong of his first fight. He watched a second cockroach scurry up and down the wall. Up and down it moved. The seconds lit cigarettes, and opened a discussion of the love-nest suit which had put the abnormal relationships of a rich old sugar daddy and a young gold digger on the front pages of the newspapers. Tucker sat and recalled the mice and cooties in the trenches in France. Up and down the cockroach moved.

When he entered the ring, he received only a small dribble of applause. The crowd knew the bum. Someone yelled at him, asking him if he had gotten his pants pressed for the tea party. Another wanted to know where his patent leather shoes were. Tucker never listened to the comments of the crowd, or its razzberries. He was past the time when he heard or was affected by boos. In France, he had lost all concern and worry when the shells landed. When he had heard one coming, he just casually flopped on the ground. A guy can get used to anything, if he just hangs around long enough. He sat in his corner, waiting, his eyes fastened on the ropes.

The crowd leaped to its feet spontaneously, and roars rose from the murkiness of faces when Dane entered the ring. He was a husky Swede with childish blue eyes, a thick square head, a bull neck, a mountainous pair of shoulders, and legs that resembled tree trunks. Tucker did not look at him.

A slit-mouth of an announcer bellowed out the names of the contending fighters, pointing to their respective corners as he briefly described trumped-up reputations. They shook hands in the center of the ring and returned to their corners. A gong clanged.

The arc lights glared down upon them, revealing a contrast between the fighters that was almost vicious. Dane was strong and full of youth; Tucker worn out and with a paunch of a belly. Both fighters were wary; and the crowd was perfunctory. It wanted Dane to make a corpse of the big fat ham. They faced each other, feinted, tapped, and blocked as they continuously circled around and around. Tucker could see that the kid was nervous; but he had learned to be a bit cautious of shaky young fighters when they looked as powerful as Dane. Dane led with a few light lefts. Tucker caught them easily with his gloves. His confidence perked up, and he retaliated with a straight left. It slid off Dane's jaw. They lumbered, feeling for openings. They clinched and their interlocked bodies made one swaying ugliness in the white glare of the arc lights. The referee danced in and parted them. They clinched again. They broke. Dane hesitantly attacked, and Tucker clumsily skipped backward.

Roars and boos grew out of the sordidness that surrounded the ring.

"Come on, Kayo. He's only a bum!"

"In the bread basket, you Swede! The bread basket!"

"Lam one in the bread basket, you squarehead, and he's through!"

"Come on, fight!"

"This ain't no party!"

"Hey, how about doin' your sleepin' at home? Huh?"

"Siddown in front!"

"Siddown, Tucker, and take a load off your feet!"

"No guts!"

"Murder the sonofabitch!"

"Kill the sonofabitch!"

"Fight, you hams. Fight!"

"Come on, you Swede boy, in the bread basket!"

Dane connected with a few inconsequential left jabs. He was clumsy, and when he led, he stumbled about, losing his balance. A good fighter with a willingness to take a chance, and a heart to mix and trade punches, could have cut him up and polished him off in short order. But Tucker kept backing away out of range, pausing to jab out with a few untimed, ineffective left-handed stabs. Dane danced about him in confusion, and when his opponent retreated, he stood in the center of the ring, hands lowered ungainly, a stupid expression of indecision on his face.

The crowd roared, and suddenly above the disgruntled roaring and booing there rose a throaty-voiced suggestion that sleeping quarters were upstairs. The bell saved them from further exertion.

The razzing increased during the one-minute intermission. Tucker sat heedless of the mob. He rinsed his mouth out from the water bottle, and puffed slightly. The seconds pointed out that Dane was leaving himself so open that a five-ton truck could be driven through his guard; Tucker said he would watch it, and catch the kid in the next round. He waited. He had five more rounds to go. He wondered if he could slip one through when Dane was off balance and stun him, or put him away. If he wanted to last through, he couldn't take many chances, and the kid looked like he had a punch that could kill a mule. He glanced toward the Dane's corner, where the latter's handlers were instructing him with emphatic gestures. He eyed the ropes.

Round two was duller and more slow than the first round. It was a clinching party. A fan called out that they were like Peaches and Daddy. Another suggested a bed. A third asked was it a track meet or a six-day bike race. The crowd grumbled. And repeatedly someone yelled to kill the sonofabitch.

A pimply-faced punk of a kid arose from his chair, yawned, ignored the commands from behind to sit down, and in a moment of quiet, shouted:

"I tank I go home!"

The crowd laughed, and he sat down.

Near the close of the round, Dane connected with a wild but solid right. The accidental wallop had echoed with a thud, and the mob was brought to its feet, yelling for blood and a knockout. Dane hesitated a moment, and stared perplexedly at his opponent. Then he went for Tucker with a look of murderous, if formal and melodramatic, intent stamped on his face.

The bell ended the round. There was a buzz of excitement. Dane was not such a dud after all. That right had been a beaut. Now he was getting

warmed up, and he would do his stuff. He'd crush a lemon like Kid Tucker dry; he'd put him away in a hurry. Watch that Swede boy go now; watch him knock that Tucker bastard out now! One to the bread basket, and one on the button, and the fights would go out for that has-been.

Tucker was a trifle groggy as the seconds started working over him. They whispered that he should fake weariness. That would bring Dane in, wide open. Then one solid punch might turn the trick. Tucker nodded his head as if to indicate that he knew the whole story. But when he found himself in there punching and taking them, he found himself unable to put anything behind his punches. In France, he had gone through two days of a terrific bombardment. Then he had caved in. He had gone on like an automatic man. He could not give himself. It was the same with fighting. He wanted to go in and take a chance trading punches. He told himself that he would. The haze was now cleared from his mind, and he was determined. But things had all happened like this before. Tucker, willing and determined, and then being unable to carry out his will, incapable of giving himself. He couldn't go in and fight. The war and the prize ring had taken all the fight out of him. His nerves and muscles wouldn't respond to his will. There had been too many punches. He awaited the bell, determining in vain. Tucker's state was called being yellow, having no guts. He sat out his final seconds of rest.

Just before the bell, Levison appeared, and told one of the Kid's seconds to warn him that he had to fight if he wanted his dough. Then, the clang of the gong. Some people in the crowd noticed Levison, but their curiosity was drowned by the roar greeting the new round. They were going to watch Dane take the bum for sure in this one.

The tired Tucker backed away. Dane pursued him, determined. His handlers had persuaded him into a state of self-confidence. He unscrewed an awkward left which flushed on Tucker's button. Tucker reeled backwards. The crowd leaped to its feet, yelling for blood. Dane *grew far away from Tucker*. Gloves came at the Kid like *locomotives slowly rising from the distance, coming closer and growing larger until they collided with his face. One ran into his stomach.*

"In the bread basket. Come on, you Swede!"

Tucker experienced a heaving nausea, and *far, far away there was a din of shouting.*

Instinctively, mechanically, Tucker fell into a clinch. He made a weak, hopeless effort to sew Dane up. His head swam in a daze, he was glassyeyed. Dane, *a billowing mass of flesh grew before his dimmed eyes. Something big closed his eyes.* His feet slid from under him. He was blinded for a few seconds. Then he weakly perceived through his sick daze. He arose feebly. *There was a swinging of gloves, a going around of posts, ropes, and gloves.* He floundered forward to clinch. He was off balance, and Dane came up from the floor with a haymaker that mashed into his jaw; the impact of the punch caused an audible thud. The lights went out for Tucker, and about him, dizzy darkness crashed, like a tumbling nightmarish dream. He fell backward, and his head bounced hard on the canvas. He lay there, quivering slightly, while the referee tolled off the necessary ten seconds. He bled from the mouth; blood trickling out to run in tiny rivulets and mixed with the dust and resin.

The mob rocketed approval.

"That's the ticket, Swede!"

"That's the babe!"

"You put him out for a week. Oh, you beautiful Swede!"

"You got the stuff, kid. Yay!"

"Christ, what a wallop! Dynamite!"

"Out for a week!"

"Oh, you Swede! Wahooooo!"

The punk kid with the pimply face who had yelled about going home in a Swedish accent evidently recalled Levison's visit to the ringside just before the gong. He jumped up on his chair, and shouted:

"Fake!"

As Tucker was lifted back to his corner, and set helplessly on the stool, the cry of fake was suddenly taken up, and it contagiously reverberated through the arena.

Dane left the ring, and the cheers turned to boos as feet stamped and the cry of fake loudened into a booming roar.

The seconds continued working on Kid Tucker. Levison, in the back of the building, nervously spoke with two policemen. Then, after giving hasty instructions to six burly bouncers, he walked to the ringside, climbed through the ropes and stood turning in the center of the ring, his hand raised for quiet.

"Silence, pleez!" he megaphoned.

He finally received relative silence and shouted through megaphoned hands:

"Ladies and gents! Ladies and gents! I wanna say a few words to yuh. I wancha to know I ain't never had nothin' to do with a framed fight, or a faked boxing match of any kind or classification. I wancha to know that any time Sol Levison promotes a bout, then that bout is on the square. A fight that Sol Levison promotes is one hundred per cent on the level. Now to show you all that I'm on the level, I'm gonna offer one hunerd dollars, one hunerd dollars reward to the man that can prove that this last fight was a frameup. Now some one of you spectators here has been so unkind as to insinu-ate that this here last fight has not been on the level. Now, I'm offering one hunerd dollars to the man that proves that this or that any fight that Sol Levison has ever promoted was not on the level, to the very best, I say to the very best, of his knowledge and intentions."

There was a mingling of cheers and boos.

"When one of my fights is not on the level, Sol Levison wants to know about it. This here last fight was not faked to the knowledge of Sol Levison. Kid Tucker here, he asks me for a chanct to go on so's he could make himself a little stake. I gave him his chanct, just as I always do with a boxer. Now, when I came up here just before the last round of this here last bout, it was to instruct Tucker that he had to fight if he wanted to get his purse. It was a square fight. Kid Tucker was yellah. He was just yellah. He was afraid of Kayo Dane, and refused to put up a resistance. He got just what was coming to him becuz he was too yellah to fight like a man, and like he agreed to when I agreed to pay him. He was yellah."

There were cheers. The handlers lifted Tucker down from the ring, and he was carted away to the dressing room amid many boos.

"Now, ladies and gents, to show you how I feel about this here matter, just let me tell you somethin'. When Sol Levison hires fighters, they fight. They fight or Sol Levison knows why. I guarantee that each and every bout I stage will give you your money's worth. If it don't, I guarantee that you kin get your money back at the box office. And when I hire boxers in good faith, they either fight ... or they get no purse from Sol Levison. Now, to show you how I feel, and to guarantee that you'll get your money's worth after the showing this yellah bum made here, I'm gonna take his purse that was coming to him if he had lived up to his agreement with me and stood up and fought like a man, I'm gonna take his purse because he don't deserve it for breaking the contract he made with me, and I'm gonna give it to the boy who puts up the best fight here this evening, and I'm gonna let you all choose the boy to get it by general acclaim. Now, ladies and gents, I ask you, is that fair? He was yellah and he didn't earn his purse. So, I asks you, is it not fair to give it to a boy with a real fighting heart. Now is that fair or isn't it?"

The roars of the crowd approving Levison's speech sounded like far echoes down in the mouldy dressing room where the beaten Kid Tucker lay unconscious. His handlers worked on him in vain, dousing him with water, using smelling salts, working in vain. Two bantams, one a swarthy-skinned Italian boy who had won a Golden Gloves championship before turning professional, and the other a bushy-haired Jewish lad, left to fight the next bout.

"He must have got an awful sock," the Jew said.

"He looks pretty bad," the Italian kid said to his manager.

"We'll bring him around," one of the seconds said.

They worked over Kid Tucker for an hour. Cheers echoed down from the other fights while they worked. A doctor was called in, and he could not bring Kid Tucker to consciousness. An ambulance was called, and Kid Tucker was carted out on a stretcher. As he was being put into the ambulance, the crowd was roaring acclaim, shouting out its decision that the swarthy skinned Italian bantamweight and former Golden Gloves champion, had merited Tucker's purse.

But Tucker did not need it. He was taken to the hospital and died of a cerebral hemorrhage without ever regaining consciousness.

[FICTION]

HELLO JOE

This is the best boy-meets-girl story ever written around boxing. It is also the best job of putting down on paper what it might have been like to be in there with Joe Louis.

WILLIAM FAY

We stood there under the lights, and I said, "Hello, Joe." I hadn't met him when we weighed at two o'clock. He said, "Hello, Farmer, boy." He said it soft and touched my gloves, and I could see him just the way he was. You know the way the Bomber is, a sleepyhead, and like a cat, all silk and brown, the champion of the world. The gloves he wears don't mean he don't have claws. Artie Monaghan was referee. "I want a nice clean fight," he said. "You boys have been around. You know the rules."

I know the rules, all right. I ought to know the rules. I got a small lump on my head for every rule they got. Artie knows just who I am and how I am, and talks into the ear that works. The other ear is just a muffin ear. It is a muffin that you wouldn't want to eat.

We left the hotel at eight o'clock and came to the stadium in a cab. I gave the guy a sawbuck for himself, and Lew said, gagging, to the guy, "You got a high-class load of freight." The cabby only laughed, but you could see he liked to hack a fare like us. We had two motorcycle cops up front, with Lew and me and Marty Manus sitting in the cab.

Lew taped my hands when we got there, and Marty made small strips of tape, like a doctor when he knows you will bleed. Lew put a towel around my head. I didn't want a towel around my head.

"You don't wanna lose your sweat," Lew said.

"How can I lose it? How can anybody lose his sweat? It stinks in here. It's hot!"

Lew smiled. "You're on edge, Farmer, that's all it is. How you feel?" He smiled some more. He thumped me playful on the arm.

"How the hell you think I feel at a time like this?" I said to him. I was sorry for the way I talked. I never talked like that before. "I'm sorry, Lew," I said. "It's hot, I guess. How'd the Yankees do today?"

Lew said, "How'd the Yankees make out, Marty?"

Marty said he didn't know. "They play two hours later in St. Louie," he said. "I'll ask some guy."

"Never mind," I said. "Forget it. I don't want anybody else in here."

"I can ask the cop outside the door."

"The hell with it," I said.

"He's on edge," Lew said. "That's the way you wanta be, Farmer. It's better that way."

I was on edge, all right, and I am a Yankee fan like Colonel Ruppert was a Yankee fan.

We went to our corners and Lew took the robe off me. Joe stood in his corner, with the colored boys there. It is hard to take your eyes off Joe, the way he is when the lights are shining down, when his robe is off and there's just the red gloves on his hands.

"The hell with him," said Lew, and then I took my eyes away.

The hell with me, too, was the thought I had, but Lew was being nice. He is always nice. He is a guy to have around. The ball park was black, except for where the ring was, and this is a time, it is always a time, when you're waiting for the bell and the crowd don't say a thing. The crowd just waits and feels the things you feel, except it don't get hit, tonight or any night. Lew shook my glove and said, "Go get 'im, Farmer." I did not say, "With what?" I turned around when I heard the bell, and saw that Joe was gliding easy, the way he

always glides, slick and smart, looking at me over his hands.

I know the things they said about the fight before we climbed in here, the things they wrote in the papers, and all the noise they made. The pictures they made, of Joe and me, and what we ate and what we weighed, and how I nearly beat the guy the last time that we fought. Well, that don't put the teeth back in my head if Joe should knock them out. That don't make me charming when I smile. That don't mean that I can beat one side of Joe. I'm smarter than the boys who write for the papers, though. They don't get hit by Joe, but I get hit, and I know how it feels.

He's got that left hand out. It is a hand that doesn't miss. He feeds it just a little at a time. He's got a spring inside his arm. They tell you he carries the arm too low. They tell the things that Dempsey would have done. Dempsey would take it right on his beard, just the same as me. I took it then. It wasn't hard. Just hard enough to bring the blood into my mouth. I shuffled in and watched the way he moved, his sleepy face. He doesn't have a face. He's got a mask. It doesn't say one thing at all. You don't know when the trouble's coming next.

He's got that left hand on a hinge. He is too smart to take a chance with me. He knows I hit like houses falling down, but not so good as him. He always takes it easy for a round or so, and then he gives you all the guns. Then everyone goes home. I moved in close and tried a short right to his chin. I threw it neat, but Joe just moves his kinky skull away. He chopped me with a right, like only Joe can chop, and then we punched inside a while, got tangled in a clinch. I looked and saw Lew crouching on the steps below the ring. Lew told me, "Easy," with the lips. I smiled a little smile for Lew. It's lonesome in a ring.

You've seen my picture once or twice, with Joe DiMaggio? With Lefty Gomez? With Selkirk and the boys? You know just how I feel about the Yanks. You know the way I like to see them play. I'm not a slob. I'm in the big leagues too. It's nice when you can walk down through a crowd and people say, "There's Farmer Willy Watson." It's nice to hear them all remembering how I nearly beat the champ, the first time we fought.

I was sitting with Lew in back of third base,

drinking beer and watching the Yankees. The beer was warm in the bottles. This was in May. The sun was bright all over the park and some of the boys wore glasses in the outfield. My vest was open, and it was a wonderful time. It was just three months ago last week.

Lew said, to get a rise from me, "I like Cleveland, Farmer. What'll you lay?"

"Whatta you want?" I said. "I'll lay you ten to five." We always clown around like that.

It was nice, all right, just sitting in the sun, and they'd taken my picture again that day, me with DiMaggio's glove on my hand, and him with his fists held up like he knew how to use them. A gag, it was.

"You'll lay ten to five?" said Lew. "You mean it? Cleveland's got Feller," he said.

"Ten to five," I said, and I hoped I wasn't showing off.

There was a girl on the other side of Lew. "I'll take twenty cents' worth," she said, and she had the nicest voice; her smile was white and nice and clean. She wasn't fresh. She was a friend of Lew's. We'd met her coming down the aisle.

Lew knew the girl from show business, where he used to be a stagehand, and I could see that this was a girl to know.

"Ain't seen you in ten years, Margie," Lew had said. "Ain't seen you since that Ziegfeld show." He sure was glad to see her. So was I.

The girl laughed. "Not so loud," she said.

Ten years are not so much. They didn't hang so heavy on this girl. And you could take a good ten years off me and find I'd still be shaving.

"We don't get any younger," Lew had said. "This is Farmer Watson, Margie."

"Pleased to meet you," I said, but I am strictly a slob when the ladies are around. I can open my eyes, but never my mouth.

"Siddown," said Lew, "and have a beer."

So the girl sat down and had a beer, but she drank her beer from a paper cup. I poured what was left of my beer in a cup, and Lew said, "What's the matter with the bottle, Farmer?" Leave it to Lew to say a thing like that. I kept looking around him at the girl, not so scared as I usually am. She had nice long legs and tidy feet. The clothes she wore were good. I wondered why she kept sitting around with a couple of bums like us.

I'm in the second round with Joe and we're moving

along. The crowd is screaming the things it feels. They got a right to scream, for the prices they pay, and pretty soon now Joe will get to work. It's watching his face that gets you down, as much as the things he does with his hands. I'm not afraid; don't get me wrong. It's just that Joe is the best in the world. I walked right in and hooked a left. I threw a short right hand inside that must have hurt. It's not that I can't give the man a fight. It's just he's better than I am. It's just there never was a man like Joe, and the dough I get is not enough for getting my brains messed up inside my head. He stabbed me with that long left hand again. He brought it three times to my face. I shuffled in and tossed a right; I know I must have done it wrong, because my back was on the floor. I even bounced a little bit. I've seen Galento go like that, when Louis hit him on the chin, and like Galento, I am tough, and never have been down. I heard the count. I was all right. Of course I would be getting up.

I don't know what happened to Lew at the ball game. Somebody came along, some pal, or maybe too many beers. But he was gone, that's all I know, and I was sitting with the girl.

She said, "I saw your fight last summer with the champ." They all say that—then it's not so hard to talk.

"I bet you don't like fights," I said.

"Not much," she said. "But you were really very good. You nearly won."

"Nearly's not enough though," I answered.

"It's closer than anybody else has come." She wanted me to be sure of that. "And you'll probably win the next time. A lot of people think so. I hope so, anyway." I told you she was nice.

"Thanks," I said. "But the man is murder."

"I like ball games," she said. "I really do." And she didn't fool. She always knew the score. She knew why McCarthy used so many lefthanders when a guy like Feller was pitching. She was a wonderful girl and it was easy for us to talk.

I said, "Will you have a hot dog?" And she said, "Yes, I love them." Then both of us were laughing about a lot of things, I don't know what; I didn't care, though both of us could see that I owed Lew ten bucks.

The way it is, when you are hit by Joe, it hurts more after than it does at first. The count was four, and Artie Monaghan held fingers up in front of me, first four, then five, then six. I rested on one knee. I looked around. I watched the timekeeper, standing up, hitting his club on the floor of the ring. The lights made faces clear around the ring, and some of the faces that I saw were sad. Joe never had me down before, not once in fifteen rounds the other time. I was all right, and Artie rubbed the resin off my gloves. I turned towards Joe and he came fast.

He wore no feeling on his face. No pity, fear or excitement there. No nothing there at all. But he came fast. I moved away. My legs were pretty good. I made him waste a right hand past my ear, and that's a trick that I do good. In fact, that's why the ear is tin. I grabbed Joe's arms and held him tight, and then I punched when we were on the ropes. I shook my head and waited for the bell. It wasn't long.

Lew ran a sponge across my face. He said, "You make 'im come to you." He fixed two cuts that Joe had opened just above my eyes. "You watch 'im, Farmer. Don't get hurt."

Lew knows I haven't got a chance, I thought. They know the truth when they start saying, "Don't get hurt."

I said it was the springtime. It was May, and it was warm; the trees were pretty when we walked along the street. You can thank the Rockefellers for the trees. We stood in Radio City, by the flowers. She said she liked to watch them. "So do I," I said, and then I felt so good I didn't care the Yankees lost.

That's where she worked—in Rockefeller Center, singing songs. A little beefy now, not much, she didn't dance. She said that she was thirty and I knew she didn't lie. She said Ziegfeld would do a handspring in his grave if she ever tried to dance.

"I bet you could dance like a dream," I said, which was pretty clever stuff for me.

"Willy, you're sweet," she told me then, and I was glad she called me Willy. Why they call me "Farmer" I don't know, because I never farmed so much as one potato. Sometimes they call me "the Ox," sometimes "the Plow," and a lot of silly things that are supposed to describe my style. Farmer or no Farmer, I've done all right. You'd hoe a lot of spinach to make the dough I made. A half million dollars gathering gold dust in the bank.

The place where Margie worked was built up on the roof. The Starlight Club, they call it, where a dinner costs four bucks. She sang and played the piano. The songs she sang were sweet and hot and very good. She's got a soft throb in her voice that sounds like broken hearts. Perhaps she's got a gimmick in her throat, like Crosby's got, that makes her sound so good. She sings so nice. She sings so clean and happily, then sad. The dinner trade don't slam their knives and forks around when Margie sings. I want to say it's all big league. I sat and listened quite a while, and signed some autographs for pretty girls who came along, and then I took a bow. You'd think that I gave flavor to the joint. You'd think that dinner didn't cost four bucks. I can't help wondering all the time what Margie sees in me, when she's a celebrity herself.

That night she drew my picture on a bill of fare. We were sitting in a coffee joint uptown, just off Broadway. She drew my picture, with my cauliflower ear, and I'd been trying all day long to turn my head the other way.

"I got another ear," I said.

She looked surprised. She said, "I'm sorry, Willy. But that's the ear I like. That's you."

"Don't you mind?"

"Mind what?"

"The ear," I said. "The vegetable. That's why I snap my hat down on the side."

She said, "You goose. You big goose. Why, I don't mind at all. I like you as you are."

I nearly cried. I couldn't stand to have her talk like that. I knew I loved her like I never loved my mother. Except I never knew my mother. I never met a pretty girl who didn't have me scared before.

You'll think I'm crazy. I swear you will, but I never knew about those things. The next day I bought her an automobile that cost three thousand bucks, because she'd told me she was fond of driving in the country. They brought it to her house.

I called her on the phone and said, "Hello, Margie." I waited, feeling foolish, for what she'd have to say.

She said, "That fire engine is back where it came from," and then hung up.

I sat there for the longest time. I didn't know what I should do, but I knew that I'd done something wrong. I called her on the telephone again. I said, "I'm sorry, Margie. I'm terrible sorry. You gotta see me. You don't understand."

"I understand," she said.

"Then you'll see me?"

"I don't know."

But she saw me, though. Late that afternoon.

She had a package in her hand and she smiled a little bit. She said, "You're nice, Willy. You're really nice." She handed me the package. I opened it up in the street where we met, and I saw it was a necktie.

"A present," she said. "From me to you." And then we walked along the street and she took me into a stocking store. She bought three pairs and held out her hand. "Two dollars, Willy," she told me then. "These are the kind I always wear."

"Three for two bucks?"

"Uh-huh," she said. "This is a present from you to me." We had a perfectly wonderful time, walking down the street.

Margie isn't here tonight. A girl like Margie doesn't like the blood to flow. But Joe is here. He's coming now, and Lew says, "Keep your hands up, Farmer." He shoves me off the stool.

Joe is sweating pretty good. He's oiled like a machine, and Joe is a guy who always takes a proper pride in his work. He doesn't like the last time when I went the full fifteen, and maybe he knows the year just past has slowed me up a bit. A year don't set so easy when you're thirty-two years old. But he'll have to take me the hard way. He knows I won't fold up, not like those other humpty-dumpties, not like those bums who fall right down as soon as he lifts his hands. I got pride in my work, too, except it's not as good as his. He hit me a left hook on the chin, but I held it there with my own right glove, not letting him take the hand away. I belted him clean in his body. I pushed him to the ropes. I brought my two hands up inside, the only way to fight a guy like Joe, who's smart. He got away. He stabbed me with a left. He did it again and cut me again. He cracked me a right hand high, and the way Joe hits, you always got pains for another two weeks, at least. "All right, Joe," I said to myself. "Here we go, just you and me. The way things are, they're not so good." I hooked three times, but he blocked them all. This guy is smooth and hard to find. His hands are hard. They're in my face, and then I'm on the floor again, and Artie holds three fingers up for me to see. I see them, all right, but no so clear as the last time, and I think to myself that a punchy slob is never a prize for a girl. I wonder does it pay me to get up? I hear the crowd that thinks I'm brave. They think I'm a wonderful man. They think I'm great when the going

gets tough, and how would they like it in here with Joe?

I never kissed a pretty girl until I was thirty-two years old. I just kissed her, that was all, and Margie ran her fingers through my hair. She seemed contented in my arms, counting the buttons on my vest.

She said, "I know. I understand. I'm lonely too. Everyone needs a place to rest his head. You're good, Willy, and you're brave. I always loved the people who were brave."

"I'm not so brave," I said, "It's not so smart to be so brave. That's why I got an ear like this."

"Forget the ear," she said.

I told her sometimes I get pains in my head. "That don't do any good," I said.

She understood. "You mean the champ?"

I meant the champ, all right. I told her that. "He's better than I am, Margie," I said. "I'm only second best. I thought that I should tell you that. I wanted you should get it straight."

She was worried, of course. I could see she was worried. "Do you have to fight him, Willy? Is it necessary?"

"I got a contract with Morris Weintraub," I said. "I can't run out on Morris. I never run out on anybody."

"I know, I know," she said. She thought while. "You're not second best, Willy," she told me then. "It isn't right to think that way. I'll bet it's not the way you used to think. You can beat him, Willy. You nearly beat him the last time." She don't know about the fight game, but it was nice of Margie to talk like that.

"That was the best fight I ever made," I said. "I don't have another one left like that."

"I don't care," she said, and I kissed her again. Her lips were soft and sweet and full of fire. Each man should have a woman for himself. I wondered how I ever got along all by myself before. "I don't care," she said again. "And don't you care. Win, lose or draw," she said. Her eyes were wet when I looked in them, and they were frightened too.

That's why I could stay here on the floor. "Win, lose or draw," she said. It's all the same to her. God knows he hit me hard enough to knock me out. He's stopped a dozen other bums with punches only half so good. "You're good and brave," she said. "I like you as you are," she said. There were a lot of things she said, all of them nice, that I'll remember longer than the punches I must take. . . . Okay, Artie, I'll be up. How many fingers, Artie— nine?

I'm up and on my feet. I'm goofy, just a bit. So this is sport? So you can have it, if it's sport. The champ will kill you if you let him do the punching all the time. I put my skull inside my arms. I let him punch a little while. I let my thoughts get clear. I knew my legs were not so good. We clinched, some-how, and Artie stepped between us. I said "Now!" when Joe was walking in. I throw them fast, so fast I don't know where I got the juice inside my arms. Joe slipped away, that easy way. This is the third round. He can wait, can wait forever till I'm gone inside, then bat my head right off into the bleach-ers—that's a laugh. I heard the bell and I was glad the hands belonged to Lew and not to Joe.

Lew's got collodion and stuff to stop the cuts. The kindest hands, he's got. The water is so good and cold and wonderful to feel, I wish they'd dump the bucket on my head.

"I'm all right," I said to Lew, and to myself I said, *Don't get panicky, you slob. You take it standing up.* Marty combed my hair, just for effect, and I sat straight and steady with my hands set on my knees. Marty said, "The Yankees win both games in St. Louie," and only Marty would think of that at such a time as this. I laughed. I looked around the ringside and I smiled for all my pals. I got so many pals you a need a place like this to hold them all. Lew said, "Good luck." Then I was walking back at Joe. We're in the sixth or seventh—I'm not sure. So far no trouble that a chin like mine can't take. He breaks me down a little at a time, not all at once. They told him how to fight me, not to mess around inside, where maybe he'd be cut. He's a million-dol-lar piece of chocolate. They don't want to take a chance. He's waiting till my legs give out, and then I'll get it good. He's clean. He got a mark. He's just a shadow with a ball bat in his hands. I keep my hands up and move along. They'll know at least I gave the guy a fight, a helluva fight. He didn't miss the last one that he threw. It caught me right. The best one yet. The lights swam for a minute, like a river made of gold. They come so fast you got no chance to see the punches come. I reach for Joe, but he's not there. His hands are there, but never Joe. I'd like to grab his arms and hold them still. His gloves are just like bullets from a gun.

In June I trained in Jersey, where I always train, and it was hot. This training isn't fun for me no more. Each morning I did six miles on the road, and in the afternoon, six rounds and sometimes eight, with tough guys who get twenty bucks a round. I can eat these bums I train with, but they got to make a living, too, and I see no sense. in punching the heads of guys that I can lick. Margie came, some days, and every Sunday she would come. We'd sit there on the porch, or walk along the roads when it was night, just holding hands and talking things about the two of us. The lilacs in the fields got smells you can't buy in a store. The night is soft and you can smell the grass; it all is different when you're with a girl. I always liked nice things like that, but now I know it's better with a girl. One night I said, "It would be nice if I was champ. I wouldn't fight again. We would sit and take our shoes off. We would say, 'We are the champ.' You'd be the champ same as me."

"That would be fun," she said. "But it doesn't matter, Willy. It really doesn't matter."

The hell it doesn't matter, I thought then. But I was sorry I had talked like that. The thought just got away, I guess—a foolish thought. But I had never done a thing for her. I couldn't help but think it would be nice if I was champ. What else I got to offer?

Artie stepped in between Joe and me, to look at the cuts I had in my eyes. It was the eighth, I guess, or maybe the ninth, and the round had twenty seconds more to go. He must have guessed the eye was not too bad. He clapped his hands, and Joe came bang-ing in again. He wasn't wasting time no more. Joe was teeing off.

Lew washed me up and Marty helped. Marty poured the water down my pants. He rubbed my legs and stuck the salts under my nose. I didn't need the salts. It was a bed I needed most. "Can't even see the guy," I said. I wished that I could see him. It's tough to fight a guy that you can't see. When the eye was fixed, I saw him, though, sitting there across the ring, the black boys talking in his ears, rubbing his lean brown belly, clucking soft and confident to him. Lew shoved me off the stool.

You got to admit I'm tough. I take a punch, all right. Joe hit me clean, right on the chin, and I could hear the crowd blow out its breath. They got a speaker system hanging down from over the ring.

It makes the punches sound louder than they are. You hear it loud across the radio. I wondered now did Margie hear the punch, or hear the crowd. I figured that the punches I must take hit Margie too. But what would you do? This guy is hot and getting warmer all the time. I wondered how she liked it when they said, "The Farmer's bleeding bad." That must be nice, indeed.

I ripped a fine right hand at Joe. I felt the punch go home. I tried again. I weaved as best I could from all the jabs he sent my way, those snakes with little razor blades that he's got up his arm. "I like you just the way you are," she said, and just the way I am, I never laid down yet. I hooked a short left hook at Joe when he was coming in. The punch was clean and stopped him for a while. It made him think. But then another made him mad. It made him fight twice as hard, although you couldn't tell it by his face. I knew if I just stood there I'd be killed, so I kept hitting back at Joe the best I could. You hear the crowd like thunder all the time. You know they're getting value for the dough they paid.

She told me, just this afternoon, "Willy, I won't worry. Not a bit. Just give him the evil eye, or something. I know you'll be all right."

"Whatta we got to lose?" I said, then clowned around some stupid way. Lew and Marty tried to clown around and help things out, but they knew, just as well as me, I didn't have a chance. I thought, *What kind of a hero am I? What kind of a fighter will stand around just looking at his corpse?* I could see her disappointment; I knew the way she felt. A woman will love you, win or lose, but a man should have faith when he goes to war. There were other things this afternoon.

I might go fifteen rounds, if I am smart. If my legs are good enough for me to run away. If I wrap my arms around my head and don't peek out at Joe. Just let my pride, like the rest of me, be hamburger.

I never thought of that before, when I used to fight alone. I didn't have to save my face for anybody's lips. I only had to worry for myself, and I could say, "You're okay, Willy," or "Willy, you're a bum."

The hell with Joe. She likes me the way I am. I walked on in. I took a tough one in the mouth. I shoved my left hand out and stopped him when he tried again. This is the tenth. He's strong, I see, and here the trouble comes. We stood together and we

punched. It seemed forever that we punched, and then we leaned together until Artie came along. He walked between us and we moved into the clear. Joe belted me with all he had. He wondered was I ever going down. A little worry in his eyes. Not very much, but some. It made me proud. I grinned at Joe. "How's it goin', Joe?" I asked him with the grin. But Joe didn't grin. That's not his way when the fight is on. That's why he is the champ, a classy kid. Inside, when we were working in a clinch, I heard him sigh a little sigh. I felt him hold a little bit. He's only human after all. I got it then. I got it good. He brought the fight to me with every gun he had. We stood and fought ourselves to pieces, Joe and me, and then I wasn't standing any more. My gloves were shoving at the floor. . . . Don't show me any fingers, Artie. I don't want to see no fingers. I'll get up. I'll go the whole fifteen.

I'm getting up and grinning back at Joe. His chest is going up and down. I never saw him heave like that before.

This afternoon, before we weighed, before I went with Marty and Lew to the Boxing Commission, there was a little church, downtown, and a priest that Margie knew when she was a kid. A long while ago, she said. She said she liked it best this way. She likes it, win or lose. It wasn't in the papers, not today. Nobody knows but Marty, Lew and Marty's wife, and Marty said he'd cut her heart out if she talked, if the thing got in the papers before the fight. She cried and held some flowers in her hand. She said that Margie was so beautiful today. Any day, I said.

Well, Joe, it's you and me. You're getting pretty tired. But not so tired you couldn't kill a horse with that left hook. It's round thirteen.

Joe hit me in the mouth with that left hand, but he was slow, a little bit. Not many guys have ever made Joe travel thirteen rounds. Not any guy will make me travel thirteen rounds again. I don't feel bad. Don't feel so bad I can't stand up.

This Joe is dangerous all the time. His mouthpiece shows. His mouth is open just a little bit. He's breathing through his teeth. He brought one home, downstairs, and that is not so good. Not when I'm getting set to do some tricks myself. He's trying now; he's trying hard; the effort's in his face and eyes. It never was before. He belts me twice and I belt him. When Artie breaks us, I can hear the crowd, the way they yell. It isn't often I can hear the crowd. There's always other things to do.

Joe brings his arms up slow. They must be awful tired. He hits me with another right-hand punch. I bring my own arms up; that's not so hard, because I've traveled more times to the wars than Joe. He's gone; he's tired inside; he isn't any faster than myself.

Well, Joe is young, and he can try again. A guy like me don't get a second chance. There is no other time for me. I'd like to nail him flat against the ropes. But Joe is smart. He's hard to catch. He's smooth and clever in his way. But I'm no dope. I've been around. I'm only starting in to punch. I hit Joe with a left hook on the chin. He wobbled some and didn't like the punch a bit. We've got this round and then two more, and Dempsey stopped Jess Willard in three rounds.

Just let me belt you, Joe. Just once or twice like that again. I've got a chance. A lousy little chance. I wonder what would Margie think, if I should bring the title home—a slob like me.

[REPORTING]

TITLE BATTLE IN TYPHOON

No other noncombatant has contributed as much to boxing as Nathaniel Stanley Fleischer. Over more than fifty-five years he wrote fifty-three books on the subject, donated 190 championship belts and officiated at more than a thousand fights, including two dozen championship contests. Starting in 1922 he was editor and publisher 'of *The Ring*, boxing's foremost magazine, and between 1941 and 1987 his *Ring Record Book and Encyclopedia* was the standard reference work. Born in 1887, he died in 1972.

This account of the Jimmy Carruthers–Chamrern Songkitrat bantam-weight championship fight in Bangkok on May 2, 1954, appeared in *The Ring*. Of it Fleischer said: "This was the most dramatic fight I ever saw—even more dramatic, because of the circumstances, than Dempsey-Firpo."

NAT FLEISCHER

In a scene unparalleled in the history of the bantamweight division, a scene that rivaled that in the Dempsey-Tunney fight in Philadelphia, before a gathering of 59,760 persons who paid 5,000,700 ticals, totaling $227,304.90 in U. S. currency, in an arena especially built for the occasion, Jimmy Carruthers of Australia defeated Chamrerm Songkitrat by a hairline margin in defense of the Australian's crown. The bout, unlike championship matches staged in our country or in Europe, was scheduled for twelve rounds, the only distance Jimmy would agree upon.

Fortunate for Carruthers that the fight was not a fifteen-rounder, as otherwise, in my opinion, he would have been shorn of his title. Bleeding badly from a deep cut above the right eye and tiring perceptibly, Jimmy used up all his energy in the final session to pull the chestnuts out of the fire, while his opponent, almost as fresh and strong as when he started, could have gone on for several more rounds without tiring. Carruthers was a lucky boy to hold on to his title. Although referee Bill Henneberry, imported from Down Under, gave the verdict to the champion by a margin of 31½ to 27½, I figured the fight much closer. Scoring the New York system, I had Carruthers ahead by one round and one point, and in the Australian system, used by the only official in the fight, I gave the decision to Jimmy by 31 to 29 points. The fight definitely was that close. In fact the majority of the spectators and many scribes had the local champion ahead at the end of the fight.

Carruthers' jabbing won the fight for him. In

hitting, especially body punching, he was outscored by Chamrern.

Those who witnessed the Tunney-Dempsey ten-round title bout in Philadelphia can imagine what was encountered here by picturing a terrific tropical storm that started hours before the fight, increased in intensity as the bout progressed, drenched the spectators and made a lake out of the ring. Bulbs from the overhead lighting system crashed to the canvas every now and then forcing temporary halts while the broom brigade rushed into the ring to sweep it clear, since the fighters, by agreement, were permitted to fight in their bare feet due to the slippery conditions. Carruthers stepped on glass in the eleventh round and cut his foot.

Carruthers, with the height and reach in his favor, figured to have an advantage, but with equal weights at 117¼ pounds and the conditions more suitable for Chamrern, who is accustomed to barefoot fighting, Jimmy found himself at a disadvantage. Once, in attempting to toss his right for the jaw as Chamrern stepped out of range, Carruthers hit the canvas with a thud and a splash, face down, spun back, and cracked his chin against the floor; his mouth bled from then on. Several times he lost his balance and almost went down, and in the second round, Songkitrat slipped and landed on his back.

But, despite the conditions, the fight was well fought with plenty of action by both lads who put on a splendid performance considering the torrent. Carruthers and his mentor, Dr. McGirr, thought that the champ had won easily and that if the weather had been favorable, he would have scored a knockout, but I didn't agree. He didn't show as much punching power as did his rival. The Australian pair the morning after the fight announced that they were satisfied that had they not imported their own referee, the championship would have changed hands, but that statement carried no weight with me since I found the Siamese most fair in their treatment.

The fight warrants a repeat, especially in view of the throng that packed the new National Stadium, and the thousands who clamored unsuccessfully for admission. Bangkok is definitely the place for the return engagement for which a contract was signed in my presence, with me a witness, but if it takes place, according to Brigadier General Pichai Kullavanijya, who arranged the title match, he will ask the World Championship Committee to appoint a neutral referee to avoid any squawks. It is certain that Dr. McGirr will oppose such a move.

Regarding the next move of the champion, Dr. McGirr stated that he prefers to have Robert Cohen of France get the next shot at the title, but insists that the Frenchman must accept terms offered by the champ. He asked me to present the champion's challenge to the French contender at the European Boxing Union Convention at Monte Carlo. He is willing to have Jack Solomons act as a partner in staging the bout.

Discussing Carruthers' future, Dr. McGirr said: "I know that Solomons has something to say in Cohen's promotions. We offered to have Jimmy fight the Frenchman but he seems to think he, not my Jimmy, is the champion. He wants even more than Jimmy can get out of the fight. If he turns down my offer now, I shall shunt him to the side lines and give Songkitrat the next championship match."

However, since then Carruthers, who has had difficulty making weight, has officially made known his retirement as undefeated world bantamweight champion.

Despite his hairline defeat by Carruthers, Songkitrat definitely continues to fit into the championship picture. He earned the right to another shot at the crown and remains the number two contender, the post he occupied before the fight here.

Carruthers received 175,000 Australian pounds tax free, round-trip tickets for himself and wife, his trainer and his manager, and all expenses for the entire outfit.

The Bangkok fight in more than one way established a record. It was the first championship bout, or for that matter any other important contest, in which women seconded the title holder. Mrs. Myra Carruthers and Mrs. McConnell, wife of Carruthers' trainer, took their place as aides to Bill during the entire contest.

Dressed in specially made white garments draped with Australian flags, they worked as would our Whitey Bimstein or the Florio brothers when handling the corner of a champion or challenger. Within a few minutes after entering the ring and discarding their huge Siamese umbrellas, the women were drenched by the continuous cloudbursts, but they were game to the core and stuck to their task to the end.

Add to the above the record attendance for a

bantam championship match, and that for the first time in ring history champion and challenger fought in their bare feet, and you have something by which to remember the Bangkok affair.

For a city that had never seen a championship bout before, and where Thai or foot-and-hand fighting, of which I shall write in the next issue, is the national pastime, Bangkok's Police Department which staged the bout for the Police Hospital Fund under the direction of General Pichai, as he is commonly known, did itself proud. Except for the storm and the thousands who had to be turned away due to the shortage of accommodations at the vast arena, the gigantic affair was carried out without a flaw.

Since I was the guest of the Thailand government and the official representative of both the National Boxing Association and the European Boxing Union at the fight, the principals in the contest and the Thailand government officials appointed me to supervise the weigh-in to see that the championship regulations were adhered to, and made me the official arbiter in any dispute. There was no need for the latter since at no time did a point arise that required special considerations, so well did General Pichai handle his end of the program.

In every respect, this was a fight crowd such as seldom if ever in my long experience has been seen at the ringside of a world title bout. Dignitaries from Thailand and other nations in this Far Eastern land, most of them in native garb, nobility from many lands, fight fans who traveled by bicycle, train, auto and by foot for many miles—they all headed for the National Stadium hours before the first bout, a hand-and-foot mill, got under way.

Traffic was so congested that it took more than an hour to cover less than a mile from my Government Residence to the arena. But it was little different in that respect from what we ordinarily encounter in any big city when a champion match is being staged, except for the color offered by the mass of humanity of many nations, trudging through the street high in mud, unmindful of the downpour or the ruination of their clothes. As for the latter, all types that give the Far East its picturesqueness, were in evidence, from that of the Hindus, Japs, coolies, Australians and Americans, many of whom were present, to the native garb of the Siamese.

It was a sight to behold—one I shall never forget.

Picture the old Garden Bowl in Long Island, but to a greater depth, with about 20,000 additional seats, and you have a pretty good idea of how the National Stadium of Bangkok looked on this night of all nights. Throughout the day the radio kept announcing that the fight was a sellout but that didn't halt those who had no tickets from flocking to the scene and adding to the congestion. Their national hero, the Jack Dempsey of Thailand, was to fight for a world title, and his admirers were determined to see him.

The lusty cheers that greeted his appearance in the ring, the many gifts that were showered on him after he had bowed in native custom to Buddha, were evidence of the admiration the people of Thailand have for their boy. He is to the Siamese youth what Dempsey is to the American youth, and in his close defeat he became even more of a national figure because he had gone the limit with a fighting champion.

Songkitrat, known as the "Fiery Lizard," is a handsome Thai boy of twenty-four, who took his name from a boxing school he attended. He toughened himself for Siamese-style fighting by plowing behind a water buffalo in the rice paddies as a youth, and so clever was he in the Thai rough-and-tumble style of fighting that he was urged to turn his talents to the European and American style, in which he has met with success.

Though he was defeated on points by the Orient champion, Larry Bataan, in 1952 after he had floored his opponent, he won the Orient lightweight title from Speedy Cabanella that same year in a Bangkok fight. He then whipped Masahi Akiyama, Japanese bantam title holder, Vic Herman of Scotland, Jimmy Pearce of England, Kevin James of Australia and our own Pappy Gault, to gain the title shot at Carruthers.

At the weigh-in, with me in charge, I urged that the bout be postponed for a day. But since we had had three successive days of this Oriental typhoon in which the rain came down like pellets, Brigadier General Pichai, speaking for his government, urged that no postponement be made. "We have arranged half fares on all trains from every part of the country to enable our people to come to see Chamrern fight for the title, and we have no accommodations to handle the throng that is flooding the city," the General said. "The fight I think should be held regardless of the weather.

106

Our people are accustomed to such storms."

Before acting, since the final decision was left to me, I gave each of the fighters an opportunity to express his opinion. They were in favor of going on with the show.

Then came the request of Carruthers to be permitted to fight without shoes. "The ring will be too slippery to fight with regular boxing boots on," he said.

I gave consent after the same request had been made by Chamrern, and thus the stage was set for this historic ring contest. Dr. McGirr, manager of Carruthers, like Brigadier General Pichai, remarked, "Since we have had this heavy downpour for three days, there is no assurance that there will be a clearance by tomorrow and I agree that the fight must go on tonight."

Between weighing-in time and the fight, thousands of visitors went to the various Buddha temples to pray for the rain to halt and the success of their hero. In the national temple, the beautiful Emerald Buddha temple, the scene was most impressive. There hundreds of fight fans from the North and South who had never been to the famous historic building, knelt in prayer with shoes off, the native custom. The National Museum and the King's Palace grounds, all open for the occasion, likewise were jammed with visitors.

It was a picture to behold, to see fight fans, men, women and children, many carrying bags of food, coming to the fight in their gayest festival garments, paying respects to Buddha and their latest national idol, Chamrern Songkitrat.

As for the fight itself, one round followed the other in pattern. Carruthers would flip his right, a stinging sort of jab that knocks his opponent off balance when it lands, while Songkitrat, following instructions, rushed forth to play an attack on Jimmy's body. In the majority of rounds, Chamrern was the aggressor, but Jimmy caught him time and again with effective rights; but he couldn't defend himself against a vicious two-handed body attack that often caused the champ to gasp.

Entering the ninth round, the fight was anyone's. I had Carruthers ahead by only one point. It was in the ninth that Jimmy turned the tide somewhat more in his favor with quickened speed and more effective punching. He was good in that round, which he won.

Then came the tenth in which Songkitrat, urged by his handler to rush his man and attack the head

instead of body, opened a deep gash over the champion's right eye, a new cut, which bled profusely. Carruthers, face red with claret, showed signs of weariness as he tried to halt the assault of his opponent, who was widely cheered as his partisan rooters figured he now had the fight in hand and would win. The round belonged to Songkitrat.

The rally by the Thai boy continued in the next round in which he kept piling in blows, giving his opponent no quarter. He pummeled away at the injury above the eye, often forcing Carruthers to jump into a clinch from which he quickly broke and tried desperately to stab his vaunted right, his best punch, to the face of the challenger. Some landed but most failed to reach their objective.

The fight on my card was now even in rounds, with the champion one point ahead in that method of scoring.

The gong sounded for the final round. Chamrern hadn't heard it and stood waiting while Jimmy rushed out of his corner to shake and resume the warfare. Referee Henneberry waved the Thailand boy to the center of the ring, the shake was over and out went Carruthers to clinch the narrow-margin victory. In desperation, apparently realizing his plight, he met the body attack of his rival with equal blows but couldn't avoid punches to the head that kept the blood flowing freely from the wound above the eye.

Carruthers slowed up Songkitrat with punches to the jaw and several good lefts to the body but his best attack in this final session was his effective right, tossed out like one throwing a dart; and though he was hurt several times during the round, he did more damage, landed the more effective blows in that frame and was more effective in the many body exchanges.

That, in my opinion, won the fight for him. It was the round that clinched the victory, but Jimmy knew that he had been in a battle, and from both him and his handlers we learned that it was his toughest fight.

Make no mistake about judging Songkitrat. He's a good fighter who is courageous as all Thai fighters are, has a heavy wallop and is exceedingly fast. All he lacks is some science and this he'll gain as he continues to fight the top men of his division. He would make a good addition to the bantams and feathers of America, but he can make much more money in the Orient than he could in a country where we are short of men of his weight who possess drawing power.

With the fight over, and many boos penetrating the air when the decision was rendered, Songkitrat grabbed the microphone and standing in the center of the ring, said:

"I am very proud to have been able to bring fame to my country by being the first Thai boxer to contend for the world bantamweight title, and I am personally satisfied that the decision was fair and beyond doubt. If I am not sorry, my friends and my countrymen, why are you?"

Thus in Songkitrat, Thailand has a boxer who lives up to the tradition of fair play and sportsmanship for which his country is noted.

The day following the bout, General Phao Sriyanonda, Director General of National Police and Deputy Minister of the Interior and Minister of Finance, at a banquet tendered in honor of Commissioner of Police Delaney of New South Wales and me, asked me to obtain an American trainer for Thailand boxers. He requested me to sign someone for six months in an effort to boom the sport in Siam and to help organize a Police Athletic League boxing team.

This I shall do upon my return to America.

[PORTRAIT]

PITY THE POOR GIANT

In the career of Primo Carnera the fight game reached its nadir, and Paul Gallico found, in the facts of it, a story surpassing anything that he could invent as a fiction writer. As a footnote, it should be recorded that, in 1946, Carnera returned to the United States, flourished financially as a wrestler and became an American citizen.

PAUL GALLICO

There is probably no more scandalous, pitiful, incredible story in all the record of these last mad sports years than the tale of the living giant, a creature out of the legends of antiquity, who was made into a prize fighter. He was taught and trained by a wise, scheming little French boxing manager who had an Oxford University degree, and he was later acquired and developed into a heavyweight champion of the world by a group of American gangsters and mob men; then finally, when his usefulness as a meal ticket was outlived, he was discarded in the most shameful chapter in all boxing.

This unfortunate pituitary case, who might have been Angoulaffre, or Balan, or Fierabras, Gogmagog, or Gargantua himself, was a poor simple-minded peasant by the name of Primo Carnera, the first son of a stonecutter of Sequals, Italy. He stood six feet seven inches in height, and weighed two hundred and sixty-eight pounds. He became the heavyweight champion, yet never in all his life was he ever anything more than a fourth-rater at prize fighting. He must have grossed more than two million dollars during the years that he was being exhibited, and he hasn't a cent to show for it today.

There is no room here for more than a brief hasty glance back over the implications of the tragedy of Primo Carnera. And yet I could not seem to take my leave from sports without it. The scene and the story still fascinate me, the sheer impudence of the men who handled the giant, their conscienceless cruelty, their complete depravity toward another human being, the sure, cool manner in which they hoaxed hundreds of thousands of people. Poor Primo! A giant in stature and strength, a terrible figure of a man, with the might of ten men, he was a helpless lamb among wolves who used him until there was nothing more left to use, until the last possible penny had been squeezed from his big carcass, and then abandoned him. His last days in the United States were spent alone in a hospital. One leg was paralyzed, the result of beatings taken around the head. None of the carrion birds who had picked him clean ever came back to see him or to help him.

No one who was present in Madison Square Garden the night that Primo Carnera was first introduced to American audiences will ever forget him as he came bounding down the aisle from the dressing room and climbed into the ring. It was a masterpiece of stage management.

He wore black fighting trunks on the side of which was embroidered the head of a wild boar in red silk. He disdained the usual fighter's bathrobe and instead wore a sleeveless vest of a particularly hideous shade of green, and on his head a cap of the same shade, several sizes too large for him and with an enormous visor that made him look even larger than he was. Leon See, the Frenchman, then his manager, was a small man. The bucket carriers and sponge wielders were chosen for size, too— diminutive men; everything was done to increase the impression of Primo's size.

Carnera was the only giant I have ever seen who was well proportioned throughout his body for his height. His legs were massive and he was truly thewed like an oak. His waist was comparatively small and clean, but from it rose a torso like a Spanish hogshead from which sprouted two tremendous arms, the biceps of which stood out like grapefruit. His hands were like Virginia hams, and his fingers were ten red sausages.

His head was large, even for the size of his body, and looking at him you were immediately struck with his dreadful gummy mouth and sharp, irregular, snaggle teeth. His lips were inclined to be loose and flabby. He had a good nose and fine, kind brown eyes. But his legs looked even more enormous and treelike than they were, owing to the great blue bulging varicose veins that wandered down them on both sides and stuck out far enough so

that you could have knocked them off with a baseball bat. His skin was brown and glistening and he invariably smelled of garlic.

This was the horror that came into the Madison Square Garden ring and sent a sincere shudder through the packed house. That is to say, he was horrible until he commenced to fight, when he became merely pitiful and an object demanding sympathy. Behind what passed for the wild battle blaze in his eyes and the dreadful gummy leer, emphasized by the size of the red rubber mouthpiece (tooth protector) with which they provided him, there was nothing but bewilderment and complete helplessness. The truth was that, handicapped by rules and regulations, a sport he did not understand and was not temperamentally fitted for, and those silly brown leather bags laced to his fingers, never at any time could he fight a lick. His entire record, with a few exceptions, must be thrown out as one gigantic falsehood, staged and engineered, planned and executed by the men who had him in tow and who were building him up for the public as a man-killer and an invincible fighter.

But I think the most dreadful part of the story is that the poor floundering giant was duped along with the spectators. He was permitted, in fact encouraged, to believe that his silly pawings; and pushings, when they connected, sent men staggering into unconsciousness and defeat. It was not until late in his career, when in spite of himself he learned something through sheer experience and number of fights, that he ever knocked anyone out on the level. But he never could fight, and never will. In spite of his great size and strength and his well-proportioned body, he remained nothing but a glandular freak who should have remained with the small French traveling circus from which Leon See took him.

This big, good-natured, docile man was exhibiting himself in a small wandering cirque in the south of France as a strong man and Greco-Roman wrestler, engaging all comers and local talent in a nightly show, having found that it paid him more and offered a better life than that of his chosen profession of mosaic-worker. Here he was discovered by a former French boxing champion who signed him up and apprenticed him to one Monsieur Leon See to be taught the rudiments of *la boxe*. It is highly probable that the time spent as a wrestler set his muscles and prevented him from ever becoming a knockout puncher. But Monsieur Leon See was taking no chances. He taught and trained Carnera strictly as a defensive boxer.

Now, it must be understood that Leon See was one of the most intelligent, smart and wily men that ever turned a fighter loose from his corner. He was not much more scrupulous than the bevy of public enemies who eventually took Carnera away from him simply by muscling him, but he was much more far-seeing and he had certain well-thought-out notions and theories about the ridiculous game of boxing. Among them was the excellent and sensible thought that the human head was never intended by nature to be punched, and that secondly, from the manner of its construction out of hundreds of tiny, delicately articulated bones, the closed fist was never meant to be one of man's most effective weapons. In this last idea, Monsieur See was not alone. The coterie of tough guys and mobsters who eventually relieved him of his interest in Carnera rarely used the fist, reckoning it, as did See, an inefficient weapon. The boys always favored the pistol or Roscoe, also known as the Difference, the Equalizer, the Rod, and the Heat.

See was a keen student of the human body—for a prize-fight manager—and he knew something about men. He was aware that abnormalities of size were usually compensated for by weaknesses elsewhere. He found out—exactly how is not known—that Primo Carnera would never be able to absorb a hard punch to the chin. He may have had some secret rehearsal in a gymnasium somewhere in Paris and, having ordered some workaday heavyweight to clout Primo one just to see what would happen, saw that the giant came all undone, wobbled and collapsed. Be that as it may, Monsieur See knew. And never at any time while he was connected with Carnera would he permit anyone to punch Primo in the head—neither his sparring partners nor his opponents. Since both received their pay from practically the same source, this was not so difficult to arrange as might be imagined. But See also had something else. He was a Frenchman and so he had a heart. He loved big Carnera.

Years later See proved to be right. When Carnera, through exigent circumstances, was forced to fight without benefit of prearrangement, and the heavyweights began to sight along that big, protruding jaw of his and nail him for direct hits, he was slaughtered. He was brave and game and apparently could take punches to the body all the night long. But one hard, true tap on the chin and he fell down goggle-eyed. For a long time during the early years, however, nobody was permitted to hit him there, and Carnera himself began to think he was invincible.

Primo's first trip to the United States was arranged through an American contact man and importer of foreign fighting talent, a character from Tin Ear Alley named Walter Friedman or, as Damon Runyon nicknamed him, Walter (Good-Time Charley) Friedman. See was smart enough to know that without an American "in ," without cutting in an American manager, he would not get very far in America. What he was not quite smart enough to know was how deep his "in" took him, that the ramifications of Friedman's business and other connections were to lead through some very rough and rapacious parties.

Carnera's first fight in New York involved him with a lanky Swede named Big Boy Peterson. In this fight poor Carnera was hardly able to get out of his own way and caused his opponent the most frightful embarrassment through not being able to strike a blow that looked sufficiently hard to enable him to keep his end of the bargain, if there was one. Eventually Peterson succumbed to a push as Carnera lumbered and floundered past him, and to make assurance doubly sure, the Swede hit himself a punch on the jaw as he went down. Someone had to hit him.

Now, this was a shameless swindle from start to finish one way or another. If Peterson was making an honest effort to fight he never should have been permitted to enter the ring. The press unanimously announced beforehand that it would probably be a sell and a fake, and when it was over, suggested strongly that it had been. But it said so in a gay and lighthearted manner as though the whole thing were pretty funny (as indeed it was), and there was no one on the New York State Athletic Commission either sufficiently intelligent or courageous enough to throw Primo and his handlers and fixers right out of the ring and thence out of the country. The Peterson fight in Madison Square Garden, the stronghold of professional boxing, was a sort of test case by the Carnera crowd to see how much they could get away with. On that score it was a clean-cut success. They found out that they could get away with anything. And so they proceeded to do just that. Primo's first American tour was organized, a tour that grossed something like $700,000, of which handsome piece of money Carnera received practically nothing. He was barnstormed across the country in the most cold-blooded, graceless, shameful series of fixed, bought, coerced, or plain out-and-out tank acts ever. If one of them was contested on its merits it was only because the opponent by no possible stretch of the imagination or his own efforts could harm Carnera or even hit him.

Where the fight could not be bought—that is to say, where the fighter was unwilling to succumb to a tap on the elbow for a price—guns were produced by sinister strangers to threaten him; and where neither threats nor money were sufficient to bag the fight, he was crossed or tricked, as in the case of Bombo Chevalier, a big California Negro who was fascinated by the size of Carnera's chin, and nothing would do but he was going to hit it, just to see what would happen. Between rounds one of Chevalier's own attendants rubbed red pepper or some other inflammatory substance into his eyes so that he lost all interest in tapping anybody's chin.

In Newark, New Jersey, a Negro was visited in his dressing room before the bout by an unknown party not necessarily connected with Carnera's management, and was asked to inspect shooting irons, and in Philadelphia another Negro, Ace Clark, was amusing himself readying up Carnera for a knockout—he had already completely closed one of Primo's eyes—when somebody suggested he look down and see what the stranger beneath his corner was holding under his coat, and what caliber it was.

Every known build-up fighter was lined up for this tour, including faithful old hands like K.O. Christner, Chuck Wiggens, and poor Farmer Lodge. Political and gangster friends in the cities visited volunteered with their private heavyweights for quick splashes that might look well on the record books. It was all for the cause. The more money Carnera made, the more the boys would have to cut up amongst themselves. It was all just one big happy family. It seemed almost as though every scamp in the boxing game contributed his bit somehow to that Carnera build-up.

Friedman, as has been indicated, was the go-between, and although Leon See was quite capable of all the planning necessary to keep Carnera in the victory columns, nevertheless it would have been considered bad form, and downright dangerous, if See had not cut the local boys in. And, at that, I suspect the said local boys showed the amiable and gifted Frog a few things about building up a potential heavyweight champion that made the two Stribling fights arranged by Monsieur See, one in Paris and the other in London and both ending in fouls, look like Holy Gospel.

An adviser and co-director of the tour, Broadway Bill Duffy was cut in. Bill was then in the night-club and fight-managing business, but in his youth he had been convicted of a little al fresco burgling and had been sent away for a spell. He was still to achieve the highest pinnacle of fame that can come to an American—to be named a Public Enemy. It is a curious commentary upon the conduct of boxing around New York that Duffy was allowed to operate as a manager and a second when there was a rule on the books of the State Athletic Commission, if indeed it was not written directly into the boxing law, that no one ever convicted of a felony was to be eligible for any kind of a license.

Duffy usually split even on things with his dearest friend, Owen Madden, better known as Owney, who had also been away for a time in connection with the demise of a policeman. Owney was out on parole at the time—he was sent back later—making beer (and very good beer it was, too) and acting as silent partner in the operation of a number of prize fighters. Also in this crowd was a charming but tough individual known as Big Frenchy De Mange who made news one evening by getting himself snatched and held for ransom by Mad-Dog Vincent Coll. The Mad Dog was subsequently rubbed out in a West Side drugstore telephone booth. But the subject, after all, is Primo Carnera and not gangsters and racket men, though pretty soon it was all one subject and all one sweet and fragrant mess. The boys had their connections in every town. The Philadelphia underworld collaborated through the medium of the always friendly and helpful Maxmillian Boo-Boo Hoff, and the same courtesies were extended all the way through to the Pacific Coast, where occurred the Bombo Chevalier incident, which was too nauseous even for the local commission there to stomach. There was an investigation resulting in the suspension of a few unimportant people. But Carnera and his swindle went merrily onward.

And it continued until he won the heavyweight championship of the world by ostensibly knocking out Jack Sharkey, then world's champion, in the sixth round, with a right uppercut. I say "ostensibly" because nothing will ever convince me that that was an honest prize fight, contested on its merits.

Sharkey's reputation and the reputation of Fat John Buckley, his manager, were bad. Both had been involved in some curious ring encounters. The reputation of the Carnera entourage by the time the Sharkey fight came along in 1933 was notorious, and the training camps of both gladiators were simply festering with mobsters and tough guys. Duffy, Madden, *et Cie.*, were spread out all over Carnera's training quarters at Dr. Bier's Health Farm at Pompton Lakes, New Jersey. A traveling chapter of Detroit's famous Purple Gang hung out at Gus Wilson's for a while during Sharkey's rehearsals. Part of their business there was to muscle in on the concession of the fight pictures.

If the fight was on the level, it wasn't like either of the companies operating the two pugs. If it was honest, the only explanation was that the boys were going sissy. As far as Primo knew, the right uppercut with which he tagged Sharkey in the sixth round was enough to kill a steer. He had knocked out many men with the same punch. Now he was the heavyweight champion of the world, and even if he didn't have any money to show for it, Italy and Mussolini were going to be very pleased. I have often wondered how long he remained innocent, how long it was before he began to catch on.

For instance, it must have been a terrible surprise and considerable of an eye-opener to Carnera the night he fought Tommy Loughran in Miami as heavyweight champion of the world. It was a no-decision match and a bad one for the gang to make, but they had to do something because they were desperate for money at the time. If the Sharkey fight was crooked, it is probable that the entire end of Primo's purse had to be paid over for the fix.

The Loughran fight had to go on the level because no one had ever managed to tamper with Loughran, and neither he nor his manager was afraid of guns. And Tommy had another curious and valuable protection. He was a good Catholic, and many priests were his friends. The gunmen were a little shy of those padres, who might usually be found in twos and threes at Tommy's home or his training camps. But the mob figured that with a hundred-pound advantage in weight Carnera could take care of Loughran, who was, little more than a

light heavyweight and never was a hard hitter. During the fight Carnera hit Loughran more than a dozen of the same upper cuts that had stretched Sharkey twitching on canvas, and never even reddened Tommy's face. Loughran was a cream-puff puncher and yet staggered Carnera several times with right hands and was himself never in any kind of danger from a punch. He merely got tired from having Carnera leaning on him for half an hour. If nothing else, that fight beneath the Miami moon exposed how incompetent Carnera was as a bruiser, and how utterly false were the stories about his invincibility, besides casting fresh suspicion upon his knockout of Sharkey. We had all seen Loughran put on the floor by a 175-pounder. If a man weighing around 280 pounds, as Primo did for that fight, hit him flush on the jaw and couldn't drop him, and yet had knocked out one of the cleverest heavyweights in the business, it wasn't hard to arrive at a conclusion. It was obvious that he was a phony and the first stiff-punching heavyweight who was leveling would knock him out.

Max Baer did it the very next summer. The following summer Joe Louis did it again, and then an almost unknown Negro heavyweight by the name of Leroy Haynes accomplished the feat for the third time. And that was the beginning of the end of Primo.

His lucrative campaigns and the winning of the heavyweight championship had enriched everyone connected with him except poor Primo, who saw very little of the money he earned. There were too many silent partners and "boys" who had, little pieces of him. Monsieur Sée had long since been dispensed with and shipped back to France for his health; he had served his purpose. But it was an evil day for Carnera when they chased Leon back to Paris, for Leon never would have permitted anyone to belt Carnera on his vulnerable chin. As suggested, the little Frenchman had a love for the big fellow whom he had taught and trained and watched over so carefully. The Duffy crowd had no love for anything. Fighters' chins were made to be smacked and they might just as well get used to taking the punches there.

It seemed as though their power was beginning to lose some of its effectiveness, exhausted perhaps by its own virus and viciousness, shortly after they had made Carnera champion. Primo escaped to Italy with his title and nothing else and later returned here for the disastrous fight with Loughran under the guidance of a little Italian banker by the name of Luigi Soresi, who appeared to be genuinely trying to get and keep for poor Carnera some of the money he was making.

The by-products of the Miami affair were typical and pathetic. Duffy and company were living over a Miami night club in style and spending money like water—Primo's money. Carnera was relegated to a cheap cottage back of the town with a trainer. No one really looked after him. No one cared particularly whether he trained or not. He came into the ring against Loughran twenty pounds overweight. Shortly after that, Duffy was clapped into the jug for a spell for some boyish pranks with his income tax, and from the cooler he wrote pleading letters at the time that Carnera was preparing to defend his title against Baer, maintaining that he was needed to guide, advise, and teach Primo, to prime him for the first serious defense of his title, and that he should be given furlough from quod to attend to this matter. Carnera vigorously denied that he needed him. He was only too delighted to have Duffy held in durance vile. Of course what was really killing Uncle Will was that he was where for the first time he couldn't get his fingers on a nice big slice of the sugar that big, stupid Wop would make for boxing Baer.

It is difficult to bag or fix a heavyweight championship prize fight, though it has been done. But in the postwar sports renaissance there was so much money at stake in a heavyweight championship fight that it took more cash than most could produce to purchase either champion or challenger. It stood to reason that if the champion figured to make a million dollars or more out of his title he wasn't going to sell out for any less. Too, the power of the gangs was weakening. Repeal dealt them a terrible blow and took away their chief source of revenue. Three or four years before, Carnera's title would have been safe because his handlers would not have accepted any challenger for the title unless he agreed to preserve the state of the champion's health throughout the encounter. And there were always ways and means of keeping a challenger from double-crossing.

But Duffy was in the sneezer, as the boys sometimes quaintly called the jailhouse, Carnera was broke and needed money. He could only get it by fighting Baer. And the Baer fight could not be fixed. Baer's reputation was good; at least, he had not been caught out in any shady fights. He was a

powerful hitter and it was apparent that now at last the rest of us were going to be made privy to what it was that happened when Carnera was struck forcefully on the chin. We didn't have to wait long. He was knocked down three times in the first round, and lost his championship in the eleventh round on a technical knockout when he was helpless, having been knocked down a total of thirteen times during the ten and a half rounds.

Not, however, until he fought and was knocked out by Joe Louis was it apparent what a dreadful thing had been done to this great hulk of a man. Strange to feel pity and sympathy excited for one so gross and enormous and strong. But the outsizes of the world are not the happy men, and their bulk is often of little use or help to them. If anything, it is a handicap when up against the speed and timing and balance of a normal man. Carnera's great strength was practically useless to him in the ring. The hardest blow he could strike was little more than a push. True, if he caught you in a corner he could club you insensible, but no smart fighter is caught in corners, and the big man was never fast enough anyway to catch anyone but out-and-out tramps.

When he fought Joe Louis he was defensively but little better than he was the first time I saw him, which, as it happened, was not in Madison Square Garden, but in the smoky, stuffy, subterranean Salle Wagram, a little fight club in Paris where I happened to be one evening when Jeff Dickson was promoting a fight between Primo Carnera, who had then been fighting a little less than a year, and one Moise Bouquillon, a light heavyweight who weighed 174 pounds. Monsieur See was experimenting a little with his giant. It was obvious that Bouquillon was going to be unable to hurt him very much, but what I noted that evening and never forgot was that the giant was likewise unable to hurt the little Frenchman. Curiously, that fight was almost the exact duplicate of the one that Carnera as champion later fought with Loughran. Walter (Good-Time Charley) Friedman was there too. Many years later he told me quite frankly: "Boy, was that a lousy break for us that you come walking into that Salle Wagram that night and see that the big guy can't punch! Just that night you hadda be there. Leon wanted to see if he could go ten rounds without falling down. And you hadda be there. We coulda got away with a lot more if you don't walk in there and write stories about how he can't punch."

Joe Louis slugged Carnera into bleating submission, cruelly and brutally. Handsome Uncle Will Duffy was back in his corner again, jawing angrily at him when he was led trembling and quivering back to his chair after the referee had saved him again, one side of his mouth smashed in, dazed and dripping blood. The very first right-hand punch Louis hit him broke Carnera's mouth and hurt him dreadfully.

Here, then, was the complete sell. He had nothing. His title was gone, his money squandered by the gang. And the one thing he thought he had, an unbeatable skill in defense and an irresistible crushing power in attack that no man living could withstand, never existed. It was a fable as legendary as the great giants of mythology that he resembled. The carrion birds that had fed upon this poor, big, dumb man had picked him clean. They had left him nothing, not even his pride and his self-respect, and that probably was the cruelest thing of all.

In his last fight, the one with Haynes, he was again severely beaten about the head. One of his legs refused to function. The fight was stopped. While he lay in the hospital in New York for treatment, as I have said, he lay alone.

I often wonder what that hulk of a man thinks today as he looks back over the manner in which he was swindled, tricked and cheated at every turn, as he recalls the great sums of money that he earned, all of it gone beyond recall. The world has no place for him, not even as a freak in a circus, from whence he emerged and where he might happily have spent his life and become prosperous. Because as a giant, a terror and a horror, he stands exposed as a poor, unwilling fraud who was no man-killer at all, but a rather helpless, sad creature who, when slugged by a 185-pound mortal, either toppled stricken to the floor or staggered about or bled or had to be saved from annihilation by a third man who obligingly stepped between him and his tormentors.

He was born far, far too late. He belonged to the twelfth or thirteenth century, when he would have been a man-at-arms and a famous fellow with mace and halberd, pike or bill. At least he would have fought nobly and to the limit of his strength, properly armed, because Carnera was a courageous fellow to the limit of his endurance, game and a willing fighter when aroused. In those days he would have won honor afield and would have got himself decently killed, or, surviving, would have been retired by his feudal lord to round out his days and talk over the old brave fights.

Today there is nothing left for this man but reflection upon his humiliations. He was just a big sucker whom the wise guys took and trimmed. What an epitaph for one who came from the ancient and noble race of giants.

All this took place in our country, *Anno Domini* 1930–1935.

ROBERTO DURAN AND THE WISE OLD MEN

Leonard Gardner, whose fine fight novel *Fat City* was filmed in 1972 under John Huston's direction, brought his superior perceptive and descriptive powers to Montreal for the 1980 Roberto Durán–Sugar Ray Leonard welterweight championship mixing. It was the best of their three meetings, as in the second a frustrated Durán quit in the eighth round, and in the third Leonard handled him even more easily. This account, not only of the fight but of the scene surrounding it, is about as good as boxing reporting ever gets.

LEONARD GARDNER

As a child I had no doubt that Joe Louis was a greater man than Franklin D. Roosevelt, and in the tales I heard of great heroes, Corbett, Jeffries, Gans, Ketchel, and Dempsey ranked right along with Perseus and Daniel Boone. I put myself to sleep reciting the order of champions, and to the end of my father's life the subject of boxing kept the two of us from ever reaching that lonely gulf where child and parent no longer have anything of passionate interest to say to one another. My father's last words to me, in fact, an hour or two before his death, were, "Do you think Big Train Liston can win the title again?"—a confusion of two heavyweights, Amos Lincoln and Sonny Liston, that was as definite an indication of his failing powers as any medical test could have provided. In his mid-seventies he had a speed bag in the attic he could still punch into a rhythmic blur, and in his early eighties he had his last fight, on State Street in Santa Barbara, with a panhandler who put his hand in my father's pocket. "I gave him the Fitzsimmons shift," my father said. His hands were badly bruised.

The shift was the arcane maneuver with which Bob Fitzsimmons had conquered Jim Corbett in 1897 and won the heavyweight championship, and which had apparently become lost to the body of modern boxing technique. In my childhood we practiced it with the gloves on in the backyard, and my father, no longer a young man, executed it with confusing speed. He would feint at my head with his left, feint with his right, shoot his right foot in front of his left foot and let go a left hook he would pull up short at my solar plexus, reenacting a turning point in history.

The idea was to put the same weight of the body behind the left as you got behind the right, through a sudden shift to southpaw. Sometimes the punch wasn't pulled quite short enough, and I got a sense of how Corbett was undone by the gangly, baldheaded Fitz, who my father swore weighed only 157 pounds. It was a peculiar series of moves, that shift, and a little alarming when the whole works, came swirling at you. But nobody I saw at that time used it, and I don't recall having seen a version of it until Roberto Durán came on the scene and tore through a decade of lightweights.

I first saw Durán in 1972, on television, when he won the lightweight title from Ken Buchanan with an electrifying attack. It was unfortunate that the bout ended after the thirteenth round, with Buchanan on the floor from a low blow, Buchanan was ruled unable to continue, and, so Durán became champion.

It was a sour ending to the bout, but Buchanan had been overwhelmed from the opening bell and there was no doubt of Durán's superiority. He had fought as if possessed. Over the years Durán acquired finesse, but without losing any of that unrelenting aggressiveness that gave his fights such excitement. In his final defense of his lightweight title he showed fine ring skills, knocking out Esteban DeJesus in twelve rounds. Durán then retired as undisputed lightweight champion, in an era so overpopulated with WBA and WBC champions that the concept of a true world champion is eroding.

Durán had epitomized the old-fashioned hungry fighter, but with wealth he ate too well and his appetite cost him his title. He had to move up to the welterweights, and now he was getting a shot at a media hero and new champion, Sugar Ray Leonard. Leonard was a 9-to-5 favorite. The consensus, when the bout was announced, was that a lightweight's frame couldn't stay in there with a welterweight's frame, especially if the welterweight had the fastest hands in the business and could punch.

Before leaving for Montreal I called a friend who for many years had contributed to the cultural stature of the city of Stockton, California, by matching the right Mexican with the right Filipino. We talked over the old argument that a good big man beats a good little man.

"What about Fitzsimmons?" he said.

In the restaurant of the Hotel Bonaventure, I was eating an early supper when Durán appeared. With him were his Panamanian bodyguards, some Panamanian friends, and one of his two elderly trainers, Freddie Brown, who is seventy-three and was smoking a cigar and looking disgusted. They were accompanied by a terrific din of Latin music out of Durán's tape deck, which was the size of a small suitcase. Trumpet blasts, voices, thumps, clacks, strums, ringings, and high-pitched whistles poured from the box at a volume close to that favored by campaign cars cruising neighborhoods before election day.

Durán put his tape deck on the table, sprawled in, a chair, and began loudly beating time on the table. He was bearded, wore a T-shirt in praise of Panama, jeans, a white cap, and a pair of rainbow suspenders. His black eyes gazed vacantly, his head and shoulders rocked, and he appeared a captive of his own restless energy. He let out a few sharp cries, then took up a knife and spoon, beating them together even as the waitress took the orders. When he spoke his voice filled the room.

At the table next to mine a couple was speaking with raised voices.

"Why do they let people like that in here? Why don't they throw him out?"

"They must be some of Durán's crowd," the man said.

"That *is* Durán," I told him.

"Is *that* Durán? Is that really Durán?" he called back. "Then I've just decided who I'm pulling for. The other guy."

When Durán's steak arrived, Brown intercepted it and with a look of scorn dumped the french-

fried potatoes onto his own plate. Durán cut the steak into large chunks which he held up on his fork and gnawed hastily. Within a very few minutes he had finished his meal and was walking out with his bodyguards and his music.

Out in the lobby, Durán was signing autographs with careful block printing, while Brown stood gazing into space, chewing his cigar. Slightly stooped, he wore red and gray checkered trousers high over a small paunch, and a multicolored sport coat with a zigzag pattern. Brown had worked with Marciano and many other champions, acquiring a degree of immortality as the cut man who closed the rip in Rocky's nose in his second bout with Ezzard Charles. Brown's own nose had been hammered flat. I had heard that fifty years ago he had considered plastic surgery, but then had decided to hell with it.

"Roberto sure looks up for this one," I said.

Brown kept gazing and chewing. "He hasn't been in this good a shape since the second DeJesus fight six years ago."

"Is that why he didn't work out today? Are you afraid of overtraining him?"

"Overtrain?" he said, staring at me with utter exasperation. "How can you get overtrained? You're either in shape or you're not. What does overtrained mean? I never heard of such a thing. You got to work hard. If you don't you're not in shape to fight. This is the most talked about fight of all time. " He relit his cigar. "Let me tell you something," he said. "There's a lot of tension in this fight. But it favors experience. Durán's been through all this before. But the tension's getting to Leonard. He's worried. Leonard didn't want this fight. The commission made him take it. He wanted to fight Cuevas."

This was a source of confidence for the Durán camp, which included Don King. King was copromoting the bout with his rival, Bob Arum, whom he has been known to call The Snake. Arum's headquarters were across the street in Le Régence Hyatt and he always managed to appear without King at press conferences, where he predicted record-breaking sums from the closed-circuit telecast. King had been trying to make the match for some time. Leonard had been ordered by the WBC to defend against Durán, the number one contender, or risk being stripped of his tide. Negotiations began, instead, between Leonard and Pipino Cuevas, who holds the WBA version of the title.

But Durán is such a national hero in Panama that the president himself is his friend, and so officials in the government of Panama, specifically Colonel Rubén Paredes, a commander of the Panamanian national guard, interceded with the WBA, whose president, Rodrigo Sanchez, is Panamanian.

The result was that negotiations broke down between Cuevas and Leonard, who was then forced to sign with Durán. Arum claimed Leonard would gross $8 to $10 million. As the bout drew near he was calling it "the dream fight of the century." And Don King declared himself "ecstatic with delight."

"Dundee didn't want this fight," Brown said. "They did everything they could to avoid this fight."

Angelo Dundee, Leonard's manager, gave me his line on Durán in the bar at the top of the Hyatt. A singer was singing as he spoke. "Durán's a heel-to-toe guy," he said. "He takes two steps to get to you. So the idea is don't give him the two steps. Don't move too far away. The more distance you give Durán, the more effective he is. What you don't do against aggression is run from it, because then he picks up momentum. My guy won't run from him.

"Durán waves at you with his hand. He gives you movement of his body, slipping from side to side. He won't come straight in. He'll try to feint you. He misses you with an overhand right. He turns southpaw, comes back with a left hook to the body. My guy's going to be moving side to side. And he's going to go to the body. Nobody ever hit Durán in his weak spot." Dundee poked his fingers under his ribs. "He doesn't do his homework on the table. He's soft. Leonard's the puncher in this fight. I think Leonard's going to knock him out in ten or eleven rounds. Because Durán hasn't destroyed anybody as a welterweight. The reason being that he's hitting on bigger guys and the bigger guys are able to absorb it more than the little guys. He was devastating as a lightweight, but he never was one of those one-punch knockerouters. He was a grinder. Ray's going to nail him. Ray's going to stop him in his tracks with the jab. Leonard's got so much talent they haven't seen it yet."

Dundee, who has the manner and appearance of a gentle professor, didn't like the singer's moves. He pointed out her whole repertoire of mechanical gestures. He liked her songs well enough to sing a few lines himself, but he particularly disliked the way she kept handling her hair. As we rode down to the lobby, Dundee went into a reflective mood often observed in elevators. "I got the greatest respect for Durán," he said. "I've known him for years. I talk Spanish with him and I know what kind of a guy he is. He's a sweetheart and he's a great fighter. I don't take anything away from him. He's great at what he does, but he's a heel-toe guy."

Both Durán and Leonard worked out at a hockey arena converted to a gym. Leonard boxed brilliantly, hitting on the move, slipping punches and countering with combinations that seemed to flow from him effortlessly. Once he knocked down a sparring partner so picturesquely that the young man, from Leonard's hometown boxing club, got up with what seemed a smile of aesthetic appreciation. At intervals, while Leonard skipped rope, a trainer would mop his sweat from the floor with a towel. Sweating in the dressing room, he talked with newsmen, some of his statements sounding rehearsed, with an eye toward boosting the gate. At the close of the session he took up a newspaper and looked it over while an aide knelt and removed his boxing shoes.

Durán held few press conferences, and his dressing room was filled with noisy friends from Panama. He was indeed a heel-toe man, but he got around the ring quickly, occasionally sending a sparring partner reeling from a right hand thrown with an authority and form that stirred memories of great right-hand punchers of the past. He tugged and hauled, bulled his man into the ropes, and swung viciously to the body. He clowned, beating the speed bag with his head, skipping rope like a drunk, then leaping high, then hopping while in a squat, whirling the rope flamboyantly. And all through the workout, in the ring and on the bag and rope, he emitted strange shrill cries. They were not snorts and grunts many boxers make when punching. They were oohs and aahs, wailed in a sharp, high-pitched staccato, like cries of birds, and seemed to strike an emphasis, set a rhythm or express exuberance. He was an appealing eccentric.

Three days before the fight Durán shadowboxed two ten-minute rounds, and energy poured from him. Joyously he prowled the ring, swaying and bobbing. He squatted, leaped high, and turned. He punched the ropes, the corner pads, circled the ring and, like a child or a cat, tapped the hands of the men grasping the ropes. Brown leaned on the top strand, trying to smile as punches shot past his face. Weaving and punching, emitting his cries and shrieks, exchanging insults with his friends in the bleachers, Durán seemed possessed by the wild joy of his own vitality. After nine weeks of training, the nearness of the fight seemed to fill him with happiness. He ducked through the ropes, and just as he was about to jump to the floor, his eighty-one-year-old co-trainer, Ray Arcel, stepped quickly over and reached up and lifted him down from the ring.

"He gets so excited he doesn't know what he's doing," said Arcel. "I had a fighter jump out of the ring once and he hurt his leg and couldn't fight."

I remembered Arcel from my childhood, when he handled a long procession of Louis's victims.

Back in the lobby of the Hotel Bonaventure I found Arcel relaxing in a chair. His eyes are dark and impenetrable, his mouth set, his prominent nose well-shaped despite fights in New York streets and rings that preceded his career as a trainer. He wore a dark tie, a striped shirt, and a navy blue sport coat, and had the stem, dignified appearance of a retired judge. He had trained Ross, Braddock, Zale, and more than a dozen other champions, and had been in Charles's corner the night he sliced up Marciano's nose. But Benny Leonard was the gem of all his fighters. He had worked with Leonard in 1931 and 1932 when the stock market crash forced the great lightweight champion out of retirement.

I asked his opinion of the new Leonard.

"We'll find out what this guy has to offer in the first round," Arcel said. "Leonard's a master craftsman. I don't underestimate him, but I'm going to find out early how much stamina he has. I want to see if he can take a body beating and stand up for the first six or seven rounds. He looks good but who's he fought? Durán was in against good opposition in the lightweights. Guys like Buchanan and Lampkin and DeJesus were good boxers. That guy Bizzarro was like a deer. But could they keep it up for fifteen rounds?

"The only reason Durán was ineffective as a welterweight was because he wasn't in condition. The fights meant nothing to him, except Palomino. He could still be a lightweight. He won't listen. A fighter's got to have some kind of self-control. He can't just eat every kind of crap. He's like a kid. He didn't have to be a welterweight

but now that he is, he's still good enough to beat everybody. He's strong enough to handle the bigger men."

"Mickey Walker did it," I said. "He even beat heavyweights."

"Mickey Walker was a drunk," said Arcel. "Jack Kearns made a drunk out of him. Tunney was a terrible drunk, too, after he retired. Disgusting. Liquor is a terrible thing. Did you know it was Benny Leonard who taught Tunney how to beat Greb? I was right there in the gym and I saw what he showed him. Leonard was a great student of boxing. He could do it all."

"I've wondered about the no-decision bouts in those days," I said. "You take a look at Benny Leonard's record and he's got a lot of knockouts in the important bouts but a lot of the no-decision bouts went the limit. Did they go all out in those no-decision bouts or did they have an understanding to go easy?"

In an instant Arcel came out of his chair and was facing me, his eyes combative.

"The fighter never lived that Benny Leonard would have to ask to go easy on him!"

"I didn't mean it that way," I said. "I meant did *he* go easy on *them?*"

"He *had* to go easy! He couldn't get anybody to fight him if he didn't agree to carry them."

In the men's room of the Hotel Bonaventure, sports pages with the daily fight news in English and French were tacked on a bulletin board above the urinals. Panamanians crowded the lobby. When Durán passed through they went along with him and sometimes Arcel had to shove them away. "If you love this guy so much, leave him alone!" he yelled.

Arcel and Brown were upset. Carlos Padilla had been named referee by Jose Sulaiman, president of the WBC, who was staying across the street in Leonard's hotel. Padilla had been the referee who stopped Wilfred Benitez with six seconds to go when he lost the championship to Sugar Ray Leonard. More recently, he had worked the first Antuofermo-Minter middleweight tide bout.

"He breaks you before you get in there," complained Arcel. "Remember what he did to Antuofermo? He prevented a man from defending his title successfully. Then what recourse do you have? You lose a fight, then two days later it's all forgotten. I want a referee in there that'll let my fighter fight, that's all."

To a tremendous roar, Durán came up the steps and through the ropes. As he moved restlessly around the ring he appeared loose and confident and charged with a predatory intensity. The rain that had fallen during the preliminaries had stopped now, but many of the ringside spectators still sat encased in the black plastic rubbish bags distributed by the Olympic Stadium staff.

Although the ring was under a canopy, wet spots showed along the apron of the blue canvas. Holding the ropes, Durán worked his feet in the resin box and Brown and Arcel had a moment to speak to Padilla before the roar came up again and Leonard approached the ring, surrounded by a large entourage of friends and his cornermen— Dundee and the two trainers who have been with him since his first amateur fights, Dave Jacobs and Janks Morton.

The instructions took place without delay. The seconds ducked out through the ropes and the fighters stood facing one another across the ring. When the two came out at the bell, Durán looked short by comparison, with short, powerful legs and the thick neck that helps a fighter absorb the force of blows to the head. As he advanced on Leonard, feinting with his head and shoulders, his disadvantage in reach was evident. Yet he stepped in almost immediately to hit Leonard solidly to the head with his right and left. Standing flat-footed, both men landed hard jabs. Then Durán attacked with a rush, driving Leonard to the ropes, where he hit him some terrible blows to the body and established what was to be the pattern of the fight.

Leonard fought back and when he had punching room, drove in his jab. But Durán was fighting with the fierceness of a man whose whole being willed one thing. He swarmed over Leonard with startling violence. When his right missed he banged in with his head and he kept Leonard on the ropes with the fury of his attack. When Leonard covered up, arms tied against his body and gloves shielding his face, Durán beat on his arms as if in a frenzy to take something out of him, some resilience or sense of control, and in that first round he took some of his strength, too. He landed a hook to the liver that might've put another fighter on the canvas in a knot of pain.

Through the first five rounds Durán overpow-ered him. With quick and unpredictable moves he hit hard at long range. In close, he grabbed and mauled, chopping hooks to Leonard's ribs and head, grappling and hitting, while Leonard covered and fought back in flurries. But Leonard was taking heavy punishment. His jab, so quick and accurate in other bouts, seemed to have deserted him. Often, at long range, he stood flat-footed as Durán stalked him, and he hesitated until Durán led and was swarming over him again, and then he would open up and trade with him, but this was Durán's kind of fight and he excelled at it.

Arcel and Brown had no more worries about Padilla. He stood back and let the battle rage in the clinches. Sometimes, instead of separating the two, Padilla would simply slap away a grasping hand, allowing the infighting to go on. When he did push them apart, Leonard would move toward him, putting him in the line of Durán's charge and gaining a moment of respite. Durán came in without fear of Leonard's power, and took what he had to take, but his feints were deceptive and he was ducking and slipping and rolling with punches. He had moves Leonard was unable to solve. Again and again Leonard's back was against the ropes. He seemed unable to slip and sidestep as he had against the twenty-seven professionals he had fought previously. Durán, with the experience of seventy-one bouts, was showing him the roughest secrets of the trade.

Leonard proved to have extraordinary durability and gameness in those rounds. There were times when I doubted he could survive them. In the middle rounds Leonard began to come back. He fought head to head with Durán, slamming him with hard combinations that had no apparent effect. Durán kept coming. Between rounds, Dundee, his face grave, was shouting at Leonard to move and box, but Leonard went on slugging as if unable to move.

It became a contest of fighting heart, and resulted in exchange after fierce exchange, a slugfest between two men with great speed and punching skills. Leonard was hurt on the ropes in the eleventh, a round of bitter trading, and in the thirteenth his knees were buckled by a left hook. Still he fought back, taking lefts and rights on the jaw and coming back with hard, quick flurries in a round of almost constant exchanges. With disregard of danger, their bodies steaming in the misty, humid air, both fighters traded punches in the fastest and most stubbornly fought round of the fight. Drawing on the depths of his stamina, Leonard finished strong enough to win the last two rounds. In the final seconds, Durán dropped his arms and stuck out his chin in a taunt that may have come from frustration over the unyielding toughness he had encountered in Leonard.

The fight was Durán's, although the judges made it close. One scored ten rounds even. With that kind of judging, there seemed the possibility of a draw, but the voting, after a correction in addition, was unanimous: 145–144, 148–147, 146–144. Durán had taken the title, but both men had fought with such fire that the fight would rank with the great ones.

The ring filled with excited fans and security guards. Several fights broke out and it appeared Durán was scuffling with somebody, too. His interpreter, Luis Henriquez, was squared off with Wilfred Benitez, the former champion, who was asked by Howard Cosell to comment on the fight, and had abandoned his post to yell insults at Durán. A security guard picked him up and was about to throw him over the ropes into the press section when I convinced him that Wilfred was a valuable commodity.

Afterward, in the press room, a jubilant Durán, his chest bare, was asked what had made the difference for him, and he placed his hand over his heart.

His heart indeed had been indomitable. However, there was enough controversy in the press room to ensure that the lawyers and promoters would be talking about a rematch. Dundee was displeased with the refereeing. He called the fight a wrestling match. There were debates over why Leonard had slugged and not boxed. The opinion was offered that he had chosen the wrong strategy. But I believed what I had seen—a good man giving his best while outfought. By pressuring him, crowding him and hurting him, Durán had taken away Leonard's advantages.

At three o'clock that morning, Arcel was leaving the hotel with Carlos Eleta, Durán's manager, and other friends to look for an all-night restaurant, and I walked along with them. We talked about the fight, and I asked Arcel if he was satisfied with the refereeing.

"Yes, I thought Padilla did a good job," he said. "Freddie and I had a talk with him. I told him the whole world was watching. This was the fight everybody wanted to see, and he should let the fighters fight."

Someone asked if Durán was the greatest fighter he had ever trained. For a while Arcel didn't answer, as if unwilling to compromise his devotion to the legendary Benny Leonard, whom he considered the greatest he had ever seen. But then the past seemed to give up its hold on him. He was tired, and he told me that Benny Leonard was all used up by the time he had worked with him. At last, Arcel said, "Yes," and a moment later added, "Durán is the best fighter in the world."

THE USEFUL SCIENCE OF DEFENCE

Captain John Godfrey was a patron of Figg's Amphitheater, where he practiced fencing, cudgeling and boxing. In 1747 he published *The Useful Science of Defence,* the two final chapters, reprinted here, being the first treatment of boxing in a book. The work sold out two large printings and was, Pierce Egan noted sixty-five years later, "now extremely scarce."

CAPTAIN JOHN GODFREY

BOXING

Boxing is a combat, depending more on Strength than the Sword: But Art will yet bear down the Beam against it. A less Degree of Art Will tell for more than a considerably greater Strength. Strength is certainly what the Boxer ought to set out with, but without Art he will succeed but poorly. The Deficiency of Strength may be greatly supplied by Art; but the want of Art will have but heavy and unwieldy Succour from Strength.

Here it may not be amiss to make some little anatomical Enquiry into the advantageous Disposition of the Muscles by the just Posture of the Body, and the acting Arm. I will venture to dabble a little in it; but cry Mercy all the while. If I make a Piece of Botch-Work of it, forgive the poor Anatomist through the Swords-Man.

The Strength of Man chiefly consists on the Power of his Muscles, and that Power is greatly to be increased by Art. The Muscles are as Springs and Levers, which execute the different Motions of our Body; but by Art a Man may give an additional Force to them.

The nearer a Man brings his Body to the Center of Gravity, the truer Line of Direction will his Muscle act in, and consequently with more resisting Force. If a Man designs to strike a hard Blow, let him shut his Fist as firm as possible; the Power of his Arm will then be considerably greater, than if but slightly closed, and the Velocity of his Blow vastly augmented by it. The Muscles which give this additional Force to the Arm, in shutting the Fist, are the Flexors of the Fingers, and the Extensors are the opposite Muscles, as they open or expand the same; yet in striking, or using any violent Efforts with your Hand, these different Orders of the Muscles contribute to the same Action. Thus it will appear, that when you close the Fist of your left Arm, and clap your right Hand upon that Arm, will plainly feel all the Muscles of it to have a reciprocal Swelling. From hence it follows, that Muscles, by Nature designed for different Offices, mutually depend on each other in great Efforts. This Consideration will be of much Advantage in that artificial Force in Fighting, which beats much superior Strength, where Art is wanting.

The Position of the Body is of the greatest Consequence in Fighting. The Center of Gravity ought to be well considered, for by that the Weight of the Body being justly suspended, and the true Equilibrium thereby preserved, the Body stands much the firmer against opposing Force. This depends upon the proper Distance between the Legs, which is the first Regard a *Boxer* ought to have, or all his manly Attempts will prove abortive. In order to form the true Position, the left Leg must be presented some reasonable Distance before the Right, which brings the left Side towards the Adversary; this right-handed Man ought to do, that, after having stopped the Blow with his left Arm, which is a Kind of Buckler to him, he may have the more Readiness and greater Power of stepping in with his right Hand's returning Blow. In this Posture he ought to reserve an easy Flexion in the left Knee, that his Advances and Retreats may be the quicker. By this proper Flexion, his Body is brought so far forward, as to have a just Inclination over the left Thigh, insomuch that his Face makes a perpendicular or straight Line with the left Knee; whilst the right Leg and Thigh in a slanting Line, strongly prop up the whole Body, as does a large Beam an old Wall. The Body by this means is supported against all violent Efforts, and the additional Strength acquired by this Equilibrium, is greatly to the Purpose. How much greater Weight must not your Adversary stand in need of, to beat you back from this forward inclining of the Body, than the so much less resisting Reclination of it? By this disposed Attitude you find the whole Body gently inclining forward with a slanting Direction, so that you shall find from the *Outside* of the right Ankle all the way to the Shoulder, a straight Line of Direction, somewhat inclining, or slanting upward, which Inclination is the strongest Position a Man can contrive; and it is such as we generally use in forcing Doors, resisting Strength or pushing forward any Weight with Violence: For the Muscles of the left Side, which bend the Body gently forward, bring over the left Thigh the gravitating Part, which by this Contrivance augments the Force; whereas, if it was held erect or upright, an indifferent Blow on the Head, or Breast, would overset it. The Body by this Position has the Muscles of the right Side partly relaxed, and partly contracted, whilst those of the Left are altogether in a State of Contraction; but the Reserve made in the Muscles of the right Side, is as Springs and Levers to let fall the Body at Discretion.

By delivering up the Power to the Muscles of the left Side, which, in a very strong Contraction, brings the Body forward, the Motion which is communicated, is then so strong, that, if the Hand at that Time be firmly shut, and the Blow at that Instant pushed forward, with the contracting Muscles, in a straight Line with the moving Body, the Shock given from the Stroke will be able to overcome a Force, not thus artfully contrived, twenty times as great.

From this it is evident, how it is in our Power to give an additional Force and Strength to our Bodies, whereby we may make ourselves far superior to Men of more Strength, not seconded by Art.

Let us now examine the most hurtful Blows, and such as contribute most to the Battle. Though very few of those, who fight, know, why a Blow on such a Part has such Effects, yet by Experience they know it has; and by these evident Effects, they are directed to the proper Parts; as for Instance, hitting

under the Ear, between the Eye-brows, and about the Stomach. I look upon the Blow under the Ear to be as dangerous as any, that is, if it light between the Angle of the lower Jaw and the Neck; because in this Part there are two Kinds of Blood Vessels considerably large; the one brings the Blood immediately from the Heart to the Head, whilst the other carries it mediately back. If a Man received a Blow on these Vessels, the Blood proceeding from the Heart to the Head, is partly forced back, whilst the other Part is pushed forwards vehemently to the Head: The same happens in the Blood returning from the Head to the Heart, for part of it is precipitately forced into the latter, whilst the other Part tumultuously rushes to the Head; whereby the Blood Vessels are immediately overcharged, and the Sinus's of the Brain so overloaded and compressed, that the Man at once loses all Sensation, and the Blood often runs from his Ears, Mouth and Nose, altogether owing to it's Quantity forced with such Impetuosity in to the smaller Vessels, the Coats whereof being too tender to resist so great a Charge, instantly break, and cause the Effusion of Blood through these different Parts.

This is not the only Consequence, but the Heart being overcharged with a Regurgitation of Blood (as I may say with respect to that forced back on the succeeding Blood coming from it's left Ventricle) stops it's Progress, whilst that Part of the Blood coming from the Head, is violently pushed into it's right Auricle; so that as the Heart labours under a violent Surcharge of Blood, there soon follows a Cardiaca or Suffocation, but which goes off as the Parts recover themselves and push the Blood forward. The Blows given between the Eye-brows contribute greatly to the Victory: For this Part being contused between two hard Bodies, *viz* The *Fist*, and *Os frontale*, there ensues a violent Ecchymosis, or Extravasation of Blood, which falls immediately into the Eye-lids; and they being of a lax Texture incapable of resisting this Influx of Blood, swell almost instantaneously; which violent Intumescence soon obstructs the Sight. The Man thus indecently treated, and artfully hoodwinked, is beat about at his Adversary's Discretion.

The Blows on the Stomach are also very hurtful, as the Diaphragm and Lungs share in the Injury. The Vomitions produced by them I might account for, but I should ran my anatomical Impertinences too far.

I would recommend to those who Box, that on

the Day of Combat they charge not their Stomachs with much Aliment: for by observing this Precaution, they will find great Service. It will help them to avoid that extraordinary Compression on the *Aorta Descendens,* and in a great measure preserve their Stomachs from the Blows, which they must be the more exposed to, when distended with Aliments. The Consequence of which may be attended with a Vomiting of Blood, caused by the Eruption of some Blood Vessels, from the overcharging of the Stomach: Whereas the empty Stomach, yielding to the Blow, is as much less affected by it, as it is more by it's Resistance, when expanded with Food. Therefore I advise a Man to take a little Cordial Water upon an empty Stomach, which, I think, would be of great Service, by its astringing the Fibres, and contracting it into a smaller Compass.

The Injury the Diaphragm is subject to from Blows, which light just under the Breast-bone, is very considerable; because the Diaphragm is brought into a strong convulsive State, which produces great Pain, and lessens the Cavity of the Thorax, whereby the Lungs are a great Measure deprived of their Liberty, and the Quantity of Air retained in them, from the Contraction of the Thorax through the convulsive State of the Diaphragm, is so forcibly pushed from them, that it causes a great Difficulty of Respiration, which cannot be overcome till the convulsive Motion of the Diaphragm ceases.

The artful Boxer may, in some Degree, render the Blows less hurtful on this Part, by drawing in the Belly, holding his Breath and bending his Thorax over his Navel, when the Stroke is coming.

I have mentioned Strength and Art as the two Ingredients of a Boxer. But there is another, which is vastly necessary; that is, what we call a Bottom. We need not explain what it is, as being a Term well understood. There are two Things required to make this Bottom, that is, Wind and Spirit, or Heart, or wherever you can fix the Residence of Courage. Wind may be greatly brought about by Exercise and Diet; but the Spirit is the first Equipment of a Boxer. Without this substantial Thing, both Art and Strength will avail a Man but little. This, with several other Points, will appear more fully in the Characters of the Boxers.

CHARACTERS OF THE BOXERS

Advance, brave BROUGHTON! Thee I pronounce Captain of the *Boxers.* As far as I can look

back, I think, I ought to open the Characters with him: I know none so fit, so able to lead up the Van. This is giving him the living Preference to the rest; but, I hope, I have not given any Cause to say, that there has appeared, in any of my Characters, a partial Tincture. I have throughout consulted nothing, but my unbias'd Mind, and my Heart has known no Call but Merit. Wherever I have praised, I have no Desire of pleasing; wherever decried, no Fear of offending. BROUGHTON, by his manly Merit, has bid the highest, therefore has my Heart. I really think all will poll with me, who poll with the same Principle. Sure there is some standing Reason for this Preference. What can be stronger than to say, that for seventeen or eighteen Years, he has fought every able Boxer that appeared against him, and has never yet been beat? This being the Case, we may venture to conclude from it. But not to build alone on this, let us examine farther into his Merits. What is it that he wants? Has he not all that others want, and all the best can have? Strength equal to what is human, Skill and Judgement equal to what can be acquired, undebauched Wind, and a bottom Spirit, never to pronounce the word ENOUGH. He fights the Stick as well as most men, and understands a good deal of the Small-Sword. This Practice has given him the Distinction of *Time* and *Measure* beyond the rest. He stops as regularly as the Swords-Man, and carries his Blows truely in the Line; he steps not back, distrusting of himself to stop a Blow, and piddle in the Return, with an Arm unaided by his Body, producing but a kind of flyflap Blows; such as the Pastry-Cooks use to beat those Insects from their Tarts and Cheesecakes. No, BROUGHTON steps bold and firmly in, bids a Welcome to the coming Blow; receives it with his guardian Arm; then with a general Summons of his swelling Muscles, and his firm Body, seconding his Arm, and supplying it with all it's Weight, pours the Pile-driving Force upon his Man.

That I may not be thought particular in dwelling too long upon BROUGHTON, I leave him with this Assertion, that as he, I believe, will scarce trust a Battle to a warning Age, I never shall think he is to be beaten, till I see him beat.*

About the Time I first observed this promising Hero upon the Stage, his chief Competitors were

* Three years after Capt. Godfrey's book was published Jack Broughton, on April 11, 1750, lost his title to Jack Slack.—ED.

PIPES and GRETTING. He beat them both (and I thought with ease) as often as he fought them.

PIPES was the neatest Boxer I remember. He put in his Blows about the Face (which he fought at most) with surprising Time and Judgement. He maintained his Battles for many Years by his extraordinary Skill, against Men of far superior Strength. PIPES was but weakly made; his Appearance bespoke Activity, but his Hand, Arm, and Body were but small. Though by that acquired Spring of his Arm he hit prodigious Blows; and I really think, that at last, when he was beat out of his Championship, it was more owing to his Debauchery than the Merit of those who beat him.

GRETTING was a strong Antagonist to PIPES. They contended hard together for some Time, and were almost alternate Victors. GRETTING had the nearest way of going to the Stomach (which is what they call the Mark) of any Man I knew. He was a most artful Boxer, stronger made than PIPES, and dealt the straightest Blows: But what made PIPES a Match for him, was his rare Bottom Spirit, which would bear a deal of Beating, but this, in my Mind, GRETTING was not sufficiently furnished with; for after he was beat twice together by PIPES, *Hammersmith* JACK, a meer Sloven of a Boxer, and every Body that fought him afterwards, beat him. I must, notwithstanding, do that Justice to GRETTING'S Memory, as to own that his Debauchery very much contributed to spoil a great *Boxer;* but yet I think he had not the Bottom of the other.

Much about this Time, there was one WHITAKER, who fought the *Venetian* GONDELIER. He was a very strong Fellow, but a clumsy *Boxer.* He had two Qualifications, very much contributing to help him out. He was very extraordinary for his throwing, and contriving to pitch his weighty Body on the fallen Man. The other was, that he was a hardy Fellow, and would bear a deal of Beating. This was the man pitched upon to fight the *Venetian.* I was at *Slaughter's* Coffee-House when the Match was made, by a Gentleman of an advanced Station; he sent for FIG to produce a proper Man for him; he told him to take care of his Man, because it was for a large Sum; and the *Venetian* was a Man of extraordinary Strength, and famous for breaking the jaw-bone in *Boxing.* FIG replied, in his rough Manner, I do not know, Master he may break one of his own Countrymen's jaw-bones with his Fist; but, I will bring him a

Man, and he shall not break his Jaw-bone with a Sledge Hammer in his Hand.

The Battle was fought at FIG's Amphitheatre, before a splendid Company, the politest House of that kind I ever saw. While the GONDELIER was stripping, my Heart yearned for my Countryman. His Arm took up all Observation; it was surprisingly large, long, and muscular. He pitched himself forward with his right Leg, and Arm full extended, and, as WHITAKER approached, gave him a Blow on the Side of the Head, that knocked him quite off the Stage, which was remarkable for it's Height. WHITAKER'S Misfortune in his Fall was then the Grandeur of the Company, on which account they suffered no common People in, that usually sit on the Ground and line the Stage round. It was then all clear, and WHITAKER had nothing to stop him but the bottom. There was a general foreign Huzza on the Side of the *Venetian,* pronouncing our Countryman's Downfall; but WHITAKER took no more Time than was required to get up again, when finding his Fault in standing out to the length of the other's Arm, he, with a little Stoop, ran boldly in beyond the heavy Mallet, and with one *English* Peg in the Stomach (quite a new Thing to Foreigners) brought him on his Breech. The Blow carried too much of the *English* Rudeness for him to bear, and finding himself so unmannerly used, he scorned to have any more doings with his slovenly Fist.

So fine a House was too engaging to FIG, not to court another. He therefore stepped up, and told the Gentlemen that they might think he had picked out the best Man in *London* on this Occasion: But to convince them to the contrary, he said, that, if they would come that Day se'nnight, he would bring a Man who should beat this WHITAKER in ten Minutes, by fair hitting. This brought very near as great and fine a Company as the Week before. The man was NATHANIEL PEARTREE, who knowing the other's Bottom, and his deadly way of Flinging, took a most judicious Method to beat him.—Let his Character come in here—He was a most admirable *Boxer,* and I do not know one he was not a Match for, before he lost his Finger. He was famous, like PIPES, for fighting at the Face, but stronger in his Blows. He knew WHITAKER'S Hardiness, and doubting of his being able to give him Beating enough, cunningly determined to fight at his Eyes. His Judgement carried in his Arm so well, that in about six

Minutes both WHITAKER'S Eyes were shut up; when groping about a while for his Man, and finding him not, he wisely gave out, with these odd Words—Damme—I am not beat, but what signifies my fighting when I cannot see my Man?

We will now come to Times a little fresher, and of later Date.

GEORGE TAYLOR, known by the Name of GEORGE the BARBER, sprang up surprisingly. He has beat all the chief Boxers, but BROUGHTON. He, I think, injudiciously fought him one of the first, and was obliged very soon to give out. Doubtless it was a wrong Step in him to commence a Boxer, by fighting the standing Champion: For GEORGE was not then twenty, and BROUGHTON was in the Zenith of his Age and Art. Since that he has greatly distinguished himself with others; but has never engaged BROUGHTON more. He is a strong able Boxer, who with a Skill extraordinary, aided by his Knowledge of the Small and Back-Sword, and a remarkable Judgement in the Cross-Buttock-Fall, may contest with any. But, please or displease, I am resolved to be ingenuous in my Characters. Therefore I am of the Opinion, that he is not over-stocked with that necessary Ingredient of a Boxer, called a Bottom; and am apt to suspect, that Blows of equal strength with his, too much affect him and disconcert his Conduct.

Before I leave him, let me do him this Justice to say, that if he were unquestionable in his Bottom, he would be a Match for any Man.

It will not be improper, after GEORGE the BARBER, to introduce one BOSWELL, a Man, who wants nothing but Courage to qualify him for a compleat *Boxer*. He has a particular Blow with his left Hand at the Jaw, which comes almost as hard as a little Horse kicks. Praise be to his Power of Fighting, his excellent Choice of *Time* and *Measure*, his superior Judgement, dispatching forth his executing Arm! But fye upon his dastard Heart, that marrs it all! As I knew that Fellow's Abilities, and his worm-dread Soul, I never saw him beat, but I wished him to be beaten. Though I am charmed with the Idea of his Power and Manner of Fighting, I am sick at the Thoughts of his Nurse-wanting Courage. Farewell to him, with this fair Acknowledgement, that, if he had a true *English* Bottom (the best fitting Epithet for a Man of Spirit) he would carry all before him, and be a Match for even BROUGHTON himself.

I will name two Men together, whom I take to be the best Bottom Men of the modern Boxers: And they are SMALLWOOD, and GEORGE STEVENSON, the Coachman. I saw the latter fight BROUGHTON, for forty Minutes. BROUGHTON I knew to be ill at that Time; besides it was a hasty made Match, and he had not that Regard for his Preparation, as he afterwards found he should have had. But here his true Bottom was proved, and his Conduct shone. They fought in one of the Fair-Booths at *Tottenham* Court, railed at the End towards the Pit. After about thirty-five Minutes, being both against the Rails, and scrambling for a Fall, BROUGHTON got such a Lock upon him as no Mathematician could have devised a better. There he held him by this artificial Lock, depriving him of all Power of rising or falling, till resting his Head for about three or four Minutes on his Back, he found himself recovering. Then loosed the Hold, and on setting to again, he hit the Coachman as hard a Blow as any he had given him in the whole Battle; that he could no longer stand, and his brave contending Heart, though with Reluctance, was forced to yield. The Coachman is a most beautiful Hitter; he put in his Blows faster than BROUGHTON, but then one of the latter's told for three of the former's. Pity—so much Spirit could not inhabit a stronger Body!

SMALLWOOD is thorough game, with Judgement equal to any, and superior to most. I know nothing SMALLWOOD wants but Weight, to stand against any Man; and I never knew him beaten since his fighting DIMMOCK (which was in his Infancy of Boxing, and when he was a perfect Stripling in Years) but by a Force so superior, that to have resisted longer would not have been Courage but Madness. If I were to chuse a Boxer for my Money, and could but purchase him Strength equal to his Resolution, SMALLWOOD should be the Man.

JAMES I proclaim a most charming Boxer. He is delicate in his Blows, and has a Wrist as delightful to those who see him fight, as it is sickly to those who fight against him. I acknowledge him to have the best Spring of the Arm of all the modern Boxers; he is a compleat Master of the Art, and, as I do not know he wants a Bottom, I think it a great Pity he should be beat for want of strength to stand his Man.

I have now gone through the Characters of the

most noted Boxers, and finished my whole Work. As I could not praise all in every Article, I must offend some; but if I do not go to Bed till every Body is pleased, my Head will ake as bad as Sir *Roger's*. I declare that I have not had the least Thought of offending throughout the whole Treatise, and therefore this Declaration shall be my quiet Draught.

Let me conclude with a general Call to the true British Spirit, which, like purest Gold, has no Alloy. How readily would I encourage it, through the most threatening Dangers, or severest Pains, or Pledge of Life itself! Let us imitate the glorious Example we enjoy, in the saving Offspring of our King, and blessed Guardian of our Country. Him let us follow with our keen Swords, and warm glowing Hearts, in Defence of our Just Cause, and Preservation of *Britain's* Honour.

[COMMENT]

FROM: THE WORLD I KNEW

In this the English novelist and poet supports boxing as one of the arts, and does it bravely and well.

LOUIS GOLDING

And there was boxing. Thank the Lord, despite the thousand barriers, there was boxing. For I have been a boxing fan just as much as I have been a ballet fan, and for similar reasons, as I will explain. Whenever I had anything to celebrate, I would go to see boxing. And, as a matter of fact, I would go to see boxing when I had nothing to celebrate too—when I wanted to get away from myself, from my books, from my friends. . . .

I was saying I went boxing on my big nights. I also went boxing on my small nights, quite often two or three nights a week, and an occasional Sunday afternoon, too. It is a seduction to which, of course, infinitely more portentous men of letters than I have been prone, and these have devoted to boxing some of their most inspired writing.

Were they, I among them, mere sadists? That is a reproach I need not waste much time over. I have known gentle insurance clerks who play no more violent game than dominoes who are much more academically sadistic than any bullfight *aficionado*. I have had it said often enough to me: "Oh, yes. We know all about *you*. Boxing, eh? Blood and teeth, eh? Your real heaven would be to horsewhip gangs of naked Negroes with a rhinoceros-hide whip."

Well, it would not. That is enough of that. I found it exciting, I found it beautiful. I found it exciting, not merely when a Big Fight came along and filled countless columns of the newspapers with its vast melodrama. I found it exciting in the most subfusc little hall in the dimmest suburb.

And beautiful, too, not less than painting or dancing or drama. The assertion will sound pretentious only to those who have never seen a boxing match. Or at least only a bad one. And it can be bad, right enough. It can be as slow as waiting in a drizzle for a local train two hours late. It can be as heavy as the sight of two doped seals wallowing about gloomily in a tank. It can be as messy as a butcher's counter. It is not fair to judge boxing, which is at the same time a fine sport, a fine science, and a fine art, from one or two shoddy specimens—any more than one should condemn the cinema and all its works because one once saw a rotten film.

Now about the pure aesthetics of boxing. Clearly there is something magnificent in the spectacle itself. Here are two young fellows in the very pink of physical perfection. Their training has eliminated the last half-ounce of superfluous flesh from every muscle of their body. You can say you prefer tennis or swimming or cycling as a sport, but you cannot get away from the fact that the training that boxing involves makes the male body as perfect as it knows how to be. We know that the job involves more often than not a flattened nose and a thickened ear. But I hardly think that matters unless a boxer has ambitions to be a musical-comedy star, which happens now and again, but not frequently. They have had to forswear delights and live laborious days to attain that condition. You might feel that £50, or £5,000, is a disproportionate payment for a job of work which might last forty-five minutes and might not last two. But it would be like saying that a great violinist is overpaid for his half-hour on the platform, which has only attained that dazzling perfection through heartbreaking application, hour upon hour, year upon year.

The boxers have worked hard, too. They have been as Spartan in their self-denial as monks. There have been strenuous months of work in the gymnasium, topwork, groundwork, skipping, punch-balling, shadowboxing. They have been plugging out on the roads, up hill and down dale, in thick sweaters and flannels. They have attained the taut perfection of a machine.

And then—and then, their great moment comes.

As they stand isolated in the chalky glare from the arc lights, the smoky darkness which frames them makes a picture out of them which has something of the quality of a Michelangelo. But they are something more than canvas. They might stand immobile for one tense moment, each trying to sum up his opponent, to read his mind. In that moment they are superb statuary. You forget—if it is a Big Fight night—you forget the thousands of spectators seething around you, from the journalists just under the canvas, the dinner-jacketed (fancy) in the ringside seats, all the way up, tier beyond tier, to the enraptured errand boys just under the roof. You forget the torrents of newspaper publicity, you forget the purses, the side bets, the commercial angle of it all. It is for that one moment as if you were in a quiet art gallery. They are Greek athletes you are gazing on, molded in bronze to last for all time.

Then the moment snaps. They are not Greek athletes. They are a Cornish miner and a Pimlico greengrocer who have become professional boxers. They are not marble and motionless. They are flesh and blood, and they move. And it is in the nature of their movement that one will often find, in first-rate boxing, at any rate, the quality of ballet, almost as vigorously controlled within the framework of its own patterns.

Then, finally, there is its drama. For boxing is, after all, not merely a contest between two spendidly developed bodies. You will frequently see a boxer of inferior physique make rings round a young Hercules, because he has established a complete intellectual and moral ascendancy over him. The fact is, boxing is also a contest between two minds and two characters—and that is exactly what great drama is. It is an art that both creates character and reveals it. Of course, a fight in the higher levels of the art requires two artists. A Yehudi needs his Stradivarius, a Massine composing his ballet needs his Lichine and his Baronova. But once you have your Jimmy Wilde, your Fidel la Barba, matched against the opponent decreed for him by the stars in their courses, then the rhythm is achieved, that definite musical line, which makes the supreme fights in one's memory abide like the hearing of symphonies.

[FACT]

ALL THE WAY TO THE GRAVE

For more than a quarter of a century Frank Graham wrote the cleanest prose to appear in a newspaper and the most accurate dialogue to appear anywhere. No one has ever written more beautifully about boxing. This column, which appeared in the *New York Journal American,* was written on his return home from the funeral of his friend and favorite manager, Joe Gould. His favorite fighter was Jim Braddock.

FRANK GRAHAM

One of Joe Gould's favorite stories was about the time Tex Rickard was building up Luis Firpo and wanted Italian Jack Herman as an opponent for him in Havana and Joe, who managed Herman, accepted the match and, on looking for his fighter, found him in a hospital.

"What's the matter with you?" he asked.

"I had a pain in the belly," Herman said, "and the doctor says I'm going to get appendicitis."

"Are you?" Joe asked.

"I don't think so," Herman said. "I feel great."

"Then what are you laying here for," Joe said, "when you are boxing Firpo in Havana on Wednesday?"

"I am?" Herman yelled.

And, the way Joe used to tell it, Herman jumped out of bed and pulled on his pants.

They knew the story well in the fight mob and now some of them were standing in the rain outside the Riverside Memorial Chapel. Funeral services for the little man who guided Jim Braddock to the heavyweight championship were just over and they were standing there, talking about him, and Ernie Braca said:

"He was a very game guy and he gave it a great fight but I knew he was gone when I went into Mt. Sinai to see him a couple of weeks ago. His wife, Lucille, asked me if I couldn't drop in to try and cheer him up and when I walked in, I said to him: 'What are you laying here for when you're boxing Firpo in Havana on Wednesday?'

"I thought it would get a laugh out of him but he couldn't give. He just lay there looking at me and I knew he was a goner."

One of them stood there talking with the others about Joe for a while and then he went away and he was thinking about Joe and the time when Joe and Braddock were broke and the last thing either of them could have figured was that one day Jim would be the heavyweight champion.

But in that time Joe was hustling for him, not knowing where he would be able to take him, but determined that Jim would not stay on the docks and the relief rolls because Jim was too nice a guy for that and he had a wife and children and they rated a better shake than that. Joe's own furniture was in hock and he was sleeping on the bare floor of his apartment and hoping the landlord wouldn't come around looking for the rent too soon, but he never said anything about that to anybody but kept talking Braddock and trying to get a shot for him and finally he got it from Jimmy Johnston.

It was a preliminary bout on the Baer-Carnera card in the Garden Bowl in June of 1934. Braddock was in with a fellow named Corn Griffin, out of Georgia, and knocked him out in the third round. They were on their way back to the dressing room, Joe and Jim, and Jim said to Joe:

"I did that on hash. Get me a couple of steaks and there is no telling what I will do."

A year later they were at Evans Loch Sheldrake, Jim training for the fight with Max Baer in which he was to win the championship. There was a day when Jim, having finished his work, was sitting on the veranda of the main house with Joe and Francis Albertanti. No one could have asked for a more beautiful day. A blue sky a setting sun ...

trees green … flowers in bloom … birds … bees … butterflies.

Francis, who hates the country, glared through the haze of his cigar smoke at Jim.

"- - - - you, Braddock," he said. "If it wasn't for you, I wouldn't be here."

Joe laughed.

"If it wasn't for Braddock," he said, "you know where we'd be, don't you?"

"On relief," Francis said.

"Right," Joe said.

Jim laughed with them and he looked at Joe and you could see he was thinking about a lot of things they had gone through together and how it was Joe who was always out there in front of him, showing him the way.

There was the night in the Garden Bowl when Jim took the championship from Max Baer … and the night in Chicago when he lost it to Joe Louis.

Louis giving him a frightful beating, and at the end of the sixth round, Joe saying to Jim:

"I'm going to stop it."

Jim, sitting in his corner, looking up at him through the haze of blood in his eyes and saying:

"If you do, I'll never speak to you again as long as I live."

Joe, knowing Jim meant it, let the fight go on and, in the eighth round, Louis hit him on the chin, splitting the flesh on his chin and Jim fell on his face. And, as he lay there, his blood made little pools on the canvas. And when the count was over, Joe helping to lift him and get him back to his corner.

Joe wanting Jim to quit after that but Jim begging for a shot at Tommy Farr and Joe giving in and making the match for him and, in the Garden, Jim coming back to his corner at the end of the eighth round of a ten-round fight and asking Joe:

"How am I doing?"

Joe saying:

"You're losing, Jim."

And Jim saying:

"Watch me do the big apple in the next two rounds."

And going out there and beating Farr in the next two rounds and getting the decision and, in the dressing room, Joe saying:

"That was great, Jim. And that was all. You'll never fight again. But I don't have to tell you we'll still be together, like we have been."

It was raining and the one who had been thinking about this was on his way home and now he was thinking back, just a little while ago, to the funeral services and Rabbi Morris Goldberg intoning in Hebrew. He didn't know what it was then the Rabbi was saying but he knew now, because somebody had told him:

"The Lord is my shepherd: I shall not want. He maketh me to lie down in green pastures; He leadeth me beside the still waters. He restoreth my soul; He leadeth me in the paths of righteousness for His name's sake. …"

And then he had seen the funeral cars starting for Mount Neboh Cemetery in Brooklyn and Jim getting into one of the cars.

STILLMAN'S GYM

The best description of Stillman's, the most famous of all fight gyms, appeared in the best of the boxing autobiographies, *Somebody Up There Likes Me.*

ROCKY GRAZIANO (WRITTEN WITH ROWLAND BARBER)

Ma took my word for it that I was in no kind of trouble. I just got in a simple mix-up with the Army, and someday everything will get straightened out. I am off the hook there, but I still got to pick up some scratch, and how to make any money has got me stumped. I don't want to go on any jobs with Romolo. Benjy is away and so is Sammy. Tommy is waiting trial on a federal rap. I can't locate Big Sal to get back in touch with Eddie Coco.

After all the years Terry Young kept needling me about being a fighter, I didn't want to give him the satisfaction of coming around. But I didn't have no other out. I go to Terry's house. Terry gets all steamed up.

"Jeez, Rocky!" he says. "Howja get outa the Army?"

I just shrugged my shoulders. "I'm out, ain't I?"

"You better get rid of that uniform. Let's see what I got that fits you. I'll take you up to the gym this afternoon and maybe Irving Cohen will give a look at you."

So I get rigged out in an old zoot suit that was too big for Terry, a sweat shirt, and a porcupine hat, and that is how I look when I first walk into Stillman's Gym.

Stillman's Gym don't look no better to me than I do to Stillman's. Up at the end of a long, dark stairway is this barn of a place. In the middle are two regulation-size rings, with big lights over them. It's a good thing there are big lights because the windows look like they haven't been washed in years. Even the pigeons that hang around out there have give up looking in for free at the fighters.

On one side of the rings is a hot-dog stand which don't sell hot dogs, a row of telephone booths which are never empty long enough to clear out the day before's cigar smoke, the door to the locker room, and the stairs up to the balcony where they punch the bags. On the far side of the rings is some exercise space and some training tables. On the left side of the rings is Lou Stillman.

One thing I like about this joint my first day there. I see that everybody spits on the floor at Stillman's, and spitting is an old habit I got.

What I do not like is everything else that is going on. In the ring to the left a couple of guys are slugging each other. They're wearing headgear, but one of the guys is taking a beating in the face and bleeding out of his nose. You can hear his gloves land where he pounds the other guy in the ribs. They're grunting and wheezing with every punch. And nobody is paying much attention to them, except a trainer who leans on the edge of the ring, looking bored and chewing on an old cigar stub.

There must be thirty or forty guys in the room, bundled up in hats and overcoats. They're all talking to each other like they're making big deals, instead of watching the workouts. In ring number two, a half dozen guys are galloping around shadowboxing. Behind the rings, some guys in trunks are shadowboxing, others are doing pushups. From up on the balcony comes the noise of the punching bags—whappity, whappity, whappity. The phones keep ringing and guys keep yelling for guys who ain't there to answer them. Every third and fourth minute the bell rings for the rounds. Guys in overcoats come, make their deals, and go. Or they take their coats off and sit in one of the folding chairs and read the paper or the racing form.

And under the clock, off to the left, is Lou Stillman, who is more bored than anybody else, keeping track of who's in the ring and who's due in next like a checker in a parking lot.

This is the famous Stillman's Gym I heard about all my life. Why, if this joint was down on the East Side, it would be condemned; that was my first thought. And if it was condemned, it wouldn't even be worth our trouble to strip out the lead pipe. What do Lulu and Terry and everybody see in this place?

I go back into the locker room with Terry. This is some cockroach trap, the locker room. There is only one little shower for all the guys with lockers there. It stinks of sweat and old socks and mouthwash and liniment. Guys dressing back there are all mixed, colored and white, but this don't seem to bother Terry. He throws a jock strap and an old pair of trunks at me. "Here, see if these pants fit you."

I threw the things right back at him. "Who you kidding?" I say. "I'm getting out of here."

"What's the matter?" says Terry. "You ain't even met Irving Cohen yet."

"You tell him if he wants to match me in a bout, O.K., I'm ready. But I ain't going to go through none of this shit." I waved towards the training rings outside. "How much they pay you for fighting out there?"

"What you mean, how much they pay you? You crazy? This is only a gymnasium."

"I don't fight no place, gymnasium or no place, unless I get paid," I said. "I come up here with you because I got to make some scratch."

"Just do me a favor. Just stick around until Irving comes. Will ya?"

I sit on the bench there resigning myself to the fact I may have to go back with Romolo to make any money, while Terry puts on his trunks. He throws on this robe that has "Terry Young" on the back of it, and we go outside. Everybody is swarming all around Terry. He is a real important fighter, there's no doubt about it, and probably the next lightweight champion of the world. There's even guys there writing down what Terry is saying. I stand in the corner, under the balcony stairs,

thinking that if I beat it out of there, Terry would never know the difference.

Before I can make it, he comes up to me with this short guy with a round face and a big smile, a polite-looking little guy. "This here is Irving Cohen, Rocky," says Terry. "This here is my friend Rocky, Irving."

"Terry told me a lot about you," says the manager in his quiet voice. "He—" Irving stopped like maybe he said the wrong thing and turned to Terry. "This is your friend Rocky, the *fighter,* isn't it?"

"You ain't kidding he's the fighter," says Terry. "You ask anybody was ever in the ring with him in the amateurs." He stepped away, leaving me and Irving alone.

Still smiling, Irving looked me up and down. I must have been some sight for a fight manager—a wise-looking kid with a face still pasty from the can, hair sticking out like a mop under the flattop hat, wearing this sharp green suit that was too long for me with the pants pegged too tight like the year before's style, a ragged sweat shirt under the jacket, and big, stiff GI shoes.

He put his hand on my shoulder. "Kid," he said, "you don't want to be a fighter, do you? A good-looking kid like you?"

"I tell you the truth, Mr. Cohen," I said. "Terry said I could make fifty dollars a fight, that's the only reason."

"Let me tell you straight, Rocky," he says to me, and he talked real soft, like a priest. "You aren't in any shape to fight professional, kid. If you knew what it was like, you wouldn't want to be a fighter. Take my advice. You look like a good kid, a smart fellow. You go find yourself a job that pays fifty a week and you'll be thankful you listened to me." He smiled and shook his head slowly. "Just forget there's any easy dough in fighting. And remember what a favor I'm doing you by telling you this."

"Mr. Cohen," I said. "I give it a chance. Get me a fight and I'll take the chance."

He pointed across the gym. "Rocky," he says, "see the guy in the brown sweater over there, drinking the coffee? See him? He was a nicelooking, clean-cut boy like you once. See his busted nose, smashed all over his face? See the scars over his eyes, where they had to sew him up? You see his right ear? But the worst part you can't see. You just watch the guy the next time the bell rings. You watch him spill his coffee."

Terry comes back then. "You going to take a look at Rocky today, Irving?" he says.

"I'm not sure Rocky wants to go in the ring."

I was confused. I did and I didn't. I had to have that money. Terry saw I was mixed up about what to say. He put his arm around Irving and took him away. Finally Irving stops smiling and holds up his hands, like he was saying, "All right, if that's what you want."

So Terry talked Irving into it, and I went back to put on the trunks. What the hell, I will show them what I can do with some bum there in the training ring—once. I will show them once, and if they don't want to give me no fifty-dollar bout, that's all they will ever see of me.

Irving says do I want to warm up a little first and I say no, let's get this over with. He introduces me to my opponent. I don't get his name, something Spanish. A dark, strong-looking guy, older than me.

Lou Stillman announces to the crowd that Rocky Bob and Antonio what's-his-name will box two rounds in the first ring, and we climb in. Nobody listens to the announcement. Terry and Irving are the only ones who are looking at us. The bell rings.

When we touch gloves, I look down below. A couple guys are sleeping at ringside with newspapers over their faces. There's a bunch of guys talking by the sandwich stand, and another bunch over by the telephone booths. Lou Stillman is clowning around for the newspaper guys.

This is the first time I have been in the ring in over a year since I fought the four-rounder in the Bronx Coliseum under the name of Robert Barber. I felt a little funny up there with my legs bare, the gloves on, the mouthpiece under my lip. Then this guy stung my cheek with a left hook, and I stopped feeling funny. I went after him, swinging for his head. I kept missing and he kept jabbing that left in my face. He ducked my right and I crashed into the ropes. He ducked another right and I almost went down on my knees. Then I caught him in the corner and begun to give it to him.

In the back of my head, I knew that the guys down below were watching me now. Somebody was yelling. Terry was pounding on the canvas, on the apron of the ring. I finished the guy off with a shot to the temple. He sat there against the post, in a daze. All the characters in the overcoats were crowding in down by the ring. All the phones were ringing and nobody paid no attention. I hopped out through the ropes. Some trainer jumped into the ring to tend to the guy with the Spanish name. The joint was kind of jumping there for a minute. Terry was whacking me on the back.

"That guy you knocked out," he said, "that guy used to be the middleweight champeen of Argentina!"

Irving Cohen had stopped talking softly.

"Whitey! Whitey!" he was yelling. "Whitey! You got to teach this guy!"

He grabs my arms and pumps them. "Where'd you learn to punch like that, Rocky?" he said. Before I could give him an answer, this wiry guy with thin, blond hair come up to us. "Rocky," said Irving, "this is Whitey Bimstein. He's going to train you, Rocky."

"Yah, hi ya, Whitey," I said. I turned to Irving. "You gonna get me a bout for fifty bucks, Mr. Cohen?"

"Don't you worry, Rocky," said Irving. "You start working out with Whitey here, and I'll get you a bout."

I went and had a shower and got dressed in a hurry and almost beat it out of the gym when Irving stopped me at the top of the stairs. "Rocky," he says, "where you going? Whitey's waiting for you."

"You tell Terry when you got a bout for me and Terry will let me know, Mr. Cohen," I said.

"But you got work to do, kid."

"Ya din like that I done to that bum in there today?"

"You landed some good punches, Rocky. But I don't know if your legs will hold up for even four rounds under a pace like that. You got to box a little bit, Rocky. You can't go in swinging like that with every boy you fight."

"That's the way I do it, Mr. Cohen. If you don't like it, I'm sorry. If you do like it, then I'd like to fight somebody." I start down the stairs.

"Will I see you tomorrow, Rocky?" says Irving. He gives me a little smile, like he's hoping and praying I'll say yes.

"I don't know," I tell him. "Depends if I find any better way to pick up a little dough."

It winds up Irving Cohen give me a ten-spot right there on the gymnasium stairs. It looks like he's trying to bribe me to come back the next day to work out with this Whitey guy, the trainer. But a sawbuck looks big when you got an empty pocket, and I took it and told him goodbye and took off down the East Side without even telling Terry so long or thanks.

By the time I reached home and changed back to my uniform, I figured I earned the ten for knocking out this bum. I give all them characters a show, didn't I? I made Lou Stillman's eyes pop out of his head and all the boxers stop shadow-boxing and all the customers stop talking and sleeping, and I had Terry pounding the canvas and Irving yelling to blow his top. Sure I earned the ten.

[FACT]

THE FIGHT

In the 178 years since Bill Neat (not Neate) fought Tom Hickman and Hazlitt took his only fling at fight writing, this has been extolled as the all-time, all-around classic. It did get boxing into the English textbooks and the literature courses.

WILLIAM HAZLITT

"...The fight, *the* fight's *the thing*
Wherein I'll catch the conscience of the King."

Where there's a will, there's a way,—I said to myself, as I walked down Chancery-lane, about half-past six o'clock on Monday, the 10th of December, to inquire at Jack Randall's where the fight the next day was to be; and I found "the proverb" nothing "musty" in the present instance. I was determined to see this fight, come what would, and see it I did, in great style. It was my *first fight*, yet it more than answered my expectations. Ladies! it is to you I dedicate this description; nor let it seem out of character for the fair to notice the exploits of the brave. Courage and modesty are the old English virtues; and may they never look cold and askance on one another! Think, ye fairest of the fair, loveliest of the lovely kind, ye practisers of soft enchantment, how many more ye kill with poisoned baits than ever fell in the ring; and listen with subdued air and without shuddering, to a tale tragic only in appearance, and sacred to the Fancy!

I was going down Chancery-lane, thinking to ask at Jack Randall's where the fight was to be, when looking through the glass-door of the *Hole in the Wall*, I heard a gentleman asking the same question *at* Mrs. Randall, as the author of *Waverly* would express it. Now Mrs. Randall stood answering the gentleman's question, with the authenticity of the lady of the Champion of the Light Weights. Thinks I, I'll wait till this person comes out, and learn from him how it is. For to say a truth, I was not fond of going into this house of call for heroes and philosophers, ever si ce the owner of it (for Jack is no gentleman) threatened once upon a time to kick me out of doors for wanting a mutton-chop at his hospitable board, when the conqueror in thirteen battles was more full of *blue ruin* than of good manner. I was the more mortified at this repulse, inasmuch as I had heard Mr. James Simpkins, hosier in the Strand, one day when the character of the *Hole in the Wall* was brought in question, observe—"The house is a very good house, and the company quite genteel: I have been there myself!"

Remembering this unkind treatment of mine host, to which mine hostess was also a party, and not wishing to put her in unquiet thoughts at a time jubilant like the present, I waited at the door, when, who should issue forth but my friend Joe Toms, and turning suddenly up Chancery-lane with that quick jerk and impatient stride which distinguishes a lover of the Fancy, I said, "I'll be hanged if that fellow is not going to the fight, and is on his way to get me to go with him." So it proved in effect, and we agreed to adjourn to my lodgings to discuss measures with that cordiality which makes old friends like new, and new friends like old, on great occasions. We are cold to others only when we are dull in ourselves, and have neither thoughts nor feelings to impart to them. Give a man a topic in his head, a throb of pleasure in his heart, and he will be glad to share it with the first person he meets. Toms and I, though we seldom meet, were an *alter idem* on this memorable occasion, and had not an idea that we did not candidly impart; and "so carelessly did we fleet the time," that I wish no better, when there is another fight, than to have him for a companion on my journey down, and to return with my friend Jack Pigott, talking of what was to happen or of what did happen, with a noble subject always at hand, and liberty to digress to others whenever they offered. Indeed, on my repeating the lines from Spenser in an involuntary fit of enthusiasm,

"*What more felicity can fall to creature,*
Than to enjoy delight with liberty?"

My last-named ingenious friend stopped me by saying that this, translated into the vulgate, meant "*Going to see a fight.*"

Joe Toms and I could not settle about the method of going down. He said there was a caravan, he understood, to start from Tom Belcher's at two, which would go there *right out* and back again the next day. Now, I never travel all night, and said I should get a cast to Newbury by one of the mails. Joe swore the thing was impossible, and I could only answer that I had made up my mind to it. In short, he seemed to me to waver, said he only came to see if I was going, had letters to write, a cause coming on the day after, and faintly said at parting (for I was bent on setting out that moment)— "Well, we meet at Philippi!" I made the best of my way to Piccadilly. The mail-coach stand was bare. "They are all gone," said I; "this is always the way

with me—in the instant I lose the future—if I had not stayed to pour out that last cup of tea, I should have been just in time"; and cursing my folly and ill-luck together, without inquiring at the coach-office whether the mails were gone or not, I walked on in despite, and to punish my own dilatoriness and want of determination. At any rate, I would not turn back: I might get to Hounslow, or perhaps farther, to be on my road the next morning. I passed Hyde Park corner (my Rubicon), and trusted to fortune. Suddenly I heard the clattering of a Brentford stage, and the fight rushed full upon my fancy. I argued (not unwisely) that even a Brentford coachman was better company than my own thoughts (such as they were just then), and at his invitation mounted the box with him. I immediately stated my case to him—namely, my quarrel with myself for missing the Bath or Bristol mail, and my determination to get on in consequence as well as I could, without any disparagement or insulting comparison between longer or shorter stages. It is a maxim with me that stage-coaches, and consequently stage-coachmen, are respectable in proportion to the distance they have to travel: so I said nothing on that subject to my Brentford friend. Any incipient tendency to an abstract proposition, or (as he might have construed it) to a personal reflection of this kind, was however nipped in the bud; for I had no sooner declared indignantly that I had missed the mails, than he flatly denied that they were going along, and lo! at the instant three of them drove by in rapid, provoking, orderly succession, as if they would devour the ground before them. Here again I seemed in the contradictory situation of the man in Dryden who exclaims: "I follow fate, which does too hard pursue!" If I had stopped to inquire at the White Horse Cellar, which would not have taken me a minute, I should now have been driving down the road in all the dignified unconcern and *ideal* perfection of mechanical conveyance. The Bath mail I had set my mind upon, and I had missed it, as I miss everything else, by my own absurdity, in putting the will for the deed, and aiming at ends without employing means. "Sir," said he of the Brentford, "the Bath mail will be up presently, my brother-in-law drives it, and I will engage to stop him if there is a place empty." I almost doubted my good genius; but, sure enough, up it drove like lightning, and stopped directly at the call of the Brentford Jehu. I would not have believed this possible, but the brother-in-law of a mail-coach driver is himself no mean man. I was transferred without loss of time from the top of one coach to that of the other, desired the guard to pay my fare to the Brentford coachman for me as I had no change, was accommodated with a great coat, put up my umbrella to keep off a drizzling mist, and we began to cut through the air like an arrow. The mile-stones disappeared one after another, the rain kept off; Tom Turtle, the trainer, sat before me on the coach-box, with whom I exchanged civilities as a gentleman going to the fight; the passion that had transported me an hour before was subdued to pensive regret and conjectural musing on the next day's battle; I was promised a place inside at Reading, and upon the whole, I thought myself a lucky fellow. Such is the force of imagination! On the outside of any other coach on the 10th of December, with a Scotch mist drizzling through the cloudy moonlight air, I should have been cold, comfortless, impatient, and, no doubt, wet through; but seated on the Royal mail, I felt warm and comfortable, the air did me good, the ride did me good, I was pleased with the progress we had made, and confident that all would go well through the journey. When I got inside at Reading, I found Turtle and a stout valetudinarian, whose costume bespoke him one of the Fancy, and who had risen from a three months' sick bed to get into the mail to see the fight. They were intimate, and we fell into a lively discourse. My friend the trainer was confined in his topics to fighting dogs and men, to bears and badgers; beyond this he was "quite chapfallen," had not a word to throw at a dog, or indeed very wisely fell asleep, when any other game was started. The whole art of training (I, however, learnt from him) consists in two things, exercise and abstinence, abstinence and exercise, repeated alternately and without end. A yolk of an egg with a spoonful of rum in it is the first thing in the morning, and then a walk of six miles till breakfast. This meal consists of a plentiful supply of tea and toast and beef-steaks. Then another six or seven miles till dinner-time, and another supply of solid beef or mutton with a pint of porter, and perhaps, at the utmost, a couple of glasses of sherry. Martin trains on water, but this increases his infirmity on another very dangerous side. The Gas-man takes now and then a chirping glass (under the rose) to console him, during a six-weeks' probation, for the absence of Mrs. Hick-

man—an agreeable woman, with (I understand) a pretty fortune of two hundred pounds. How matter presses on me! What stubborn things are facts! How inexhaustible is nature and art! "It is well," as I once heard Mr. Richmond observe, "to see a variety." He was speaking of cock-fighting as an edifying spectacle. I cannot deny but that one learns more of what is (I do not say of what ought to be) in this desultory mode of practical study, than from reading the same book twice over, even though it should be a moral treatise. Where was I? I was sitting at dinner with the candidate for the honours of the ring, "where good digestion waits on appetite, and health on both." Then follows an hour of social chat and native glee; and afterwards, to another breathing over healthy hill or dale. Back to supper, and then to bed, and up by six again— Our hero

"Follows so the ever-running sun,
With profitable ardour—"

to the day that brings him victory or defeat in the green fairy circle. Is not this life more sweet than mine? I was going to say; but I will not libel any life by comparing it to mine, which is (at the date of these presents) bitter as coloquintida and the dregs of aconitum!

The invalid in the Bath mail soared a pitch above the trainer, and did not sleep so sound, because he had "more figures and more fantasies." We talked the hours away merrily. He had faith in surgery, for he had had three ribs set right, that had been broken in a *turn-up* at Belcher's, but thought physicians old women, for they had no antidote in their catalogue for brandy. An indigestion is an excellent commonplace for two people that never met before. By way of ingratiating myself, I told him the story of my doctor, who, on my earnestly representing to him that I thought his regimen had done me harm, assured me that the whole pharmacopeia contained nothing comparable to the prescription he had given me; and, as a proof of its undoubted efficacy, said, that "he had had one gentleman with my complaint under his hands for the last fifteen years." This anecdote made my companion shake the rough sides of his three great coats with boisterous laughter; and Turtle, starting out of his sleep, swore he knew how the fight would go, for he had had a dream about it. Sure enough the rascal told us how the first three rounds went off, but "his dream," like others, "denoted a foregone conclusion." He knew his men. The moon now rose in silver state, and I ventured, with some hesitation, to point out this object of placid beauty, with the blue serene beyond, to the man of science, to which his ear he "seriously inclined," the more as it gave promise *d'un beau jour* for the morrow, and showed the ring undrenched by envious showers, arrayed in sunny smiles. Just then, all going on well, I thought on my friend Toms, whom I had left behind, and said innocently, "There was a blockhead of a fellow I left in town, who said there was no possibility of getting down by the mail, and talked of going by a caravan from Belcher's at two in the morning, after he had written some letters." "Why," said he of the lapells, "I should not wonder if that was the very person we saw running about like mad from one coach-door to another, and asking if any one had seen a friend of his, a gentleman going to the fight, whom he had missed stupidly enough by staying to write a note." "Pray, Sir," said my fellow-traveler, "had he a plaid-cloak on?" "Why, no," said I, "not at the time I left him, but he very well might afterwards, for he offered to lend me one." The plaid-cloak and the letter decided the thing. Joe, sure enough, was in the Bristol mail, which preceded us by about fifty yards. This was droll enough. We had now but a few miles to our place of destination, and the first thing I did on alighting at Newbury, both coaches stopping at the same time, was to call out, "Pray, is there a gentleman in that mail of the name of Toms?" "No," said Joe, borrowing something of the vein of Gilpin, "for I have just got out." "Well!" says he, "this is lucky, but you don't know how vexed I was to miss you; for," added he, lowering his voice, "do you know when I left you I went to Belcher's to ask about the caravan, and Mrs. Belcher said very obligingly, she couldn't tell about that, but there were two gentlemen who had taken places by the mail and were gone on in a landau, and she could frank us. It's a pity I didn't meet with you; we could then have got down for nothing. But *mum's the word.*" It's the devil for any one to tell me a secret, for it's sure to come out in print. I do not care so much to gratify a friend, but the public ear is too great a temptation to me.

Our present business was to get beds and a supper at an inn; but this was no easy task. The public-houses were full, and where you saw a light at a private house, and people poking their heads out of the casement to see what was going on, they instantly put them in and shut the window, the moment you seemed advancing with a suspicious overture for accommodation. Our guard and coachman thundered away at the outer gate of the Crown for some time without effect—such was the greater noise within; and when the doors were unbarred, and we got admittance, we found a party assembled in the kitchen round a good hospitable fire, some sleeping, others drinking, others talking on politics and on the fight. A tall English yeoman (something like Matthews in the face, and quite as great a wag)—

"A lusty man to ben an abbot able,"—

was making such a prodigious noise about rent and taxes, and the price of corn now and formerly, that he had prevented us from being heard at the gate. The first thing I heard him say was to a shuffling fellow who wanted to be off a bet for a shilling glass of brandy and water—"Confound it, man, don't be insipid!" Thinks I, that is a good phrase. It was a good omen. He kept it up so all night, nor flinched with the approach of morning. He was a fine fellow, with sense, wit, and spirit, a hearty body and a joyous mind, free-spoken, frank, convivial—one of that true English breed that went with Harry the Fifth to the siege of Harfleur—"standing like greyhounds in the slips," &c. We ordered tea and eggs (beds were soon found to be out of the question) and this fellow's conversation was *sauce piquante*. It did one's heart good to see him brandish his oaken towel and to hear him talk. He made mince-meat of a drunken, stupid, red-faced, quarrelsome, frowsy farmer, whose nose "he moralized into a thousand similes," making it out a firebrand like Bardolph's. "I'll tell you what, my friend," says he, "the land-lady has only to keep you here to save fire and candle. If one was to touch your nose, it would go off like a piece of charcoal." At this the other only grinned like an idiot, the sole variety in his purple face being his little peering grey eyes and yellow teeth; called for another glass, swore he would not stand it; and after many attempts to provoke his humourous antagonist to single combat, which the other turned off (after working him to a ludicrous pitch of choler) with great adroitness, he fell quietly asleep with a glass of liquor in his hand, which he could not lift to his head. His laughing persecutor made a speech over him, and turning to the opposite side of the room, where they were all sleeping in the midst of this "loud and furious fun," said, "There's a scene, by G—d, for Hogarth to paint. I think he and Shakespeare were our two best men at copying life." This confirmed me in my good opinion of him. Hogarth, Shakespeare, and Nature, were just enough for him (indeed for any man) to know. I said, "You read Cobbett, don't you? At least," says I, "you talk just as well as he writes." He seemed to doubt this. But I said, "We have an hour to spare: if you'll get pen, ink and paper, and keep on talking, I'll write down what you say; and if it doesn't make a capital 'Political Register,' I'll forfeit my head. You have kept me alive tonight, however. I don't know what I should have done without you." He did not dislike this view of the thing, nor my asking if he was not about the size of Jem Belcher; and told me soon afterwards, in the confidence of friendship that "the circumstance which had given him nearly the greatest concern in his life, was Cribb's beating Jem after he had lost his eye by racket-playing." —The morning dawns; that dim but yet clear light appears, which weighs like solid bars of metal on sleepless eyelids; the guests drop down from their chambers one by one—but it was too late to think of going to bed now (the clock was on the stroke of seven), we had nothing for it but to find a barber's (the pole that glittered in the morning sun lighted us to his shop), and then a nine miles' march to Hungerford. The day was fine, the sky was blue, the mists were retiring from the marshy ground, the path was tolerably dry, the sitting-up all night had not done us much harm—at least the cause was good; we talked of this and that with amicable difference, roving and sipping of many subjects, but still invariably we returned to the fight. At length, a mile to the left of Hungerford, on a gentle eminence, we saw the ring surrounded by covered carts, gigs and carriages, of which hundreds had passed us on the road; Toms gave a youthful shout, and we hastened down a narrow lane to the scene of action.

Reader, have you ever seen a fight? If not, you have a pleasure to come, at least if it is a fight like that between the Gas-man and Bill Neate. The crowd was very great when we arrived on the spot; open carriages were coming up, with streamers flying and music playing, and the country-people were pouring in over hedge and ditch in all directions, to see their hero beat or beaten. The odds were still on Gas, but only about five to four. Gully had been down to try Neate, and had backed him considerably, which was a damper to the sanguine confidence of the adverse party. About two hundred thousand pounds were pending. The Gas says, he has lost £3,000, which were promised him by different gentlemen if he had won. He had presumed too much on himself, which had made others presume on him. This spirited and formidable young fellow seems to have taken for his motto the old maxim, that "there are three things necessary to success in life—*Impudence! Impudence! Impudence!*" It is so in matters of opinion, but not in the Fancy, which is the most practical of all things, though even here confidence is half the battle, but only half. Our friend had vapoured and swaggered too much, as if he wanted to grin and bully his adversary out of the fight. "Alas! The Bristol man was not so tamed!"—"This is *the grave-digger*," would Tom Hickman exclaim in the moments of intoxication from gin and success, shewing his tremendous right hand, "this will send many of them to their long homes; I haven't done with them yet!" Why should he—though he had licked four of the best men within the hour, yet why should he threaten to inflict dishonourable chastisement on my old master Richmond, a veteran going off the stage and who has home his sable honours meekly? Magnanimity, my dear Tom, and bravery, should be inseparable. Or why should he go up to his antagonist, the first time he ever saw him at the Fives Court, and measuring him from head to foot with a glance of contempt, as Achilles surveyed Hector, say to him, "What, are you Bill Neate? I'll knock more blood out of that great carcase of thine, this day fortnight, than you ever knocked out of a bullock's!" It was not many, 'twas not fighter-like. If he was sure of the victory (as he was not), the less said about it the better. Modesty should accompany the *Fancy* as its shadow. The best men were always the best behaved. Jem Belcher, the Game Chicken (before whom the Gas-man could not have lived), were civil, silent men. So is Cribb, so is Tom Belcher, the most elegant of sparrers, and not a man for every one to take by the nose. I enlarged on this topic in the mail (while Turtle was asleep), and said very wisely (as I thought) that impertinence was a part of no profession. A boxer was bound to beat his man, but not to thrust his fist, either actually or by implication, in every one's face. Even a highwayman, in the way of trade, may blow out your brains, but if he uses foul language at the same time, I should say he was no gentleman. A boxer, I would infer, need not be a blackguard or a coxcomb, more than another. Perhaps I press this point too much on a fallen man— Mr. Thomas Hickman has by this time learnt that first of all lessons, "That man was made to mourn." He has lost nothing by the late fight but his presumption; and that every man may do as well without! By an over-display of this quality, however, the public had been prejudiced against him, and the *knowing-ones* were taken in. Few but those who had bet on him wished Gas to win. With my own prepossessions on the subject, the result of the 11th of December appeared to me as fine a piece of poetical justice as I had ever witnessed. The difference of weight between the two combatants (14 stone to 12) was nothing to the sporting men. Great, heavy, clumsy, long-armed Bill Neate kicked the beam in the scale of the Gas-man's vanity. The amateurs were frightened at his big words, and thought that they would make up for the difference of six feet and five feet nine. Truly, the *Fancy* are not men of imagination. They judge of what has been, and cannot conceive of any thing that is to be. The Gasman had won hitherto; therefore he must beat a man half as big again as himself—and that to a certainty. Besides, there are as many feuds, factions, prejudices, pedantic notions in the *Fancy* as in the state or in the schools. Mr. Gully is almost the only cool, sensible man among them, who exercises an unbiassed discretion, and is not a slave to his passions in these matters. But enough of reflections, and to our tale. The day, as I have said, was fine for a December morning. The grass was wet, and the ground miry, and ploughed up with multitudinous feet, except that, within the ring itself, there was a spot of virgin-green closed in and unprofaned by vulgar tread, that shone with dazzling brightness in the mid-day sun. For it was now noon, and we had an hour to wait. This is the trying time. It is then the heart sickens, as you think what the two champions are about, and how short a time will determine their fate. After the first blow is struck, there is no opportunity for nervous apprehensions; you are swallowed up in the immediate interest of the scene—but

"Between the acting of a dreadful thing
And the first motion, all the interim is
Like a phantasma, or a hideous dream."

I found it so as I felt the sun's rays clinging to my back, and saw the white wintry clouds sink below the verge of the horizon. So, I thought, my fairest hopes have faded from my sight!—so will the Gasman's glory, or that of his adversary, vanish in an hour. The *swells* were parading in their white boxcoats, the outer ring was cleared with some bruises on the heads and shins of the rustic assembly (for the *cockneys* had been distanced by the sixty-six miles); the time drew near, I had got a good stand; a bustle, a buzz ran through the crowd, and from the opposite side entered Neate, between his second and bottle-holder. He rolled along swathed in his loose great coat, his knock-knees bending under his huge bulk; and, with a modest cheerful air, threw his hat into the ring. He then just looked round, and began quietly to undress; when from the other side there was a similar rush and an opening made, and the Gas-man came forward with a conscious air of anticipated triumph, too much like the cock-of-the-walk. He strutted about more than became a hero, sucked oranges with a supercilious air, and threw away the skin with a toss of his head, and went up and looked at Neate, which was an act of supererogation. The only sensible thing he did was, as he strode away from the modern Ajax, to fling out his arms, as if he wanted to try whether they would do their work that day. By this time they had stripped, and presented a strong contrast in appearance. If Neate was like Ajax, "with Atlantean shoulders, fit to bear" the pugilistic reputation of all Bristol, Hickman might be compared to Diomed, light, vigorous, elastic, and his back glistened in the sun, as he moved about, like a panther's hide. There was now a dead pause—attention was awe-struck. Who at that moment, big with a great event, did not draw his breath short—did not feel his heart throb? All was ready. They tossed up for the sun, and the Gasman won. They were led up to the *scratch*—shook hands, and went at it.

In the first round every one thought it was all over. After making play a short time, the Gasman flew at his adversary like a tiger, struck five blows in as many seconds, three first, and then following him as he staggered back, two more, right and left, and down he fell, a mighty ruin. There was a shout, and I said, "There is no standing this." Neate seemed like a lifeless lump of flesh and bone, round which the Gasman's blows played with the rapidity of electricity or lightning, and you imagined he would only be lifted up to be knocked down again. It was as if Hickman held a sword or a fire in that right hand of his, and directed it against an unarmed body. They met again, and Neate seemed, not cowed, but particularly cautious. I saw his teeth clenched together and his brows knit close against the sun. He held out both his arms at full length straight before him, like two sledge-hammers, and raised his left an inch or two higher. The Gas-man could not get over this guard—they struck mutually and fell, but without advantage on either side. It was the same in the next round; but the balance of power was thus restored—the fate of the battle was suspended. No one could tell how it would end. This was the only moment in which opinion was divided; for, in the next, the Gas-man aiming a mortal blow at his adversary's neck, with his right hand, and failing from the length he had to reach, the other returned it with his left at full swing, planted a tremendous blow on his cheek-bone and eyebrow, and made a red ruin of that side of his face. The Gas-man went down, and there was another shout—a roar of triumph as the waves of fortune rolled tumultuously from side to side. This was a settler. Hickman got up, and "grinned horrible a ghastly smile," yet he was evidently dashed in his opinion of himself; it was the first time he had ever been so punished; all one side of his face was perfect scarlet, and his right eye was closed in dingy blackness, as he advanced to the fight, less confident, but still determined. After one or two rounds, not receiving another such remembrancer, he rallied and went at it with his former impetuosity. But in vain. His strength had been weakened—his blows could not tell at such a distance—he was obliged to fling himself at his adversary, and could not strike from his feet; and almost as regularly as he flew at him with his right hand, Neate warded the blow, or drew back out of its reach, and felled him with the return of his left. There was little cautious sparring—no half-hits—no tapping and trifling, none of the *petit-maître-ship* of the art—they were almost all knock-down blows: the fight was a good stand-up fight. The wonder was the half-minute time. If there had been a minute or more allowed between each round, it would have been intelligible how they should by degrees recover strength and resolution; but to see two men smashed to the ground, smeared with gore, stunned, senseless, the breath

beaten out of their bodies; and then, before you recover from the shock, to see them rise up with new strength and courage, stand ready to inflict or receive mortal offence, and rush upon each other "like two clouds over the Caspian"—this is the most astonishing thing of all: this is the high heroic state of man! From this time forward the event became more certain every round; and about the twelfth it seemed as if it must have been over. Hickman generally stood with his back to me; but in the scuffle, he had changed positions, and Neate just then made a tremendous lunge at him, and hit him full in the face. It was doubtful whether he would fall backwards or forwards; he hung suspended for a second or two, and then fell back, throwing his hands in the air, and with his face lifted up to the sky. I never saw any thing more terrific than his aspect just before he fell. All traces of life, of natural expression, were gone from him. His face was like a human skull, a death's head, spouting blood. The eyes were filled with blood, the nose streamed with blood,the mouth gaped blood. He was not like an actual man, but like a preternatural, spectral appearance, or like one of the figures in Dante's *Inferno.* Yet he fought on after this for several rounds, still striking the first desperate blow, and Neate standing on the defensive, and using the same cautious guard to the last, as if he had still all his work to do; and it was not till the Gas-man was so stunned in the seventeenth or eighteenth round, that his senses forsook him, and he could not come to time, that the battle was declared over. Ye who despise the Fancy, do something to shew as much *pluck,* or as much self-possession as this, before you assume a superiority which you have never given a single proof of by any one action in the whole course of your lives! When the Gas-man came to himself, the first words he uttered were, "Where am I? What is the matter?" "Nothing is the matter, Tom, you have lost the battle, but you are the bravest man alive." And Jackson whispered to him, "I am collecting a purse for you, Tom." Vain sounds, and unheard at that momentl Neate instantly went up and shook him cordially by the hand, and seeing some old acquaintance, began to flourish with his fists, calling out, "Ah, you always said I couldn't fight. What do you think now?" But in all good humour, and without any appearance of arrogance; only it was evident Bill Neate was pleased that he had won the fight. When it was over, I asked Cribb if he did not think it was a good one? He said, *"Pretty well!"* The carrier-pigeons now mounted into the air, and one of them flew with the news of her husband's victory to the bosom of Mrs. Neate. Alas, for Mrs. Hickman!

Mais au revoir, as Sir Fopling Flutter says. I went down with Toms; I returned with Jack Pigott, whom I met on the ground. Toms is a rattlebrain; Pigott is a sentimentalist. Now, under favour, I am a sentimentalist too—therefore I say nothing, but that the interest of the excursion did not flag as I came back. Pigott and I marched along the causeway leading from Hungerford to Newbury, now observing the effect of a brilliant sun on the tawny meads or moss-coloured cottages, now exulting in the fight, now digressing to some topic of general and elegant literature. My friend was dressed in character for the occasion, or like one of the *Fancy;* that is, with a double portion of great coats, clogs, and overhauls: and just as we had agreed with a couple of country-lads to carry his superfluous wearing-apparel to the next town, we were overtaken by a return post-chaise, into which I got, Pigott preferring a seat on the bar. There were two strangers already in the chaise, and on their observing they supposed I had been to the fight, I said I had, and concluded they had done the same. They appeared, however, a little shy and sore on the subject; and it was not till after several hints dropped, and questions put, that it turned out they had missed it. One of these friends had undertaken to drive the other there in his gig: they had set out, to make sure work, the day before at three in the afternoon. The owner of the one-horse vehicle scorned to ask his way, and drove right on to Bagshot, instead of turning off at Hounslow: there they stopped all night, and set off the next day across the country to Reading, from whence they took coach, and got down within a mile or two of Hungerford, just half an hour after the fight was over. This might be safely set down as one of the miseries of human life. We parted with these two gentlemen who had been to see the fight, but had returned as they went, at Wolhampton, where we were promised beds (an irresistible temptation, for Pigott had passed the preceding night at Hungerford as we had done at Newbury), and we turned into an old bow-windowed parlour with a carpet and a snug fire; and after devouring a quantity of tea, toast, and eggs, sat down to consider, during an hour of philo-

sophic leisure, what we should have for supper. In the midst of an Epicurean deliberation between a roasted fowl and mutton chops with mashed potatoes, we were interrupted by an inroad of Goths and Vandals—*O procul este profani*—not real flashmen, but interlopers, noisy pretenders, butchers from Tothill-fields, brokers from Whitechapel, who called immediately for pipes and tobacco, hoping it would not be disagreeable to the gentlemen, and began to insist that it was a *cross.* Pigott withdrew from the smoke and noise into another room, and left me to dispute the point with them for a couple of hours *sans intermission* by the dial. The next morning we rose refreshed; and on observing that Jack had a pocket volume in his hand, in which he read in the intervals of our discourse, I inquired what it was, and learned to my particular satisfaction that it was a volume of the "New Eloise." Ladies, after this, will you contend that a love for the Fancy is incompatible with the cultivation of sentiment? We jogged on as before, my friend setting me up in a genteel drab great coat and green silk handkerchief (which I must say became me exceedingly), and after stretching our legs for a few miles, and seeing Jack Randall, Ned Turner, and Scroggins, pass on the top of one of the Bath coaches, we engaged with the driver of the second to take us to London for the usual fee. I got inside, and found three other passengers. One of them was an old gentleman with an aquiline nose, powdered hair and a pigtail, and who looked as if he had played many a rubber at the Bath rooms. I said to myself, he is very like Mr. Windham; I wish he would enter into conversation, that I might hear what fine observations would come from those finely-turned features. However, nothing passed, till, stopping to dine at Reading, some inquiry was made by the company about the fight, and I gave (as the reader may believe) an eloquent and animated description of it. When we got into the coach again, the old gentleman, with a graceful exordium, said he had, when a boy, been to a fight between the famous Broughton and George Stevenson, who was called the *Fighting Coachman,* in the year 1770, with the late Mr. Windham. This beginning flattered the spirit of prophecy within me, and rivetted my attention. He went on—"George Stevenson was coachman to a friend of my father's. He was an old man when I saw him some years afterwards. He took hold of his own arm and said, 'There was muscle here once, but now it is no more than this young gentleman's.' He added, 'Well, no matter; I have done no more harm than another man.' Once," said my unknown companion, "I asked him if he had ever beat Broughton? He said Yes; that he had fought with him three times, and the last time he fairly beat him, though the world did not allow it. 'I'll tell you how it was, master. When the seconds lifted us up in the last round, we were so exhausted that neither of us could stand, and we fell upon one another, and as Master Broughton fell uppermost, the mob gave it in his favour, and he was said to have won the battle. But,' says he, 'the fact was, that as his second (John Cuthbert) lifted him up, he said to him, "I'll fight no more, I've had enough," which,' says Stevenson, 'you know gave me the victory. And to prove to you that this was the case, when John Cuthbert was on his death-bed and they asked him if there was any thing on his mind which he wished to confess, he answered, "Yes, that there was one thing he wished

to set right, for that certainly Master Stevenson won that last fight with Master Broughton; for he whispered him as he lifted him up in the last round of all, that he had had enough." "This," said the Bath Gentleman, "was a bit of human nature;" and I have written this account of the fight on purpose that it might not be lost to the world. He also stated as a proof of the candour of mind in this class of men, that Stevenson acknowledged that Broughton could have beat him in his best day; but that he (Broughton) was getting old in their last recounter. When we stopped in Piccadilly, I wanted to ask the gentleman some questions about the late Mr. Windham, but had not courage. I got out, resigned my coat and green silk handkerchief to Pigott (loth to part with these ornaments of life), and walked home in high spirits.

P.S. Toms called upon me the next day, to ask me if I did not think the fight was a complete thing? I said I thought it was. I hope he will relish my account of it.

[FACT]

THE DAY OF THE FIGHT

This is a behind-the-scenes look on September 27, 1946 at one of the contestants in the first part of one of the great trilogies of boxing. In the ring after the second, nine months later in Chicago, Rocky Graziano would exult, "Somebody up there likes me!" From that would evolve the similarly titled best-selling autobiography and the 1956 film starring the thirty-one-year old Paul Newman in only his second screen appearance.

W.C. HEINZ

The window was open from the bottom and in the bed by the window the prizefighter lay under a sheet and a candlewick spread. In the other bed another prizefighter slept, but the first one lay there looking at the ceiling. It was nine-thirty in the morning and he would fight that night.

The name of the first prizefighter is Rocky

Graziano, but you don't have to remember that. The thing to remember is that he is a prizefighter, because they said this was to be a piece telling what a fighter does, from the moment he gets up in the morning until the moment he climbs into the ring, on the day when he must fight.

"All right, Rock," Whitey Bimstein, his trainer,

said. "If you don't want to sleep you can get up."

The suite is on the twelfth floor of a hotel in New York's West Eighties, off Central Park. In the other bedroom Eddie Coco, one of the fighter's managers, still slept. On the soiled striped sofa in the sitting room a young lightweight named Al Pennino lay on his right side, facing the room, a blanket over him and a pillow under his head.

"If he don't feel like sleepin'," Whitey said, "there's no sense of him lyin' there if he wants to get up."

He was walking around the sitting room, picking up newspapers and putting them on the table, fussing around the doors of the closet-like kitchenette. Graziano and Whitey had been living there in the long weeks Graziano had been training for this one. They do not let a fighter live at home when he is in training for a fight.

"What time is it?" Graziano said. He had come out of the bedroom and was standing just inside the sitting room. He was wearing a pair of brown checked shorts and that was all. There was sleep in his face and the black hair was mussed on his head.

"Nine thirty-five," Whitey said.

Pennino and Coco were awake and walking around now. The other fighter, Lou Valles, a welterweight, came out of the bedroom in a shirt and a pair of slacks.

"You sleep?" Coco said to Graziano.

"Yeah," Graziano said. "All right."

"We got a nice day."

Outside the window the sun shone a pale yellow and in the distance over the park there was a blue-gray haze. This one was to be held in Yankee Stadium and the weather is one of the things they worry about when they have an outdoor fight.

As they sat around the small sitting room now they said little, seeming reluctant to break the sleep that was still in their heads. Finally Valles got up and walked over to the table by the wall and picked up the morning newspapers. They were opened to the sports sections because Graziano was going to fight Tony Zale, the middleweight champion, and this one was an important fight.

"You see?" he said, showing one of the papers to Pennino. "That Rocky takes a good picture. Right?"

Graziano did not say anything.

"He's a good-looking guy," Pennino said.

"You know what I'm going to do if I win the title tonight?" Graziano said. "If I win the title,

I'm gonna get drunk. You know what I mean by that?"

"Yeah," Whitey said. "I know what you mean. You remind me of another fighter I had. He said if he won the title he'd get drunk. He won the title and he had one beer and he was drunk."

"Who?" Graziano asked.

"Lou Ambers," Whitey said.

Graziano went to the bedroom and when he came out he had on a pair of gray sharkskin slacks, turned once at the cuffs, a basque shirt with narrow blue stripes, and over this a gray-blue sleeveless sweater. He had washed and his hair was combed back. At ten-thirty Jack Healey came in. He is another of Graziano's managers, a suave but nervous type they call "The Mustache."

"You all right?"

"Sure," Graziano said. "Relax. I'm all right."

They waited for Pennino and Coco to finish dressing and they sat around talking about Stanley Ketchel, Bob Fitzsimmons, and Joe Dundee, Healey and Whitey talking and the fighters gazing around the room and out the window.

They were ready to leave then because it was eleven-fifteen. At the door the maid, in a blue dress with white cuffs and collar, said she wished them luck, and the woman who ran the elevator smiled at them in a way implying that she knew it was a special day.

Graziano's car was waiting in front of the hotel. It is blue and buff, new, and on the front doors the small letters read "Rocky." They got in, Healey driving, Graziano in the middle, and Coco on the outside, Whitey and Pennino and Valles in the back.

When they reached Fifty-fourth Street they turned west and stopped in front of the side door to Stillman's Gym. They got out and left Pennino to watch the car and went upstairs and into the gym, gray and, but for Lou Stillman and a couple of others, deserted.

"Hey," Stillman said, coming across the floor from the front. "What you guys want anyway?"

"You know what we want," Whitey said.

"I'll punch you in the nose," Stillman said to Graziano. "I'll knock you out before tonight."

"You'll what?" Graziano said, feigning annoyance and taking a fighting pose.

"What's the matter?" Stillman said, smiling. "Can't you take a joke?"

They went back into a small partitioned room in

the back. There was a scale and Graziano started stripping and they shut the door. In a couple of minutes they came out, Graziano fastening his belt.

"I'll bet you down there he'll weigh fifty-three and a half," Whitey said "I'll bet you'll see."

"What did he weigh here?" Healey said.

"A little over fifty-four," Whitey said, "but he'll go to the toilet."

"He looks great," Healey said. "You can tell from his eyes."

In the car again they started around the block. Graziano shut off the radio which Pennino must have turned on while the rest were in the gym.

"You should listen to that," Healey said. "They might tell you about the fight."

Graziano said nothing. They drove west to the West Side Highway and South past the North River docks.

"Rock," Whitey said, "your old man still working down here?"

"No," Graziano said. "He's workin' down at the Fish Market instead."

It was 11:48 A.M. when they were looking ahead down the street to the mob around the rear entrance to the New York State building where Graziano and Zale would weigh in. There were about two hundred people there, men, kids, photographers, and even a few women standing on and around the steps.

"We'll park down in front of your grandmother's," Healey said.

He drove slowly across the intersection past the park and pulled up at the curb on the right in front of the building where Graziano, as a kid, had lived. This was his neighborhood, and when they got out of the car there was a cop standing there and he stuck out his hand to Graziano and shook his head.

"Well," he said, "you're still the same, aren't you?"

Graziano said something but by now some of the crowd, running, had caught up. They were men, young and middle-aged and a lot of kids, and one of the men had his left arm in a sling.

"You see this?" he was shouting at Graziano from the back and waving his right fist. "You see this? Think of this tonight."

"All right. All right," the cop was shouting. "Stand back."

They hustled the fighter, then, into the narrow doorway between two stores and, with the fighter leading, they climbed up three flights. He opened a

door and there they followed him into the kitchen of an apartment.

"Hello," he said to the man standing there and then pausing and looking around. "Where's Grandma?"

"In the park maybe," the man, Graziano's uncle, Silvio, said. "Maybe shopping. She went out about half an hour ago."

Graziano sat on a chair by the window, his right elbow on the windowsill. He looked around the room and through the door and into one of the bedrooms and his uncle watched him.

"How you feel, Rocky?" Silvio said.

"I feel fine," Graziano said.

That was all they said. He sat there waiting, looking around occasionally, not saying anything to the others who had followed him in. The door to the hall was open and presently a couple of photographers came in.

"Do you mind, Rocky?" one of them said. "We'd just like to get a picture of you and your grandmother."

"That's all right," Graziano said. "She'll be in soon."

He looked out the window again and, leaning forward, at the street below.

"Here she comes now," he said.

An old woman hurried across the street carrying a brown paper bag in one arm. She had been stout once and she had on a gray print house dress and a small black hat and when she came in, breathing heavily from climbing the stairs, she walked across the room, smiling, and took Graziano by the hands and the two of them stood there speaking in Italian and smiling.

Graziano took her then by the arms and led her to the chair by the window and she sat down and put her bundle on the floor and took off her hat. She sat there smiling at Graziano and looking occasionally at the others and nodding her head.

"Do you mind now?" the photographer said to Graziano.

"Oh," Graziano said, and then he turned to the old woman. "They want to take a picture for the newspapers of you and me."

"Picture?" the old woman said, and her face changed. "That's why you come?"

"Oh no," Graziano said, and his own face had changed and he was shaking his head. "Oh no. I'd have come anyway. They just came in."

"I put on black dress," the old woman said.

"No," the photographer said to Graziano. "Tell her no. We'll only take a minute. We haven't got time."

"No," Graziano said to her. "That dress is all right."

"I put on nice black dress," the old woman said.

They took several pictures, then, of Graziano showing his grandmother, in the house dress, his right fist, and then Graziano said good-by to her, taking her by the hands, and he and those who had followed him went downstairs where there was a crowd waiting.

They pushed through the crowd, kids grabbing at Graziano and trying to run along at his side, and men shouting at him, things like: "Hey, Rocky!"... "Good luck, Rocky!" ... "Flatten him for me, Rocky!"

They swarmed, half-running, down the street and the bigger crowd around the steps of the State building shouted and pushed, the cops shoving them back, and the photographers' bulbs flashing and many in the crowd making fists. Inside they hurried into an elevator that was waiting. The room upstairs was a big one. It was crowded with men, some of them standing on chairs, and at the end of the room by the desk there was a scale and around that the crowd was tight-packed.

They pushed the fighter through, the crowd quiet, and when he got to the desk there was some milling around and conversation and then he started taking off his clothes and tossing them on the desk. The crowd stood back and watched him, and he stripped and took off even his wristwatch and his ring, and put on a pair of purple boxing trunks.

Mike Jacobs, the promoter, Nat Rogers, the matchmaker, Eddie Eagan, the chairman of the New York State Athletic Commission, Irving Cohen, another of Graziano's managers, Art Winch and Sam Pian, Zale's managers, Healey and Coco and Whitey—they all were there on the inside of the crowd. Outside of them were newspapermen and photographers and more commissioners, and then Graziano stepped on the scale and Eagan leaned forward and adjusted the weight on the bar and watched the bar settle slowly to rest.

"The weight," Eagan said, announcing it, "is exactly one hundred fifty-four. Graziano, one hundred fifty-four pounds."

Several of the newspapermen were crowding out to find telephones and there was the noise of conversation in the crowd.

"How much did Zale weigh?" Healey asked.

"A hundred and sixty," somebody said.

"Black trunks for Zale," Harry Markson, Jacobs' press agent, said, announcing it. "Purple trunks for Graziano."

Graziano sat on the desk and Dr. Vincent Nardiello, the commission physician, put a stethoscope to Graziano's chest. Then the doctor took the fighter's blood pressure and announced the heartbeat and blood pressure figures to the press.

"All right, Zale," Eagan said, raising his voice. "All right, Zale. Come out."

The other fighter, Zale, who would fight Graziano, came out through a doorway to the left of the desk. He was naked except for the black trunks and tan street shoes. The crowd moved back and he walked to the scales where Graziano stood. They did not look at each other.

"Take a pose. Make them pose," the photographers were hollering and Zale and Graziano faced each other, Graziano's arms cocked wide at the sides of his chest, Zale's arms drawn up in a fighting pose in front of his chest. They stood there holding the pose while the bulbs flashed again and their eyes met. Graziano smiled once and nodded; Zale smiled back.

The photographers were still working away, shouting for one more, swearing at each other, when Eagan stepped between the fighters and moved them over beside the desk.

"Now, I understand you're both good rugged fighters," Eagan said, "but I want a clean fight. I want no hitting in the breaks and that's one rule I'm going to caution the referee to observe."

He talked with them for another moment and then he turned and Zale went back through the door and Graziano went back to the desk and they both dressed. When they were finished dressing they walked, each with his group around him, through the crowd down the hall to another office where, in separate corners of the room, they tried on the gloves and alternate sets of gloves. One of the commissioners marked with a pen each fighter's name on the white lining of his gloves.

"He's got a bad eye," someone said to Graziano, nodding toward Zale who was waiting while the commissioner marked his set. "It's his left."

"No," Graziano said, looking over at Zale. "I noticed that. It's his right, not his left."

There were crowds again in the hall and outside the building, running after him and shouting the same things, a few of them different things, but most of them over and over again: "Hey, Rock!" … "Good luck, Rock!" … "I prayed for you last night."

They hurried down the street, photographers running ahead of them, and pausing to snap them, and the crowd pushed on behind. They passed the car parked at the curb and went into a small bar and restaurant on the right where a cop stood by the door to keep the crowd out.

They walked through the bar quickly into a small restaurant in the back. There were a half-dozen tables with red and white striped tablecloths on them and Graziano sat down at a table at the right. In the corner at the left there were two men and two women at a table, and one of the men said something to the others and they turned around quickly and watched Graziano as he sat there fingering a fork and waiting while the others, eight or ten, pulled up chairs around the table or stood in back.

"Look, Rock," Healey said, and he shoved a photograph of Graziano in a fighting pose across the table, "autograph this, will you?"

"Okay, Jack," Graziano said, looking at him and then reaching around for the pen someone handed him from in back. "Don't get excited. Relax."

"I know," Healey said, "I'm more excited than you are. I'll relax."

"Autograph it to Pete," someone said. "Pete is his first name. Pasca is the last. P-A-S-C-A."

Graziano wrote something on the photograph and Healey put another down in front of him.

"Sign that to Pat," he said. "P-A-T."

"What is it, a girl or a fella?" Graziano said.

"I don't know," Healey said. "Put 'Best Wishes, Rocky.' It don't matter. That covers it."

In the arched doorway they stood watching, about fifteen or twenty of them, and then the waitress came from the back, carrying on a tray a cup of tea with a slice of lemon on the saucer. She put those down and went away and when she came back she had toast and a soft-boiled egg broken into a cup.

Graziano sat there eating the egg and the toast, blowing on the tea and trying it. They had let those from the bar into the restaurant now and they stood, three and four deep around the table, not saying anything or speaking only in whispers, watching in almost complete silence the fighter as he finished the egg and toast.

There were the crowds outside again, then, shouting the same things and the cop had to clear a path through them to the car. There were many faces at the windows of the car, faces shouting and fists, and Healey pulled the car away from the curb and drove east and then north on Second Avenue and at Forty-ninth Street he turned west.

On Forty-ninth Street at Seventh Avenue they had to stop for a light. They sat there, not saying anything and waiting for the light to change, when a guy in a white shirt, in his twenties, came off the sidewalk and thrust his face into the open front window of the car where Graziano sat between Healey and Coco.

"Hey, Rock," he said, making a fist, "if you win I get married. If you lose she'll have to wait a couple more years."

He turned as if to leave the car and then he saw them inside starting to smile.

"I ain't kiddin'," he said, turning back and reaching into his pants pocket and coming out with a fist full of bills. "Fresh dough I just got from the bank."

Graziano said nothing. Healey drove over to Ninth Avenue where he had to swerve the car out to avoid a bus pulling wide from the curb.

"You see?" he said. "These bus guys think they got a license to do anything they want."

"Watch," somebody said. "He's gonna yap."

The bus driver was shouting out of the window at his side.

"Hey, Rock!" he was shouting. "Good luck tonight. I know you can flatten that guy."

"What do you make of that?" Healey said. "How do you like that?"

In front of the hotel they sat in the car waiting while Whitey went up to get a leather bag containing Graziano's robe, his boxing shoes, his trunks, and the other things he would need in the fight. While they waited Healey went across the street to a newsstand and came back with the afternoon newspapers. He tossed them down on the front seat and Graziano picked up the first one and turned to the sports page where the banner headline read: "Zale Picked to Knock Out Graziano in Eight Rounds."

"Look at this," he said to Healey, flatly, without emotion.

"That's okay," Healey said. "What a guy thinks, he should write."

They drove to Coco's house, which is in the Pelham Bay section of the Bronx. They parked the car in front of the house and walked down the concrete driveway to the back where there were eight or ten men and women and a couple of kids on the back porch.

"Rocky," Mrs. Coco said, "these are friends of ours from Utica. They'd like to meet you and they came down for the fight."

Graziano shook hands with them and they all smiled and tried not to look at him steadily. They studied him furtively, the way some men study an attractive girl on the subway. He sat there on the porch for a few minutes while the others talked around him and they took him downstairs for the dinner on which he would fight.

There was a bar at one end of the wood-paneled room and there was a long table set for twelve. He sat at the head of the table and some of the others sat watching him while they brought him his dish of spinach, his plate of lettuce, his toast, and his steak.

Graziano ate quickly, cutting large pieces, using his fork with his left hand, always holding the knife in his right. When he said he wanted some water, Whitey said he could have a little without ice. He had some hot tea and lemon and then he said he did not want to eat any more, pushing away the plate on which there was still a small portion of steak.

"That's all right," Whitey said. "If you feel satisfied, don't force yourself." He went upstairs, then, and sat on the porch while the others ate. When they had finished, a half hour later, it was four-twenty and Whitey said they would take a short walk before Graziano took a nap.

They walked—Graziano and Pennino in front and Whitey and Healey in back—down the street and across the street under the elevated to the park. They walked through the park until four-thirty and then Whitey told them it was time to turn back. They walked past a barbershop where they saw Coco sitting down for a shave. Whitey said he would stop in the drugstore down the block and that he would be right back. Graziano and Pennino went into the barbershop and Graziano sat down in the barber chair next to the one in which Coco sat.

"I'll get a trim, Eddie," he said. "Is it all right if I just get a trim in the back?" "Sure," Coco said. "Why not?"

A couple of girls in their teens and wearing sweaters and skirts came in then and stood by the chair looking at Graziano as he looked back at them.

"Are you Rocky Graziano?" one of them said.

"Yeah," Graziano said. "That's right."

"I could tell by your nose," one of them said. "You gonna win tonight?"

"Sure," Graziano said, smiling. "Why not?"

By now Whitey had come back.

"What are you doin' in the chair?" he said.

"I'm gettin' a trim," Graziano said.

"A what?"

"A trim. A trim just in the back."

"Listen," Whitey said, "get up out of there. It's time for you to rest."

"Look, Whitey," Graziano said, "I'm restin' here."

"C'mon," Whitey said.

When they got back to Coco's house they sat in the living room. At ten minutes to five Graziano went in the next room and phoned his wife and at five o'clock Whitey said it was time for Graziano to go upstairs and lie down.

"What difference does it make?" Healey said. "He'll flatten the guy anyway." "I know," Whitey said, "but he goes upstairs and takes his nap."

Graziano and Whitey went upstairs then and Mrs. Coco showed them a small room with maple furniture and a single bed. When Mrs. Coco had turned the covers back she left and Graziano stripped down to his shorts and sat on the bed.

"See if they got any comic books, will you, Whitey?" he said. "Go downstairs and see, hey?"

Whitey went downstairs and came back with one comic book. Graziano took it and looked at the cover.

"Go out, hey Whitey?" he said, looking up. "Go out and get some others."

Whitey and Coco walked up the street to a candy store where they picked out ten books from the rack—"Buzzy"… "Comic Capers"… "Captain Marvel, Jr." … "Whiz Comics" … "Sensation Comics".… "Ace Comics"… "All-Flash."

When they came back and opened the door to the bedroom Graziano was lying on his back under the covers reading the comic book and there was a towel over the pillow under his head.

"Hey!" Coco said. "What about that towel?"

"Yeah," Graziano said. "I got some grease on my hair."

"What of it?" Coco said. "We're gonna wash the sheets and pillow case."

They went downstairs, then, and left him. It was five-twenty and for the next hour and a half the men sat in the driveway at the back on chairs they had brought from the porch and the kitchen and they talked about fights.

At six-fifty Whitey got up and went into the house. He heard someone on the stairs and Graziano came into the kitchen, dressed, his hair combed back.

"Hey," Whitey said. "I was just gonna get you up. You sleep?"

"I don't know," Graziano said. "I think maybe I dropped off a little."

They went out into the back yard, then, and Graziano sat down on one of the chairs. Dusk was setting in, so one of them lighted the garage light so they could see a little better and they sat around waiting and not saying much. At seven twenty-five Whitey said they had to go.

The driveway, dark, seemed full of people. Some of them wanted to shake his hand and the rest kept calling the word "luck."

"If you hear any noise from section thirty-three," one woman yelled, "that's us."

"We've got an undertaker with us from Utica," another woman said, "so you don't have to worry and you can hit him as hard as you like."

"Excuse me, Rocky," Mrs. Coco said, "but this is my delivery boy and he wants to meet you."

"Sure. Hello," Graziano said.

They walked out the dark driveway and pushed through a lot of kids who had been waiting there all afternoon and got into the car. It took them twenty minutes to drive to Yankee Stadium. On the way Pennino, in the back seat, sang songs and Whitey told a couple of old jokes.

When they reached the Stadium, Healey pulled the car up in front of Gate Four and stopped.

"You can't stop here," a cop said.

"This is Graziano," Healey said.

"I can't help it," the cop said.

Healey did not argue with the cop but eased the car down a few feet in front of another cop. Now someone in the crowd had spotted Graziano in the front seat and the crowd stopped moving forward and started to gather around the car.

"This is Graziano," Healey said to the cop.

"You shouldn't stop here," the cop said.

"I know it," Healey said, "but we gotta stop somewhere. He's fightin' tonight."

"You better see the lieutenant," the cop said.

"C'mon," Whitey said. "Let's get out. Leave it here."

They got out and the cops were pushing the crowd back now and those in the crowd were calling the same things the other crowds had called before. The cops were clearing a way through and Whitey gave Pennino the bag and they pushed through to the gate.

Along the tunnel under the stands they led Graziano now into the clubhouse used by the visiting teams. It was divided lengthwise down the middle by a wood-framed partition covered with cheap lavender cloth. Just inside the door a half-dozen preliminary fighters were in various stages of preparation, getting into their ring clothes, having their hands taped, warming up. They led Graziano past them and, parting a heavy dark blue drape, into his own part of the room.

"What time is it now?" he said, looking around.

"Eight o'clock," somebody said.

He sat down on one of the folding chairs to wait. Whitey had opened the leather bag and was taking out the equipment—the ring shoes, the boxing trunks, the protective cup—and placing them on the rubbing table, when Commissioner Eagan and Commissioner Bruno came in. They shook Graziano's hand as he stood up and stood talking with him for a minute or so and then they left.

"You better warm up, Rock," Whitey said. "Just warm up a little."

Graziano moved around the room, clothed, throwing short punches for about five minutes, and then sat down again.

"Let's go," a voice outside said, calling to the preliminary fighters. "The first two bouts."

Graziano stood up again. He took off his sweater and his basque shirt and went to a locker and hung them up. He came back and sat down on the table, and took off his shoes and socks. He got off the table and put them in the locker and then he took off his trousers and shorts and hung them up. He came back and sat down, naked now, on the table, and Whitey handed him a new pair of white woolen socks. He put them on and then put on his boxing shoes. He started moving around the room again, throwing short punches, weaving and bobbing a little as he went. He did this for a couple of minutes and then Whitey called to him and he went over and tried on a pair of the purple trunks. He took them off and tried on another pair, which he seemed to like better.

Sol Bimstein, Whitey's brother, came in and walked over to the table and picked up a pair of the purple trunks.

"Ain't these a nicer color purple?" he said.

"I like these best," Graziano said.

"Whichever he likes best," Whitey said.

Graziano put on his basque shirt, then, and began shadowboxing around the room again. A couple of deputy commissioners came in to stand there and watch him and then Whitey took Graziano's robe—white with a green trim and with Graziano's name in green block letters on the back—and spread it over half the table. Graziano stopped the shadowboxing and took off his trunks and shirt and walked to the table and lay down on his back.

Whitey worked first over his upper body. He rubbed coco oil on Graziano's chest. Then he put a towel across Graziano's chest and Graziano turned over and lay facedown and Whitey rubbed the oil on his back. Then he sat up and Whitey went over his legs with rubbing alcohol. Whitey was sweating and he took off his own shirt. He worked hard on Graziano's legs and then he went back at his shoulders and chest. When he was finished Graziano got off the table and, once again stripped but for his shoes and socks, moved around throwing punches until Whitey stopped him and took him over to a corner where they talked together quietly and Whitey showed Graziano a move with his left. Then he told Graziano to sit down and put his feet up on the table and he put a towel across Graziano's back and another across his legs.

"What time is it?" Graziano said.

"Eight fifty-five," Sol Bimstein said.

"I thought it was later than that," Graziano said.

"How do you feel?" Whitey said.

"Tired," Graziano said.

At nine o'clock a couple of commissioners and Art Winch, one of Zale's managers, came in.

"Is it time?" Whitey said.

"Yes," Winch said. "We might as well get started."

Graziano got up, then, and Whitey helped him into the white and green satin robe. He sat on the table, his legs hanging over, and Whitey started bandaging Graziano's right hand, Winch and the commissioners watching. It took him about seven minutes to do the right hand. When he was starting the left hand Winch said something and Whitey raised his voice.

"Just what I'm allowed," he said. "No more. No less."

"All right. All right," Winch said.

They stood there watching until the job was done and then Sam Pian, Zale's other manager, came in.

"You stayin'?" Winch said.

"Right," Pian said. He sat down on a chair by the lockers and Winch and the commissioners went out. Graziano, the tape and gauze a gleaming white on his hands now, started moving around, shadowboxing again.

"I'm spying," Pian said as Graziano passed near him.

"Yeah. Sure," Graziano said. "I know."

He stopped throwing punches.

"This tape stinks," he said, looking at his hands.

"I know it does," Pian said.

"It peels off," Graziano said. He started moving around again, the leather of his shoes squeaking in the quiet room, the satin of his robe rustling. Mike Jacobs came in and Graziano stopped and spoke with him and then Jacobs went out and Healey came in.

"You got half an hour," he said.

"All right," Graziano said. He walked out through the drape.

"Where's he goin'?" Pian asked.

"Some of the preliminary fighters want to see him," Healey said. "They can't come in so he went out to see them."

"Oh," Pian said.

"He's a nice kid, ain't he, Sam?" Healey said.

"Yes," Pian said. "I guess he's a nice kid."

He got up to follow Graziano as Graziano came back in. Healey started out, and put his head back in between the curtains.

"I'll see you after, Rock," he said.

"Scram," Graziano said, looking up from where he was sitting by the table, his feet on the table, his hands on his lap. "Get out."

"I'll punch you in the eye," Healey said. He threw a kiss and pulled his head out as Sol Bimstein came in. "Main bout next," Sol said. "There's two rounds to go in the semifinal."

"Is it warm out?" Graziano said.

"Just nice," Sol said.

Graziano sat there waiting and Whitey came over to him and rubbed a little Vaseline on Graziano's face. It was ten minutes to ten. Whitey said something to him and he got up and went out. In a minute he came back and Whitey helped him off with his robe. He helped him into his protector and his trunks and then Graziano stood there rotating his shoulders, bending at the waist. When he stopped Whitey gave him a short drink from the water bottle. Then Whitey rubbed Graziano's chest and his stomach and his shoulders and Graziano took several deep breaths. Then Graziano began pacing back and forth, throwing short punches, breathing hard through his nose. He was doing this when a couple of the commissioners came in.

"Hey, Rock," one of them said to him. "What are you going to do with all the dough you get? The place is packed."

"All right," a voice shouted in from outside. "Main bout. Main bout."

"All right, Rocky," Whitey said. He moved over to his fighter and put the towel around his fighter's neck, crossing the ends in front, and he helped him back into his robe. Somebody took the pail and Whitey had his first-aid kit and, with Pian still watching them and following them, they moved out.

In the tunnel there were special cops and a couple of preliminary fighters who shouted something at Graziano. They moved quickly through the tunnel and down the steps to the lower level. Whitey's hand was on Graziano's back. Graziano kept exercising his arms, jigging a little now and then. They were close around him and they moved quickly along the lower level and then up the steps of the dugout where they hit him with the sound.

There were 39,827 people there and they had paid $342,497 to be there and when Graziano's head came up out of the dugout they rose and made their sound. The place was filled with it and it came from far off and then he was moving quickly down beneath this ceiling of sound, between the two long walls of faces, turned toward him and yellow in the artificial light and shouting things, mouths open, eyes wide, into the ring where, in one of the most brutal fights ever seen in New York, Zale dropped him once and he dropped Zale once before, in the sixth round, Zale suddenly, with a right to the body and a left to the head, knocked him out.

[FICTION]

FIFTY GRAND

The fixed fight is the most popular device in boxing fiction, but this surmounts it and is, of course, the best piece of fight fiction ever written. It was first printed in the *Atlantic Monthly*, after having been rejected by *Cosmopolitan* and the *Saturday Evening Post*.

ERNEST HEMINGWAY

"How are you going yourself, Jack?" I asked him.

"You seen this Walcott?" he says.

"Just in the gym."

"Well," Jack says, "I'm going to need a lot of luck with that boy."

"He can't hit you, Jack," Soldier said.

"I wish to hell he couldn't."

"He couldn't hit you with a handful of birdshot."

"Bird-shot'd be all right," Jack says. "I wouldn't mind bird-shot any."

"He looks easy to hit," I said.

"Sure," Jack says, "he ain't going to last long. He ain't going to last like you and me, Jerry. But right now he's got everything."

"You'll left-hand him to death."

"Maybe," Jack says. "Sure. I got a chance to."

"Handle him like you handled Kid Lewis."

"Kid Lewis," Jack said. "That kike!"

The three of us, Jack Brennan, Soldier Bartlett, and I were in Handley's. There were a couple of broads sitting at the next table to us. They had been drinking.

"What do you mean, kike?" one of the broads says. "What do you mean, kike, you big Irish bum?"

"Sure," Jack says. "That's it."

"Kikes," this broad goes on. "They're always talking about kikes, these big Irishmen. What do you mean, kikes?"

"Come on. Let's get out of here."

"Kikes," this broad goes on. "Whoever saw you ever buy a drink? Your wife sews your pockets up every morning. These Irishmen and their kikes! Ted Lewis could lick you too."

"Sure," Jack says. "And you give away a lot of things free too, don't you?"

We went out. That was Jack. He could say what he wanted to when he wanted to say it.

Jack started training out at Danny Hogan's health farm over in Jersey. It was nice out there but Jack didn't like it much. He didn't like being away from his wife and the kids, and he was sore and grouchy most of the time. He liked me and we got along fine together; and he liked Hogan, but after a while Soldier Bartlett commenced to get on his nerves. A kidder gets to be an awful thing around a camp if his stuff goes sort of sour. Soldier was always kidding Jack, just sort of kidding him all the time. It wasn't very funny and it wasn't very good, and it began to get Jack. It was sort of stuff like this. Jack would finish up with the weights and the bag and pull on the gloves.

"You want to work?" he'd say to Soldier.

"Sure. How you want me to work?" Soldier would ask. "Want me to treat you rough like Walcott? Want me to knock you down a few times?"

"That's it," Jack would say. He didn't like it any, though.

One morning we were all out on the road. We'd been out quite a way and now we were coming back. We'd go along fast for three minutes and then walk a minute, and then go fast for three minutes again. Jack wasn't ever what you would call a sprinter. He'd move around fast enough in the ring if he had to, but he wasn't any too fast on the road. All the time we were walking Soldier was kidding him. We came up the hill to the farmhouse.

"Well," says Jack, "you better go back to town, Soldier."

"What do you mean?"

"You better go back to town and stay there."

"What's the matter?"

"I'm sick of hearing you talk."

"Yes?" says Soldier.

"Yes," says Jack.

"You'll be a damn sight sicker when Walcott gets through with you."

"Sure," says Jack, "maybe I will. But I know I'm sick of you."

So Soldier went off on the train to town that same morning. I went down with him to the train. He was good and sore.

"I was just kidding him," he said. We were waiting on the platform. "He can't pull that stuff with me, Jerry."

"He's nervous and crabby," I said. "He's a good fellow, Soldier."

"The hell he is. The hell he's ever been a good fellow."

"Well," I said, "so long, Soldier."

The train had come in. He climbed up with his bag.

"So long, Jerry," he says. "You be in town before the fight?"

"I don't think so."

"See you then."

He went in and the conductor swung up and the train went out. I rode back to the farm in the cart. Jack was on the porch writing a letter to his wife. The mail had come and I got the papers and went over on the other side of the porch and sat down to read. Hogan came out the door and walked over to me.

"Did he have a jam with Soldier?"

"Not a jam," I said. "He just told him to go back to town."

"I could see it coming," Hogan said. "He never liked Soldier much."

"No. He don't like many people."

"He's a pretty cold one," Hogan said.

"Well, he's always been fine to me."

"Me too," Hogan said. "I got no kick on him. He's a cold one, though."

Hogan went in through the screen door and I sat there on the porch and read the papers. It was just starting to get fall weather and it's nice country there in Jersey, up in the hills, and after I read the paper through I sat there and looked out at the country and the road down below against the woods with cars going along it, lifting the dust up. It was fine weather and pretty nicelooking country. Hogan came to the door and I said, "Say, Hogan, haven't you got anything to shoot out here?"

"No," Hogan said. "Only sparrows."

"Seen the paper?" I said to Hogan.

"What's in it?"

"Sande booted three of them in yesterday."

"I got that on the telephone last night."

"You follow them pretty close, Hogan?" I asked.

"Oh, I keep in touch with them," Hogan said.

"How about Jack?" I says. "Does he still play them?"

"Him?" said Hogan. "Can you see him doing it?"

Just then Jack came around the corner with the letter in his hand. He's wearing a sweater and an old pair of pants and boxing shoes.

"Got a stamp, Hogan?" he asks.

"Give me the letter," Hogan said. "I'll mail it for you."

"Say, Jack," I said, "didn't you used to play the ponies?"

"Sure."

"I knew you did. I knew I used to see you out at Sheepshead."

"What did you lay off them for?" Hogan asked.

"Lost money."

Jack sat down on the porch by me. He leaned back against a post. He shut his eyes in the sun.

"Want a chair?" Hogan asked.

"No," said Jack. "This is fine."

"It's a nice day," I said. "It's pretty nice out in the country."

"I'd a damn sight rather be in town with the wife."

"Well, you only got another week."

"Yes," Jack says. "That's so."

We sat there on the porch. Hogan was inside in the office.

"What do you think about the shape I'm in?" Jack asked me.

"Well, you can't tell," I said. "You got a week to get around into form."

"Don't stall me."

"Well," I said, "you're not right."

"I'm not sleeping," Jack said.

"You'll be all right in a couple of days."

"No," says Jack, "I got the insomnia."

"What's on your mind?"

"I miss the wife."

"Have her come out."

"No. I'm too old for that."

"We'll take a long walk before you turn in and get you good and tired."

"Tired!" Jack says. "I'm tired all the time."

He was that way all week. He wouldn't sleep at night and he'd get up in the morning feeling that way, you know, when you can't shut your hands.

"He's stale as a poorhouse cake," Hogan said. "He's nothing."

"I never seen Walcott," I said.

"He'll kill him," said Hogan. "He'll tear him in two."

"Well," I said, "everybody's got to get it some time."

"Not like this, though," Hogan said. "They'll think he never trained. It gives the farm a black eye."

"You hear what the reporters said about him?"

"Didn't I! They said he was awful. They said they oughtn't to let him fight."

"Well," I said, "they're always wrong, ain't they?"

"Yes," said Hogan. "But this time they're right."

"What the hell do they know about whether a man's right or not?"

"Well," said Hogan, "they're not such fools."

"All they did was pick Willard at Toledo. This Lardner, he's so wise now, ask him about when he picked Willard at Toledo."

"Aw, he wasn't out," Hogan said. "He only writes the big fights."

"I don't care who they are," I said. "What the hell do they know? They can write maybe, but what the hell do they know?"

"You don't think Jack's in any shape, do you?" Hogan asked.

"No. He's through. All he needs is to have Corbett pick him to win for it to be all over."

"Well, Corbett'll pick him," Hogan says.

"Sure. He'll pick him."

That night Jack didn't sleep any either. The next morning was the last day before the fight. After breakfast we were all out on the porch again.

"What do you think about, Jack, when you can't sleep?" I said.

"Oh, I worry," Jack says. "I worry about property I got up in the Bronx, I worry about property I got in Florida. I worry about the kids. I worry about the wife. Sometimes I think about fights. I think about that kike Ted Lewis and I get sore. I got some stocks and I worry about them. What the hell don't I think about?"

"Well," I said, "tomorrow night it'll all be over."

"Sure," said Jack. "That always helps a lot, don't it? That just fixes everything all up, I suppose. Sure."

He was sore all day. We didn't do any work. Jack just moved around a little to loosen up. He shadowboxed a few rounds. He didn't even look good doing that. He skipped rope a little while. He couldn't sweat.

"He'd be better not to do any work at all," Hogan said. We were standing watching him skip rope. "Don't he ever sweat at all any more?"

"He can't sweat."

"Do you suppose he's got the con? He never had any trouble making weight, did he?"

"No, he hasn't got any con. He just hasn't got anything inside any more."

"He ought to sweat," said Hogan.

Jack came over, skipping the rope. He was skipping up and down in front of us, forward and back, crossing his arms every third time.

"Well," he says. "What are you buzzards talking about?"

"I don't think you ought to work any more," Hogan says. "You'll be stale."

"Wouldn't that be awful?" Jack says and skips away down the floor, slapping the rope hard.

That afternoon John Collins showed up out at the farm. Jack was up in his room. John came out in a car from town. He had a couple of friends with him. The car stopped and they all got out.

"Where's Jack?" John asked me.

"Up in his room, lying down."

"Lying down?"

"Yes," I said.

"How is he?"

I looked at the two fellows that were with John.

"They're friends of his," John said.

"He's pretty bad," I said.

"What's the matter with him?"

"He don't sleep."

"Hell," said John. "That Irishman could never sleep."

"He isn't right," I said.

"Hell," John said. "He's never right. I've had him for ten years and he's never been right yet."

The fellows who were with him laughed.

"I want you to shake hands with Mr. Morgan and Mr. Steinfelt," John said. "This is Mr. Doyle. He's been training Jack."

"Glad to meet you," I said.

"Let's go up and see the boy," the fellow called Morgan said.

"Let's have a look at him," Steinfelt said.

We all went upstairs.

"Where's Hogan?" John asked.

"He's out in the barn with a couple of his customers," I said.

"He got many people out here now?" John asked.

"Just two."

"Pretty quiet, ain't it?" Morgan said.

"Yes," I said. "It's pretty quiet."

We were outside Jack's room. John knocked on the door. There wasn't any answer.

"Maybe he's asleep," I said.

"What the hell's he sleeping in the daytime for?"

John turned the handle and we all went in. Jack was lying asleep on the bed. He was face down and his face was in the pillow. Both his arms were around the pillow.

"Hey, Jack!" John said to him.

Jack's head moved a little on the pillow. "Jack!" John says, leaning over him. Jack just dug a little deeper in the pillow. John touched him on the shoulder. Jack sat up and looked at us. He hadn't shaved and he was wearing an old sweater.

"Christ! Why can't you let me sleep?" he says to John.

"Don't be sore," John says. "I didn't mean to wake you up."

"Oh no," Jack says. "Of course not."

"You know Morgan and Steinfelt," John said.

"Glad to see you," Jack says.

"How do you feel, Jack?" Morgan asks him.

"Fine," Jack says. "How the hell would I feel?"

"You look fine," Steinfelt says.

"Yes, don't I," says Jack. "Say," he says to John.

"You're my manager. You get a big enough cut. Why the hell don't you come out here when the reporters was out! You want Jerry and me to talk to them?"

"I had Lew fighting in Philadelphia," John said.

"What the hell's that to me?" Jack says. "You're my manager. You get a big enough cut, don't you? You aren't making me any money in Philadelphia, are you? Why the hell aren't you out here when I ought to have you?"

"Hogan was here."

"Hogan," Jack says. "Hogan's as dumb as I am."

"Soldier Bartlett was out here wukking with you for a while, wasn't he?" Steinfelt said to change the subject.

"Yes, he was out here," Jack says. "He was out here all right."

"Say, Jerry," John said to me. "Would you go out and find Hogan and tell him we want to see him in about half an hour?"

"Sure," I said.

"Why the hell can't he stick around?" Jack says. "Stick around, Jerry."

Morgan and Steinfelt looked at each other.

"Quiet down, Jack," John said to him.

"I better go find Hogan," I said.

"All right, if you want to go," Jack says. "None of these guys are going to send you away, though."

"I'll go find Hogan," I said.

Hogan was out in the gym in the barn. He had a couple of his health-farm patients with gloves on. They neither one wanted to hit the other, for fear the other would come back and hit him.

"That'll do," Hogan said when he saw me come in. "You can stop the slaughter. You gentlemen take a shower and Bruce will rub you down."

They climbed out through the ropes and Hogan came over to me.

"John Collins is out with a couple of friends to see Jack," I said.

"I saw them come up in the car."

"Who are the two fellows with John?"

"They're what you call wise boys," Hogan said. "Don't you know them two?"

"No," I said.

"That's Happy Steinfelt and Lew Morgan. They got a poolroom."

"I been away a long time," I said.

"Sure," said Hogan. "That Happy Steinfelt's a big operator."

"I've heard his name," I said.

"He's a pretty smooth boy," Hogan said. "They're a couple of sharpshooters."

"Well," I said. "They want to see us in half an hour."

"You mean they don't want to see us until a half an hour."

"That's it."

"Come on in the office," Hogan said. "To hell with those sharpshooters."

After about thirty minutes or so Hogan and I went upstairs. We knocked on Jack's door. They were talking inside the room.

"Wait a minute," somebody said.

"To hell with that stuff," Hogan said. "When you want to see me I'm down in the office."

We heard the door unlock. Steinfelt opened it.

"Come on in, Hogan," he says. "We're all going to have a drink."

"Well," says Hogan. "That's something."

We went in. Jack was sitting on the bed. John and Morgan were sitting on a couple of chairs. Steinfelt was standing up.

"You're a pretty mysterious lot of boys," Hogan said.

"Hello, Danny," John says.

"Hello, Danny," Morgan says and shakes hands.

Jack doesn't say anything. He just sits there on the bed. He ain't with the others. He's all by himself. He was wearing an old blue jersey and pants and had on boxing shoes. He needed a shave. Steinfelt and Morgan were dressers. John was quite a dresser too. Jack sat there looking Irish and tough.

Steinfelt brought out a bottle and Hogan brought in some glasses and everybody had a drink. Jack and I took one and the rest of them went on and had two or three each.

"Better save some for your ride back," Hogan said.

"Don't you worry. We got plenty," Morgan said.

Jack hadn't drunk anything since the one drink. He was standing up and looking at them. Morgan was sitting on the bed where Jack had sat.

"Have a drink, Jack," John said and handed him the glass and the bottle.

"No," Jack said, "I never liked to go to these wakes."

They all laughed. Jack didn't laugh.

They were all feeling pretty good when they

left. Jack stood on the porch when they got into the car. They waved to him.

"So long," Jack said.

We had supper. Jack didn't say anything during the meal except, "Will you pass me this?" or "Will you pass me that?" The two health-farm patients ate at the same table with us. They were pretty nice fellows. After we finished eating we went out on the porch. It was dark early.

"Like to take a walk, Jerry?" Jack asked.

"Sure," I said.

We put on our coats and started out. It was quite a way down to the main road and then we walked along the main road about a mile and a half. Cars kept going by and we would pull out to the side until they were past. Jack didn't say anything. After we had stepped out into the bushes to let a big car go by, Jack said, "To hell with this walking. Come on back to Hogan's."

We went along a side road that cut up over the hill and cut across the fields back to Hogan's. We could see the lights of the house up on the hill. We came around to the front of the house and there standing in the doorway was Hogan.

"Have a good walk?" Hogan asked.

"Oh, fine," Jack said. "Listen, Hogan. Have you got any liquor?"

"Sure," says Hogan. "What's the idea?"

"Send it up to the room," Jack says. "I'm going to sleep tonight."

"You're the doctor," Hogan says.

"Come on up to the room, Jerry," Jack says.

Upstairs Jack sat on the bed with his head in his hands.

"Ain't it a life?" Jack says.

Hogan brought in a quart of liquor and two glasses.

"Want some ginger ale?"

"What do you think I want to do, get sick?"

"I just asked you," said Hogan.

"Have a drink?" said Jack.

"No, thanks," said Hogan. He went out.

"How about you, Jerry?"

"I'll have one with you," I said.

Jack poured out a couple of drinks. "Now," he said, "I want to take it slow and easy."

"Put some water in it," I said.

"Yes," Jack said. "I guess that's better."

We had a couple of drinks without saying anything. Jack started to pour me another.

"No," I said, "that's all I want."

"All right," Jack said. He poured himself out another big shot and put water in it. He was lighting up a little.

"That was a fine bunch out here this afternoon," he said. "They don't take any chances, those two."

Then a little later, "Well," he says, "they're right. What the hell's the good in taking chances?"

"Don't you want another, Jerry?" he said. "Come on, drink along with me."

"I don't need it, Jack," I said. "I feel all right."

"Just have one more," Jack said. It was softening him up.

"All right," I said.

Jack poured one for me and another big one for himself.

"You know," he said, "I like liquor pretty well. If I hadn't been boxing I would have drunk quite a lot."

"Sure," I said.

"You know," he said, "I missed a lot, boxing."

"You made plenty of money."

"Sure, that's what I'm after. You know I miss a lot, Jerry."

"How do you mean?"

"Well," he says, "like about the wife. And being away from home so much. It don't do my girls any good. 'Who's your old man?' some of those society kids'll say to them. 'My old man's Jack Brennan.' That don't do them any good."

"Hell," I said, "all that makes a difference is if they got dough."

"Well," says Jack, "I got the dough for them all right."

He poured out another drink. The bottle was about empty.

"Put some water in it," I said. Jack poured in some water.

"You know," he says, "you ain't got any idea how I miss the wife."

"Sure."

"You ain't got any idea. You can't have any idea what it's like."

"It ought to be better out in the country than in town."

"With me now," Jack said, "it don't make any difference where I am. You can't have any idea what it's like."

"Have another drink."

"Am I getting soused? Do I talk funny?"

"You're coming on all right."

"You can't have any idea what it's like. They ain't nobody can have an idea what it's like."

"Except the wife," I said.

"She knows," Jack said. "She knows all right. She knows. You bet she knows."

"Put some water in that," I said.

"Jerry," says Jack, "you can't have an idea what it gets to be like."

He was good and drunk. He was looking at me steady. His eyes were sort of too steady.

"You'll sleep all right," I said.

"Listen, Jerry," Jack says. "You want to make some money? Get some money down on Walcott."

"Yes?"

"Listen, Jerry," Jack put down the glass. "I'm not drunk now, see? You know what I'm betting on him? Fifty grand."

"That's a lot of dough."

"Fifty grand," Jack says, "at two to one. I'll get twenty-five thousand bucks. Get some money on him, Jerry."

"It sounds good," I said.

"How can I beat him?" Jack says. "It ain't crooked. How can I beat him? Why not make money on it?"

"Put some water in that," I said.

"I'm through after this fight," Jack says. "I'm through with it. I got to take a beating. Why shouldn't I make money on it?"

"Sure."

"I ain't slept for a week," Jack says. "All night I lay awake and worry my can off. I can't sleep, Jerry. You ain't got an idea what it's like when you can't sleep."

"Sure."

"I can't sleep. That's all. I just can't sleep. What's the use of taking care of yourself all these years when you can't sleep?"

"It's bad."

"You ain't got an idea what it's like, Jerry, when you can't sleep."

"Put some water in that," I said.

Well, about eleven o'clock Jack passes out and I put him to bed. Finally he's so he can't keep from sleeping. I helped him get his clothes off and got him into bed.

"You'll sleep all right, Jack," I said.

"Sure," Jack says. "I'll sleep now."

"Good night, Jack," I said.

"Good night, Jerry," Jack says. "You're the only friend I got."

"Oh, hell," I said.

"You're the only friend I got," Jack says, "the only friend I got."

"Go to sleep," I said.

"I'll sleep," Jack says.

Downstairs Hogan was sitting at the desk in the office reading the papers. He looked up. "Well, you get your boy friend to sleep?" he asks.

"He's off."

"It's better for him than not sleeping," Hogan said.

"Sure."

"You'd have a hell of a time explaining that to these sports writers, though," Hogan said.

"Well, I'm going to bed myself," I said.

"Good night," said Hogan.

In the morning I came downstairs about eight o'clock and got some breakfast. Hogan had his two customers out in the barn doing exercises. I went out and watched them.

"One! Two! Three! Four!" Hogan was counting for them. "Hello Jerry," he said. "Is Jack up yet?"

"No. He's still sleeping."

I went back to my room and packed up to go into town. About nine-thirty I heard Jack getting up in the next room. When I heard him go downstairs I went down after him. Jack was sitting at the breakfast table. Hogan had come in and was standing beside the table.

"How do you feel, Jack?" I asked him.

"Not so bad."

"Sleep well?" Hogan asked.

"I slept all right," Jack said. "I got a thick tongue but I ain't got a head."

"Good," Hogan said. "That was good liquor."

"Put it on the bill," Jack says.

"What time you want to go into town?" Hogan asked.

"Before lunch," Jack says. "The eleven-o'clock train."

"Sit down, Jerry," Jack said. Hogan went out.

I sat down at the table. Jack was eating a grapefruit. When he'd find a seed he'd spit it out in the spoon and dump it on the plate.

"I guess I was pretty stewed last night," he started.

"You drank some liquor."

"I guess I said a lot of fool things."

"You weren't bad."

"Where's Hogan?" he asked. He was through with the grapefruit.

"He's out in front in the office."

"What did I say about betting on the fight?" Jack asked. He was holding the spoon and sort of poking at the grapefruit with it.

The girl came in with some ham and eggs and took away the grapefruit.

"Bring me another glass of milk," Jack said to her. She went out.

"You said you had fifty grand on Walcott," I said.

"That's right," Jack said.

"That's a lot of money."

"I don't feel too good about it," Jack said.

"Something might happen."

"No," Jack said. "He wants the title bad. They'll be shooting with him all right."

"You can't ever tell."

"No. He wants the title. It's worth a lot of money to him."

"Fifty grand is a lot of money," I said.

"It's business," said Jack. "I can't win. You know I can't win anyway."

"As long as you're in there you got a chance."

"No," Jack says. "I'm all through. It's just business."

"How do you feel?"

"Pretty good," Jack said. "The sleep was what I needed."

"You might go good."

"I'll give them a good show," Jack said.

After breakfast Jack called up his wife on the long-distance. He was inside the booth telephoning.

"That's the first time he's called her up since he's out here," Hogan said.

"He writes her every day."

"Sure," Hogan says, "a letter only costs two cents."

Hogan said goodbye to us and Bruce, the nigger rubber, drove us down to the train in the cart.

"Goodbye, Mr. Brennan," Bruce said at the train, "I sure hope you knock his can off."

"So long," Jack said. He gave Bruce two dollars. Bruce had worked on him a lot. He looked kind of disappointed. Jack saw me looking at Bruce holding the two dollars.

"It's all in the bill," he said. "Hogan charged me for the rubbing."

On the train going into town Jack didn't talk. He sat in the corner of the seat with his ticket in his hatband and looked out of the window. Once he turned and spoke to me.

"I told the wife I'd take a room at the Shelby tonight," he said. "It's just around the corner from the Garden. I can go up to the house tomorrow morning."

"That's a good idea," I said. "Your wife ever see you fight, Jack?"

"No," Jack says. "She never seen me fight."

I thought he must be figuring on taking an awful beating if he doesn't want to go home afterward. In town we took a taxi up to the Shelby. A boy came out and took our bags and we went in to the desk.

"How much are the rooms?" Jack asked.

"We only have double rooms," the clerk says. "I can give you a nice double room for ten dollars."

"That's too steep."

"I can give you a double room for seven dollars."

"With a bath?"

"Certainly."

"You might as well bunk with me, Jerry," Jack says.

"Oh," I said, "I'll sleep down at my brother-in-law's."

"I don't mean for you to pay for it," Jack says. "I just want to get my money's worth."

"Will you register, please?" the clerk says. He looked at the names. "Number two thirty-eight, Mr. Brennan."

We went up in the elevator. It was a nice big room with two beds and a door opening into a bathroom.

"This is pretty good," Jack says.

The boy who brought us up pulled up the curtains and brought in our bags. Jack didn't make any move, so I gave the boy a quarter. We washed up and Jack said we better go out and get something to eat.

We ate lunch at Jimmy Handley's place. Quite a lot of the boys were there. When we were about half through eating, John came in and sat down with us. Jack didn't talk much.

"How are you on the weight, Jack?" John asked him. Jack was putting away a pretty good lunch.

"I could make it with my clothes on," Jack said. He never had to worry about taking off weight. He was a natural welterweight and he'd never gotten fat. He'd lost weight out at Hogan's.

"Well, that's one thing you never had to worry about," John said.

"That's one thing," Jack says.

We went around to the Garden to weigh in after lunch. The match was made at a hundred forty-seven pounds at three o'clock. Jack stepped on the scales with a towel around him. The bar didn't move. Walcott had just weighed and was standing with a lot of people around him.

"Let's see what you weigh, Jack," Freedman, Walcott's manager, said.

"All right, weigh him then," Jack jerked his head toward Walcott.

"Drop the towel," Freedman said.

"What do you make it?" Jack asked the fellows who were weighing.

"One hundred and forty-three pounds," the fat man who was weighing said.

"You're down fine, Jack," Freedman says.

"Weigh him," Jack says.

Walcott came over. He was a blond with wide shoulders and arms like a heavyweight. He didn't have much legs. Jack stood about half a head taller than he did.

"Hello, Jack," he said. His face was plenty marked up.

"Hello," Jack said. "How you feel?"

"Good," Walcott says. He dropped the towel from around his waist and stood on the scales. He had the widest shoulders and back you ever saw.

"One hundred and forty-six pounds and twelve ounces."

Walcott stepped off and grinned at Jack.

"Well," John says to him, "Jack's spotting you about four pounds."

"More than that when I come in, kid," Walcott says. "I'm going to go and eat now."

We went back and Jack got dressed. "He's a pretty tough-looking boy," Jack says to me.

"He looks as though he'd been hit plenty of times."

"Oh, yes," Jack says. "He ain't hard to hit."

"Where are you going?" John asked when Jack was dressed.

"Back to the hotel," Jack says. "You looked after everything?"

"Yes," John says. "It's all looked after."

"I'm going to lie down awhile," Jack says.

"I'll come around for you about a quarter to seven and we'll go and eat."

"All right."

Up at the hotel Jack took off his shoes and his coat and lay down for a while. I wrote a letter. I looked over a couple of times and Jack wasn't sleeping. He was lying perfectly still but every once in a while his eyes would open. Finally he sits up.

"Want to play some cribbage, Jerry?" he says.

"Sure," I said.

He went over to his suitcase and got out the cards and the cribbage board. We played cribbage and he won three dollars off me. John knocked at the door and came in.

"Want to play some cribbage, John?" Jack asked him.

John put his kelly down on the table. It was all wet. His coat was wet too.

"Is it raining?" Jack asks.

"It's pouring," John says. "The taxi I had got tied up in the traffic and I got out and walked."

"Come on, play some cribbage," Jack says.

"You ought to go and eat."

"No," says Jack. "I don't want to eat yet."

So they played cribbage for about half an hour and Jack won a dollar and a half off him.

"Well, I suppose we got to go eat," Jack says. He went to the window and looked out.

"Is it still raining?"

"Yes."

"Let's eat in the hotel," John says.

"All right," Jack says. "I'll play you once more to see who pays for the meal."

After a little while Jack gets up and says, "You buy the meal, John," and we went downstairs and ate in the big dining room.

After we ate we went upstairs and Jack played cribbage with John again and won two dollars and a half off him. Jack was feeling pretty good. John had a bag with him with all his stuff in it. Jack took off his shirt and collar and put on a jersey and a sweater, so he wouldn't catch cold when he came out, and put his ring clothes and his bathrobe in a bag.

"You all ready?" John asks him. "I'll call up and have them get a taxi."

Pretty soon the telephone rang and they said the taxi was waiting.

We rode down in the elevator and went out through the lobby, and got in a taxi and rode around to the Garden. It was raining hard but there was a lot of people outside on the streets. The Garden was sold out. As we came in on our way to the dressing room I saw how full it was. It looked like half a mile down to the ring. It was all dark. Just the lights over the ring.

"It's a good thing, with this rain, they didn't try and pull this fight in the ball park," John said.

"They got a good crowd," Jack says.

"This is a fight that would draw a lot more than the Garden could hold."

"You can't tell about the weather," Jack says.

John came to the door of the dressing room and poked his head in. Jack was sitting there with his bathrobe on, he had his arms folded and was looking at the floor. John had a couple of handlers with him. They looked over his shoulder. Jack looked up.

"Is he in?" he asked.

"He's just gone down," John said.

We started down. Walcott was just getting into the ring. The crowd gave him a big hand. He climbed through between the ropes and put his two fists together and smiled, and shook them at the crowd, first at one side of the ring, then at the other, and then sat down. Jack got a good hand coming down through the crowd. Jack is Irish and the Irish always get a pretty good hand. An Irishman don't draw in New York like a Jew or an Italian but they always get a good hand. Jack climbed up and bent down to go through the ropes and Walcott came over from his corner and pushed the rope down for Jack to go through. The crowd thought that was wonderful. Walcott put his hand on Jack's shoulder and they stood there just for a second.

"So you're going to be one of these popular champions," Jack says to him. "Take your goddam hand off my shoulder."

"Be yourself," Walcott says.

This is all great for the crowd. How gentlemanly the boys are before the fight! How they wish each other luck!

Solly Freedman came over to our corner while Jack is bandaging his hands and John is over in Walcott's corner. Jack puts his thumb through the slit in the bandage and then wrapped his hand nice and smooth. I taped it around the wrist and twice across the knuckles.

"Hey," Freedman says. "Where do you get all that tape?"

"Feel of it," Jack says. "It's soft, ain't it? Don't be a hick."

Freedman stands there all the time while Jack bandages the other hand, and one of the boys that's going to handle him brings the gloves and I pull them on and work them around.

"Say, Freedman," Jack asks, "what nationality is this Walcott?"

"I don't know," Solly says. "He's some sort of a Dane."

"He's a Bohemian," the lad who brought the gloves said.

The referee called them out to the center of the ring and Jack walks out. Walcott comes out smiling. They met and the referee put his arm on each of their shoulders.

"Hello, popularity," Jack says to Walcott.

"Be yourself."

"What do you call yourself 'Walcott' for?" Jack says. "Didn't you know he was a nigger?"

"Listen" says the referee, and he gives them the same old line. Once Walcott interrupts him. He grabs Jack's arm and says, "Can I hit when he's got me like this?"

"Keep your hands off me," Jack says. "There ain't no moving pictures of this."

They went back to their corners. I lifted the bathrobe off Jack and he leaned on the ropes and flexed his knees a couple of times and scuffed his shoes in the rosin. The gong rang and Jack turned quick and went out. Walcott came toward him and they touched gloves and as soon as Walcott dropped his hands Jack jumped his left into his face twice. There wasn't anybody ever boxed better than Jack. Walcott was after him, going forward all the time with his chin on his chest. He's a hooker and he carries his hands pretty low. All he knows is to get in there and sock. But every time he gets in there close, Jack has the left hand in his face. It's just as though it's automatic. Jack just raises the left hand up and it's in Walcott's face. Three or four times Jack brings the right over but Walcott gets it on the shoulder or high up on the head. He's just like all these hookers. The only thing he's afraid of is another one of the same kind. He's covered everywhere you can hurt him. He don't care about a left hand in his face.

After about four rounds Jack has him bleeding bad and his face all cut up, but every time Walcott's got in close he's socked so hard he's got two big red patches on both sides just below Jack's ribs. Every time he gets in close, Jack ties him up, then gets one hand loose and uppercuts him, but when Walcott gets his hands loose he socks Jack in the body so they can hear it outside in the street. He's a socker.

It goes along like that for three rounds more. They don't talk any. They're working all the time. We worked over Jack plenty too, in between the rounds. He don't look good at all but he never does much work in the ring. He don't move around much and that left hand is just automatic. It's just like it was connected with Walcott's face and Jack just had to wish it in every time. Jack is always calm in close and he doesn't waste any juice. He knows everything about working in close too and he's getting away with a lot of stuff. While they were in our corner I watched him tie Walcott up, get his right hand loose, turn it and come up with an uppercut that got Walcott's nose with the heel of the glove. Walcott was bleeding bad and leaned his nose on Jack's shoulder so as to give Jack some of it too, and Jack sort of lifted his shoulder sharp and caught him against the nose, and then brought down the right hand and did the same thing again.

Walcott was sore as hell. By the time they'd gone five rounds he hated Jack's guts. Jack wasn't sore; that is, he wasn't any sorer than he always was. He certainly did used to make the fellows he fought hate boxing. That was why he hated Kid Lewis so. He never got the Kid's goat. Kid Lewis always had about three new dirty things Jack couldn't do. Jack was as safe as a church all the time he was in there, as long as he was strong. He certainly was treating Walcott rough. The funny thing was it looked as though Jack was an open classic boxer. That was because he had all that stuff too.

After the seventh round Jack says, "My left's getting heavy."

From then he started to take a beating. It didn't show at first. But instead of him running the fight it was Walcott was running it, instead of being safe all the time now he was in trouble. He couldn't keep him out with the left hand now. It looked as though it was the same as ever, only now instead of Walcott's punches just missing him they were just hitting him. He took an awful beating in the body.

"What's the round?" Jack asked.

"The eleventh."

"I can't stay," Jack says. "My legs are going bad."

Walcott had been just hitting him for a long time. It was like a baseball catcher pulls the ball and takes some of the shock off. From now on Walcott commenced to land solid. He certainly was a socking machine. Jack was just trying to block everything now. It didn't show what an awful beating he was taking. In between the rounds I worked on his legs. The muscles would flutter under my hands all the time I was rubbing them. He was sick as hell.

"How's it go?" he asked John, turning around, his face all swollen.

"It's his fight."

"I think I can last," Jack says. "I don't want this bohunk to stop me."

It was going just the way he thought it would. He knew he couldn't beat Walcott. He wasn't strong any more. He was all right though. His money was all right and now he wanted to finish it off right to please himself. He didn't want to be knocked out.

The gong rang and we pushed him out. He went out slow. Walcott came right out after him. Jack put the left in his face and Walcott took it, came in under it and started working on Jack's body. Jack tried to tie him up and it was just like trying to hold on to a buzz saw. Jack broke away from it and missed with the right. Walcott clipped him with a left hook and Jack went down. He went down on his hands and knees and looked at us. The referee started counting. Jack was watching us and shaking his head. At eight John motioned to him. You couldn't hear on account of the crowd. Jack got up. The referee had been holding Walcott back with one arm while he counted.

When Jack was on his feet Walcott started toward him.

"Watch yourself, Jimmy," I heard Solly Freedman yell to him.

Walcott came up to Jack looking at him. Jack stuck the left hand at him. Walcott just shook his head. He backed Jack up against the ropes, measured him and then hooked the left very light to the side of Jack's head and socked the right into the body as hard as he could sock, just as low as he could get it. He must have hit him five inches below the belt. I thought the eyes would come out of Jack's head. They stuck way out. His mouth come open.

The referee grabbed Walcott. Jack stepped forward. If he went down there went fifty thousand bucks. He walked as though all his insides were going to fall out.

"It wasn't low," he said. "It was a accident."

The crowd were yelling so you couldn't hear anything.

"I'm all right," Jack says. They were right in front of us. The referee looks at John and then he shakes his head.

"Come on, you polack son-of-a-bitch," Jack says to Walcott.

John was hanging onto the ropes. He had the towel ready to chuck in. Jack was standing just a little way out from the ropes. He took a step forward. I saw the sweat come out on his face like somebody had squeezed it and a big drop went down his nose.

"Come on and fight," Jack says to Walcott.

The referee looked at John and waved Walcott on.

"Go in there, you slob," he says.

Walcott went in. He didn't know what to do either. He never thought Jack could have stood it. Jack put the left in his face. There was such a hell of a lot of yelling going on. They were right in front of us. Walcott hit him twice. Jack's face was the worst thing I ever saw—the look on it! He was holding himself and all his body together and it all showed on his face. All the time he was thinking and holding his body in where it was busted.

Then he started to sock. His face looked awful all the time. He started to sock with his hands low down by his side, swinging at Walcott. Walcott covered up and Jack was swinging wild at Walcott's head. Then he swung the left and it hit Walcott in the groin and the right hit Walcott right bang where he'd hit Jack. Way low below the belt. Walcott went down and grabbed himself there and rolled and twisted around.

The referee grabbed Jack and pushed him toward his corner. John jumps into the ring. There was all this yelling going on. The referee was talking with the judges and then the announcer got into the ring with the megaphone and says, "Walcott on a foul."

The referee is talking to John and he says, "What could I do? Jack wouldn't take the foul. Then when he's groggy he fouls him."

"He'd lost it anyway," John says.

Jack's sitting on the chair. I've got his gloves off and he's holding himself in down there with both hands. When he's got something supporting it his face doesn't look so bad.

"Go over and say you're sorry," John says into his ear. "It'll look good."

Jack stands up and the sweat comes out all over his face. I put the bathrobe around him and he holds himself in with one hand under the bathrobe and goes across the ring. They've picked Walcott up and they're working on him. There're a lot of people in Walcott's corner. Nobody speaks to Jack. He leans over Walcott.

"I'm sorry," Jack says. "I didn't mean to foul you."

Walcott doesn't say anything. He looks too damned sick.

"Well, you're the champion now," Jack says to him. "I hope you get a hell of a lot of fun out of it."

"Leave the kid alone," Solly Freedman says.

"Hello, Solly," Jack says. "I'm sorry I fouled your boy."

Freedman just looks at him.

Jack went to his corner walking that funny jerky way and we got him down through the ropes and through the reporters' tables and out down the aisle. A lot of people want to slap Jack on the back. He goes out through all that mob in his bathrobe to the dressing room. It's a popular win for Walcott. That's the way the money was bet in the Garden.

Once we got inside the dressing room Jack lay down and shut his eyes.

"We want to get to the hotel and get a doctor," John says.

"I'm all busted inside," Jack says.

"I'm sorry as hell, Jack," John says.

"It's all right," Jack says.

He lies there with his eyes shut.

"They certainly tried a nice double cross," John said.

"Your friends Morgan and Steinfelt," Jack said. "You got nice friends."

He lies there, his eyes are open now. His face has still got that awful drawn look.

"It's funny how fast you can think when it means that much money," Jack says.

"You're some boy, Jack," John says.

"No," Jack says. "It was nothing."

THE HIGHER PRAGMATISM

The O. Henry ending, like George La Blanche's pivot blow, should have been outlawed in 1889.

O. HENRY

"Say," said Mack, "tell me one thing—can you hand out the dope to other girls? Can you chin 'em and make matinee eyes at 'em and squeeze 'em? You know what I mean. You're just shy when it comes to this particular dame—the professional beauty—ain't that right?"

"In a way you have outlined the situation with approximate truth," I admitted.

"I thought so," said Mack grimly. "Now, that reminds me of my own case. I'll tell you about it."

I was indignant, but concealed it. What was this loafer's case or anybody's case compared with mine? Besides, I had given him a dollar and ten cents.

"Feel my muscle," said my companion suddenly, flexing his biceps. I did so mechanically. The fellows in gyms are always asking you to do that. His arm was hard as cast iron.

"Four years ago," said Mack, "I could lick any man in New York outside of the professional ring. Your case and mine is just the same. I come from the West Side—between Thirteenth and Fourteenth—I won't give the number on the door. I was a scrapper when I was ten, and when I was twenty no amateur in the city could stand up four rounds with me. 'S a fact. You know Bill McCarty? No? He managed the smokers for some of them swell clubs. Well, I knocked out everything Bill brought up before me. I was a middleweight, but could train down to a welter when necessary. I boxed all over the West Side at bouts and benefits and private entertainments, and was never put out once.

"But say, the first time I put my foot in the ring with a professional I was no more than a canned lobster. I dunno, how it was—I seemed to lose heart. I guess I got too much imagination. There was a formality and publicness about it that kind of weakened my nerve. I never won a fight in the ring. Lightweights and all kinds of scrubs used to sign up with my manager and then walk up and tap me on the wrist and see me fall. The minute I seen the crowd and a lot of gents in evening clothes down in front, and seen a professional come inside the ropes, I got as weak as ginger ale.

"Of course, it wasn't long till I couldn't get no backers, and I didn't have any more chances to fight a professional—or many amateurs, either. But lemme tell you—I was as good as most men inside the ring or out. It was just that dumb, dead feeling I had when I was up against a regular that always done me up.

"Well, sir, after I had got out of the business, I got a mighty grouch on. I used to go round town licking private citizens and all kinds of unprofessionals just to please myself. I'd lick cops in dark streets and car conductors and cab drivers and draymen whenever I could start a row with 'em. It didn't make any difference how big they were, or how much science they had, I got away with 'em. If I'd only just have had the confidence in the ring that I had beating up the best men outside of it, I'd be wearing black pearls and heliotrope silk socks today.

"One evening I was walking along near the Bowery, thinking about things, when along comes a slumming party. About six or seven they was, all in swallowtails, and these silk hats that don't shine. One of the gang kind of shoves me off the sidewalk. I hadn't had a scrap in three days, and I just says, 'De-lighted!' and hits him back of the ear.

"Well, we had it. That Johnnie put up as decent a little fight as you'd want to see in the moving pictures. It was on a side street and no cops around. The other guy had a lot of science, but it only took me about six minutes to lay him out.

"Some of the swallowtails dragged him up against some steps and began to fan him. Another one of 'em comes over to me and says:

"'Young man, do you know what you've done?'

"'Oh, beat it,' says I. 'I've done nothing but a little punching-bag work. Take Freddy back to Yale and tell him to quit studying sociology on the wrong side of the sidewalk.'

"'My good fellow,' says he, 'I don't know who you are, but I'd like to. You've knocked out Reddy Burns, the champion middleweight of the world! He came to New York yesterday, to try to get a match on with Jim Jeffries. If you—

"'But when I come out of my faint I was laying on the floor in a drugstore saturated with aromatic spirits of ammonia. If I'd known that was Reddy Burns, I'd have got down in the gutter and crawled past him instead of handing him one like I did. Why, if I'd ever been in a ring and seen him climbing over the ropes, I'd have been all to the sal volatile.

"So that's what imagination does," concluded Mack. "And, as I said, your case and mine is simultaneous. You'll never win out. You can't go up against the professionals. I tell you, it's a park bench for yours in this romance business."

[FACT]

A RADIO MAN REMEMBERS

When George Hicks first spoke into a radio microphone in 1928 he had already been, among other things, a college student, logger, sawmill hand, factory worker, truck driver and seaman. He became one of the most respected of all radio reporters, covering much of the history of the thirties and forties, including the combat in Europe during World War II. His D-Day broadcast of the Normandy invasion is a classic. He is now finding expression in painting, but because of his sensitivity not only to sights but also to sounds and, above all, to people, he was asked to write what has remained with him from the adolescent years of the radio coverage of fights. He later found expression in painting.

GEORGE HICKS

When Primo Carnera defended his heavyweight championship against Max Baer in the Madison Square Garden Bowl on Long Island in June of 1934, the Blue Network of the National Broadcasting Company attempted an experiment. Whether it worked or not was not too important, because they had Graham McNamee doing the blow-by-blow at ringside, but they assigned two of us, an engineer and me, to the champion's dressing room.

I went into the dressing room early with the engineer because I was afraid that I might other-wise be barred. In those days radio had few credentials, and at least the engineer had his equipment to prove what he was.

While the engineer set up in the corner I walked over to Carnera. He was sitting on the rubbing table with one of his handlers standing next to him.

"Excuse me, Champ," I said, "but will it be all right if I interview you over the radio right after the fight?"

Carnera said nothing. He just looked at me with those big, round, brown eyes.

"Maybe," the handler said, shrugging. "We can't say right now."

I watched them prepare the big man then and, finally, when the call came, lead him out. I was afraid to leave the room, afraid that I would not be able to get back in, but after the fight had started and I could hear the roar of the crowd I spoke to the uniformed guard at the door and walked through the tunnel to the beginning of an aisle.

The open arena seemed to me to be the site of an explosion. Under the lights at the bottom of it Carnera was down and the whole pit was filled with a shattering violence of sound. I stood there and watched Carnera get up and, as it went on, get knocked down ten more times, until it ended in the eleventh round.

I was waiting in the dressing room when they brought Carnera back. The big man was breathing heavily but, as they sat him down, he did not seem badly hurt. I stood back, waiting until those who had followed him in had left and only the two handlers still remained with him. Then I walked over to him, the microphone in my hand and the lead line trailing behind me to where the engineer knelt over his portable amplifier in the corner.

"Mr. Carnera," I said, "would you care to speak over the radio now?"

He was sitting on the rubbing table with his head down, still breathing heavily, his robe hanging loose from his shoulders. He lifted that big head and looked at me, and he seemed startled and confused.

"No," one of the handlers said. "He don't want to talk. Beat it."

Then the door behind us opened again, and in walked a short, strutting man followed by several others. I recognized the man, for he was one of this country's best-known sports columnists.

"Hello, Champ," he said, walking up to Carnera. Carnera's head came up again and he stared out of those brown, hurt eyes. He looked at the man and then he looked away.

"How do you feel about losing it?" the short man said.

Carnera dropped his head and shook it slowly.

"You mean you liked being champion?" the sports writer said.

Carnera lifted his head and looked again at the man. The sweat was still coming out of his forehead and now it was running down and dripping off his nose.

"What do you think the people in Italy will think of you now?" the sports writer said.

"I don't know," Carnera said, and his eyes were starting to fill with tears and he looked away from the man.

"You think Mussolini will like this?" the sports writer said.

Carnera dropped his head, dripping with his sweat.

"Well," the sports writer said, turning, "so long, Champ."

In the silence that followed I put on my earphones and, in them, I could hear McNamee's voice from ringside. I could hear that excited, breathless speech of his slowing down now and beginning to replay the best moments of the fight. In the almost emptiness of that dressing room I walked my microphone back to Carnera.

"Would you care to speak over the radio now?" I said.

Carnera looked up at me and nodded. I signaled the engineer to call Control Room. Now in the earphones I could hear the 11 p.m. correct time and the station break. I got the go-ahead, and I started to speak with the large, suffering man with the injured pride as he sat on the rubbing table, asking him how he felt, if he was physically hurt, about what hopes he might have now.

I no longer remember what Carnera said, but suddenly, answering my questions, he began to cry. No big tears came, but it was the simple, small crying of a boy who has never wished harm. to anyone and who has just been terribly mistreated. As it was ending I could hear, in my earphones, McNamee.

"For Christ's sake!" McNamee was shouting. "Get this on the air! It's great! Primo Camera is crying!"

It never did get on the air. Someone at Radio City had decided not to switch-return to the Bowl. Only those few of us—we in the dressing room, McNamee and his engineer and perhaps those in Control Room—heard Primo Carnera crying. The dressing-room experiment had failed.

Joe Louis was not unfriendly but he was an impenetrable man. Perhaps he himself did not know what motivated him. It was a wonderfully warm late summer day, while he was training at Pompton Lakes for the Max Baer fight in 1935, when I was able to stop him as he rounded a corner of the gym. He slouched, bland, quizzical, the sun in his eyes causing him to squint, silently waiting.

I asked how he felt and what his weight was, writing down the answers for a spot I would put on the air later. I was actually afraid to ask him the next question.

"Baer," I said, finally, "says he's going to knock you into the eighth row. What do you think of that?"

Joe changed without moving. Something happened to his eyes.

"Every dog got a right to wag his own tail," Joe said.

He spoke it so fast I could not, at first, understand it, let alone write it down, but it all came back to me years later when I had an appointment with an executive in his hotel room. His wife answered my knock and let me in. She seemed nervous, alone with me, and we were still standing there when her husband came in. When he saw us he moved toward us and, for just that instant, our eyes met and I saw there what I had seen just that once in Joe's. Then it was gone and he apologized for being late.

Al Ettore was a big, blond Italian-American with pink skin, and that night in 1936 when he fought Joe Louis in Philadelphia he came into the ring healthy and smiling and nodding to those he knew in the press rows. He must have thought he had a chance, but by the fifth round his body was being shocked backward with every punch. The speed and rhythm with which Louis punched at that time made of Joe a brown blur, and there began to settle over Ettore's face a quiet look, a kind of resigned expression. His eyes closed as if he were falling asleep, and Louis made one more blurred move and the flesh on Ettore's left cheek split downward in the same direction as his nose, and he fell forward.

Eight years later, in Belgium, I saw another such face. A young man I knew was killed by a bomb. When I looked down at him, lying there on his back on the frozen ground, his face was also split open, and life had so newly left him that a small, steady breath of steam was still rising from the split into the damp, cold air. A long time later, thinking about that, I remembered Ettore.

[POETRY]

FROM: THE ILIAD

This is the first fight story. During the last year of the siege of Troy, and at the funeral games of Petroclus, the bout followed the chariot races and preceded the wrestling and running. Achilles was the promoter, Epeus the attraction, Euryaus the opponent and Tydides was the well-meaning amateur who overmatched his boy.

In 1982 Carlo Rotella, then a student at Wesleyan University, discovering the "Sweet Science" by A.J. Liebling, became a fight fan and subsequently found, in this Robert Fagles' translation of the epic, Epeus bragging, "I am the greatest" while complaining "So what if I'm not a world-class man of war?" Muhammad Ali's self celebrations and Vietnam protestations naturally came to mind.

HOMER (TRANSLATED BY ROBERT FAGLES)

He savored every word of Nestor's story.
Then Achilles made his way through crowds of troops
and set out prizes next for the bruising boxing-match.
He fetched and tethered a heavy-duty mule in the ring,

six years old, unbroken—the hardest kind to break—
and offered the loser a cup with double handles.
He rose up tall and challenged all the Argives:

"Son of Atreus—all you Achaean men-at-arms!
We invite two men—our best—to compete for these.
Put up your fists, fight for what you're worth.
The man that Apollo helps outlast the other—
clearly witnessed here by Achaea's armies—
he takes this beast of burden back to his tents
but the one he beats can have the two-eared cup."

And a powerful, huge man loomed up at once,
Panopeus' son Epeus, the famous boxing champion.
He clamped a hand on the draft mule and shouted,
"Step right up and get it—whoever wants that cup!
This mule is mine, I tell you. No Achaean in sight
will knock me out and take her—I am the greatest!
So what if I'm not a world-class man of war?
How can a man be first in all events?
I warn you, soldiers—so help me it's the truth—
I'll crush you with body-blows, I'll crack your ribs to splinters!
You keep your family mourners near to cart you off—
once my fists have worked you down to pulp!"

Dead silence. So the armies met his challenge.
Only Euryalus rose to take him on, heroic volunteer,
bred of Talaus' blood and a son of King Mecisteus
who went to Thebes in the old days, when Oedipus fell,
and there at his funeral games defeated all the Thebans.
The spearman Diomedes served as the man's second,
goading him on, intent to see him win.
First he cinched him round with the boxer's belt
then taking rawhide thongs, cut from a field-ox,
wrapped his knuckles well.

Both champions, belted tight,
stepped into the ring, squared off at each other and let loose,
trading jabs with their clenched fists then slugged it out—
flurries of jolting punches, terrific grinding of jaws,
sweat rivering, bodies glistening—suddenly Euryalus
glanced for an opening, dropped his guard and Epeus hurled
his smashing roundhouse hook to the head—a knockout blow!
He could keep his feet no longer, knees caved in on the spot—
as under the ruffling North Wind a fish goes arching up
and flops back down on a beach-break strewn with seaweed
and a dark wave blacks him out. So he left his feet
and down he went—out cold—but big-hearted Epeus
hoisted him in his arms and stood him upright.
A band of loyal followers rushed to help him,
led him out of the ring, his feet dragging,

head lolling to one side, spitting clots of blood . . .
still senseless after they propped him in their corner,
and they had to fetch the two-eared cup themselves.

[FICTION]

FROM: THE MAN WHO LAUGHS

Phelem-ghe-madone was the predecessor of all those large and lethargic heavyweights. He was, Victor Hugo wrote in 1869, "all surface more than anything else, and seemed to enter boxing-matches rather to receive than to give." Had Lady Josiana been French instead of English she would have been the Madame Defarge of *la boxe*.

VICTOR HUGO (TRANSLATED BY ISABEL F. HAPGOOD)

The finest boxing-matches then took place at Lambeth, a parish where the Lord Archbishop of Canterbury has a palace—although the air there is unhealthy—and a rich library which is open at certain hours to respectable people. Once, it was in the winter, there took place there, in a field which was closed with lock and key, a match between two men, at which Josiana, escorted by David, was present. She had inquired: "Are women admitted?" And David had replied: "*Sunt feminae magnates.*" Free translation: "Not women of the middle class." Literal translation: "Great ladies are." A duchess enters everywhere. That is why Lady Josiana saw the boxing-match.

Lady Josiana merely made the concession of dressing like a cavalier, a thing much practiced then. Women never travelled otherwise. Out of six persons which the Windsor coach held, it was rare that there were not one or two women in male attire. It was a sign of belonging to the gentry.

Lord David, being in the company of a woman, could not take part in the match, and was obliged to remain a simple spectator.

Lady Josiana only betrayed her quality by looking through an opera glass, which was the act of a gentleman.

The "noble encounter" was presided over by Lord Germaine, great grandfather or grand uncle of that Lord Germaine who, towards the end of the eighteenth century, was colonel, took to his heels in battle, was afterwards minister of war, and escaped the carbines of the enemy only to fall under the sarcasms of Sheridan, a worse sort of shot. Many gentlemen laid bets: Harry Bellew, of Carleton, who had claims on the extinct peerage of Bella-Aqua, against Henry, Lord Hyde, member of Parliament for the borough of Dunhivid, which is also called Launceston; the Honorable Peregrine Bertie, member for the borough of Truro, against Sir Thomas Colpepper, member for Maidstone; the Laird of Lamyrbau, which is on the borders of Lothian, against Samuel Trefusis, of the borough of Penryn; Sir Bartholomew Gracedieu, of the borough of Saint Ives, against the very Honorable Charles Bodville, who is called Lord Robartes, and who is Custos Rotulorum of the county of Cornwall; and others.

The two boxers were an Irishman from Tipperary, called from the name of his native mountain, Phelem-ghe-Madone, and a Scotchman named

Helmsgail. This placed two national prides face to face. Ireland and Scotland were about to fight; Erin was going to deal blows to Gajothel. Hence the bets exceeded forty thousand guineas, without counting the stakes.

The two champions were naked, with very short breeches, buckled round their hips, and shoes with hobnailed soles, laced round their ankles.

Helmsgail, the Scotchman, was a little fellow, barely nineteen years of age, but he had his forehead already stitched up; that is why they laid two and a third to one on him. A month previously, he had smashed in a rib and put out the eyes of the boxer Sixmileswater, which explains the enthusiasm.

There had been a gain for those who had bet on him of twelve thousand pounds sterling. In addition to his scarred brow, Helmsgail's jaw was minus some of its teeth. He was alert and quick. He was about the height of a small woman, squat, thickset, of a low and menacing stature, and none of the materials of which he was made had been wasted; not a muscle which did not answer the end— pugilism. There was compactness in his firm torso, as brown and shining as bronze. He smiled, and the three teeth which he lacked added to his smile.

His adversary was large and overgrown, that is to say, weak.

He was a man of forty. He was six feet high, with the chest of a hippopotamus, and a gentle air. The blow of his fist could split the deck of a ship, but he did not know how to deliver it. The Irishman, Phelem-ghe-Madone, was all surface more than anything else, and seemed to enter boxing-matches rather to receive than to give. Only, one felt that he would last a long time. A sort of underdone beef, difficult to chew, and impossible to swallow. He was what is called in local slang "raw flesh." He squinted. He seemed resigned.

These two men had passed the preceding night side by side in the same bed, and had slept together. They had each drunk three fingers of port wine from the same glass.

Each had his group of supporters, people rude of aspect, threatening the umpires at need. In the group for Helmsgail, John Gromane was to be seen, famous for carrying an ox upon his back, and a certain John Bray, who had one day taken upon his shoulders ten bushels of flour, of fifteen gallons to the bushel, plus the miller, and with this burden he had walked more than two hundred paces. On the side of Phelem-gheMadone, Lord Hyde had brought from Launceston a certain Kilter, who lived at Green Castle, and could throw over his shoulder a stone weighing twenty pounds, higher than the highest tower of the castle. These three men, Kilter, Bray and Gromane, were from Cornwall, which does honor to the county.

The other supporters were brutal fellows, with solid backs, bow legs, big, knotty fists, clumsy faces, in rags, and fearing nothing, being almost all returned convicts. Many of them understood admirably how to render the members of the police force drunk. Each profession must have its talent.

The field chosen was further away than the Bear Garden, where bears, bulls, and dogs had been made to fight in former days, beyond the last buildings in process of construction, beside the edifice of the priory of Saint Mary Overy, ruined by Henry VIII. North wind and hoar frost was the weather; a fine rain was falling, quickly congealed into sleet. Among the gentlemen present some were to be recognized as fathers of families, because they opened their umbrellas.

On the side of Phelem-ghe-Madone, Colonel Moncreif, umpire, and Kilter, to lend him a knee. On the side of Helmsgail, the honorable Pughe Beaumaris, umpire, and Lord Desertum, from Kilcarry, to lend his knee.

The two boxers stood motionless for a few moments in the enclosure while the watches were compared. Then they walked up to each other and shook hands.

Phelem-ghe-Madone said to Helmsgail: "I should like to go home."

Helmsgail replied, honestly, "The gentry must have something, after putting themselves out."

In their naked condition they were cold. Phelem-ghe-Madone shivered. His jaws chattered. Doctor Eleanor Sharpe, nephew to the Archbishop of York, cried to them, "Tap each other, you knaves. That will warm you up."

These kindly words thawed them. They attacked each other.

But neither of them was angry. They had three feeble rounds. The Reverend Doctor Gumdraith, one of the forty Fellows of All Souls' College, shouted, "Pour some gin into them."

But the two referees and the two seconds, all four judges, adhered to the rule. It was very cold, however.

The cry was heard, "First blood!" They were soon replaced face to face with each other.

They looked at each other, approached, stretched out their arms, touched fists, then retreated. All at once Helmsgail, the little man, gave a bound. The real combat began.

Phelem-ghe-Madone was struck full in the forehead between his eyes. His whole face dripped with blood. The crowd shouted, "Helmsgail has tapped his claret!" They applauded. Phelem-ghe-Madone, whirling his arms as a windmill whirls its sails, began to throw his fists about at haphazard.

The honorable Peregrine Bertie said, "Blinded, but not yet blind."

Then Helmsgail heard this encouragement burst forth on all sides—"Bung his peepers!"

In short, the two champions were really well chosen, and although the weather was not very favorable, it was understood that the match would prove a success. The quasi-giant, Phelem-ghe-Madone, had the inconveniences of his advantages, he moved heavily. His arms were clubs, but his body was a mass. The little man ran, struck, leaped, gnashed his teeth, redoubled vigor by swiftness, knew ruses. On one side was the primitive, savage, uncultivated blow with the fist, in a state of ignorance; on the other, the blow of civilization. Helmsgail fought as much with his nerves as with his muscles, and as much with his malice as with his strength; Phelem-ghe-Madone was a sort of inert slaughterer, somewhat slaughtered himself, as a preliminary. It was art against nature. It was the ferocious man against the barbarian.

It was clear that the barbarian would be beaten. But not very soon. Hence the interest. A small man against a large man. The chances in favor of the small man. A cat gets the better of a dog. The Goliaths have always been vanquished by Davids.

A hail of shouts fell upon the combatants— "Bravo, Helmsgail! Good! Well done, highlander! Now, Phelem!"

And Helmsgail's friends kindly repeated to him the exhortation: "Bung his peepers!"

Helmsgail did better. Suddenly ducking and rising again with the undulation of a reptile, he struck Phelem-ghe-Madone on the breast bone. The Colossus tottered.

"Foul blow!" cried Viscount Barnard.

Phelem-ghe-Madone sank back on Kilter's knee saying: "I am beginning to get warmed up."

Lord Desertum consulted the referees, and said: "There will be a suspension of five minutes."

Phelem-ghe-Madone was weakening. Kilter wiped the blood from his eyes, and the sweat from his body with a piece of flannel, and put the neck of the bottle to his mouth. They had reached the eleventh round. Phelem-ghe-Madone, besides the wound on his forehead, had his pectoral muscles disfigured with blows, his abdomen swollen, and his sinciput bruised. Helmsgail had sustained no injury.

A certain tumult arose among the gentlemen.

Lord Barnard repeated, "Foul blow."

"Bets off," said the Laird of Lamyrbau.

"I recall my stake," chimed in Sir Thomas Colpepper.

And the honorable member for the borough of Saint Ives, Sir Bartholomew Gracedieu added, "Give me back my five hundred guineas, I'm off."

"Stop the fight," shouted the spectators.

But Phelem-ghe-Madone rose staggering almost like a drunken man, and said, "Let us continue the fight, on one condition—I am also to have the right to deal a foul blow."

On all sides arose the cry: "Agreed!"

Helmsgail shrugged his shoulders.

At five minutes past, the fight was resumed.

The combat, which was agony for Phelem-ghe-Madone, was play for Helmsgail. What a thing is science! the little man found means to put the big one in chancery, that is to say, Helmsgail suddenly took Phelem-ghe-Madone's big head under his left arm, curved like a crescent, and held it there under his armpit, with the neck bent, and the nape of the neck low, while with his right falling again and again, like a hammer upon a nail, but from below and underneath, he smashed the latter's face at his leisure. When Phelem-ghe-Madone, finally released, raised his head, he had no longer any face.

What had been nose, eyes, and mouth, appeared now only like a black sponge soaked in blood. He spat. Four teeth were seen on the ground. Then he fell, Kilter received him on his knee.

Helmsgail was hardly touched. He had a few insignificant bruises, and a scratch on one collarbone.

No one was cold any longer. They were laying sixteen and a quarter to one for Helmsgail against Phelem-ghe-Madone.

Harry Carleton shouted: "There's no longer a

Phelem-ghe-Madone. I bet on Helmsgail my peer-age of Bella-Aqua, and my title of Lord Bellew against the Archbishop of Canterbury's old wig."

"Give me your muzzle," said Kilter to Phelem-ghe-Madone, and thrusting his flannel into the bottle, he wiped him off with gin. His mouth became visible once more, and Phelem-ghe-Madone opened one eyelid. His temples seemed cracked.

"One round more, my friend," said Kilter. And he added, "For the honor of the low town."

The Welshman and the Irishman understand each other; but Phelem-ghe-Madone gave no sign which could indicate that he had any intelligence left.

Phelem-ghe-Madone rose, Kilter supporting him. It was the twenty-fifth round. By the way in which this Cyclops, for he had now but one eye, placed himself in position, all understood that the end had come, and no one entertained any doubt that he was lost. He placed his guard above his chin, the sign of a failing man. Helmsgail, hardly perspiring, exclaimed: "I bet on myself. A thousand to one."

Helmsgail raised his arm and struck, and, what was strange, both fell. A gay growl of content was heard.

It was Phelem-ghe-Madone who was content.

He had taken advantage of the terrible blow which Helmsgail had given him on the skull, to deal him a foul blow in the navel.

Helmsgail lay and rattled in his throat.

The spectators looked at Helmsgail as he lay on the ground and said: "Paid back."

Every one applauded, even those who had lost.

Phelem-ghe-Madone had returned a foul blow for a foul blow, and acted according to his right.

Helmsgail was carried off on a stretcher. The general opinion was that he would not recover. Lord Robartes exclaimed: "I win twelve hundred guineas." Phelem-ghe-Madone was crippled for life.

As they came out, Josiana took Lord David's arm, which is tolerated between the "engaged." She said to him, "It is very fine. But—"

"But what?"

"I should have thought it would have driven away my ennui. Well, it has not."

[FICTION]

STOP THE FIGHT!

This is completely believable, and thus one of the best.

NORMAN KATKOV

She had been at him since early morning, and now, during supper, Gino Genovese played with the spaghetti on his plate as he sat at the kitchen table, facing his wife.

"I had enough prize fighters in my family," she said. "My husband was a prize fighter. Not my son. Not while I live; you hear me, Gino?"

"Anna, I told you a thousand times." He spoke quietly and he was very patient. "Young Gino won't fight after tonight. Take my word."

"He's a baby," she said, and Gino realized she hadn't heard him at all.

"He's eighteen, Anna; finished with high school. Young Gino is a man."

"No!" she shouted. She brought her hand down flat on the oilcloth covering the table. "He's not a man." Her voice rose. "He's not a man to me!"

Gino looked at the open window and grimaced. "Anna, please. The neighbors."

"The neighbors," she repeated dully, and pushed her hair back from her forehead. "Is there someone on Water Street who doesn't know my baby is a fighter?"

Some fighter, Gino thought. The kid had won the Golden Gloves and had six pro matches, so that made him a fighter already. He leaned over to close the window, and when he had settled back in his chair, he saw that his wife was staring at nothing, her elbow on the table and her hand to her cheek; her head moving back and forth, back and forth, as though she were in mourning.

"Anna," he said gently, and reached out to touch her. "The spaghetti will get cold, sweetheart," Gino said, but she didn't see him and at last he bent over his plate.

I should have gone to work today instead of taking off, he said to himself, thinking of Marinkov and Stein and Annalora, and the rest of the Park Department crew of which he was foreman. *What good did I do her by staying home?* he thought, as he wound the spaghetti around his fork. *She's like the old women with the kerchiefs over their heads who sit in the sun on Clara Street. She's forty years old and she acts eighty years.*

"Why couldn't he sleep home?" Anna demanded. "Answer me that? My own son. What's the matter with his bed?" she asked, pointing toward Young Gino's room.

Gino sat motionless, the spaghetti trailing from his fork to the plate. "I told you, Anna, his manager wants him to rest. His manager says we would make him excited."

"His manager says," Anna replied. "Who is his manager—chief of police?"

"Anna, what do you want, sweetheart?" He dropped the fork and raised his hands over the plate. "Did I tell Young Gino to fight? Did I go see him fight in the Golden Gloves or since the Golden Gloves? When he came to me and wanted to turn pro, did I tell him yes? When he asked me to be his manager, did I say yes?" Gino reached for a glass of water. "So he went and got Len Farrell for a manager, what should I do then? Should I throw Young Gino out of the house, or turn him

over and paddle him because he got my old manager?" He bent forward. "Listen to me, Anna, baby, Young Gino won't fight after tonight. It's the last time tonight."

"He didn't need the boxing gloves," Anna said.

Gino closed his eyes for a moment, and shook his head slowly. "That's five years ago, sweetheart."

"He didn't need them," she said.

Gino sucked in breath and bit his lip. He set the glass down on the table. "Your brother bought him the gloves, Anna."

"My brother, you, Len Farrell, you're all the same." She held the table with both hands, her hair now loose from the pins and falling in disarray about her neck and over her ears and down her cheeks. "You won't be satisfied until they make him a cripple. Then you'll be satisfied. True, Gino?"

And he got up from his chair and walked out of the kitchen. He went through the hall into the living room, and stood with his hands in his pockets, his knees against the cold radiator, looking out onto Water Street.

I did the right thing, he thought, as he felt the soft curtain brush against his face. *That Pete Wojick will give Young Gino a good licking, and then finish—the kid won't have a stomach for fighting after tonight, that's all.*

Gino had seen it happen enough times: a lad starting out; being overmatched; getting a beating that took the heart out of him for always. You had to bring a kid along very careful when he started, building up his confidence.

All right, Gino thought, and he grimaced again, *it's done with. At least I won't have to listen to her any more after tonight.* He remembered how Len Farrell had protested the match; he remembered pleading with his old manager, agreeing that Wojick was too seasoned for Young Gino, too tricky and wise, with a right hand that could strike like a poleax.

"I've got to stop him fighting, Len," Gino had said. "My wife—she's making me crazy. Let Wojick give him the deep six once and the kid will quit." Gino had gone one afternoon a month ago to the Rose Room Gym downtown to watch his son work out, standing far back among the spectators, so the boy wouldn't see him. "Young Gino's a boxer, a cutie. He won't like getting hurt, Len." He had gone on, talking and talking, until at last Farrell had agreed to make the match—eight rounds in the semifinal at the ball park tonight.

Gino heard Anna moving around in the kitchen, and suddenly, for no reason that he knew, turned away from the window, crossed the living room and went into his son's bedroom.

Gino touched the bed and smoothed the spread, and on the wall above the headboard saw the farm scene Young Gino had painted when he was seven. Anna had taken it to be framed. She had framed the Palmer Method penmanship certificate, and three months ago, in June, she had framed her son's high-school diploma, hanging it there on the wall behind Young Gino's bed.

He turned away and took a step toward the chest of drawers standing at an angle beyond the windows, and knew then why he had come into Young Gino's room. There was the big, double frame that Anna had not bought, which Young Gino had brought home, and in it, the two glossy pictures: the boy on the right and the father on the left.

The boy had dug out Gino's black silk trunks and boxing shoes, and gone to the same photographer across the street from the Rose Room who, twenty years earlier, had taken the father's picture. He had posed the same: right hand high on the bare chest, and left extended; head cocked and shoulders forward.

Standing before the chest of drawers, Gino could see no difference between them, and then noticed the boy's shoulders, sloping more than his father's, and the really enormously big arms for a welterweight.

"I never weighed more than one forty-three," Gino said aloud, and remembered when he had quit. He had finished with fighting one night two blocks from here on the porch of Anna's father's house. She had said she would never see him if he fought again. He'd had thirty fights then, and Len Farrell was ready to take him to Chicago. First to Chicago, and then New York, if he was good enough. That night Gino had asked Anna to marry him.

He remembered, all right, because he had gone into Anna's house and telephoned Len Farrell to tell the manager he was finished.

"No big loss," Gino said aloud. "I wouldn't have been much; I had no punch," and heard Anna behind him; heard her breathing heavy.

"You're proud, Gino, aren't you? Your son is a fighter; you lived to see it," she said, but he would not turn. He didn't turn as he heard her cross the room, but held fast to the chest of drawers.

"You fooled me good, Gino," she said. "Used me for a real dummy, making him a fighter behind my back, lying behind my back," and she reached for the double frame and held it high over her head and flung it to the floor.

He heard the glass smash as he turned. He felt the frame hit his shoe, but didn't look down. He looked at her until her hands went to her cheeks, her lips trembling, the color leaving her face white, and her eyes wide, watching him.

But he said nothing. He went past her, out to the small back porch, taking his jacket off the hook as he pushed open the door and came down the steps. He got into the jacket as he stood beside the car parked in the driveway, and then slid in behind the wheel, turning the key, starting the motor, shifting gears in the old coupé and backing out into the street, his mind blank, not letting himself think as he turned up toward the boulevard leading to the downtown section.

He was driving into the sun, which hung low beyond the green dome of the cathedral on Dayton Avenue, and he squinted as he came into sight of the office buildings. Once he went through a red light, listening to the horns on either side of him. Once he stopped for a semaphore, waiting until long after the light had changed to green and a trailer truck behind him blasted its horn.

Gino came into Kellogg Circle and turned, driving down Washington Street to the bus depot and around it to the alley behind the Rose Room. He parked behind a supermarket and got out of the car, slamming the door behind him and walking out to Exchange Place. He never smoked, but now he went into a drugstore, bought a pack of cigarettes and lit one, inhaling too deeply and coughing as the unfamiliar smoke seared his throat and mouth. He held the cigarette awkwardly and walked toward the newsstand on Seventh Street, but saw Tots Todora, and Bubbling-Over Norris, and Joey Richards, all of them fight fans, and he didn't want to talk with them. He didn't want to see them. He had a feeling to see Young Gino.

He had a feeling to talk to his son or touch him. He remembered, as he walked faster, the years when Young Gino was growing up, sleeping in his own bedroom.

Gino would wake in the night and know—really know—that his son was not sleeping. Gino would get out of bed real slow and careful, not to disturb Anna. Walking in his bare feet, he would turn on the light in the hall, tiptoe into his son's room and stand beside his son's bed and watch him asleep. He would stand there for he never knew how long, looking down at his son, and always, before he left, he would move the covers around his son, and move the hair from his son's forehead, and bend forward to kiss Young Gino.

He never told Anna and he never told his son, and now, turning into the hotel lobby, he had the same feeling he had to see Young Gino. He walked past the room clerk to the house phones and asked for Len Farrell's room.

"Five-o-two, I'm ring ... ging," the operator said, and in a moment Gino heard Farrell say hello.

"Len?" Gino said. "Gino. I'm downstairs."

"Hello, lieutenant," Farrell said.

"I want to come up, Len."

"Sure, lieutenant; I held out two tickets for you," Farrell said.

"Len, it's Gino. Where's the kid? I want to see the kid."

"I'll bring them down myself, lieutenant. A pleasure. For the police department, any time," Farrell said.

"Len. Len!"

"I'll be down right away," Farrell said, and hung up.

After a moment, Gino dropped the receiver on the cradle. He saw the room clerk watching him, and moved away from the row of telephones, out into the lobby.

He walked to the newsstand near the doors and bought a paper and was looking at the front page when Len Farrell appeared.

"You must be crazy," Len said.

"I'm crazy?" Gino folded the paper and pushed it under his arm. "What's the matter with you? Lieutenant. Police force."

Farrell shook his head. He was a tall thin man with slick black hair, combed straight back. "What if the kid had answered the phone?" he asked. "I've had him quiet all day, and all he'd need would be to talk to you. A good thing I can still think, which is more than you can do.

"How is he, Len?"

"He's fine."

"How does he feel?" Gino asked.

"Like a tiger. How do you expect him to feel? He thinks he can lick the world."

"Yeah."

"I must have been out of my mind to make this match," Farrell said.

"He'll get over it," Gino said.

"Sure," Farrell said. "You just keep telling yourself that."

"What else could I have done?" Gino asked.

Farrell shook his head and carefully buttoned his jacket. "Don't ask me. Don't bring me in this. You're the mastermind," Farrell said. "Wojick. If it was my way, I wouldn't let Young Gino near Wojick for a year."

"You told me that already. Give me a ticket, Len."

"Oh, no," Farrell said, and stepped back, but Gino took the manager's arm. He held the arm, his fingers bunching the coat sleeve, looking at Farrell until the older man reached into his pocket. "Let go of my arm," Farrell said.

"I want a ticket. If I don't get it from you, I buy one," Gino said. "I want to see that fight, Len."

Farrell took a long white envelope from his pocket. "You're not sitting ringside," he said. "The kid might see you. I'll have enough trouble with him as it is."

"Fifteen rows back," Gino said. "I can't see good any more if I'm any farther away from the ring."

He took the ticket from Farrell and shoved it into his rear pants pocket. "Take care of him, Len," Gino said.

"Yes. Yes, I'll take care of him." Farrell slipped the flap into the envelope. He held the envelope to his lips like a child with a blade of grass, and he whistled softly. "He could have been a real good fighter, Gino. A real classy fighter."

"He'll live without it," Gino said, and didn't want to talk about the kid any more.

He said goodbye to Farrell and left the lobby, walking out into the early evening. The street lights were glowing, the sun was gone from the heavens and the sky was a dull orange, turning black. He went into a diner and ordered a sandwich and a glass of milk and ate it. That took twenty minutes. In the basement of the bus depot he had his shoes shined. That took ten minutes. He watched a Chicago-bound bus load and leave, and afterward found an empty bench and sat down in a corner of it. He squirmed around on the bench, sitting in one position for a moment and then changing to another, and a third, and a fourth, until at last he was bent forward, his legs uncrossed, his elbows on his knees and one hand massaging the other.

Gino heard the dispatcher announce the arrival

of a Kansas City bus and got off the bench. "Get it over with," he said aloud, and left the depot, crossing the deserted Federal Building Plaza to the alley where he had left his car.

It was complete night now. Driving out to the ball park, Gino remembered the hours before his own fights. He had been very nervous always, and in the afternoon, when Farrell had put him to bed, Gino had never been able to sleep, but lay motionless, his eyes closed, trying not to think of the fight.

"I wasn't yellow," he said aloud as he came into Lexington Avenue, a mile from the ball park. It was his chief worry always—that the referee, or Farrell, or the sports writers, or those at ringside and those beyond, would think him without courage. Often he would fight with complete abandon, standing toe to toe with an opponent who could hit much harder, in a desperate need to convince everyone of his fearlessness.

He saw the lights of the ball park and drove slowly until a youth standing beside a crudely lettered sign gestured at him. Gino turned into the lad's back yard, converted into a parking lot for the night. He paid the boy and walked along the road until he was across the street from the dark walls of the ball park.

He wasn't going in at the main gate, so that he would have to pass the long refreshment counter behind home plate; he'd made up his mind to that. Gino could see them standing there now: Ernie Fliegel and a few of the Gibbons family; maybe My Sullivan and Billy Light, whom Gino had boxed once in Milwaukee. They would be on him about Young Gino, teasing and baiting him, and he didn't want any of it tonight. He'd had all he could take for one day.

Gino saw the open doors near right field and crossed Lexington Avenue, handing his ticket to the gateman and walking ahead quickly, turning away from the foul line as he neared the stands, crossing out onto the playing field.

The ring was set up on the pitcher's mound. As he crossed second base, Gino could see the permanent stands, spreading in a huge V from home plate. There were twenty rows of chairs around the ring. Gino stood well back from the last row, looking at a couple of inept heavyweights, moving awkwardly through four dull rounds.

Once, during the second four-rounder, an usher asked him if he wanted to sit down, but Gino shook his head. Once, during the six-round bout that followed, Gino saw Frankie Battaglia, who had boxed as a middleweight when he was fighting. Gino turned his back, waiting until he'd heard the bell sound for the end of a round before he looked back at the ring.

It came too soon. One second the ring was clear and Gino could see the cigarette smoke drifting toward the lights, and the next instant Pete Wojick was in the ring, manager and trainers around him.

"He's big. He's too big," Gino said, as Wojick's manager took the robe from the fightee's shoulders and the welterweight began moving about in the corner, punching short lefts and rights, hooks and jabs and uppercuts, into the night air.

The referee stood in a neutral corner, arms resting on the ropes. Across the ring, the announcer looked toward the visiting-team dugout from which the boxers entered the ball field. Gino saw the heads turning, the men standing up in front of their seats, and remembered it was a practice of Farrell's to keep the opponent waiting. He heard the murmurs of the impatient crowd, and saw his son come out of the dugout. Young Gino was wearing his father's old robe, which he had found in the trunk in the front closet. He came down the aisle toward the ring, his gloves pushed against each other and resting on his chest.

Gino lit a cigarette and held it in his hand. He saw Farrell step on the bottom rope and pull up on the middle one for Young Gino. He saw the boy come into the ring and stand absolutely still, arms at his sides, looking across at Wojick. He saw Farrell put his hand in under the robe and massage Young Gino's back, and then he heard the announcer who had come to the center of the ring:

"... the fighting son of a fighting father, Young Gino Genovese!" as Gino moved to the aisle and bent almost double, hurrying to his seat in the fourteenth row, the cigarette dropping from his hand. He said, "Pardon me," and started moving down the row, holding the backs of the seats in front of him, saying, "Excuse," and "Sorry," until he dropped into the empty folding chair, hearing the bell and raising his head in the darkness to see the two fighters come toward the middle of the ring.

Just let it be quick, Gino said to himself, sitting with his hands in his lap, his legs tucked under the chair and his ankles crossed, as he watched the kid jab above Wojick's ear with his left hand.

He fights like the picture he took, Gino thought as he watched his son, boxing straight up and down in the classic manner, the left arm out, the right carried high on the chest, the head cocked just a little to one side and the feet far apart.

Wojick took two more lefts and came forward, hooking to the stomach and then to the kidneys as he closed with Young Gino, holding until the referee separated them. Wojick was shorter, carrying absolutely no weight in his legs, with the body of a middleweight.

Young Gino moved around him, jabbing all the time, holding the right on his chest and waiting. They regarded each other carefully for maybe forty-five seconds, circling each other, and then Wojick hooked hard to the stomach.

And again to the stomach, so that Young Gino went back a step and Wojick was on top of him. He came forward all in a rush, his head low, moving in and mauling with both hands, driving Young Gino into the ropes and holding him there. Wojick was in close now, so the kid couldn't punch at all, pushing his head in under Young Gino's chin. He used Young Gino's body as leverage, punching with both hands to the stomach and the kidneys and the stomach again, until at last the kid's arms came down for an instant and Wojick brought the right up and over.

But Young Gino had slipped out, taken a step to his left and moved clear and away from Wojick, out toward the middle of the ring, his stomach pink now from the pounding he'd taken.

Wojick came out to meet him, moving his arms as he shuffled forward, and Young Gino jabbed him. He hit Wojick six times running, long jabs that held the older fighter off balance, moving very carefully, keeping to the center of the ring.

He boxed beautifully, and as Wojick started to hook with his left, Young Gino came in, jabbing short and hard in a perfectly executed counterpunch and bringing the right hand over flush to Wojick's chin.

And Wojick went down as the entire ball park went up on its feet. Young Gino moved to a corner and Wojick took a six count. The referee wiped Wojick's gloves on his shirt, and Young Gino was there swinging. Wojick was in trouble, the legs still wobbly and his eyes glassy, but he had his arms up.

"Wait!" Gino yelled at his son. "Find him!" he yelled, but they were screaming in the ball park, wanting the knockout, and the kid was swinging

and punching wildly, as Wojick kept his head down and his forearms covering his face and waited for the bell.

And lasted until the bell, as the crowd settled down slowly, almost one by one, and all around him Gino could hear them shouting at one another and grinning and talking about the kid and how great he was, except they hadn't seen what Gino had seen—that Wojick had not taken another punch, but had caught all the kid's blows on his arms and shoulders and gloves.

Near Gino somebody said, "How do you like that kid, Louie? A champ, isn't he?"

Somebody said, "The best since McLarnin."

And somebody said, "I seen the old man. The kid's better. The kid got the punch the old man never had," and in the darkness Gino rubbed one hand with the other and heard the bell and looked up at the ring.

Young Gino came out very fast, the water from the sponge glistening on his hair and shoulders. He went almost across the ring and jabbed twice and tried the right, missing with the right, as Gino cursed Farrell.

That Farrell must be nuts, he thought, *not telling the kid to wait.* He looked over at Young Gino's corner for Farrell, and heard the crowd suck in breath and turned quickly to the ring to see his son against the ropes.

"What happened?" Gino asked. He had the arm of the man next to him. "What happened?" he asked, watching Wojick follow his son around the ring.

"Wojick belted him a right hand," the man next to him said, and Gino saw his son staggering.

He saw Wojick following Young Gino, fighting cautiously now, out of the crouch, the left arm no more than six inches from his chest and the right pulled back next to the stomach.

Young Gino tried to clinch, but Wojick stepped away and hooked. He hooked twice to the body and then to the head. In the fourteenth row Gino watched Wojick very carefully and saw him push his left foot forward. He saw him weave and he saw Wojick's left glove drop just a couple of inches as the right started down at the stomach and whistled in and caught Young Gino high in the face.

"Down," Gino whispered. "Go down, kid," he said. "Go down!" he said, as he felt the pain in his heart, and saw Wojick jab twice more and get set and drop his left glove again and bring the right hand in along Young Gino's jaw.

"It's over," Gino whispered. "At least, it's finished fast," but his son clinched. Held on and hooked his arms in Wojick's, gaining ten seconds' rest before the referee separated them.

Clinched again immediately, and Gino saw his son straighten up when they were split once more and saw him keep the left out, staying away from Wojick until just before the bell, when he took another right to the chin that spun him clear around so that he fell against the ropes, hanging there until the gong sounded and Farrell was in the ring to lead him to the corner.

The doctor came then. He went into the ring, and Gino whispered, "Stop it. Just stop it."

But the crowd yelled "No!" at the doctor. They yelled, "Let the kid alone!" and "He's okay, doc!" and, "That kid's tough!" until at last the doctor nodded at the referee and left the ring, while Farrell worked over Young Gino.

The kid got up at the ten-second buzzer. He pulled his arm free of Farrell and rose, standing away from the stool in the comer, his arms hanging, looking across at Wojick.

The crowd loved it. They loved it that Young Gino went across the ring to carry the fight to Wojick. They loved it when Young Gino landed a right to Wojick's heart that stopped the older fighter for a few seconds. They loved it that the kid was anxious, and all the time Gino watched Wojick and Wojick's left glove, waiting for it to drop until, after a minute of the round was gone, Young Gino missed with his right and was open.

Gino saw the left glove drop. He saw Wojick get set, the shoulders drooping, and he felt the right when it landed on his son's chin.

Gino waited for the kid to fall. He watched Young Gino helpless. He saw his son get hit with a second right and a third, and while the boy staggered around the ring, refusing to fall, taking whatever Wojick could deliver, Gino said, "That's enough." He said, "That's all," and got out of his chair.

He heard them yelling "Sit down!" but he started pushing his way toward the aisle, bent forward, feeling the hands against him, as he was shoved from one man to the next until he was in the aisle at last, running toward the ring.

An usher reached for Gino, but missed him. A cop grabbed him, holding his arm, as Gino watched the ring and prayed for the bell, hearing the cop's voice, but not what the cop said, while the kid held on to Wojick, beaten and out on his feet, and nothing holding him up except heart.

"Let me alone," Gino said. "That's my kid," he said to the cop. "Ask Farrell," he said, pointing with his free arm. He turned toward the cop. "My kid," Gino said to the cop. "Let me in my kid's corner," he said, as the bell sounded and the cop released him.

Gino pulled at his jacket as he ran. He got the jacket off and dropped it there at the foot of the three steps leading to the ring, and then he was in the ring, kneeling before his son as Farrell worked on Young Gino.

"Don't talk," Gino warned. "Breathe deep and let it out slow. Wojick's left. It drops when he's going to use the right. The left drops maybe an inch when he shoots the right! You got that? Nod if you got that," and watched his son nod as he rubbed the boy's legs. "Stay away this round. It's only the fourth. Stay away and box him and watch the left. You're a winner, kid; you got that knockdown going for you. Watch the left and bring your right in over it. Remember," as the warning buzzer sounded, and Gino rose, putting his hand flat against his son's chest. "Now you rest, big shot. Rest and watch the left," and Young Gino smiled at him.

Gino felt the smile warming him. He felt the smile all through him, and reached out to brush the kid's hair away from the forehead, and then he had the stool as the bell sounded and Young Gino went out to the center of the ring.

Gino held the stool as he came down the steps. *Let him fight,* Gino decided. *If he wants it that much, let him do what he wants. She'll have to take it, that's all. I'll do what I can, be good and listen to her, but she'll have to get used to it.*

Me, I'm her husband, she had a right to tell me to quit. Not the kid, she can't tell the kid what to do with his life; and he turned to look at his son in the ring.

LAWDY, LAWDY, HE'S GREAT!

Muhammad Ali and Joe Frazier, with their conflicting styles and convictions, were made for each other, as their trio of matches brought out. This ringside-inside coverage does their final meeting justice as one of the greatest of all hevyweight championship fights.

MARK KRAM

It was only a moment, sliding past the eyes like the sudden shifting of light and shadow, but long years from now it will remain a pure and moving glimpse of hard reality, and if Muhammad Ali could have turned his eyes upon himself, what first and final truth would he have seen? He had been led up the winding, red-carpeted staircase by Imelda Marcos, the First Lady of the Philippines, as the guest of honor at the Malacañang Palace. Soft music drifted in from the terrace as the beautiful Imelda guided the massive and still heavyweight champion of the world to the long buffet ornamented by huge candelabra. The two whispered, and then she stopped and filled his plate, and as he waited the candles threw an eerie light across the face of a man who only a few hours before had survived the ultimate inquisition of himself and his art.

The maddest of existentialists, one of the great surrealists of our time, the king of all he sees, Ali had never before appeared so vulnerable and fragile, so pitiably unmajestic, so far from the universe he claims as his alone. He could barely hold his fork, and he lifted the food slowly up to his bottom lip, which had been scraped pink. The skin on his face was dull and blotched, his eyes drained of that familiar childlike wonder. His right eye was a deep purple, beginning to close, a dark blind being drawn against a harsh light. He chewed his food painfully, and then he suddenly moved away from the candles as if he had become aware of the mask he was wearing, as if an inner voice were laughing at him. He shrugged, and the moment was gone.

A couple of miles away in the bedroom of a villa, the man who has always demanded answers of

Ali, has trailed the champion like a timber wolf, lay in semi-darkness. Only his heavy breathing disturbed the quiet as an old friend walked to within two feet of him. "Who is it?" asked Joe lifting himself to look around. "Who is it? I can't see! I can't see! Turn the lights on!" Another light was turned on, but Frazier still could not see. The scene cannot be forgotten; this good and gallant man lying there, embodying the remains of a will never before seen in a ring, a will that had carried him so far—and now surely too far. His eyes were only slits, his face looked as if it had been painted by Goya. "Man, I hit him with punches that'd bring down the walls of a city," said Frazier. "Lawdy, Lawdy, he's a great champion." Then he put his head back down on the pillow, and soon there was only the heavy breathing of a deep sleep slapping like big waves against the silence.

Time may well erode that long morning of drama in Manila, but for anyone who was there those faces will return again and again to evoke what it was like when two of the greatest heavyweights of any era met for a third time, and left millions limp around the world. Muhammad Ali caught the way it was: "It was like death. Closest thing to dyin' that I know of."

Ali's version of death began about 10:45 a.m. on Oct. 1 in Manila. Up to then his attitude had been almost frivolous. He would simply not accept Joe Frazier as a man or as a fighter, despite the bitter lesson Frazier had given him in their first savage meeting. Esthetics govern all of Ali's actions and conclusions; the way a man looks, the way he moves is what interests Ali. By Ali's standards, Frazier was not pretty as a man and without semblance of style as a fighter. Frazier was an affront to beauty, to Ali's own beauty as well as to his precious concept of how a good fighter should move. Ali did not hate Frazier, but he viewed him with the contempt of a man who cannot bear anything short of physical and professional perfection.

Right up until the bell rang for Round One, Ali was dead certain that Frazier was through, was convinced that he was no more than a shell, that too many punches to the head had left Frazier only one more solid shot removed from a tin cup and some pencils. "What kind of man can take all those punches to the head?" he asked himself over and over. He could never come up with an answer. Eventually he dismissed Frazier as the embodiment of animal stupidity. Before the bell Ali was subdued in his corner, often looking down to his manager, Herbert Muhammad, and conversing aimlessly. Once, seeing a bottle of mineral water in front of Herbert, he said, "Watcha got there, Herbert? Gin! You don't need any of that. Just another day's work. I'm gonna put a whuppin' on this nigger's head."

Across the ring Joe Frazier was wearing trunks that seemed to have been cut from a farmer's overalls. He was darkly tense, bobbing up and down as if trying to start a cold motor inside himself. Hatred had never been a part of him, but words like "gorilla," "ugly," "ignorant"—all the cruelty of Ali's endless vilifications—had finally bitten deeply into his soul. He was there not seeking victory alone; he wanted to take Ali's heart out and then crush it slowly in his hands. One thought of the moment days before, when Ali and Frazier with their handlers between them were walking out of the Malacañang Palace, and Frazier said to Ali, leaning over and measuring each word, "I'm gonna whup your half-breed ass. "

By packed and malodorous Jeepneys, by small and tinny taxis, by limousine and by worn-out bikes, 28,000 had made their way into the Philippine Coliseum. The morning sun beat down, and the South China Sea brought not a whisper of wind. The streets of the city emptied as the bout came on public television. At ringside, even though the arena was air-conditioned, the heat wrapped around the body like a heavy wet rope. By now, President Ferdinand Marcos, a small brown derringer of a man, and Imelda, beautiful and cool as if she were relaxed on a palace balcony taking tea, had been seated.

True to his plan, arrogant and contemptuous of an opponent's worth as never before, Ali opened the fight flat-footed in the center of the ring, his hands whipping out and back like the pistons of an enormous and magnificent engine. Much broader than he has ever been, the look of swift destruction defined by his every move, Ali seemed indestructible. Once, so long ago, he had been a splendidly plumed bird who wrote on the wind a singular kind of poetry of the body, but now he was down to earth, brought down by the changing shape of his body, by a sense of his own vulnerability, and by the years of excess. Dancing was for a ballroom; the ugly hunt was on. Head up and unprotected, Frazier stayed in the mouth of the cannon, and the big gun roared again and again.

Frazier's legs buckled two or three times in that first round, and in the second he took more lashing as Ali loaded on him all the meanness that he could find in himself. "He won't call you Clay no more," Bundini Brown, the spirit man, cried hoarsely from the corner. To Bundini, the fight would be a question of where fear first registered, but there was no fear in Frazier. In the third round Frazier was shaken twice, and looked as if he might go at any second as his head jerked up toward the hot lights and the sweat flew off his face. Ali hit Frazier at will, and when he chose to do otherwise he stuck his long left arm in Frazier's face. Ali would not be holding in this bout as he had in the second. The referee, a brisk workman, was not going to tolerate clinching. If he needed to buy time, Ali would have to use his long left to disturb Frazier's balance.

A hint of shift came in the fourth. Frazier seemed to be picking up the beat, his threshing-blade punches started to come into range as he snorted and rolled closer. "Stay mean with him, champ!" Ali's corner screamed. Ali still had his man in his sights, and whipped at his head furiously. But at the end of the round, sensing a change and annoyed, he glared at Frazier and said, "You dumb chump, you!" Ali fought the whole fifth round in his own corner. Frazier worked his body, the whack of his gloves on Ali's kidneys sounding like heavy thunder. "Get out of the goddamn corner," shouted Angelo Dundee, Ali's trainer. "Stop playin'," squawked Herbert Muhammad, wringing his hands and wiping the mineral water nervously from his mouth. Did they know what was ahead?

Came the sixth, and here it was, that one special moment that you always look for when Joe Frazier is in a fight. Most of his fights have shown this: you can go so far into that desolate and dark place where the heart of Frazier pounds, you can waste his perimeters, you can see his head hanging in the public square, may even believe that you have him but then suddenly you learn that you have not. Once more the pattern emerged as Frazier loosed all of the fury, all that has made him a brilliant heavyweight. He was in close now, fighting off Ali's chest, the place where he wants to be. His old calling card—that sudden evil, his left hook—was working the head of Ali. Two hooks ripped with slaughterhouse finality at Ali's jaw, causing Imelda Marcos to look down it her feet, and the President to wince as if a knife had been stuck in his back. Ali's legs seemed to search for the floor. He was in serious trouble, and he knew that he was in no-man's-land.

Whatever else might one day be said about Muhammad Ali, it should never be said that he is without courage, that he cannot take a punch. He took those shots by Frazier, and then came out for the seventh, saying to him, "Old Joe Frazier, why I thought you were washed up." Joe replied, "Somebody told you all wrong, pretty boy."

Frazier's assault continued. By the end of the 10th round it was an even fight. Ali sat on his stool like a man ready to be staked out in the sun. His head was bowed, and when he raised it his eyes rolled from the agony of exhaustion. "Force yourself, champ!" his corner cried. "Go down to the well once more!" begged Bundini, tears streaming down his face. "The world needs ya, champ!" In the 11th, Ali got trapped in Frazier's corner, and blow after blow bit at his melting face, and flecks of spittle flew from his mouth. "Lawd have mercy!" Bundini shrieked.

The world held its breath. But then Ali dug deep down into whatever it is that he is about, and even his severest critics would have to admit that the man-boy had become finally a man. He began to catch Frazier with long right hands, and blood trickled from Frazier's mouth. Now, Frazier's face began to lose definition; like lost islands reemerging from the sea, massive bumps rose suddenly around each eye, especially the left. His punches seemed to be losing their strength. "My God," wailed Angelo Dundee. "Look at 'im. He ain't got no power, champ!" Ali threw the last ounces of resolve left in his body in the 13th and 14th. He sent Frazier's bloody mouthpiece flying into the press row in the 13th, and nearly floored him with a right in the center of the ring. Frazier was now no longer coiled. He was up high, his hands down, and as the bell for the 14th round sounded, Dundee pushed Ali out saying, "He's all yours!" And he was, as Ali raked him with nine straight right hands. Frazier was not picking up the punches, and as he returned to his corner at the round's end the Filipino referee guided his great hulk part of the way.

"Joe," said his manager, Eddie Futch, "I'm going to stop it."

"No, no, Eddie, ya can't do that to me," Frazier pleaded, his thick tongue barely getting the words out. He started to rise.

"You couldn't see in the last two rounds," said Futch. "What makes ya think ya gonna see in the 15th?"

"I want him, boss," said Frazier.

'Sit down, son," said Futch, pressing his hand on Frazier's shoulder. "It's all over. No one will ever forget what you did here today."

And so it will be, for once more had Frazier taken the child of the gods to hell and back. After the fight Futch said: "Ali fought a smart fight. He conserved his energy, turning it off when he had to. He can afford to do it because of his style. It was mainly a question of anatomy, that is all that separates these two men. Ali is now too big, and when you add those long arms, well … Joe has to use constant pressure, and that takes its toll on a man's body and soul." Dundee said: "My guy sucked it up and called on everything he had. We'll never see another one like him." Ali took a long time before coming down to be interviewed by the press, and then he could only say, "I'm tired of bein' the whole game. Let other guys do the fightin'. You might never see Ali in the ring again."

In his suite the next morning he talked quietly. "I heard somethin' once," he said. "When somebody asked a marathon runner what goes through his mind in the last mile or two, he said that you ask yourself why am I doin' this. You get so tired. It takes so much out of you mentally. It changes you. It makes you go a little insane. I was thinkin' that at the end. Why am I doin' this? What am I doin' here in against this beast of a man? It's so painful. I must be crazy. I always bring out the best in the men I fight, but Joe Frazier, I'll tell the world right now, brings out the best in me. I'm gonna tell ya, that's one helluva man, and God bless him."

THE GREAT ALMOST WHITE HOPE

Before the latest "Golden Boy" worked his way through the weight classes to the welterweight title and *The Ring* magazine's best-pound-for-pound knighting, a writer outstanding in his own field produced this revealing account of the personality and pursuits of an American barrio hero.

MARK KRIEGEL

You need more than a map to make it from the barrio to Brentwood as Oscar De La Hoya has, arriving this summer morning at the Riviera Country Club for a celebrity golf outing. It's not that there aren't any homeboys in the house, just that most of them are parking cars or cutting grass or busing tables. The Spanish stucco clubhouse stands like a monument to all that's supposed to be good and gracious in southern-California society. And Oscar fits right in.

Over brunch in the ballroom, the twenty-three-year-old champion—I have to keep reminding myself he's a fighter—is receiving a steady stream of well-wishers. Most of them are colonels and captains in the corporate culture—Peerless Faucet, Sherwin-Williams, Owens Corning—clean-shaven, backslapping gentlemen calling one another amigo.

The occasion is to benefit local Boy Scout chapters. The tournament chairman and his wife thank Oscar profusely. Like De La Hoya, most of the scouts are from East L.A. They're just not as blessed. Some live below the poverty line, explains the chairman's wife, and others are in wheelchairs. "It's a worthy cause," she says.

Oscar nods gravely. He knows the drill. He's "giving back to the Community"—the phrase you hear again and again—though it's never quite clear what community these people mean.

Now he's introduced to a woman who runs a "Hispanic advertising agency," as it's described for my benefit. "So nice of you," she gushes, a flutter in her lashes. "Young men need role models."

And grown men need autographs. Even here, the signature sharks and memorabilia mercenaries are never far behind, armed with their indelible markers, glossies, and spongy red Everlast gloves. Can you sign, Oscar, please . . . and this one for my girl; she's a big fan. Next, there's some guy doing a boxing movie. The stars are already attached, but what he'd really like is for Oscar to do a cameo.

De La Hoya indulges each request with equal earnestness. He's more of a sales rep than anybody in the room. He's selling an image. In an aside, he confesses, "Gotta go along with it. Gotta be the perfect person. Somebody's always watching."

So he gives them that shy smile, that teenager's voice still the slightest bit soprano. His manners are precious. And he's as pretty as he is polite. In his khakis and his baseball cap, Oscar De La Hoya could be one of those freshfaced kids in ads for the Gap or Benetton. At another angle, he could be Speed Racer, the perversely perfect creation of Japanese animators. And still another take: In another time and place, in another movie, he'd have played the matador opposite Ava Gardner. Oscar De La Hoya looks like anything but what he is.

I saw him last at Caesars Palace in Las Vegas, where he won the 140-pound superlightweight championship by dispatching a deity of Mexican machismo named Julio Cesar Chavez. There was so much blood in the ring, and every drop of it Chavez's, that a custodial worker was sent in with a mop before the walkout bout could begin. When I mention the mop, De La Hoya leans closer to shield himself from the glad-handers. His eyes have become animated. Suddenly, he's all there.

"A mop?" he asks. "Really, a mop? Wow."

De La Hoya opened a gash above Chavez's left eye a minute into the fight. It was like a razor cut, a red thread. But De La Hoya attacked the wound until it was the size of a baby's mouth. Then, in the fourth and final round, came a left hand thrown from an acute angle, something between a hook and an uppercut, a punch that seemed to explode Chavez's nose, making shrapnel of cartilage and tissue and blood.

"Oh, that felt good," says De La Hoya, now dreamy with delight. He's never had a sip of liquor, but blood, even the recollection of blood, gets him high. "I wish he had two noses," he says.

So it turns out our sugarcoated salesman has a sadist in his soul. But that's only the first in a collection of contradictions that define Oscar De La Hoya: He's the pretty boy of an ugly business; a child star spinning in a constellation of has-beens; Mexican by his blood, American in his inclinations; barrio by birth, country club by preference.

He lives in a condo in Whittier, the town that gave us Richard Nixon. But now he's talking of moving again. Maybe Bel Air. Maybe South Pasadena.

"I read it's even more exclusive than Beverly Hills."

And back in East L.A., he will again be called an aspiring white boy, charged with selling out and abandoning the Community. In fact, that's not the case. De La Hoya isn't nearly old enough to forget where he came from. If that's not enough, there's the food stamp he keeps in his wallet to remind him. Then there are the scholarships in his name. He even renovated the old Resurrection gym on Lorena Street. Now it's the Oscar De La Hoya Boxing Youth Center.

Yes, he's giving back. But that misses the point.

Here in the ballroom, as a busboy refills Oscar's water glass, something becomes clear: There's already an incalculable calculable distance between De La Hoya and the barrio of his birth. He knows better than these mere businessmen that greed is good. This latest and greatest of Golden Boys has an intimate, almost philosophical comprehension of Reverend Ike's old theorem—the best way to help the poor is not to be one of them. Still, that misses the point, too.

Oscar is a fighter. It is not the barrio he avoids but another place. Call it what it's been called before: Palookaville, that punchers' purgatory where broken boxers live in poverty and chagrin.

They all seem to get there, one way or another, traveling the pug's path from Kid to Bum. In Palookaville, the Ali Shuffle is a palsied jig. Mando Ramos, of Palookaville by way of East L.A., would shoot up and shiver with junk. And Bobby Chacon, another erstwhile Golden Boy from the 'hood, collects cans and bottles for deposit.

Chacon was there, poor and punchy and picking up cans in the back of the Olympic Auditorium in L.A. as Chavez and De La Hoya kicked off their publicity tour all those months ago.

That's a role model.

"I learned from him," says De La Hoya. "I learned from them all."

Oscar De La Hoya may prove to be the greatest fighter of his time, even great enough to save his sorry-ass sport. He has time and talent on his side, but also instincts as old as his blood. His grandfather Vicente was an amateur featherweight in Durango, Mexico. His father, Joel, arrived in Los Angeles when he was sixteen and went on to a brief pro career. He was 9-3-1 as a lightweight before finding steadier, less perilous work in a warehouse of an air-conditioning manufacturer.

Joel De La Hoya would lace the gloves for Oscar's first fight at a local boys' Club. Oscar was six. And though these earliest stories are apocryphal—did Oscar draw blood or just tears?—one detail is absolutely clear, that which he recalls again and again: He got money for winning.

His first purses were dollar bills, bestowed by the men of the neighborhood. They kept passing him dead presidents, too, just as long as he kept winning. So he augmented his instinct, conditioning himself to smell money with blood. Where Oscar was going, there'd be a lot of both.

He trained at the Hollenbeck Youth Center on First Street and at Resurrection, an old church itself resurrected as a gym. De La Hoya provided a new take on an old character: the fighter as a child star.

In a way, he saw the barrio through a bubble. He walked the streets, but the streets never walked on him. Strange for a boy from the 'hood, but stranger still for that boy to be a fighter. He has none of the macho mannerisms. Even in the ring, he has no bop. No wiggle. No funky step. No profane homeboy homilies for Oscar De La Hoya.

"I was taught to have manners," he sniffs.

De La Hoya's arrogance is beyond idiom. He

had neither a streetfight ("never, not once," he says) nor a skateboard. But he had ambition in abundance. Oscar De La Hoya was fed aspirations the way other kids are fed Frosted Flakes. Everybody had high hopes—the father, the family, the neighborhood. Listen long enough to all the happy horseshit about the Community and role models and you'd believe that physicality combined with the vaguest virtue is enough to gentle the conditions in the slums.

"Ever since I was a little kid," he says, "I had to be some kind of example."

He'd never be one of the boyz. But there was always the sense that his success would be shared by all of East Los Angeles. Even the gang bangers knew enough not to mess with him. Everybody was rooting for Oscar. Do it for us, *ese.* Do it for us.

At the age of eleven, Oscar watched on TV as another East L.A. fighter did it for us. His name was Paul Gonzales, and he won a gold medal in the 1984 Olympics.

"I remember cheering for him on TV," says De La Hoya. "He was the hero for us—all of us."

But then, quite abruptly, De La Hoya suffered his first and final attack of rebellion. Perhaps he understood then what Gonzales admits only now, that "the pressure of representing my country was nothing compared to representing my neighborhood." Or perhaps, as De La Hoya says, "I was just tired. I just wanted to be in the street, playing football or baseball, whatever. I wanted, you know, a normal life." But something about normal life, that discrepancy between a child star's expectation and a real kid's reality, just didn't feel right.

"After a few months, I realized what I had to lose," he says. It wasn't a difficult decision, going back to the gym. "I didn't have chat many friends, anyway."

Besides, what he had was more than an aptitude for hitting people. And none of the men watching from ringside understood quite so well as a woman. Cecilia De La Hoya, a seamstress and occasional singer, was the first to recognize a spooky duality in her boy.

"She used to say she didn't recognize me, her own son, when I went in the ring," he says. "She said she saw red in my eyes. She said she saw a beast. And she was right, always right. When I see blood, I want to see more."

He had the body to enable his bloodlust. The fighter you see today looks much like the fighter

he's always been. Then, as now, he had cobra quickness, an unnaturally strong lead hand (he does everything lefty except fight), and the advantage of superior reach and leverage. He was always tall—he'd grow to almost five eleven—a stick figure except for the shoulders, chose puncher's engines. He's built as if jets had been mounted on a biplane.

Joel De La Hoya, chief architect of his son's ambition, looked to Paul Gonzales as a blueprint. Gonzales recalls Oscar's father coming to the Resurrection, where a former vice cop named Al Stankie was wrapping his hands. Stankie had trained Gonzales for the '84 games. There was even supposed to be a Gonzales movie, *The Cop and the Kid.*

"Train my son, Oscar," said the elder De La Hoya. "Make him a gold medalist, too." So for a time, the two Golden Boys shared a trainer. But while Gonzales's career was already in decline, De La Hoya was beginning an ascent unlike any the neighborhood had seen. For a while, he had a private tutor to help make up for all the school he missed while competing on the amateur circuit. But, really, how many kids with tutors could knock opponents unconscious—two of them in an afternoon? Oscar was 225 wins against 5 losses as an amateur, winning more championships, titles, and trophies than he could count.

"Now win the gold medal," Gonzales told him, "and you'll always have pussy."

You imagine that sheepish smile—embarrassed, perhaps, but never quite innocent—in response. There wasn't much time for girls. Oscar missed the prom at Garfield High to fight a Cuban at Fort Bragg, North Carolina. He vowed to throw himself a prom. After the Olympics. It was always after the Olympics.

In 1990, Cecilia De La Hoya watched the beast in her son win his weight class at the Goodwill Games in Seattle. Oscar had no idea she'd missed a week of radiation treatment to be there. It wasn't until they'd returned that she tried to explain about breast cancer, showing him the burns on her back left by the treatments.

She died on October 28 of that year. To honor her, Oscar vowed to win a gold medal at the Barcelona Olympics and present it at her grave. He did just that, against an unholy pressure. He was a role model, a soldier for God and country, for family and friends, for East L. A., and for the memory of his mother. He was nineteen. Oscar's Story, as some movie producers were now calling it, had acquired elements that were meaningful, maudlin, and, most of all, marketable.

Understand what made for such fame and fortune, what made a Latin boxer so mainstream. The most improbable blessing of all, that which made Oscar De La Hoya separate and singular, that which he got from his mother, is his face. Let's hear nothing of narcissism; pretty boy is the beast's best disguise. But also, the telltale sign of uncanny resilience.

Consider a fighter's years in the ring. Try to quantify the punishment and pain. Impossible. There's only the physical evidence, what precedes slurred speech and thick thoughts: blunted features, ridges of scar tissue, a wandering eye, cauliflower ear. There's a school of thought, much of it Mexican, that regards these various uglinesses as ennobling. There's an expectation that the fighter be willing to take a lot just to give a little.

"If I was scarred, if my nose was all busted up, they'd love me," De La Hoya says. "But I'm not going to apologize to the Mexican fans for not getting hit. I'm not going to apologize for being better than my opponents."

Don't mistake the fighter with heart for an eager masochist. And don't misunderstand his wounds—tattoos acquired on the road to Palookaville. De La Hoya even fired a trainer on account of ugliness. His name was Carlos Ortiz. He was once the lightweight champion of the world. But his face told Oscar of that place he did not want to go. "His nose had been broken, and he'd been cut up so many times," says De La Hoya. "I did not want to have that face."

He'd rather have the face that can make his fights feel like Menudo concerts, what with all the young girls in the crowd. His is the face boyfriends hate. And his is the face fighters wish to ruin, especially Mexican fighters.

Such good looks inspire not just envy but terror. As the punches accumulate—already seventeen years in the ring for Oscar—the still-pretty face can be construed in terms almost metaphysical. A pretty face means the mathematics of macho do not apply. And from one fighter to another, it also means this: I'll treat her real good when you're in Palookaville.

Trying to gauge the various distances—between Oscar and the Community, the barrio and the country club—I'm cruising with Paul Gonzales through the Flats, a stretch of low-slung khaki-colored projects, the concrete pueblos of East L.A. Deserted courtyards are dotted with metal crosses, clothesline posts that have the effect of a soldiers' cemetery. Kiddie gangstas in shades stand sentry, arms crossed. This week's cool is black high-top Converse, no laces. Driving Fourth Street now, domain of the Quatro Flats crew, its graffiti tags like hieroglyphics on an endless stretch of wall: Wicked and Whisper, Spooky and Smiley, Lilo and Cuko. Moving along, there's a "Stop the Violence" mural. Then the black Aztec eagle made popular by Cesar Chavez and the United Farm Workers.

Now look up: the billboard. There he goes, million-dollar smile. EL CAMPEON DE LA PROTECCION EN GEL! Buy gel antiperspirant. Be like Oscar.

"Snake," says Gonzales, gesturing at the billboard. "Just 'cause he grew up in East L.A. don't mean he's from the 'hood."

After all these years, Gonzales is positioned for the counterpunch, the perfect spokesman to articulate these resentments against the Golden Boy. After all, Paul Gonzales was once a Golden Boy himself. But also, Kid Barrio.

He was eleven, riding in the backseat of a Chevy Impala, when the fragments of buckshot and glass embedded themselves in the back of his head. "Gang-banging?" he says. "I guess you could say I was." At thirteen, he was stabbed while beating down a grown man who'd called him a punk. That was right in front of his house, 129 Paseo Los Alisos Unit 56. That's Primera Flats, kid. No private home like where Oscar grew up.

Paul Gonzales won the gold at nineteen, same age as Oscar. Only he was not nearly so blessed. It was said of Gonzales that a lion's heart beat within a sparrow's body. Even as he accepted his medal, he had three broken bones in his right hand, dislocations of the elbow and shoulder, and a broken toe. That would be the story of his pro career as well. He'd grow only to bantamweight, and it seemed as though every time he hit somebody, he broke something else. Today, Gonzales tells kids at the Hollenbeck Youth Center to stay in school and stay off drugs. At thirty-one, he has long since retired, without a championship or big money, without any of what Kid Barrio once expected.

He began calling Oscar a "snake" after a 1993 Los Angeles Times piece in which his former protege charged him with, of all things, forgetting where he came from. "He'd tell everybody he wasn't Mexican," Oscar told the paper. "He was cocky and rude. I'll never make a mistake like that."

Now Gonzales says, "I met him at the airport when he came back from Barcelona. I told him, 'Don't forget where you came from.' And look at him now. Thinks just 'cause he's got money, he can get pussy whenever he wants. Thinks his shit smells rosy."

Gonzales became another guy from East L.A. who found himself rooting for De La Hoya's opponents. Let's see: There was Rafael Ruelas, then 43–1, who had to sneak across the border from the mountain village of Yerba Buena, Mexico, at the age of seven before settling in the San Fernando Valley. Oscar called him "a good little fighter," then knocked him senseless in the second round.

"Oscar's people are picking them right," says Gonzales, unimpressed.

Then there was Genaro "Chicanito" Hernandez, from South-Central L. A. He was 32-0-1. Before the fight Oscar returned to Garfield High School, his alma mater, where he donates money for scholarships. The kids threw eggs at him. It hurt, though not nearly as much as he would hurt his opponent. What De La Hoya did to Hernandez's nose was enough to make Chicanito quit.

"I thought Chicanito would win," Gonzales shrugs.

Then, of course, there was Julio Cesar Chavez, 97-1-1, of Culiacan, the hardscrabble town known as Mexico's Medellin, for its reputation for drugs and violence. The publicity tour began with boos as Oscar was introduced to his hometown crowd at the Olympic Auditorium. But Oscar turned those boos into blood and money.

"Oscar beat a great fighter," says Gonzales. "But that great fighter was already on his way down."

Gonzales's envy is as palpable as his sweat during our sweltering tour of the barrio. He leans forward, an urgent look in his eyes, wanting me so much to understand. "Oscar got lucky, see. Serious luck. Am I ugly? My face ain't scarred and people like me. I play golf, I live in the suburbs, but I come around and help out the kids. There was supposed to be a movie, *The Cop and the Kid*. I don't know what happened. They're selling Oscar to white America. … I was sellable. My story was sellable."

He's giving himself up now, but in doing so he defines another distance, this one almost infinitesimal, but far enough to divide riches from regret. I feel for Gonzales but now admire De La Hoya even more. So close is Palookaville, even for the Golden Boys.

Oscar De La Hoya lives alone in a guarded, gated community. He's got a two-car garage and two bedrooms overlooking the pool. But I couldn't tell you the difference between Oscar's condo and the others. They all have that prefab look. Out front, there's a white Lamborghini and a black BMW, also a license plate mounted on the garage wall, ELA GOLD.

Inside, Oscar sits in a living room adorned with a framed poster of Marilyn Monroe, James Dean, and Humphrey Bogart drinking at a bar. He's watching Entertainment Tonight on a fifty-inch screen. The cast of *Friends* is holding out for more money. "How much are they asking for?" the champ wants to know.

Jennifer Aniston's father, himself an actor, explains that, show business being what it is, he wants his daughter to get all she can while she can. Besides, says Mr. Aniston, "I'd like to keep living in the manner to which I've grown accustomed."

Oscar nods at the screen, as if he knows from experience how this will play out.

Soon, the limousine arrives to take him to Television City to do *The Late Late Show* with Tom Snyder. "I feel blessed," he says. "Nothing has gone wrong. Even things that went wrong went right. I truly feel my mother is looking out for me."

He's said this before. It's part of his routine. But then he surprises me. He says he visits her grave before and after each fight. "That's how I know the round I'll knock them out," he says. "I'm just sitting there, talking to her, and it comes to me. I call out a round. I feel that's the round she wants me to end it. It's been like that for the last eight or nine fights. A number just pops into my head."

It's difficult to imagine Oscar, such a rational kid, so square with common sense, having a discourse with the dead. I ask if he had Chavez losing in the fourth.

"Actually, I had five," he says. "Before the fifth round."

"That's what she told you?"

He shrugs.

The freeway arcs over East Los Angeles, past King Taco. He once told me of meeting his ex-fiancee there. Her name was Veronica. She was a schoolteacher and a beauty queen. "Like someone you'd see on TV," Oscar once said.

I saw them nestling in a booth at Planet Hollywood after the Chavez fight. It seemed as if the whole neighborhood, certainly all those who had dogged him, was falling over one another to pay their respects to the new champ and his girl. "She was a nice girl and everything," he says. "But I can't trust a bit. Not a girl. Can't trust a woman, not at all."

There's a distant look on his face as he stares out the window. The subject is closed. After a beat, he thinks to add, "Now I'm free like a bird. Girls, girls, girls."

He does his own monologue with Tom Snyder, wiping the sweat from his palms just before he goes on. He smiles the right smile, says the right things. Perfection is born of practice, and Oscar De La Hoya knows all the answers, even how to look like he gives a shit. I'm reminded of what he said, almost apologetically, in the country-club ballroom: "Gotta go along with it."

Snyder asks about the Chavez fight.

"I would have loved for it to continue," says De La Hoya. "Just one more round, another minute."

Sure, another minute and the beast would have won by hemorrhage.

Now let's open up the phone lines—North Bergen, New Jersey, you're on. Sounds like a girl up past her bedtime. "You look good to be a boxer," she coos.

Next caller, a teenybopper from Vancouver. "What do you look for in a girl?" she asks.

Oscar flashes the smile that sells deodorant. "Patience and understanding."

The next morning De La Hoya attends a press conference to announce his upcoming fight with Miguel Angel Gonzalez, another Mexican champion, forty-one wins without a loss. And after Gonzalez, there's supposed to be a January rematch with Chavez. Then he's expected to come up to 147 pounds to fight a great if aging welterweight in Pernell Whitaker. Three fights, $25 million.

And a lot more where that came from.

As he suffers no deficiency in attitude or preparation, De La Hoya, now 22–0, figures to run the table. All that's unknown is his chin. But right now, he looks to be what Sugar Ray Leonard was more than a decade ago—the star bright enough to illuminate others, to clarify a new constellation.

"He can make $100 million in purses, easy," says his promoter, Bob Arum.

He can make twice that. The business of boxing is business. But what goes down behind closed doors is far colder than what goes on in the ring. Remember that fighters are typically owned in "pieces," as if investors can buy the piece of their choosing: heart or hands or balls. Remember that the next time a promoter runs over the body of his own broken boxer to crown the new Kid on whom he now has options. Or the next time you hear of rankings purchased in bribe money. Remember it when some sportscaster declares that Ali's mind is "sharp as ever." And in considering this Golden Boy, remember the generations of can't-miss kids now sipping methadone or collecting cans or nursing on that witch's tit called regret.

The great Julio Cesar Chavez sucks on it, too. He supported a whole neighborhood back in Culiacan, his Community. But the whole time, he was borrowing against his next purse. Now he finally gets paid—the De La Hoya fight was twice his biggest payday—and what happens? The IRS takes $2.6 million in current and back taxes. The sanctioning bodies get another $200,000. And Don King, the promoter who had him on allowance all those years, sues for the $1.35 million he says Chavez still owes. Soon after the fight, his wife files for divorce, and the Mexican treasury department wants him for tax fraud.

Not too long ago, he was the greatest fighter in the world. But no one would ask Julio Cesar Chavez, who speaks only Spanish, to smile and sell deodorant. After all, he still stinks of the streets.

"It took him ninety-nine fights to realize what the business of boxing was all about," says De La Hoya.

And by then it was too late.

Chavez was already being escorted to Palookaville, by a pretty boy, no less.

Most fighters go entire careers, wrecking themselves in the process, without ever knowing what De La Hoya somehow knows in his blood. It's a blessing, a survival skill, but also a malignancy. In commerce, as in love, he's bound by suspicion, not sentiment.

"I can't trust anyone," he says. "Sometimes, I don't trust myself."

He'll cut you off and not look back. Al Stankie brought him through the amateur ranks. But before the Olympics, Al Stankie was busted for drunken driving, so he had to go.

Shelly Finkel, a manager especially esteemed by boxing standards, bankrolled De La Hoya's amateur career. Finkel spent more than $100,000 on the fighter and his family. "His father came to me, physically crying, and said, 'My wife is dying, would you help me?'" Finkel recalls. "So I paid for what was necessary. I paid for Oscar's mother's chemotherapy and her burial."

But just after the Olympics, Finkel learned that his services would no longer be needed. Team De La Hoya had a better deal.

The management duo of Steve Nelson and Robert Mittleman had offered a $1 million bonus in return for the standard one-third piece of the fighter. But the money went quickly. Joel De La Hoya bought a new house in Montebello, a suburb of East L.A. His old friend Robert Alcazar—the man who succeeded Stankie as trainer—took his cut. And Oscar bought the Lamborghini. His only reckless period—spending up to $10,000 a week—would last until he fired Nelson and Mittleman in December 1993.

Oscar said he hadn't received his payments on time. But in fact, he never much cared for Mittleman and Nelson. Their final offense was insisting on the palooka-faced trainer, Ortiz. The parties would reach an out-of-court settlement. But things haven't been quite the same between the fighter and his father, who initially sided with the managers.

Today, De La Hoya listens to other grown-ups. There's Mike Hernandez, a respected Chevrolet dealer from East L.A. whom he calls "my adviser." And there's Alcazar's replacement as head trainer, Jesus Rivero, the "Professor," a venerable Mexican who insists that his student study the two Williams: Shakespeare and Pep. Oscar knows the bard even better than the boxer. He's obsessed with betrayal. "Trust?" he says. "I guess I trust my brother, Joel, my little sister, Ceci, my father."

"Your father?"

"What happened caused friction. … But we stuck together."

He doesn't want to talk about his father.

"Do you trust the Professor?"

"Can't say I do, can't say I don't," he says. "I trust him in the ring."

"Your adviser?"

"He's my adviser."

"Yes, but do you trust him?"

"It's tough to say, do you trust somebody."

No, he doesn't trust. And he plays along, using a press agent's patter to guard the interiors of his emotional life. He keeps his distance. But he keeps his dignity, too. And that's the most difficult thing for a fighter to do. I can't say what will become of Oscar De La Hoya, but I can swear what won't. He won't be caught grabbing ass at the bar. He won't make a "comeback" to satisfy various debts to the IRS or an ex-wife or his own unfulfilled promise. He won't go out drooling or shaking. He won't be sold off in pieces, either.

"I own 100 percent of Oscar De La Hoya." His eyes narrow, just a hint of that beast who smells blood with money. "What fighter can say that?"

"Do me a favor, amigo. Get me a picture of Oscar and the boys."

So it begins, the Boy Scout benefit at the Riviera, known for years as "Hogan's Alley" but more recently as "O.J.'s old club." De La Hoya plays with a group from Owens Corning. The caddie is Flip Wilson's son. Oscar has been golfing just a year and a half, minus the months spent in training, and already shoots in the mid-eighties. But more than that is his natural ease in country-club society, so far from the culture of boxing. It's not just the hushed etiquette or the breeze rustling through the eucalyptus trees. Golf is a bloodless sport. And it's difficult to reconcile this kid lining up his putt with the sadist who felt some sort of ecstasy in making homeboy Hernandez "bleed like a fountain."

He sinks a twenty-footer.

"That," he says, "is what makes it all worth it."

The groundskeepers and maintenance men, also born to the barrio, shoot odd sidelong glances his way, not unlike the stare of that sentry back in Quatro Flats. But the look on the women preparing lunch is pure adoration. A blushing volunteer tracks him down on the fairway. She says they met back in '92. He doesn't remember but goes along with it anyway.

The De La Hoya autograph is requested without respite, those autograph hounds still sniffing around. The guys from Owens Corning have gloves and posters for him to sign, too. The club pro apologizes even as he hands Oscar a golf ball.

"I've signed smaller," says Oscar. "Try signing a G-string."

Was that a wink? I can't tell. Soon, he'll have his

picture taken with the crippled Boy Scouts. Finally, when he comes in off the course, an old man rushes to give him a big hug. "Anytime you want to be my guest here, please let me know. Just stay the way you are, young man."

"Excuse me," says Oscar. "I have a previous appointment."

He gives a shrug but not her name. And for a mere moment, his sheepish smile gives way to a shit-eating grin. Then he gets in the tinted cockpit of his six-figure ride, the black BMW, to indulge his secret solitary extravagance: speed. Pedal hits the metal as he heads down Sunset, past all chose brown-faced kids selling maps to the stars, putting all the distance he can between himself and Palookaville.

[PORTRAIT]

TWO VISITS WITH SAM LANGFORD

Sam Langford fought during that period when the art and science of boxing reached an all-time high, and met the best from lightweights through heavyweights. On January 10, 1944, Al Laney found him as he describes in the first of these two columns from the *New York Herald Tribune*. The second column appeared on Christmas Day, 1944, after Laney had conducted a campaign that resulted in the establishment of a $10,000 trust fund for Langford. Langford died in Cambridge, Massachusetts, on January 12, 1956.

AL LANEY

About two weeks ago we began a search through Harlem for Sam Langford, the old Boston Tar Baby. Inquiries up and down Lenox and Seventh Avenues in bars and grills, cigar stores, newsstands and drugstores failed to turn up a lead. Zoot-suited youths accosted on street corners invariably looked blank and asked, "Who he?" A dozen times we were told positively that Sam was dead.

This is the man competent critics said was the greatest fighter in ring history, the man the champions feared and would not fight, the man who was so good he never was given a chance to show how good he really was. You'd think he'd be a hero to every youth in Harlem.

Sam is not dead. We found him at last in a dingy hall bedroom on 139th Street. He was just sitting there on the edge of his bed listening to the radio. That is all there is for Sam to do now, for he is old and blind and penniless. The Negro woman who admitted us said Mr. Langford's room was the third door down a corridor so dark you had to feel your way. Sam stood up when we entered and fumbled for a string attached to a pale bulb in the ceiling. There was a look of surprise on his flat, broad face.

"You come to see me?" he asked with wonder in his low melodious voice. Sam has been sitting there in the dark for a long time and there have been no visitors. It took him some time to understand that this was an interview and there would be a story in the paper.

"What you want to write about old Sam for?" he said. "He ain't no good any more. You ever see me fight?"

We lied to Sam, said we had and that he was the greatest we ever saw. That seemed to please him mightily and he laughed loud. Anyone who never saw Sam in the ring is bound to be surprised at his height. He is only 5 feet 6 1/2 inches and yet at 165 pounds he brought down such giants as Jack Johnson, Harry Wills and the towering Fred Fulton. His short legs, long arms, great shoulders and wide girth give him a curiously gnomelike appearance. All of his 210 pounds now seems to be above the hips. But he is a gnome with a prodigiously broad flat nose, a cauliflower ear and an immense amiability.

Sam receives a few dollars a month from a foundation for the blind. It is not enough but he makes it do. His days are all alike. He rises early and two small boys lead him to a restaurant for breakfast. He is back in his room by one o'clock and then he just sits in the dark until late in the afternoon when he goes out to eat again.

This would seem to be a dreary existence, but Sam never was addicted to thinking or to brooding over his fate in the days when they told him he was lucky to get fights at all, and he does not brood now. We had been led to believe by what we had read that this stepchild of fistiana was a stupid man who had been plucked clean by the thieves and then thrown out to starve. A child of the jungle, they used to call him.

It was therefore a surprise to find that Sam is not stupid. He is even intelligent, though ignorant by the world's standards. He never went to school a day in his life and certainly he is a simple creature, almost childlike. His memory is good, he is an excellent mimic, and you would go far to find a more interesting storyteller.

And all the stories Sam tells are amusing ones. He will not be drawn into telling the other kind. He remembers them, but if you ask him about the old days when he was given the business by all and sundry he chuckles and tells another funny story. He laughs all the time he is talking and his laugh is so infectious, his face so expressive, you forget he is blind. When he tells his stories and laughs he seems almost a happy man. There is no drop of hate in his soul for anyone.

Sam said he was born March 4, 1886, in Weymouth, Nova Scotia, but that is just a date he thought up. He admits he doesn't know, and since he was fighting before 1900 he probably is in the middle sixties. He asked about his old friends among the boxing writers and said be sure to get in that he remembered them and sent his greetings. He said he didn't want anybody to feel sorry for him.

In a way Sam is right. His joviality and cheerfulness in adversity envelop you in sadness but he does not inspire pity. He has somehow achieved the feat of rising above it with simple dignity.

"Don't nobody need to feel sorry for old Sam," he said. "I had plenty good times. I been all over the world. I fought maybe three, four hundred fights and every one was a pleasure. If I just had me a little change in my pocket I'd get along fine."

"Chief," said Sam Langford yesterday, "this gonna be the best Christmas I ever had. Maybe you could put it in the paper."

What Sam wanted was to convey to all his thousands of friends the fact that he is happy and that he understands quite well that it is they who have made it possible. He has a simple faith in the power of the press and he believes that if it is in the paper everyone will see it.

Sam's faith is justified. It is almost a year now since his story was told in this newspaper. At that time Sam was blind and penniless and hungry and he was very lonely indeed. Now he is a man fixed for life so that he never again will be hungry. His friends to the number of several thousand sent money for him, and this money, gathered into a fund, was used to take care of Sam modestly as long as he will live.

Many of these friends never have seen Sam. That is one of his remarkable qualities. You do not have to -know him to be his friend and know the kind of man he is. But Sam's friends did not just contribute months ago and then forget that Christmas was coming. Sam wishes this column to acknowledge, besides greetings by mail, the following gifts:

A fine guitar, three boxes of cigars, two of which were purchased by GIs in post exchanges; a pair of gloves, a bottle of gin, several neckties, an anonymous gift of $5 with which he is to buy the best Christmas dinner he can find; a quantity of hard candy, of which someone remembered that he is immensely fond; and various other items good to eat at Christmastime.

All of these things Sam had around him last night. He had friends around him, too, and there will be friends with him today. A year ago Sam's total wealth was twenty cents. With it he bought a meager breakfast and then he sat the day out on the side of his bed, all alone. No one came to see him, for no one knew he was there. He had been a great man in his day, the famous Boston Tar Baby, the greatest fighter of them all, but now he was long since forgotten, believed by many to be dead.

But this is another Christmas Day. He is not

alone any more, his dingy room is gay with Christmas decorations, and a candle burned in it last night. His belly will be stuffed with turkey and fixin's today and he will play his guitar and sing and he will laugh. To hear Sam laugh and sing is one of the most profound Christmas experiences a man can have.

He cannot see the decorations or the candle's light, but they make a very great difference to him. Sam is by no means a religious man in the conventional sense, but we were wondering last night how many men there are who understand so well as he the real meaning of Christmas.

Sam wants all of his friends to know that he is happy today and we would like them to know, too, that he is the most completely happy man we have ever seen. Not many are able to be completely happy. For most of us there always are reservations of one kind or another. But not for Sam. He is like a child in the enjoyment of his presents and the remembrance of his friends. He is celebrating Christmas in that spirit.

"You see that bottle, Chief?" he said last night.

"If you come back here on the Fourth of July it'll still be some in it. But tomorrow I'm gonna have myself a couple of good belts. Oil myself up some for a little geetar playin'. Boy! Listen to that thing talk. She shore talk sweet, don't she?

"You tell all my friends I'm the happiest man in New York City. I got a geetar and a bottle of gin and money in my pocket to buy Christmas dinner. No millionaire in the world got more than that or anyhow they can't use any more. Tell my friends all about it and tell 'em I said God bless 'em."

SHELBY, 1923

No one else has ever written as well of the backstage, nonathletic or under-the-table aspect of boxing as did John Lardner. It was his opinion that the art of the fight manager reached its zenith when Jack Kearns took Shelby, Montana, in 1923. As Kearns turned in the classic job, so did Lardner when he reconstructed it a quarter of a century later.

JOHN LARDNER

Jack Kearns, a boxing manager who became almost legendary in the prize-fight business between the two World Wars because of his ability to make money in large, bold scoops without recourse to manual labor, visited New York a while back with his current heavyweight fighter. The fighter, Joey Maxim, will not add luster to Kearns' name in history books. He is just a footnote sort of fighter—pedestrian, the critics say, and practically punchless. There was something like boredom in Kearns' voice as he sat on a desk in the offices of the Twentieth Century Sporting Club, in Madison Square Garden, shortly before Maxim's bout with the Swedish champion, Olle Tandberg, and delivered a routine hallelujah to his latest means of support. "This kid is better than Dempsey in most ways," said Kearns. His soft blue eyes stared vacantly at the floor. "He don't hit quite as hard as Dempsey, but otherwise he's better." Since Kearns managed Jack Dempsey when the latter was heavyweight champion of the world, it may be that he holds a lifetime dispensation from some celestial chamber of commerce to misuse Dempsey's name for advertising purposes. At any rate, no thunderbolt split the ceiling to strike him down for his blasphemous words. His audience, composed of managers, trainers, reporters, and press agents, shifted its feet and withheld comment. There was nothing to be said—nothing polite. Then one of the managers, an old-time boxing man, began to warm to the recollection of the team of Dempsey and Kearns. He turned the talk to happier times. "Remember Shelby, Doc?" be asked. (Kearns is known to his contemporaries as Doc.) "You and Dempsey broke three banks in Montana." Kearns' eyes came to life. "We broke four banks," he said. With rising enthusiasm, he went on to describe his withdrawal after the sack of Shelby, Montana, in 1923, with two bags of silver in a railroad caboose. His listeners drew closer. The career and prospects of Joey Maxim were, for the time being and without regrets, tabled.

To boxing people who have heard of the place, the memory of Shelby is precious for many reasons, one of them being that it brought a man of their own profession—namely, Kearns—into single-handed combat with a state 146,997 square miles in area, producing copper, gold, silver, zinc, lead, manganese, oil, coal, grain, and livestock. No one who was involved in the Shelby affair, including Kearns and Dempsey, is any longer a perfectly reliable authority on the facts of the story, owing to the blurring influence of the autobiographical instinct on boxing memoirs. However, investigation shows that Kearns' performance compared favorably—for tenacity, at least—with those of the predatory railroad barons Jay Gould, Daniel Drew, Commodore Vanderbilt, and James J. Hill. As it happened, it was on Hill's Great Northern Railway, which opened up the north of Montana, in the eighteen-eighties, that Kearns rode into the state, with a fiery purpose, and out of it again, with great haste, in 1923. The scope of Kearns' raid has been exaggerated somewhat by his admirers, himself among them, but there is no doubt that it had a profound effect on no fewer than two Montana counties, Toole and Cascade. Furthermore, the name, spirit, and wealth of the whole state were invoked by those Montanans who struggled with Kearns first-hand. They stated more than once at the time that "the honor of all Montana" was at stake. Montana today is perhaps in a sounder financial condition than Kearns, but that only goes to show the extent of its natural resources. It took

an oil strike to draw Kearns to Shelby, in Toole County, in the first place, and it took another oil strike, years later, to complete Toole County's recovery from Kearns.

The raider, who was born John L. McKernan, is now sixty-five years old. He is still a dapper figure when dressed for pleasure, but his hair is thin and a paunch shows at the conjunction of his pants and sweater when he climbs into the ring on business, as he did at the meeting of his man Maxim with Tandberg, in which Maxim won a close decision and both heavyweights disqualified themselves as white hopes for the championship by their gentle work. The bout netted Kearns and his fighter approximately fifteen hundred dollars. The loser, by the terms of an arrangement based on his drawing power, got fifteen thousand dollars. The bout between Dempsey and Tom Gibbons at Shelby on July 4, 1923, brought Kearns and Dempsey nearly three hundred thousand dollars. The loser got nothing whatever. In those days, though, Kearns was forty years old and at the height of his genius.

A good many people in 1923, including writers of newspaper editorials, likened Shelby after the fight to a Belgian village ravaged by the Huns. They ignored or overlooked the fact that Shelby, like no Belgian village on record, had opened the relationship by begging to be taken. Kearns and Dempsey had never heard of Shelby before its citizens went to the trouble of raising a hundred thousand dollars to entice them there. In the popular view, Dempsey was the archfiend of the episode. His reputation as a draft dodger in the First World War, carefully cultivated by managers of rival fighters like Fightin' Bob Martin, the A.E.F. heavyweight champion, made a strong impression on the public; during the Shelby crisis, people were quite willing to consider him a profiteer as well as a slacker. They lost sight of Kearns in Dempsey's shadow. It was only the men directly concerned with financing the Dempsey-Gibbons match who realized that Kearns was the brains and backbone of the visiting party. In language that will not bear repeating, these men marveled at Kearns' almost religious attachment to the principle of collecting all the cash in Montana that was not nailed down.

It was the booster spirit that got Shelby into trouble—the frontier booster spirit, which seems to have been a particularly red-blooded and chuckle-headed variety. Up to 1922, Shelby had been a village populated by four or five hundred cowhands, sheepherders, and dry-dirt farmers. In 1922, oil was struck in the Kevin-Sunburst field, just north of town. The population rose to over a thousand. It was not much of a jump; the significant difference was that all the new citizens had money. Some of them were oil speculators, some of them were real-estate men from the West Coast buying up land to sell to oil speculators. A few were merchants selling standard boomtown merchandise, much of it liquid, to the oilmen and the real-estate men. Kearns had not yet seen Shelby with his own eyes when he first tried to describe it to skeptics in the East a year later, but his description was not far wrong. "It's one of these wide-open towns," he said spaciously. "Red Dog Saloon, gambling hells—you know, like you see in the movies." It was old Blackfoot country. South of Shelby, the Marias River wound toward the site of a vanished fur-trading post on the Missouri. Not far north was the Canadian border. The Great Northern Railway ran west from Shelby to Glacier Park and the Pacific, east to Duluth and the Twin Cities, south a hundred miles to the nearest real town, Great Falls. In Shelby proper, there were the railroad depot, a few stores, a few houses, a couple of new banks, the Silver Grill Hotel, where fifty extra beds filled the lobby at the height of the boom, and half a dozen saloons.

In one of the saloons, on an evening in January 1923, a bunch of the boys, all of them leading citizens, were whooping it up in a civic-minded way. The party was headed by Mayor James A. Johnson, a large man of fifty-eight who had made a comfortable fortune ranching and had added to it in the boom through oil leases and the ownership of the First State Bank of Shelby. Sitting around him were men named Zimmerman, Sampson, Dwyer, and Schwartz. It was Sam Sampson, a storekeeper and landowner, who first suggested that the best way to make the nation and the world Shelby-conscious—that being the object of everyone in town who owned property—would be to stage a fight there for the heavyweight championship of the world. Dempsey was champion. The two most talked-of contenders for his title at that time were Harry Wills, a Negro, and Tom Gibbons, a white man from St. Paul. The barroom committee skipped lightly over Wills. Gibbons was its choice on two counts: the color of his pelt and the fact that he was a Northwestern man, from a state with which Montana had close commercial connections. The committee toasted Gibbons, Shelby, and itself.

Then Sampson began to send telegrams in all directions. He wired Dempsey and Gibbons and their managers, and received no replies, which was not surprising, in view of Shelby's overwhelming anonymity. He also sent a telegram to Mike Collins, a journalist and boxing matchmaker in Minneapolis. Collins, a friend of Gibbons, agreed to come to Shelby at the committee's expense and study the possibilities. His reaction on stepping off the train at the Shelby depot was recorded by himself at a later date. "I was startled," he said. Shelby was small and raw beyond the power of a city man's imagination. Mayor Johnson and Sampson led Collins across a few roads of the Great Plains to a saloon, where the Mayor gave Collins the impression that Mose Zimmerman, another committeeman who owned land, was ready to finance the championship fight out of his own pocket. To substantiate this, the Mayor rounded up Zimmerman, who denied indignantly that he was ready to contribute anything but a small, decent, proportionate piece of the total. The Mayor looked sad. Collins walked back to the depot to catch the 8 p.m. train for Minneapolis. As things turned out, he was the first of a series of people who started to wash their hands of Shelby by catching a train. They were all called back at the last minute. A Fate straight out of Sophocles had matters in her grip.

Before the eight-o'clock train arrived, Mayor Johnson arranged a mass meeting of citizens in a saloon. Collins was persuaded to address it. He said starkly that Shelby had no boxing arena, no population, and, as far as he could see, no money. "You would need a hundred thousand dollars before you even talk to Dempsey and Gibbons," he added. At this point, Shelby startled him for the second time. The Mayor and his friends raised twenty-six thousand dollars on the spot, the contributors receiving vouchers for ringside tickets to the fight in exchange. Collins noted that the vouchers were marked July 4. The Phantom battle already had a date and a ticket sale. This show of *sang-froid* won him over. A short time afterward, he set out, in the company of a gentleman named Loy J. Molumby, state commander of the American Legion, to stump Montana for the balance of the money. Traveling from town to town in Molumby's private airplane, they brought the total of cash on hand to a hundred and ten thousand dollars in a little more than a week's time. The moment had come, Collins freely admitted, to let Dempsey and Gibbons in on the secret. It was now, he said, just a matter of convincing them that there was such a place as Shelby and showing them the money.

The two things were achieved in reverse order. It was after seeing the money that Dempsey and Gibbons—or, rather, their managers, Kearns and Eddie Kane—brought themselves to believe in Shelby. The rest of the country, having seen no money, did not believe in Shelby for some time to come. At the beginning of May, the boxing critic of the New York *Tribune,* Jack Lawrence, spoke of a meeting that would take place soon at Madison Square Garden between the Dempsey and Gibbons parties. "There," he wrote scornfully, "they will probably hear a counterproposition from the lips of Tex Rickard that will waft Shelby, Montana, back to the pastoral obscurity from which it emerged so suddenly."

Lawrence was wrong. Kearns and Kane bypassed New York and Rickard and went to Chicago to inspect the cash and negotiate the Shelby deal with Molumby and Collins, who were now the accredited agents of Mayor Johnson's town. It is apparent that both managers were remarkable for the grandeur of their vision. Kane showed it by agreeing to let Dempsey and Kearns have everything the bout drew, up to three hundred thousand dollars, at the box office in Shelby, if there was a Shelby, before taking a percentage for Gibbons. The Gibbons share was to be fifty per cent of the receipts from three hundred thousand to six hundred thousand dollars, and twenty-five per cent of everything above that. Three hundred thousand dollars was exactly what Kearns and Dempsey had made from a spectacular million-dollar-gate fight with Georges Carpentier, which Tex Rickard had promoted two years before on the threshold of New York City. Kearns was now counting on gouging the same sum from an infinitesimal cowtown that had no boxing ring, no grandstand, no professional promoter, and no large city within five hundred miles. At least, he said he was counting on that. Almost no one in New York believed there would be a fight. Kearns' friends suspected, with characteristic misanthropy, that Doc was up to some sort of practice ruse to keep his hand in and his brain lean and sharp for coming campaigns. Rickard, the most famous promoter of the day, who did not think much of either Gibbons or Wills as an opponent for Dempsey, having sped Kearns West with a tolerant wink, went on with plans for his own notion of a Dempsey match with the Argentine Luis Firpo, for autumn delivery.

Kearns, however, was in earnest. It pleased his fancy to undertake this Western adventure on his own. He wanted for once to be free from Eastern entanglements, free from his professional peers. Gibbons and Kane, the parties of the second part, would be amateurs at Shelby in everything but name. At Shelby, every power, privilege, and bargaining weapon would belong to Kearns. If he could carry three hundred thousand dollars out of a town of one thousand population, he would become immortal in his profession. If he couldn't, he had dictated terms that said firmly that all money paid to him and Dempsey in advance was theirs to keep. If they got three hundred thousand dollars, there would be a fight; if they didn't, there would be no fight, and no rebate. Molumby agreed, on behalf of Mayor Johnson, to deliver a second installment of a hundred thousand to Kearns on June 15, and a third, and last, on July 2, two days before the fight. This was Molumby's last major gesture in connection with the Dempsey–Gibbons match. Like half a dozen other Montanans who tried to learn the boxing business in the next few weeks, he flunked the course.

A slight difficulty occurred in the secondary negotiations between Kearns and Kane. The difficulty was that they had not spoken to each other for four years and had no wish to start speaking now. Kearns says today that he does not remember the reason for the breach, which may or may not be true; boxing men are usually shy about revealing the causes of their Grade A feuds—the ones that last anywhere from a year to life. Quartered two floors apart in the Morrison Hotel in Chicago, Kane and Kearns conferred by messenger. The messenger was Collins. One question was who was to referee the fight. It was purely nominal, for Kearns had already decided on his good friend Jim Dougherty, sometimes known as the Baron of Leiperville, Pennsylvania. After four trips by Collins up and down the hotel's emergency stairway, Kane accepted Dougherty. He had no choice. Kearns, as the champion's manager, was in command. Kane, managing the challenger—and a poorly recommended challenger, at that, in the opinion of most critics— could consider himself lucky to have gained a chance at the title for Gibbons. That chance was something, though Gibbons was older and smaller than Dempsey. Beyond it, there was a possibility of making some money if the fight was highly successful, which was the dream that Mayor Johnson had sold to Collins and Collins to Kane. Kane and Gibbons were gambling, like the men of Shelby and the men of the rest of Montana who backed them. That explains, in part, the deep affection Montana came to feel for Gibbons as the time of the fight drew near.

A few days after the terms were signed, Collins, as "matchmaker," or supervisor of arrangements, announced the ticket price scale: from fifty dollars, ringside, to twenty dollars for the rear seats. There were no seats at the moment, but Mayor Johnson had persuaded Major J. E. Lane, a local lumber merchant, to build an arena at the edge of town to accommodate forty thousand people. There was no money for Major Lane, but the Mayor got him to take a seventy-thousand-dollar chattel mortgage on the arena. Training camps were staked out for both fighters. On May 16, Kearns entrained for Montana with a staff of sparring partners for Dempsey, who made his own way there from his home in Salt Lake City. Kearns was glad to leave the decadent cities of the East, where the newspapers, when they mentioned Shelby at all, still questioned the reality of the fight and half questioned the reality of Shelby. He found Shelby in a holiday mood. The Mayor and his friends had recovered from the strain of getting up the first hundred thousand dollars and had not yet begun to worry about finding the remaining two hundred thousand. The ticket sale would take care of that. Kearns beamed upon these unsophisticated burghers with boots on their feet and guns in their belts. He addressed them at a Chamber of Commerce luncheon at the Silver Grill. With all the sincerity he could muster on short notice, he told them that Gibbons was a great fighter, "the best boxer in the world." "I would not be surprised," Kearns told the meeting lovingly, "if the winner of this contest fought Harry Wills right here in Shelby on Labor Day. You will be the fight capital of the nation. We have come here," he added, "at something of a sacrifice, since we were offered half a million dollars for the same fight in New York. However, Shelby spoke first, and Shelby wins out." Then Kearns took a rapid look at Shelby, whose facilities could all be seen at a glance with the naked eye, and caught the six o'clock train to Great Falls. All Montana, and Shelby in particular, was well pleased with itself at this point. It is hard to say at just what hour between then and June 15, the first day of open crisis, misgivings began to set in. They must have come soonest to Johnson and Molumby, who were in

charge of the ticket sale and the cashbox. Kearns ostensibly had no notion of how things were going. When he was told, Montana was stunned by the change in the manner of the free-and-easy stranger.

Kearns had made his base in Great Falls, partly because it was a town of thirty thousand, which offered some freedom of movement, and partly because Dempsey was training there, at Great Falls Park, a mile or so outside the city limits. Before June 15, Dempsey trained well and seemed happy. The park, in a hollow in the hills of Cascade County, just east of the Missouri River and in sight of the Little and Big Belt Mountains and the Birdtail Divide, was a pleasant place surrounded by cottonwood trees and had formerly been a scene of revelry. Dempsey lived and sparred in a roadhouse that prohibition and repeated government raids had closed down. Sometimes the champion fished in the Missouri. He had a pet cow, a Hereford bull, a wolf cub, and a bulldog in camp, as well as two of his brothers, Johnny and Bernie; his trainer, Jerry (the Greek) Luvadis; and his stooge, Joe Benjamin, with whom he played pinochle. His sparring partners ranged from giants like Big Ben Wray, seven feet two inches tall, to small, clever middleweights who could simulate Gibbons' style. Gibbons trained in Shelby. He lived with his wife and children in a house on the great, treeless plain, not far from the arena. If anything more was needed to make Gibbons a favorite and Dempsey unpopular in Shelby after June 15, Gibbons' choice of training quarters did it. The town saw him and his family every day. Gibbons at that time was thirty-four, six years older than Dempsey. He had had a long and fairly successful career among middleweights and light heavyweights, though the gifted little Harry Greb had beaten him just the year before. He was a polite and colorless man, with a slim waist, a big chest, and a high shock of pompadoured hair.

On June 15, the day appointed for the payment of the second hundred thousand dollars to Kearns and Dempsey, Kearns went to the Great Falls station to take a train to Shelby. He says now that he was going, in all innocence, to ask Mayor Johnson for the money, that he did not know that the Mayor and Molumby were at that moment wretchedly chewing cigars in a room in the Park Hotel in Great Falls, having just confessed to George H. Stanton, the leading banker of Great Falls, that the day of reckoning found them approximately ninety-eight per cent short. They asked him what to do. Stanton, like all Montanans, had followed the Shelby adventure closely. As the principal capitalist of that part of the state, he had followed it more closely than most, and he probably had a fair notion of the truth before he heard it from the unhappy promoters. However, he told them it was a hell of a note, and he sent someone to get Kearns off the train. Kearns came to the hotel room, looking hopeful. It was his first business contact with Stanton; it would have been better for Stanton if it had been his last. The promoters explained the situation, or what they could understand of it. They admitted frankly that it confused them. It seemed that a great many tickets that had been mailed out, unbonded, to various parts of the state and country were not yet paid for. It seemed that expenses were unexpectedly large. It appeared that there was sixteen hundred dollars in cash on hand for Kearns and Dempsey. Whatever suspicions Kearns may have had before this, the cold facts undoubtedly shocked him. He flew into a rage.

"Why don't *you* take over the promotion and the sale?" suggested Stanton. "From all I can see, you own the fight right now."

"I won't promote!" screamed Kearns. "These guys are the promoters. I'm trying to train a fighter. Let them get our money up or there won't be any fight."

Kearns left the room in a black mood. He went back to the hotel that evening, at Stanton's invitation, and found that most of the money in Great Falls was represented there: Stanton, president of the Stanton Trust & Savings Bank; Dan Tracey, hotel owner; Russell and Arthur Strain, department-store owners; J. W. Speer, lawyer and former judge; and Shirley Ford, vice-president of the Great Falls National Bank. From there on, Kearns was told, the honor of Montana was at stake. The fight would have new promoters. The money would be raised. It was raised, within twenty-four hours. At 5:15 p.m. the next day, June 16, the press was summoned to see Stanton present Kearns with a check for a hundred thousand dollars, seventeen hours and a quarter after the deadline of midnight, June 15. Kearns put the check in his pocket and congratulated Montana. "A dead-game state," he said. Stanton accepted his kind words modestly, though it must be said that the newspapermen present got the impression that he himself had put up seventy-three thousand dollars of the money, which was not strictly true. He had supplied cash in that amount,

but it was underwritten almost entirely by Mayor Jim Johnson, of Shelby, with land and oil leases from his own estate. The Strain brothers and the O'Neill brothers, Lou and John, who were oilmen, made up the balance. While Molumby and Mayor Johnson sat humbly by—the latter quite silent about his contribution to the salvation of Montana's honor—Dan Tracey delivered a tough speech. The Great Falls committee had appointed Tracey head man of the fight. The old promoters, he said, were through as head men. He would protect the interest of his Great Falls friends. He would see that they got every nickel back. He would countersign all checks from now on. He paused, and Kearns advanced to shake him by the hand. "This reassures me," said Kearns. "I will stick by Shelby and ignore the countless offers I have got from other states for this fight. I am sure," he added thoughtfully, "that we won't have any trouble with the last hundred thousand dollars—due midnight, July second." Mayor Johnson mopped his brow with a handkerchief. "This is a great relief," he told the press. "I wasn't cut out to be a boxing promoter." Molumby had nothing to say. Earlier that day, he had been denounced by an American Legion post in St. Louis for involving the Legion in Dempsey's affairs.

The reign of Tracey as head man lasted eleven days. It was a time of stress and brooding. The backers of the fight knew that since raising the second hundred thousand dollars had been like pulling teeth, the collection of the third hundred thousand would be on the order of a major amputation. The advance sale of tickets brought in no money to speak of. People could not be expected to buy tickets unless they were sure the fight would take place, and the promoters could not persuade the strong-minded Kearns to guarantee a fight before he was sure of the money. The Great Northern canceled a plan to run special trains from the East and the Pacific Coast. The promoters and their friends snarled at Kearns whenever they saw him, and nervously fondled the butts of their guns. Frank Walker, of Butte, Montana, a lawyer and later Postmaster General under Franklin Roosevelt, came to Great Falls to add weight to the heckling of Kearns. Kearns, however, rode his choppy course serenely and nonchalantly, true to his lofty principle of three hundred thousand dollars or no contest. The strain was much harder on Dempsey than on Dempsey's manager. If Kearns was Public

Enemy No. I to the financiers of Montana, Dempsey was the people's choice for the part. He was sharply aware of it and of the artillery on the hip of nearly everyone he saw. He said later that he pleaded with Kearns, to no avail, at this time to waive the final payment, to promise a fight, and to take over the box-office management. The champion's state of mind showed in his work. He looked slow and easy to hit in training, and his sparring partners complained of his viciousness when he hit them. On his twenty-eighth birthday, June 24, seemingly angry at his failure to catch Jack Burke, a middleweight, he knocked down another sparring partner seven times in five rounds and broke the jaw of the giant Wray, who subsequently took his meals through a tube.

The crises came fast now. On June 26, Stanton, conferring in Shelby with Tracey and Mayor Johnson, who had been reduced to assistant promoter, was told that the lumber merchant and the contractors were about to foreclose their mortgage on the arena. Stanton stalked angrily to the railroad station, but he was called back into conference, inevitably, at the last minute. Half an hour later, he announced that the creditors had agreed to accept payment on a pro-rata basis from the gate receipts. He said that all was well. Tracey, the tough talker of June 16, could not bring himself to share this view. The mortgage crisis had broken his spirit. On June 27, he resigned his job. "The money my people put up is nowhere in sight that I can see," he said. "I can't be sure they'll get it back, and I'm through." Shelby was excited the next day by a telegram received by Mayor Johnson from Minneapolis signed "Louis W. Till," which it assumed to be from Louis Hill, board chairman of the Great Northern, assuring the Mayor that he was "on way with cash and securities so Tom can have chance to put profiteering Dempsey in hospital." The wire turned out to be a hoax. On June 29, Stanton made a final, desperate move. After consulting with Great Falls leaders on a list of names and sending telegrams to all parts of the state, he proclaimed that "twenty lifelong friends" had pledged five thousand dollars each to meet the final payment to Kearns and "save the honor of Montana." The announcement was given out now, Stanton said, to dispel doubts that the fight would be held, but the payment to Kearns would not be made until the agreed date of July 2, because, he went on sulkily, some of the new sponsors "are disposed to follow the lead taken by the champion's manager and adhere rigidly to the condi-

tions of the contract." It was their opinion, he said, that Kearns "would get out of the fight if he could." Enlarging on the patriotism of his twenty lifelong friends, Stanton said that cancelation of the bout "would have cast reflections on the state that would have been far-reaching in effect." The Northwest, he added, would now save the fight; the Dakotas, Wyoming, Idaho, Washington, Oregon, and western Canada would send at least fifteen thousand people. The members of the committee would take a loss but "are game enough to see this thing through."

Kearns, ignoring the slurs in this manifesto upon his good faith, expressed satisfaction. Dempsey forced a smile and acknowledged the gameness of all Montanans. But on July 2, facing the press, with Kearns present, in Great Falls, Stanton revealed that he had been unable to cash the pledges of his lifelong friends. Eight of them had come through as advertised, he said, but in the circumstances he did not feel like keeping their money. He looked defiantly at Kearns. Kearns shrugged and retired to discuss things with a lieutenant of his from New York, Dan McKetrick. Then he told Stanton that he would make the "gamble" that had been forced on him. He would take over the fight, and the gate receipts with it. From that moment, the concern about paying Kearns was outweighed by a vivid fear that Kearns and Dempsey would slip across the border before July 4 with the money they had already collected, leaving Shelby to whistle for its world-championship fight. There is no evidence that either man contemplated doing this, but practically everyone in Montana was convinced that both of them did contemplate it. Kearns says he remembers Frank Walker, in a state of deep emotion, shaking his fist beneath his nose on July 3, and warning him not to attempt to escape.

Shelby had built up to the fight, within its limits. There were concession booths and stands all the way from Main Street to the arena. Entertainers had come from every corner of the state. A tent show called the Hyland-Welty Comedians was playing the town; it starred a certain Patricia Salmon, the toast of the out-of-town reporters, who for fifty dollars a week did three song spots a day, yodeled in front of the curtain, and played the lead in *Which One Shall I Marry, Thorns and Orange Blossoms, The Tie That Binds,* and *The Sweetest Girl in Dixie.* An acquaintance of mine from Billings, Montana, drove to Shelby for the fight with his father, an early patriotic ticket buyer. The sign he remembers best on Main Street was "Aunt Kate's Cathouse." All tourists slept in their automobiles the night of July 3. The great Northwestern migration to Shelby had not materialized, but there were enough cars parked on the plain by the arena to show that there was interest in the fight. Part of this interest was speculative; many people had not bought tickets, but they counted on getting in anyway.

Dempsey came from Great Falls in a private railroad car on July 4, arriving in the early afternoon. A switch engine pulled his car to a siding near the arena, where a crowd of men instantly surrounded it. "There were no cheers," recalls Dempsey. His party, which included a Chicago detective named Mike Trant and a celebrated hanger-on of the time, "Senator" Wild Bill Lyons, both strongly and ostentatiously armed, took counsel. Some of the crowd was trying to climb aboard. Lyons told the engineer to keep the engine hooked on and to run the car up and down the siding till it was time for Dempsey to get off. When that time came, the crowd pressed close around the champion, but there were, according to Dempsey, no gunshots or blows. "Trying to run out, were you?" called some of the men. An emissary from the ringside reported that it was too early for Dempsey's entrance, since the program had been delayed. The crowd, however, got solidly behind Dempsey in a physical sense and pushed him firmly to the arena doors, where he waited with half a dozen retainers by a soft-drink stand, listening to the comments on his character and lineage.

The reason for the delay was the public's reluctance to pay the official prices for tickets. Kearns had opened the gates in the morning, after surrendering five hundred dollars from the advance sale for the privilege to a crew of federal revenue men who were on hand looking closely and hungrily after their country's interests. At noon, however, there were only fifteen hundred people in the grandstand to watch the first preliminary bout. Thousands milled around outside the gates, many of them shouting, "We'll come in for ten dollars!" These were the aristocrats of the mob, and Kearns began to accommodate them at two-thirty, while people inside pushed down from high seats to empty ringside seats, the working press sweltered over typewriters almost too hot to touch, and two bands—the Montana State Elks band on one side of the ring and the Scottish Highlanders of Calgary on the other—alternately administered soothing music. A blind war veteran was singing a ballad in the ring when Kearns finally was overrun by the rest of the crowd outside, which came in free. Dempsey entered at three-thirty-six, thirty-six minutes late. "It was the most hostile crowd a heavyweight champion ever faced," he said a few years later, through a ghost writer, and he was probably right. There was some hissing, he recalls, but mostly "sullen silence." Gibbons made it harder for him by delaying his arrival till three forty-five and taking ten minutes to have his hands taped in the ring. A few empty bottles descended near Dempsey's corner, tossed by spectators who blamed the champion for the delay. Dodging glassware in the corner with Dempsey were Kearns and Bill Lyons, who wore chaps and a sombrero as well as his arsenal. A number of what Kearns called "my Chicago hard guys" sat watchfully at the ringside just below.

It was a very bad fight. Dempsey, outweighing Gibbons—a hundred and eighty-eight pounds to a hundred and seventy-four—but stale and nervous, could not land his punches squarely. It was widely said later that he would not, out of fear for his safety, but that theory conflicts with the character and testimony of Dempsey and the opinion of expert eyewitnesses. Gibbons won a few of the early rounds. He opened a cut over Dempsey's eye in the second, and Dempsey complained afterward that Kearns, never the most sure-handed of seconds, poured cut medicine into the eye between rounds, making him half blind until the seventh. From the sixth round on, it was Dempsey's fight, easily. The crowd stopped crying "Kill him, Tommy!" and cried "Hang on!" That was all Gibbons tried to do—he had every reason to know he was working for nothing, and Dempsey's strength had soon made him sure he couldn't win. Gibbons scored one moral triumph when he survived the twelfth round, a new record against Dempsey, and another when he survived the fifteenth, and last, and forced the bout to a decision. The last round was one long clinch; Gibbons wrapped his arms around Dempsey, and the onlookers shouted derisively at the champion and threw cushions. Gibbons made no objection to Referee Dougherty's decision for Dempsey. Neither did the crowd.

Dempsey got out with the utmost dispatch when the verdict had been given. The Chicago hard guys, led by Detective Trant, hustled him aboard the private car on the siding. At the Shelby station, his car was hooked to a train for Great Falls. He spent the night at the Park Hotel in Great Falls and caught a regular train the next day for Salt Lake City. Both of Dempsey's eyes were slightly discolored when he boarded the Salt Lake train and exchanged a few last words with residents of Great Falls who came to see him off. "Don't hurry back!" called his well-wishers. "I won't, boys!" said Dempsey sincerely.

Kearns' departure from Montana was a little more complicated. To this day, he holds to the colorful view that he narrowly escaped injury or death from the guns of the West in getting out with the money. The money, the proceeds of the last day's ticket sale, amounted to about eighty thousand dollars in silver and bills. Kearns and McKetrick counted it in the presence of the federal tax men and stuffed it into a couple of canvas sacks. It is altogether possible that if Kearns had then honored an earlier promise to meet with certain fight fans and Shelby citizens in a saloon to talk things over before saying goodbye, he and the cash would not have left the state intact. The temper of Shelby needed only a sprinkling of ninety-proof rye to boil over. But Kearns, holding to his higher purpose, which was to keep all the money, less tax, broke the date. He and McKetrick made straight from the box office for a caboose attached to a locomotive that stood waiting in the twilight at the station. The getaway transportation had been chartered with the help of the federal men. As Kearns and McKetrick boarded the caboose, they observed in the street nearby the shadowy figure of a small man with a ukelele. This was the late Hype Igoe, a New York sportswriter with a turn for minstrelsy, who, having written his fight piece and lingered in Shelby to take on fuel, was delicately strumming chords for his own entertainment. "This is the New York Special, Hype," called Kearns. Igoe accepted the invitation and got aboard, and the special rolled out of Shelby.

Still playing a cautious game, the Kearns party spent the rest of the night in the cellar of a barbershop in Great Falls. Kearns passed up the Salt Lake City express the next day, and for five hundred dollars, out of one of the canvas bags, hired a locomotive and coach from the Great Northern's Great Falls agent. He and his friends joined Dempsey the next day.

On July 9 began a series of events that canonized Kearns in the boxing business. The Stanton Trust & Savings Bank of Great Falls closed its doors that day. Stanton insisted that the closing had no connection with the Dempsey–Gibbons fight; he blamed it on postwar conditions in general. However, all other reports from Montana then and later agreed that the public knowledge of Stanton's association with the fight caused a run on the bank, which the banker could not meet because of the temporary withdrawal of seventy-three thousand dollars in cash from his own account to pay Kearns on June 16. The state bank examiner, L.Q. Skelton, came to Great Falls to take over the bank. He saved himself an extra trip to the neighborhood by taking over Mayor Johnson's First State Bank of Shelby as well, Johnson having stopped payments to depositors on the morning of July 10. It was now revealed for the first time that much of the cash paid by Stanton to Kearns had been secured by Johnson with his personal property, which he began making over to Stanton after the fight. On July 11, the First State Bank of Joplin, Montana, an affiliate of Stanton's bank, closed down. Newspaper reports from Joplin stated that all closings to date were "generally accredited" to the championship boxing bout in Shelby. Boxing people never doubted this for a moment. Kearns and Dempsey have been pointed out ever since as winners over three Montana banks. The better informed students of the situation, like Kearns, feel that the score should be four, for on August 16 of the same year, almost unnoticed by the press, the First National Bank of Shelby was closed by order of its board of directors, following withdrawals of something like a hundred thousand dollars in the first month after the fight. This left Shelby with, for the time being, no banks at all and practically no assets. The oil boom subsided not long afterward. The arena was torn down and the lumber salvaged by the mortgage holders.

Kearns says that Mayor Johnson wrote to Dempsey and himself that summer asking for a loan of twenty-five thousand dollars, and that it was granted, and repaid within a year. It is certain that the Mayor was comfortably off when he died, in 1938, thanks mainly to another strike in the Kevin-Sunburst oil field a few years after the first one, which reanimated the town. The career of Patricia Salmon, the tent-show actress, took an opposite course. Her New York press reviews from Shelby in 1923 won her a contract with Florenz Ziegfeld and a season in the "Follies." It was thought for a time that she, Dempsey, and Kearns (and the United States government) were the beneficiaries of the Shelby fight. But Miss Salmon was a one-year wonder. Her star declined as Johnson's rose, and in 1928 she was towed off the floor of Madison Square Garden with a set of swollen feet after performing consecutively for a hundred and thirty-five hours and forty minutes in a dance marathon that she had hoped would bring her publicity and another job in the theater.

A word should be said about the early unpopularity of Dempsey, for it contributed much to his discomfort at Shelby and to the public's reaction in Montana and elsewhere. Like other entertainers in both World Wars, Dempsey, in 1918, did a certain amount of morale building among war workers. There is evidence that he was popular with sports followers, including some Army and Navy men, in 1919, when he won the championship, and that the change did not set in until after managers of heavyweights with war records, all of them outclassed as prize fighters by Dempsey, began to play up their wartime service in their interviews and advertisements. A photograph was widely circulated of Dempsey striking a pose in a shipyard during the war with a workman's tool in his hands and patent-leather shoes on his feet. He was formally acquitted of draft evasion in 1920. From the time he lost the championship to Gene Tunney, in 1926, he was immensely popular in America and abroad. However, it was plain to anyone who knew him that he never forgot certain aspects of his public life between 1919 and 1926. He was commissioned as a physical director in the Coast Guard in the last war. I saw him during preparations for the Okinawa landing in 1945. He had obtained leave to go to Okinawa on a Coast Guard ship and could hardly control his excitement; in fact, it was almost necessary to gag him to maintain security before the operation began. He went ashore on the Marines' sector of the front shortly after D Day. He did not stay long, since he served no military purpose there, but it probably helped to compensate him for an hour spent with a sharp-tongued crowd outside the wooden arena at Shelby in 1923. Shelby paid as it went for its attitude toward Dempsey, but, like Kearns, he was not an easy man to satisfy.

[FICTION]

CHAMPION

Ring Lardner, rightly, never thought this one of his better stories. In Midge Kelly he drew a caricature, not a character, and yet, largely because a successful boxing movie was made from it, it became Lardner's best-known work.

RING LARDNER

Midge Kelly scored his first knockout when he was seventeen. The knockee was his brother Connie, three years his junior and a cripple. The purse was a half dollar given to the younger Kelly by a lady whose electric had just missed bumping his soul from his frail little body.

Connie did not know Midge was in the house, else he never would have risked laying the prize on the arm of the least comfortable chair in the room, the better to observe its shining beauty. As Midge entered from the kitchen, the crippled boy covered the coin with his hand, but the movement lacked the speed requisite to escape his brother's quick eye.

"Watcha got there?" demanded Midge.

"Nothin'," said Connie.

"You're a one-legged liar!" said Midge.

He strode over to his brother's chair and grasped the hand that concealed the coin.

"Let loose!" he ordered.

Connie began to cry.

"Let loose and shut up your noise," said the elder, and jerked his brother's hand from the chair arm.

The coin fell onto the bare floor. Midge pounced on it. His weak mouth widened in a triumphant smile.

"Nothin', huh?" he said. "All right, if it's nothin' you don't want it."

"Give that back," sobbed the younger.

"I'll give you a red nose, you little sneak! Where'd you steal it?"

"I didn't steal it. It's mine. A lady give it to me after she pretty near hit me with a car."

"It's a crime she missed you," said Midge.

Midge started for the front door. The cripple picked up his crutch, rose from his chair with difficulty, and, still sobbing, came toward Midge. The latter heard him and stopped.

"You better stay where you're at," he said.

"I want my money," cried the boy.

"I know what you want," said Midge.

Doubling up the fist that held the half dollar, he landed with all his strength on his brother's mouth. Connie fell to the floor with a thud, the crutch tumbling on top of him. Midge stood beside the prostrate form.

"Is that enough?" he said. "Or do you want this, too?"

And he kicked him in the crippled leg.

"I guess that'll hold you," he said.

There was no response from the boy on the floor. Midge looked at him a moment, then at the coin in his hand, and then went out into the street, whistling.

An hour later, when Mrs. Kelly came home from her day's work at Faulkner's Steam Laundry, she found Connie on the floor, moaning. Dropping on her knees beside him, she called him by name a score of times. Then she got up and, pale as a ghost, dashed from the house. Dr. Ryan left the Kelly abode about dusk and walked toward Halsted Street. Mrs. Dorgan spied him as he passed her gate.

"Who's sick, Doctor?" she called.

"Poor little Connie," he replied. "He had a bad fall."

"How did it happen?"

"I can't say for sure, Margaret, but I'd almost bet he was knocked down."

"Knocked down!" exclaimed Mrs. Dorgan. "Why, who——?"

"Have you seen the other one lately?"

"Michael? No, not since mornin'. You can't be thinkin——"

"I wouldn't put it past him, Margaret," said the doctor gravely. "The lad's mouth is swollen and cut, and his poor, skinny little leg is bruised. He surely didn't do it to himself and I think Ellen suspects the other one."

"Lord save us!" said Mrs. Dorgan. "I'll run over and see if I can help."

"That's a good woman," said Dr. Ryan, and went on down the street.

Near midnight, when Midge came home, his mother was sitting at Connie's bedside. She did not look up.

"Well," said Midge, "what's the matter?"

She remained silent. Midge repeated his question.

"Michael, you know what's the matter," she said at length.

"I don't know nothin'," said Midge.

"Don't lie to me, Michael. What did you do to your brother?"

"Nothin'."

"You hit him."

"Well, then, I hit him. What of it? It ain't the first time."

Her lips pressed tightly together, her face like chalk, Ellen Kelly rose from her chair and made straight for him. Midge backed against the door.

"Lay off'n me, Ma. I don't want to fight no woman."

Still she came on, breathing heavily.

"Stop where you're at, Ma," he warned.

There was a brief struggle and Midge's mother lay on the floor before him.

"You ain't hurt, Ma. You're lucky I didn't land good. And I told you to lay off'n me."

"God forgive you, Michael!"

Midge found Hap Collins in the showdown game at the Royal.

"Come on out a minute," he said.

Hap followed him out on the walk.

"I'm leavin' town for a w'ile," said Midge.

"What for?"

"Well, we had a little run-in up to the house. The kid stole a half buck off'n me, and when I went after it he cracked me with his crutch. So I nailed him. And the old lady came at me with a chair and I took it off'n her and she fell down."

"How is Connie hurt?"

"Not bad."

"What are you runnin' away for?"

"Who the hell said I was runnin' away? I'm sick and tired o' gettin' picked on; that's all. So I'm leavin' for a w'ile and I want a piece o' money."

"I ain't only got six bits," said Happy.

"You're in bad shape, ain't you? Well, come through with it."

Happy came through.

"You oughtn't to hit the kid," he said.

"I ain't astin' you who can I hit," snarled Midge. "You try to put somethin' over on me and you'll get the same dose. I'm goin' now."

"Go as far as you like," said Happy, but not until he was sure that Kelly was out of hearing.

Early the following morning, Midge boarded a train for Milwaukee. He had no ticket, but no one knew the difference. The conductor remained in the caboose.

On a night six months later, Midge hurried out of the "stage door" of the Star Boxing Club and made for Duane's saloon, two blocks away. In his pocket were twelve dollars, his reward for having battered up one Demon Dempsey through the six rounds of the first preliminary.

It was Midge's first professional engagement in the manly art. Also it was the first time in weeks that he had earned twelve dollars.

On the way to Duane's he had to pass Niemann's. He pulled his cap over his eyes and increased his pace until he had gone by. Inside Niemann's stood a trusting bartender, who for ten days had staked Midge to drinks and allowed him to ravage the lunch on a promise to come in and settle the moment he was paid for the "prelim."

Midge strode into Duane's and aroused the napping bartender by slapping a silver dollar on the festive board.

"Gimme a shot," said Midge.

The shooting continued until the wind-up at the Star was over and part of the fight crowd joined Midge in front of Duane's bar. A youth in the early twenties, standing next to young Kelly, finally summoned sufficient courage to address him.

"Wasn't you in the first bout?" he ventured.

"Yeh," Midge replied.

"My name's Hersch," said the other.

Midge received the startling information in silence.

"I don't want to butt in," continued Mr. Hersch, "but I'd like to buy you a drink."

"All right," said Midge, "but don't overstrain yourself."

Mr. Hersch laughed uproariously and beckoned to the bartender.

"You certainly gave that wop a trimmin' tonight," said the buyer of the drink, when they had been served. "I thought you'd kill him."

"I would if I hadn't let up," Midge replied. "I'll kill 'em all."

"You got the wallop all right," the other said admiringly.

"Have I got the wallop?" said Midge. "Say, I can kick like a mule. Did you notice them muscles in my shoulders?"

"Notice 'em? I couldn't help from noticin' 'em," said Hersch. "I says to the fella sittin' alongside o' me, I says: 'Look at them shoulders! No wonder he can hit,' I says to him."

"Just let me land and it's good-bye, baby," said Midge. "I'll kill 'em all."

The oral manslaughter continued until Duane's closed for the night. At parting, Midge and his new friend shook hands and arranged for a meeting the following evening.

For nearly a week the two were together almost constantly. It was Hersch's pleasant role to listen to Midge's modest revelations concerning himself, and to buy every time Midge's glass was empty. But there came an evening when Hersch regretfully announced that he must go home to supper.

"I got a date for eight bells," he confided. "I could stick till then, only I must clean up and put on the Sunday clo'es, 'cause she's the prettiest little thing in Milwaukee."

"Can't you fix it for two?" asked Midge.

"I don't know who to get," Hersch replied. "Wait, though. I got a sister and if she ain't busy, it'll be O.K. She's no bum for looks herself."

So it came about that Midge and Emma Hersch and Emma's brother and the prettiest little thing in Milwaukee foregathered at Wall's and danced half the night away. And Midge and Emma danced every dance together, for though every little onestep seemed to induce a new thirst of its own,

Lou Hersch stayed too sober to dance with his own sister.

The next day, penniless at last in spite of his phenomenal ability to make someone else settle, Midge Kelly sought out Doc Hammond, matchmaker for the Star, and asked to be booked for the next show.

"I could put you on with Tracy for the next bout," said Doc.

"What's they in it?" asked Midge.

"Twenty if you cop," Doc told him.

"Have a heart," protested Midge. "Didn't I look good the other night?"

"You looked all right. But you aren't Freddie Welsh yet by a consid'able margin."

"I ain't scared of Freddie Welsh or none of 'em," said Midge.

"Well, we don't pay our boxers by the size of their chests," Doc said. "I'm offerin' you this Tracy bout. Take it or leave it."

"All right: I'm on," said Midge, and he passed a pleasant afternoon at Duane's on the strength of his booking.

Young Tracy's manager came to see Midge the night before the show.

"How do you feel about this go?" he asked.

"Me?" said Midge. "I feel all right. What do you mean, how do I feel?"

"I mean," said Tracy's manager, "that we're mighty anxious to win, 'cause the boy's got a chanct in Philly if he cops this one."

"What's your proposition?" asked Midge.

"Fifty bucks," said Tracy's manager.

"What do you think I am, a crook? Me lay down for fifty bucks. Not me!"

"Seventy-five, then," said Tracy's manager.

The market closed on eighty and the details were agreed on in short order. And the next night Midge was stopped in the second round by a terrific slap on the forearm.

This time Midge passed up both Niemann's and Duane's, having a sizable account at each place, and sought his refreshment at Stein's farther down the street.

When the profits of his deal with Tracy were gone, he learned, by first-hand information from Doc Hammond and the matchmakers at the other "clubs," that he was no longer desired for even the cheapest of preliminaries. There was no danger of his starving or dying of thirst while Emma and Lou Hersch lived. But he made up his mind, four

months after his defeat by Young Tracy, that Milwaukee was not the ideal place for him to live.

"I can lick the best of 'em," he reasoned, "but there ain't no more chance for me here. I can maybe go east and get on somewheres. And besides—"

But just after Midge had purchased a ticket to Chicago with the money he had "borrowed" from Emma Hersch "to buy shoes," a heavy hand was laid on his shoulder and he turned to face two strangers.

"Where are you goin', Kelly?" inquired the owner of the heavy hand.

"Nowheres," said Midge. "What the hell do you care?"

The other stranger spoke:

"Kelly, I'm employed by Emma Hersch's mother to see that you do right by her. And we want you to stay here till you've done it."

"You won't get nothin' but the worst of it, monkeying with me," said Midge.

Nevertheless, he did not depart for Chicago that night. Two days later, Emma Hersch became Mrs. Kelly, and the gift of the bridegroom, when once they were alone, was a crushing blow on the bride's pale cheek.

Next morning, Midge left Milwaukee as he had entered it—by fast freight.

They's no use kiddin' ourself any more," said Tommy Haley. "He might get down to thirtyseven in a pinch, but if he done below that a mouse could stop him. He's a welter; that's what he is and he knows it as well as I do. He's growed like a weed in the last six months. I told him, I says, 'If you don't quit growin' they won't be nobody for you to box, only Willard and them.' He says, 'Well, I wouldn't run away from Willard if I weighed twenty pounds more.'"

"He must hate himself," said Tommy's brother.

"I never seen a good one that didn't," said Tommy. "And Midge is a good one; don't make no mistake about that. I wisht we could of got Welsh before the kid growed so big. But it's too late now. I won't make no holler, though, if we can match him up with the Dutchman."

"Who do you mean?"

"Young Goetz, the welter champ. We mightn't not get so much dough for the bout itself, but it'd roll in afterward. What a drawin' card we'd be, 'cause the people pays their money to see the fella with the wallop, and that's Midge. And we'd keep the title just as long as Midge could make the weight."

"Can't you land no match with Goetz?"

"Sure, 'cause he needs the money. But I've went careful with the kid so far and look at the results I got! So what's the use of takin' a chanct? The kid's comin' every minute and Goetz is goin' back faster'n big Johnson did. I think we could lick him now; I'd bet my life on it. But six mont's from now they won't be no risk. He'll of licked hisself before that time. Then all as we'll have to do is sign up with him and wait for the referee to stop it. But Midge is so crazy to get at him now that I can't hardly hold him back."

The brothers Haley were lunching in a Boston hotel. Dan had come down from Holyoke to visit with Tommy and to watch the latter's protégé go twelve rounds, or less, with Bud Cross. The bout promised little in the way of a contest, for Midge had twice stopped the Baltimore youth and Bud's reputation for gameness was all that had earned him the date. The fans were willing to pay the price to see Midge's haymaking left, but they wanted to see it used on an opponent who would not jump out of the ring the first time he felt its crushing force. Bud Cross was such an opponent, and his willingness to stop boxing gloves with his eyes, ears, nose and throat had enabled him to escape the horrors of honest labor. A game boy was Bud, and he showed it in his battered, swollen, discolored face.

"I should think," said Dan Haley, "that the kid'd do whatever you tell him after all you've done for him."

"Well," said Tommy, "he's took my dope pretty straight so far, but he's so sure of hisself that he can't see no reason for waitin'. He'll do what I say, though; he'd be a sucker not to."

"You got a contrac' with him?"

"No, I don't need no contrac'. He knows it was me that drug him out o' the gutter and he ain't goin' to turn me down now when he's got the dough and bound to get more. Where'd he of been at if I hadn't listened to him when he first came to me? That's pretty near two years ago now, but it seems like last week. I was settin' in the s'loon acrost from the Pleasant Club in Philly, waitin' for McCann to count the dough and come over, when this little bum blowed in and tried to stand the house off for a drink. They told him nothin' doin' and to beat it out o' there, and then he seen me and

come over to where I was settin' and ast me wasn't I a boxin' man and I told him who I was. Then he ast for money to buy a shot and I told him to set down and I'd buy it for him.

"Then we got talkin' things over and he told me his name and told me about fight'n' a couple o' prelims out of Milwaukee. So I says, 'Well, boy, I don't know how good or how rotten you are, but you won't never get nowheres trainin' on that stuff.' So he says he'd cut it out if he could get on in a bout and I says I would give him a chanct if he played square with me and didn't touch no more to drink. So we shook hands and I took him up to the hotel with me -and give him a bath and the next day I bought him some clo'es. And I staked him to eats and sleeps for over six weeks. He had a hard time breakin' away from the polish, but finally I thought he was fit and I give him his chanct. He went on with Smiley Sayer and stopped him so quick that Smiley thought sure he was poisoned.

"Well, you know what he's did since. The only beatin' in his record was by Tracy in Milwaukee before I got hold of him, and he's licked Tracy three times in the last year.

"I've gave him all the best of it in a money way and he's got seven thousand bucks in cold storage. How's that for a kid that was in the gutter two years ago? And he'd have still more yet if he wasn't so nuts over clo'es and got to stop at the good hotels and so forth."

"Where's his home at?"

"Well, he ain't really got no home. He came from Chicago and his mother canned him out o' the house for bein' no good. She give him a raw deal, I guess, and he says he won't have nothin' to do with her unless she comes to him first. She's got a pile o' money, he says, so he ain't worryin' about her."

The gentleman under discussion entered the café and swaggered to Tommy's table, while the whole room turned to look.

Midge was the picture of health despite a slightly colored eye and an ear that seemed to have no opening. But perhaps it was not his healthiness that drew all eyes. His diamond horseshoe tie pin, his purple cross-striped shirt, his orange shoes and his light-blue suit fairly screamed for attention.

"Where you been?" he asked Tommy. "I been lookin' all over for you."

"Set down," said his manager.

"No time," said Midge. "I'm goin' down to the w'arf and see 'em unload the fish."

"Shake hands with my brother Dan," said Tommy.

Midge shook with Holyoke Haley.

"If you're Tommy's brother, you're O.K. with me," said Midge, and the brothers beamed with pleasure.

Dan moistened his lips and murmured an embarrassed reply, but it was lost on the young gladiator.

"Leave me take twenty," Midge was saying. "I prob'ly won't need it, but I don't like to be caught short."

Tommy parted with a twenty-dollar bill and recorded the transaction in a small book the insurance company had given him for Christmas.

"But," he said, "it won't cost you no twenty to look at them fish. Want me to go along?"

"No," said Midge hastily. "You and your brother here prob'ly got a lot to say to each other."

"Well," said Tommy, "don't take no bad money and don't get lost. And you better be back at four o'clock and lay down a w'ile."

"I don't need no rest to beat this guy," said Midge. "He'll do enough layin' down for the both of us."

And laughing even more than the jest called for, he strode out through the fire of admiring and startled glances.

The corner of Boylston and Tremont was the nearest Midge got to the wharf, but the lady awaiting him was doubtless a more dazzling sight than the catch of the luckiest Massachusetts fisherman. She could talk, too—probably better than the fish.

"O you Kid!" she said, flashing a few silver teeth among the gold. "O you fighting man!"

Midge smiled up at her.

"We'll go somewheres and get a drink," he said. "One won't hurt."

In New Orleans five months after he had rearranged the map of Bud Cross for the third time, Midge finished training for his championship bout with the Dutchman.

Back in his hotel after the final workout, Midge stopped to chat with some of the boys from up north, who had made the long trip to see a champion dethroned, for the result of the bout was so nearly a foregone conclusion that even the experts had guessed it.

Tommy Haley secured the key and the mail and ascended to the Kelly suite. He was bathing when Midge came in, half an hour later.

"Any mail?" asked Midge.

"There on the bed," replied Tommy from the tub.

Midge picked up the stack of letters and post-cards and glanced over them. From the pile he sorted out three letters and laid them on the table. The rest he tossed into the wastebasket. Then he picked up the three and sat for a few moments holding them, while his eyes gazed off into space. At length he looked again at the three unopened letters in his hand; then he put one in his pocket and tossed the other two at the basket. They missed their target and fell on the floor.

"Hell," said Midge, and stooping over picked them up.

He opened one postmarked Milwaukee and read:

DEAR HUSBAND:

I have wrote to you so many times and got no anser and I dont know if you ever got them, so I am writeing again in the hopes you will get this letter and anser. I dont like to bother you with my trubles and I would not only for the baby and I am not asking you should write to me but only send a little money and I am not asking for myself but the baby has not been well a day since last Aug. and the dr. told me she cant live much longer unless I give her better food and thats impossible the way things are. Lou has not been working for a year and what I make dont hardley pay for the rent. I am not asking for you to give me any money, but only you should send what I loaned when convenient and I think it amts. to about $36.00. Please try and send that amt. and it will help me, but if you cant send the whole amt. try and send me something.

Your wife,
EMMA

Midge tore the letter into a hundred pieces and scattered them over the floor.

"Money, money, money!" he said. "They must think I'm made o' money. I s'pose the old woman's after it too."

He opened his mother's letter:

DEAR MICHAEL:

Connie wonted me to rite and say you must beet the dutch-man and he is sur you will and wonted me to say we wont you to rite and tell us about it, but I guess you havent no time to rite or we herd from you long beffore this but I wish you would rite jest a line or 2 boy because it wuld be better for Connie then & barl of medisin. It wuld help me to keep things going if you send me money now and then when you can spair it but if you cant send no money try and fine time to rite a letter onley a few lines and it will please Connie. jest think boy he hasent got out of bed in over 3 yrs. Connie says good luck.

Your Mother,
ELLEN F. KELLY

"I thought so," said Midge. "They're all alike." The third letter was from New York. It read:

HON:

This is the last letter you will get from me before your champ, but I will send you a telegram Saturday, but I can't say as much in a telegram as in a letter and I am writing this to let you know I am thinking of you and praying for good luck.

Lick him good hon and don't wait no longer than you have to and don't forget to write me as soon as its over. Give him that little old left of yours on the nose hon and don't be afraid of spoiling his good looks because he couldn't be no homlier than he is. But don't let him spoil my baby's pretty face. You won't will you hon.

Well hon I would give anything to be there and see it, but I guess you love Haley better than me or you wouldn't let him keep me away. But when your champ hon we can do as we please and tell Haley to go to the devil.

Well hon I will send you a telegram Saturday and I almost forgot to tell you I will need some more money, a couple hundred say and you will have to wire it to me as soon as you get this. You will won't you hon.

I will send you a telegram Saturday and remember hon I am pulling for you.

Well goodbye sweetheart and good luck.

GRACE

"They're all alike," said Midge. "Money, money, money."

Tommy Haley, shining from his ablutions, came in from the adjoining room.

"Thought you'd be layin' down," he said.

"I'm goin' to," said Midge, unbuttoning his orange shoes.

"I'll call you at six and you can eat up here without no bugs to pester you. I got to go down and give them birds their tickets."

"Did you hear from Goldberg?" asked Midge.

"Didn't I tell you? Sure; fifteen weeks at five hundred, if we win. And we can get a guarantee o' twelve thousand, with privileges either in New York or Milwaukee."

"Who with?"

"Anybody that'll stand up in front of you. You don't care who it is, do you?"

"Not me. I'll make 'em all look like a monkey."

"Well you better lay down awhile."

"Oh, say, wire two hundred to Grace for me, will you? Right away; the New York address."

"Two hundred! You just sent her three hundred last Sunday."

"Well, what the hell do you care?"

"All right, all right. Don't get sore about it. Anything else?"

"That's all," said Midge, and dropped onto the bed.

"And I want the deed done before I come back," said Grace as she rose from the table. "You won't fall down on me, will you, hon?"

"Leave it to me," said Midge. "And don't spend no more than you have to."

Grace smiled a farewell and left the café. Midge continued to sip his coffee and read his paper.

They were in Chicago and they were in the middle of Midge's first week in vaudeville. He had come straight north to reap the rewards of his glorious victory over the broken-down Dutchman. A fortnight had been spent in learning his act, which consisted of a gymnastic exhibition and a ten minutes' monologue on the various excellences of Midge Kelly. And now he was twice daily turning 'em away from the Madison Theater.

His breakfast over and his paper read, Midge sauntered into the lobby and asked for his key.

He then beckoned to a bellboy, who had been hoping for that very honor.

"Find Haley, Tommy Haley," said Midge. "Tell him to come up to my room."

"Yes, sir, Mr. Kelly," said the boy, and proceeded to break all his former records for diligence.

Midge was looking out of his seventh-story window when Tommy answered the summons.

"What'll it be?" inquired the manager.

There was a pause before Midge replied.

"Haley," he said, "twenty-five per cent's a whole lot o' money."

"I guess I got it comin', ain't I?" said Tommy.

"I don't see how you figger it. I don't see where you're worth it to me."

"Well," said Tommy, "I didn't expect nothin' like this. I thought you was satisfied with the bargain. I don't want to beat nobody out o' nothin', but I don't see where you could have got anybody else that would of did all I done for you."

"Sure, that's all right," said the champion. "You done a lot for me in Philly. And you got good money for it, didn't you?"

"I ain't makin' no holler. Still and all, the big money's still ahead of us yet. And if it hadn't of been for me, you wouldn't of never got within grabbin' distance."

"Oh, I guess I could of went along all right," said Midge. "Who was it hung that left on the Dutchman's jaw, me or you?"

"Yes, but you wouldn't been in the ring with the Dutchman if it wasn't for how I handled you."

"Well, this won't get us nowheres. The idear is that you ain't worth no twenty-five per cent now and it don't make no difference what come off a year or two ago."

"Don't it?" said Tommy. "I'd say it made a whole lot of difference."

"Well, I say it don't and I guess that settles it."

"Look here, Midge," Tommy said, "I thought I was fair with you, but if you don't think so, I'm willin' to hear what you think is fair. I don't want nobody callin' me a Sherlock. Let's go down to business and sign up a contrac'. What's your figger?"

"I ain't namin' no figger," Midge replied. "I'm sayin' that twenty-five's too much. Now what are you willin' to take?"

"How about twenty?"

"Twenty's too much," said Kelly.

"What ain't too much?" asked Tommy.

"Well, Haley, I might as well give it to you straight. They ain't nothin' that ain't too much."

"You mean you don't want me at no figger?"

"That's the idear."

There was a minute's silence. Then Tommy Haley walked toward the door.

"Midge," he said, in a choking voice, "you're makin' a big mistake, boy. You can't throw down your best friends and get away with it. That damn woman will ruin you."

Midge sprang from his seat.

"You shut your mouth!" he stormed. "Get out o' here before they have to carry you out. You been spongin' off o' me long enough. Say one more word about the girl or about anything else and you'll get what the Dutchman got. Now get out!"

And Tommy Haley, having a very vivid memory of the Dutchman's face as he fell, got out.

Grace came in later, dropped her numerous bundles on the lounge and perched herself on the arm of Midge's chair.

"Well?" she said.

"Well," said Midge, "I got rid of him."

"Good boy!" said Grace. "And now I think you might give me that twenty-five per cent."

"Besides the seventy-five you're already gettin'?" said Midge.

"Don't be no grouch, hon. You don't look pretty when you're grouchy."

"It ain't my business to look pretty," Midge replied.

"Wait till you see how I look with the stuff I bought this mornin'!"

Midge glanced at the bundles on the lounge.

"There's Haley's twenty-five per cent," he said, "and then some."

The champion did not remain long without a manager. Haley's successor was none other than Jerome Harris, who saw in Midge a better meal ticket than his popular-priced musical show had been.

The contract, giving Mr. Harris twenty-five per cent of Midge's earnings, was signed in Detroit the week after Tommy Haley had heard his dismissal read. It had taken Midge just six days to learn that a popular actor cannot get on without the ministrations of a man who thinks, talks and means business. At first Grace objected to the new member of the firm, but when Mr. Harris had demanded and secured from the vaudeville people a one-hundred dollar increase in Midge's weekly stipend, she was convinced that the champion had acted for the best.

"You and my missus will have some great old times," Harris told Grace. "I'd of wired her to join us here, only I seen the Kid's bookin' takes us to Milwaukee next week, and that's where she is."

But when they were introduced in the Milwaukee hotel, Grace admitted to herself that her feeling for Mrs. Harris could hardly be called love at first sight. Midge, on the contrary, gave his new manager's wife the many times over and seemed loath to end the feast of his eyes.

"Some doll," he said to Grace when they were alone.

"Doll is right," the lady replied, "and sawdust where her brains ought to be."

"I'm liable to steal that baby," said Midge, and he smiled as he noted the effect of his words on his audience's face.

On Tuesday of the Milwaukee week the champion successfully defended his title in a bout that the newspapers never reported. Midge was alone in his room that morning when a visitor entered without knocking. The visitor was Lou Hersch.

Midge turned white at sight of him.

"What do you want?" he demanded.

"I guess you know," said Lou Hersch. "Your wife's starvin' to death and your baby's starvin' to death and I'm starvin' to death. And you're dirty with money."

"Listen," said Midge, "if it wasn't for you, I wouldn't never saw your sister. And, if you ain't man enough to hold a job, what's that to me? The best thing you can do is keep away from me."

"You give me a piece o' money and I'll go."

Midge's reply to the ultimatum was a straight right to his brother-in-law's narrow chest.

"Take that home to your sister."

And after Lou Hersch had picked himself up and slunk away, Midge thought: "It's lucky I didn't give him my left or I'd of croaked him. And if I'd hit him in the stomach, I'd of broke his spine."

There was a party after each evening performance during the Milwaukee engagement. The wine flowed freely and Midge had more of it than Tommy Haley ever would have permitted him. Mr. Harris offered no objection, which was possibly just as well for his own physical comfort.

In the dancing between drinks, Midge had his new manager's wife for a partner as often as Grace. The latter's face as she floundered round in the arms of the portly Harris belied her frequent protestations that she was having the time of her life.

Several times that week, Midge thought Grace was on the point of starting the quarrel he hoped to have. But it was not until Friday night that she accommodated. He and Mrs. Harris had disappeared after the matinee and when Grace saw him again at the close of the night show, she came to the point at once.

"What are you tryin' to pull off?" she demanded.

"It's none o' your business, is it?" said Midge.

"You bet it's my business; mine and Harris's. You cut it short or you'll find out."

"Listen," said Midge, "have you got a mortgage on me or somethin'? You talk like we was married."

"We're goin' to be, too. And tomorrow's as good a time as any."

"Just about," said Midge. "You got as much

chanct o' marryin' me tomorrow as the next day or next year and that ain't no chanct at all."

"We'll find out," said Grace.

"You're the one that's got somethin' to find out."

"What do you mean?"

"I mean I'm married already."

"You lie!"

"You think so, do you? Well, s'pose you go to this here address and get acquainted with my missus."

Midge scrawled a number on a piece of paper and handed it to her. She stared at it unseeingly.

"Well," said Midge, "I ain't kiddin' you. You go there and ask for Mrs. Michael Kelly, and if you don't find her, I'll marry you tomorrow before breakfast."

Still Grace stared at the scrap of paper. To Midge it seemed an age before she spoke again.

"You lied to me all this w'ile."

"You never ast me was I married. What's more, what the hell difference did it make to you? You got a split, didn't you? Better'n fifty-fifty."

He started away.

"Where you goin'?"

"I'm goin' to meet Harris and his wife."

"I'm goin' with you. You're not goin' to shake me now."

"Yes, I am, too," said Midge quietly. "When I leave town tomorrow night, you're going to stay here. And if I see where you're goin' to make a fuss, I'll put you in a hospital where they'll keep you quiet. You can get your stuff tomorrow mornin' and I'll slip you a hundred bucks. And then I don't want to see no more o' you. And don't try and tag along now or I'll have to add another K.O. to the old record."

When Grace returned to the hotel that night, she discovered that Midge and the Harrises had moved to another. And when Midge left town the following night, he was again without a manager, and Mr. Harris was without a wife.

Three days prior to Midge's Kelly's ten-round bout with Young Milton in New York City, the sporting editor of the *News* assigned Joe Morgan to write two or three thousand words about the champion to run with a picture layout for Sunday.

Joe Morgan dropped in at Midge's training quarters Friday afternoon. Midge, he learned, was doing road work, but Midge's manager, Wallie

Adams, stood ready and willing to supply reams of dope about the greatest fighter of the age.

"Let's hear what you've got," said Joe, "and then I'll try to fix up something."

So Wallie stepped on the accelerator of his imagination and shot away.

"Just a kid; that's all he is; a regular boy. Get what I mean? Don't know the meanin' o' bad habits. Never tasted liquor in his life and would prob'bly get sick if he smelled it. Clean livin' put him up where he's at. Get what I mean? And modest and unassumin' as a schoolgirl. He's so quiet you wouldn't never know he was round. And he'd go to jail before he'd talk about himself.

"No job at all to get him in shape, 'cause he's always that way. The only trouble we have with him is gettin' him to light into these poor bums they match him up with. He's scared he'll hurt somebody. Get what I mean? He's tickled to death over this match with Milton, 'cause everybody says Milton can stand the gaff. Midge'll maybe be able to cut loose a little this time. But the last two bouts he had, the guys hadn't no business in the ring with him, and he was holdin' back all the w'ile for the fear he'd kill somebody. Get what I mean?"

"Is he married?" inquired Joe.

"Say, you'd think he was married to hear him rave about them kiddies he's got. His fam'ly's up in Canada to their summer home and Midge is wild to get up there with 'em. He thinks more o' that wife and them kiddies than all the money in the world. Get what I mean?"

"How many children has he?"

"I don't know, four or five, I guess. All boys and every one of 'em a dead ringer for their dad."

"Is his father living?"

"No, the old man died when he was a kid. But he's got a grand old mother and a kid brother out in Chi. They're the first ones he thinks about after a match, them and his wife and kiddies. And he don't forget to send the old woman a thousand bucks after every bout. He's goin' to buy her a new home as soon as they pay him off for this match."

"How about his brother? Is he going to tackle the game?"

"Sure, and Midge says he'll be a champion before he's twenty years old. They're a fightin' fam'ly and all of 'em honest and straight as a die. Get what I mean? A fella that I can't tell you his name come to Midge in Milwaukee onct and wanted him to throw a fight and Midge give him such a trimmin' in the street that he couldn't go on that night. That's the kind he is. Get what I mean?"

Joe Morgan hung around the camp until Midge and his trainers returned.

"One o' the boys from the News," said Wallie by way of introduction. "I been givin' him your fam'ly hist'ry."

"Did he give you good dope?" he inquired.

"He's some historian," said Joe.

"Don't call me no names," said Wallie smiling. "Call us up if they's anything more you want. And keep your eyes on us Monday night. Get what I mean?"

The story in Sunday's News was read by thousands of lovers of the manly art. It was well written and full of human interest. Its slight inaccuracies went unchallenged, though three readers, besides Wallie Adams and Midge Kelly, saw and recognized them. The three were Grace, Tommy Haley and Jerome Harris, and the comments they made were not for publication.

Neither the Mrs. Kelly in Chicago nor the Mrs. Kelly in Milwaukee knew that there was such a paper as the New York News. And even if they had known of it and that it contained two columns of reading matter about Midge, neither mother nor wife could have bought it. For the News on Sunday is a nickel a copy.

Joe Morgan could have written more accurately, no doubt, if instead of Wallie Adams, he had interviewed Ellen Kelly and Connie Kelly and Emma Kelly and Lou Hersch and Grace and Jerome Harris and Tommy Haley and Hap Collins and two or three Milwaukee bartenders.

But a story built on their evidence would never have passed the sporting editor.

"Suppose you can prove it," that gentleman would have said. "It wouldn't get us anything but abuse to print it. The people don't want to see him knocked. He's champion."

BOXING WITH THE NAKED EYE

For some 25 years, on and off until his death in 1963, Joe Liebling wrote boxing pieces for *The New Yorker* that remain distinguished examples of scholarship, sagacity, wit and intimate knowledge. Thus one of the most fortunate blows ever struck in behalf of the sport was a left-jab landed on Liebling's nose by his Uncle Mike in 1917, when Joe was 13 years old.

Uncle Mike was a boxing buff and also, to quote Liebling, "a sound teacher and a good storyteller, so I got the rudiments and the legend at the same time." In the pursuit of further knowledge Joe was subsequently struck by Philadelphia Jack O'Brien, who had been hit by Bob Fitzsimmons, who had been hit by Jim Corbett, Corbett by John L. Sullivan, he by Paddy Ryan, Ryan by Joe Goss, and Goss by Jem Mace. "I wonder," Liebling wrote, introducing his *The Sweet Science*, "if Professor Toynbee is as intimately attuned to his sources."

A.J. LIEBLING

Watching a fight on television has always seemed to me a poor substitute for being there. For one thing, you can't tell the fighters what to do. When I watch a fight, I like to study one boxer's problem, solve it, and then communicate my solution vocally. On occasion my advice is disregarded, as when I tell a man to stay away from the other fellow's left and he doesn't, but in such cases I assume that he hasn't heard my counsel, or that his opponent has, and has acted on it. Some fighters hear better and are more suggestible than others—for example, the pre-television Joe Louis. "Let him have it, Joe!" I would yell whenever I saw him fight, and sooner or later he would let the other fellow have it. Another fighter like that was the late Marcel Cerdan, whom I would coach in his own language, to prevent opposition seconds from picking up our signals. *"Vas-y, Marcel!"* I used to shout, and Marcel always *y allait*. I get a feeling of participation that way that I don't in front of a television screen. I could yell, of course, but I would know that if my suggestion was adopted, it would be by the merest coincidence.

Besides, when you go to a fight, the boxers aren't the only ones you want to be heard by. You are surrounded by people whose ignorance of the ring is exceeded only by their unwillingness to face facts—the sharpness of your boxer's punching, for instance. Such people may take it upon themselves to disparage the principal you are advising. This disparagement is less generally addressed to the man himself (as "Gavilan, you're a bum!")

than to his opponent, whom they have wrongheadedly picked to win. ("He's a cream puff, Miceli!" they may typically cry. "He can't hurt you. He can't hurt nobody. Look—slaps! Ha, ha!") They thus get at your man—and, by indirection, at you. To put them in their place, you address neither them nor their man but your man. ("Get the other eye, Gavilan!" you cry.) This throws them off balance, because they haven't noticed anything the matter with either eye. Then, before they can think of anything to say, you thunder, "Look at that eye!" It doesn't much matter whether or not the man has been hit in the eye; he will be. Addressing yourself to the fighter when you want somebody else to hear you is a parliamentary device, like "Mr. Chairman . . ." Before television, a prize-fight was to a New Yorker the nearest equivalent to the New England town meeting. It taught a man to think on his seat.

Less malignant than rooters for the wrong man, but almost as disquieting, are those who are on the right side but tactically unsound. At a moment when you have steered your boxer to a safe lead on points but can see the other fellow is still dangerous, one of these maniacs will encourage recklessness. "Finish the jerk, Harry!" he will sing out. "Stop holding him up! Don't lose him!" But you, knowing the enemy is a puncher, protect your client's interests. "Move to your left, Harry!" you call. "Keep moving! Keep moving! Don't let him set!" I sometimes finish a fight like that in a cold sweat.

If you go to a fight with a friend, you can keep up unilateral conversations on two vocal levels— one at the top of your voice, directed at your fighter, and the other a running *expertise* nominally aimed at your companion but loud enough to reach a modest fifteen feet in each direction. "Reminds me of Panama Al Brown," you may say as a new fighter enters the ring. "He was five feet eleven and weighed a hundred and eighteen pounds. This fellow may be about forty pounds heavier and a couple of inches shorter, but he's got the same kind of neck. I saw Brown box a fellow named Mascart in Paris in 1927. Guy stood up in the top gallery and threw an apple and hit Brown right on the top of the head. The whole house started yelling, 'Finish him, Mascart! He's groggy!' " Then, as the bout begins, "Boxes like Al, too, except this fellow's a southpaw." If he wins, you say, "I told you he reminded me of Al Brown," and if he loses, "Well, well, I guess he's no Al Brown. They don't make fighters like Al any more." This identifies you as a man who (a) has been in Paris, (b) has been going to fights for a long time, and (c) therefore enjoys what the fellows who write for quarterlies call a frame of reference.

It may be argued that this doesn't get you any-where, but it at least constitutes what a man I once met named Thomas S. Matthews called communi-cation. Mr. Matthews, who was the editor of *Time*, said that the most important thing in journalism is not reporting but communication. "What are you going to communicate?" I asked him. "The most important thing," he said, "is the man on one end of the circuit saying 'My God, I'm alive! You're alive!' and the fellow on the other end, receiving his message, saying 'My God, you're right! We're both alive!' " I still think it is a hell of a way to run a news magazine, but it is a good reason for going to fights in person. Television, if unchecked, may carry us back to a pre-tribal state of social devel-opment, when the family was the largest conversa-tional unit.

Fights are also a great place for adding to your repertory of witty sayings. I shall not forget my adolescent delight when I first heard a fight fan yell, "I hope youse bot' gets knocked out!" I thought he had made it up, although I found out

later it was a cliché. It is a formula adaptable to an endless variety of situations outside the ring. The only trouble with it is it never works out. The place where I first heard the line was Bill Brown's, a fight club in a big shed behind a trolley station in Far Rockaway.

On another night there, the time for the main bout arrived and one of the principals hadn't. The other fighter sat in the ring, a bantamweight with a face like a well-worn coin, and the fans stamped in cadence and whistled and yelled for their money back. It was thirty years before television, but there were only a couple of hundred men on hand. The preliminary fights had been terrible. The little fighter kept looking at his hands, which were resting on his knees in cracked boxing gloves, and every now and then he would spit on the mat and rub the spittle into the canvas with one of his scuffed ring shoes. The longer he waited, the more frequently he spat, and I presumed he was worry-ing about the money he was supposed to get; it wouldn't be more than fifty dollars with a house that size, even if the other man turned up. He had come there from some remote place like West or East New York, and he may have been thinking about the last train home on the Long Island Rail-road, too. Finally, the other bantamweight got there, looking out of breath and flustered. He had lost his way on the railroad—changed to the wrong train at Jamaica and had to go back there and start over. The crowd booed so loud that he looked embarrassed. When the fight began, the fellow who had been waiting walked right into the new boy and knocked him down. He acted impa-tient. The tardy fellow got up and fought back gamely, but the one who had been waiting nailed him again, and the latecomer just about pulled up to one knee at the count of seven. He had been hit pretty hard, and you could see from his face that he was wondering whether to chuck it. Somebody in the crowd yelled out, "Hey, Hickey! You kept us all waiting! Why don't you stay around awhile?" So the fellow got up and caught for ten rounds and probably made the one who had come early miss his train. It's another formula with multiple applications, and I think the man who said it that night in Far Rockaway did make it up.

The Fives Court in London, early nineteenth century
A popular hangout for fighters and their followers is shown during a sparring session between
lightweights Jack Randall and Ned Turner.

Jack Johnson (right) vs. James J. Jeffries, July 4, 1910 *(See page 209)*

Jack Dempsey (right) vs. Georges Carpentier, July 2, 1921 *(see page 58)*

Jack Dempsey (left) vs. Luis Firpo, September 14, 1923 *(See page 240)*

Abe Attell, 1924 *(See page 347)*

Gene Tunney, 1927 *(See page 298)*

Gene Tunney (right) vs. Jack Dempsey, "the long count," September 22, 1927
Tunney receives valuable extra seconds to recover while Dempsey hovers nearby, unaware that he must move to a neutral corner before referee Dave Barry can begin the count.

Joe Louis (left) vs. Tami Mauriello, September 18, 1946
(See page 50 for tribute to Louis.)

Rocky Graziano (right) vs. Tony Zale, June 10, 1948
(See page 141 for pre-fight coverage of the 1946 Zale–Graziano bout.)

Rocky Marciano (right) vs. Jersey Joe Walcott, September 23, 1952 *(See page 78)*

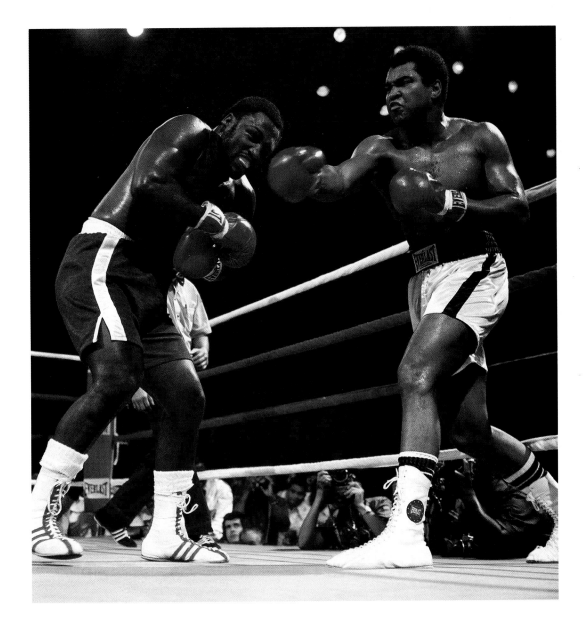

Muhammad Ali (right) vs. Joe Frazier, October 1, 1975 *(see page 176)*

Sugar Ray Leonard (right) vs. Roberto Durán, June 20, 1980 *(See page 115)*

Marvin Hagler (standing) vs. Thomas Hearns, April 15, 1985 *(See page 281)*

Marvin Hagler (right) vs. Sugar Ray Leonard, April 6, 1987 *(See page 15)*

Oscar De La Hoya (left) vs. Julio Cesar Chavez, June 7, 1996 *(See page 179)*

Evander Holyfield (right) vs. Mike Tyson, June 28, 1997 *(See page 283)*

JACK JOHNSON V. JIM JEFFRIES

In Sydney, Australia, on the day after Christmas, 1908, Jack London watched Jack Johnson toy with Tommy Burns and win the heavyweight championship of the world. In the last paragraph of his story in *The New York Herald* he started the bigoted ballyhoo that brought Jim Jeffries back, after six years without a fight.

"But one thing remains," London wrote, bravely. "Jeffries must emerge from his alfalfa farm and remove the golden smile from Johnson's face. Jeff, it's up to you!"

In Reno, Nevada, eighteen months later, he watched a fat alfalfa farmer try and, for the first time in a ring, fail.

JACK LONDON

Reno, Nevada, July 5, 1910—Once again has Johnson sent down to defeat the chosen representative of the white race and this time the greatest of them. And as of old, it was play for Johnson. From the opening round to the closing round he never ceased his witty sallies, his exchanges of repartee with his opponent's seconds and with the audience. And, for that matter, Johnson had a funny thing or two to say to Jeffries in every round.

The golden smile was as much in evidence as ever and neither did it freeze on his face nor did it vanish. It came and went throughout the fight, spontaneously, naturally.

It was not a great battle after all, save in its setting and significance. Little Tommy Burns, down in far-off Australia, put up a faster, quicker, livelier battle than did Jeffries. The fight today was great only in its significance. In itself it wasn't great. The issue, after the fiddling of the opening rounds, was never in doubt. In the fiddling of those first rounds the honors lay with Johnson, and for the rounds after the seventh or eighth it was more Johnson, while for the closing rounds it was all Johnson.

Johnson played as usual. With his opponent not strong in attack, Johnson, blocking and defending in masterly fashion, could afford to play. And he played and fought a white man, in the white man's country, before a white man's audience. And the audience was a Jeffries audience.

When Jeffries sent in that awful rip of his the audience would madly applaud, believing it had gone home to Johnson's stomach, and Johnson, deftly interposing his elbow, would smile in irony at the audience, play-acting, making believe he thought the applause was for him—and never believing it at all.

The greatest fight of the century was a monologue delivered to twenty thousand spectators by a smiling Negro who was never in doubt and who was never serious for more than a moment at a time.

As a fighter Johnson did not show himself a wonder. He did not have to. Never once was he extended. There was no need. Jeffries could not make him extend. Jeffries never had him in trouble once. No blow Jeffries ever landed hurt his dusky opponent. Johnson came out of the fight practically undamaged. The blood on his lip was from a recent cut received in the course of training and which Jeffries managed to reopen.

Jeffries failed to lead and land. The quickness he brought into the fight quickly evaporated, and while Jeffries was dead game to the end, he was not so badly punished. What he failed to bring into the ring with him was his stamina, which he lost somewhere in the last seven years. Jeffries failed to come back. That's the whole story. His old-time vim and endurance were not there. Something has happened to him. He lost in retirement outside of the ring the stamina that the ring itself never robbed him of. As I have said, Jeffries was not badly damaged. Every day boys take worse lacings in boxing bouts than Jeffries took today.

Jeffries today disposed of one question. He could not come back. Johnson, in turn, answered

---

another question. He has not the yellow streak. But he only answered that question for today. The ferocity of the hairy-chested caveman and grizzly giant did not intimidate the cool-headed Negro. Many thousands in the audience expected the intimidation, and were correspondingly disappointed. Johnson was not scared, let it be said here, and beyond the shadow of any doubt, not for an instant was Johnson scared. Not for a second did he show the flicker of fear that the Goliath against him might eat him up.

But the question of the yellow streak is not answered for all time. Just as Johnson has never been extended, so has he never shown the yellow streak. Just as any man may rise up, heaven alone knows where, who will extend Johnson, just so may that man bring out the yellow streak; and then again he may not. So far the burden of proof all rests on the conclusion that Johnson has no yellow streak.

And now to the battle and how it began! All praise to Tex Rickard, the gamest of sports, who pulled off the fight after countless difficulties and who, cool, calm and quick with nervous aliveness, handled the vast crowd splendidly in his arena and wound up by refereeing the fight.

Twenty thousand filled the great arena and waited patiently under the cloud-flecked, wide Nevada sky. Of the many women present some elected to sit in the screened boxes far back from the ring, for all the world like old-time Spanish ladies at the theater. But more, many more women, sat close to the ringside beside their husbands or brothers. They were the wiser by far.

Merely to enumerate the celebrities at the ringside would be to write a sporting directory of America—at least a directory of the four-hundred sportsmen, and of many more hundreds of near four-hundreds. At four minutes to two Billy Jordan cleared the ring amid cheers and stood alone, the focal point of twenty thousand pairs of eyes, until the great William Muldoon climbed through the ropes to call ringing cheers from the twenty thousand throats for the state of Nevada, the people of Nevada and the governor of Nevada.

Beginning with Tex Rickard, ovation after ovation was given to all the great ones, not forgetting Bob Fitzsimmons, whom Billy Jordan introduced as "The greatest warrior of them all." And so they came, great one after great one, ceaselessly, end-

lessly. Until they were swept away before the greatest of them all, the two men who were about to do battle.

It was half past two when Johnson entered. He came first, happy and smiling, greeting friends and acquaintances here and there and everywhere in the audience, cool as ice, waving his hand in salute, smiling, smiling, ever smiling with eyes as well as with lips, never missing a name nor a face, placid, plastic, nerveless, with never a signal of hesitancy or timidity. Yet he was keyed up, keenly observant of all that was going on, ever hearing much of the confused babble of the tongues about him—hearing, aye, and understanding, too.

There is nothing beary or primitive about this man Johnson. He is alive and quivering, every nerve fiber in his body, and brain. Withal that it is hidden so artfully or naturally under that poise of facetious calm of his. He is a marvel of sensitiveness, sensibility and perceptiveness. He has the perfect mechanism of mind and body. His mind works like chain lightning and his body obeys with equal swiftness.

But the great madness of applause went up when Jeffries entered the ring two minutes later. A quick, superficial comparison between him and the Negro would have led to a feeling of pity for the latter. For Jeff was all that has been said of him. When he stripped and his mighty body could be seen covered with mats of hair, all the primordial adjectives ever applied to him received their vindication. Nor did his face belie him. No facial emotion played on that face, no whims of the moment, no flutterings of a lighthearted temperament.

Dark and somber and ominous was that face, solid and stolid and expressionless, with eyes that smoldered and looked savage. The man of iron, grim with determination, sat down in his corner. And the carefree Negro smiled and smiled. And that's the story of the fight. The man of iron, the grizzly giant, was grim and serious. The man of summer temperament smiled and smiled. That is the story of the whole fight. It is the story of the fight by rounds.

At the opening of the first round they did not shake hands. Knowing the two men for what they are, it can be safely postulated that this neglect was due to Jeffries or to the prompting from Jeffries' corner. But it is not good that two boxers should not shake hands before a bout. I would suggest to those protagonists of a perishing game, if they wish to preserve the game, that they make the most of these little amenities that by custom grace their sport and give it the veneer of civilization.

Both men went to work in that first round very easily. Johnson smiling, of course; Jeffries grim and determined. Johnson landed the first blow, a light one, and Jeffries in the clinches gave a faint indication of his forthcoming tactics by roughing it, by crowding the Negro around and by slightly bearing his weight upon him. It was a very easy round, with nothing of moment. Each was merely feeling the other out and both were exceedingly careful. At the conclusion of the round, Johnson tapped Jeffries playfully on the shoulder, smiled good-naturedly and went to his corner. Jeffries, in the first, showed flashes of catlike quickness.

Round Two—Jeffries advanced with a momentary assumption of famous crouch, to meet the broadly smiling Johnson. Jeffries is really human and good-natured. He proved it right here. So friendly was that smile of Johnson's, so irresistibly catching, that Jeffries, despite himself, smiled back. But Jeffries' smiles were doomed to be very few in this fight.

And right here began a repetition of what took place down in Australia when Burns fought Johnson. Each time Burns said something harsh to Johnson in the hope of making him lose his temper, Johnson responded by giving the white man a lacing. And so today. Of course, Jeffries did not talk to Johnson to amount to anything, but Corbett, in his corner, did it for Jeffries. And each time Corbett cried something in particular, Johnson promptly administered a lacing to Jeffries.

It began in the second round. Corbett, in line with his plan of irritating the Negro, called out loudly:

"He wants to fight a little, Jim."

"You bet I do," Johnson retorted, and with that he landed Jeffries a stinger with his right uppercut.

Both men were tensely careful, Jeffries trying to crowd and put his weight on in the clinches, Johnson striving more and more than the other to break out of the clinches. And at the end of this round, in his corner Johnson was laughing gleefully. Certainly Jeffries showed no signs of boring in, as had been promised by his enthusiastic supporters.

It was the same story in the third round, at the conclusion of which the irrepressible Negro

was guilty of waving his hands to friends in the audience.

In this fourth round Jeffries showed up better, rushing and crowding and striking with more vim than hitherto shown. This seemed to have been caused by a sally of Johnson's, and Jeffries went at him in an angry sort of way. Promptly Jeffries rushed, and even ere they came together Johnson cried out: "Don't rush me, Jim. You hear what I'm telling you?"

No sign there of being intimidated by Jeffries' first dynamic display of ferocity. All he managed to do was to reopen the training cut in Johnson's lip and to make Johnson playful. It was most anybody's round and it was certainly more Jeffries' than any preceding one.

Round five brought Jeffries advancing with his crouch. The blood from Johnson's lip had turned his smile to a gory one, but still he smiled, and to balance things off he opened Jeffries' lip until it bled more profusely than his own. From then until the end of the fight, Jeffries' face was never free from blood, a steady stream, later flowing from his right nostril, added to by an open cut on his left cheek. Corbett's running fire of irritation served but to make Johnson smile the merrier, and to wink at him across Jeffries' shoulder in the clinches.

So far, no problems have been solved, no questions answered. The yellow streak had not appeared. Neither had Jeffries bored in, ripping awfully, nor put it over Johnson in the clinches. Yet one thing had been shown. Jeffries was not as fast as he had been. There was a shade of diminution in his speed.

Johnson signalized the opening of the sixth round by landing stinging blows to the face in one, two, three order. Johnson's quickness was startling. In response to an irritating remark from Corbett, Johnson replied suavely, "Too much on hand right now," and at the same instant he tore into Jeffries. It was Johnson's first real aggressive rush. It lasted but a second or two, but it was fierce and dandy. And at its conclusion it was manifest that Jeff's right eye was closing fast. The round ended with Johnson fighting and smiling strong, and with Jeff's nose, lip and cheek bleeding and his eye closed. Johnson's round by a smile all the way through.

The seventh round was a mild one, opening with Jeff grim and silent and with Johnson leading and forcing. Both were careful and nothing happened, save that once they exchanged blows right niftily. So far Jeff's roughing and crowding and bearing in of weight had amounted to nothing; also he was doing less and less of it.

"It only takes one or two, Jeff," Corbett encouraged his principal in the eighth round. Promptly Johnson landed two stingers. After a pause he landed another. "See that?" he chirruped sweetly to Corbett in the corner. Jeff perceptibly showed signs of slowing down in this round, rushing and crowding less than ever. Jeff's slowing down was not due to the punishment he had received, but to poorness of condition. He was flying the first signals of fatigue. He was advertising, faintly, it is true, that he had not come back.

The ninth round was introduced by a suggestion from Corbett, heroically carrying out the policy that was bringing his principal to destruction. "Make the big stiff fight," was Corbett's suggestion.

"That's right. That's what they all say," was Johnson's answer, delivered with the true Chesterfield grace across his adversary's shoulder. In the previous rounds Johnson had not wreaked much damage with the forecasted cut, the right uppercut.

In this round he demonstrated indubitably that he could drive the left hand in a way that was surprising. Be it remembered that it had long been denied that he had any sort of punch in that left of his. Incidentally, in this round, it led all the others, and he landed a blow near Jeffries' heart that must have been discouraging.

The tenth round showed Johnson with his unexpected left, as quick as ever, and Jeffries going slower and slower. The conclusion of the first ten rounds may be summed up as follows:

The fight was all in favor of Johnson, who had shown no yellow, who had shown condition, who had shown undiminished speed, who had not used his right uppercut much, who had developed a savage left, who had held his own in the clinches, who had gotten the best of the infighting and all the outfighting, who was unhurt, and who was smiling all the way.

Jeff was in bad shape: He was tired, slower than ever, his rushes had been futile, and the sports who had placed their money against him were jubilant.

There were men who proclaimed they saw the end. I refused to see this end, for I had picked Jeff to win, and I was hoping hugely—for what I did not know, but for something to happen, for anything that would turn the tide of battle. And yet I could not hide from myself the truth, that Jeff slowed down.

The eleventh round looked better for Jeff. Stung by a remark of Corbett's, Johnson rushed and provoked one grand rally from Jeff. It was faster fighting and more continuous than at any time in the preceding ten rounds, culminating in a fierce rally in which Jeff landed hard.

Round twelve found Johnson, if anything, quicker and more aggressive than ever. "Thought you were going to have me wild?" Johnson queried sweetly of Corbett. As usual every remark of Corbett's brought more punishment to Jeffries. And by the end of this round the second of the two great questions was definitely answered. Jeff had not come back.

The thirteenth round was the beginning of the end. Beginning slowly enough, but stung by Corbett, Johnson put it all over him in the mouth fighting, and all over Jeff in the outfighting and the infighting. From defense to attack and back again and back and forth Johnson flashed like the amazing fight mechanism he is. Jeff was silent and sick, while as the round progressed Corbett was noticeably silent.

A few entertained the fond hope that Jeff could recuperate, but it was futile; there was no comeback in him. He was a fading, heartsick, heartbroken man.

"Talk to him, Corbett," Jeff's friends appealed in the fourteenth round, but Corbett could not talk. He had long since seen the end. And yet through this round Johnson went in for one of his characteristic loafing spells. He took it easy and played with the big gladiator, cool as a cucumber, smiling broadly as ever, and yet, as careful as ever. "Right on the hip," he grinned out once as Jeff in a desperate dying flurry managed to land a wild punch in that vicinity.

Corbett, likewise desperate, ventured a last sally. "Why don't you do something?" he cried to the loafing, laughing Johnson. "Too clever, too clever, like you," was the reply.

Round fifteen and the end. It was pitiful. There happened to Jeff the bitterness that he had so often made others taste, but which for the first time, perforce, he was made to taste himself.

He who had never been knocked down was knocked down repeatedly. He who had never been knocked out was knocked out. Never mind the technical decision. Jeff was knocked out and through the ropes by the punch he never believed Johnson possessed—by the left and not by the right. As he lay across the lower rope while the seconds were tolled off, a cry that had in it tears and abject broken pride went up from many of the spectators.

"Don't let the Negro knock him out! Don't let the Negro knock him out!" was the oft-repeated cry.

There is little more to be said. Jeff did not come back. Johnson did not show the yellow streak. And it was Johnson's fight all the way through. Jeff was not the old Jeff at all.

Even so, it is to be doubted if this old Jeff could have put away this amazing Negro from Texas, this black man with the unfailing smile, this king of fighters and monologists.

Corbett and Berger and the others were right. They wanted Jeff to do more boxing and fighting in his training. Nevertheless, lacking the come-back, as he so patently did, this preliminary boxing and fighting would have profited him nothing. On the other hand, it would have saved his camp much of the money with which it backed him.

It was a slow fight. Faster, better fights may be seen every day of the year in any of the small clubs in the land. It is true these men were heavyweights, yet for heavyweights it was a slow fight.

It must be granted that plucky Tommy Burns put up a faster fight with Johnson a year and a half ago. Yet the American fight followers had to see this fight of today in order to appreciate what Burns did against this colored wonder.

Johnson is a wonder. No one understands him, this man who smiles. Well, the story of the fight is the story of a smile. If ever man won by nothing more fatiguing than a smile, Johnson won today.

And where now is the champion who will make Johnson extend himself, who will glaze those bright eyes, remove that smile and silence that golden repartee?

EPIGRAMS

Lucilius, the Latin satirical poet of the second century B.C., was the first of the "boxing-is-legalized-brutality" boys.

LUCILIUS [TRANSLATED BY W. R. PATON]

I

This Olympicus who is now such as you see him, Augustus, once had a nose, a chin, a forehead, ears and eyelids. Then becoming a professional boxer he lost all, not even getting his share of his father's inheritance; for his brother presented a likeness of him he had and he was pronounced to be a stranger, as he bore no resemblance to it.

II

Having such a mug, Olympicus, go not to a fountain nor look into any transparent water, for you, like Narcissus, seeing your face clearly, will die, hating yourself to death.

III

When Ulysses after twenty years came safe to his home, Argos the dog recognized his appearance when he saw him, but you, Stratophon, after boxing for four hours, have become not only unrecognizable to dogs but to the city. If you will trouble to look at your face in the glass, you will say on your oath, "I am not Stratophon."

IV

Your head, Apollophanes, has become a sieve, or the lower edge of a worm-eaten book, all exactly like ant-holes, crooked and straight, or musical notes Lydian and Phrygian. But go on boxing without fear; for even if you are struck on the head you will have the marks you have—you can't have more.

V

Cleombrotus ceased to be a pugilist, but afterwards married, and now has at home all the blows of the Isthmian and Nemean games, a pugnacious old woman hitting as hard as in the Olympian fights, and he dreads his own house more than ever he dreaded the ring. Whenever he gets his wind, he is beaten with all the strokes known in every match to make him pay her his debt; and if he pays it, he is beaten again.

VI

His competitors set up here the statue of Apis the boxer, for he never hurt anyone.

VII

I, Androleos, took part in every boxing contest that the Greeks preside over, every single one. At Pisa I saved one ear, and in Platæa one eyelid, but at Delphi I was carried out insensible. Damoteles, my father, and my fellow-townsmen had been summoned by herald to bear me out of the stadium either dead or mutilated.

VIII

Onesimus the boxer came to the prophet Olympus wishing to learn if he were going to live to old age. And he said, "Yes, if you give up the ring now, but if you go on boxing, Saturn is your horoscope."

DEATH

(From "10,000 Words a Minute")

Norman Mailer is the Henry Armstrong of the literary establishment. Armstrong, as the fancy well know, was a swarmer, crowding his adversary, throwing punches from all angles and inventing some as he went along. Mailer crowds his reader, overwhelming him with unexpected wordage, unconventional structures and surprising images. This technique won Armstrong three titles which he held at the same time while introducing "simultaneously" into the lexicon of the fight game. Similarly it has won Mailer a Pulitzer Prize in journalism, and wide acclaim as a novelist. Regretfully he is not as keen an observer of boxing as he is of the rest of society.

The Patterson–Liston fight, here described, was a no-contest going in, as it was throughout. The knowing among the gymnasium gentry knew Patterson couldn't take Liston's punch, nor could he punch hard enough to hurt Liston, as confirmed in their second go.

NORMAN MAILER

But then there is nothing else very much like being at a Heavyweight Championship fight. It is to some degree the way a Hollywood premiere once ought to have been; it's a big party with high action—there is the same rich flush of jewelry, bourbon, bare shoulders, cha-cha, silk, the promise that a life or two will be changed by tonight; it is even a bit like a political convention; it is much more like an event none of us will ever see—conceive of sitting in a classic arena waiting for a limited war with real bullets to begin between a platoon of Marines and two mounted squads of Russian Cossacks—you'd have the sensation of what a Heavyweight Championship can promise. A great heavyweight fight could take place in the center of a circus.

Ideally, it should take place in New York. Because Broadway turns out and Hollywood flies in with Las Vegas on the hip, and many of the wings and dovecotes and banlieues of what even a couple of years ago was called Café Society is there, and International Set (always seeing their first fight), and Big Business, and every good-looking call girl in New York, and some not so good-looking, and all the figures from the history pages of prizefighting in America, as well as ghosts there are some to claim—the ghost of Benny Leonard, the ghost of Harry Greb. Plus all the models, loose celebrities, socialites of high and lower rank, hierarchies from the racetrack, politicians, judges, and—one might offer a prayer if one really cared—one sociologist of wit and distinction ought to be there to capture for America the true status of its conflicting aristocracies: does Igor Cassini rate with Mickey Rooney or does Roger Blough get a row in front of Elizabeth Taylor? Is Frank Sinatra honored before Mrs. Woodward? Does Zsa Zsa Gabor come in ahead of Mayor Wagner? The First Sociologists of America are those professionals who sell the hot seats for a big fight in New York.

In Chicago, there was little of this. If there are nine circles to Hell, there were nine clouds over this fight. D'Amato was not licensed to manage in New York. Small matter. Patterson once again would fight in New York without him. But Liston was not cleared to fight by the State Boxing Commission—the shadow of the Establishment lay against him. So the fight was transferred to Chicago which promptly took fire. If Patterson–Liston was not clean enough for New York, it was not cool enough for Chicago. The local newspapers gave the kind of publicity one tastes in cold canned food. The stories on training were buried. Interest was greater outside the city than within. Yet little of Broadway arrived and less of Hollywood. You cannot get producers and movie stars to travel a distance to watch two Negroes fight. A bitch lives to see a white man fight a black man. She's not prejudiced—depending on the merits, she'll root for either, but a Negro against a Negro wets no juice.

And then there was poor weather. The day before the fight was misty, chilly. It rained on and off, and cleared inconclusively on Tuesday, which was cold. Fight night was cold enough to wear a topcoat. Comiskey Park was far from filled. It could hold fifty thousand for a big fight; it ended with less than twenty in paid admissions. Twenty-six thousand people showed. Proportions were poor. Because of theatre television, Patterson would make more money on this fight than any fighter had ever made, and there was much local interest in cities all over America. Parties were got up to go to the theatre, see it on television. The press coverage was larger than average, larger let us say than any of the three Johansson fights or the Marciano–Walcott fights. It was the biggest fight in ten years, it was conceivably the biggest fight since Louis fought Schmeling the second time, and yet nobody in the city where it was fought seemed to care. Radio, with its roaring inside hysteria, had lost to television, that grey eminence which now instructed Americans in the long calm of Ecclesiastes: vanity of vanities, all events are vanity.

So for a celebrity hunter, ringside was nothing formidable at this fight. The good people of Chicago turned out modestly. The very good people—which is to say, the very rich—turned out for ringside, and had a chance to cross the outfield grass, luminous green in the half-light of the base-ball towers, and walk to their seats under the great folded wings of the grandstand. Ever since the Romans built the Colosseum, arenas take on a prehistoric breath at night—one could be a black ant walking inside the circle a pterodactyl must have made with its wing as it slept. Or is it hills like dark elephants of which we speak?

I had a seat in the working press five rows from the ring. An empty seat away was Jimmy Baldwin. There had been a chill between us in the last year. Not a feud, but bad feeling. We had been glad, however, to see each other in Chicago. Tacitly, settling no differences, not talking about it, we had thought to be friendly. But the unsettled differences were still there. Two nights ago, at a party, we had had a small fight. We each insulted the other's good intentions and turned away. Now we sat with a hundred-pound cake of ice on the empty seat between us. After ten minutes, I got up and went for a walk around the ring.

The Press section occupied the first six rows. Back of us was an aisle which made a larger square around the square of the ring. On the other side of this aisle was the first row of ringside seats. This was as close as you could come to the fight if you had entered by buying a ticket. So I took a sampling of the house as I walked around the square. If this had been New York, you would expect to find twelve movie stars in the front row. But this was Chicago. Behind us were a muster of local Irish politicians, big men physically in the mold of Jimmy Braddock, not unhappy tonight with their good seats.

The front row to my right and the front row across the ring from me was given over in part to the Mob. They were the most intricate faces one would find this side of Carpaccio or Bellini, chins with books and chisels, nostrils which seemed to screw the air up into the head, thin-lipped mouths like thinnosed pliers, eyes which behind their dark glasses scrutinized your interior until they could find the tool in you which would work for them, and then would flip away like the turning of a card. Yes, those two rows of seats made up a right angle of *don capos* and a few very special Catholic priests, thin, ascetic, medieval in appearance, as well as a number of field officers dressed in black like subalterns, but older, leaner, with more guilds at their command. They were well-seated. They filled close to every seat around the corner.

It proved to be Patterson's corner.

That was art. They did not have to do much more. Sitting there, they could devote their study to Patterson. He would see them when he came back to his corner, his seconds would be obliged to look at them each time a new round began and they climbed down the steps from the corner. The back of the cornermen's necks would be open to detailed inspection, the calves of Patterson's leg, as he sat resting on the stool, would be a ready target for mental arrows. Like Lilliputians they could shoot thousands of pins into Gulliver.

I completed the tour. The last row, Liston's corner, was routine: musclemen, mobsters, business-sporting, a random sample. Turning the angle I came back to my seat, and sat watching a preliminary, shivering a little in the cold. It was much too cold for a fight. The sensitivity to magic I had felt earlier in the evening would not come back. There was just a dull sense of apprehension. Everything was wrong.

The preliminaries ended. Visiting fighters were called up from the crowd to take a bow. Archie Moore drew a large hand: he was wearing a black-silk cape with a white lining and he twirled the cape with éclat. It said: "Go away, all solemn sorcerers, the magic man is here."

Patterson and Liston arrived within a minute of each other. The visiting fighters who were gathered in the ring said hello to each man, shook their gloves, and went back to their seats.

The Star-Spangled Banner was played. Liston stood in his corner with his handlers, the referee stood in the middle of the ring, and Cus D'Amato stood alone, eight feet away from Patterson and his seconds. Since D'Amato was across from me, I could see his face clearly. It was as pale as his white sweater. His face was lifted to the sky, his eyes were closed. While the anthem played, D'Amato held his hand to his heart as if he were in anguish. I had the impression he was praying with fear.

The anthem ended, the fighters took their instructions from the referee, and stripped their robes. Their bodies made a contrast. Liston, only an inch taller than Patterson, weighed 214 pounds to Patterson's 189. But the difference was not just in weight. Liston had a sleek body, fully muscled, but round. It was the body of a strong man, but the muscles looked to have been shaped by pleasure as much as by work. He was obviously a man who had had some very good times.

Whereas Patterson still had poverty in his muscles. He was certainly not weak, there was whipcord in the way he was put together, but it was still the dry, dedicated body of an athlete, a track man, a disciplinarian: it spoke little of leisure and much of the gym. There was a lack eating at it, some misery.

The bell rang.

Liston looked scared.

Patterson looked grim.

They came together with no vast impact, trying for small gains. Each was moving with large respect for the other. Liston had the unhappy sweaty look in his eye of the loudest-talking champion on a city block—he has finally gotten into a fight with one of the Juniors, and he knows this Junior can fight. If he loses he's got much to lose. So Liston was trying to make Junior keep distance.

Patterson was not doing much. He threw a fast left hook which missed, then he circled a bit, fighting from a crouch. He lunged in once very low, try-

ing to get under Liston's long jab and work to the stomach, but his timing was not acute and he drew back quickly. There had been no inspiration, no life, and a hint of clumsiness. But it had been intellectually sound. It caused no harm. Then he tried again, feinting a left hook, and slipping Liston's left jab, but as he came in close, Liston grabbed him with both arms, and they bulled back and forth until the referee separated them. Now, they each had an unhappy look on their faces as if they were big men who had gotten into an altercation in a bar, and didn't like the physical activity of fighting. Each of them looked like it would take three or four rounds to warm up.

All this had used a minute. Liston seemed to have gained the confidence that he was stronger, and he began crowding Patterson to the rope, throwing a good many punches, not left hooks, not left jabs, not uppercuts or straight rights, just thick, slow, clubbing punches. None of them landed on Patterson's body or head, they all banged on his arms, and occasionally Patterson would bang Liston back on the arm. It is a way of fighting. A strong slow fighter will sometimes keep hitting the other man on the shoulder or the biceps until his arms go dead. If the opponent is in condition, it is a long procedure. I was surprised at how slow Liston's punches were. From ringside, they looked easy to block. He had a way of setting himself and going "ahem" before he threw the punch. It is, of course, one thing to block punches from your seat at ringside, and another to block them in a ring, but when a fighter is punching with real speed and snap, you can't block the punches from where you sit. Even from thirty feet away, you are fooled.

All that was fooling me now was Patterson. He seemed sluggish. He was not getting hit with Liston's punches, but he was not hitting back, he seemed to miss one small opportunity after another. He was fighting like a college heavyweight who has gone in to work with a professional and is getting disheartened at the physical load of such sparring. He had the expression on his face of somebody pushing a Cadillac which has run out of gas.

Then occurred what may have been the most extraordinary moment ever seen in a championship fight. It was very spooky. Patterson, abruptly, without having been hurt in any visible way, stood up suddenly out of his crouch, his back a foot from the ropes, and seemed to look half up into the sky as if he had seen something there or had been struck by something from there, by some transcendent bolt, and then he staggered like a man caught in machine-gun fire, and his legs went, and he fell back into the ropes. His left glove became tangled in the top rope, almost as Paret's arm had been tangled, and that murmur of death, that visitation which had passed into Madison Square Garden on the moment Paret began to die, seemed a breath from appearing now, Patterson looked at Liston with one lost look, as if somehow he had been expecting this to happen ever since the night it happened to Paret; it was the look of a man saying, "Don't kill me," and then Liston hit him two or three ill-timed punches, banging a sloppy stake into the ground, and Patterson went down. And he was out. He was not faking. He had started to pass out at the moment he stood straight on his feet and was struck by that psychic bolt which had come from wherever it had come.

Patterson rolled over, he started to make an attempt to get to his feet, and Baldwin and I were each shouting, "Get up, get up!" But one's voice had no force in it, one's will had no life.

Patterson got up somewhere between a quarter and a half second too late. You could see the critical instant pass in the referee's body, and Patterson was still getting his glove off the ground. The fight was over: 2:06 of the First. It must have been the worst fight either fighter had ever had.

Liston looked like he couldn't believe what had happened. He was blank for two or three long seconds, and then he gave a whoop. It was an artificial, tentative whoop, but it seemed to encourage him because he gave another which sounded somewhat better, and then he began to whoop and whoop and laugh and shout because his handlers had come into the ring and were hugging him and telling him he was the greatest fighter that ever lived. And Patterson, covered quickly with his bathrobe, still stunned, turned and buried his head in Cus D'Amato's shoulder.

From the stands behind us came one vast wave of silence. Here and there sounded cheers or applause, but you could hear each individual voice or pair of hands clapping into the silence.

"What happened?" said Baldwin.

[SELF-PORTRAIT]

HOW IT FEELS TO BE CHAMP

Rocky Marciano had some help, of course, on this one, but it remains his—the feelings, the thoughts and how it was. One year and two fights later, he retired—49 fights, 49 wins, 43 by knockout—the only retired undefeated heavyweight champion in history.

ROCKY MARCIANO

At about 8:30 on the morning of September 24, 1952, I woke up in a hotel room in Philadelphia. You know how it is when you wake up in a strange place, and at first you don't know where you are.

"Something nice happened to me," I thought to myself, and then I remembered. "That's right. Last night I won the heavyweight championship of the world."

When I tried to turn it seemed like my whole body was sore. I had cuts that had been stitched over both eyes and another on the top of my head, but I was as happy as I think anybody can be. Jersey Joe Walcott had given me the toughest fight I'd ever had, but I'd knocked him out in the thirteenth round, and I was heavyweight champion of the world.

I've had the title now for almost three years. In that time I've found out that, in most ways, it's everything you think it's going to be, and in other ways it's very different.

It's easy for me to remember what I thought it would be like to be champion, because I can remember the first night I ever thought I had a chance. On December 19, 1949, I had Phil Muscato down five times and knocked him out in five rounds in Providence. This was my twenty-fourth win without a loss as a pro and my twenty-second knockout, and after the fight I drove back to Brockton, like I always did after my Providence fights, with my pals Ali Colombo and Nicky Sylvester and Snap Tartarlia.

It was a nice night, clear and cold, but as soon as I got into the car I felt something was different. Usually on the way home after a fight we laughed and kidded a lot, but this night everybody was very serious.

"You know, Rock," one of the guys said while we were driving along, "you haven't got very far to go now."

I said, "To go where?"

"For the title," one of the others said.

"Ali," I said. "Take it easy."

"No," somebody said. "Figure it out. About five good wins and you can be on top of the heap."

Then we started figuring who I'd have to get by— Roland LaStarza, Rex Layne, Joe Louis, if he made a comeback, Jersey Joe Walcott and Ezzard Charles—and when they dropped me off at my house and I went to bed I couldn't sleep. I was a kid who never dreamed he could be heavyweight champion. I wanted to be a major-league catcher, but then I threw my arm out and I started to fight just to help my Pop support the family. Now I got to thinking what it would be like if I could be champion.

I remembered the night Primo Carnera won the title from Jack Sharkey. I was nine years old at the time, and in the Italian section of Brockton they had big bonfires burning and they sang and shouted around them almost all night long. I could remember those fires in the James Edgar playground right across the street from our house and I figured that gee, if I could win the title, I'd come back to Brockton and I'd throw a big party for the whole town and every kid would be invited and get an expensive gift.

Right after he won the title Carnera came to Brockton to referee at the old Arena that was across Pleasant Street from the Brockton Hospital. My uncle, John Piccento, took me that night to see him, and on the way out Carnera walked right by us and I reached out and I touched his arm.

"I saw Carnera and I touched him," I told my Pop when I got home. "I really did."

"How big is he?" my Pop asked me.

"Bigger than this ceiling," I said, "and you should see how big his hands are."

The year before I licked Muscato and was lying there thinking about what it might be like to be the champion of the world I had met Joe Louis for the first time. He was boxing an exhibition with Arturo Godoy in Philadelphia, and I was fighting Gilly Ferron on the card. We were all in the dressing room for the weigh-in when Joe came in.

"Say, Joe," my manager, Al Weill, said, "I want you to shake hands with my heavyweight."

Joe stuck out his hand and we shook. He looked like a mountain, and he had on a big, beautiful overcoat and a mohair hat, light-brown with a nice feather in it. I figured that hat alone must have cost fifty dollars, and now I got to thinking about the money he must have made.

When Louis knocked out Max Schmeling in 2 minutes and 4 seconds in their second fight, Ali Colombo and I were talking about all that dough. We were just kids talking, but it said in the paper that, figuring the purse Louis got for the fight, he made over $150,000 a minute, which is more than the President of the United States gets paid a year.

I got to imagining now what it would mean to have money like that, not just for clothes but the security and what I could do for my family and my friends and others. I thought that boy, when you're the heavyweight champion of the world it means you can lick any man in the world, and wherever you go in the world everything must stop and what an influence you must have.

There were a lot of things I didn't know then that I know now that I'm champion. I didn't know that my life would be threatened a couple of times. I didn't know that, although you do make a lot of money, it isn't what people think it is, expenses and taxes being what they are, and that you can't begin to do the things with it that you dreamed about. I didn't know that being heavyweight champion of the world is almost a full-time job, and that the influence you have on people is sometimes so strong that it worries you and can even bring tears to your eyes.

After I knocked out Joe Louis, for example, my mother got a letter that said that, if I came home to Brockton for the celebration that was planned, I'd be shot. Then, just before my first fight with Charles last June, my folks got another note from a man who said he was a Charles rooter and that if I beat Charles I'd be killed, because Charles is a gentleman and I'm a bully.

The Brockton police found the first letter was written by a thirteen-year-old girl. I don't know, or care, who wrote the second one, but although letters like that don't worry me, they worry my mother.

After that first letter my sisters had to take her to Dr. Rocco Del Colliano, in Brockton, and now every time I fight he picks her up at the house and drives her around all evening until the fight is over. I never imagined I'd put my family through anything like that, because I never realized how many people's lives are tied up in a fight.

I had a friend in Brockton named Miles Dempsey, and he was my first real fan. He used to go to all my amateur fights, and he was the first guy who asked me to arrange for him to buy good seats when I started to fight pro. During the excitement of the sixth round of that June fight with Charles he died at ringside of a heart attack. In my mind this is a part of that fight.

When you're the heavyweight champion the money, of course, is the big thing you're going for, because that's why you became a fighter in the first place. Before I started fighting, the most I ever made was $1.25 an hour as a manual laborer. When I retire, if I'm lucky, I should never have to worry about money again, but it isn't what you think it is, and your security is still a problem.

Last year, for example, I fought Charles twice. At the end of the year, after expenses and taxes, I came out with a lot less than $100,000. When I fight twice in a year I don't figure to net more than about $15,000 out of the second fight, and that's not a lot when you've only got four or five more years of fighting and when, each time you go into the ring, you're risking the heavyweight championship of the world.

I'm not complaining, because I couldn't make that kind of money doing any other thing, and when you come from a poor family you know it's a privilege to pay taxes. It's just that you feel that other people don't understand.

I'll never, you see, be able to afford that big party for all the kids in Brockton. That's not important, just kind of a foolish dream, but the important thing is that you can't do all you want for charities and churches and just good people, and you have a feeling that they go away not liking you because of it. You want to be liked by everybody, not just for yourself, but because when you're heavyweight champion of the world you represent boxing and boxing did everything for you.

There'll be a church that needs $10,000 or a hospital that needs that much to help build a new ward. I'll get a letter from a woman I don't even know but she'll write that if I'd give her $1,500 her little boy could be made well again. How do you think I feel?

They run at you, too, with all kinds of business schemes, but that's only a nuisance, and not like the others. There are people who want me to sign notes for them or loan them money or sponsor them on singing or acting careers. One guy wanted to start a band, and another I had never heard of wanted me to go halves with him in a night club in Buffalo.

They've tried to sell me uranium and copper and oil wells, a dairy and an oil route. Any salesman near Brockton, where I'm home only about two months a year, tries to get me to buy whatever he's handling, and it might be a carving machine or a salad mixer, books, furniture, a car or a horse.

Some of the things you do with your money don't pan out the way you dreamed, either. I always said that, if I became champion, one of the first things I'd do would be to send my Mom and Pop back to their home towns in Italy, and I used to think a lot about what a great time that would be for them.

I did it, right after the first Walcott fight. There were so many things pulling at me at the time, though, that I couldn't even see them off on the plane, and some of the pleasure was lost there. Then, instead of staying three months, they came back after one month, and they never did get to my mother's little town of San Bartholomeo, near Naples. They went only to my Pop's town, Ripi-atitina, in Abruzzi, on the Adriatic coast, and it took a couple of months before my mother would tell me why.

"Too much sadness there," she said, and you should understand that my mother is the kind of a woman who can't stand to see suffering and wants to help everybody. "Every place we went they had nothing, and they looked to us and how much could we do? I did not want to go to my own town."

It took my mother that long to tell me about the trip because, when you become heavyweight champion, something comes between you and other people, even your family. Everybody stands back a little, not because of anything you do but because of what you are, even though you try so hard to prevent it. You end up a lonesome guy in a crowd.

"Rocco, there is something I would like to talk with you about," my mother said not long ago while we were at Grossinger's, in the Catskill Mountains of New York, where I always do my training and where I was getting ready for this coming fight with Don Cockell.

"Sure, Mom," I said. "I wish you'd talk to me any time you want."

"You are so important now," she said. "I don't like to bother you."

"Please, Mom," I said. "You can never bother me. I'm your son."

"I have been thinking," she said, and she had probably been carrying this around in her mind for a year or more, "that there is so much pleasure you miss. When your sister has a baby and when somebody gets married it is a beautiful thing. This is a happiness you should enjoy. The most wonderful things in life you cannot enjoy because you are so busy and a big man."

I knew this before she even said it, because it is part of being champion. My sister Concetta's baby is going on two years old now, and I didn't see her until she was almost six months old. When my old friend Nicky Sylvester got married I couldn't even get to the wedding. My own baby, Marianne, is two, and they tell me this is the time when it's the most fun to be with your child, that she's walking around the house now and that every day she's picking up a new word. Instead, I'm with my wife Barbara and the baby about four months a year.

When I get together with my old friends in Brockton it isn't the same, either. They never start a conversation. They answer my questions quickly, and I never do find out how they feel and what they're thinking, and we never have the laughs about the little things we used to have before. They no sooner get out to our house than they're starting for the door, because they're afraid they're bothering me, and I try to tell them they're not.

That's what it's like to be heavyweight champion, when you look at one side. You have to give up something for everything you get, I guess, and when it gets me down and I lie in bed at night and feel a little depressed I think about all the good that there is in it, and it's more than you can imagine.

Take what it has meant to my Pop. He's sixty-one years old now, and came to this country in 1916. He was gassed in World War I fighting with the Second Marines at Chateau Thierry, and he was never really well after that. For over thirty years he worked in the shoe shops in Brockton at the Number 7 bed-laster, which is one of the tough ones. Four years ago I could see to it that he retired.

My Mom was telling me that when I was a kid, day after day would go by when Pop wouldn't say a word. With six kids to support on that little money at that tough job his life was a real drag. Just a few months ago Ali Colombo and I were looking at some old pictures of Pop, and he was skin and bones. Now he's gained about ten pounds, and he has a great time in his quiet way, sitting there and cutting out stories about me and helping around the camp.

Outside of your own family, you can make the title mean so much for other people. One of my greatest pleasures is meeting some nice little guy, like my kind of people, and, when I can make it, going into his town with him. This is a real honest, hard-working quiet little guy that nobody ever paid much attention to, and he takes me around and introduces me to everybody in the town and this makes him somebody important where he works and lives.

Once I made a speech at a dinner in Boston of the big shoe manufacturers. Everybody who spoke was telling jokes and I'm not good at that, so I thought I'd try to make a point in a light way.

I told them that if I was a good fighter, I thought they should take some of the credit for it. I said my Pop worked in the shoe shops for thirty years and I used to carry his lunch to him and I saw how tough it was. I told them that sometimes I saw his pay and I saw how little he got. I said: "He used to tell me, 'I want you to stay out of the shoe shops.' So, to keep away from them, I became a fighter instead, and therefore I think you men had a part in making me a fighter."

I don't know if I got it across. I just thought it was worth a try.

221

The influence you have and that you can use for good without being a crusader goes so far beyond what you think, that sometimes it frightens you. Right after I won the title from Walcott, Al Weill, Charley Goldman, two sparring partners—Bob Golden and Toxie Hall—and I made a five-week, 30,000-mile exhibition tour of the Pacific, and when they say you're heavyweight champion of the whole world they mean it.

In Manila there were mobs wherever we went. Whenever I'd come out of the hotel for my walk there'd be a hundred people waiting just to look at me. One day I went into a store to buy souvenirs, and there were five hundred people watching for me outside. When I got in a cab, dozens of them ran after it.

Out there they don't look for autographs. All they want is to feel the muscles in your arms. One day I was walking along the street and a little guy stopped his car in the middle of heavy traffic, got out, ran up to me, felt my muscle and got back in his car and drove off.

I tell this to explain something else that happened. I was scheduled to box on a Thursday, but it rained that day and the next two days. Then the promoter suggested I box on Sunday.

"No," I said, "I'm a Roman Catholic, and I go to church on Sunday."

When I'm training for a fight, I have to train on Sundays, too, but I don't have to box exhibitions on Sunday.

I didn't think anything of it, but it was a big front-page story in the newspapers. A little later we went out to visit a leper colony, and a priest spoke to me.

"Rocky," he said, "these people out here are great sports enthusiasts, and we try to get them to be better church people. You've done more for the Catholic religion in that one move than anyone has done here in my time."

That's what I mean when I say that sometimes it frightens you. You might, without realizing it, say a wrong thing. Ali Colombo and I have been taking long walks together since we were kids, and he still goes out on the road with me, and many times when we're walking we work out what I'll say in a speech or how I'll answer if a certain question is asked.

Before we went to the leper colony we were a little nervous, because we didn't know what it would be like. There was a woman who explained that we couldn't contract the disease, and she told us how

the poor people in the colony never see anyone important and have so little to look forward to.

There were, maybe, 1,200 people in the place, and when we got there and started to walk through them they just moved back to make a path for us without anyone saying anything to them, and it was one of the saddest things I ever saw. I went up on a stage and they asked if they could see my muscles and how I train, so I took off my shirt and I shadowboxed a couple of rounds.

Then we started out. Again they pulled away to make that path, and they began to call to me.

"God bless you, Rocky," they were calling. "God bless you. May you reign long."

If you think that being heavyweight champion of the world is all happiness you're wrong. In Los Angeles, before we went to the Pacific, we visited the iron-lung patients in a hospital named Rancho Los Amigos, and maybe it was there more than any other place that I realized what being champion of the world means.

We went to the men's polio ward first and there was one kid lying there who knew everything about me, from my earliest fights, and we'd catch each other's eyes in his mirror while we talked. There was another guy who'd been there as long as anybody could remember, and there was one big kid who'd been a basketball player for Loyola, and when I looked in his mirror to talk with him I saw he had my picture pasted on it. They say I had guts in the Walcott fight, but this kid was telling me how he'd lick it and play basketball again.

After that we went to the women's ward, where there were a lot of fourteen and fifteen-year-old kids, and the nurse told us that all that day they'd had all the nurses busy primping them up because I was coming. With us was a friend of mine, Ernie Clivio, who has a dairy in Stoneham, Massachusetts, and when we got out we just looked at one another and I thought we might both cry.

Shortly after I won the title, Al Weill and I received a letter from the White House saying that the President doesn't get to see many sports events and so he was having a sports luncheon to meet some of the sports figures. They wanted to know if we'd be kind enough, if you can imagine, to attend.

I was more nervous than I've ever been going into a fight. Joe DiMaggio, Ty Cobb, Cy Young, Clark Griffith, Ben Hogan, Gene Sarazen, Florence Chadwick and about forty others were there, and to begin with we were all formed in a semicircle in the White House when the President came in.

"So you're the heavyweight champion of the world," he said, when he came to me, and then he stepped back and looked at me and smiled.

"Yes, sir," I said.

"You know," he said, "somehow I thought you'd be bigger."

"No, sir," I said.

After the luncheon we posed on the White House steps, and one of the photographers who's a real fight fan took a picture of the President looking at my right fist. Can you imagine me, Rocco Marchegiano, a shoe worker's son and a PFC in the Army, posing with a five-star general who became the President of the United States?

Everybody, of course, isn't for you when you're champion. There are people who resent you and make remarks, and very often you find that women don't understand.

"What makes you enjoy hurting people?" an elderly woman said to me one night at a dinner party in Milton, Massachusetts.

"I don't enjoy hurting them," I said.

"Then why do you do it?" she said. "Is it some sadistic impulse?"

I dropped it then, but I think it's important for people to understand what you feel about an opponent. I don't want them to think that the heavyweight champion of the world is just a pug.

When I train for a fight I devote eight to twelve weeks getting ready to fight another man. The sports writers say I live a monk's life, because I put all my thoughts and all my efforts into it, and all those around me devote themselves to the same thing.

There are a number of key people who are very important to a fighter getting ready for a fight. They are his wife and family, if he's married, his manager, his trainer and his best friend. In all of these I've been very lucky.

That's the usual thing to say, but I mean it. When a fighter goes into camp for those two or three months his mind should be free and no problems should move in on it. My wife Barbara and I find that even in the four months we have together we don't have the freedom we want, but she has yet to make one complaint. We talk on the phone regularly while I'm in camp, but two weeks before a fight she'll always say that I'm not to call her again until the fight is over, and my family is the same.

I couldn't have made it without Al Weill and Charley Goldman, who trains me. On the way up Al got me opponents who, with only one exception and he got timid after I hit him a good punch, gave me a good fight for as long as it went.

"You see, you're learnin' while you're earnin'," Charley used to tell me.

I'll never forget the first day seven years ago when I met Al and Charley. Ali Colombo and I had bummed down from Brockton with our lunch in a paper bag, and I wanted Al to manage me and I was scared.

"If I manage you," he said, "you got to remember this. With me, I'm the boss. I do the managing and all you do is the fightin'. You don't ask me who you're fighting or where you're fightin' or how much you're gettin'. When you go to the gym you do what Charley tells you, and after the fight you get your share."

That's the way it should be with a fighter, really. I don't have any of the money worries, and I was a real crude kid as a young fighter and Charley taught me everything I know.

Ali Colombo is a guy who thinks and feels just like I do. Camp could get pretty grim at the end if you didn't have somebody like that to talk with.

The last month before a fight I don't even write a letter. The last ten days I see no mail and get no telephone calls and meet no new acquaintances. The week before the fight I'm not allowed to shake hands or go for a ride in a car. Nobody can get into the kitchen, and no new foods are introduced. Even the conversation is watched.

By that I mean that the fellas keep it pleasant, with not too much fight talk. My opponent's name is never mentioned, and I don't read the write-ups because, as Charley explained it, somebody might write one idea that might stick in my mind.

"Besides," he said, "think what fun it will be to read the clippings after the fight and see who was right and who was wrong."

For two or three months, then, every minute of my life is planned for one purpose. I don't even think about what I'm going to do the day after the fight, because that's going to be like an adventure and exciting. Everything on my part and on the part of everybody else in camp is directed toward one goal—to lick the other man. I see him in front of me when I'm punching the bag. When I run on the road I've got him in my mind, and always I'm working on certain moves and punches that I hope will lick him.

Take the second Walcott fight. Willie Wilson, one of my sparring partners, had Walcott's moves down very good. He'd feint me and pull away or, after I'd hit him a punch, he'd pull down and try to tie me up. The big problem was to figure out what I was going to hit him with for a second punch, and one night Ali and I were talking about it, walking for about forty-five minutes after dinner, and then we talked it over with Charlie and Al.

We decided to try right-hand uppercuts after a left hook, and I practiced it a lot on the big bag and then against Wilson. As it happened, the fight went less than a round, but the 3-D movies showed why very well. I hit him with a hook, but as he ducked to take it high on the head he moved right into the power of that uppercut, because, with an uppercut, the power is right after you start it.

When he went down I moved to a neutral corner. I listened for the count, and when it got to eight I said to myself: "You know, this fella isn't going to get up."

For the second LaStarza fight—the one with my title on the line—we knew he carried his left high, and always brought it back high. I had to bring that hand down to get to his head, so I practiced throwing right hands to the heart. Finally, along around the tenth round, I got his arm down and I stopped him in the eleventh.

When you work and work like that with only one purpose in mind for weeks on end there's only one thing you want to do—and that's get out there and try it in a fight. Of course, to begin with, you enjoy the fight itself, or you wouldn't be a fighter.

What it comes down to in the ring is that it's the other guy or you. Anybody in there with me is there to get me and I'm in there to get him, but the one thing that people don't seem to understand is that there's nothing personal about it and you don't carry this over outside the ring. You get rid of it in there.

Walcott is an example. I never wanted to lick a man more, because I had to lick him to get his title. Coming up to the second fight his manager was complaining that I'm a dirty fighter and that I hit low and butted Joe in our first fight. One night on television in Chicago he even had a billygoat on with him to represent me, but you know that's only part of the publicity.

When I was training for LaStarza, Walcott came up to see me work in the hangar where I train at the Grossinger airfield. After the photographers had finished posing us, Joe and I got to talking, with nobody listening, over behind the bags.

"Joe," I said, "how's the motel going out there in Jersey?"

"Fine," he said. "Very good."

"I hope you make a lot of money with it," I said. "I really do."

"Rock," he said, "I want to say this. I liked that title. I didn't want to lose it to anybody, but if I had to lose it, I'm glad I lost it to you. You're a good fighter and you're gonna be a great champ."

"I appreciate that, Joe," I said, "and I think you're a great guy."

This was a real warm thing, and why not? Walcott fought his greatest fight against me, and I fought my greatest against him. This is something that people are going to talk about for the rest of our lives, and we can be proud of it. It took two of us to do this together. One can't do it alone.

I have the same kind of fondness for other guys I fought. On the way up I knocked out Johnny Pretzie in five rounds, Gino Buonvino in ten rounds and then in two in a return, and Bernie Reynolds in three. After I became champ I wondered what they were doing and I wrote them post cards.

Reynolds didn't answer me, but I had a nice letter from Buonvino and his wife and one from Pretzie. Buonvino is a carpenter in New York now, and he and his wife sent me their best. Pretzie wrote me that he had a young fighter he was training, and he recalled our fight.

"But don't you think somebody might lick you?" I get asked quite often. "Don't you ever worry about it?"

I don't want to seem like I'm bragging but I don't think anybody in the world can lick me. I've never been defeated in forty-seven fights as a pro, and right now I hope maybe I can hold the title, if I'm lucky, four or five more years and retire undefeated. At the same time, once in a while, maybe seven or eight times when I'm building up to a fight, the thought comes to me on the road or while I'm resting: "Suppose this guy licks me? What will happen to all my plans?"

That's as far as it gets. I never believe it can happen, really. It's just one of the things that come to your mind.

I can remember, though, the night that Joe Louis and Jersey Joe Walcott fought for the first time and Walcott had Louis down twice but didn't get the decision. I had had one pro fight ten months before, and I was working for the Brockton Gas Company and I was sitting on the bed at home listening to the fight.

It never occurred to me that I would be the guy to knock out Louis and retire him and then knock out Walcott and take the heavyweight championship of the world. Now that I'm champion I wonder, once in a while, if there is some other kid nobody ever heard of sitting someplace and listening to one of my fights, or watching it on television, who might, in a few years, do the same thing to me.

Out on the West Coast there's this big, young heavyweight named Charley Powell. He put together a lot of knockouts last year, and they were touting him as a real good prospect. The night last fall when he fought Charley Norkus I watched on television, and when the fight got under way I could see that he was a big guy and boxed nice and could punch.

"You know," I thought to myself, "this might be the guy."

Norkus finally knocked Powell out, but he's still a prospect. I'm heavyweight champion of the world, but is there some young fighter somewhere who wants it as much as I did? The champion never knows.

[POETRY]

FROM: THE EVERLASTING MERCY

This is the opening of the verse narrative of the redemption of Saul Kane written in 1911 by the poet laureate and boxing buff. In this fight Kane behaved like a semipro Floyd Patterson. He had the instincts of a fighter and the compassion of a priest.

JOHN MASEFIELD

From '41 to '51
I was my folks' contrary son;
I bit my father's hand right through
And broke my mother's heart in two.
I sometimes go without my dinner
Now that I know the times I've gi'n her.

From '51 to '61
I cut my teeth and took to fun.
I learned what not to be afraid of
And what stuff women's lips are made of;
I learned with what a rosy feeling
Good ale makes floors seem like the ceiling,
And how the moon gives shiny light

To lads as roll home singing by't.
My blood did leap, my flesh did revel,
Saul Kane was tokened to the devil.

From '61 to '67
I lived in disbelief of Heaven.
I drunk. I fought, I poached, I whored,
I did despite unto the Lord.
I cursed, 'twould make a man look pale,
And nineteen times I went to gaol.

Now, friends, observe and look upon me,
Mark how the Lord took pity on me.
By Dead Man's Thom, while setting wires,

Who should come up but Billy Myers,
A friend of mine, who used to be
As black a sprig of hell as me,
With whom I'd planned, to save encroachin',
Which fields and coverts each should poach in.
Now when he saw me set my snare,
He tells me, "Get to hell from there.
This field is mine," he says, "by right;
If you poach here, there'll be a fight.
Out now," he says, "and leave your wire;
It's mine."
                    "It ain't."
                              "You put."
                                        "You liar."
"You closhy put."
"You bloody liar."
"This is my field."
"This is my wire."
"I'm ruler here."
"You ain't."
"I am."
"I'll fight you for it."
"Right, by damn.
Not now, though, I've sprained my thumb,
We'll fight after the harvest hum.
And Silas Jones, that bookie wide,
Will make a purse five pounds a side."
Those were the words, that was the place
By which God brought me into grace.

On Wood Top Field the peewits go
Mewing and wheeling ever so;
And like the shaking of a timbrel
Cackles the laughter of the whimbrel.
In the old quarry-pit they say
Head-keeper Pike was made away.
He walks, head-keeper Pike, for harm,
He taps the windows of the farm;
The blood drips from his broken chin,
He taps and begs to be let in.
On Wood Top, nights, I've shaked to hark
The peewits wambling in the dark
Lest in the dark the old man might
Creep up to me to beg a light.

But Wood Top grass is short and sweet
And springy to a boxer's feet;
At harvest hum the moon so bright
Did shine on Wood Top for the fight.

When Bill was stripped down to his bends

I thought how long we two'd been friends,
And in my mind, about that wire,
I thought, "He's right, I am a liar.
As sure as skilly's made in prison
The right to poach that copse is his'n.
I'll have no luck tonight," thinks I.
"I'm fighting to defend a lie.
And this moonshiny evening's fun
Is worse than aught I've ever done."
And thinking that way my heart bled so
I almost stept to Bill and said so.
And now Bill's dead I would be glad
If I could only think I had.
But no. I put the thought away
For fear of what my friends would say.
They'd backed me, see? O Lord, the sin
Done for the things there's money in.

The stakes were drove, the ropes were hitched,
Into the ring my hat I pitched.
My corner faced the Squire's park
Just where the fir trees make it dark;
The place where I begun poor Nell
Upon the woman's road to hell.
I thought of 't, sitting in my corner
After the time-keep struck his warner
(Two brandy flasks, for fear of noise,
Clinked out the time to us two boys).
And while my seconds chafed and gloved me
I thought of Nell's eyes when she loved me,
And wondered how my tot would end,
First Nell cast off and now my friend;
And in the moonlight dim and wan
I knew quite well my luck was gone;
And looking round I felt a spite
At all who'd come to see me fight;
The five and forty human faces
Inflamed by drink and going to races,
Faces of men who'd never been
Merry or true or live or clean;
Who'd never felt the boxer's trim
Or brain divinely knit to limb,
Nor felt the whole live body go
One tingling health from top to toe;
Nor took a punch nor given a swing,
But just soaked deady round the ring
Until their brains and bloods were foul
Enough to make their throttles howl,
While we who Jesus died to teach
Fought round on round, three minutes each.

And thinking that, you'll understand
I thought, "I'll go and take Bill's hand.
I'll up and say the fault was mine,
He shan't make play for these here swine."
And then I thought that that was silly,
They'd think I was afraid of Billy;
They'd think (I thought it, God forgive me)
I funked the hiding Bill could give me.
And that thought made me mad and hot.
"Think that, will they? Well, they shall not.
They shan't think that. I will not.
I'm Damned if I will. I will not."
      Time!

From the beginning of the bout
My luck was gone, my hand was out.
Right from the start Bill called the play,
But I was quick and kept away
Till the fourth round, when work got mixed,
And then I knew Bill had me fixed.
My hand was out, why, Heaven knows;
Bill punched me when and where he chose.
Through two more rounds we quartered wide,
And all the time my hands seemed tied;
Bill punched me when and where he pleased.
The cheering from my backers eased,
But every punch I heard a yell
Of "That's the style, Bill, give him hell."
No one for me, but Jimmy's light
"Straight left! Straight left—!" and "Watch his
      right."

I don't know how a boxer goes
When all his body hums from blows;
I know I seemed to rock and spin,
I don't know how I saved my chin;
I know I thought my only friend
Was that clinked flask at each round's end
When my two seconds, Ed and Jimmy,
Had sixty seconds' help to gimme.
But in the ninth, with pain and knocks
I stopped: I couldn't fight nor box.
But missed his swing, the light was tricky,
But I went down, and stayed down, dicky.
"Get up," cried Jim. I said, "I will."
Then all the gang yelled, "Out him, Bill.
Out him." Bill rushed ... and Clink, Clink,
      Clink.
Time! and Jim's knee, and rum to drink.
And round the ring there ran a titter:
"Saved by the call, the bloody quitter."

They drove (a dodge that never fails)
A pin beneath my finger nails.
They poured what seemed a running beck
Of cold spring water down my neck;
Jim with a lancet quick as flies
Lowered the swellings round my eyes.
They sluiced my legs and fanned my face
Through all that blessed minute's grace;
They gave my calves a thorough kneading,
They salved my cuts and stopped the bleeding.
A gulp of liquor dulled the pain,
And then the two flasks clinked again.
Time!
      There was Bill as grim as death,
He rushed, I clinched, to get more breath,
And breath I got, though Billy bats
Some stinging short-arms in my slats.
And when we broke, as I foresaw,
He swung his right in for the jaw.
I stopped it on my shoulder bone,
And at the shock I heard Bill groan—
A little groan or moan or grunt
As though I'd hit his wind a bunt.
At that, I clinched, and while we clinched,
His old time right-arm dig was flinched,
And when we broke he hit me light
As though he didn't trust his right,
He flapped me somehow with his wrist
As though he couldn't use his fist,
And when he hit he winced with pain.
I thought, "Your sprained thumb's crocked again."
So I got strength and Bill gave ground,
And that round was an easy round.

During the wait my Jimmy said,
"What's making Billy fight so dead?
He's all to pieces. Is he blown?"
"His thumb's out." "No? Then it's your own.
It's all your own, but don't be rash—
He's got the goods if you've got cash,
And what one hand can do he'll do,
Be careful this next round or two."

Time. There was Bill, and I felt sick
That luck should play so mean a trick
And give me leave to knock him out
After he'd plainly won the bout.
But by the way the man came at me
He made it plain he meant to bat me;
If you'd a seen the way he come
You wouldn't think he'd crocked a thumb.

With all his skill and all his might
He clipped me dizzy left and right;
The Lord knows what the effort cost,
But he was mad to think he'd lost,
And knowing nothing else could save him
He didn't care what pain it gave him
He called the music and the dance
For five rounds more and gave no chance.

Try to imagine if you can
The kind of manhood in the man,
And if you'd like to feel his pain
You sprain your thumb and hit the sprain.
And hit it hard, with all your power
On something hard for half-an-hour,
While someone thumps you black and blue,
And then you'll know what Billy knew.
Bill took that pain without a sound
Till halfway through the eighteenth round,
And then I sent him down and out,
And Silas said, "Kane wins the bout."

When Bill came to, you understand,
I ripped the mitten from my hand
And went across to ask Bill shake.

My limbs were all one pain and ache,
I was so weary and so sore
I don't think I'd a stood much more.
Bill in his corner bathed his thumb,
Buttoned his shirt and glowered glum.
"I'll never shake your hand," he said.
"I'd rather see my children dead.
I've been about and had some fun with you,
But you're a liar and I've done with you.
You've knocked me out, you didn't beat me;
Look out the next time that you meet me,
There'll be no friend to watch the clock for you
And no convenient thumb to crock for you,
And I'll take care, with much delight,
You'll get what you'd a got tonight;
That puts my meaning clear, I guess,
Now get to hell; I want to dress."

I dressed. My backers one and all
Said, "Well done you," or "Good old Saul."
"Saul is a wonder and a fly 'un,
"What'll you have, Saul, at the Lion?"
With merry oaths they helped me down
The stony wood path to the town.

[FACT]

THE TIME OF RUBY ROBERT

Edgar Lee Masters (1869–1950) was not only a major poet, best known for his *Spoon River Anthology,* but also a biographer and most fortunately for our purposes an avid admirer and keen observer of boxing. Here he makes his pitch for Bob Fitzsimmons, the Cornishman who held the middleweight, heavyweight and light-heavyweight titles in that order.

EDGAR LEE MASTERS

I saw Bob Fitzsimmons a good many times, both in action, and when he was ambling on the streets of Chicago, sometimes leading his pet lion. His hair was reddish, but he wasn't so very ruby after all, and as for freckles, though he was cartooned with a great back covered with freckles, the size of a quarter, he wasn't very freckled either. Sports writers must have something sensational. When it isn't at hand they make it up, and often out of scant materials. Fitz's clothes always seemed too tight for him, too tight in the shoulders. He dressed rather flashily, not in taste like "Gentleman" Jim Corbett. He talked like a Cockney, pronouncing "half," "arf," and the like. As he walked along you could see that his legs were not of the same giant proportions as his shoulders. The latter were simply huge.

You will find in the twenty-third book of *The Iliad* old Homer's description of the fight between the boxer Epeius and the boxer Euryalus, in which Epeius smote Euryalus, so that his legs sank beneath him. They fought in those days with thongs of ox-hide fitted about their hands. There may have been critics of the game, but they did not indulge for years in comparative analyses, and in fanciful reasons for the defeat of one or the other. The Homeric fight reminds one of the contests of Fitz, for when he smote an antagonist the latter's "glorious limbs" sank beneath him.

I have been interested in pugilism all my life. I have seen many of the greatest of the pugilists. The reports of fights have a strange fascination for me, and I have always studied them, as later I have followed the explanations and criticisms and guesses of the men who follow the sport for the newspapers. If you will consider that many of them were not born when Corbett defeated Sullivan in 1892, or even when Fitzsimmons defeated Corbett in 1897, you will see that when these judges of the sport indulge in comparisons, and say that Louis is a greater puncher than Jeffries was, or that Peter Maher was a harder hitter than Louis, they are manifestly venturing an opinion without the facts having been gathered by the eyes. One thing that stands out is the constant cry that Louis was knocked down by Schmeling, and later by Galento, and that shows that he is not all that he is cracked up to be. They don't take into account that many of the greatest boxers were knocked down somewhere along the path of their career. The great Sullivan was knocked down by Charley Mitchell, who was a middleweight. Jack Johnson was knocked down by Stanley Ketchell, a middleweight. Fitzsimmons was knocked down many times. Corbett was knocked down and knocked out. Dempsey was knocked out of the ring by Firpo. Tunney was knocked down for a long count by Dempsey. The list could be amplified. This is enough to prove that the most skilled boxer can get it and that it does not speak much one way or the other as to his standing. Certainly

and plainly Sullivan was a better man than Mitchell; Jack Johnson was a better man than Ketchell, and Fitzsimmons was a better man than the men who floored him. Dempsey demonstrated his superiority over Firpo on the spot. And Tunney, though knocked down, got the decision, and I have never heard any great howl that he did so. The case against Louis passes out when the facts are considered which should enter into a judgment of him as a champion. No one who knows anything would say that Galento is a better man than Louis. A big awkward fighter can get in a blow sometimes, and for that matter an ordinary man could knock Louis down, or Sullivan in his best days, if he got the right sock on the right spot. I have a memory of Sullivan being knocked down in barroom scraps. I am surprised to see experts give so much attention to the knock down that Louis received at the hands of Schmeling. Schmeling is a big man and when he got in the right blow on Louis, Louis had to go down, as great fighters did before him. There is nothing to this.

I could put up a good argument to the effect that Fitzsimmons, all things considered, was the greatest fighter who ever lived, but it would be a long argument and intricate with comparisons back and forth. Along the way I'd have to get Dempsey out of the way, who at Toledo in his fight with Willard was a whirlwind of power and skill. I have felt that Fitz could have defeated Sullivan. But I'll not indulge in such speculations. I'll only say that Fitz never had a superior, and rest the case upon some salient facts. In this connection I might mention first the matter of his age when he won battles, this has bearing upon his strength and vitality. He was never anything more than a light heavyweight, a class created in 1903 when George Gardner defeated Jack Root. Fitz defeated Gardner in the fall of 1903. So that when he defeated Corbett in 1897 he was only the middleweight champion.

Sullivan called Fitz a fighting machine on stilts, in reference to his spindling legs and his enormous shoulders and arms. But be it observed I don't recall an instance where Fitz's legs gave out on him. They seemed to have the endurance of steel. As to age he was thirty-five when he won the championship of the world over Corbett; he was forty-one when he gave the giant Jeffries with his 220 pounds of bone and muscle a terrible beating, and conceivably might have won the fight if his hands had not been turned to pulp by hammering the bronze head and jaws of Jeffries. On the other hand Corbett was towards thirty-one when he lost to Fitzsimmons; Dempsey was thirty-one when he lost to Tunney; Sullivan was thirty-four when he lost to Corbett. I differ from experts on fighting as to this age matter. A man at thirty-one or thirty-four is good enough for any man of any age. It may be that dissipation will lower a fighter's effective strength, but the mere matter of years, which have not advanced beyond thirty or so, will not do so. The case of Fitzsimmons proves this, and I stress it to make the point in favor of the Cornishman as a fighter with no superior. He had what no one can explain: he had strength, as Sullivan had, strength that can endure, that can rush and deliver great blows, strength that can stand up when beaten and bloody and fight on, as Sullivan did in his fight with Corbett. There was a report about that Sullivan was drunk the night before that fight. It is likely true, for Sullivan had been drinking heavily for years. And they say that is bad for the muscles and the wind—but look at Sullivan lasting for 21 rounds, chasing Corbett around the ring, and at last sinking in exhaustion in his corner. The standard reports of this fight say that Corbett defeated Sullivan; they do not say that Sullivan was knocked out.

Corbett was a boxer. He cut his foes to pieces, and as for himself he was hard to hit. He cut Fitzsimmons to ribbons, but it did not avail him, as it did in his fight with Sullivan. Fitz stayed on, though several years older than Corbett, and older than Sullivan was when Corbett defeated him. These points are well to remember.

I saw Fitzsimmons in action several times, first with a fighter named Ed Dunkhorst, who was called the "Human Freight Car." He was the Carnera of his day. When the two stepped into the ring it looked like a fight between a grasshopper and a rat. You can well suppose that if Dunkhorst's weight had sent a blow to Fitz's jaw that Fitz would have gone down. Why not? Dunkhorst must have weighed towards three hundred. But Fitz almost murdered this huge slugger, as he waltzed around Dunkhorst planting terrible punches that made Dunkhorst grunt and double up. Before this time Fitz had defeated Peter Maher, and the first Jack Dempsey and a long list of fighters of all weights. He took them all on, saying that the bigger they were the harder they fell.

Then I saw the fight between Fitzsimmons and the champion of South Africa, a heavyweight named Jeff Thorne, or Jim Thorne, the name is differently reported. Thorne greatly outweighed Fitz, perhaps by twenty pounds anyway. Thorne was not to be despised. There had been so much talk by this time of Fitz's short punch, a kind of corkscrew it was, that I was very glad of the chance to see him use it on this Jeff Thorne. I wanted to see how it was that Fitz could put a man down so that he could not get up. In this connection you must admit that many champions didn't put their men down so that they could not get up; they wore them out, or cut them to pieces, or covered them with blood and bruises, or put them down as Dempsey put down Tunney—who got up. Fitz put them down for good. He did it with Corbett, and many others.

Malachy Hogan, a referee long remembered as an honest man and a good, fellow, met me on the street one day in Chicago and gave me a ringside seat to this fight between Fitz and Thorne. It was held at Tattersall's, and I was there on time, sitting within a few feet of the ring, waiting to see Fitz do the trick.

Pretty soon the fighters entered the ring amid great applause. Fitz in a manner ambled into the ring, though he was quick and nimble enough. His indifference was laughable. He looked about as if he knew what the result was going to be, as if he wanted to get at the business and have it over. His legs were slender, but not too much so, not as much so as the cartoons of the time led one to believe that they were. He was bald, but what hair he had was not so ruby after all. The arresting thing about him was his shoulders, which were huge, with no ridges of muscles, but as it seemed with long thin muscles slipping and gliding smoothly and easily beneath his skin, not so freckled after all. His arms were the most powerful to look at that I ever saw, and without bulges. They were long symmetrical cables of muscle, like a python's body, like the legs of a large man. He probably weighed about 160, a good deal less than Thorne, that was clear.

Fitz sat in his corner unconcerned, waiting for the bell, while Malachy Hogan stepped about getting ready to judge the fight. At last the bell! Fitz ambled over to the center of the ring, and there met Thorne coming on fast, full of fight, and striking out viciously over and over. He tried for Fitz's jaw. Fitz lifted up one of those huge shoulders, and sent the blow harmlessly to one side. He tried for Fitz's stomach. Fitz just drew in his stomach, and the blow fanned the air. Meantime Fitz did not strike a blow; and meantime I was watching every movement with concentrated eyes. The round ended with no damage. Thorne had not hit Fitz, Fitz had not tried to hit Thorne. I was wondering what cunning plan Fitz was nursing in that small bald head of his, I was watching to see the famous corkscrew.

Well, the second round, with Thorne after Fitz as in the first round, to no result! Then they got close together, and I looked and watched. Then this is what I saw: Fitz twisted a short blow to Thorne which caught him on the chin. The blow was not over six inches in delivery—but what a sock! You could tell that from the way that Thorne crumpled. He sank down to the resin. Malachy counted him out. He did not get up. He lay there limp and helpless. Malachy with the help of some others carried him to his corner. When he was put into his chair his head fell over on his breast. They rubbed him with ammonia. They sprayed champagne upon him. Still he did not come to. He was dead to the world. I wish I had held a watch on all this. But it was a good deal more than 18 seconds. It seemed to me several minutes before Thorne awoke to the realities. He had received one of Fitz's twists from one of those python-like arms. Can you think of another fighter who did the like, or did what Fitz did at Carson City to Corbett? Does this count in measuring what Fitz was when compared to other fighters?

No championship should be decided on ten rounds. I indulge that judgment based upon what I have seen, for outside of Fitz and others, Choynski included, and Jack Johnson in a sparing match, I saw Young Griffo, Terry McGovern, Tommy West, Benny Leonard, Harry Wills, Firpo, and in the old days Joe Goddard, Jim Hall, a marvelous boxer, whom Fitz defeated with some difficulty, and once a few years before Sullivan died I saw him spar with Jake Kilrain. A fighter can be very bad off in the tenth round, or even in the fifteenth round, and then come on and score the victory. That's what it means to have strength, that enigmatic X. That's what it means to fight 75 rounds, as Sullivan did with Jake Kilrain. That's what it means to be bleeding and reeling, as Fitz was in the 13th round at Carson City, and then in the 14th round to score a terrible knockout. Which shows

that a man's strength and punching power can be on tap when he is bleeding. In these days a technical knockout is awarded when a man is blind and bleeding. Not in the old days, not in the days of Homer, nor in the days when Jeffries was blind from Fitz's blows at Coney Island.

One time in a conversation with Corbett, not many years before his death, I asked him how it was that he had fought sixty rounds, and others had fought as many in former days, and then in these later days 15 rounds were considered a long fight, long enough to test the superiority of one of the contestants. His reply was that fighters grew to be trained for speed and terrific strength, quickly exerted; while formerly they were trained for endurance, trained by running and other exercises that make for wind. There is something to this, but it doesn't quite convince. Later than this I read a statement by Tunney in which he said that ten rounds were not enough upon which a championship should pass. And I believe that in the second fight between him and Dempsey, Dempsey might have scored a knockout if the fight had gone to fifteen rounds. The matter comes back to that enigmatic thing called strength, to which I have already referred. In this talk I furnish material for experts to argue, but I am an expert myself, since I have done for years what experts do, namely, I have watched fights, read the reports of fights, and talked to experts who have seen fights that I did not see.

Fitz's fight with Corbett at Carson City helps to prove my point. I didn't see this fight, but I have talked by the hour about it with Bob Davis, who was in Fitz's corner there, representing the New York *Journal*, and as a coach to Fitz. You will find descriptions of this fight in plenty, but none so vivid as that Bob Davis can give at the luncheon table. It was a fierce fight, animated by hate on Corbett's part, and by cool ambition on Fitz's. Corbett kept dancing about jabbing and cutting Fitz, and dodging Fitz's blows. He hit Fitz enough. He covered him with blood. In the sixth round Fitz was down. It seemed that Fitz was through. In the thirteenth round Fitz presented a spectacle as terrible as Galento did in his recent fight with Louis. But the fight was not stopped. It had to go on to a finish.

Bob Davis told me that Fitz came back to his corner at the end of the thirteenth round with his chest streaming with blood, with his face covered with blood, with his eyes half-blinded. He sat down and his seconds began to sponge him off, to work on him. Then Fitz said coolly and as a matter of fact that he would get Corbett in the next round and to put up money on it, to tell the boys to bet. Think of that! When Bob heard Fitz say this he turned to his fellows and told them to put their money on Fitz. That was the amount of confidence that Bob Davis had in Fitz, sitting there covered with blood. More than that he sent a wire to his paper, saying that Fitz had won in the fourteenth round. This before the round was fought! But it was soon fought. Fitz worked what was called "the fatal shift," some kind of a placing and bracing of his feet in which all his bulk and strength were put into leverage, and he delivered the solar plexus, a blow to the midriff, which sent Corbett writhing and helpless, defeated and counted out. Everybody knows what it is to get a blow in the pit of the stomach. That was what Fitz gave Corbett. He had studied it out, and it did the trick. That made Fitz heavyweight champion of the world, at thirty-five years of age, weighing about 160 pounds. He began then to tour the country heralded as the champion of champions. He was thus heralded, but his name lacked magic somehow. He didn't clean up. He was not a gentleman, a Shakespearean amateur; he was a fighter. Six years after this time he won the light heavyweight championship. He was only the world's middleweight champion when he defeated Corbett.

In 1898 Jeffries after a bruising fight in San Francisco with Tom Sharkey, gaining the decision in the 20th round, was after Fitz. Fitz told him to go and get a reputation. Finally when the match was made Jeffries took on Tommy Ryan as a trainer, a very foxy and able fighter. He trained Jeffries so that Fitz would have difficulty in hitting him. That is he trained him to a kind of crouch, with the head down and one fist thrust forward. The great hulk, Jeffries, with his 220 pounds of bronze-like flesh, did not want to be hit by a fist with only 160 pounds back of it, seeing that those pounds were Fitz's. Fitz gave Jeffries everything he had. He was then thirty-seven years of age. Jeffries was twenty-four. In the 11th round Jeffries knocked old Fitz out.

Fitz turned forty and challenged Jeffries. In the meantime Jeffries had fought Tom Sharkey 25 rounds and had won the decision. There was no knock down. For the first time that I know any-thing about, pictures were made of the fight. I saw them and studied them, watching the short Sharkey and the tall bear-like Jeffries fight toe to toe, round after round. You couldn't tell from the pictures that either one had any advantage. They toed the mark and slugged. Often Jeffries' head went back, often Jeffries soaked Sharkey with terrific blows. But it turned out that Sharkey's ribs were smashed. The fight looked like a draw. But after observation at the hospital it was not difficult for doctors to say that Sharkey was badly punished, even if not knocked out.

At this time there was a huge fellow named Gus Ruhlin, called the giant grip-man, as he had run a grip-car. In the week before Fitz fought Jeffries the second fight, Fitz took on this Ruhlin, defeating him handily in a few rounds. Also in this week he took on Sharkey, knocking him out in two rounds, as I remember the facts. True, Sharkey had been badly macerated in that fight with Jeffries, but what do you think of the trick that Fitz turned in actually knocking out the tough Tom Sharkey? Then came Fitz's second fight with Jeffries. It took place at San Francisco.

As I am writing this article a magazine is on my desk with a piece in it by Hype Igoe, in which he says that Fitz gave Jeffries the most awful beating that he ever saw a man take in the ring, and that Dempsey's destruction of Willard or Firpo cannot be compared to it. I have heard the same thing from men who were on the ground, from Louis Houseman, a sports writer for Chicago papers, from Malachy Hogan already mentioned. Fitz was over forty, and Jeffries twenty-six. Fitz was a light heavyweight, Jeffries was one of the heaviest of the heavyweights.

Houseman told me that Jeffries at the last was nothing but bloody pulp, he was blinded, reeling. In these days the fight might have been stopped to save the life of Jeffries. Fitz had the fight won by a large margin until the strange end of things in the eighth round. Then suddenly Jeffries, out of his blindness, delivered a blow which sent Fitz sprawling to the mat. It turned out that what happened was this: Fitz walked close to Jeff, saying, "Hit me, Jeff." That's what he told Houseman, and Houseman told this to me. Spectators did not realize at the time that Fitz had nothing on which to continue the fight. His hands were just mush, bloody mush. That's why he said to Jeffries, "Hit me, Jeff," and exposed himself so that Jeffries could do it. When Fitz was in his dressing room they had to cut the gloves from his bands. His endurance had not deserted him, he was simply without weapons. Can any fight by Sullivan, by Dempsey, by anyone be compared to this? To me it puts Fitz at the top. For courage, for power, for skill, for fighting will, there is nothing in the record of Sullivan down to Joe Louis that holds a candle to it.

After this fight Fitz drifted around, sometimes fighting, but not notably. He got to be fifty and wanted to fight. The authorities would not let him. His purse was thin, and finally it came out that he had died in Chicago, aged fifty-six. Like other men he had to leave it to posterity to judge of him, to decide how good he was; and as in the case of other men, experts argue about him, and lie about him, and misvalue his record. So far as I am concerned I think he was a wonder in every way.

[PORTRAIT]

NEWS OF A CHAMPION

W.O. McGeehan was the founder of the "Aw nuts" school of sports writing. He referred to boxing as "the cauliflower industry" and "the manly art of modified murder" and named the members of the New York State Athletic Commission "The Three Dumb Dukes." He wrote this column about Ad Wolgast in 1927 for the *New York Herald Tribune,* for which he worked from 1914 until he died of a heart attack in 1933 at the age of 54.

Adolph (Ad) Wolgast was lightweight champion of the world from 1910 to 1912. He died, at the age of 67, on April 14, 1955, in a sanitarium in Camarillo, California, still believing that he would someday fight Joe Gans again. Gans had died on August 10, 1910.

W.O. McGEEHAN

Ad Wolgast, once lightweight champion of the world, is in the news again briefly. Friends who have been caring for him in California have made application to have him committed to an asylum as hopelessly insane.

For more than ten years Wolgast has been living in a phantom world populated by old prize-ring ghosts. His mind failed him shortly after he lost his championship, and he labored under the hallucination that he was to meet Joe Gans (long since dead) for the lightweight championship. Jack Doyle, a Los Angeles promoter, with more heart than most of the men who make their money out of the manly art of modified murder, took pity on him and assumed full charge of him.

Through Doyle's generosity Ad Wolgast was provided with a little gymnasium, where he did his training. He seldom used to miss a morning on the road. It was his hallucination that he was to meet Joe Gans, dead even before Wolgast's mind went into the fog, in a championship bout. For years he settled down into this routine with only the idea that he must be in condition for the championship bout.

Sometimes they would take him to boxing matches. He always used to say, "I could whip either of them." But he never insisted on meeting any of the fighters he saw. He was concentrating on the phantom bout with Gans. Physically Wolgast seemed to be all that he ever had been, but his mind was gone forever.

I saw Wolgast win the lightweight championship from Battling Nelson in a ring pitched in the adobe mud near Port Richmond, California. For concentrated viciousness, prolonged past forty rounds, that was the most savage bout I have ever seen. Both men were badly enough battered, for in giving Nelson a beating, Wolgast was forced to take almost as much as he gave. It was inevitable that the effects would tell.

Somewhere around the thirtieth round I think it was, Wolgast was dropped by a body blow and it looked like the end. But he was up in an instant, snarling and lashing at Nelson. After that it was Nelson, the Durable Dane, who showed signs of weakening and whose face began to look like a raw slab of steak. The features were obliterated and only the slit of one eye remained open.

In the forty-second round Nelson was pressing feebly forward while Wolgast's gloves were hurling crimson splashes around the ring every time they struck the battered face. The Dane would not yield an inch, but it had become so cruel that the most hardened ringsiders were calling upon the referee to stop it.

Finally Eddie Smith stepped between the men and pushed Nelson to his corner. The Dane snarled at him, then tried to protest through the twisted and battered mouth. The only sound that came was one such as might have been made by an exhausted and terribly wounded wild animal. Nelson's seconds caught him and pushed him onto the stool in the corner. The referee raised Wolgast's hand. He had become the lightweight champion of the world.

Not so long after I saw him lose this title to Willie Ritchie of California, then a young graduate from the amateur ranks. It started out as though Wolgast would rush Ritchie off his feet. The "Cadillac Bearcat" was beating the Californian from the start, when Ritchie landed a wild swing that caught Wolgast flush on the jaw. Wolgast dropped to his knees, all but out. As he was about to collapse he drove two foul punches upward at the Californian. He had the rattlesnake's instinct to strike, even when mortally hurt.

It was Wolgast's fate to have won the championship in one of the hardest fights ever staged only to have lost it through almost a chance blow—if there is such a thing as a chance blow.

Said one of Wolgast's former managers, "He was one of the greatest fighters I ever knew, and it was a pleasure to manage him. He never cared whom he fought or how often. He would fight anybody I signed him up with.

"Once I tried him out for fun. I knew that he was in his hotel room so I rang him up and told him I had signed him as a substitute boxer for some bouts that night. The schedule called for him to appear in three hours. 'All right,' he said. 'Wake me up in a few hours, and I'll get ready to go into the ring.'

" 'But you haven't asked who it is that you are going to fight,' I said. 'No,' said Wolgast, 'and I don't care. Just wake me up so that I won't be late getting into the ring.' He was that way all the time. He would say, 'Get me anybody for any time, and I'll fight him any time you say.'

"You do not meet that kind of fighter these days, the fellow you can have hop into a ring on a few hours' notice. The boys are very careful, particularly the topnotchers, as to the kind of matches you make for them. They never want to take a chance with any of the rough ones. Can you picture any of the later lightweights being careless about whom they are signed up with?"

From the point of view of the manager there is no doubt that Wolgast was the ideal prize fighter. He always was willing to step into the ring at the command of the mastermind, to take a beating, and to listen to the voice of the manager shouting, "Go on in. He can't hurt us!"

Nearly all of Wolgast's former managers have their health and are in no danger of the almshouse or the insane asylum. Oh yes. There is no doubt that Ad Wolgast was the ideal prize fighter from the manager's point of view. But poor little Wolgast will be taken to a state insane asylum shortly. The blows that the managers did not feel seem to have had effect upon Wolgast. Perhaps the fighter was just a trifle more sensitive than the manager.

THE SOUR TASTE IN JACK BODELL'S POP

Hugh McIlvanney may well be the best boxing writer not only of his time but any time on either side of the ocean. Working out of England he has followed the milling coves from continent to continent, and here, back in London, on March 24, 1970, he covered Jack Bodell vs. Henry Cooper.

HUGH McILVANNEY

The sneering denigration of Jack Bodell has gone beyond a joke. After he had fought unyieldingly through 15 painful rounds against the superior class of Henry Cooper last week, striving to compensate with fitness and heart for his acknowledged deficiencies in skill, Bodell was jeered out of the ring at Wembley Pool. "Get back among the pig swill," he was told by a bunch of characters who looked as if they might have more than a passing acquaintance with the stuff. They came jostling out of those seats where all the best fights are fought and yelled at the big man as he squinted sadly past discoloured swellings at the emotional tumult greeting Cooper's restoration to the British heavyweight championship. A cacophony of animal noises made extravagant allusion to the few chickens Bodell keeps at home in Derbyshire. "You're a clown, Bodell. You wasted your bloody time coming here, you big mug."

It can be said that the only sensible reaction to such inanities is that of George Walker, who manages his brother Billy's career as a heavyweight. "When you go into the fight game you go in for the cash. These are the people you despise. They're nothing. All they are good for is buying tickets. If that sort of thing gets under your skin, you shouldn't be in the business." Of course, George was always a hard man for whom the rustle of bank notes drowned most other annoying sounds. But even in boxing not everyone can develop that kind of skin. Tougher men than Bodell have been hurt by such spiteful assaults on their dignity. The former champion's wife has already said publicly that she has been distressed by the endless baiting.

She senses that her man has been subjected to more than the normal callousness of the fight crowd. He has been chosen as the victim of a sustained, sadistic joke. Professional boxers readily learn to live with the antagonism of the mob, to ignore its ill-tempered disapproval. But to fight your heart out and then be met with derisive laughter must be peculiarly sickening. Many fighters have made a good living by playing the clown in the ring but Bodell has always struggled to be taken seriously.

Obviously, when the public, or even a moronic section of it, decides spontaneously to ridicule someone there is not much to be done. In this case, however, the relentless emphasis of London promoters on Bodell's failure to sell tickets, on the unattractiveness of his crude southpaw methods and unglamorous persona, encouraged a contemptuous attitude. The computerised charade between Muhammad Ali and the late Rocky Marciano was enacted behind closed doors, leaving an eerie greyness where the spectators should have been, and when it was shown here one famous matchmaker said: "Some crowd. Jack Bodell must have been on the bill." It was a mildly amusing insult, in the same category as the suggestion that Bodell's supporters travel to fights on the back of one motorbike.

Some of the other jibes are made inevitable by Bodell's determination to carry a piece of south Derbyshire around with him wherever he goes. He is a dedicated hick, often dressing in the kind of suits middle-aged men remember encountering at demobilisation centres, and arranging his tie in an elaborate left-handed Windsor that still leaves the knot no bigger than a two-shilling piece. His raw, big-jawed face, and the short hair thinning into single strands where once it made an oily quiff above his forehead accentuate what most Londoners regard as an agricultural appearance, though he started working life as a collier. An accent that seems to broaden as he enters the Home Counties completes the picture of a man who is less than a ready-made hero for metropolitan audiences. All this would be overlooked, indeed its exoticism might be an advantage, if he could fight brilliantly or dramatically. He cannot. His boxing is amateurishly clumsy. His head still jerks into an exposed position as he lunges in with his ponderous right lead, his left is predictable and only modestly damaging and his footwork gives the impression of having been acquired at a school for deep-sea divers.

The statistical healthiness of his record—only ten defeats in 63 contests—can be traced largely to the barging strength of the headlong rush that is his principal tactic, to conscientious industry and to admirable courage. These last qualities are not as commonplace as many imagine, and at two points in the match with Cooper on Tuesday they might have earned a great deal. In the sixth round Cooper, having applied conspicuous pressure in the previous three minutes, began to show evidence of his 36 years, and Bodell took the round easily. But he could never again overcome the difference in technical equipment and punching authority. When Cooper's legs tired noticeably in the 14th the younger man, too, was weary and could not exploit the chance. So Cooper was left, as most of us had suspected he would be, with another great night to remember. Anyone who questions his right to it must have spent the past decade on another planet. To establish how exceptional he is it is not necessary to stress the excitement of his punching, the contrast between the gentle charm of his demeanour outside the ring and the violent courage of his performances inside, or the consistency that has enabled him to hold the British title for more than ten years. It is only necessary to say that on the brink of his 36th birthday he left home to train for six weeks, isolated from the family that is the genuine centre of his life. More than anything else, all those hours of running in cold Kent dawns kept the old man just young enough on Tuesday night.

At home in Wembley some time later, pouring champagne for a small party that included the recruited cut expert Eddie Thomas, Cooper said he was likely to meet the South African Jimmy Richards, and then José Urtain, the Basque heavyweight whose record suggests he has faced a long line of plaster gnomes. These are acceptable names—that of Joe Frazier is patently not—but most of us would take special satisfaction from seeing Cooper retire to enjoy a lifetime of untarnished prestige. Tuesday showed that while he is still too much for any British heavyweight he no longer hooks with the deadliness to worry the best in the world. In short, all that is left for him in the game is money, and he has enough of that to get by.

With Jack Bodell, everything is different. After telephoning home from the ringside on Tuesday, he strode cheerily into his dressing-room, stripped to his boxing boots and shouted for drinks. Someone produced a bottle of lemonade. "Gimme that bleeder," said Bodell. "That's your real south Derbyshire pop. Best in the world." He drank it down eagerly, telling us between gulps that he hadn't seen the last of the British title and we hadn't seen the best of him. Half an hour afterwards, as Cooper and the rest of us were preparing to leave the other dressing-room along the corridor, Bodell suddenly appeared in his overcoat and plonked himself down in a chair just inside the door of the small ugly room. He had two bottles of beer and was obviously in a mood to be sociable. It was impossible not to feel a warmth for this large, simple-natured, likeable man.

In that strange moment the mindless mocking of him seemed to amount to real cruelty. All of us hesitated, sensing he should have company, but Cooper had a party to host and with a last mumble of inadequate pleasantries we filed out, leaving the loser sitting alone in the winner's dressing-room.

THE NONPAREIL'S GRAVE

This is boxing's most famous poem. Jack Dempsey, "The Nonpareil," was born John Kelly in County Kildare, Ireland, on December 15, 1862. He won the middleweight title in 1884, and was undefeated in sixty-one fights when he was knocked out by George LaBlanche, with an illegal pivot punch, in 1889. Two years later he lost the title to Bob Fitzsimmons, and he died on November 2, 1895, ten months after his last fight, in Portland, Oregon, at the age of 32.

M. J. McMahon, of Portland, Dempsey's lawyer, was so disturbed by the neglect of his idol's grave that he wrote this poem and circulated 1,000 copies of it anonymously. One of these reached the *Portland Oregonian,* which printed the poem on December 10, 1899. Dempsey's friends then erected a tombstone, on which the poem is inscribed.

M. J. McMAHON

I

Far out in the wilds of Oregon,
　On a lonely mountain side,
Where Columbia's mighty waters,
　Roll down to the ocean tide;
Where the giant fir and cedar
　Are imaged in the wave,
O'ergrown with firs and lichens,
　I found Jack Dempsey's grave.

II

I found no marble monolith,
　No broken shaft, or stone,
Recording sixty victories,
　This vanquished victor won;
No rose, no shamrock could I find,
　No mortal here to tell
Where sleeps in this forsaken spot
　Immortal Nonpareil.

III

A winding wooden canyon road
　That mortals seldom tread,
Leads up this lonely mountain,
　To the desert of the dead.

And the Western sun was sinking
　In Pacific's golden wave,
And those solemn pines kept watching
　Over poor Jack Dempsey's grave.

IV

Forgotten by ten thousand throats,
　That thundered his acclaim,
Forgotten by his friends and foes,
　Who cheered his very name.
Oblivion wraps his faded form,
　But ages hence shall save
The memory of that Irish lad
　That fills poor Dempsey's grave.

V

Oh, Fame, why sleeps thy favored son
　In wilds, in woods, in weeds,
And shall he ever thus sleep on,
　Interred his valiant deeds?
'Tis strange New York should thus forget
　Its "bravest of the brave"
And in the fields of Oregon,
　Unmarked, leave Dempsey's grave.

[FACT]

FROM: STREET FIGHTING TO FAME

Daniel Mendoza, called "The Light of Israel," was born on July 5, 1764, at Aldgate, London. He stood five feet seven inches, weighed 160 pounds and participated in thirty-seven bouts, the last when he was 56. He was the first Jewish champion of the world, the first proponent of scientific boxing, and his treatise *The Art of Pugilism* was the first technical tract to appear on the subject. He made a fortune, enjoyed it, failed at business, did time in debtor's prison and was constantly on the run from his creditors. He died on September 3, 1836, at the age of 72, leaving a wife, eleven children, no money, but a great name.

The following excerpts are from *The Memoirs of the Life of Daniel Mendoza*, the first such by any champion, published in 1826 and edited anew in 1951 by Paul Magriel. They tell of his penchant, before his two victories over Richard Humphries made him famous, for street fighting, of his visit with King George III, with whom no other Jew had ever spoken, and of an experience not uncommon to fighters whose reputations make them targets.

DANIEL MENDOZA

Shortly after my return to town, I was induced to engage in another pugilistic contest, for being present one day in company with a man at a fight at Kentish Town, my friend happened to be grossly insulted by a man whom I challenged in consequence, and we accordingly set to, when after a contest of about half an hour, he was forced to give in, being so severely beaten as to be scarcely able to stand, and indeed, he was obliged to be carried off the field.

Some short time after this I fought three battles in one day, which were occasioned by the following circumstances:

Being at this time out of employment, I was enabled to devote a day or two to amusement and therefore availed myself of the opportunity to go to Barnet to see a battle there between Johnson and Love; and accordingly set out walking, but on reaching Highgate I was overtaken by an old man who was going to the fight in a cart with some friends and being invited to make one of their party, I accompanied them.

On our arrival at Barnet, we were greatly disappointed, for, instead of witnessing a contest of skill between the combatants, Johnson obtained the victory over his opponent in less than five minutes.

On our return, we overtook a young man driving a cart, who boasted greatly of the swiftness of his horse, and invited us to run against him, to which we agreed, and to his great disappointment gained the victory, upon which he was so much out

of humor, that he began to vent his spleen upon us. At this moment a gentleman happened to ride up, who, on the circumstance being mentioned to him, declared it would afford him the greatest gratification to see such a fellow well thrashed, and promised to reward anyone who would set about it. Upon which I expressed my determination of having a trial with him myself, for though he appeared to be superior to me in strength, I felt sufficient confidence in my own powers to be but very little dismayed at the circumstance.

Having alighted, therefore, we stripped and set to in an adjoining field, and having fought nearly an hour, the battle ended in my favor.

At the conclusion of the contest, the gentleman by whose persuasion I was induced to fight, being highly pleased, presented me with a guinea and raised a subscription for me among the spectators of between five and six pounds.

The success of this battle and the unexpected pleasure of receiving a few pounds put me in high spirits, and I determined to spend the rest of the day with my companions. We proceeded on the road with great triumph when we were accosted at Finchley by a party of butchers who seemed desirous of provoking a quarrel. A sporting gentleman who was passing by at that time expressed his surprise that I did not get out of the cart and thrash the butchers for their insolence; upon which I acquainted him with the circumstance of my having just fought, but on his promise of a guinea if I again came off victorious I set to with the butcher, who after a battle of half an hour gave in. The gentleman gave me two guineas and also raised a subscription, which with what I had received before amounted to fourteen pounds. I was highly elated and anxious to get to town to spend some of the money which I considered as the honorable reward of my exertions.

I set off to town on horseback but soon found that my day's work was not yet finished, for I had not proceeded far before the disorder of my dress and my awkward manner of riding happened to attract the notice of a fellow who was passing, and who remarked to his companions that I had the appearance of a tailor. They began to shout with a view to frightening the horse and making me the butt of their sport. I immediately dismounted and having singled out the instigator of the disturbance and insisted on his fighting me on the spot, I convinced him in half an hour that he had much better have let me alone.

He found that though I could not ride very well, I could fight quite well enough to give him as severe a thrashing as perhaps he ever received, and from the condition in which I left him, I have no doubt that he was too much in need of ease and rest himself to molest anyone else that evening. I came off this contest as from the two others without receiving a scratched face, or even any blow of material consequence.

I now remounted, and no one offering me any further interruption, proceeded on my journey; on reaching town I determined (notwithstanding the fatiguing exertions of the day) to go to a dance which I knew was to be held in a certain house I was in the habit of frequenting; and accordingly, not choosing to leave my horse in the street, I introduced him into the dancing room, to the surprise and entertainment of the company, chiefly consisting of sailors and their lasses, and having remained here for about two hours, and it drawing near midnight, I thought it high time to quit this place of mirth.

When my health was improving, I frequently used to indulge myself with excursions into the country for the purpose of taking the air. On one of these occasions, I went for a few days to Windsor, and, during my stay in that town, had the honor of being introduced to a great personage. This happened one evening on the terrace, where I was

walking, and was suddenly surprised at being accosted by a nobleman, who, in a very abrupt manner, mentioned his intention of introducing me to His Majesty. He had scarcely spoken when the King, attended by some lords in waiting, approached the spot, upon which I was introduced, and had a long conversation with His Majesty, who made many ingenious remarks on the pugilistic art, such as might naturally be expected to be made by a person of so comprehensive a mind and such transcendent abilities, as that illustrious personage is generally believed to possess!

Before I quitted the terrace, the Princess Royal (now queen of Württemberg) brought one of the younger branches of the royal family to me, and asked my permission (which I of course readily granted) for this young gentleman to strike me a blow, in order that he might have to boast at a subsequent opportunity of having at an early period of his life, struck a professed pugilist on Windsor terrace.

My creditors having now discovered that I had arrived in London, seemed resolved to harass and persecute me. A few mornings after my arrival I was arrested for an old debt, which it was not then in my power to discharge, and was consequently obliged to give bail to the action, which I was at length, with considerable difficulty, enabled to settle. In numerous other instances, I was subjected to great expense and inconvenience, but in consequence of a great many gentlemen taking lessons of me, and paying me liberally for my trouble, I contrived to settle many of their demands.

About this time I was introduced to Lord Camelford, whose impetuosity of temper is well known to have led him into many difficulties, and finally to have proved fatal to him. When I attended his lordship, he requested me to spar with him, which I accordingly did, and he professed to feel highly gratified at my exertions, and intimated that he would show me an original attitude of his own, in which he had attained a degree of perfection that would counteract any assault that could be made on him. At his request, therefore, I aimed several blows at him, one of which took place, and in consequence of his lordship's throwing back his head with great violence, he thrust it through the glazed door of a bookcase.

This accident irritated him greatly, and as soon as he was extricated, which was not done without difficulty, he asked, whether I had ever played at the game of single-stick? On my answering I was not entirely unacquainted with the sport, he insisted on my engaging with him; and having procured a pair of weapons from an adjoining room, we set to. At this game I found his lordship a better proficient than myself; he struck with a great force as well as skill, and I speedily received a violent blow over the ear, which caused great pain at the time. However, I was resolved not to yield, and therefore continued till he was tired, when he again proposed to change the amusement to fencing, and though I candidly told him, I knew nothing of this art, he insisted upon my engaging with him, to which I was with reluctance induced to consent. On one of the foils happening to break, he very coolly observed, we might as well change them for a pair of small swords, with which, he said, if we took proper care, we could not possibly injure each other.

To this proposal I at first strongly objected, and declared my determination not to engage with weapons of such a dangerous nature; upon which my noble antagonist appeared highly irritated, and I began to apprehend the violent effects of his anger; therefore with the view of appeasing his wrath, I pretended to assent to his proposal, merely expressing a wish that he would take care of my family, in case of any accident happening to me. This he promised to do, and left me for the purpose of fetching the swords.

As soon as the coast was clear, I rushed out of the room, and flew down stairs, with all the rapidity in my power: such was my impatience to depart, that I never stopped till I had reached the bottom of the staircase, when I found I had descended too low, and had got to the cellar door; consequently I was obliged to return, and having, at last, reached the street door, departed abruptly from the house, and, as may be imagined, never felt the least inclination to re-enter it.

[REPORTING]

DEMPSEY—FIRPO

Frank Menke was a good newspaperman, but a more successful ghost writer and encyclopedist. This piece would be an example of gross overwriting, except that it describes the most dramatic of all glove fights and, written more than twenty years after the event, is the best wrap-up of what happened.

FRANK G. MENKE

Never in the history of American pugilism was there staged a battle so sensational as the Jack Dempsey–Luis Firpo affair in New York on the night of September 14, 1923.

From the moment that the first gong banged until the Argentine warrior lay a crumpled heap upon the canvas—total time: 3 minutes, 57 seconds—there was action so rapid, so cyclonic that the eye could not follow, nor the brain record the exact details.

It was not a boxing match—not a civilized fistic encounter. Two wild men were tossed into the same ring, each with an intent to murder the other—or be murdered in his failure. And 85,000 persons, imbibing the spirit of madness, arose to their feet, and 85,000 voices howled and shrieked in a delirium that made a din which rivaled a thousand Niagaras.

Its like in ring battling had never been seen before—and never will be known again. The story is the epic of ringdom—the fight of all the ages.

With the clang of the first gong, Dempsey fairly catapulted from his comer to meet a huge, hairy giant from the pampas of South America; rushed, crouched, swirled upward and swung a terrific left-hand punch to his foeman's jaw.

It was short—by two inches.

As Dempsey steadied, to try again, Firpo's powerful right hand whistled through the night and struck Dempsey full and solid upon the point of the chin. Every ounce of the South American's gigantic body was concentrated in that blow—one of the hardest ever landed in ring annals.

The knees of the world's champion buckled under him; a world's champion pitched forward. He was toppling, face forward, to dethronement. One punch—the first of the fight—seemed to have sent him to his doom!

If Firpo had been six inches farther away at that very fraction of a second, Dempsey probably would have crumpled into the resin dust, either to rise no more, or, in rising, to be met by a fusillade of blows which probably would have crushed the consciousness from him.

But as Dempsey pitched forward, Firpo was so close that the champion fell against the body of the giant. Instinct made him grab—and hold. Desperately, wildly, Firpo tried to shake off Dempsey. Before he could achieve his purpose, the brief rest saved Dempsey.

Strength and a little power came back to Dempsey's legs; the floodgates of reserve energy opened, revived him, refreshed him—refreshed and revived, however, only the body of him, because Dempsey afterward said he remembered nothing about that first round after he had been hit with that first pile-driver blow.

He had been hit and hurt by the rushing, tearing, lunging form before him. And that form must be destroyed. Such was the prompting of savage instinct. Everything that Dempsey had learned in years of boxing was forgotten; his clear reasoning power, his coolness and calmness were gone. There was nothing left but the fighting fury which made him known as the Tiger Man of the prize ring.

Urged on only by a wild and blazing rage, the champion ripped and tore into the giant and, as he did so, he put into his blows every bit of killing power which he could summon. He was relentless, merciless, forgetful of the ethics of the fighting game; a cruel monster, determined that the man before him must be hammered and pounded into absolute helplessness.

Dempsey, loose from the first clinch, rushed at Firpo, both hands working with the power and speed of a locomotive piston rod. A left hand landed with mighty force upon the chin of Firpo. The Argentinian went down in a heap—perhaps 30 seconds after the round had started.

The official proceeded to drone the count. He had reached "nine" when Firpo started to rise. Then he stopped counting—when he should have gone on, for Firpo was not in a boxing position and should have been counted out then and there. It was at least 13 full seconds before Firpo was back in fighting pose.

Another flurry of blows met Firpo—and again he toppled. He arose, dealt a right-hander to Dempsey's chin and was rewarded with a right to his own, which floored him again. Once more Firpo arose, but Dempsey hurled himself at the huge Argentinian. Even as Dempsey whirled through the air, Firpo steadied on wobbling legs, swung his world-famous right and again caught Dempsey on the rim of the jaw! Dempsey's body quivered, his legs buckled, he stumbled forward, his hands went to the floor.

As the referee raced over, expecting to begin the count, Dempsey pulled himself together, straightened up, lunged at Firpo and caught him on the jaw with a punch that didn't travel more than eight inches. Firpo dropped almost upon the spot where Dempsey, a few seconds before, had been sprawled.

Again Firpo beat the count and rushed at Dempsey. The champion backed to the ropes, more because he was jockeying to get a newer shot at Firpo's jaw than because of fear of the South American's charge.

Then something happened which forms one of the most astonishing chapters in the entire annals of the prize ring. A world's champion, a challenger, a referee were in the ring one second. A second later only two figures were visible. The king of kings of the fistic realms suddenly disappeared as though a trap door had opened and swallowed him.

Over 85,000 persons saw the fight—and perhaps 85,000 different accounts have been given as to how Dempsey went out of the ring—and how he got back. Of the 85,000, perhaps no more than fifty persons in the first row of the ringside press seats actually saw what happened. My seat was in the first row—alongside Jim Corbett. My view was wholly unobstructed.

This is what I saw:

Dempsey was backed to the ropes with Firpo crowding with the left side of his body. Firpo's right arm was free. Six times in succession he hit Dempsey on the chin or head without a return, because Dempsey was in such a position that his arms were practically handcuffed.

Realizing his peril, Dempsey decided to slide out of the trap. Bending his head low toward his own right arm, he attempted to move along the ropes until he was clear of Firpo.

At the exact moment that Dempsey's head was below the upper strand, and at the exact fraction of a second that his right foot was off the floor, Firpo hit the champion on the chin with a right. The middle of Dempsey's body was up against the middle strand of the ropes at that very second.

The result was this:

Dempsey's legs shot off the ground, and his head shot backward. A world champion spun around much as does the piece of wood one uses in playing tiddlywinks. And in a headfirst backward dive, Jack Dempsey, ruler of the fistic world, went into the press row—while 85,000 persons looked on in hushed amazement.

Much has been written about how reporters saved Dempsey in his fall—and how they helped him back into the ring. The real truth is that the reporters handicapped, more than helped, Dempsey in his ring re-entry.

When 194 pounds of humanity came hurtling through the air directly at their heads, those reporters did only the natural thing. They pushed up their hands to protect themselves; they summoned all the power they could to keep Dempsey from falling upon them and breaking their necks. Their thought was to save themselves—not to aid Dempsey, who suddenly had become a 194-pound menace to their existence.

Dempsey landed among the group. Squirming, twisting, lunging with arms, kicking with legs, he strove to get himself steered in the right direction so that he could climb back through the ropes. In one of his wild lurches, his fist hit Kid McPart-

land, one of the judges, in the eye—and blackened it for ten days.

It is true that reportorial hands shoved Dempsey as he climbed back through the ropes. But they weren't hands of friendship. The men who pushed him did so because they wanted to be sure Dempsey didn't kick them in the face or body. They were passing Dempsey back and forth, because they wanted none of him floundering on their heads and frail necks.

Never did a man look more bewildered, more "all gone," than Dempsey, back in the ring just as the referee counted "nine," flat-footed, legs spread wide for balance, against the ropes. His hands were helpless at his sides. His eyes showed no brain light. His whole body slumped.

This was Firpo's second golden opportunity for world conquest—and for the second and final time it slipped from him.

Had Firpo closed in on Dempsey and thrown every ounce of his titanic power into one punch, Dempsey would have gone down—and his reign would have ended. But Firpo, not sure whether Dempsey was faking, decided to take no chances. He went in cautiously. Precious seconds flew onward into eternity. He finally decided to strike. He swung—and missed—because Dempsey instinctively ducked, as energy came back to him.

The action of Firpo galvanized Dempsey into a new attack. He went forward—revived by some mysterious force. The arms that had been helpless suddenly began whirling through the air. He drove Firpo back—back—and back with his furious charge and, under the avalanche of leather, Firpo crumpled again to the floor. As Dempsey tore at him, Firpo braced and fought back. Toe-to-toe the two men stood, no quarter asked—none given.

The bell banged—the round had passed into official history. But Dempsey never heard it. As Firpo turned to go to his corner the champion's foggy brain construed the act as a new retreat. He went racing after the Wild Bull of the Pampas, showering blows on head, neck and shoulders.

Firpo whirled, a look of surprise on his face—then one of insane rage. He closed in and began slugging viciously, until the referee was able, by locking their arms, to stop the sluggery and tell Dempsey the round was over.

It was a round without dramatic equal in the annals of boxing. Firpo had been down five times; Dempsey had staggered once, was down on his hands later, and out of the ring upon another occasion.

Perhaps a hundred blows had been swung—and about ninety had landed, each with force and power enough to batter any other giant into an hour of unconsciousness. But these were super-men that night.

When the referee finally had stopped the after-bell battling, Dempsey stood in mid-ring. He did-n't know the location of his own corner. Jack Kearns, his manager, leaped through the ropes, grabbed Dempsey by the arms, hauled him to his chair, flopped him down, picked up a bucket of ice water and hit Dempsey with its contents. The shock revived Dempsey—brought him back to consciousness for the first time since he was hit with that pile-driver smash in the first round.

There was wild confusion in Dempsey's corner because Kearns couldn't find the smelling salts. They were in the pocket of his shirt. He had forgotten he had placed them there. Kearns was roaring condem-nation at Jerry (The Greek) Luvadis, the trainer, and Jerry was trying to grab at Kearns' pocket to get the salts because Kearns was shouting so loudly he couldn't hear Jerry. Kearns hit Jerry in the nose. Jerry grabbed the bottle from Kearns' pocket. Kearns poked the fumes under Dempsey's nose.

The buzzer announced ten seconds before the bell. Kearns leaned over, yelled at Dempsey.

"Quit taking chances—cover—cover! He's a murderer!"

"What round?" asked Dempsey.

"Second," answered Kearns—and the bell rang.

Dempsey came out—cautiously. This time Firpo did the rushing. Dempsey, a keen fighter once again now that his mental faculties were restored, crouched, weaved, feinted, and Firpo lashed out with his right. Dempsey had miscalcu-lated Firpo's nearness, and the blow, a murderous drive, crashed into Dempsey's body, under the heart.

Dempsey sagged back. Firpo "cocked" his right and started to let it go, when, like the flight of a meteor, Dempsey's short left crashed against Firpo's jaw. The South American staggered and fell to the floor with a sickening crash. It seemed that this must be the end. But it wasn't. At "eight" Firpo was up—and Dempsey was upon him.

Scorning a defense, Dempsey pumped lefts into Firpo's face and body with the precision of drum beats. Firpo, in desperation, swung a right, missed, and the momentum carried him close to Dempsey. The champion's short left caught Firpo on the point of the jaw. As he started to fall, Dempsey put all he had into a lifting right hook—and Firpo, in falling, went down as if driven by some terrific explosive force.

For six seconds he lay there inert, seemingly lifeless. Blood streamed from his nose and mouth. His eyes were open—but glazed. At "eight" he made a feeble attempt to rise, lifted himself a few inches—and then toppled back.

"Ten," droned the referee and Dempsey was still the world's champion.

MR. JOHN JACKSON: 1788–1795

After forty years of observing and reporting the events of the English ring, Henry Downes Miles authored *Pugilistica,* a three-volume history, published in 1863, covering 144 years of British boxing. He was a conscientious researcher, or heavy borrower, who milked all available sources including Pierce Egan, for whom, he was constantly reminding his reader, he had little respect. This is from his chapter on Mr. John Jackson, that remarkable gentleman who was the first to overcome completely the stigma of being a professional pugilist.

HENRY DOWNES MILES

John Jackson was born in London, in 1768, and was the son of an eminent builder, by whom the arch was thrown over the Old Fleet Ditch, near the mouth of the River Fleet, flowing from the Hampstead and Highgate Hills, and crossed by bridges at Holborn and Ludgate. This forms the great sewer of Blackfriars from the north into the new Low Level, over which run Farringdon Street (the site of the old Fleet Market), and Bridge Street, leading to the splendid bridge by Cubitt, with its ugly iron companion carrying the L.C. & D.R. John Jackson's uncles were farmers, and tenants of the Duke of Bedford and the Marquis of Hertford. Nature had bestowed upon him all those athletic requisites which constitute the *beau ideal* of perfect manhood. There was a happy combination of muscular development with proportionate symmetry in his frame (his height was five feet eleven, and his weight fourteen stone), which rendered him a fitting model for the sculptor, and excited the admiration of all those by whom these qualities are appreciated. At the age of nineteen he became a frequenter of the sparring schools, and displayed such talents as proved that he was destined to eclipse the most favoured of his contemporaries; added to which, possessing as he did the *suaviter in modo* as well as the *fortiter in re,* he soon found patrons of the highest grade.

It is stated that a conversation with Colonel Harvey Aston led to his first encounter in the prize ring. Fewterel, a Birmingham boxer, as yet unbeaten, had been the conqueror, says "Pancratia," in eighteen battles. The meeting took place at Smitham Bottam, near Croydon, June 9th, 1788. We copy the report:

"This day there were decided three boxing matches, which had been long depending, and great bets were depending on. The first was between Jackson, a fine young man of nineteen years only, and Fewterel, of Birmingham. Tom Johnson seconded Jackson, and Bill Warr, Fewterel; Humphries and Dunn were the bottle-holders. Fewterel is a man of extremely great bulk, so much so that, at first setting-to, it was doubted whether Jackson would level such an opponent. Yet this he never failed to do when he could plant his blows at distance. The contest had lasted one hour and seven minutes; its decision being very much procrastinated by Fewterel fighting shifty, getting down to avoid a blow, and then remaining so long on the floor as often to require the interposition of the umpires to remind his seconds of 'time.' Fewterel at last gave up the contest, and Major Hanger, by command of the Prince of Wales, who was present, gave young Jackson a bank note."

Jackson's next contest (March 12th, 1789) was with George Ingleston, the brewer. It closed by an untoward accident, by which Jackson broke the small-bone of his leg, as will be seen under the head of Ingleston, in the Appendix to Period II.

Jackson's next contest was one of the greatest interest to the pugilistic world. The victories of Mendoza had placed him on the pinnacle of fame; and the attempt to defeat the conqueror of Sam

Martin, of Humphries (twice), of Bill Warr (twice), to say nothing of minor boxers, was viewed as indeed a bold flight of young ambition. On April 15th, 1795, the men met at Hornchurch, in Essex, for a stake of 200 guineas aside. We copy the contemporary report:—

"A twenty-four-feet stage was erected in a most advantageous hollow, which accommodated upwards of three thousand spectators, and so excellently adapted that no one could claim a superiority of situation. All the eminent patrons and amateurs were present: the Duke of Hamilton, Lord Delaval, Sir John Phillipson, Mr. Clark, Mr. Bullock, Mr. Lee, Mr. Fawcett, etc.; and among the pugilists of note were Jackling, Will Warr and Joe Warr, George the Brewer, Tom Tyne, Fearby (the Young Ruffian), etc.

"At one o'clock Mendoza mounted the spot of combat, accompanied by his second, Harry Lea, and Symonds (the Old Ruffian), as his bottle-holder. Jackson immediately followed, with Tom Johnson as his second, and Wood, the coachman, for his bottle-holder. The chosen umpires were Mr. Alexander and Mr. Allen.

"They each politely bowed to the people, and were received with general acclamations. About five minutes after one they, as usual, saluted each other by shaking hands, and immediately set-to. Bets five to four in favour of Mendoza.

THE FIGHT

"Round I.—Both having assumed their attitude, displayed the greatest caution; full a minute expired before a blow was struck, when Jackson made a hit, and his antagonist fell.

"2.—Mendoza guarded with great science, avoided the blows of his opponent, and put in several severe ones.

"3.—In this round there was much hard fighting. Odds rose two to one in favour of Mendoza, but the round terminated by Mendoza falling.

"4.—This was the most severely contested round throughout the battle. Jackson seemed to hold his opponent's manoeuvres in contempt, followed him up with great resolution, and put in some dreadfully severe blows, by the last of which Mendoza fell, and his right eye was much cut; Jackson now evidently had the advantage.

"5.—In this round Jackson caught his opponent by the hair, and holding him down, gave him several severe blows, which brought him to the ground; Mendoza's friends called 'foul' but the umpires decided on the contrary. Odds had now changed two to one on Jackson.

"6, 7, 8.—Throughout these three rounds Jackson supported his superiority. Mendoza acted entirely on the defensive.

"9.—This was the last round. Jackson manifestly displayed astonishing advantage; he several times struck his adversary, when he fell quite exhausted, and gave in.

"The battle only lasted ten minutes and a-half, and was acknowledged by every spectator to be the hardest contested that ever was fought in so short a time. Jackson was very little hurt, leaping from the stage with great agility, but Mendoza was quite cut up.

"A subscription purse was made and fought for between a Jew called Black Baruk, who was seconded by Symonds (the Old Ruffian), and Burk a glass-blower, seconded by James the waterman. It was very well contested for half an-hour, when a dispute arose about a foul blow, and it was terminated by sharing the money between them."

Nearly seven years after his combat with Mendoza, a "gag" paragraph having appeared in the newspaper, announcing a forthcoming fight as in arrangement between Mendoza and Jackson, the latter inserted the following letter to the Editor of the *Oracle and Daily Advertiser* of Wednesday, December 1, 1801:—

"*SIR,—I was somewhat astonished on my return to town on Saturday, to learn that a challenge was inserted in your paper on Thursday last, as if from Mr. Mendoza. Should I be right in my conclusion, by believing that it came from that celebrated pugilist, I beg you will inform the public through the medium of your paper, that for some years I have entirely withdrawn from a public life, and am more and more convinced of the propriety of my conduct by the happiness which I enjoy in private among many friends of great respectability, with whom it is my pride to be received on terms of familiarity and friendship: goaded, however, as I am to a petty conflict. I hope that it will not be considered too much arrogance on my part simply to observe, that, after waiting for more than three years to accept the challenge of any pugilist, however dexterous in the science, and however highly flattered by his friends, I think it rather extraordinary that Mr. Mendoza should add a silence of four years to those three, it being nearly seven years since I had the satisfaction of chastising him; but Mr. Mendoza derived one great good from the issue of that contest—he was taught to be less hasty in forming his resolutions, more slow in carrying them into effect.*

"This cautious and wise principle of action deserves much commendation; and having served an apprenticeship of seven years to learn a certain portion of artificial courage, he now comes forward with a stock of impudence (the only capital which during that time he seems to have acquired) to force me to appear once more in that situation which I have for years cheerfully avoided.

"Reluctant, however, as I am to attract again, even for a moment, the public attention, I shall have no objection to vindicate my character by a meeting with Mr. Mendoza when and where he pleases, PROVIDED he'll promise to fight, and provided he'll also promise not to give previous information to the magistrates at Bow Street, or elsewhere.

"I am, Sir, yours and the public's most respectfully,
"JOHN JACKSON"
Nov. 20, 1801

Need we say that this was on the part of Mendoza a mere piece of that absurd system of gagging then so much in vogue, and on which we have elsewhere commented.

Independent of his pugilistic prowess, Mr. Jackson was distinguished for his extraordinary powers as a runner of a short distance, and as a leaper no man of his day was equal to him at a standing jump, of which many extraordinary feats are on record. His muscular strength was equal to his bodily activity, and in the presence of Mr. Harvey Coombe, and other gentlemen, he lifted ten hundred weight and one quarter, and wrote his own name with eighty-four pounds weight suspended from his little finger!

One of the most able and experienced sporting writers, the late Vincent George Dowling, Esq., the founder, and for more than thirty years the editor of *Bell's Life in London,* has left on record a graceful tribute to the memory of his friend of many years, John Jackson, in the form of an obituary notice. From this we shall here make a few extracts.

"John Jackson was an instance of the glorious truth which this country is constantly evolving—that if a man be true to himself, he may defy the obloquy and malice of millions. No matter in what grade of life a creature be thrown; no matter whether from necessity or choice he mingles with the learned or the illiterate, the high or the low; give him the attribute of genius, or, if that be denied, honesty and perseverance, and he must dis-

tinguish himself. The choice of a profession is the puzzle of boyhood—be it so. *A profession never degraded a man, if that man took care not to degrade his profession."* This last axiom deserves to be written in letters of adamant; it contains the philosophy we hope to inculcate by our pages. Mr. Dowling continues: "As there always have been, and always will be, ruffians loose upon society, who can only be met and quelled by the arguments such brutes can appreciate; and as

Heads, nineteen in twenty, 'tis confest,
Can feel a crabstick quicker than a jest,

it is essential that boxing, as an art, should not fall into desuetude. It empowers the little man to defend himself against the big one; makes the weaker man, to a considerable extent, able to protect himself against the onset of the stronger one, and, in some cases, to punish his want of skill and his presumption. Doubtless much has been done in our great cities by gas and an improved police; but even now things do occasionally occur to call upon every man to know how with his own hands to defend his own head, or, what is doubtless of more consequence, the heads of those near and dear to him, or under his protection. Such a power is a *corps de reserve,* which, though it *may* never be called into action, it is valuable and assuring to possess. So thought our grandfathers' fathers in the days of Fielding. Boxing, to a gentleman, was a more modern and practical application of knight-errantry; it enabled a man to protect himself against aggression, and yet more, to defend an insulted woman. 'Good,' exclaims the anti-pugilist, 'but what say you to the prize-fighter?' The response is plain: He is the exemplar, the professor, the demonstrator of a practice, of an exercise. Could or can the sword or the bow be taught without professors, and can they teach without exemplifying? . . ." After a few facts, which will be found embodied in our *Memoir,* Mr. Dowling concludes: "From 1795, Mr. Jackson ceased to be a public pugilist, having fought but three battles, winning two, and not gaining (for it cannot be called losing) the third by an accident. On what basis, then, rests his fame as a thoroughly tried boxer? On none whatever; the pedestal of his popularity was conduct, the keystone to fortune in every grade of life. There is a singular similarity in the career of John Jackson and John Gully: the latter fought but thrice, was beaten once, won the other two, and then retired to enjoy a better fortune in a higher sphere of society."

Ere quitting the more active sporting career of Mr. Jackson, it may be as well to state that as a runner his speed was extraordinary, but he could not last: he also excelled as a jumper until the celebrated Ireland "tooke the shine out of all England."

The opening of "Jackson's Rooms, 13, Old Bond Street," was literally an era in the gymnastic education of the aristocracy. Not to have had lessons of Jackson was a reproach. To attempt a list of his pupils would be to copy one-third of the then peerage. Byron, who was proud of being thought a pugilist, has in his correspondence spoken highly of his tutor; but the fact is, from lameness, the poet could neither hit nor stop effectively. When Jackson taught the author of "Childe Harold," he was forty-four, Byron about twenty-three; the latter therefore stood a boy before a veteran. In a note to the 11th Canto of "Don Juan," we find this: "My friend and corporeal pastor and master, John Jackson, Esquire, professor of pugilism, who I trust still retains the strength and symmetry of his model of a form, together with his good humour, and athletic as well as mental accomplishments."

And in his diary we read:—"Jackson has been here; the boxing world much as usual, but the club increases (*i.e.* Pugilistic Club). I shall dine at Cribb's tomorrow."

He records going to this dinner thus: "Just returned from dinner with Jackson (the Emperor of Pugilism), and another of the select, at Cribb's, the Champion's."

The next extract shows the author of "Childe Harold" actually in training: "I have been sparring with Jackson for exercise this morning, and mean to continue and renew my acquaintance with my muffles. My chest, and arms, and wind are in very good plight, and I am not in flesh. I used to be a hard hitter, and my arms are very long for my height (5 feet 8½ inches); at any rate exercise is good, and this the severest of all; fencing and the broad-sword never fatigued me half so much." This latter is dated the 17th of March, 1814.

"Got up, if anything, earlier than usual; sparred with Jackson *ad sudorem*, and have been much better in health for many days."

Byron kept at his work, for we find him writing thus on the 9th of April, 1814: "I have been boxing for exercise for the last month daily."

In returning to the younger days of the "finest formed man in Europe," we shall take the liberty of borrowing a graphic colloquial sketch from the lips of a veteran: "There were the Lades, the Hangers, the Bullocks, the Vernons, but give me Jack Jackson, as he stood alone amid the throng. I can see him now, as I saw him in '84, walking down Holborn Hill, towards Smithfield. He had on a scarlet coat, worked in gold at the button-holes, ruffles, and frill of fine lace, a small white stock, no collar (they were not then invented), a looped hat with a broad black band, buff knee-breeches, and long silk strings, striped white silk stockings, pumps, and paste buckles; his waistcoat was pale blue satin, sprigged with white. It was impossible to look on his fine ample chest, his noble shoulders, his waist (if anything too small), his large, but not too large hips (the fulcrum of the human form, whether male or female), his limbs, his balustrade calf and beautifully turned but not over delicate ankle, his firm foot, and peculiarly small hand, without thinking that nature had sent him on earth as a model. On he went at a good five miles and a half an hour, the envy of all men, and the admiration of all women."

As regards his face nature had not been bountiful; his forehead was rather low, and the mode he wore his hair made it peculiarly so. His cheek bones were high, and his nose and mouth coarse. His ears projected too much from his head, but his eyes were eyes to look at rather than look with; they were full and piercing, and formed a great portion of his power as a pugilist—with them he riveted his men.

Anatomists of the first standing examined Jackson, and artists and sculptors without number took sketches and models of his arm; but it was the extraordinary proportion of the man throughout that formed the wonder.

After 1795 Mr. Jackson resolved to teach others the art in which he himself excelled. For an instructor he had that invaluable requisite, temper; he was never too fast with his pupils. This made his initiatory lessons tedious to young gentlemen who go ahead, and it may readily be conceived that amid the aristocracy of England he had plenty of rough assailants to deal with. But he was always on his guard; there was no chance of rushing suddenly in and taking Jackson by surprise—he could not be flurried. Amid the other qualifications he had studied Lavater, and managed to reckon up his customers at first sight, and knew what he had to trust to. It has been said "he defied any man to hit him"; this is the truth, but not the whole truth—he defied any man to hit him whilst he (Jackson) stood merely on the defensive; in a fight, of course, it is impossible to avoid being hit.

"His sparring was elegant and easy. He was peculiarly light upon his feet, a good judge of distance, and when he indulged his friends with a taste of his real quality, the delivery of his blow was only observable in its effect. It literally came like lightning, and was felt before it was seen. Most big men are comparatively slow, but he was as rapid as Owen Swift or Johnny Walker, and this, too, when upwards of fifty years of age.

"Jackson not only told you what to do, but why you should do it; in this essential point many capital instructors are and have been deficient. The want of this power of explaining the purpose of an action made Young Dutch Sam and Richard Curtis bad instructors, though they were finished pugilists, and, which does not always follow, capital sparrers.

"Jackson was not unmindful of the fact that art never ends. If there was anything new in the gymnastic, equestrian, or pedestrian way, there be assured was Jackson; not merely witnessing the exhibition, but examining the means by which the effects were produced. He was consequently often at Astley's and at the Surrey, when Ireland, the jumper, was there, and knew all the famous fencers, funambulists, dancers, and riders of his day, and his day was a long one.

"Of his private character, what can be said more than that all his pupils became his friends. Save with Dan Mendoza, it is not known that he ever had a quarrel. He was a careful man, not a mean man—saving, but not penurious. It is to be remembered, too, from his peculiar situation, continued calls were made upon his purse by the ruffianly and profligate, who claimed a brotherhood that he utterly and properly repudiated."

In 1811, he procured a benefit at the Fives Court, in aid of the subscription for the suffering Portuguese; it realized £114. Next year he did the same for the British prisoners in France; this benefit amounted to £132 6s. He also aided the benefit for the Lancashire weavers (1826).

One old boxer (but who was not of Jackson's day) pestered him incessantly for money. 'No, said Jackson, "I'll give you no money; but you may go to the Horse and Groom, and you will find a clean bed, three meals, and a pot of beer a day; stay there until matters mend." The man was thankful in the extreme; but a week had not elapsed ere he was found in the taproom bartering his dinner for gin!

Of course a "lion" like Jackson could not avoid being made a "show" of on particular occasions; accordingly, when the allied sovereigns were in England, his aid was required. On the 15th of June, 1814, at the house of Lord Lowther, in Pall Mall, a pugilistic fete came off in the presence of the Emperor of Russia, Platoff, Blucher, etc. The display so delighted those illustrious fighting men that it was resolved to carry the thing out on a grander scale; accordingly, the King of Prussia, the Prince Royal, Prince of Mecklenburgh, and others assembled. Jackson, Cribb, Belcher, Oliver, Painter, and Richmond, were the principal performers. The foreign nobility now wanted a peep, and at Angelo's rooms some splendid displays took place. It was said that Jackson had inoculated them with a pugilistic fever, but it is believed he never obtained a single pupil from among them. If this be a fact, it is an extraordinary one.

At the coronation of George the Fourth, 1821, Mr. Jackson was applied to to furnish an unarmed force "to preserve order." Cribb, Spring, Belcher, Carter, Richmond, Ben Burn, Harmer, Harry Lee, Tom Owen, Joshua Hudson, Tom Oliver, Harry Holt, Crawley, Curtis, Medley, Purcell, Sampson, and Eales, with Jackson at their head, formed the corps, dressed as Royal Pages.

One gold coronation medal was given to the boxers—they raffled for it at a dinner. Tom Belcher won and wore it.

In 1822, a number of noblemen and gentlemen, admirers of the gymnastic sports of their country, with a Royal Duke (Clarence) at their head, presented John Jackson with a service of plate. The salver, which bears the subjoined inscription, is of magnificent workmanship, weighing one hundred and eighty-seven ounces.

THIS SALVER
(With other Plate)
Was purchased by Subscriptions from
A ROYAL DUKE
and Several of the Nobility and Gentry,
And presented to
JOHN JACKSON, ESQ.

The Most Noble the Marquis of Worcester,
Admiral Tollemache, Major General Barton,
Henry Smith, Bart, M.P., and John Harrison,
Esq.

Mr. Jackson had for many years been stakeholder, frequently referee, and was always ready to go round personally to solicit a subscription for the beaten man—and who could refuse John Jackson? A match was made in 1822, between Randall and Martin for 500 guineas a side, but Mr. Elliot, Martin's backer, "cried for his toy again," in fact, demanded his money back. Mr. Jackson declared he would never again be a stakeholder, and he kept his word. Thus virtually he retired from the ring, and from that moment the ring declined. Its progress downwards has been checked, now and then, by men of good conduct, and battles of great interest. Spring and Langan (1824) revived the hopes of many. Dutch Sam, from 1827 to 1839, rallied a few of the right sort around him, so did Bum and Owen Swift. A sort of reaction took place when Broome fought Bungaree; another, when Caunt fought Bendigo; again on the occasion of the great resultless battle of Farnborough between Sayers and Heenan in 1861; and lastly, the Benicia Boy's pulley-hauley match with Tom King, awakened attention; but down, down, down, the ring seems doomed to go, unless some thorough reform in the *etiquette* of fights is introduced, or some "Fair Play," or "Pugilistic Club," of respectability, energy, influence, and numbers, can be formed to check its rapid descent. Let us hope to see it revive like "a giant refreshed," to the utter confounding of unmanly, cruel, and bloodthirsty foreign methods of resenting insults by retorting fatal injuries.

John Jackson lived for many years at the house in which he died, No. 4, Lower Grosvenor Street West. The Old "Tattersall's" may be said to have divided his residence from that of another great artist, the late John Liston. "It is with pleasing melancholy we remember," says his old friend Vincent Dowling, "the Yarmouths, the Coombes, the Lades, the Ashtons, wending their way to the house of the one, while the Kembles, with perhaps Charles Mathews and Charles Taylor, Theodore Hook and Young, were standing in converse near, or visiting the low-roofed house of the latter."

There is little more to say. Loved by many, respected by all, enjoying a large circle of excellent society, John Jackson passed his later days. Affluent, but not rich in the vulgar sense, he wanted less than he had, and his income exceeded his expenditure. He was a cheerful companion, sang a good song, told his anecdotes with great tact, and never obtruded them. For the last year or two before his death his health declined, but until then he rarely had a day's illness. Peacefully and trustfully, with his hand in that of his niece (whom he loved, and had assisted as a daughter), John Jackson expired on the 7th of October, 1845, in the seventy-seventh year of his age. His death was as calm and resigned as his life had been exemplary.

The remains of John Jackson rest in Brompton Cemetery, beneath a handsome monument, by Mr. Thomas Butler, of which we give a faithful representation. On the side of the mausoleum nearest to the entrance is inscribed on each side of a medallion portrait of the deceased:

HERE LIE THE	Born, Sept. 28,
REMAINS OF	1769,
JOHN JACKSON,	Died, Oct. 7, 1845.

HIC VICTOR CAESTUS
ARTEMQUE REPONO.

On the opposite side to the footpath is a nude gladiator, holding a laurel wreath, and plunged in grief. On the top is a lion couchant, and on the farther end we read the following:—

"Stay, traveller," the Roman records said,
To mark the classic dust beneath it laid;—
"Stay, traveller," this brief memorial cries,
And read the record with attentive eyes.
Hast thou a lion's heart, a giant's strength?
Exult not, for these gifts must yield at length.
Do health and symmetry adorn thy frame?
The mouldering bones below possessed the same.
Does love, does friendship every step attend?
This man ne'er made a foe, ne'er lost a friend.
But death too soon dissolves all human ties,
And, his last combat o'er, here Jackson lies.

This Monument was erected by the subscriptions
of several noblemen and gentlemen,
to record their admiration of one
whose excellence of heart and incorruptible worth
endeared him to all who knew him.

EPISTLE FROM TOM CRIB TO BIG BEN[1]

Concerning some foul play in a late transaction[2]

This bit of political satire was turned out by the Irish bard who wrote, among much else, "Believe Me If All Those Endearing Young Charms," " 'Tis the Last Rose of Summer" and "The Harp That Once Through Tara's Halls." A great friend of Byron's, he never shared the latter's enthusiasm for boxing but he did report in his diary meeting Gentleman John Jackson and attending with him the Jack Randall-Ned Turner fight at Crawley on December 4, 1818. He found it "altogether not so horrid as I expected."

THOMAS MOORE

"Ahi, mio Ben!"—METASTASIO[3]
What! Ben, my old hero, is this your renown?
Is *this* the new *go?*—kick a man when he's down!
When the foe has knock'd under, to tread on him then—
By the fist of my father, I blush for thee, Ben!
"Foul! foul!" all the lads of the Fancy exclaim—
CHARLEY SHOCK is electrified—BELCHER spits flame—
And MOLYNEUX—ay, even BLACKY cries "shame!"

Time was, when JOHN BULL little difference spied
'Twixt the foe at his feet, and the friend at his side:
When he found (such his humour in fighting and eating)
His foe, like his beefsteak, the sweeter for beating.
But this comes, Master Ben, of your curst foreign notions,
Your trinkets, wigs, thingumbobs, gold lace and lotions:
Your Noyaus, Curaçaos, and the Devil knows what—
(One swig of Blue Ruin[4] is worth the whole lot!)

 Your great and small *crosses*—(my eyes, what a brood!
A *cross*-buttock from me would do some of them good!)
Which have spoilt you, till hardly a drop, my old porpoise,
Of pure English *claret* is left in your *corpus;*
And (as JIM says) the only one trick, good or bad,
Of the Fancy you're up to, is *fibbing,* my lad.
Hence it comes—BOXIANA, disgrace to thy page!—
Having floor'd, by good luck, the first *swell* of the age,
Having conquer'd the *prime one,* that *mill'd* us all round,
You kick'd him, old Ben, as he gasp'd on the ground!
Ay—just at the time to show spunk, if you'd got any—
Kick'd him, and jaw'd him, and *lag'd*[5] him to Botany!
Oh, shade of the *Cheesemonger!*[6] you, who, alas,
Doubled up, by the dozen, those Mounseers in brass,
On that great day of *milling,* when blood lay in lakes,

250

When Kings held the bottle, and Europe the stakes,
Look down upon Ben—see him, *dunghill* all o'er,
Insult the fall'n foe, that can harm him no more!
Out, cowardly *spooney!*—again and again,
By the fist of my father, I flush for thee, Ben.
To *show the white feather* is many men's doom,
But, what of *one* feather?—Ben shows a *whole Plume.*

---

1 A nickname given, at this time, to the Prince Regent.
2 Written soon after Bonaparte's transportation to St. Helena.
3 Tom, I suppose, was "assisted" to this motto by Mr. Jackson,
   who, it is well known, keeps the most learned company going.
4 Gin.
5 Transported.
6 A Life Guardsman, one of the Fancy, who distinguished
   himself, and was killed in the memorable set-to at Waterloo.

[PORTRAIT]

FROM: THE MONGOOSE

Archie Moore, in 228 fights over twenty-nine years, was the last of the great ring craftsmen of our time. As times go, and especially as they continue to go for boxing, he may have been the last of all time. His final public appearances were as an actor, and he is best remembered in that calling for his role as Jim, the runaway slave in Sam Goldwyn Jr.'s movie version of *The Adventures of Huckleberry Finn.* He passed away in 1998. Fortunately, his international adventures as a fighter were chronicled by the talented sportswriter to whose memory the San Diego–Jack Murphy Stadium was dedicated.

JACK MURPHY

Archibald Lee Moore, the light-heavyweight boxing champion of the world, is forty-four years of age by his own account and forty-seven by his mother's. She says that he was born on December 13, 1913, in Benoit, Mississippi, but he insists that the year was 1916 and, on occasion, that the place was somewhere in Missouri, or perhaps Illinois. "My mother should know, she was there," he has conceded. "But so was I. I have given this a lot of thought, and have decided that I must have been three when I was born." Whoever is right, Moore is the most elderly champion in the history of boxing. By all the rules of the game, he should have faded into retirement long ago, like his contemporaries Joe Louis, Joe Walcott, Ezzard Charles and Rocky Marciano, all of whom have settled into a sedentary life appropriate to their gray hairs and accumulating paunches. Moore's hair is gray and he is often grievously overweight, but he just doesn't seem to age. "I don't worry about growing old, because worrying is a disease," he says. Not long ago, he was chatting with a friend in a Los Angeles gymnasium after a workout when he chanced to overhear a couple of young fighters discussing

251

him. "That old man should quit," said one of the apprentices, nodding toward Moore. "He should get out and let us take over. Look at him with his old gray head!" Moore walked lightly over to where the two fighters were standing, tapped the nearer one on the shoulder, and said, smiling, "It isn't this old gray head that worries you young fellows, it's this old gray fist."

Moore has been a professional boxer for twenty-six years, starting as a middleweight, winning his championship as a light heavyweight in 1952, by beating Joey Maxim in fifteen rounds, and on two occasions fighting for the heavyweight title—first, in 1955, against Rocky Marciano, and then, in 1956, against Floyd Patterson, both of whom knocked him out. He has had two hundred and fourteen fights to date, and has won a hundred and eighty-three, a hundred and thirty-one of them by knock-out—a record unmatched in pugilism. However, because his build is undistinguished and his countenance unscarred, there is nothing about his appearance that hints at the violent nature of his trade, and he affects a wispy bebop goatee that gives him more the look of a jazz musician than of a fighter. His taste in wearing apparel is something less than severe—he usually goes into the ring draped in a gold or silver silk dressing gown festooned with sequins, and he has been photographed at Epsom Downs in England wearing a gray topper, striped pants, and a cutaway, and on Fifth Avenue strolling along, cane in hand, in a white dinner jacket and Bermuda shorts—but his natural poise and his almost regal bearing enable him to carry off such trappings with dignity. Moore calls himself "the Mongoose," but although he is sharp-sighted and agile and fearless, like a mongoose, he has practically none of the irritable nature of that ferocious little animal. Moore's warm personality and rough-and-ready wit make friends for him everywhere. People come up to him on the street to shake his hand, and motorists wave to him. He can go unannounced into a night club in Harlem or its Los Angeles counterpart and soon the management will have him on the bandstand, entertaining the customers with his light patter. Children respond to him enthusiastically. "Wouldn't it be awful if a man had to go through a day—even one day—without a little music and laughter!" he once said when somebody complimented him on his happy disposition.

Moore is probably the most widely travelled boxer of all time—largely because there was a period of some years when it was impossible for him to get fights in this country with anyone near his class—and he is proud of the attention he has received from Toronto to Tasmania. "I have passed the time of day with President Eisenhower and if you will pardon me, several dictators," he remarked some time ago. "I was once criticized for some newspaper pictures showing Juan Peron with his arms around me. I can only reply that when the head of a government invites me to meet him, I think it is judicious to do so. I have been to Germany, too. I posed with all the West German politicians, policemen, generals, and fighters. When I ran out of dignitaries, I went to the parks and posed with the statues. I really dig that historic stuff, you know. However, I am not a political person. I am an ambassador of good will."

In actuality, Moore isn't quite the political innocent he often pretends to be. He is a registered Democrat and, as a San Diego resident of some twenty years' standing, has worked in behalf of several California office seekers. Moreover, in 1960 he ran for a lame-duck term as assemblyman in California's Seventy-ninth Assembly District, but he was beaten, probably because he didn't bother to train—a tendency that he had carried over from his professional life. (Instead of campaigning for the office, Moore went off to Rome and rounded up a suitable challenger for his championship—an Italian fighter named Giulio Rinaldi, who outpointed him in a non-title bout.) When Moore took out his nominating papers, he listed Mississippi as his birthplace on one affidavit and Missouri on another. Advised that he'd have to make a choice, he protested, on the ground that both states deserved this honor. Eventually, he decided in favor of Mississippi. (In Nat Fleischer's "The Ring," though, he is quoted as having said he was born in Collinsville, Illinois.) He also listed his occupation as "the light-heavyweight champion of the world," but a deputy registrar pointed out that California law permits only a three-word description on the ballot, so he reluctantly settled for "light-heavyweight champion."

If the deputy registrar had chosen to make a point of it, he might have questioned that capsule description as well, for although Moore is the recognized champion where it counts—in New York, Massachusetts, and California, and abroad—the

National Boxing Association, which presides over the small-time, or remaining forty-seven states, decided late last year that he was not defending his championship often enough and declared the title vacant. Moore, who has had a running feud with the National Boxing Association for years, appealed to the United Nations. It hadn't previously occurred to anybody that the United Nations had jurisdiction over boxing, but when Moore's camp sent a telegram to Ambassador Henry Cabot Lodge asking him to help a "great internationalist," the N.B.A. backed up and granted Moore an additional period of grace in which to contract for a championship fight. Moore paid no heed. "When I wanted the N.B.A. to recognize me as a challenger, they let me wither for five solid years," he said. "I think I've made a definite contribution to boxing; if everybody is going to forget that, why, I'll get a job or go into the movies or something." When the deadline was up, the N.B.A. defrocked Moore a second time and arranged for a fight between the two leading contenders—Jesse Bowdry, a twenty-three-year-old St. Louis fighter, and Harold Johnson, whom Moore had fought five times and defeated four times, the last fight being a championship bout at Madison Square Garden in 1954, when Moore knocked him out in fourteen rounds. Johnson knocked out Bowdry in nine rounds, and the N.B.A. said he was champion. The fact remains that Moore is in the big money and Johnson is not.

Johnson currently declares that he is no longer interested in fighting Moore. "Archie is an old man, and they can put you in jail for beating up old men," he said not long ago. "Why, Johnson is my protégé," Moore countered. "I have always looked after Harold and said nice things about him. The trouble with Harold is that he is under the impression the clock of time has stopped. As soon as the young man"—Johnson is thirty-three—"makes a reputation for himself, I'll be glad to give him another shot at my title." At various times, Moore has announced that he intends to keep his championship for sixteen years or until 1968 ("That would help me get even for the sixteen years I waited until they finally let me fight Maxim"), and that he will continue to defend his title until he can pass it along to his son Hardy Lee. Hardy Lee recently observed his first birthday.

Moore loves to talk. "I am a great sidewalk talker," he once said. "I can talk Mexican-fashion, squatting on my heels, or big-city style, with my spine up against a lamppost or a building, or even garment-center technique, with my backside at the edge of a curb." He is a frequent after-dinner speaker, and he plans his post-fight speeches, which are usually addressed to a nationwide radio and television audience, with loving care. "When I am invited to speak at a prison, I usually accept, because nobody walks out in the middle of my speech, and there is no heckling," he says. Moore sometimes talks while he is fighting too. In 1957, when he knocked out Tony Anthony in the seventh round of a championship fight in Los Angeles, Anthony's manager, Ernie Braca, complained that his man had been befuddled by Moore's line of chatter. "Archie is a smart old guy," he said. "He talked his way to victory." "Please remind Mr. Braca that I mixed a few punches into the conversation," Moore responded. And not only does Moore like to talk but he also has a knack of getting his utterances into print, as he demonstrated on the occasion of a fight with Willi Besmanoff at Louisville in 1958. The fight was scheduled for the night before the Kentucky Derby, and when Moore arrived, several days ahead of time, he made the horrifying discovery that while the town was full of journalists, most of them had their minds on horses rather than on boxers. A day or two before the fight, he showed up in the stable area at Churchill Downs early in the morning and chatted amiably with his friends among the sportswriters as they made their rounds of the Derby horses. "I want to thank all of you gentlemen for coming to Louisville to see me fight," he said sounding genuinely pleased. Then, his eyes twinkling, he added, "Oh, by the way, why don't you stay over and see the Kentucky Derby? I understand it's an excellent race."

Moore acknowledges certain defects in his conversation. "I'd rather use six little words than one big one," he says. "I tend to draw a pitch out. I say this to say that. Eventually, however, my meaning comes clear. Like the night I was fighting Bobo Olson. I hit him in the belly with a left hook and followed with a right to the head. The right was slightly high, but Bobo got the message. Still, there is, I fear, that one chink in my armor. I am inclined to waste words. In fact, I throw them away. It is my only excess." The last statement is not entirely accurate. Moore has such a tremendous fondness for food that he regularly eats himself out of shape—so far out that every time he has defended his championship he has been obliged to take off from twenty-five to forty pounds in order to reach a hundred and seventy-five pounds, the weight limit of his class. The sports columnist Jimmy Cannon once accused him of gluttony, to which he replied, with all possible solemnity, "no, Jimmy, I am not a glutton—I am an explorer of food." According to his associates, the difficulty is that he chooses the wrong terrain to explore, and Moore himself admits that "the things I like to eat are not becoming to a fighter." He is particularly attracted to starches and to fried foods, and between meals he finds an icebox irresistible. Some months ago, when he was in New York with his lawyer on business, the two men shared a hotel room, and one night, a couple of hours after they had retired, following a seven-course dinner, the lawyer, awakened by a stealthy noise in the room, turned on the light just in time to see Moore walking in his sleep through the door. Leaping out of the bed, the attorney grabbed him by an arm and steered him back into the room. "Archie! What are you doing?" he demanded. Moore mumbled sleepily, "Where is the icebox in this house?" He then awakened, ate a bagel he had bought that evening from a street vender, and slept quietly until it was time for breakfast.

Although Moore contends that "fat is just a three-letter word that was invented to confuse people," his battles with the scales have often provided more excitement and suspense than the ring battles they prefaced. He always waits until the last possible minute to start reducing. "In order to lose weight, I must get myself into the proper frame of mind," he once said when he was facing such an ordeal. "I'm circling the problem now, looking it over carefully. I may pounce at any time." When Moore pounces, the mongoose in him comes out. He believes in trimming down the hard way, by means of a low-calorie diet and savage exercise—a combination that would almost certainly hospitalize a lesser man—and the regimen makes him a bit snappish. In the summer of 1955, while Moore was training for his championship fight with Bobo Olson at the Polo Grounds, he took off twenty-three pounds, the last few at Ehsan's Training Camp, a dreary, unpainted sweatpit in Summit, New Jersey. His trainers closed the doors and windows of the gymnasium early every afternoon, quickly transforming it into a steam cabinet, and in this suffocating atmosphere Moore, swaddled in a skintight rubber costume, went through his ritual of shadowboxing, sparring, bag-punching, rope-skipping, giving off sprays of water like a revolving lawn sprinkler. The close air was almost unbearable, but he drove himself furiously, and during the last twenty-four hours before the weigh-in had nothing to eat or drink except half a lemon. The method seemed extreme, particularly for a middle-aged athlete, but it was effective. Moore made the weight by two pounds, and knocked out Olson in three rounds.

Last May, when Moore started training for his most recent title defense—on June 10th, at Madison Square Garden, against Rinaldi, the man who had outpointed him in a non-title match in Rome the year before—he weighed a hundred and ninety-eight pounds. For the Rome fight, Moore had agreed to weigh in at a maximum of a hundred and eighty-five pounds or forfeit a thousand dollars. He started taking off surplus weight, mostly in steam cabinets, only six days before the match, and the best he could do was a hundred and ninety, so he lost the thousand. Furthermore, Rinaldi took the decision. For the New York match with Rinaldi when the title was at stake, Moore diminished himself with such a desperate crash diet ("You can eat as much as you like, as long as you don't swallow it," he was fond of saying at the time) that the fight crowd began speculating on whether he would have enough strength left to mount the steps into the ring. Rocky Marciano, who visited Moore's training camp, called Kutsher's In the Catskills was appalled by his training methods. "I don't believe Rinaldi can lose the fight," he said. "The weight-making will beat Archie—that's the big thing." The promoters of the bout, alarmed by the possibility that the star would either collapse from exhaustion or be disqualified by excess poundage, invited the *alter* champion, Harold Johnson, to serve as a standby. "Hasn't Harold always stood by?" Moore asked when he was told about it. Moore made the weight by half a pound, and Dr. Alexander Schiff, who examined him for the New York State Athletic Commission, marvelled at his condition. "I don't know his age, but he has the body and the reflexes of a man of thirty or thirty-two," the Doctor said. A great sigh of relief was heard from Harry Markson, general manager of boxing for Madison Square Garden. "I feel as though I had lost that weight myself," he said, beaming. Johnson was not surprised. "I knew he'd make it," he said. "Archie wasn't going to let me have all that money." Moore won an overwhelming fifteen-round decision, and seemed as fresh at the finish as he had at the start. Fascinated by this time with the whole subject of weight removal, he issued an invitation to newspapermen: "Come to my home town a year from now and you won't find a fat man in San Diego. I'm going to open a chain of health studios." He hasn't got around to it yet, but at last report he was still thinking about it.

A self-styled expert on nutrition, Moore frequently speaks of a "secret diet" that he says he obtained from an Australian aborigine in the course of his travels. ("Did you ever see a fat aborigine?" he asks.) He declares that he got the diet in exchange for a red turtleneck sweater, and he regarded it as a professional secret up until last year when he included it in his autobiography, "The Archie Moore Story," written in collaboration with Bob Condon and Dave Gregg, and published by McGraw-Hill. The diet proved to be about like most other diets except that it placed uncommon emphasis on the drinking of hot sauerkraut juice for breakfast—an idea that the aborigine had somehow overlooked. Unfortunately the appearance of the diet coincided with the embarrassing disclosure that Moore was asking postponement of a fight with Erich Schoeppner, a German light heavyweight, because he was unable to make the weight.

Moore's alternating periods of feast and famine subject his physique to such drastic restyling that he finds it convenient to buy clothes in three sizes. There's one rack of suits for the heavyweight Moore, at around two hundred and fifteen pounds; another for the junior-heavyweight Moore, at a hundred and ninety; and still another for the championship weight. Moore tends to regard his smallest self as something of a stranger. Studying his profile in a mirror before one of his title fights, he said critically, "I look sort of funny when I get down to seventy-five. I'm not skinny, exactly, but I don't look like me."

Once a fight is over, it doesn't take long for Moore to become recognizable to himself again. When he is in residence in San Diego, he likes to entertain his friends with cookouts at which the staple item is barbecued spare-ribs, and when he is fooling

around at his rural fight camp, a small ranch situated on a ridge of rocky but oak-shaded hills thirty miles northeast of San Diego, and known as the Salt Mine, he often takes a skillet in hand and fries up a tasty batch of chicken, which is one of his favorite dishes. "Fried chicken has a personality of its own," he says. "You can eat it hot or cold, with a fork or freehand style." As a matter of fact, Moore's home, a two-story brick house on the edge of downtown San Diego, was built on the site of a restaurant that he owned and operated for a number of years and that was called the Chicken Shack. Under his personal supervision, the house has been remodelled and expanded, at a reported cost of a hundred and fifty thousand dollars, until it has become one of the show places of the city. The creature comforts include a swimming pool in the shape of a boxing glove; a poolside cabana that is equipped, fittingly, with both a barbecue pit and a steam room; a soundproof music studio where he plays piano or a bass fiddle in occasional jam sessions, or listens to an extensive collection of jazz records; and three rumpus rooms—one for himself, one for his wife, and one for his children. In his rumpus room, Moore has a regulation-size pool table, imported from England. "I play piano, but will shoot pool with tone-deaf guests," he says. "After all, a man can't spend his whole life just fightin' and fiddlin'."

He is also an expert pistol shot (he practices frequently on targets at the Salt Mine), a skilled angler, a student of boxing history, and a handyman who is equally at ease with an electric drill or behind the steering levers of a bulldozer. "The main secret of true relaxism is diversion," he says. "A person who has no hobby has no life." He is devoted to the current Mrs. Moore—the former Joan Hardy—a tall, attractive, light-complexioned woman, who has borne him two daughters and two sons in six years of marriage. Because she is a sister-in-law of the actor Sidney Poitier, she is not much awed by her husband's celebrity, and she cheerfully makes allowances for artistic temperament. She didn't complain, for example, when Moore insisted that she shorten the heels on her shoes by a full inch. He is five feet eleven inches tall, and she is only an inch less. The champion didn't want his wife towering over him, and he refused to wear elevator shoes. Since he wouldn't go up, she agreed to come down. (When Moore first sprouted his goatee, along with a light mustache, a reporter asked him if his wife didn't object to the new growth when he kissed her. Moore smiled indulgently and replied, "A girl doesn't mind going through a little bush to get to a picnic.") Mrs. Moore—she is his fifth wife—has been a stabilizing influence on her husband. Not only has she given him domestic happiness but her quiet efficiency has brought a measure of order to his once disorganized social and business affairs. Until she assigned herself the duties of secretary, bookkeeper, and business manager, Moore was surrounded by clutter and chaos. Well-meaning but irresponsible, he would accept half a dozen speaking engagements for the same date and ignore them all. Now his appointments are cleared through his wife, and he usually shows up on schedule.

Mrs. Moore is also secretary of Archie Moore Enterprises, Inc., a firm that was established two years ago for the purpose of supervising the champion's investments and maintaining amicable relations with the Director of Internal Revenue. Moore is the president of the corporation; the vice-president is Bill Yale, a young San Diego attorney; and the treasurer is Clarence Newby, a San Bernardino C.P.A. who serves as Moore's accountant and tax expert. The president's income from boxing and related activities goes to the corporation, which pays him a salary. Moore doesn't like to talk about his financial affairs. "I am wealthy in terms of happiness, because I have a wonderful wife and fine children," he says, "but I still must scratch for a living."

Moore's professional entourage, whose members wear uniform blue coveralls as they go about their various duties at the Salt Mine, includes an odd assortment of friends. There is for instance, Redd Fox, a sort of court jester, whose admiration for Moore is so extravagant that he once had his hair barbered to form the letter "M." There is a wizened little man in his late seventies, known as Poppa Dee (his real name is Harry Johnson), whom Moore calls "the medicine man of boxing." "I like to have Poppa in my camp because he makes me feel good," Moore says. Then, there is a sparring partner called Greatest Crawford, who has made a substantial reputation in the ring on his own hook, and a masseur called the Big Bopper (his real name is Richard Fullylove), who stands six feet two and weighs two hundred and ninety-eight and who used to play football for a small Negro college in Texas. At one time, Moore planned to farm him out between fights to the San Diego Chargers, of the American Football League, but the Big Bopper was unable to pass the Charger physical examination. He had high blood pressure. Moore has had three trainers in recent years—Cheerful Norman, Hiawatha Grey, and the incumbent, Dick Saddler. Cheerful Norman left the Moore entourage five years ago, and Hiawatha has quit several times after minor disputes with Moore, but the two men remain firm friends. Hiawatha, like Archie's other trainers, and like Archie himself, is a Negro. "He is a very wise old owl," Moore has commented. "It would be wise to be married to him fourteen years before you call him Hiawatha, because he doesn't like the name. Most people just call him Hi. He goes his own way." Saddler has been the most enduring of Moore's trainers, and his staying power can probably be attributed as much to a happy nature and a talent for playing the piano as to his technical qualifications. Moore's authority is unquestioned when he's in training, but Saddler's clowning relaxes him, and when he's relaxed, he willingly takes orders. (Nevertheless, Moore insists on taping his own hands before a workout or a fight—he is the only pugilist of stature to do so—and won't wear protective headgear while sparring in the gymnasium, lest he come to depend on it.) When Moore is skipping rope, a routine that invariably attracts a crowd at training headquarters, Saddler accompanies him on the piano, usually pounding out a boogie-woogie beat. "My only trouble with Dick is he is a ham," says Moore. "He tries to upstage me. I put the piano behind a curtain, but he insists on being seen." Saddler is satisfied with the relationship. "I guess Archie hired me because I can play piano," he says, "but he admits I know a little about fighting, too." Another long-time friend and camp follower is Norman Henry, a drowsy sort of man who is always welcome at the Salt Mine, even though he is a fight manager and fight managers, collectively, are anathema to Moore. Moore simply enjoys his company. One afternoon when Henry was cat-napping in a chair, Moore nodded toward him and remarked to a visitor, "At the dawn of civilization there were three men. One, watching lightning strike, saw the possibilities of fire. Another invented the wheel. Norman? Well, Norman was asleep. He had already invented the bed."

Last winter, Moore's Salt Mine sparring partners included a handsome young boxer out of Dallas named Buddy Turman, who a short time later turned up as Moore's opponent in a ten round non-title bout in Manila. (Fighting one's sparring partners, it should be explained, is an old and cherished custom in the fight game. Rocky Marciano fought a series of harmless exhibitions with one of his relatives a few years ago, and Young Stribling, a fighter of an earlier era, was—until Moore deposed him—the all-time knockout champion, thanks in no small measure to his custom of flattening his chauffeur in one small town after another.) Moore usually has two or three rookie fighters on tap at his training camp, and for a brief period the cast included a distinguished young man named Cassius Marcellus Clay, who, having made a reputation by winning the Olympic light-heavyweight championship in Rome the summer before last, had decided to learn what he could at the feet of the Master. Accompanied by a woman lawyer, Clay flew to San Diego last fall and announced that since he planned to turn professional, he was going to spend at least a month studying under Archie Moore at the Salt Mine. Clay said he admired the Mongoose more than any other fighter in the world and would gladly do anything asked of him—that no sacrifice would be too great, no chore too mean or small. He devoutly hoped that Moore would become his manager. It sounded like an ideal arrangement, but within two weeks Clay had turned in his blue coveralls and left, saying, "I wanted Archie to teach me to fight, but the only thing I learned was how to wash dishes. Who ever heard of a fighter with dishpan hands?" Clay is now fighting under other management and remains unbeaten after eight bouts. He is considered a long-range threat to Patterson.

It was at the age of fifteen that Moore determined to become a fighter. His color was chiefly responsible for this decision, because boxing was the only way he could see for a Negro to rise above the kind of poverty he grew up in. He was born Archie Lee Wright, but his parents were separated shortly after his birth, and he and his sister Rachel and his half brothers Louis and Jackie were all brought up in a St. Louis slum by his Uncle Cleveland and his Aunt Willie Moore, whose surname he adopted as a convenience. His uncle died when Archie was fourteen, leaving only a small insurance policy, and it was up to Aunt Willie to support the family. "We had a tie of affection in our home—oh, it was so beautiful," Moore recalls fondly. "As they say, we were too poor to paint and too proud to whitewash, so we kept everything spotless. We had bare wood floors, and on Saturday we scrubbed them with lye soap. We kept our house so clean it was like a hospital. My auntie taught us that we might not have the best furniture or wear the best clothing, but we sure could keep them clean." Despite the best Aunt Willie could do to bring them up properly, however, both Archie and Louis had brushes with the law in their teens (as Moore recalled in his autobiography, "Louis was light-fingered by nature and somehow a man's watch got tangled up in his hand, and the man sent the police to ask Louis what time it was"), and Archie spent a twenty-two-month term in the Missouri reformatory at Booneville for hooking coins from a streetcar motorman. Of the reformatory experience, he says, "I don't say I enjoyed it, but I'm grateful for what it did for me. It was a glorious thing in my life, because it forced me to get eight to ten hours of sleep every night; it gave me an opportunity to have three hot meals a day; it gave me a lesson in discipline I would never have got at home. They used to pay me a little something for the work I did, but it should have been the other way around. I should have paid them for what they did for me."

Shortly after Archie returned home form Booneville, he and his aunt had a conference about his future. "I had a thought about what I could do, and I told my auntie I wanted to fight," he said recently. "I had to fight. For a Negro starting a career, that was the only way. It was the only way. It was the last road. I considered the other possibilities. I could get an education and become a postman or a teacher; I could become a policeman or a fireman; I could play baseball. There weren't many opportunities then, even for an educated Negro. As a teacher, the most I could become was a school principal. As a policeman, I couldn't advance beyond the rank of lieutenant or captain. I couldn't be a police chief or a fire chief; my color made that impossible. Professional baseball didn't offer much, because at that time all the colored ballplayers were in the Negro leagues and Satchel Paige was the only one of them who was making big money. He had a reputation and his big drawing power, so he took a percentage of the gate. The other colored ballplayers were lucky to earn three hundred dollars a month. Remember, this was right in the middle of the depression. I began to read in the newspapers about the boxers. Kid Chocolate was my first hero. I suppose I like him because his name sounded so sweet. His skin was ebony; he was like patent leather. Most of all, the money intrigued me. I read that Kid Chocolate was fighting for a gate of ten thousand dollars, and that seemed like all the money in the world. I knew Kid Chocolate got twenty-five per cent of the purse. According to my figures, that was around twenty-five hundred dollars, and he was a rich man. *Twenty-five hundred dollars!* Do you know what kind of money that was then? Do you know how much it was to a family that depended on the government for a basket of food each week—for a family that waited for a government check each month to pay the rent? It was fabulous. It was my way out."

It was unlikely that any fighter has ever put more thought and effort into learning the boxing trade than Moore did. He was skinny as a boy, but he developed unusual strength with exercises of his own invention. One of his stunts was walking on his hands. He'd go up and downstairs on his hands, and sometimes around the block, or around several blocks. The boy also developed his arms and shoulder by exercising phenomenally on a chinning bar. While still in his teens, he once chinned himself two hundred and fifty-five times, and he used to shadowbox hour after hour in front of a mirror. "The idea was to take myself out of Archie and put me into my image," he says. "I tried to visualize what I would do to Archie if I were the fellow in the mirror. I wanted to anticipate the reaction to my moves. I learned boxing from beginning to end and from end to beginning." To develop his jab, he got the idea of practicing before a mirror with a five-pound weight in each hand. He would wrap his fists around a pair of his Aunt Willie's flatirons and spar for six minutes without a rest. Then he'd pause for breath and repeat the procedure. "I knew I'd be wearing six-ounce gloves in the ring," he explains. "if I could spar with five-pound weights, the six-ounce gloves would feel as light as feathers. I'd never have to worry about becoming arm-weary." He credits his stinging jab to the flatirons. "I had the best jab in the business, Joe Louis notwithstanding," he says proudly.

In the course of events, Moore went to work in one of the Civilian Conservation Corps camps, at Poplar Bluff, Missouri, and there had a chance to take part in the Golden Gloves competitions, which gave him excellent training. After a while, he was fighting and winning what are known in the trade as "bootleg fights," in which technically amateur fighters make a little side money fighting anybody they can get a match with. One of the earliest such bouts he remembers was with Bill Simms, at Poplar Bluff, in 1935. Moore knocked him out in two rounds. This sort of campaigning—in Missouri, Arkansas, Oklahoma, and Illinois—kept him on the go, and he was learning fast. "When I was fighting as an amateur, I used to ride the freight trains, and once I had an experience I'll never forget," Moore recalls. "I was on a freight returning to St. Louis when a brakeman got after me. I had been standing there on the side of a tank car—it had molasses in it, I think—and I was daydreaming, without a care in the world, when a sixth sense told me I was in danger. I pulled back just as the brakeman swung at me with a club. He missed, and the club splintered on the handrail of the car. It would have killed sure if he had hit me. I was scared and excited, but I got away from him. I ran. I was as surefooted as a goat. I've always wondered why that fellow wanted to kill me. I was just a harmless hobo; I wasn't bothering anybody. I suppose that brakeman will never know the grief he caused me. When he swung that club, I dropped the little bag I was carrying. I lost all my fighting equipment. I had a pair of nice white trunks, a pair of freshly shined shoes, and my socks all neatly rolled. Those things meant alot to me, and I was heartbroken over losing them."

Moore's first professional fight, to the best of his recollection, was against Murray Allen, in 1936 at Quincy, Illinois, and he won a decision, breaking his right hand in the process. His share of the gate was three dollars, which was two dollars less than the sum required for a boxing license. ("The commission was very generous," says Moore. "When they told me that I'd have to take out the license, they agreed to waive the other two dollars. I didn't fight in that state again until 1951. By then, I guess the license had expired.") The newspapers and the record books had not yet deigned to take notice of young Archie Moore, but before the year was out he had begun to establish himself. According to he latest edition of "The Ring," Moore won thirteen fights in a row that year, all by knockouts, and then lost the next three, by decisions, and won the seventeenth, by a decision. The first of the recorded knockouts was over Kneibert Davidson. The following year, 1937, he fought a dozen times and won the middleweight championships of Kansas, Oklahoma, and Missouri, all twelve bouts by knockout.

Early in 1938, Moore headed for California, where he hoped to establish himself by fighting the prominent middleweights of the day—Harold Romero, Eddie Booker, Swede Berglund, and others. He was riding in an automobile driven by a St. Louis mechanic named Felix Thurman, who was his manager at the time, when, near Bartlesville, Oklahoma, a car in the opposite lane suddenly bore down upon them. Thurman had a split-second choice—meet the other car head on or pile into an irrigation ditch. He chose the ditch. The car flipped over and landed on its roof, knocking Thurman unconscious. Moore, unharmed but frightened, tried to pry open the door, but it wouldn't budge. Then he heard the sound of dripping liquid. It was water dribbling from the upturned wheels, but Moore thought it was gasoline, and was afraid the car would catch fire. In a panic, he smashed a window with his right fist, and then crawled out through the jagged, glass, cutting an artery in his right wrist. Unaware that the cut was bleeding badly, he made a desperate effort to lift his unconscious companion from the wreckage, but he couldn't, so he stood beside the road, helpless and bewildered, until a car came along—carrying, as luck would have it, two internes. They quickly administered first aid to Moore and revived Thurman, who was not seriously injured. "Do you know how long you would have lived with the bood spurting like that?" one of the internes asked Moore. "About fourteen minutes!" Moore still speaks with awe about the kindness of the two men who saved his life. "It was almost too much for me to understand," he said some years later. "I figured that anybody in Oklahoma seeing two Negroes overturned in a ditch would drive on. Yet the first car stopped and came to my aid. I don't know whether God is a white man or a black man, but I knew then He truly made us all."

Fortunately, the automobile, once it had been turned right side up and towed to a filling station, proved to be still navigable. Thurman straightened the dented top with a mallet he had brought along in his tool chest, and the two resumed their journey. The tow job had cost them twelve dollars,

leaving them with a capital of twenty-three dollars, and this was reduced by five dollars the next day, when Thurman developed a toothache and was obliged to go to a dentist and have the tooth pulled. When they ran out of money completely, Thurman began trading his expensive mechanic's tools for gasoline, yielding his treasures piece by piece. A spray gun got them their last tank of gasoline, and they arrived in La Jolla, where Thurman's wife had preceded them, at three o'clock in the morning, weary and hungry, having driven several hundred miles and eaten only a sack of peanuts and two oranges in the past twenty-four hours. Moore, always an early riser, awoke at six-thirty and went for a pre-breakfast sprint along the beach, in the course of which he noticed a great column of smoke arising from the direction of nearby San Diego. He wondered idly where the fire was, and later that morning, when he and Thurman called on a San Diego boxing promoter named Linn Platner, he learned that it was at the Coliseum. The aspiring young fighter had arrived in San Diego on the day the boxing arena had burned down.

For the next several years, Moore moved around a great deal but moved upward in the boxing world only a little. He toured Australia and Tasmania and came off very well, winning four of his seven fights there by knockout and the others by decision, but when he returned to this country, there still seemed to be no place for him in the big time. Not long ago, Moore was asked whether he thought racial bias had kept him out, and he said, "I would rather believe it didn't. In fact, I would be making excuses for myself if I blamed my troubles on color. Joe Louis, Henry Armstrong, and John Henry Lewis were Negroes, and they all won championships during that period. Racial prejudice couldn't have been the main reason. My problem was that the people who handled me didn't have good enough connections. Looking back though, I'm glad that's the way it was. The people who handled me did not deliver me to the element that controlled boxing. I don't want to talk about that element; I'm just happy I never came under the control of those people. I'm not saying, mind you, that I have any affection for fight managers. If it weren't for managers, a lot of fighters would have been millionaires. I have emancipated myself from the pit of boxing, and am no longer tied down by managers." Moore was particularly aggrieved, it seems, because the last manager to hold his contract—Charlie Johnston, with whom he parted company in July of 1958—insisted on doing some of the talking for the firm. "Charlie was the sort who always wanted to speak for his tiger," Moore says. "But he didn't bother to call when our contract ended; he knew better. I have finally earned the right to meet the press and public the way a fighter should." Not long ago, Moore outlined a plan for turning his ranch into a haven for aged and indigent managers. "Every day, I would come in with a black-snake whip and get them up. Then I'd have them do five miles of roadwork around the ranch. That would be good for their health and also give them a chance to understand their fighters a little better. But I wouldn't be altogether harsh. I'd furnish them with cheap cigars, and give them plenty of time to lie and boast to each other. Of course, I'd have a small problem remembering all their names, because most fight managers look alike to me. But I'd over-come that. I'd have a commom name for them—Bum. That's what they spend their lives calling the kids they live off."

Moore's current manager, Jack (Doc) Kearns, has the official title of boxing representative, because the champion can't stand the word "man-ager." A veteran of the boxing world, Kearns gives his age as sixty-nine, though eighty is probably closer to the mark. He has been part of Moore's life since Moore won the championship from Maxim, in 1952. Maxim was then managed by Kearns, and Moore had to guarantee Maxim a hundred thou-sand dollars for the fight. This gave Moore a clear idea of the value of the championship and of the value of Kearns, and when the title changed hands, Kearns came along with the franchise. Moore, who received only eight hundred dollars for winning the championship, not only adopted Kearns but adopted his policy of demanding a hundred-thou-sand-dollar guarantee for putting his title at stake. The only contract between him and Kearns is a handshake. "I cut my purses with Doc because I like him," says Moore. "Doc is for his fighter. He made my big matches with Olson, Marciano, and Patterson. We've had a fine relationship. Doc is a promoter, a talker, a guy who knows how to maneuver. You could give Doc two hundred pounds of steel wool and he'd knit you a stove."

In 1941, Moore was industriously beating his way through thickets of contenders on his way to the middleweight title, and had achieved the eminence of fifth rank in that division, when, in March, he collapsed on the sidewalk in San Diego and was taken unconscious to a hospital. His illness was diagnosed as a perforated ulcer, and an emergency operation was necessary to save his life. The news-papers reported that if Moore survived, which seemed doubtful, he would never fight again. He was in the hospital thirty-eight days, and spent an even longer period convalescing, and then came down with appendicitis, which necessitated another operation. Then, late in the summer, gaunt and wasted, he appeared in the office of Milt Kraft, who at that time was overseer of a gov-ernment housing project that was about to get under way in San Diego, and asked for work as an unskilled laborer. "When Archie came to see me, he was so weak he could barely stand," says Kraft, who now owns a wholesale sporting-goods busi-ness in San Diego. "Three different kids who were working for me put in a word for him, separately. They all said he was sickly but a good worker. 'Don't worry about this guy—we'll see that his work gets done,' they said, but I didn't want it that way. If I hired a man, he had to be able to do a job, to pull his own load. Archie obviously wasn't in shape for heavy work, but I decided to find some-thing for him. You don't turn away a man when three people speak up for him. When that hap-pens, the fellow is pretty sure to be something spe-cial. I had an opening for a night watchman, and I offered the job to Archie. We had a big trailer camp where the workmen were going to live, and about five hundred and fifty empty trailers to look after. I gave Archie a key to one of the trailers, and told him to lie down and rest. I asked only one thing—he'd have to get out every hour during the night and check the trailer area. 'I'll do anything,' he said. 'I'm desperate.'" Moore had been on the job about a week when Kraft began receiving reports of strange activity in the trailer camp. Peo-ple in the neighborhood complained of a phantom runner in the night, and investigating, Kraft found Moore jogging along among the trailers as he made his rounds. "My association with Archie was the most inspiring experience of my life," Kraft says. "I've never seen a man with such determina-tion. Here was Archie, down on his luck, a physical wreck, the doctors telling him he would never fight again—yet he was positive in his own mind that he'd become a champion."

Kraft and Moore soon became firm friends,

and the fighter got into the habit of reporting early for work each evening. "Archie came early because he wanted to talk," says Kraft. "He told me about himself and he wanted to know about me. Somebody told him I had won the national bait-and-fly-casting championship in 1939, and he began examining me like a trial lawyer. He had to know everything about me. He asked me if I had been confident before the tournament, if I had been sure I was going to win. He wanted to know at what point I became sure of myself, whether I had been afraid or excited. I told him I had been very confident, and positive that I would finish high among the leaders. That made his eyes shine. He told me, 'Mr Kraft, I feel exactly the same way. I'm absolutely certain I'll be champion of the world someday.'"

Many years later, after Moore had indeed become champion of the world, the two men went fishing on the Colorado River, in California. It was the first time Moore had ever held a casting rod. Kraft showed him how to grip it and where to throw the plug. "When he reeled it in, he had *two* bass, weighing two pounds apiece," Kraft says, smiling happily at the memory. "Imagine catching two bass with one cast the first time you wet the hook! A man who can do that can do anything."

Moore, disqualified for military service because of his two operations, returned to the ring early in 1942, and won his first five fights by knockout, but it was not until eleven years and fifty-four knockouts later that he got a chance at a world's title, and by this time he was officially a light heavyweight and was occasionally taking on heavyweights. He met Maxim, the light-heavyweight champion, in St. Louis on December 17, 1952, won a decisive victory on points, pocketed his eight hundred dollars, and shook hands with Doc Kearns. Prosperity was just around the corner. During the next nineteen months, he won thirteen fights, including two more with Maxim, and he was just beginning to get his share of the big money when, in the course of a routine physical examination for the California Athletic Commission before a scheduled bout with Frankie Daniels in San Diego, in April, it was discovered that something was wrong with Moore's heart. The boxing world was stunned. The Daniels fight, which was called off, was to have been a warmup for a bout at Las Vegas between Moore and Nino Valdes, who

was then the No. 2 ranking heavyweight. Moore was ordered to bed in a San Diego hospital, and the diagnosis was confirmed by a heart specialist. The doctors held little hope. Moore's heart ailment was organic; he would never fight again, and he would have to forfeit his championship. Friends who visited him in the hospital at the time found him close to despair. "This is so cruel," he said, clenching his fists in anguish. "I've been fighting all these years and I've never made any real money. Now I've got a chance to cash in, and this happens." He turned away, rolling on his side to face the wall. For the first time that anybody could remember, he seemed utterly defeated.

Doc Kearns was the only person who didn't lose courage. With nothing to go on but faith in his fighter (the title "Doc" was conferred on him by Jack Dempsey, not by a medical school), he convinced himself that Moore's heart condition was correctable. At any rate, he was certainly not going to accept the judgment of two local doctors as final. He obtained Moore's release from the San Diego hospital and flew with him to San Francisco to consult another specialist. The verdict there was the same: Moore had a heart murmur, and fighting was out of the question. Then Kearns, Moore, and a friend named Bob Reese—an automobile dealer from Toledo, Ohio—took off for Chicago, where they went to Arch Ward, sports editor of the *Chicago Tribune*, for advice. Ward himself, as they knew, was receiving treatment for a heart ailment, and he recommended that they see the Chicago specialist who was treating him. Once more the news was bad: Moore dare not fight; no commission would license him. Ward, who later died of a heart attack, wrote a column urging Moore to retire. Then Moore and Kearns decided to go to the Ford Hospital, in Detroit, for an examination by Dr. John Keyes, of the cardiology department. "Detroit was our last hope," Kearns recalls. "I'd been told that they had the greatest heart doctors in the world at the Ford Hospital. If they couldn't help Archie, I knew he was finished." Dr. Keyes' findings brought the sun up again for Moore and Kearns. The heart condition wasn't organic, after all; Moore had a fibrillation—an irregular heart rhythm that was correctable with medication. "They put me in bed, and I began receiving medication every two hours," Moore says. "This continued for four days. On the fifth day, I had another electrocardiogram, and the heartbeat was

261

regular again. The doctor gave me a clean bill of health, and I got my walking papers."

A month and a half later, on May 2, 1955, Moore fought Valdes as scheduled, in the Las Vegas ballpark. Many of Moore's friends thought that he was foolish to fight so soon after recovering from a heart ailment, and some sports columnists were ghoulishly speculating that he might die in the ring; they warned the Nevada State Athletic Commission against assuming responsibility for the bout. Sportswriters arriving in Las Vegas a couple of days before the fight found Moore exercising before a paying audience in a ballroom above the Silver Slipper gambling casino. He looked terrible. Free to enter the ring at whatever his weight happened to be on the day of the fight, he had allowed himself to balloon to two hundred pounds, and he was in such poor shape that he had difficulty lasting three minutes with a sparring partner. He spat out his mouthpiece after thirty seconds in the ring because he could barely get his breath. The fight itself was scheduled for fifteen rounds. When it began, Valdes was as trim as a panther, and Moore looked like the winner of a pie-eating contest. Silhouetted against the evening sky, he shuffled about the ring, his long trunks flopping in the breeze. He landed few blows and was clearly exerting himself as little as possible. The crowd began to jeer him, and Valdes steadily piled up a lead on points. Then, starting in the eighth round, the old man suddenly became the aggressor. He began scoring with his left hook, he jolted the Cuban with right-hand leads, and now and then he banged Valdes with stinging combinations. It became obvious that Moore was using the bout as a training fight—that this was merely the first step in his preparations for bigger bouts later in the year, with Olson and Marciano. As the contest progressed, Moore became stronger and Valdes faded. There were scattered boos when the referee, Jim Braddock, who was the only official, awarded the decision to Moore; but most of the working press at ringside agreed with Braddock.

Seven weeks later and twenty-five pounds lighter, Moore defended his light-heavyweight championship against Olson at the Polo Grounds, and knocked him out in three rounds. In September, back up to a hundred and eighty-eight pounds, Moore attempted to take the heavyweight title away from Rocky Marciano, at Yankee Stadium, and succeeded in flooring him with a short right uppercut in the second round, but Marciano got up, and pounded Moore down and out in the ninth. (A year or so later, the two were reminiscing about the fight, and Marciano said, "When you had me down in the second round there, Archie, it was too close." Moore replied graciously, "Rocky, it's like I've always said—it was a pleasure to fight you.") Marciano never fought again. The next spring—in April, 1956—he announced his retirement from the ring, and on November 30th of the same year Moore and Floyd Patterson, who had been adjudged the ranking contenders, met in the Chicago Stadium for the vacant title. Moore's best fighting weight is between a hundred and eighty-two and a hundred and eighty-five pounds, but he came into the ring at a hundred and ninety-six pounds, looking like a Buddha in boxing gloves. He was thirty-nine (or forty-two) years old. Patterson, at a trim hundred and eighty-two and a quarter, and twenty-one years old, knocked him out in the fifth round with a looping left hook that Moore, normally an extremely clever defensive fighter, should have avoided easily. It was probably the worst performance of Moore's career, but when the writers trooped into his dressing room after the fight, he received them with his customary aplomb. Instead of sulking, he stood on a bench and courteously answered questions during a long interview, but his lame explanation that he was overtrained obviously failed to satisfy the critics. Nevertheless, when the inquisition finally ended, he thanked the writers for their time and their company. "God bless you, Archie, you're wonderful!" shouted the late Caswell Adams, then boxing writer for the *New York Journal-American*. Boxing writers are a cynical breed and seldom applaud anybody, but this time they cheered.

BROOKLYN MICK

This is here for the shop talk and the beginnings of a sparring partner—all in the first half. The second half is about Nathan Hale and Patrick Henry.

EDDIE ORCUTT

The Mick was supposed to be resting, getting ready to fight the Argentine at the Coliseum that night. He had stripped to his shorts and he was sitting up on his bed in this dollar-a-day hotel room, with a blanket over his legs. He had hung his sweat clothes in the window to get a little sun before he packed them, and the air in the room had a bitter smell. This Brooklyn Mick was a black Irishman, sailor-tattooed on his arms and big chest, and he had grown a one-day stubble of beard to protect his face against glove cuts. His face had two deep lines down the cheeks, and they curved along his jaw and made an inverted U over the deep cleft in his chin. These lines wreathed his wide mouth when he laughed, but when he looked serious, the lines hardened and his chin had the character that a bulldog's jowls have.

"Hype Igoe put a piece in the newspapers about me, and he called me the Dean of Sparring Partners. I been sparring partners to five world champions. Six, because Tommy Loughran was the light-heavy champ. You can put in your story that I probably boxed more rounds with Mr. Joe Louis than any other white man in the world.

"You don't have to go yet," the Mick said.

They had picked the Mick up in Los Angeles, working out with Maxie Rosenbloom, earning a couple dollars a round and trying to get back in some kind of shape. The Mick was tough and he knew his way around, but he was twelve pounds overweight and he had not had a ring fight in six months, and so he was exactly what they wanted for the Argentine. They were pointing the Argen-

tine for big money, so, naturally, they would not give him anybody who was in shape to make trouble for him. The Mick would go in and take a beating. He was broke and a long way from home, and he needed the money.

"You don't have to go yet." This thing was on his mind, this jam that he was in back East, and finally he wanted to give me the story. If it had not been for this trouble, he would have been in New York right then, working for Joe Louis or Tommy Farr. He saw where the Garden had signed Max Baer and Jim Braddock, too, and either of them would have been glad to have him, he said. He had boxed each of them. The year before, when Schmeling began training at Napanoch for Joe Louis, the Mick had been the second man to arrive in Schmeling's camp, and the last to leave. Schmeling had paid him thirty-five dollars a day, all expenses and a bonus. The Mick had been tops at his trade.

"Schmeling told me: 'Make yourself at home. If there is anything you don't see, ask for it. You'll get it.' He was tanned and brown. He had a solid grip and his eyes were clear. He looked like a real clean-living man, which he was.... But I hadda take it on the duffy outa New York," the Mick said. "Wit' a wife an' two kids, I couldn't stay back there, see, because you can't tell what these guys will do. Like I told you," he said, "they got something wrong wit' their mind."

This trouble was bad.

"Wit' a wife an' two kids, I couldn't stay back there—"

On this last afternoon, resting up for his hundred-dollar pasting, the Mick wanted to spill his trouble to somebody. To understand it, though, you would have to get some of this talk that he gave me about his trade. Because if the Mick had never taken up a good trade, if he had not worked hard at it and then been good at it, he never would have been in this jam.

The Mick was a good Irish talker with a tang of Brooklyn in his brogue, and I ribbed him to talk shop because I liked to hear it.

"Sparrin' wit' a guy," the Mick said, "you learn him like a book. Carnera couldn't let go his right, bein' muscle-bound, see, but if you run into his left, it would knock your teeth out. He was always holdin' it out, stickin' wit' it, an' stickin' an' stickin'. He could stick good wit' it."

You had to watch out for that left, and you had to ride him in the clutches, not try to rassle with him. If you watched those things, the Mick said, you could give Primo a good workout without getting hurted.

"Workin' wit' these champeens," he explained, "you got to be kind of a cutie. You got to give 'em what they're payin' you for, but you don't wanta just let 'em punch you up. You got to learn 'em." If they wanted to punch somebody around, they could hire some has-been or some punk that didn't know any better, but a real sparring partner was not just a punching dummy.

The Mick had gone with Carnera back in '31, when Da Preem was prepping for his first Sharkey fight. The Mick had been down on his luck then, because it was right after they killed Kid Ritchie, the Mick's first manager. He had been glad to go with Carnera for fifteen dollars a day. Carnera had hired him again for the second Sharkey fight, then taken him on a stage tour, and then brought him back to camp again when Carnera began readying up for Max Baer.

"I will never forget the first time I seen this Carnera. He was out on the lawn at Doc Bier's place, playin' wit' a little brown dog. He sure was very big. He looked like a sea sperrint playin' wit' a goldfish."

Max Baer had hired him next. "But I only worked wit' him a week, on account they said I was not the type." The Mick laughed. He had a sort of hell-may-care, chuckling laugh. "He was a good guy, though. He was all right. He would be always trying to knock your brains out, but if he hurt you, he would clown around an' give you time to stall out of it."

Carnera's left hand had been made to order for Baer, the Mick said, but Braddock's was not. "Baer was a sucker for a left—but he was a smart sucker, see? Carnera goes in stickin' wit' his left, but he moves back after a jab, like most guys do. Well, if you jab Max Baer and pull back, you are going to pull back into his right hand, see, an' he'll hit you so hard wit' it that you bust an ankle. 'At's what this Carnera did. But Braddock was always movin' in behind his left, an' if you swing the right you just wrapped it around his neck. Braddock was awful tough, too, in them days," the Mick said. "Awful tough. But a nice guy, though. A prince."

Most of the guys that get up around the top are nice guys, the Mick said, no matter how they were raised. "They been places, see, an' they met high-class people," he explained. "It all adds up. It's education," the Mick said. "Even watchin' 'em an' workin' wit' 'em, it's kind of an education.

"This Carnera was like a kid. Always happy, an' we even hadda save the funny papers for 'im. But when you was introduced to him, he would make a good impression on you."

The Mick was glad to talk shop, I think. When he was telling about rowboat riding with Max Schmeling at Napanoch, or explaining what Tommy Loughran used the thumb of his glove for, or trying to tell me how it felt to be in with Joe Louis that first time, it was easier to forget all this about being broke and in a jam and a long way from home. Schmeling and Mr. Joe Louis interest him most.

"After bein' wit' Mr. Joe Louis so much, when he was first sensational, see," the Mick explained, "I sure was interested in workin' wit' Schmeling. I knew right away that Schmeling was no bum, because he had plenty of brains. A big heart too. The last day Schmeling worked, it began rainin' an' we hadda box indoors. I boxed 'im third. In the second round he was really fightin', an' I hit 'im square under the eye wit' the hardest punch I ever throwed. I didn' go to do it. It raised a bump under his eye. 'Are you hurted?' I asked him. 'Nah! Nah! Come on in! I feel good!' he said. Gee, I liked that guy. An' I knew he was right for Mr. Joe Louis too.

"The night before Schmeling–Louis," the Mick said, "I went on the radio, which Francis Albertanti got me into, for two hundred and fifty dollars. When I said Schmeling would win, everybody laughed. 'Schmeling by a knockout,' I said, 'on account of his big heart an' a good right hand!' Everybody in the studio laughed."

It was funny, but the Mick had not seen the fight itself. He and his wife had had another young couple in, and they had sat around the Mick's living room with a pitcher of beer, listening to the radio.

"In the second, remember how the Dutchman's eye began swelling? Oh-oh, did I feel bad," the Mick said, "because it was me that started that eye!" But pretty soon the radio gave off a *Boff* and they said the German was reaching Joe Louis with his right.

"I jumped outa me chair! I leapt in the air! An' you shoulda seen the way me wife got laughing at me!" the Mick said.

The Mick's black eyes twinkled with his grin, because that had been one of the big nights of his life, and it was funny to think of him sitting there in his home with his wife and friends and getting this big bang over the radio.

"Certain'y, I had tickets to the fight. I had two tickets, but I hadda give 'em away," he said. "I didn't wanta see the fight—I was too excited!" The Mick laughed at himself. "I had been sparring partners wit' both these guys, see?

"Mr. Joe Louis hired me for one week when he was training for Carnera. He hired me for three weeks when he was training for Max Baer. I and three other fighters then accompanied him on an exhibition tour of Canada and New England, staying at the best hotels everywhere, and nothing was too good for us, and we boxed Mr. Joe Louis in twelve different cities. He stopped me once. This was in Bangor, Maine, on account of a cut over me eye which Mr. Mushkey Jackson feared might result in a permanent injury, him being the referee."

Talking about Louis, the Mick made sentences carefully, the way he believed they would look good in a newspaper story. He referred to the colored boy as "Mister."

"They was four sparrin' partners. Stanley Ketchell, two-twenty pounds, which Mr. Joe Louis knocked out nine times. Andy Wallace, two-ten, which Mr. Joe Louis knocked out seven times. Me, which Mr. Joe Louis did not knock out, but he stopped me in Bangor, Maine, on account of this eye. And Paul Cavalier, which Mr. Joe Louis did not knock out at all."

They had opened in Montreal; then going to a place called Ottawa, the Mick said. He told me how the four sparring partners had spent a day loafing around Montreal, and it seems that the town was full of Frenchies, talking French. Talking back to them, the fighters gave them the double-talk. "Look, will you or me get me that two-three on the outside, inside, over here, see, so the inside over the outside—" The Mick said that the Frenchies went nuts.

Talking about Mr. Joe Louis as a fighter or as a boxer, the Mick was very earnest and respectful, but he was full of chuckles about the tour. The crowds had mobbed in everywhere to see Joe Louis, because he was supposed to be dynamite and murder, but the sparring partners had made a picnic out of it. In Bangor, after the show, a friend had thrown a party for Louis, and the Mick gave me a long story about the doings. Afterwards, in the hotel room, he and Cavalier had short-sheeted Andy Wallace's bed, and the four two-hundred-pounders had wound up with a big towel fight. "Wit' wet towels too!"

"We returned to Boston, and here Mr. Joe Louis swang over to go back to Detroit, and we came on home. Before leaving, Mr. Joe Louis bought us presents. Mine was a swell wrist watch, and you can say it is a sacred piece, which I will never part with. I did not question the other boys the extent to which Mr. Louis gave them presents, but you can put it in that he sure done so."

Well, this was the shop talk of the Mick's trade, and he had added it all up in his mind. "It's a good business," he told me. "It's a good business for a guy that was raised tough." At another time he said: "If I hadda do it all over again, I would do the same. I think I done right."

On this last afternoon, even when he got to thinking about this trouble that he was in, the Mick said the same thing.

"I was raised tough. I been knocked around all me life," he said. "I don't go out easy." You had to be tough, he explained, if you were going to earn your thirty-five a day off Max Schmeling, or Mr. Joe Louis, or any of the good ones. When you got him to talking about this angle of it, though, you began to understand about the choice this Brooklyn Mick had made.

The Mick had been born down on Sands Street, in the Williamsburg district of Brooklyn, near the Navy Yard, and his first playground had been the city dump. "In them days, I t'ought it was the biggest place in the world." Al Capone and Johnny Torrio had started in that district. Vincent Coll, the baby killer, nicknamed Mad Dog Coll, had been the Mick's friend when they were going to grammar school. "Him and me was raised kids together," the Mick said. He had gone to school there, too, with Barney Souza, the boy who talked too much. Telling me this, giving me these names, the Mick would go somber, deadpan, and his voice held a tone that I tried, in my mind, to label. It was not terror, because it was blank and quiet, but it had some recollection of terror in it. Kids grew up on fighting in this neighborhood.

"You hadda fight. You hadda learn to fight good," the Mick said. Even these tough kids knew, though, that there were things there that you could not fight. The Mick said: "There was big guys, see?" And he watched me to see if I got it. That meant Coll, or Capone, or such names, and their shadow was on the rats and the hoodlums and the lesser tough guys of the district.

"But even when I was a kid, sometimes I would get away from the neighborhood and live different for a day. That does a guy good. I would play like I was explorin' around in the country, wit' tree forests an' hills an' lakes, an' stuff like that.

"The city dump was a good place," the Mick told me, "an' when I was maybe nine or ten I would play hooky there. I would get up before daylight, an' I would find bread an' maybe half a bottle of port wine on the table from me folks havin' a party the night before. So I would cop it an' beat it over to the city dump, see, an' I would stay there all day. Not go to school, not go home or nuttin'. There was places like hills or caves, because there was all kinds of junk on this dump, see? I would go explorin' around all day.

"An' they was always dumpin' cans there by the millions, but some of these cans from the restaurants would not be opened yet. If I would find a full can, I would open it an' eat whatever was in it. Maybe beans, maybe salmon—whatever was in it, I would eat it, see?

"You know how I would open them cans? I wouldn' swipe a can opener from home, because that would be, like you say, civilized. I would get me a big rusty nail an' a brick, an' I would hammer holes all around under the edge of the can till I could bust the top off!" The Mick had a laugh at these things he did when he was little. "That's a kid for you!" he said.

In the neighborhood, though, the Mick said, there were some very tough guys, and the smaller kids would imitate them. They would gang up and fight, or they would prowl around on the clip, like these older guys, and the best fighters would very likely grow up to be hoodlums.

"I had a good reputation in street fightin', but I never would be a hoodlum, because what kind of a heart do them guys have? How could I stand a guy up against the wall and punch him around and tell him he has to do business with my boss or I will hurt him? Maybe he might be an old fella—old enough to be my father. Guys that do that, what do they have for a heart?"

Fighting was natural, but this other business was not. The Mick told me about this Barney Souza, and how the cops finally fished him out from the foot of Bridge Street, swollen from a couple of days in the East River and with his lips mottled green from copper wire. "They sewed his mouth wit' wire, see, so's to show he shouldn'a talked so much. If you can do things like that, your mind is not right."

The Mick went on a beer truck when he was seventeen, working nights and making good money, because it was prohibition times. After that he did a two-year hitch in the Navy. He went on a coal truck when he got out. It was not much money, but jobs were scarce, and this job kept him from getting mixed up in anything.

"In me spare time, I would go over to New York, an' would hang around the fight gyms—the Pioneer, see, or Stillman's. This prevented me hangin' around wit' any neighborhood guys." The Mick twinkled his wide grin at me, and added a word.

"Ambition," he said. "See what I mean?"

And then it seems that the Mick really got a break, because old Kid Ritchie picked him up at the Pioneer and liked the look of him. Kid Ritchie took him off the coal truck and made a fighter of him. Kid Ritchie was high-class, the Mick said. In the old days he had been a fighter, and a good one, and he had saved his money. He had bought property, raised a family and settled down to running a good saloon, and when the Mick knew him, he was well-to-do and a respected man.

"Me, I could fight," the Mick said, "but I didn't know nuttin'. This Kid Ritchie knew everything. He showed me how to live right an' take care of meself, see, an' goin' in the ring he wouldn' leave me bust in sluggin' an' take a lot of punches. He would make me be smart. He never got me no fights until I was ready, an' then he got me main events in these neighborhood clubs. I was wit' him a year an' a half," the Mick said. "I win twelve straight knockouts. You know," the Mick told me, "I begun feelin' like a real prize fighter, see?"

This ended when Kid Ritchie got killed. The old man had eased a drunk out of the saloon one night, talking nice to him, in the way that old-timers have, but the drunk had come back with a gun. Kid Ritchie never had a chance.

"He used to take me home to dinners in his own house, like he was me own father," the Mick said. And then, mourning Kid Ritchie, he added it up in words that he had made careful and formal, out of respect to the Kid's memory. "He survived all me workouts," the Mick said. "I was continuously in his company all the time wit' 'm."

All this about Kid Ritchie had a bearing on what the Mick wanted to tell me about, on this last afternoon, so he went over it again. It was five years after Kid Ritchie died, he said, before he began really getting ambition again.

"Sure, I boxed on me own," he said. "I would take this fight, or that fight; sometimes win an' sometimes lose. If the other guy would be nice. I've took the handcuffs, also, when I had to. I done all right," he said, "but I was not like I was when Kid Ritchie had me, see?" The Mick watched me carefully, to make sure I would get all this. "After I finished wit' Schmeling, though," he said, "I got ambition again. Bein' wit' high-class people, see, it makes you want to be high-class yourself."

So it was this ambition, the Mick said, that got him into the trouble. He made a couple of good fights. He got himself a manager who had strong connections. And then—

"Last December—the sixt' of last December," the Mick said, "I got pinched by the Feds in Baltimore for transportin' twenty-five ounces of heroin." He said it in a flat voice. He looked square at me. The reckless Irish grin swaggered into his face for a second, but his eyes were dead black, intent, watching me. I waited.

"Ever hear of George Kubel?" the Mick asked. I said, "No."

"When I made a couple good fights, George Kubel come around to me," the Mick said, "an' asked me how about him handling me business. He tol' me what he could do for me. I knew he had good connections, see, an' I hadda have somebody with the ins, so I said okay. George Kubel was kind of big, but he was a racket guy," the Mick told me. "I knew that, but I never knew what his racket was, see?" The Mick was still watching me. "It was none of my business. I said okay, an' he started han'ling me. Look," the Mick said, "I would of had a lotta nerve to go askin' 'm if maybe he was peddling coke. He's never been pinched, see, and I don't go askin' 'm what his racket is." The Mick's eyes were dead black, somber. 'There was big guys mixed up wit' 'm, see?"

But the Mick said it looked like a good break, because Kubel started getting him work right away. He got him a bout in Boston. He got him one in Detroit. He sent the Mick over to Paterson for a couple of fights. They were not big fights—$600 was the best, the Mick said—but the Mick had this ambition in him again, and he began to go good. George Kubel had all kinds of dough and he rolled around New York in a limousine with a Filipino chauffeur, and the Mick knew that Kubel was not interested in just taking his cut out of $600 purses. Kubel had something bigger in mind.

"I figured he really went for me," the Mick explained. "The way this Kid Ritchie had. I figured he was takin' me up into money. Maybe I never got over Kid Ritchie tellin' me I would be champion of the world. Sometimes it would make me laugh. But workin' wit' Mr. Joe Louis or Schmeling or them, sometimes I would remember it. Bein' wit' high-class people, see, it makes you want to be high-class yourself.

"George got me these fights, but he never went wit' me, see? He got me this one in Detroit," the Mick said. "He sent me—he didn't go wit' me. In Boston, he sent me—he didn' go wit' me. He got me a fight in Chicago. A good fight. But he sent me— he didn't go wit' me." The Mick watched to see if I was getting it. He said, "In New York, I went around wit' him a lot, ridin' in this big limousine, see? Like I was a bodyguard. I always dressed good an' I would stick around an' keep my mouth shut, an' so George would take me along when he was goin' around, meeting guys. Some of them was plenty big. But when he set me for a fight, he wouldn't go out of town wit' me. He just sent me."

The payoff came early last December, when George Kubel got the Mick a fight in Richmond, Virginia. This time he told the Mick that they would take the big car and go down together. Naturally, the Mick thought that Kubel figured he was about ready for big money. "So I was gonna show'm a hell of a fight," the Mick said.

He finished a light workout on a Sunday noon, and Kubel drove around to the gym and picked him up. "Put your bag in the car," Kubel told him, "and go out and grab some lunch. I got an errand to do; I'll pick you up in half an hour."

The Mick did it, of course. He left his training bag in Kubel's car and packed away a meal while Kubel was doing his errand. Then Kubel called for him again, and they got away on schedule. They stopped somewhere in Jersey for a cup of coffee several hours later, and got into Baltimore at about ten o'clock that night. George Kubel had another errand in Baltimore. He had to see a guy at a certain hotel, he said. "But I guess you're good and hungry," he told the Mick. "You hop out at this restaurant and get some grub. I'll meet you here inside an hour." This time, though, he had the Mick take his bag with him.

The training bag was just a big black leather satchel with the Mick's boxing things in it, and the Mick lugged it with him into the restaurant. He set the bag down beside the counter where he could watch it, and ordered up a square meal. He ate fast, expecting Kubel to be back soon.

Kubel didn't come.

"An' so I guess now you know what the racket was," the Mick told me. "Dope, see? George went to talk to a guy about a deal, but the guy he talked to was a stool pigeon," the Mick explained. "When George came down out of the hotel, the cops closed in an' made the pinch. Me, I was waitin' for 'm an' waitin' for 'm, an' he never showed up," the Mick said. "So finally I asked the boss if I could leave this bag in the restaurant while I went up to this hotel to look for me manager."

Two blocks down the street, a couple of tough Government cops walked up to the Mick, shoved a gun at him.

George Kubel and the Filipino chauffeur were already in this room in the Baltimore post-office building when the cops threw the door open and shoved the Mick in. Right behind them there was another guy with the Mick's bag. When George Kubel looked at the bag, the Mick said, he turned the same color as the chauffeur, which was kind of a yellowish tan.

"They set this bag on the desk, an' the head man of the office was there. These cops give me plenty of rough talk, but the head guy was quiet. He was high-class. College, an' like that. 'What's in your bag, buddy?' he asked me. I told 'm. 'Is that all?' 'Yes, sir,' I says. So the boss asked these cops if I had give 'em my name when they asked me. They told him I had. He asked if I told 'em where me bag was when they asked me. They said, 'Yes.' Then he pushed a button an' a stenographer come in. It must of been midnight, see, but she was there, waitin'. So this guy says to me: 'Set down an' talk to this stenographer. Tell her everything that you got in that bag.' I set down. I thought of everything I put in that bag. I give her the list—"

The Mick told it to me earnestly. He named the things he carried in this bag, and he told me how the stenographer took them down, *chck-chck-chck-chck*, on the typewriter. When he had finished, the head man asked him again if that was all. The Mick said it was. Then the cops opened this bag. The Mick's things were there. "Me mout'piece, me boxin' helmet, bandages, bag-punchin' gloves, protector, shoes, trunks—everything I told 'em about was there. Only down at the bottom there was this package like a cigar box wrapped in paper." The Mick watched me.

"Remember," he asked, "how George had me put this bag in his car while I got me lunch that noon?"

The head man said: "There's twenty-five ounces of heroin in that package. You transported it from New York to Baltimore. What's your story?"

The Mick gave it to him.

"An' this guy believed me. He said so," the Mick told me.

But they kept the Mick eleven days in the Baltimore city jail, because a narcotics charge is dynamite, and the Government will check all the angles on any guy that gets mixed up in it. The Mick had been on edge for this fight, and the jail food—what with worry and all, he said—poisoned him. He bought three sandwiches and a can of coffee every day from a place across the street, but he got good and sick. He was in bad shape when he got out. And he had to stick around Baltimore an extra day, trying to get his bag and his boxing gear back.

They kept his bag. He finally got them to give him his ring equipment, seeing that he needed it to earn a living with, but they kept the bag for an exhibit. So then the Mick borrowed eight dollars off George Kubel to get back to New York with. Kubel had $18,000 cash on him when he was pinched, and the Mick tried to borrow ten dollars, but eight dollars was all Kubel let him have.

"So it was a fine way to get home, see?" the Mick said. "Me sick, me wife sick wit' worryin', an' me wit' the change out of eight dollars in me pockets. I felt like crawlin' in a hole. The funny thing is that if I had been a hoodlum or a racket guy, this George Kubel would never of picked me up. I wouldn' of been no use to him. If I hadn' of got me a good reputation, I never would of been in this jam. That's funny, ain't it?"

Two months later, the Government sent him a letter. It said that if he would go to the Federal building in New York City, he could get his bag. The Mick went.

"It was a good bag," the Mick said, "an' it was mine."

Everything was all right by that time, of course, and the Government had nothing on the Mick; but when he got inside the Federal building, and went to the property office to claim his bag, they told him that the Major wanted to see him. "Major? What Major?" the Mick asked. They told him who the Major was. They steered him to the Major's office, and the next thing the Mick knew, he was talking to the head of the Government's narcotics division for the whole New York district.

"He was a swell guy. High-class. When he talked to you, you could believe in him," the Mick said.

But the Major asked this Brooklyn Mick a hard question—a question that might be tough on any of us, but a very strange one to put up to a boy raised where the Mick was. They were alone in the Major's office, and after they had talked for a while, the Major asked his question.

"How good a citizen are you?" the Major asked.

Telling me about it, the Mick's grin was twisted. "That makes you stop an' think, don't it? That's a hell of a question!" he said. But in the Major's office he had finally figured an answer. "I guess I am as good as I want to be," he told the Major. "I try to be good."

Well, you will understand what the Major wanted. Down in the Baltimore jail, George Kubel had cracked. The Government had him dead to rights, of course, and Kubel had asked for a deal. He had talked. He had named names and he had

signed affidavits. He had been big, but there were others that were bigger, and Kubel had even named the biggest guy of all. The Government had pinched this big guy.

"All right," the Major said, "you can help us."

"How can I help you?" the Mick asked. The Major's office was part of the United States Government, and the Major and the Federal cops and agents were a part of it. The Mick felt funny, having the United States Government ask him for help.

"You went around a lot with Kubel. He used you for kind of a bodyguard."

"That's right," the Mick said.

Doing business in New York, a big dealer had to buy direct from the higher-ups. The Major named them. "You saw Kubel meet these men, one time and another?" "I might of," the Mick admitted. Then the Major named the big guy himself. He named a time and a place that Kubel had put in an affidavit.

"You saw him hand Kubel these packages?"

"I might of. I didn' know what was in them, though." Since he was a kid, the Mick had known enough not to see what he was not supposed to see. "George never told me," the Mick said. "I never asked."

The Major nodded. He was no country boy. "But you see what I want," he said.

The Major could have put George Kubel on the stand, perhaps, and Kubel might have spilled everything he had. But the big guy's lawyers would have made him look bad. They would have called him a rat and a squealer, and they would have claimed that he would say anything to cut time off his own rap.

If the Government could get the Mick on the witness stand, though, it would be different. The Mick was no rat. He was no peddler, no racket guy, and he had a good record. The Government could prove what he did for a living, and they could show that he was high up in his trade—sparring partner to six world champions. When the Mick told what he had seen, a jury would believe him.

"Will you do that?" the Major asked.

The Mick said: "Oh-oh!"

So, in this cheap hotel room where he was resting for his fight, the Mick held his answer and waited, and there was a kind of suspense in the room. This prize fighter from the Navy Yard district, born on Sands Street, raised kids with Vincent Coll, had made his choice long before the Major ever got him into the Federal building and asked him how good a citizen he was. He had made his choice when he got that job on the coal truck. He had made his choice when he began hanging around the fight gyms in New York, getting away from the neighborhood guys. Watching him in this hotel room, I knew what answer he had had to give the Major, but suspense tightened while I waited for him to name it. The Mick leaned forward, resting his arms on his knees and staring at the window where his sweat clothes were catching the last of the afternoon sun.

"Ever see a cokie?" the Mick asked.

I said I had, and the Mick nodded. "They showed me one," he said.

Then he shrugged. He spoke flatly, almost indifferently, the suspense ended and the story finished. "What the hell else could I do?" he said. "I told the Major: 'All right, I will do it.'" He kept on staring at the window. "A thing like that," he said, "is your duty. You hafta do it."

So, at the big guy's trial, the Mick took the stand for the United States Government, in a courtroom where the big guy's torpedoes watched him, and where some of the Mick's own friends gave him the eye and pretended that they had never seen him before. He faced men who had done murder for hire, and men who had paid hire for murder. He gave his name and his record and described his trade. The judge on the bench questioned him, asking him what money he earned at this trade, about the family he supported and his home, and about the champions he had worked for. "I believe this man's word," the judge said. When the Government asked questions, the Mick answered them and the judge and jury believed him. They did not have to depend on any frightened squealer, any stoolie or spy, because this Brooklyn Mick was an American citizen testifying under oath. You could say that he was a special kind of citizen that day. A citizen by choice.

The dope racket's big guy went to the Federal prison at Leavenworth.

"So I come out here for me health," the Mick said. He gave me his grin again suddenly. "After it was over, I was not a Gover'ment witness any more, an' I didn' know how soon somebody might start ringin' me doorbell. So I took it on the duffy outa New York. I come out here, bummin' around."

It was not very funny. I told him so.

"Gee, it's late all of a sudden," the Mick said. "I better lay back an' take me a nap." He still sat there, though, while I stood up. "You've got plenty of heart, kid," I told him, but he was not listening. He sat with his knees hunched up, his arms resting on them, and he stared thoughtfully at this window where he had hung up his sweat clothes. The sun was almost gone. The Mick still wanted to tell me something, and he was thinking it out.

"You know," he said finally, "it's all right. Stuff like that is your duty." He gave it to me soberly and confidentially, the way he had told me about Carnera's invisible uppercut and how Max Baer had acted at the weigh-in for Braddock. "You got to do it." Then he broke out this wide Irish grin of his, but he looked at me almost bashfully, because he was telling me something I should have known from a long time ago, when I was a kid in school.

"That's how our country got like it is," the Brooklyn Mick said. "People doing something for their gover'ment. Nat'an Hale. Patrick Henry. Guys like them."

He gave me those names.

Nat'an Hale. Patrick Henry. Guys like them.... People doing something for their gover'ment.... That's how our country got like it is.

After I had shaken hands with the Mick and wished him good luck, and left him to rest up for his beating, I went down into the streets and saw an unaccustomed thing. This Mick, and the Brooklyn city dump where he played when he was a kid, were a part of what I saw. I went out and walked through ordinary streets, and I looked at the ordinary people in them, and what I saw was the United States of America.

I WENT TO SEE TONY GALENTO

No other writer has ever been as avidly read by the members of the fight mob as Dan Parker. This column, which appeared in 1938, or fourteen years after Parker joined the New York *Mirror,* is typical of him in his dual roles as judge and jester.

DAN PARKER

Oh, Tony Galento, he trains on pimento
And gargles the ale when it's cool.
My pronunciamento concerning Galento Is:
"Switch to that pasta fazoole!"
　　—From Oscar O'Ginsburg's "Odes of Orange"

Orange, New Jersey, which likes to consider itself a suburban community, became a tank town Wednesday night when Charley Massera played the role of a barrel of beer to Bartender Tony Galento's bung starter. Ordinarily, under the same circumstances, the whole town would be asking: "Did he fall or was he pushed?" but these little technical points bother residents of Orange not at all. The end always justifies the means with them where the sainted Galento is concerned.

They say a left hook
To the chops closed the book
Of the prize fighter, Charley Massera.
Though it may not have landed
It left Charley stranded.
(And how is your dear old Aunt Sarah?)
　　—From Moses McGillicuddy's "Musings of
　　Massera"

The whole thing was a fifteen-minute interlude in Tony's career as a boniface. One minute he was slicing layers of foam off scuttles of suds with the bone cleaver in his tonsil-irrigating studio down the block. The next thing you knew, he was in the ring, covered all over from head to foot, covered all over with Vaseline, like the greased pig at the annual field day of the Iron Puddlers' Local No. 365. There was majesty in his manner as he clasped his gloved hands and held them aloft in acknowledgment of the applause with which his public greeted him.

And may I be vouchsafed permission to say that no sovereign, replying to expressions of fealty from his subjects, ever acknowledged them with more regal dignity?

They seen their duty and they done it
They cheered for Tony and he won it.
He put Massera on the shelf
And proved it's "everyone for THEIR self!"
　　—From Gabriel Googarty's "Gurgles of
　　Galento"

Nor did he stop at this all-embracing acknowledgment, as your fly-by-night celebrities of the prize ring might have done. Some of the beer he has drunk in his day may have gone to Tony's head, but success hasn't. He's still the same Democratic Tony who has always voted for Mayor Hague's candidate. Didn't he prove it by acknowledging every greeting from a galleryite or ringsider, individually, after having taken care of his public as a unit?

He bowed to the left and he bowed to the right
And came close to bowing right out of the fight.
Next he dropped 'em a curtsy, a regular wow,
And he would have salaamed had he only known how.
　　—From Murgatroyd the Mope's "Murdering the
　　Muse"

Finally the fight was on—the epic clash that had caused the biggest turnout of Orangemen since the Battle of the Boyne. The armory was packed to the last available inch and the halitosis quotient was dreadful. Tony's admirers and customers were everywhere. They hung by their toes from above, literally, as the girders across the drillshed were infested with them. Outside thousands lingered, hoping to hear the thud. Everyone knew Massera was going out like an empty beer barrel, the only element of doubt being "when?"

> Tony's belly rolled like jelly
> And Massera's fist
> Bounced into it—almost through it—
> Right up to the wrist.
> —From "Mendel's Mutterings"

As a boxer, Tony uses the Ely Culbertson, or approach system. He approaches an opponent wide open, as if inviting a liver massage. After getting what he wants, he switches to the Irish attack, better known as "The back of me fisht to you!"

Next, he tries "The Shoemaker's Revenge," or "Giving It the Heel." Two rounds of this and Tony decided the customers had had enough. Did I say Tony? I meant Charley. One of Tony's left hooks landed somewhere—no one is quite sure—and Charley landed on his haunches. He's up. He's down. He's out. It all happened in 45 seconds. Yussel Jacobs, in Tony's corner, summed it up succinctly when he warbled: "He certainly stood down the second time when you let him have that left."

Some of the boys said Charley almost choked on his mouthpiece after he had been counted out. If he did, it was from laughing.

Tony was back behind the bar in his white apron, with most of the grease wiped off him, in about ten minutes, and from then until dawn his cash register burned out six bearings handling the biggest night's trade in the history of the jernt.

[COMMENT]

SIKI AND CIVILIZATION

Louis Phal, called Battling Siki, was born in 1897 in Senegal, French West Africa. On September 24, 1922, he knocked out Georges Carpentier in six rounds in Paris to become the light-heavyweight champion of the world. Six months later he made the classic error of boxing Mike McTigue on St. Patrick's Day in Dublin, Ireland, and lost the title on a twenty-round decision. He was killed in a street brawl in New York City on December 15, 1925.

James Westbrook Pegler was born in 1894 in Minneapolis, Minnesota. He was a war correspondent for the United Press from 1916 through 1918, and a great sports commentator for the UP from 1919 to 1925 and for the *Chicago Tribune* from 1925 to 1933. Then he gave up his title and deserted the division to campaign among the heavies as a pugnacious political and general columnist.

WESTBROOK PEGLER

New York, December 17, 1925—Battling Siki, who tried hard to understand civilization but never quite got the idea, will be trundled out over the roads of Long Island tomorrow and buried in the civilized way without a single thump of the tom-tom. A Negro minister will commend him to the mercy of the Christian God, and Negroes will shoulder the casket, but there will be nobody there who really understood the Mohammedan-born Siki because the difference was no mere matter of complexion.

The one person who knew Battling Siki best and loved him as a man loves a friendly but mischievous pet was a white man, Bob Levy, his manager. Siki called him Papa Bob and often assaulted him with moist kisses in the same conciliatory way a chicken-killing Airedale with feathers in his whiskers might slap his master on the cheek with a sopping tongue.

Siki had heard a lot about the virtues of civilization in a dozen years of exposure to its decorous influence, but in the last minute of his life, when he fell in a dirty gutter in Hell's Kitchen, where the lights of Broadway throw deep shadows and churches face speakeasies across the street, civilization must have been a puzzle and a josh to him. As Siki stumbled over the curb and his dented plug hat bounced away, he may have laughed at the irony of it all, for he had come all the way from the jungle to the haunts of civilization and chivalry to be shot in the back.

Siki was one who could giggle with his last gasp, too. He laughed in Paul Berlenbach's face throughout their fight in the old Garden, and the harder Paul slugged him the more he seemed to enjoy the joke.

As Siki got the idea, civilization was something supposed to make men do things they didn't want to do and to curtail their natural enjoyment of life. Civilization was a good thing in theory, but it didn't work, and Siki saw proof it didn't work.

For one thing, under civilization, if a man stole your woman or your ox you were not allowed to go over to that man's house and razor his head off in person. It was against the rules to kill people. And then civilization fell out with itself and Siki was given a gun with a knife on the end of it and invited to kill everyone he saw wearing a certain uniform.

Under civilization a man was allowed just one wife at a time. But Siki rattled around Paris enough to learn civilization was, in civilized language, the bunk in this respect.

Siki came to the United States, and they told him civilization had made a law whereby it was wrong to drink liquor. And then Siki toured half of the country and found civilized men everywhere, white and black, who would sell him liquor and get him stewed contrary to the statutes.

Siki went to night clubs and, to the weird squealing of the wood winds and the muffled thump of tom-toms, the music of civilization, he saw half-naked black-and-tans wiggling and squirming in the dances of an enlightened tribe.

He fought in the ring, and when blood showed, the civilized crowds came up from their chairs, roaring approbation.

So, from what he saw of it, Siki frankly didn't get the plot of this business called civilization. The whole thing was too much for this simple mind of a primitive African who got a late start at the racket.

FROM: THE DIALOGUES

Since Socrates and Gorgias (and Plato) found in boxing a universal reference, no other form of athletic endeavor has supplied such a stockpile of simile and metaphor.

PLATO (TRANSLATED BY BENJAMIN JOWETT)

GORGIAS   *Socrates and Gorgias*

And in a contest with a man of any other profession the rhetorician more than any one would have the power of getting himself chosen, for he can speak more persuasively to the multitude than any of them, and on any subject. Such is the nature and power of the art of rhetoric! And yet, Socrates, rhetoric should be used like any other competitive art, not against everybody; the rhetorician ought not to abuse his strength any more than a pugilist or pancratiast or other master of fence; because he has powers which are more than a match either for friend or enemy, he ought not therefore to strike, stab, or slay his friends. Suppose a man to have been trained in the palestra and to be a skillful boxer—he in the fullness of his strength goes and strikes his father or mother or one of his familiars or friends; but that is no reason why the trainers or fencing-masters should be held in detestation or banished from the city; surely not. For they taught their art for a good purpose, to be used against enemies and evildoers, in self-defense not in aggression, and others have perverted their instructions, and turned to a bad use their own strength and skill. But not on this account are the teachers bad, neither is the art in fault, or bad itself; I should rather say that those who make a bad use of the art are to blame. And the same argument holds good of rhetoric; for the rhetorician can speak against all men and upon any subject.

REPUBLIC   *Socrates and Adeimantus*

Here, then, is a discovery of new evils, I said, which the guardians will have to watch, or they will creep into the city unobserved.

What evils?

Wealth, I said, and poverty; for the one is the parent of luxury and indolence, and the other of meanness and viciousness, and both of discontent.

That is very true, he replied; but still I should like to know, Socrates, how our city will be able to go to war, especially against an enemy who is rich and powerful, if deprived of the sinews of war.

There may possibly be a difficulty, I replied, in going to war with such enemy; but there is no difficulty where there are two of them?

How so? he asked.

In the first place, I said, our side will be trained warriors fighting against an army of rich men.

That is true, he said.

And do you not suppose, Adeimantus, that a single boxer who was perfect in his art would easily be a match for two stout and well-to-do gentlemen who were not boxers?

Hardly, if they came upon him at once.

What, not, I said, if he were able to run away and then turn and strike at the one who first came up? And supposing he were to do this several times under the heat of a scorching sun, might he not, being an expert, overturn more than one stout personage?

Certainly, he said, there would be nothing wonderful in that.

And yet rich men are probably not so inferior to others in boxing as they are in military qualities.

Likely enough.

Then probably our athletes will be able to fight with three or four times their own number?

I agree with you, for I think you right.

LAWS

Athenian Stranger: . . . . The regulations about war, and about liberty of speech in poetry, ought to apply equally to men and women. The legislator may be supposed to argue the question in his own mind:—Who are my citizens for whom I have set in order the city? Are they not competitors in the greatest of all contests, and have they not innumerable rivals? To be sure, is the natural reply. Well, but if we were training boxers, or pancratiasts, or any other sort of athletes, would they never meet until the hour of contest arrived; and should we do nothing to prepare ourselves previously? Surely, if we were boxers, we should have been learning to fight for many days before, and exercising ourselves in imitating all those blows and wards which we were intending to execute in the hour of conflict; and in order that we might come as near to reality as possible, instead of cestuses we should put on boxing gloves, that the blows and the wards might be practiced by us to the utmost of our power. And if there were a lack of competitors, the fear of ridicule would not deter us from hanging up a lifeless image and practicing at that. Or if we had no adversary at all, animate or inanimate, should we not venture in the dearth of antagonists to spar by ourselves? In what other manner could we ever study the art of self-defense?

Cleinias: The way which you mention, Stranger, would be the only way.

Athenian Stranger: And shall the warriors of our city, who are destined when occasion calls to enter the greatest of all contests, and to fight for their lives, and their children, and their property, and the whole city, be worse prepared than boxers? And will the legislator, because he is afraid that their practicing with one another may appear ridiculous, abstain from commanding them to go out and fight; will he not ordain that soldiers shall perform lesser exercises without arms every day, making dancing and all gymnastic tend to this end; and also will he not require that they shall practice some gymnastic exercises, greater as well as less, as often as every month; and that they shall have contests one with another in every part of the country, seizing upon posts and lying in ambush, and imitating in every respect the reality of war; fighting with boxing gloves and hurling javelins, and using weapons somewhat dangerous, and as nearly as possible like the true ones, in order that the sport may not be altogether without fear, but may have terrors and to a certain degree show the man who has and who has not courage; and that the honor and dishonor which are assigned to them respectively, may prepare the whole city for the true conflict of life? If any one dies in these mimic contests, the homicide is involuntary, and we will make the slayer, when he has been purified according to law, to be pure of blood, considering that if a few men should die, others as they will be born; but that if fear is dead, then the citizens will never find a test of superior and inferior in desert, which is a far greater evil to the state than the loss of a few.

Cleinias: We are quite agreed, Stranger, that we should legislate about such things, and that the whole state should practice them.

FROM: SHADOW BOX

George Plimpton, editor of *The Paris Review*, in his books and magazine pieces has managed to maintain literary excellence without out-distancing the sports reader. In his best work, using the Walter Mitty approach, he has taken on some of the best at their specialties, even sparring a few rounds with Archie Moore to end up, in the third round, like the rest of Archie's 140 KO victims. Here he takes us with him in Zaire for Foreman–Ali.

GEORGE PLIMPTON

I preceded Ali out to the ring. The night was soft. The giant illuminated portrait of President Mobutu glowed above the rim of the stadium. As I walked through the infield toward the ring, I wondered how Hunter Thompson's plans were coming along. He would be out on the boulevards somewhere in his strange car that only steered when he jiggled the light dimmer. The crowd was huge and noisy. I wanted to check quickly under the ring to see if I could find any little fetish bags. I imagined dozens of them under there, their necks tied with thongs to keep the chicken claws and the clay figurines and whatever else was in them from spilling out. The photographers were packed in and around, arranging their equipment; their legs set up a formidable picket barrier.

"Can I get through, please?"

"Where are you going, man?"

"Under. I'd like to get under. . . ."

I don't recall that any of them were startled; perhaps they thought that I was an electrician of some kind. Underneath, I crouched below a criss-cross of wooden beams. The earth was soft and cool to the touch. What an odd place from which to cover a fight, I thought—to try to gauge from the shuffle of feet, the thump of a body, what was going on up above on the canvas. I put my fingertips up and I could feel the tremor of feet against the drumhead surface. Officials were up there, walking around. Under, it was dark. No sign of the pouches. I ran my hand across the grass, feeling for them. Then I had the sense that someone was down there with me . . . the glint of a hand, perhaps the shine of a robe. A witch doctor on

the other side of the beam? perhaps two of them?

One would not want to be discovered fooling around with fetish bags, trespassing among them, and the enormity of trying in the surreal darkness to reason with an aggrieved witch doctor crossed my mind.

"Coming out, please."

I pressed forward against the photographer's legs, appearing from between them like an animal emerging from its burrow, just as the roar went up from the crowd's greeting one of the fighters coming out of the tunnel leading back to the dressing rooms.

I sat next to Norman. He was fine and valuable company because so often he caught a mood up there in the ring that he would share; he paid tremendous attention; it was disconcerting, too, because when a fight began and settled into its course, he would begin to sway, and the rhythm and motion of the fighter seemed to activate him like puppet strings, so that he bobbed and weaved and ducked, just as they did, occasionally snuffling like a fighter clearing his nostrils. I suppose the ultimate of this would be if his head snapped back at a good left hook and he fell backward over his press-section chair. Well, it wasn't as sympathetic as that, but he did seem plugged in to the fighters. Only after the round was done would he reach up and adjust his school-marm spectacles; he would scrawl some notes in a foldback notebook, and chat until the bell sounded for the next round, when he would stiffen slightly, as if a master puppeteer up above the ring had picked up his sticks.

But certainly neither of us—nor anyone else in

that huge crowd—expected to see what happened in the first round. The mental image of Ali *dancing* was what everyone expected. He had kept telling us that in the locker room. Not one person except for Ali himself had the slightest suspicion that at the sound of the opening bell he would take a few flat-footed steps toward the center of the ring and then back himself into a corner—with Foreman, scarcely believing his eyes, coming in after him.

For one sickening moment it looked as if a fix were on, that it had been arranged for the challenger to succumb in the first round and that it would be best if he went quickly and mutely to a corner so that Foreman could get to work on him. It was either that or Ali was going through the odd penitential rite he seems to insist on for each fight, letting himself suffer the best his opponent has to offer. In either case, the consequences were appalling to consider. We all stood. I shouted at Norman, "Oh, Christ, it's a fix,"—an echo of the fifth round of the Liston fight ten years before—hardly hearing myself in a great uproar of sound. Ali's corner men, in the shrieks reserved for warning someone walking blindly toward the edge of a cliff, urged their man to stop doing whatever he was up to and start *dancing*.

Far from obliging, Ali moved from the corner to the *ropes*—traditionally a sort of halfway house to the canvas for the exhausted fighter who hopes perhaps the referee will take pity on him and stop things. Here was Ali in the same spot, his feet square to his opponent, stretched back out over the seats at the angle of a man leaning out of a bedroom window to see if there's a cat on his roof, his eyes popping wide as if at the temerity of what he was doing, while Foreman stood in front of him and began to punch—huge, heavy blows thrown from down around the hips, street-fighter style, telegraphed, obvious, so that we watched Ali slip and block them with his elbows and arms, but it seemed inevitable that one of them would penetrate and collapse him.

With the bell coming up for the end of the round, Ali suddenly came off the ropes. While Foreman's arms were down in punching position, Ali hit him with a series of quick, smart punches in the face, the best of them a right-hand lead that knocked the sweat flying off Foreman's head in a halo. But compared to the fusillade Ali had been undergoing, it seemed the mildest sort of retribution: the crowd roared, but I suspect there were few

who sensed they were not in for a night of lunacy after all. When Ali came back to his corner, I could hear his men storm at him as he sat on his stool: "What you doin'?" "Why don' you dance?" "You *got* to dance." "Stay off the ropes."

The second and third rounds were carbon copies of the first—hugely exciting, though very few of the ingredients of scientific boxing were involved. No countering, no feinting, no moving; simply the terrifying and unique process, as it turned out, of seeing a man slowly drained of his energies and resources by an opponent swaying on the ropes, giving him—as Angelo Dundee was to say later—"a lot of nothing."

In the third round, in the midst of tremendous pressure from Foreman, Ali lurched up off the ropes and hit him some concussive shots, staggering the champion, and suddenly everyone except Foreman seemed not only to understand the plan but to see that it was working almost inexorably. Ali's corner men looked at him with eyes wide with delight—I described them on my pad as a trio of Professor Higginses looking at their Eliza and realizing they might pull it off.

In the fourth round Ali began to talk to Foreman. It is not easy to speak through a boxer's mouthpiece, but Ali began to do a lot of it, more as the rounds progressed, as if it would quicken the matter of Foreman's destruction—"Is that the best you can do?... You can't punch.... Show me something! ... That's a sissy punch!"—until Ali finally came around to what must have been a devastating thing for Foreman to hear: "Give it *back* to me! It's mine! Now it's my turn!"

There was no change in Foreman's tactics. He kept it up, this useless exhaustion of energy; he threw his punches in immense parabolas—one almost heard him sigh with futility as he began them—the punches coming slower and more ponderously, until, rising off his stool after the bell and coming across the ring to deliver them, he seemed as pathetic in the singlemindedness of his attack plan as the mummies of Ali's beloved horror films, lurching through the mists after the life-giving draughts of tana leaves. Indeed, it occurred to me as I watched transfixed that "the Mummy," one of the inspired appellatives Ali finds for his opponents ("the Washerwoman" for George Chuvalo, "the Bear" for Liston, "the Rabbit" for Floyd Patterson), had been Ali's name for Foreman, and nothing could have been more descriptive of Foreman's groping for him in the last rounds. "I am going to be the Mummy's Curse," Ali had said a few days before the fight.

By the eighth round nothing was left inside Foreman. He seemed to wobble off the stool, swayed by the shattering roar of the crowd as he advanced on Ali; he seemed a man getting off a sickbed. I yelled at Norman, "The girl with the slightly trembling hands! She's *got* to him! The succubus!" He looked over, alarmed. It occurred to me that he could not have had the slightest idea what I was talking about.

With Foreman helpless, Ali did not toy with him any more than a mongoose fools with a prey exhausted from striking. He tagged him. In the sad business of dispatching a hulk, he did it quickly and crisply. Foreman staggered, and I heard Bundini shout, "Oh my Lawdy, he on Queer Street!"—the last sound the fighter must have heard before the bruising sock that put him away, collapsing him to the canvas on his back.

Archie Moore, his face round and benign under his wool cap, came up onto the ring apron; he moved along the ropes, trying to attract Foreman's attention with arm motions, signaling him to turn on his stomach and get a knee under him to push himself up. The count went to nine. Then I saw Archie give a small wince of despair as the referee swept his arms briskly back and forth over Foreman, as if he were safe at home in a baseball game.

George Foreman's dressing room was a huge chartreuse emporiumlike parlor—like a Las Vegas anteroom. He came back into it under his own steam, but with his handlers close at his shoulders. He was wearing a red and blue robe with WORLD CHAMPION embroidered on the back in schoolboy script. Did they pack these things away, I wondered, these deposed champions? "Where's my dog?" he asked. He touched Dago on the head; the dog's tail swept back and forth. Foreman was guided to the rubbing table; he lay back on it, gold lamé towels draped over his shoulders, ice packs applied to his face. He asked Dick Sadler if he had been knocked out cold. Then, like a hand flexing a leg that had gone to sleep, he began testing his senses, counting slowly, backward from 100, and then calling out the names of everyone he could think of in his camp—the cooks, the guards, even Bill Caplan—a doleful call of more than twenty names. Caplan's name stuck in his mind. "I have a statement to make," he said. "I found true friendship tonight. I found a true friend in Bill Caplan." Caplan could not have been more surprised; he wondered if there had been neurological damage. "The Ping-Pong games. All those games." Foreman *did* seem in the grip of a euphoria. "With this fight I have found serenity in myself," he was saying. "I felt secure until my corner jumped into the ring." Everyone stared at him astonished. "I was not tired. I truly felt like I was in control of the fight. It was a privilege to fight in my ancestors' land. We have built a bridge that never will be broken again." The fists were pounding on the dressing-room door, from people outside trying to get in. "I'm still my own man. He won," he said unsurely, "but I cannot admit that he beat me. It's never been said that I have been knocked out."

He continued: "When Ali dies, he should have only the words on his headstone: 'Heavyweight Champion of the World.' Nothing else."

Then he began to repeat, at times so slowly that it seemed as if he were stumbling through a written text, what he had so often said in dressing-room statements following his victories: "When the competition is tough, there is never a loser. No fighter should be a winner. Both should be applauded."

Everyone stood around uncomfortably, knowing that it would finally sink in that for the first time in his career his generous words for a loser referred to himself.

I ran into Bundini in a corridor outside. He was subdued—perhaps by the incident with the robe. "Ali gets into trouble when he don't listen to me," he told me. "He wasn't wearing my robe for the fight when Ken Norton opened up and busted his jaw. He cursed me in Lake Tahoe and Bob Foster cut his eye. He is crazy to do that to a witch doctor like Bundini."

"What a fight tonight, though, Beau."

"Yeah," he said. "We took the butterfly and slowed him down, put wet on his wings, and more sting in his bee."

I asked him if he had given Ali any special instructions during the fight. "I told him to stop playing," he said. "The tank was empty. He had nothing in front of him."

"What a fight, though, Bundini," I said again. I knew that I was wearing an idiotic grin. "Oh, my, Bundini."

THE RING

This is a picture by the English novelist, critic and playwright of a typical London fight club of the 1920s.

J.B. PRIESTLEY

Not Wagner's but the boxing hall in the Blackfriars Road. It was once the Old Surrey Chapel, and it still suggests a chapel. I remember that when I first saw it, all that remains of my Nonconformist boyhood was wickedly thrilled at the thought of seeing some boxing matches in such a setting. Dick Burge, who was responsible for the transformation, must have been the sort of man I dreamed about when I was a boy, compelled to sit, hot and glowering, under a Children's Address. Its deaconly appearance gave me no thrill last night, however, though it was my first visit for several years. It was not a night for easy thrills. The Blackfriars Road, black and dripping, was being swept by sleet, and I trust that Mrs. Burge, now the director of The Ring, will forgive me if I say that, even after the miserable Blackfriars Road, her hall did not seem very snug and lively. The big lights above the ring itself had not been turned up, for it still wanted some minutes to eight; the place was still dim, chill, cheerless; the cries of the youths who offered us apples and bars of chocolate went echoing hollowly, forlornly; and there was nothing to see, to do. I was alone—with a whole row of ringside seats to myself—and I began to wish I had stayed at home. The program looked dull. Even the "Important 15 (3-min.) Rounds Contest" did not suggest anything very exciting.

Then the officials made their appearance. The referee climbed into his high chair, and the timekeeper sat down beside his stop watch and bell. The fat men in white sweaters brought out their pails of water, bottles, and towels, and stumped round to their corners. The announcer climbed into the ring, which was immediately flooded with hard, bright light. I like the announcer at The Ring. He looks as if he were taken over from the original chapel. He has an air of mellowed Nonconformity. His trim white hair and white mustache, his black tie, black morning coat, and dark, striped trousers—these things give him dignity; and even when he bellows "Ler-hay-dees an' Gerhentle-men, Ser-hix Rer-hound Contest," you still feel that he is probably the last of the Old Surrey Deacons.

Two thin but muscular youths, whose streetcorner faces seemed almost an insult to their excellent bodies, climbed into the ring, grinned, touched gloves, and then instantly began pummeling one another. They were poor boxers but good stouthearted fighters, and they pleased the rapidly growing audience. One of them got a cut early in the contest, with the result that both their faces were quickly crimsoned and there were marks of blood on their bodies. Somebody who knew nothing about the sport might have imagined that they were trying to kill one another and that the roaring crowd in the cheap seats was filled with a blood lust, but of course actually they were both goodhumoredly slogging away, doing little or no harm to one another, and the crowd was merely applauding their lively spirit. It ended in a draw, a great round of applause, and an astonishing shower of coppers in the ring, so many indeed that it took the announcer and an assistant several minutes to pick them up. These two novices had pleased the crowd, and so it had rained pennies on them. The man sitting in front of me—a fellow with huge shoulders, a battered face, and a professional air—had registered the general verdict when he cried: "A bloody good fight!"

The next two were not so satisfactory. They were dapper, dark lads, better boxers than the others but far less pugnacious. One of them was a trifle affected in his footwork and had a funny little trick of his own, a sort of back-kick not unlike that of a stage dancer. This amused the crowd at the back of me. They decided that these antics were effeminate, and immediately, unanimously, christened the author of them "Cissie." They indulged in waggish irony. "Oh, Cissie!" they screamed, as if in girlish terror. "Don't 'urt Cissie," they implored. In the last of their six rounds, however, these two improved and hammered one another to such a tune that the crowd was won over, dropped all talk of "Cissie," and gave them a round of applause as a benediction.

The contest that followed, though it rose to the dignity of twelve rounds, pleased nobody. The two boys appeared to be engaged in a kind of double-shadow boxing. They seemed determined to get their twelve rounds without giving one another any real trouble at all. "Oh! 'ave a fight, 'ave a fight!" cried a disgusted sportsman at the back. The referee stopped them at one point and apparently uttered words of reproof. But they did not have a fight. The crowd at the back, tired of giving them ironical congratulations, now began to stamp in unison and to whistle "All by Yourself in the Moonlight." The announcer appealed for order, but not very passionately. The timekeeper chatted with his neighbor, smoked cigarettes, and mechanically shouted "Seconds out" and sounded his bell. The referee yawned harder than ever. The two boys danced round and round the ring, went back to their corners, were slapped and toweled and massaged, returned to the center each time looking very ferocious, but did not fight. We were all glad to see the last of them. Now came the event of the evening. The fat men with cigars and the little hardbitten men with cigarettes stopped roaming up and down the corridor that led to the dressing rooms. They all came out, looking knowing and important. The lights above the ring looked harder and brighter than ever. You could not see the other side of the building; everything there was a mysterious blue haze, in which a match occasionally twinkled. "Cher-hoc-lait," cried the white-coated youth, more hopefully. "Fine Aipple," retorted the

opposition caterer, sticking his tray of green fruit under our noses. The announcer entered the ring, and there waited, grave, important. There was a cheer. Tom had come out, an old favorite and a Bermondsey lad. A grin lights up his broad flat face; he puts his two gloves together, holds them up to salute friends and patrons. He is attended by several enormous fellows with cauliflower ears, old hands. Another round of applause. The Frenchman is out, with Messieurs Dubois and Dupont in close attendance. "Ler-hay-dees an' Ger-hentlemen." Tom has cast aside his beautiful dressing gown, to reveal himself as a brown, stocky little fellow in blue shorts. The Frenchman is performing those mysterious exercises with the elastic ropes that girdle the ring. He is taller and longer in the reach than Tom, but does not look so strong or so fit—a queerly made ugly fellow, this "Froggy," as they quickly decide to call him. He does not look as if he will last more than a round or two.

At first Tom seems to have it all his own way. You hear the thump-pad-thud of his glove on Froggy's lean body. But Froggy does not seem to mind. Now and then that long left of his flashes out and sends Tom staggering. "Don't take it too easy, Tom," the crowd tells him. The other Bermondsey lads at the back are full of advice. "Poke it out, Tom," they cry; and then "Turn 'im round, Tom." And Tom's only too anxious to do all these things, but somehow the ungainly Frenchman never allows himself to be hurt. Now and then it is true, he blinks and gives a queer little grin, all of which suggests that Tom's blows to the body have made some impression, but he comes back from his corner as fresh as ever. Indeed, somewhere about the tenth round, it stops being Tom's fight, and there is now no talk of his taking it too easy. Froggy is not only very quick with that long left of his, but he is also a crafty fellow. Every time Tom rushes in, he is stopped, and you hear the dull thump of the wet glove. And there are moments when Froggy drives Tom round the ring or bounces him against the ropes. If Tom were softer, he might easily find himself on his back, with the timekeeper's voice measuring out his doom; but Tom is very tough, an old taker of punishment. The last round sees him almost as lively as ever, but now it is Froggy's glove you hear thump-pad-thudding. The final clang—and the referee jerks a thumb toward Froggy's corner. The announcer cannot be heard above the cheers. We do not know Froggy and—to speak candidly—do not like the look of him; but he has proved himself the better man; and so we give him the best cheer of the evening. (Perhaps Froggy's friends in Paris would do the same for Tom—perhaps; it is just possible.) Tom puts his gloves together, shakes them at us, still grinning, and we give him a cheer too. Everybody is good-humored.

There was more to come, but a great many people were drifting out, now that the great event was over,

and I followed them. The Blackfriars Road looked exactly as it had done when I hurried out of it earlier in the evening, a black misery, but the thought of the good humor I had left behind me kept me warm. When the old Ring is transformed into a gigantic boxing arena, where really big purses are won and lost in a few minutes under glaring film-studio lights, I hope it will keep its good humor. I hope it will, but I have my doubts.

[FACT]

EIGHT MINUTES OF FURY

A knowledgeable veteran boxing writer rises to the challenge of one of the best of middleweight championship fights and preserves a vivid word picture for posterity.

PAT PUTNAM

There was a stong wind blowing through Las Vegas Monday night, but it could not sweep away the smell of raw violence as Marvelous Marvin Hagler and Thomas Hearns hammered at each other with a fury that spent itself only after Hearns had been saved by the protecting arms of referee Richard Steele. The fight, in a ring set up on the tennis courts at Caesars Palace, lasted only a second longer than eight minutes, but for those who saw it, the memory of its nonstop savagery will remain forever.

Hagler's undisputed middleweight championship was at stake, and for the first time since he won it from Alan Minter in 1980, people had been questioning his ability to retain it. In the weeks leading up to the fight, Hagler fumed as the odds tilted back and forth before settling on the champion by the narrowest of margins. Hagler's pride was sorely stung, and a deep burning anger wrote his battle plan.

It was a simple strategy, one that could have been designed by Attila: Keep the swords swinging until there are no more heads to roll, give no quarter, take no prisoners. There would be only one pace, all-out; only one direction, forward.

It was a gamble, for Hagler would be exposing his 30-year-old body to the cannons that had knocked out 34 of the 41 men his 26-year-old challenger had faced and had earned Hearns the nickname Hit Man. "But he ain't never hit Marvin Hagler," the champion sneered. "I've taken the best shots of the biggest hitters in the middleweight division, and I've never been off my feet [Hagler considers his knockdown by Juan Roldan a slip]. And this guy isn't even a middleweight. Hit Man, my ass."

Hearns, as the challenger, came into the ring first—tall and strikingly muscular at 159¾ pounds—wearing a red robe with yellow trim. He jumped up and down to limber up his leg muscles, and then he strolled around the ring smiling. Hagler followed, in a royal-blue robe over trunks of the same color. Most champions keep challengers waiting alone in the ring as long as possible, but Hagler had warmed up well in his dressing room and he wanted to make his appearance while the sweat was still oiling his body. Entering the ring, he fixed Hearns with a scowl that never wavered, not even during Doc Severinsen's trumpet version of the National Anthem.

When the bell rang, the war was immediately on. "I think Marvin may come out so fired up that we'll just have Tommy stick and move," Emanuel Steward, the challenger's manager, had said. "Hagler will be so juiced up, after seven or eight rounds it'll rob his strength. Then we'll go for the late knockout."

But Steward underestimated just how juiced up the champ would be. Hagler never gave Hearns a chance to do anything but fight for his life. The 5' 9½" champion swept over his 6' 2" opponent like a 159¼-pound tidal wave. There were no knockdowns in the first round, but only because both men were superbly conditioned and courageous athletes. Surely each hit the other with plenty of blows powerful enough to drop lesser mortals. In all, 165 punches (by computer count) were thrown by both fighters: 82 by Hagler, 83 by the challenger.

Startled by the intensity of Hagler's assault, Hearns replied in kind. He's normally a sharpshooter from the outside, but only 22 of his 83 punches were jabs. Hagler, attacking Hearns's slender middle with his first volley, threw none. "I started slugging because I had to," Hearns admitted later. "Marvin started running in, and I had to protect myself."

It was a sensational opening round. Both fighters were rocked during the violent toe-to-toe exchanges, and midway through the round the champion's forehead over his right eye was ripped open either by a Hearns right hand or elbow. With Hagler not bothering with defense, Hearns went for the quick kill. His gloves became a red blur as he rained punch after punch on the champion's head—and it would prove his undoing.

"He fought 12 rounds in one," Steward said later. Returning to his corner, Hearns wore the drained expression of a man who had already fought for 36 minutes.

"What are you doing?" Steward screamed.

"You've got to stick and move. Jab. Don't fight with him."

In the champ's corner, Dr. Donald Romeo, the chief physician of the Nevada State Athletic Commission, was examining the cut on Hagler's forehead. Another abrasion had begun to form under the eye. Satisfied that the cut on the forehead was harmless, Romeo returned to his seat.

"Don't change," Hagler's trainer, Goody Petronelli, told the champion. "Just keep your hands up a little higher. Don't worry about the cut. Just keep charging and keep the pressure up."

"O.K.," said Hagler. "I won't worry about the cut. If you go to war, you're going to get wounded."

Hagler's pace in the second round was only slightly less relentless. "When I see blood," said the champion, "I become a bull." He came out ready to gore whatever was in his path, and although Hearns rocked him midway through the round with a strong right cross, Hagler never for an instant eased the pressure. "All that right hand did," said Hagler, "was make me even madder."

A veteran of 64 professional fights (all but two of them victories), Hagler could sense the strength seeping away from Hearns's body. As he went back to his corner after the second round, the champion knew the fight was just about over.

"This cut isn't bad but it's bleeding a lot," said Petronelli, as he worked on Hagler's forehead. "Let's not take any chances. Take him out this round."

"He's ready to go," said Hagler, spitting a mouthful of water into a pail.

"He's not going to hurt me with that right hand. I took his best, and now I'm going to knock him out."

As in the first two rounds, Hagler came out at full fury. Forcing himself up on his toes, Hearns tried to hold him off with jabs, but he had little left. Hagler waded through the challenger's jabs, pressing forward, always punching. Hearns was not backing down, but he was backing up. One of Hearns's jabs widened the cut on Hagler's forehead, and as blood came roaring down the champion's face, Steele signaled time-out and stepped in. He led Hagler back to his corner to be reexamined by Romeo.

"Can you see all right?" the physician asked over the screams of 15,088 outraged fans.

"No problem," said Hagler. "I ain't missing him, am I?"

Romeo again motioned to Steele that the fight could continue.

Deciding that he didn't want the outcome determined by anyone but himself, Hagler moved in, first firing a short left and then a smashing right to the side of Hearns's head. Dazed, the challenger floundered backward across the ring.

The pursuing Hagler unloaded a right and a left, and then leaped in with an overhand right that thundered against Hearns's head. On instinct alone, the challenger tried to clinch, but then he went down.

As Steele picked up the count, Hearns lay on his back, arms outstretched, eyes open but unseeing. With great will, Hearns rolled over and brought himself to his feet at the count of nine. But Steele, after studying the challenger's glazed eyes, wisely signaled a cease-fire. The time was 2:01 of the third round.

With blood still streaming down his face and onto his chest, Hagler leaped into the air, at least

$5.7 million richer. It was his 11th title defense, leaving him on track in his drive to surpass Carlos Monzon's middleweight record of 14.

Hearns had to be carried back to his corner, and it was several minutes before he could stand on his own two feet. Later, Hearns, who is still WBC junior middleweight champ and who stands to bank at least $5.4 million from the fight, went into Hagler's dressing room. "We made a lot of money, but we gave them a good show," Hearns said. "Tell you what. You move up and fight the light heavies, and I'll take care of the middleweights."

Hagler laughed. "You move up," he said.

After receiving four stitches for the cut in his forehead, Hagler went to a party in the Augustus Room at Caesars. He spoke briefly to the celebrators. Then, with his wife, Bertha, he watched a video replay of the fight. After seeing the knockout for the fourth time, Hagler smiled and applauded. He looked at his watch. It was midnight. "Let's go," he said to Bertha. His work was done.

[FACT]

KID DYNAMITE BLOWS UP

After winning the Pulitzer Prize for his reporting on the fall of the Soviet Union and before he ascended to the editorship of *The New Yorker*, David Remnick returned to sports long enough to cover one of the most bizarre of all heavyweight championship fights. He was there in Las Vegas on June 28, 1997, when Evander Holyfield lost parts of two ears and Mike Tyson his license to box. In this account he gives a keenly perceptive picture of not only the fight but also of the audience, reviving memories of another typical fight crowd during A.J. Liebling's nights at the old Madison Square Garden (page 207).

DAVID REMNICK

The conventions of the ring demand that a fighter in training become a monk. For months at a time, he hardens his body on roadwork and beefsteak, and practices an enforced loneliness—even (tradition has it) sexual loneliness—the better to focus the mind on war. Mike Tyson's monastery in the

Nevada desert is a mansion next door to Wayne Newton's mansion, and it could be said to lack the usual austerity. There is a chandelier worthy of Cap d'Antibes. There is a painting on silk of Diana Ross. There are books, magazines, a big television, leather couches. But the diversions are not what they could be. When Tyson is not preparing for fights, he keeps lions and tigers around as pets and wrestles with them. "Sometimes I go swimming with the tiger," he told a visitor. "But, personally, I'm a lion man. Lions are very obedient, like dogs." Tyson was keeping his pets elsewhere, though. He has estates in Ohio, in Connecticut, and off a fairway on the Congressional Country Club, in Bethesda, Maryland. The big cats are most often in Ohio. The Nevada mansion is surrounded by life-size statues of warrior heroes whom Tyson has read about and come to revere: Genghis Kahn, Toussaint-L'Ouverture, Alexander the Great, Hannibal. "Hannibal was very courageous," Tyson said. "He rode elephants through Cartilage." In a week's time, Tyson himself would be going through cartilage, too.

After spending three years in an Indiana prison for raping a teenager named Desiree Washington, Tyson went back to fighting in 1995. He denied to the end that he had ever raped anyone, but he said he was a better man now. Tyson converted to Islam— indeed, the bumper sticker on his Bentley reads "I ♥ Allah"—and he told his visitors in jail that he had spent his time studying the Koran, Machiavelli, Voltaire, Dumas, the lives of Meyer Lansky and Bugsy Siegel, "and a lot of Communist literature." He ordered up icons for his shoulders, a diptych tattoo: Arthur Ashe on one side, Mao Zedong on the other. He declared himself ready to regain his place in boxing. He would reclaim not only his title but also his image of invincibility. Iron Mike. Kid Dynamite. Once more, he would be the fighter who had expressed only disappointment after a knockout of one Jesse Ferguson, saying, "I wanted to hit him one more time in the nose so that bone could go up into his brain."

But after easily dispatching a collection of tomato cans who provided a warmup drill worth tens of millions of dollars, Tyson finally met a real fighter, if not a great one, named Evander Holyfield, who backed him down and beat him up. Holyfield took Tyson's title last November, in one of the cleverest displays of boxing guile since February, 1964, when Muhammad Ali, then Cassius Clay, stunned another invincible—Tyson's fistic precursor, Sonny Liston. Liston, like Tyson, had grown up in an environment of crime and never left it; Liston had done time for armed robbery, he mugged people, he beat up a cop, he broke heads for the Mob. And, like Tyson, he was considered a killer in the ring, unbeatable. Against Clay, Liston had been favored so strongly that the lead boxing writer for the *Times* skipped the fight and left it to a rookie in the office, Robert Lipsyte. But Clay, with his magnificent speed, dodged Liston's plodding bombs and bloodied the big man's eye. Liston quit on his stool, claiming a sore shoulder. Against Holyfield, Tyson had been similarly unmasked. "He's like any bully," said Gil Clancy, one of the game's legendary trainers. "Once Tyson saw his own blood, he backed down." The referee stopped the beating in the eleventh round. When it was over, Tyson was in such a daze that he turned to one of his handlers and asked, "What round did I knock him out in?"

The rematch with Holyfield would be worth 30 million dollars to Tyson, 35 million to Holyfield. The fight's promoter, Don King, whose good word, of course, is all one ever needs, promised record receipts for the live gate and pay-per-view television: "A hundred and fifty million, maybe two hundred million. After all, we got three billion people in Red China alone!" Whatever. If Tyson won, he would regain not only his championship but also his place as "the baddest man on the planet." Holyfield would be remembered as a fighter who on a given night had risen above himself and then, in the rematch, fell to earth.

After coming out of jail, Tyson showed signs of domestic stability. In April, he married a doctor named Monica Turner. (Turner's first husband was sentenced to ten years in prison on a cocaine-dealing charge.) Tyson and Turner have one child; another is due this summer. Until now, marriage had been a miserable topic for Tyson. His first wife, the television star Robin Givens, was famously manipulative. She had been a Sarah Lawrence girl and, even in public, treated Tyson with an airy condescension. There were, in some cynical corners, suspicions that Givens had actually married for money. Tyson was not slow to express his annoyance. The former light-heavyweight champion José Torres once asked Tyson what the best blow he had ever thrown was. "Man, I'll never forget that punch," Tyson said. "It was when I fought with Robin in Steve's apartment. She really offended me and I went *bam,* and she flew backward, hitting every fucking wall in the apartment." The marriage ended in divorce.

Unlike Givens, Turner has, for the most part,

stayed out of her husband's business affairs and out of camera range, and there have been no reports of fights, physical or otherwise. Turner mainly stayed away from Las Vegas. Tyson's most frequent visitors to his desert house were the members of his entourage, each in his own way a sterling influence: Don King, a former numbers runner from Cleveland who once stomped a man to death in a dispute over six hundred dollars and then became the greatest (and most bloviated) carnival barker since Barnum; Tyson's co-managers, Rory Holloway, an old friend, and John Horne, a failed standup comic from Albany who specializes in yelling at reporters; Tyson's trainer, Richie Giachetti, a street guy from Cleveland who worked with Larry Holmes; and a self-described "master motivator" named Steve (Crocodile) Fitch, who admits that "in another life" he spent five years in jail for manslaughter. ("But I didn't do it," he told me. "A complete setup.") Crocodile proved to be a prophetic character. During the week leading up to the fight, he could be seen in fatigues and wraparound shades, all the while screaming his suggestive war cries: "It's time for ultimate battle! Ultimate battle! Time to bite! Time to bite!"

Tyson avoided the press—especially the print press. Horne and Holloway had done a good job of convincing him that the papers were filled with nothing but lies, that the New York reporters on the boxing beat—Michael Katz, of the *News*, Wallace Matthews, of the *Post*—were out to get them. Early in the morning, before the sun was high, Tyson ran along the empty desert roads. Then he sparred in the gym. His workouts were closed. For recreation, he watched one gangster movie after another, sometimes through the night. He is partial to James Cagney, Edward G. Robinson, and John Garfield. He can recite whole scenes of *Raging Bull*, *On the Waterfront*, and—his favorite—*The Harder They Fall*.

Tyson would have preferred to be alone—or, at least, alone with his entourage and his movies—but Don King knew that in order to rouse pay-per-view orders the goat had to be fed. Tyson would not allow interviews at his house, but five days before the fight he agreed to go out to King's place to meet with a group of writers. And so on an afternoon of long shadows and hundred-degree heat a couple of white vans pulled out of the driveway of the MGM Grand Hotel, away from the

new family-friendly downtown, away from the Brooklyn Bridge and the black glass pyramid of Cheops, away from the palace of the Caesars and the Folies Bergère, out of earshot, finally, of the unending music of the city, the air-conditioned hum and the mad electronic ringing of a thousand acres of slot machines and the slushy spill of silver coins pouring into curved silver trays. Don King does not live on the Strip. He lives out where it is quiet, at the outermost edge of the city, where the desert resumes.

In all honesty, no one would ride to the edge of the desert to talk with Evander Holyfield. No one much cared about Holyfield. He was likable enough. But he was dull copy. He hadn't raped anyone. He hadn't been to jail. He talked about Jesus Christ all the time and literally sang gospel music while hitting the heavy bag. He seemed like a good fellow, but what story did he offer? He talked in the polite clichés of doing my best, having faith in my abilities and in the will of God—but what did he mean? Heavyweight-championship fights, from the days of John L. Sullivan onward, are stories, morality plays, and this story, regardless of its end, was all about Tyson. This was a war between middle-class aspiration and ghetto insolence, gospel and rap. Without Tyson there was no sense of danger, no interest, no hundred million dollars.

"People are full of shit. They want to see something dark," Tyson's former trainer Teddy Atlas told me. "People want to feel close to it and in on it, but, of course, only from the distance of their suburban homes. They want to have the benefit of comfort, security, safety, respect, and at the same time the privilege of watching something out of control—even promote it being out of control—as long as we can be secure that we're not accountable for it. With Tyson, the dark thing was always the anticipation that someone was going to get knocked out. The whole Kid Dynamite thing. But we wanted to believe that the monster was also a nice kid. We wanted to believe that Mike Tyson was an American story: the kid who grows up in the horrible ghetto and then converts that dark power into a good cause, into boxing. But then the story takes a turn. The dark side overwhelms him. He's cynical, he's out of control. And now the story is even better. It's like a double feature now, like you're getting *Heidi* and *Godzilla* at the same time."

King's minions wanted the reporters to understand that this was a special invitation—a very rare one, these days. The whole charade seemed absurd to the reporters who had been around boxing for a while. Until not so long ago, fighters before a big bout were available athletes, the least guarded of men. Like sultans, they often used to greet their visitors propped upon a few pillows in bed; reporters would sit perched at the edge of the bed or hard on the floor, notebooks out, ready to catch pearls. Archie Moore, the great light heavyweight, could unburden himself of a monologue worthy of Molly Bloom or the Duke of Gloucester. Boxers were free of the solemn self-importance of modern athletes in the team sports. They liked having people around. In the moments before fighting for the championship, Floyd Patterson napped in his dressing room, and a few writers were allowed to stay around, close enough to register the movement under the champion's eyelids, the timbre of his snore. Patterson would describe his dreams, the depths of his fear. He talked and talked, one of the great analysands of the prize ring.

Tyson used to be like that. When he was coming up as a fighter, and even as a young champion, he loved to talk to the press, tell his story. He was immensely aware of himself as the star of an ongoing Cagney movie. Some writers even saw a sweetness in him, the yearning for love and a home. Certainly it was a life beyond the imagination of the middle-class reporters who came calling. He was the kid from Amboy Street in Brooklyn's Brownsville, an especially vicious and hopeless delinquent. When he was six, his idea of a prank was to slit his big brother's arm with a razor while he slept. His father was nowhere in evidence, his mother was overwhelmed by poverty. Tyson idolized the pimps and the thieves in the neighborhood, and by the time he was 10 he was mugging old ladies and shooting into crowds for kicks. As he told his story, he could sense the titillation in the writer, and more details would pour out: "I'd shoot real close to them, skin them or something, make them take off their pants and then go run in the streets." After he had racked up dozens of arrests and was sent off to reform school, Cus D'Amato, an old and eccentric trainer who had settled upstate, along the Hudson, took him in. D'Amato was a kindly paranoiac. When he was still working out of the Gramercy Gym, in Manhat-

tan, he used to sleep in the back with nothing to keep him company but a shotgun and a dog. To his fighters, he was a kind of Father Divine, at once inspiring and full of righteous gas. He preached the value of terror, the way that all fighters faced fear and the good ones learned to harness it, to make it their friend. He was an ascetic. Money, he said, "was something to throw off the back of trains." Writers loved D'Amato, the way any writer would have loved, say, Moll Flanders had she been presented, whole, in real life, and available for quotation.

Tyson represented D'Amato's wish on dying—the chance, after Patterson and José Torres, to have a third world champion. As if to satisfy every convention of the boxing movie, D'Amato "adopted" Tyson, became his legal guardian, but he died a year before his "son" won the crown. On winning the title, Tyson wept. If only Cus had seen it, he said, if only Cus were here. It was over the top, even for Hollywood, but not for the conventions of the boxing story.

Tyson was also good copy partly because he was brutal and unabashed about being so. Unlike Ali, whose helium rants usually had more to do with camp comedy or the prophecies of Elijah Muhammad than with the violence of his profession, Tyson was blunt, clinical. He knew he had been trained to hurt other men, and he saw no good reason to deflect attention from that. He was in the beating business and he had never acquired the tact or the reflexes to say he didn't enjoy it. In his comically high voice, he spoke of throwing punches with "bad intentions to vital areas," of blows to the heart, to the kidneys, to the liver, and the pleasure he took in delivering them. He talked of his yearning to break an opponent's eardrum, to shatter his will, to make him "cry like a woman."

At the same time, Tyson was self-aware, almost academic in his regard for boxing. In a time when most baseball players hardly know the name Jackie Robinson, Tyson grew obsessed not just with all the obvious contemporaries and near-contemporaries but also with Harry Greb and Kid Chocolate, with Willie Pep and Stanley Ketchel. The writers ate that up. With boxing under attack as crippling, as atavistic and cruel, his talk made them feel that their subject was important, somehow—not merely a skein of beatings in the parking lots of betting parlors but a matter of aesthetics and history. Tyson spent hundreds of hours watching old fights, and from those films he not only learned the details of his craft but also assumed certain traits of favored precursors. He cut his hair to resemble Jack Dempsey's. He took to wearing bulky button-up sweaters because he had seen such sweaters on some of the old fighters in the old newsreels. And so, while Tyson's story was not Ali's, while he lacked that level of wit, physical improvisation, and epic, his story was a good one, good enough for half a dozen biographies, good enough, certainly, to make him the best-paid athlete in history.

We drove out Flamingo Road, past the plastic-surgery parlors, past all the clip joints and software palaces that look as if they were built last week. We arrived at a "gated community," the sort of high-security mansion neighborhoods that you see now in every city where there is sun and money and heightened fear of larceny. We rang the buzzer and the gates swung open. Don King's house is Spanish-style, perhaps—a riot of white stucco. There were Range Rovers and BMWs parked outside and an enormous satellite dish parked on the roof. We walked up the front steps and were greeted by a portrait of Don King. The real thing was in the kitchen.

"Welcome! Welcome to my home!" he boomed. King invited us in for an early dinner. He had ordered out from Popeyes.

King is the evil genius of boxing, the latest in a long line. His electrified hair is merely a way to use "personality" to hide his substance. In his way, he is even more powerful than the so-called Octopus Inc., of the 1950s—James Norris's corrupt International Boxing Club. Tyson, like so many boxers, cannot bear King. He does not especially trust King. But he does business with King, because King is the singular presence in big-time boxing. They make a lot of money together, and so Tyson is as indulgent of King's conniving as King is of Tyson's tantrums. There is no profit in judgment.

In the kitchen, King was telling me that three billion people would watch the fight. The key was penetration, he said—that is, how many people would sign up for the fifty-dollar fee and order the fight on pay-per-view. "If we get 10 percent of the universe, then we'll be fine," he added. He never quite explained what that meant. He knew I would not bother to ask. "Mike generates more capital than anyone in the history of the world. Why do they want to destroy him, the goose that laid the golden egg?"

After a long wait, Tyson showed up. He took his place on a white leather couch. As he waited for the first question, he assumed the expression of a man who has eaten a bad egg and is waiting to be sick. One by one the questions came, and Tyson answered them in a way designed to make the questioner feel like an idiot. Yes, he felt good. No, he wouldn't make the same mistakes again against Holyfield. Yes, he expected to win. But, no, it wouldn't change his life if he lost. "The way my deals are set up, I'm pretty much set." At times, he spoke as a man obsessed less with a fight than with the rational distribution of his mutual funds.

To be with Tyson even for just a couple of hours is to witness the power of a ghetto kid's fatalism. He has, his accountants would attest, all he could ever want. He will never—or should never—end up like Joe Louis, coked up on the casino floor and working as a greeter. And yet he is forever saying "My life is over" and "I am taking the blows for my children." He has a boundless sense of self-drama, of the dark future. Even here, surrounded by his co-managers Rory Holloway and John Horne, he said he had no friends, he trusted no one. And who could doubt him?

"We have to trust, but people by nature are not to be trusted," Tyson said. "That's just the way it is. I got a Machiavellian effect as far as that's concerned. I'm not a philosopher, I'm not Machiavelli in that respect, but you can't be a person always willing to do good in an environment where people are always willing to do bad. You know what I mean?

"I have no friends, man. When I got out of prison, all my old friends, they had to go. If you don't have a purpose in my life, man, you have to go. ... Why would you want someone around in your life if they have no purpose? Just to have a pal or a buddy? I got a wife. My wife can be my pal and buddy. I'm not trying to be cold, but it's something I picked up. ... If I'm gonna get screwed, I'm not gonna get screwed over by the people that screwed me before. I'm gonna get screwed by the *new* people.

"I've been taken advantage of all my life. I've been used, I've been dehumanized, I've been humiliated, and I've been betrayed. That's basically the outcome of my life, and I'm kind of bitter, kind of angry at certain people about it.... Everyone in boxing makes out well except for the fighter. He's the only one who suffers, basically. He's the only one who's on Skid Row. He's the only one who loses his mind. He sometimes goes insane, he sometimes goes on the bottle, because it's a highly intensive, pressure sport, and a lot of people lose it. There's so much you can take and then you break."

In an effort to lighten Tyson's mood and, not incidentally, the mood of this sorry conversation, some of the writers started asking about a subject close to his heart: his new family. For a few moments, he was as fuzzy as a character in *thirtysomething*.

"That's all I have, my children," he said. "Wives are known to run off and fall in love with other people, because they are human, even die. But you have to take care of children. ... The way I see it is that every fight I have is for their future. Every fight. Every fight is a different future for my children." Tyson said that he played games with his kids, ate ice cream with them. "They love *Barney*," he said. "I *hate* Barney.

"I have a stepdaughter and one day she was crying and she says, 'Mama, Jane don't want to play with me today.' And I burst out, 'She doesn't want to play with you? Then fuck her!' My wife didn't like that too much. But we're different people. She studied psychology and believes in working on a kid's mind. I believe in being strict—if you get out of line, you're getting hit! They're too young for that now, but I'm a strong believer in that. I think kids should learn discipline. If they get out of line, they should learn discipline. At what age? I don't know. Ten years old?

"See, I've been beaten all my life. My kids have parents, one's a doctor, a bright woman, and a father who's a ... a father who's rich. I had an alcoholic and a pimp for parents. So they're gonna have a great life, if they don't turn out to be bad children.... I just don't want them out on the street, because these hustlers, they can be very exciting, people gravitate to them. I survived it, but they may not be lucky enough to survive. All my real friends are in prison or dead. The ones still out are so messed up on drugs they don't know their own name."

It was as if Tyson knew something that no one else knew—not his accountants, not his managers. He was convinced of his own wretched end. Nothing, save the well-being of his kids, would please him. Last summer, Tyson threw himself a million-dollar three-day-long thirtieth-birthday party at his estate in Farmington, Connecticut. There were magnums of Cristal, and cigars rolled specially for the occasion. Tyson handed out BMWs and Range Rovers to six of his flunkies. And yet he had an awful time. "I don't know half the people here," he said as he wandered his many acres. "This isn't what I wanted."

Horne and Holloway may know nothing about boxing, but they have been expert at feeding Tyson's sense of persecution. "Nobody's on our side," Tyson told us as his co-managers nodded like proud puppeteers. "The courts are against us, the corporations are against us, the news reporters are against us, the papers—your bosses—are against us. We have nobody on our side, and we're still fighting and we're still doing well. If we had you guys on our side, we'd be a phenomenon!"

From the back of the room, King yelled, "If you would just print the truth! You write what people throw out to you as a smoke screen!"

"The fact is, they call us monsters, that we're inhuman, they want people to be afraid of us," Tyson said. (In fact, Tyson has always cultivated that image. He once told his former friend José Torres, "I like to hurt women when I make love to them. I like to hear them scream with pain, to see them bleed. It gives me pleasure.")

"Who do you mean?" one of the reporters said. "Who's calling you monsters?"

"You. Not you individually, but reporters," Tyson said. "They write that we're monsters, that we're hideous, that we commit heinous crimes."

"Let's take the Newfield book, for example," said King, referring to Jack Newfield's scrupulous biography of him. "The Newfield book is all lies, and yet everyone uses it as the defining factor on me! Everything in there is a lie! So a guy who's a good writer knows how to *speculize* and *dramatize* those lies! You know what I mean?"

"They hope it leads to you being incarcerated," said Horne, who was standing at Tyson's shoulder.

"Look," Tyson said. "Don is still a fool to have you over to his house and talk to you. He had to beg me to come over here and talk to you, because of what you guys write about me. The people that know me, love me, they read this. It feels like shit.

"And this guy, knowing you guys ain't gonna give him no justice, he still, stupidly, has you guys in his house talking to you, knowing you'll write it was a good fight and then try to put his ass in jail.

They're gonna write some madman tales, how he robbed this guy and killed this other guy. I don't know. I wasn't there when he killed the guy, but, shit, if a guy got killed he was probably doing something he wasn't supposed to be doing. You know what I mean? I'm a strong believer in that. Not in a drive-by shooting, but very few people get killed for no reason, from where I come from."

King was delighted by this moving show of support. "Just watch me prove that he attacked me," he said. "All I want is fair play! I'm still crazy enough to love America!"

We, the Americans, must have been moved to the core. There was a long silence. A European writer shyly turned to Tyson and said, "Mike, with all of that said, why don't you come out more and go on Larry King again, and go on David Letterman and set the record straight?"

Tyson's eyes narrowed. He flapped his hand in disgust. "Ah, fuck y'all. Fuck y'all," he said. "I don't have to suck your dick to justify me being a good guy. Listen, man, I'm a man! I don't go begging someone to love me."

"It's not begging," the European ventured. "It's—"

"Yes, it is!" Tyson said. "You see O. J. Simpson, he's going around all the time trying to prove his innocence. By court of law, he's innocent. Maybe common sense tells you he's not, but in a court of law he's innocent. I'm not going to go around saying, 'Well, I've done this or this for this organization.' The hell with that, man."

Now Horne started egging Tyson on. "When the intention is to destroy you from the beginning, you can't get no level playing field to set the record straight," Horne said. "Let me say one thing. All of us live different lives. None of y'all have lived the lives that we have. We have different perceptions of things.... You guys go into back rooms, you conference about everything, you help each other out, to destroy somebody who is the only reason you are all out here. No other fighter takes you out of the country, no other fighter makes your jobs so interesting."

Finally, Tyson had the presence of mind to wave Horne off, to settle King down. All he really wanted us to know was that he was unknowable. He had probably given more interviews, in his time, than Dora ever gave to Freud, but it didn't matter. "Look," he said. "I'm harder on myself than the goddam reporters. But they don't know me well enough to write what I'm about, that I'm a monster, that I'm this or that. No one knows me. ... I'd like to be written up like the old-timers. There's no doubt about it, I'm a wild man. I've had my share of the good times. but that's just part of the business, that's just who Mike is. I work hard, I live hard, I play hard, I die hard."

Like mediocre fiction, fights for the heavyweight championship of the world are invariably freighted with the solemnity of deeper meanings. It is not enough that one man shock another man's brain and send him reeling. There must be politics, too—or, at least, great lumps of symbol, historical subplots, metaphysical frosting. In team sports—in football, baseball, basketball—there are individual stars, there are rivalries, but, finally, the athletics is the thing. A team athlete's talent is usually the mastery of some peculiar and relatively recent invention: kicking a pig's bladder through a set of posts, swinging a stick of polished ash, tossing a ball through an iron hoop. Boxing is ancient, simple, lonely. There is hardly any artifice at all. Padded gloves and the gauze and tape underneath do little to protect the fighters; they merely prevent broken hands, and allow for more punching, more pain. Boxers go into the ring alone, nearly naked, and they succeed or fail on the basis of the most elementary criteria: their ability to give and receive pain, their will to endure their own fear. Since character—the will of a person stretched to extremes—is so obviously at the center of boxing, there is an undeniable urge to know the fighters, to derive some meaning from the conflict of those characters.

John L. Sullivan's triumphs were triumphs of the working class, the immigrant wave, "the people." Joe Louis fought the moral war over German fascism—fascism coming in the bruised and prostrate person of Max Schmeling. Most of all, the fights have come to be parables tinctured with the issues and conflicts of race. Indeed, some of the first boxing matches in America were held on plantations before the Civil War. White slave owners (the promoters) set up fights between their chattel. The slaves were often commanded to fight to the death. Was it such a great leap from there to the M-G-M Grand? "If [the heavyweights] become champions they begin to have inner lives like Hemingway or Dostoyevsky, Tolstoy or Faulkner, Joyce or Melville or Conrad or

Lawrence or Proust," Norman Mailer wrote twenty-six years ago in *Life*.

Dempsey was alone and Tunney could never explain himself and Sharkey could never believe himself nor Schmeling nor Braddock, and Carnera was sad and Baer an indecipherable clown; great heavyweights like Louis had the loneliness of the ages in their silence, and men like Marciano were mystified by a power which seemed to have been granted them. With the advent, however, of the great modern Black heavyweights, Patterson, Liston, then Clay and Frazier, perhaps the loneliness gave way to what it had been protecting itself against—a surrealistic situation unstable beyond belief. Being a Black heavyweight champion in the second half of the twentieth century (with Black revolutions opening all over the world) was now not unlike being Jack Johnson, Malcolm X, and Frank Costello all in one.

Black fighters found themselves fighting intricate wars over racial types, over shifting notions of masculinity, decency, and class. In 1962, with the endorsements of President Kennedy and the National Association for the Advancement of Colored People, Floyd Patterson fought in the name of the black middle class and white liberals against Liston, the gruff ex-con, who represented, as Amiri Baraka (then Le-Roi Jones) put it, "the big black Negro in every white man's hallway, waiting to do him in." But Patterson was not physically equal to his preposterous moral task. Liston flattened him in the first round. So shamed was Patterson that he fled Comiskey Park disguised in a fake beard and mustache and drove all night back to New York. He had not merely been defeated. He had let down the race, he had not fulfilled his meaning, his role in the story.

It is hard to imagine today the sense of disappointment in Patterson's loss. A columnist for the *Los Angeles Times* wrote that having Liston as champion "is like finding a live bat on a string under your Christmas tree." Some papers felt free to refer to Liston as a "jungle beast," a "gorilla." Only Murray Kempton, writing in the *Post*, was able to find an arch note of optimism in Liston's ascent. "The Negro heavyweights, as Negroes tend to do, have usually given that sense of being men above their calling," Kempton wrote. "Floyd Patterson sounded like a Freedom Rider. We return to reality with Liston. We have at last a heavyweight champion on the moral level of the men who own him. This is the source of horror which Liston has

aroused; he is boxing's perfect symbol. He tells us the truth about it. The heavyweight championship is, after all, a fairly squalid office."

Liston tried desperately to please. He promised to be a good champion, to emulate Joe Louis. He explained that he had been one of twenty-five children in rural Arkansas, that he was illiterate, abused by a violent father. He apologized for his "terrible mistakes." But the country seemed not to accept the apologies; it was hard for whites and blacks alike to countenance a man who, when asked why he would not join in the civil rights marches in the South, had answered, "I ain't got no dog-proof ass." People only laughed when Liston started associating with priests. After Cassius Clay beat Liston in Miami—and then, as Muhammad Ali, beat him again—his story took a tragic course. Liston retired to Las Vegas, where he fought a little, hung out with gangsters like Ash Resnick, and in 1971 died with a needle in his arm. The funeral procession went down the Strip. For a few minutes, people came out of the casinos, squinting in the sun and saying farewell to Liston. The Ink Spots sang "Sunny."

For a long time, especially since coming home from prison, Tyson has seen himself in Liston. Watching films of Liston working out to the old James Brown rendition of "Night Train," he said, was "orgasmic."

"Sonny Liston, I identify with him the most," he said. "That may sound morbid and grim, but I pretty much identify with that life. He wanted people to respect him or love him, but it never happened. You can't make people respect and love you by craving it. You've got to *demand* it.

"People may not have liked him because of his background, but the people who got to know him as an intimate person have a totally different opinion. He had a wife. I'm sure she didn't think he was a piece of garbage.... Everyone respected Sonny Liston's ability. The point is respecting him as a man. No one can second-guess my ability, either. But I'm going to be respected. I demand that. You have no choice. You couldn't be in my presence if you didn't."

A few weeks before the fight, I went up to Michigan to see Liston's conqueror. Muhammad Ali lives on a manicured farm in a small town near the Indiana border called Berrien Springs. It was obvious to everyone who saw him tremble as he ignited the

Olympic torch in Atlanta that Parkinson's disease has all but silenced Ali and forced him to wear a grim mask on what had been the century's most sparkling face. But out of the way of television cameras, which make him nervous and even more rigid than usual, Ali can show delight. He is especially delighted to watch himself when his body was fluid and his voice the most widely recognized in the world. We spent the better part of an afternoon watching videotapes of his fights, the early fights with Liston and then the first bout against Patterson. Ali leaned back and smiled as he watched himself, in black and white, dissect Liston, duck his blows, and sting him with jabs until Liston looked very slow and very sad.

"Ah, Sonny," Ali said. "The big ugly bear!"

Now Liston was quitting. He sat slumped on his stool. Now Ali's younger self was standing at the ropes, hysterical in his triumph, shouting down at the reporters who had dismissed him as a loudmouth and a fake, "Eat your words! Eat your words! I am the greatest!"

"They all thought I'd lose," Ali said. "Thought he'd tear me up."

After a while, I asked Ali about Tyson and whether he compared to Liston.

"Liston was faster than Tyson, but came straight ahead," he said. His voice was whispery, almost all breath.

"Could Tyson have beaten you?" I asked.

"Don't make me laugh," Ali said, and he was laughing. "Tyson don't have it. He don't *have* it." For a second, I wondered what "it" was, but then The Greatest made it clear. He pointed to his head.

About a week later, I took the ferry to Staten Island to visit Teddy Atlas, who had trained Tyson when he was learning to fight in Cus D'Amato's gym. Atlas is one of boxing's most appealing characters, the son of a doctor who used to treat patients in the ghetto for a couple of dollars. He was rebellious, a street kid who learned to box. A knife fight on Rikers Island left him with a scar on his face that runs from his hairline to his jawline. When Atlas was barely twenty, D'Amato taught him how to train fighters and then entrusted him with Tyson. Atlas last taught Tyson the catechism according to D'Amato, the peekaboo style of holding the gloves up near the face, the need to overcome the fear inside. During

one amateur fight, Tyson told Atlas between rounds that his hand was broken and he couldn't go on, but Atlas knew it was just fear, the fear of disgrace, and he pushed Tyson back out into the ring and to a victory.

Atlas, however, grew disillusioned as he saw D'Amato indulge Tyson in one ugly incident after another. Tyson harassed girls in school, beat other kids up, threatened teachers, and D'Amato nearly always found a way to make it good with the school, with the police. He would have his champion, one way or another. He was not raising a son, after all. He was raising a fighter. But in 1982, when Tyson molested Atlas's adolescent sister-in-law, Atlas lost it. He held a gun to Tyson's head and threatened him. D'Amato never punished Tyson. He did, however, get rid of Atlas.

Tyson's co-manager John Horne had told me that "the only difference between Mike Tyson and Michael Jordan is Mr. and Mrs. Jordan." But Atlas thought that was too simple, too easy on Tyson. When I asked him if he had overreacted when he held the gun to Tyson's head, he said, "This was a kid who did not hesitate to tear out the soul of another human being. He completely violated other people. And then he just moved on.

"Mike is very selfish. He was bred to be selfish. I remember sitting in the kitchen once at Cus's place and there were two plates of spaghetti, one for Mike and one for some other kid, another fighter, who hadn't sat down yet. Tyson went to take the other kids' food, too, and Camille"—D'Amato's companion—"said, 'Mike, no, don't take it.' But Cus said, 'No, go ahead, take it. You're gonna be the next champion of the world. Eat it.' Tyson was just fifteen or sixteen, and it was the wrong lesson. Listen, there are plenty of kids from Brownsville with that background and some of them are great people, people who find something in themselves to trigger a sense of accountability, the sense that someone else in the universe matters."

Atlas said Tyson was a fighter who depended solely on fast hands and the image of extreme violence. Nearly all his opponents were beaten before they ever got in the ring. Tyson never fought a truly great heavyweight (as Tunney fought Dempsey, as Ali fought Joe Frazier), and on the two occasions when an opponent stood up to him he lost: first to Buster Douglas in Tokyo in 1990, and then to Holyfield last November.

"You can lie to yourself in the ring in a hundred

different ways," Atlas said. "You can quit by degrees. You can stop punching with the idea, crazy as it sounds, that the other guy will stop if you do. Then you can make excuses to yourself, and the people around you will echo the excuses, and everything will seem to be all right. You can even foul and then claim you would have won, given the chance. Remember, this is a kid who used to hide between the walls of condemned buildings to make sure he wouldn't get beaten up. When you live like that, you learn to lie, to coax people that you are the toughest—you learn to scare people, to manipulate them. And when you can't do it you're lost.

"When I see Tyson, I see a guy who's scared, a guy who can't do it on the up and up. In his world, he was never allowed to be scared, or even honest, and so he is neither of those things. He is lost. When Tyson is alone with himself, I don't know if he believes there is one single person around him who is there because of his merits as a person. I don't even know that the women would be around without his ability to raise money. He'd have to show something independent of the ring and of his ability to send people on two-hundred-thousand-dollar shopping sprees."

On the day of the fight, I wandered the Strip. Earlier in the week, the casinos in hotels like the MGM Grand, New York New York, and Excalibur—the new family-friendly places—had been jammed with middle-class parents pushing strollers past the blackjack tables at midnight. Las Vegas is a better deal than Disney World. In Las Vegas, you can get a cheap hotel room, visit the Sphinx (at the Luxor), have your picture taken with a stuffed movie character, induce nausea on the rides, and be in the pool by lunchtime. But at the end of the week (when my room rate shot up from 79 dollars per night to $399) all the strollers were gone. The planes out at McCarran International Airport disgorged high rollers from New York, Tokyo, Taipei, and Beijing, athletes and gang-bangers, movie stars in Armani and hoochie girls in Moschino. The mind reeled—and the neck swiveled—at the effect of health clubs and silicone on the American form at century's end. All that hard work and earnest surgery. From the looks of the women at the luggage belts, there could not have been a single hooker left in the greater Los Angeles area. They had all flown in for the fight.

At the instigation of my friend Michael Wilbon, a sports columnist for the *Washington Post*, I spent the afternoon roaming the most expensive stores in town. Fight day, Wilbon instructed me, is a big shopping day, and many of the key stores—Neiman Marcus, Versace, Escada, Gucci, Armani—signed up extra seamstresses and tailors to get things ready for the evening. You don't buy a three-thousand-dollar suit and then not wear it to the main event. Even if you didn't have tickets—and that meant the vast majority who had "come in for the fight"—you showed up in the casinos looking dowdy at your peril.

At Neiman Marcus, I watched Louis Farrakhan take the Italian boutique by storm. While half a dozen of his bodyguards assumed positions near the ties and the shirt racks, the minister tried on a fine pair of mustard-colored slacks. Zegna is evidently one of his favorite designers. I watched him try on slacks for the better part of half an hour. When I asked one of his guards whether it might be possible to interview him, the guard took off his sunglasies and blinked. I took this to mean no.

The Forum Shops at Caesars Palace proved to be a nice place to hang out, too. The ceilings are painted like a cerulean sky with perfect Biblical clouds, and there is a fountain outside the Versace store that is better than the Trevi Fountain in Rome in that the Las Vegas Rome is air-conditioned.

Versace seemed to be the appointed headquarters of Tyson fans, and even Tyson himself. Before the first Holyfield fight, the managers shut down the store for Tyson. "He bought real good," a manager told me, but he declined to be more specific. The mythical figure among the boxing writers was that Tyson dropped a hundred and fifty thousand there last time. While I was fingering a blouse worth more than a decent used car, a guy with some major forearms and a purposeful stare came in: Tyson's bodyguard. Even if one did not know him by his face, there were hints: a "Team Tyson" tattoo on his arm and a "Team Tyson Rules" bomberjacket. The manager spotted him and raced over to serve. He actually rubbed his palms. Within seconds, the bodyguard was handed a suit bag. "Mike says thanks," the bodyguard said. He used his phone to order "immediate pickup" and walked out.

The fight crowd was not always thus. In the films of the big fights of the fifties and sixties, you can see that the ringside seats were taken up mainly by boxy white men in boxy blue suits—Mob guys, like Blinky Palerno and Frank Carbo, or, on a slightly higher plane, Rat Pack members. When Ali returned from exile in 1971 to fight Jerry Quarry in Atlanta, the fight crowd changed: suddenly, there were blacks at ringside. They held the same reputable and disreputable jobs as their white predecessors, but the plumage was different. The style of the hustler had shifted from Carbo's dour wool (he was known as Mr. Gray) to the iridescent suits of his black inheritors. It was as if a row of sparrows had flown the wire, to be replaced by a flock of cockatoos.

There were still plenty of white big shots around, plenty of pompadours and big-guy rings. One night at dinner at an Italian place, Trevesi, at the MGM Grand, a woman tossed her glass of wine at her big-guy boyfriend. Then she rose from her chair and, after a second of real consideration, took her glass and smashed it over the boyfriend's head. At which point there was blood on the boyfriend's skull and slivers of glass in the capellini of the woman at the next table. That would turn out to be the cleanest blow of the week.

It is customary at a big fight to surround the ring with press people, anonymous high rollers, and, most of all, "luminaries from the world of sports, politics, and the entertainment industry." In the press section, we were handed an alphabetized list of celebrities in attendance: Paul Anka, Patricia Arquette, Stephen Baldwin, Matthew Broderick, Albert Brooks, James Caan, John Cusack, Rodney Dangerfield, Lolita Davidovich, Ellen DeGeneres, Larry Flynt, Michael J. Fox, Cuba Gooding, Jr., etc. This, of course, was "subject to change," the King people warned us.

It is also customary at big fights to come late, to ignore the undercard. But I had seen about as many vermilion leather vests, chartreuse pants, and siliconed bodies as I wanted to see, and headed into the MGM Grand's arena. King had told everyone that the fight was "the greatest boxing event of all time. " It was a wonder, then, why he put together one of the grimmest undercards of all time. The highlight was surely the one women's bout, which left the canvas spotted with bloody pools. The woman in the pink shorts, Christy Martin, won the match. She had acquired all the best habits of boxing. She taunted her opponent, Andrea DeShong, at the prefight press conference, by say-

ing she was glad DeShong had finally worn a dress. "It's the first time I've seen you look respectable, like a woman," Martin said, thus proving her … manhood.

By eight-thirty, the seats were filled and the place buzzed, loud and nervous, a sound peculiar to the mass anticipation of violence, a more manic buzz than at a basketball playoff game or a political convention. Don King opened the proceedings by having the ring announcer tell us that the fight was dedicated to the memory of Dr. Betty Shabazz and to "the many, many innocent victims of crime and violence." We all stood, and the timekeeper sounded the bell ten times, boxing's equivalent of a twenty-one-gun salute.

Tyson, the challenger, came into the arena to the sound of gangsta rap. In the bowels of the arena, he had complained that he could hear Holyfield's music—electric Jesus music—and couldn't Holyfield turn it down? Tyson, as always, wore his warrior look: black trunks, black shoes, no socks. He came surrounded by Giachetti and Horne and Holloway and Crocodile and a dozen other men, all of them strung out on self-importance. They tried very hard to look dangerous.

Then Holyfield, with a far smaller entourage, came down the aisle toward the ring. He wore purple-and-white trunks with the logo "Phil 4:13" ("I can do all things through Christ which strengtheneth me"). While Tyson assumed his death mask, his intimidator's face, Holyfield was smiling. He mouthed the words to a gospel song that only he could hear. Tyson paced, and Holyfield stood in his corner, satisfied to jiggle the muscles in his arms and legs. One of his seconds massaged the ropes of muscle in his neck.

In the casino, Tyson was the favorite. You had to bet a hundred and eighty dollars on him to win a hundred. Those odds were based almost entirely on Tyson's Kid Dynamite reputation. Holyfield, however, was the pick on press row by a wide margin. And yet we knew why we were here. It was not to listen to Holyfield sing "Nearer My God to Thee."

Mills Lane, a bald and mumbly judge from Reno, was the referee. At the center of the ring, Lane reminded both fighters of their obligations to the law, to boxing, and to the Nevada State Athletic Commission, and both men nodded assent. They would, of course, not dream of trespass. So said their quick nods, the touch of the gloves.

At the opening bell, Tyson came out bobbing and weaving, but with a certain self-conscious air. He had lost the first fight not least because he had forgotten his old defensive moves. For months, Giachetti, his trainer, had been pleading with him to move his head, to jab, to forget about the one-punch knockout. But within half a minute Tyson was back to where he'd been before, throwing one huge hook at a time. Holyfield ducked the hooks easily and then held on, muscling Tyson around the ring. Last time, we had been amazed that Holyfield was stronger than Tyson, that he could push Tyson back on his heels, that he could grab Tyson's left arm in the clinches and save himself untold trauma to the kidneys and the temple. And now it was happening again. All the training, all the instructions were coming to nothing. Tyson could not intimidate Holyfield—he could not, as he had done to so many others before, terrify his man into dropping his guard, into committing a kind of boxing suicide. Holyfield had every intention of winning again, and he took the first round by controlling the pace and scoring big with two left hooks and then a right hand to Tyson's jaw.

Between rounds, as Tyson drank some water and spit in the bucket, Giachetti told him to take his time.

"Jab for the throat!" he said.

Tyson nodded, but who could tell what he was hearing—what inner voice?

In the second round, the pattern was much the same. Holyfield scored left hooks to the meat of Tyson's flank and shoved him around and back toward the ropes. Tyson jabbed occasionally, but more often he threw big, dramatic punches, and Holyfield smothered them, ducked them. Then came the crucial moment of the round—the moment that set off in Tyson some torrent of rage that would, in the end, botch the fight and possibly ruin his career. As the two men wrestled, Holyfield unintentionally rammed his skull into the sharp brow above Tyson's right eye. Within seconds, there were rivulets of blood running down the side of Tyson's face, and in the clinch he looked up at Lane and said, "He butted me." The physical side was bad enough: the gash was sure to bother Tyson throughout the fight. The blood would run in his eyes, and Holyfield, sensing his advantage, would work over the cut—punch at it, grind his head into it in the clinch—and win on a technical knockout. What was worse for Tyson

was the tremendous fear the butt stirred up in him, the way the blunt pain on his brow summoned up the last fight, his humiliation. Last time, the two men had butted heads inside, two berserk rams, and Tyson had come away the injured one, dazed and bleeding. It was as if his nightmare had come true. It was all happening again. He was in the ring, bleeding, and facing an opponent who would not back down.

Lane warned both men against excessive "roughhousing" (imagine!), but he didn't deduct any penalty points. Now, in the clinch, Tyson grew more desperate. He shoved a forearm into Holyfield's throat. But his punches, his big punches, were still missing, and they were coming in single volleys rather than in combination. Again, Holyfield won the round because of his superior strength, his ability to waltz Tyson around the ring, and the efficiency of his blows. What he threw, for the most part, landed. All three judges scored the first two rounds for Holyfield, ten to nine.

After the bell, a plastic surgeon worked on Tyson's cut.

As the doctor held a compress to Tyson's brow, the fighter jerked back.

"Aaahhh!" Tyson moaned.

"I'm sorry," the doctor said.

Tyson was breathing hard now—harder than he should have been after six minutes in the ring and months of roadwork. He said nothing. He gave no hint to anyone that something was wrong—that something had "snapped," as he put it days later. Tyson got off his stool and waited for the bell. As the two fighters stood facing each other, Holyfield suddenly pointed to his mouth, reminding Tyson that his corner had not put in his mouthpiece. Tyson walked back to Giachetti and opened his jaws; Giachetti put the mouthpiece in.

At the bell for the third round, Tyson stalked forward, and it was clear that he was enraged, desperate to end the fight before his eye failed him. He was relatively controlled at first, throwing his first sharp hooks of the fight. Holyfield was standing up to the blows and was still moving forward, crowding Tyson, but he was suddenly no longer in command. For more than two minutes of fighting, Tyson showed that he was capable of reviving his old style. Now his punches came in combinations. He kept his head moving, side to side, up and down, making it impossible for

Holyfield to flick the jab at his gash. In the clinches, however, Holyfield was still in control. He seemed to be telling Tyson that, while he could win the round, he could not win the fight, and Tyson seemed to see the sense in that. And with about forty seconds left in the round, as Holyfield was steering him around the center of the ring, Tyson suddenly spit out his mouthpiece and started gnawing on Holyfield's right ear. For a second, Holyfield seemed not to feel this lunatic attack, but then the sting hit him. He backed away, jumping up and down, pointing to his ear and the blood that now bathed it. At the same time, Tyson turned his head at an angle and spit out a half-inch chunk of ear. Lane called a time-out. Holyfield headed for his corner. Tyson chased him down and shoved him. Holyfield seemed almost to ham it up, to bounce crazily on the ropes, as if to highlight the madness of it all.

Don Turner, Holyfield's trainer, told his man to keep cool, to think about Jesus, just stay calm.

Lane said to a Nevada State Athletic Commission official at ringside that he was ready to disqualify Tyson—and he certainly would have been within his rights to do so—but first he invited the ring doctor, Flip Homansky, onto the canvas to have a look at Holyfield's ear. Homansky gravely inspected the ear and, presumably in the interests of Nevada and boxing's good name, pronounced Holyfield able to continue. Lane went to both corners and explained to the assembled handlers what had happened. He told Giachetti that Tyson "bit him on the ear."

"No, I didn't," Tyson said.

"Bullshit," Lane replied. He had already examined the ear, the teeth marks. "I thought my ear had fallen off!" Holyfield said later. "Blood was all over!" Lane deducted two points from Tyson—one for the bite, one for the shove—and, or so he claimed in a postfight interview, warned Tyson that if he did it again the fight was over.

The time-out had lasted more than two minutes, long enough for the crowd to see replays of the incident on the big screens around the arena and start booing, enough time for Tyson to decide if he had "snapped" or would do it again, and more than enough time for the jokes to begin sweeping through the press section: "Tyson's a chomp," "He's Hannibal Lecter," "a lobe blow," "pay per chew," "If you can't beat 'em, eat 'em." There would be a hundred of them.

Finally, Lane cleared the ring and resumed what little was left of the third round. The crowd, which had been fickle, swerving between chants first for Holyfield, then for Tyson, was now greatly affronted. They booed wildly. We were, of course, all prepared to see one fighter deliver a subconcussive blow to the other's brain, but a bite on the ear was beyond imagining. We were offended, disgusted, perhaps even a little thrilled. Boxing is a blood sport. Now there was blood.

Holyfield was intent on following his corner's plea to keep his cool. He marched in and connected with a stiff hook to Tyson's face. His message was delivered thus: you can do what you want, you can foul, you can threaten, you can even quit, but you will not intimidate me.

The fighters clinched again. There were about twenty seconds left in the round. And, incredibly, Tyson once more nuzzled his way into Holyfield's sweaty neck, almost tenderly, purposefully, as if he were snuffling for truffles. He found the left ear and bit. Once more, Holyfield did his jumping dance of rage and pain. The bell sounded.

Tyson's handlers now wore guilty looks; their eyes shifted. They knew what was coming.

Holyfield was not quite so sure. "Put my mouthpiece in," he told his cornermen. "I'm gonna knock him out."

But Lane could not let this go on: "One bite is bad enough. Two bites is the end of the search."

"I had to do some thinking," Lane said, reasonably, later on. "I thought about it and thought about it, and decided it was the right thing to do. Let the chips fall where they may." Tyson was disqualified. Holyfield was declared winner and "still heavyweight champion of the world." Subsequently, Tyson said that he had been forced to retaliate for the butt in the second round. After all, he said righteously, "This is my career.... I've got children to raise."

In the mayhem that followed Lane's announcement—Tyson still going berserk in the ring, pushing at the police, and then fans raining down ice cubes and curses as he headed for the locker room—in all that, one bit of business was almost forgotten. A hotel employee named Mitch Libonati found the chunk of ear that belonged to Evander Holyfield. He found it on the ring mat, wrapped it in a rubber glove, and delivered it to the champion's locker room.

"At first, they looked at me like I was pulling a prank, but I told them I had a piece of Evander's ear, and I thought he would want it," Libonati said. "It wasn't really bloody, actually. It was like a piece of sausage."

After leaving the arena and the press tent, I walked through the MGM Grand casino toward the elevators. I wanted to drop off some things in my room before heading back out to the Strip. How could one miss the victory parties? But just as I was passing some slot machines I saw a stampede of twenty or thirty people running straight at me. There were screams: "Get down!" and "There's shooting!" and "They got guns!" I had already seen some fistfights between Tyson's fans and Holyfield's fans. It was not beyond reckoning that some of the visitors could be armed. I dived behind a bank of slot machines, feeling at once terrified and ridiculous.

"Keep down!"

"Ya hear the shots!"

People were face down on the carpet, ducking under blackjack tables, roulette tables. And then it was quiet. No shots—not that we could hear, anyway. It seemed safe to walk to the elevators.

But then, as the doors opened, more people started dashing around, ducking behind slot machines and into the elevators. I went up to the fourteenth floor and then went back down in a service elevator. I had to get to the bank of elevators that would get me to the twenty-fifth floor. As I was getting out of the service elevator, Jesse Jackson and a team of police were getting in.

"It's sad. The whole thing is sad," Jackson said. "That's the one word I can think of to describe it. It's a tragedy that no one can explain. As far as Tyson is concerned, I guess the butting triggered something in him. I focus on him and what's going on in his head. And now this. They're

out there shooting with Uzis, these bad boys."

It was never entirely clear whether there had been any shooting. I doubt it. But the Nevada Highway Patrol did shut down the Strip from Tropicana Avenue to Koval Lane. No one wanted a repeat of the action after the Tyson-Seldon fight last September, when the rap star Tupac Shakur was shot to death in a car.

The rumors of Uzi fire did little to help the gambling receipts at the MGM Grand, but elsewhere on the Strip the high rollers were happy. We had all been witness to a spectacle—to the unraveling of Mike Tyson. In the days to come, he would apologize. He would reach out "to the medical professionals for help." But who now cared about him? In the ring, at his moment of greatest pressure, he had lost everything: he had proved himself to be what in gentler times would have been called a bum. Biting is certainly not unheard of in boxing—Holyfield himself once bit Jakey Winters in an amateur bout when he was eighteen—yet Tyson had done it not once but twice, in a championship fight seen by "three billion people," or however many Don King had managed to attract. The abysmal and lonely end that he had seemed to predict for himself had come so soon.

"It's over," he said in the locker room. "I know it's over. My career is over."

No one had envisioned this end more clearly than Tyson himself. On the day before the fight, he had gone out to a cemetery near the airport and laid a bouquet of flowers on the grave of Sonny Liston. The music ahead for Tyson would be not rap but something more mournful. "Someday they're gonna write a blues song just for fighters," his role model, Liston, once said. "It'll be for slow guitar, soft trumpet, and a bell."

FROM: THE FANCY

John Hamilton Reynolds was the boy wonder of English poetry. At the age of 19 he was a protégé of Byron, at 22 he was bracketed with Shelley and Keats and now he is remembered, if at all, as a friend of Keats, with whom he shared a great affection for boxing, and as an associate of Lamb, DeQuincey, Hazlitt and Hood.

In 1820, Reynolds' most celebrated book, *The Fancy*, was issued by the publishers of Keats' "Lamia." Jack Randall, eulogized in it, fought from 1815 to 1821, was the original "Nonpareil" and the most accomplished middleweight ever developed in England. Philip Samson, advised in *The Fancy* to give up the quest, four years later twice fought Jem Ward and took two beatings.

JOHN HAMILTON REYNOLDS

SONNET
On the Nonpareil
'None but himself can be his parallel!'

With marble-colored shoulders,—and keen eyes,
  Protected by a forehead broad and white,—
And hair cut close lest it impede the sight,
  And clenched hands, firm, and of punishing size,—
Steadily held, or motion'd wary-wise,
  To hit or stop,—and kerchief too drawn tight
  O'er the unyielding loins, to keep from flight
The inconstant wind, that all too often flies,—
The Nonpareil stands!—Fame, whose bright eyes run o'er
  With joy to see a Chicken of her own,
  Dips her rich pen in *claret*, and writes down

Under the letter R, first on the score,
  "Randall,—John,—Irish parents,—age not known,
  "Good with both hands, and only ten stone four!"

LINES TO PHILIP SAMSON,
The Brummagem Youth

Go back to Brummagem! go back to Brummagem!
  Youth of that ancient and halfpenny town!
Maul manufacturers; rattle, and rummage 'em;—
  Country swell'd heads may afford you renown:
Here in Town-rings, we find Fame very fast go,
  The exquisite *light weights* are heavy to bruise;
For the graceful and punishing hand of Belasco
  Foils,—and *will* foil all attempts on the Jews.

Go back to Brummagem, while you've a head on!
  For bread from the *Fancy* is light weight enough;
Moulsey, whose turf is the sweetest to tread on,
  Candidly owns you're a good *bit of stuff*:
But hot heads and slow hands are utterly useless,
  When Israelite science and caution awake;
So pr'ythee go home, Youth! and pester the Jews less,
  And work for a *cutlet*, and not for a *stake*.

Turn up the *raws* at a fair or a holiday,
  Make your fists free with each Brummagem rib;
But never again, Lad, commit such a folly, pray!
  As sigh to be one of the messmates of Crib.
Leave the P. C. purse, for others to handle,—
  Throw up no hat in a Moulsey Hurst sun;—
  Bid adieu, by the two-penny post, to Jack Randall,
  And take the outside of the coach,—one pound one!

Samson! forget there are such men as Scroggins,
  And Shelton and Carter, and Bob Burns and
Spring:
Forget *toss for sides*, and forget all the floggings,—
  While shirts are pull'd off,—to make perfect the ring.
Your heart is a real one, but skill, Phil, is wanted;
  Without it, all uselessly bravery begs:—
Be content that you've beat Dolly Smith, and been
chaunted,—
  And train'd,—stripp'd,—and pitted,—and hit
off your legs!

ON DEMPSEY AND TUNNEY

Grantland Rice was the most beloved and famous of all sports writers. From the end of World War I until he died, working at his typewriter at the age of 73 on July 13, 1954, he was also the friend and confidant of more of the sporting great than any other writer who ever lived. What follows was excerpted from his autobiography, completed twelve days before his death.

GRANTLAND RICE

In sport, you'll find there are great defensive stars and brilliant offensive competitors. Among the great offensive athletes I've studied I must include Ty Cobb, Bill Tilden, Babe Ruth, Harry Greb and Jesse Owens. But I found the greatest attacking, or pure offensive, star one June day in 1919 in Toledo, off the hot and steamy shores of Maumee Bay.

His name was Jack Dempsey. I had been in France during 1917 and 1918, so had seen no prize fights in that period. When I first met Dempsey, he was burnt purple. He had trained down to 180 pounds in getting ready for Jess Willard, the 250-pound giant. Dempsey was then twenty-four years old. He was keen and lithe, almost as fast as Cobb. It was his speed, speed of hand as well as foot, that made him such a dangerous opponent.

Dempsey was the oddest mixture of humanity I've known. In the ring he was a killer—a superhuman wild man. His teeth were frequently bared and his complete intent was an opponent's destruction. He was a fighter—one who used every trick to wreck the other fighter.

Yet, outside the ring, Jack is one of the gentlest men I know. I've seen him in his restaurant at times when some customer, with more enthusiasm than good sense, would grab his vest or part of his shirt—strictly for a souvenir—with no kickback from Jack. I've known the man closely for more than thirty years and I've never seen him in a rough argument or as anything except courteous and considerate.

Looking at Dempsey and Willard in 1919, it was hard to give Dempsey a chance. Dempsey, slightly over 6 feet, weighed 180. Willard, at 6 feet 6, weighed 250 at least.

Willard looked on Dempsey as a little boy. The night before the fight Bob Edgren and I called on Jess. He thought the fight was a joke.

"... outweigh him seventy pounds," Willard said. "He'll come tearing into me ... I'll have my left out ... and then I'll hit him with a right upper-cut. That'll be the end."

Next day when the first round opened, Dempsey circled Willard some twenty-five or thirty seconds. He was a tiger circling an ox. Finally Willard couldn't wait any longer. He jabbed at Dempsey with his left, and the roof fell in. Jack ducked under Willard's left, threw a right to the body. At the same time he nailed Willard on the right side of the head with a smashing left.

"I knew it was over then," Jack said later. "I saw his cheekbone cave in."

Lining up Georges Carpentier for the Dempsey vs. Carpentier fight, at Boyle's Thirty Acres, Jersey City, for July 1921, was a shrewd piece of work by Tex Rickard. Tex "sensed" more and better gate-building tricks in one minute than today's promoters can dream up in a year. I realize that television has taken a lot of the steam off the need for a "live" gate—what with TV rights selling for great chunks of cash. But the fact remains that Rickard, yes, and Mike Jacobs, had the kind of promotional touch that would have them storming the gates today instead of taking in the fight through a camera.

Carpentier, with a gaudy if superficial war record, had returned to Paris in one piece—and hungry. He was a pretty fair light-heavyweight, but they couldn't have ballooned the Frenchman into a bona fide heavyweight, except in the papers, with two sandbags for added ballast. At any rate, Rickard—knowing the public's love of a hero-and-villain tangle—cast Dempsey, the scowling, wire-bearded "draft dodger," as the villain, with apple-cheeked Carpentier, the amiable, personable soldier boy, as the hero. Pictures of Dempsey, riveting battleships in patent leather shoes—all at [Jack] Kearns' behest—flooded the sports pages, along with those of Carpentier, practically winning the war singlehanded.

The fight was the first to be broadcast—with Graham McNamee describing the action—and it had the whole nation taking sides for or against Dempsey....

It was all over in four rounds, but had Dempsey wanted to put the slug on Carpentier, I think he could have nailed him in the first round. From ringside, all French ships at sea received this cabled flash: "Your Frog flattened in fourth"—for a new high in international diplomacy.

I was having breakfast with Jack and Max Baer one February morning back in 1931 at the Warwick Hotel. The day before, Jack had refereed the Baer-Tommy Loughran fight at Madison Square Garden. Max had been decisioned in ten rounds.

"I've been looking at left jabs all night," Max said. "Lefts ... lefts ... lefts ... that's all I've seen!"

"The funny part," said Dempsey, "is that you could have stopped that 'Lefty' in the first round."

"How?" said Baer.

"Take off your coat," replied Jack to big Maxie, 6 feet 3 and 220 pounds. Max shucked off his coat and faced Dempsey.

"Now lead with a left, just as Loughran did," said Jack. Max led ... and there was an immediate yelp. "You broke my arm," Max howled as he backed away, holding it.

As Baer led with his left, Dempsey had dropped his huge right fist across the left biceps with paralyzing force. The left arm became useless for thirty minutes.

"I'll show you another punch," Jack said. He spun Baer and then socked him.

"You can't do that," Max said. "It's illegal."

"They'll only warn you the first time," Dempsey said.

I once asked Dempsey why college athletes never made good fighters. "Football is just as rough," I said. "They star in those games. But seldom in boxing where the big money is."

"They're too smart," Dempsey said. "The fight game is the toughest game on earth. When I was a young fellow I was knocked down plenty. I wanted to stay down. I couldn't. I had to collect that two dollars for winning—or go hungry. I had to get up. I was one of those hungry fighters. You could hit me on the chin with a sledge hammer for five dollars. When you haven't eaten for two days you'll understand.

"Few college fellers ever get that low. I had one early fight when I was knocked down eleven times before I got up to win. You think I'd have taken that beating if I had had as much as twenty-five bucks with me? No chance."

He would have.

The Giants were playing at home and Heywood Broun, covering for the *World*, and I were in the press box at the Polo Grounds when Walter Trumbull, sports editor of the old New York *Post*, appeared in our midst with a young fellow in tow. Trumbull introduced his guest, Gene Tunney, all around, and I recall that Broun made quite a fuss over the handsome youngster.

I had glimpsed Tunney several days earlier when he fought "Soldier" Jones, a tough trial horse in a supporting bout to the Dempsey–Carpentier fight at Jersey City. Tunney scored a knockout in seven rounds. He was known only as a soldier-boxer who had won the light-heavyweight title of the AEF in France. However, he had not fought as a bona fide heavyweight and certainly looked no part of one.

"What are your plans?" I asked.

"My plans are all Dempsey," he replied.

"Very interesting," I said. "But why not sharpen your artillery on Harry Greb, Carpentier or Tom Gibbons before you start hollering for Dempsey?"

"I suppose I'll have to beat them on the way up," Tunney said. "But Dempsey is the one I want."

I said no more and turned my attention back to McGraw's Giants, who with George (High Pockets) Kelly at first base, were headed for their first pennant since 1917. I recall Tunney later volunteered that he was twenty-three years old. I couldn't help thinking that this forthright young fellow would make a fine insurance salesman but certainly had no business having his features and brains scrambled by Dempsey's steel fists.

In January of 1922, Tunney defeated Battling Levinsky for the [American] light-heavyweight crown, but lost it the following May to Harry Greb in perhaps the bloodiest fight I ever covered. A great fighter—or brawler—Greb handled Tunney like a butcher hammering a Swiss steak. How the Greenwich Village Irishman with the crew haircut survived fifteen rounds I'll never know—except that Tunney always enjoyed more and better physical conditioning than anybody he ever fought. By the third round, Gene was literally wading in his own blood.

I saw Gene a few days later. His face looked as though he'd taken the wrong end of a razor fight. "You know," he said, "I must have lost nearly two quarts of blood in there."

Abe Attell, the former fighter-gambler and longtime "character" in the fight game, probably saved Tunney from bleeding to death.

"Abe was sitting near my corner—a spectator," continued Tunney. "When he saw the shape I was in after the second round, he ducked out to the nearest druggist and bought his entire supply of adrenalin chloride. Hustling back, Attell slipped the bottle to Doc Bagley. Between rounds Doc's long fingers flew. A superb 'cut' man, he'd managed to stop the bleeding only to watch Greb bust my face apart in the following round. It was discouraging."

To me, the fight was proof that Tunney meant to stick with prize fighting. I tried to tell Gene that Greb was too fast for him ... to go after a softer touch. But less than a year later they fought again and Tunney won the decision in fifteen rounds. I scored that fight for Greb, but then Tunney met Greb four times more without defeat.

In 1925 Tunney fought another fight that has never been recorded. I was the matchmaker and promoter.

Jim Corbett, the old champion and the world's greatest boxer, had written a book called *The Roar of the Crowd*. I was in the business of making sports pictures for the *Sportlight*, and I finally sold Corbett the idea of boxing three rounds, for pictures, with Gene Tunney.

My "assistant" promoter was Frank Craven, the actor. At that time Tunney had heard of Will Shakespeare and, having met Craven, he was quite keen about it all. He also knew of Corbett's reputation as a boxer and what Jim had meant from the viewpoint of science and skill. We arranged a spot in midtown Manhattan, atop the Putnam Building.

Anxious to pick up any possible tip from the old stylist, Tunney arrived at the appointed hour, ready to go and attired in trunks. Corbett took one look at them and said, "I'd like to wear long white trousers. I had a pair of good-looking legs in the old days, but they don't look so good now. I'm nearly sixty and they are kinda shriveled."

They boxed three two-minute rounds. Tunney was on the defensive. Corbett was brilliant. He feinted with his left—then punched with his left. A left feint ... a left hook; a right feint ... a left jab; a right feint; a right cross. He still had bewildering speed! He mixed up his punches better than practically any fighter I've seen since—with the possible exception of Ray Robinson.

After the exhibition, Tunney turned to me. "I honestly think he is better than Benny Leonard. It was the greatest thing I've ever seen in the ring. I learned plenty," he said.

At fifty-nine Corbett was still the master.

That winter in Florida I played golf with Tommy Armour and Tunney. Gene would hit his drive, toss aside his club and run down the fairway throwing phantom punches-left and right hooks-and muttering, "Dempsey ... Dempsey ... Dempsey."

"He's obsessed," observed Armour. "His brain knows nothing but Dempsey. I believe Jack could hit him with an ax and Gene wouldn't feel it. I don't know if Dempsey has slipped, but I'll have a good chunk down on Tunney when that fight arrives."

BRED FOR BATTLE

Damon Runyon was closer to boxing than to any other sport. He not only covered most of the major fights from the end of World War I until he died in 1946, but he owned pieces of a number of fighters and was one of a triumvirate that assisted Mike Jacobs in the formation of the Twentieth Century Sporting Club, the most powerful promotional organization in the history of the sport.

DAMON RUNYON

One night a guy by the name of Bill Corum, who is one of these sport scribes, gives me a Chinee for a fight at Madison Square Garden, a Chinee being a ducket with holes punched in it like old-fashioned Chink money, to show that it is a free ducket, and the reason I am explaining to you how I get this ducket is because I do not wish anybody to think I am ever simple enough to pay out my own potatoes for a ducket to a fight, even if I have any potatoes. Personally, I will not give you a bad two-bit piece to see a fight anywhere, because the way I look at it, half the time the guys who are supposed to do the fighting go in there and put on the old do-se-do, and I consider this a great fraud upon the public, and I do not believe in encouraging dishonesty.

But of course I never refuse a Chinee to such events, because the way I figure it, what can I lose except my time, and my time is not worth more than a bob a week the way things are. So on the night in question I am standing in the lobby of the Garden with many other citizens, and I am trying to find out if there is any skullduggery doing in connection with the fight, because any time there is any skullduggery doing I love to know it, as it is something worth knowing in case a guy wishes to get a small wager down. Well, while I am standing there, somebody comes up behind me and hits me an awful belt on the back, knocking my wind plumb out of me, and making me very indignant indeed. As soon as I get a little of my wind back again, I turn around figuring to put a large blast on the guy who slaps me, but who is it but a guy by the name of Spider McCoy, who is known far and wide as a manager of fighters.

Well, of course I do not put the blast on Spider McCoy, because he is an old friend of mine, and furthermore, Spider McCoy is such a guy as is apt to let a left hook go at anybody who puts the blast on him, and I do not believe in getting in trouble, especially with good left-hookers.

So I say hello to Spider, and am willing to let it go at that, but Spider seems glad to see me, and says to me like this: "Well, well, well, well, well!" Spider says.

"Well," I say to Spider McCoy, "how many wells does it take to make a river?"

"One, if it is big enough," Spider says, so I can see he knows the answer all right. "Listen," he says, "I just think up the greatest proposition I ever think of in my whole life, and who knows but what I can interest you in same."

"Well, Spider," I say, "I do not care to hear any propositions at this time, because it may be a long story, and I wish to step inside and see the impending battle. Anyway," I say, "if it is a proposition involving financial support, I wish to state that I do not have any resources whatever at this time."

"Never mind the battle inside," Spider says. "It is nothing but a tank job, anyway. And as for financial support," Spider says, "this does not require more than a pound note, tops, and I know you have a pound note because I know you put the bite on Overcoat Obie for this amount not an hour ago. Listen," Spider McCoy says, "I know where I can place my hands on the greatest heavyweight prospect in the world today, and all I need is the price of carfare to where he is."

Well, off and on, I know Spider McCoy twenty years, and in all this time I never know him when he is not looking for the greatest heavyweight prospect in the world. And as long as Spider knows I have the pound note, I know there is no use trying to play the duck for him, so I stand there wondering who the stool pigeon can be who informs him of my financial status.

"Listen," Spider says, "I just discover that I am all out of line in the way I am looking for heavyweight prospects in the past. I am always looking for nothing but plenty of size," he says. "Where I make my mistake is not looking for blood lines. Professor D just smartens me up," Spider says. Well, when he mentions the name of Professor D, I commence taking a little interest, because it is well known to one and all that Professor D is one of the smartest old guys in the world. He is once a professor in a college out in Ohio, but quits this dodge to handicap the horses, and he is a first-rate handicapper, at that. But besides knowing how to handicap the horses, Professor D knows many other things, and is highly respected in all walks of life, especially on Broadway.

"Now then," Spider says, "Professor D calls my attention this afternoon to the fact that when a guy is looking for a race horse, he does not take just any horse that comes along, but he finds out if the horse's papa is able to run in his day, and if the horse's mamma can get out of her own way when she is young. Professor D shows me how a guy looks for speed in a horse's breeding away back to its great-great-great-great-grandpa and grandmamma," Spider McCoy says.

"Well," I say, "anybody knows this without asking Professor D. In fact," I say, "you can look up a horse's parents to see if they can mud before betting on a plug to win in heavy going."

"All right," Spider says, "I know all this myself, but I never think much about it before Professor D mentions it. Professor D says if a guy is looking for a hunting dog he does not pick a Pekingese pooch, but he gets a dog that is bred to hunt from away back yonder, and if he is after a game chicken he does not take a Plymouth Rock out of the back yard. So then," Spider says, "Professor D wishes to know why, when I am looking for a fighter, I do not look for one who comes of fighting stock. Professor D wishes to know," Spider says, "why I do not look for some guy who is bred to fight, and when I think this over, I can see the professor is right.

"And then all of a sudden," Spider says, "I get the largest idea I ever have in all my life. Do you remember a guy I have about twenty years back by the name of Shamus Mulrooney, the Fighting Harp?" Spider says. "A big, rough, tough heavyweight out of Newark?"

"Yes," I say, "I remember Shamus very well indeed. The last time I see him is the night Pounder Pat O'Shea almost murders him in the old Garden," I say. "I never see a guy with more ticker than Shamus, unless maybe it is Pat."

"Yes," Spider says, "Shamus has plenty of ticker. He is about through the night of the fight you speak of, otherwise Pat will never lay a glove on him. It is not long after this fight that Shamus packs in and goes back to bricklaying in Newark, and it is also about this same time," Spider says, "that he marries Pat O'Shea's sister, Bridget.

"Well, now," Spider says, "I remember they have a boy who must be around nineteen years old now, and if ever a guy is bred to fight it is a boy by Shamus Mulrooney out of Bridget O'Shea, because," Spider says, "Bridget herself can lick half the heavyweights I see around nowadays if she is half as good as she is the last time I see her. So now you have my wonderful idea. We will go to Newark and get this boy and make him heavyweight champion of the world."

"What you state is very interesting indeed, Spider," I say. "But," I say, "how do you know this boy is a heavyweight?"

"Why," Spider says, "how can he be anything else but a heavyweight, what with his papa as big as a house, and his mamma weighing maybe a hundred and seventy pounds in her step-ins? Although of course," Spider says, "I never see Bridget weigh in in such manner.

"But," Spider says, "even if she does carry more weight than I will personally care to spot a doll, Bridget is by no means a pelican when she marries Shamus. In fact," he says, "she is pretty good-looking. I remember their wedding well, because it comes out that Bridget is in love with some other guy at the time, and this guy comes to see the nuptials, and Shamus runs him all the way from Newark to Elizabeth, figuring to break a couple of legs for the guy if he catches him. But," Spider says, "the guy is too speedy for Shamus, who never has much foot anyway."

Well, all that Spider says appeals to me as a very sound business proposition, so the upshot of it is,

I give him my pound note to finance his trip to Newark.

Then I do not see Spider McCoy again for a week, but one day he calls me up and tells me to hurry over to the Pioneer gymnasium to see the next heavyweight champion of the world, Thunderbolt Mulrooney.

I am personally somewhat disappointed when I see Thunderbolt Mulrooney, and especially when I find out his first name is Raymond and not Thunderbolt at all, because I am expecting to see a big, fierce guy with red hair and a chest like a barrel, such as Shamus Mulrooney has when he is in his prime. But who do I see but a tall, pale-looking young guy with blond hair and thin legs.

Furthermore, he has pale-blue eyes, and a faraway look in them, and he speaks in a low voice, which is nothing like the voice of Shamus Mulrooney. But Spider seems satisfied with Thunderbolt, and when I tell him Thunderbolt does not look to me like the next heavyweight champion of the world, Spider says like this: "Why," he says, "the guy is nothing but a baby, and you must give him time to fill out. He may grow to be bigger than his papa. But you know," Spider says, getting indignant as he thinks about it, "Bridget Mulrooney does not wish to let this guy be the next heavyweight champion of the world. In fact," Spider says, "she kicks up an awful row when I go to get him, and Shamus finally has to speak to her severely. Shamus says he does not know if I can ever make a fighter of this guy because Bridget coddles him until he is nothing but a mush-head, and Shamus says he is sick and tired of seeing the guy sitting around the house doing nothing but reading and playing the zither."

"Does he play the zither yet?" I asked Spider McCoy.

"No," Spider says, "I do not allow my fighters to play zithers. I figure it softens them up. This guy does not play anything at present. He seems to be in a daze most of the time, but of course everything is new to him. He is bound to come out okay, because," Spider says, "he is certainly bred right. I find out from Shamus that all the Mulrooneys are great fighters back in the old country," Spider says, "and furthermore he tells me Bridget's mother once licks four Newark cops who try to stop her from pasting her old man, so," Spider says, "this lad is just naturally steaming with fighting blood."

Well, I drop around to the Pioneer once or twice a week after this, and Spider McCoy is certainly working hard with Thunderbolt Mulrooney. Furthermore, the guy seems to be improving right along and gets so he can box fairly well and punch the bag and all this and that, but he always has that faraway look in his eyes, and personally I do not care for fighters with faraway looks.

Finally one day Spider calls me up and tells me he has Thunderbolt Mulrooney matched in a four-round preliminary bout at the St. Nick with a guy by the name of Bubbles Browning, who is fighting almost as far back as the first battle of Bull Run, so I can see Spider is being very careful in matching Thunderbolt. In fact, I congratulate Spider on his carefulness. "Well," Spider says, "I am taking this match just to give Thunderbolt the feel of the ring. I am taking Bubbles because he is an old friend of mine, and very deserving, and furthermore," Spider says, "he gives me his word he will not hit Thunderbolt very hard and will become unconscious the instant Thunderbolt hits him. You know," Spider says, "you must encourage a young heavyweight, and there is nothing that encourages one so much as knocking somebody unconscious."

Now of course it is nothing for Bubbles to promise not to hit anybody very hard because even when he is a young guy, Bubbles cannot punch his way out of a paper bag, but I am glad to learn that he also promises to become unconscious very soon, as naturally I am greatly interested in Thunderbolt's career, what with owning a piece of him, and having an investment of one pound in him already.

So the night of the fight, I am at the St. Nick very early, and many other citizens are there ahead of me, because by this time Spider McCoy gets plenty of publicity for Thunderbolt by telling the boxing scribes about his wonderful fighting blood lines, and everybody wishes to see a guy who is bred for battle, like Thunderbolt.

I take a guest with me to the fight by the name of Harry the Horse, who comes from Brooklyn, and as I am anxious to help Spider McCoy all I can, as well as to protect my investment in Thunderbolt, I request Harry to call on Bubbles Browning in his dressing room and remind him of his promise about hitting Thunderbolt. Harry the Horse does this for me, and furthermore he shows Bubbles a large revolver and tells Bubbles that he will be compelled to shoot his ears off if Bubbles forgets his promise, but Bubbles says all this is most unnecessary, as his eyesight is so bad he cannot see to hit anybody, anyway.

Well, I know a party who is a friend of the guy is going to referee the preliminary bouts, and I am looking for this party to get him to tell the referee to disqualify Bubbles in case it looks as if he is forgetting his promise and is liable to hit Thunderbolt, but before I can locate the party, they are announcing the opening bout, and there is Thunderbolt in the ring looking very far away indeed, with Spider McCoy behind him.

It seems to me I never see a guy who is so pale all over as Thunderbolt Mulrooney, but Spider looks down at me and tips me a large wink, so I can see that everything is as right as rain, especially when Harry the Horse makes motions at Bubbles Browning like a guy firing a large revolver at somebody, and Bubbles smiles, and also winks.

Well, when the bell rings, Spider gives Thunderbolt a shove toward the center, and Thunderbolt comes out with his hands up, but looking more far away than somewhat, and something tells me that Thunderbolt by no means feels the killer instinct such as I love to see in fighters. In fact, something tells me that Thunderbolt is not feeling enthusiastic about this proposition in any way, shape, manner, or form. Old Bubbles almost falls over his own feet coming out of his corner, and he starts bouncing around making passes at Thunderbolt, and waiting for Thunderbolt to hit him so he can become unconscious. Naturally, Bubbles does not wish to become unconscious without getting hit, as this may look suspicious to the public.

Well, instead of hitting Bubbles, what does Thunderbolt Mulrooney do but turn around and walk over to a neutral corner, and lean over the ropes with his face in his gloves, and bust out crying. Naturally, this is a most surprising incident to one and all, especially to Bubbles Browning.

The referee walks over to Thunderbolt Mulrooney and tries to turn him around, but Thunderbolt keeps his face in his gloves and sobs so loud that the referee is deeply touched and starts sobbing with him. Between sobs he asks Thunderbolt if he wishes to continue the fight, and Thunderbolt shakes his head, although as a matter of fact no fight whatever starts so far, so the referee declares Bubbles Browning the winner, which is a terrible surprise to Bubbles. Then the referee puts his arm around Thunderbolt and leads him over to

Spider McCoy, who is standing in his corner with a very strange expression on his face. Personally, I consider the entire spectacle so revolting that I go out into the air, and stand around awhile expecting to hear any minute that Spider McCoy is in the hands of the gendarmes on a charge of mayhem.

But it seems that nothing happens, and when Spider finally comes out of the St. Nick, he is only looking sorrowful because he just hears that the promoter declines to pay him the fifty bobs he is supposed to receive for Thunderbolt's services, the promoter claiming that Thunderbolt renders no service.

"Well," Spider says, "I fear this is not the next heavyweight champion of the world after all. There is nothing in Professor D's idea about blood lines as far as fighters are concerned, although," he says, "it may work out all right with horses and dogs, and one thing and another. I am greatly disappointed," Spider says, "but then I am always being disappointed in heavyweights. There is nothing we can do but take this guy back home, because," Spider says, "the last thing I promised Bridget Mulrooney is that I will personally return him to her in case I am not able to make him heavyweight champion, as she is afraid he will get lost if he tries to find his way home alone."

So the next day, Spider McCoy and I take Thunderbolt Mulrooney over to Newark and to his home, which turns out to be a nice little house in a side street with a yard all around and about, and Spider and I are just as well pleased that old Shamus Mulrooney is absent when we arrive, because Spider says that Shamus is just such a guy as will be asking a lot of questions about the fifty bobbos that Thunderbolt does not get.

Well, when we reach the front door of the house, out comes a big fine-looking doll with red cheeks, all excited, and she takes Thunderbolt in her arms and kisses him, so I know this is Bridget Mulrooney, and I can see she knows what happens, and in fact I afterwards learn that Thunderbolt telephones her the night before.

After a while she pushes Thunderbolt into the house and stands at the door as if she is guarding it against us entering to get him again, which of course is very unnecessary. And all this time Thunderbolt is sobbing no little, although by and by the sobs die away, and from somewhere in the house comes the sound of music I seem to recognize as the music of a zither.

Well, Bridget Mulrooney never says a word to us as she stands in the door, and Spider McCoy keeps staring at her in a way that I consider very rude indeed. I am wondering if he is waiting for a receipt for Thunderbolt, but finally he speaks as follows: "Bridget," Spider says, "I hope and trust that you will not consider me too fresh, but I wish to learn the name of the guy you are going around with just before you marry Shamus. I remember him well," Spider says, "but I cannot think of his name, and it bothers me not being able to think of names. He is a tall, skinny, stoop-shouldered guy," Spider says, "with a hollow chest and a soft voice, and he loves music."

Well, Bridget Mulrooney stands there in the doorway, staring back at Spider, and it seems to me that the red suddenly fades out of her cheeks, and just then we hear a lot of yelling, and around the corner of the house comes a bunch of five or six kids, who seem to be running from another kid. This kid is not very big, and is maybe fifteen or sixteen years old, and he has red hair and many freckles, and he seems very mad at the other kids. In fact, when he catches up with them, he starts belting away at them with his fists, and before anybody can as much as say boo, he has three of them on the ground as flat as pancakes, while the others are yelling bloody murder.

Personally, I never see such wonderful punching by a kid, especially with his left hand, and Spider McCoy is also much impressed, and is watching the kid with great interest. Then Bridget Mulrooney runs out and grabs the frecklefaced kid with one hand and smacks him with the other hand and hauls him, squirming and kicking, over to Spider McCoy and says to Spider like this:

"Mr. McCoy," Bridget says, "this is my youngest son Terrence, and though he is not a heavyweight, and will never be a heavyweight, perhaps he will answer your purpose. Suppose you see his father about him sometime," she says, "and hoping you will learn to mind your own business, I wish you a very good day."

Then she takes the kid into the house under her arms and slams the door in our kissers, and there is nothing for us to do but walk away. And as we are walking away, all of a sudden Spider McCoy snaps his fingers as guys will do when they get an unexpected thought, and says like this: "I remember the guy's name," he says. "It is Cedric Tilbury, and he is a floorwalker in Hamburgher's department store, and," Spider says, "how he can play the zither!"

I see in the papers the other day where Jimmy Johnston, the matchmaker at the Garden, matches Tearing Terry Mulrooney, the new sensation in the lightweight division, to fight for the championship, but it seems from what Spider McCoy tells me that my investment with him does not cover any fighters in his stable except maybe heavyweights. And it also seems that Spider McCoy is not monkeying with heavyweights since he gets Tearing Terry.

THE GREAT BENNY LEONARD

The author of *The Harder They Fall* has been a fight follower since pre-adolescence. This remembrance of Benny Leonard, his first hero, beautifully describes the importance of a boxing idol who was one of the greatest ring artists of all time and, beyond that, an ethnic standard bearer who helped his people hold their heads high.

BUDD SCHULBERG

In 1920, when my father B.P. was organizing one of the pioneer film companies and setting up shop at the (L. B.) Mayer-Schulberg Studio in downtown Los Angeles, he was a passionate fight fan. An habitue of the old Garden on Madison Square—before our western migration—his favorite fighter had been the Jewish lightweight Benjamin Leiner who fought under the nom-de-boxe of Benny Leonard. On the eve of my seventh birthday, my hero was neither the new cowboy star Tom Mix nor the acrobatic Doug Fairbanks. I didn't trade face cards of the current baseball stars like the other kids on Riverside Drive. Babe Ruth could hit fifty-four homers that year (when no one else had ever hit more than sixteen in the history of the league) and I really didn't care. The legendary Ty Cobb could break a batting record almost every time he came to the plate but no chill came to my skin at the mention of his name. That sensation was reserved for Benny Leonard.

He was doing with his fists what the Adolph Zukors and William Foxes, and soon the L. B. Mayers and the B. P. Schulbergs, were doing in their studios and their theaters, proving the advantage of brain over brawn, fighting the united efforts of the *goyim* establishment to keep them in their ghettos.

Jewish boys on their way to *schule* on the Sabbath had tasted the fists and felt the shoe-leather of the righteous Irish and Italian Christian children who crowded them, shouted, "You killed our Christ!" and avenged their gentle Savior with blows and kicks. But sometimes the young victim surprised his enemies by fighting back, like Abe Attell, who won the featherweight championship of the world at the turn of the century, or Abe Goldstein, who beat up a small army of Irish contenders on his way to the bantamweight title. But our superhero was Benny Leonard. "The Great Benny Leonard." That's how he was always referred to in our household. There was The Great Houdini. The Great Caruso. *And* The Great Benny Leonard.

My father gave me a scrapbook, with a picture of Benny in a fighting stance on the cover, and I recognized his face and could spell out his name even before I was able to read. In 1920 he was only twenty-four years old, just four years younger than my hero-worshiping old man, but he had been undefeated lightweight champion of the world ever since he knocked out the former champion, Freddie Welsh, in the Madison Square Garden.

B.P. knew Benny Leonard personally. All up-and-coming young Jews in New York knew Benny Leonard personally. They would take time off from their lunch hour or their afternoon activities to watch him train. They bet hundreds and often thousands of dollars on him in stirring contests against Rocky Kansas, Ever Hammer, Willie Ritchie, Johnny Dundee, Pal Moran, Joe Welling....He was only five-foot-six, and his best fighting weight was a few pounds over 130, but he was one of those picture-book fighters who come along once or twice in a generation, a master boxer with a knockout punch, a poised technician who came into the ring with his hair plastered down and combed back with a part in the middle, in the approved style of the day, and whose boast was that no matter whom he fought, "I never even get my hair mussed!" After his hand was raised in victory, he would run his hand back over his sleek black hair, and my father, and Al Kaufman, and Al Lichtman, and the rest of the triumphant Jewish rooting section would roar in delight, as half a century later Ali's fans would raise the decibel level at the sight of the Ali Shuffle. To share in his invincibility. To see him climb into the ring sporting the six-pointed Jewish star on his fighting trunks was to anticipate sweet revenge for all the bloody noses, split lips, and mocking laughter at pale little Jewish boys who had run the neighborhood gauntlet.

One of my old man's pals practically cornered the market on the early motion-picture insurance business. But all through his life he would be singled out as the unique amateur boxer who not only had sparred with Benny Leonard but had actually knocked Great Benny down! Every time Artie Stebbins came to our house, my father prefaced his arrival by describing that historic event. Artie Stebbins had a slightly flattened nose and looked like a fighter. He would have gone on to a brilliant professional career—B.P. had convinced himself—except for an unfortunate accident in which his opponent had died in the ring. No matter how modestly he dismissed the legendary knockdown of Benny Leonard—"I think Benny slipped..." or "I just happened to tag him right"—that knockdown remained with him as a badge of honor. My father would say with a note of awe, "He might have been another Benny Leonard!"

But when I was going on seven, there was only one Benny Leonard; my scrapbook fattened on his victories. In those days fighters fought three or four times in a single month. Benny had been an undernourished fifteen-year-old when he first climbed into the professional ring, getting himself knocked out by one Mickey Finnegan in three rounds. A year later he was knocked out again by the veteran Joe Shugrue. But from the time he reached the seasoned age of eighteen, he had gone on to win more than 150 fights, in an era in which the lightweight division was known for its class. The Great Benny Leonard had gone to the post twenty-six times in 1919 alone, and almost every one of his opponents was a name known to the *cognoscenti*. As for me, I had only one ambition, to become a world champion like The Great Benny Leonard. Or rather, two ambitions, for the second was to see The Great Benny in action.

When I asked my father if he could take me to the Joe Welling fight, he said he thought I was a little young to stay up so late. Instead he promised to tell me all about it when he came home. That night I waited for Father to bring news of the victory. In what round had our Star of the Ghetto vanquished the dangerous Joe Welling? How I wished I were in Madison Square Garden—old enough to smoke big cigars and go to the fights like my father!

I have no idea what time Daddy got home that night. Probably three or four in the morning. Where had he gone with his pals after the fight? The Screen Club? The Astor? "21"? A dozen other speaks? The apartment of a friendly young extra girl who hoped to become a Preferred feature player? When my father finally gave me the blow-by-blow next evening, he admitted that our hero had underestimated Welling's appetite for punishment. B.P. and the rest of the young Jewish fancy had bet that Welling would fall in ten, as Leonard had predicted. But Welling was nobody's pushover, and he had even fought the referee who finally stopped the fight. B.P. was out five hundred smackers. He and his pals had gone back to the dressing room to see the triumphant Benny, and the fistic Star of David, still proud of his hair-comb, apologized for leading his rooters astray. B.P. told Benny about my scrapbook, and the Great B.L. promised to autograph it for me. Then the boys went out on the town to celebrate Jewish power.

When Father told me about the Joe Welling fight and helped me paste the clippings into my bulging scrapbook, I begged him to take me with him to the next Great Benny Leonard fight. "When you're a little older," he promised.

In the early weeks of 1921, he brought me the news. Great Benny had just signed to defend his title against Richie Mitchell in the Garden! Now Richie Mitchell was no ordinary contender. He was a better boxer than Joe Welling, and a harder puncher. He was three inches taller than Benny Leonard, in the prime of his youth, strength, and ability at twenty-five, and had more than held his own against all the good ones and some of the great ones: Wolgast, Kilbane, Tendler, Dundee, Charlie White, Joe Rivers.... Only once in his impressive nine-year career had Richie Mitchell been knocked out. The Great Benny Leonard had turned the trick when I was three years old. My old man had taken the train to Milwaukee to see it, and had come back flushed with victory and victory's rewards.

Now it was time for the rematch, and Richie Mitchell had come to New York confident of reversing the only loss on his record. The day of the fight I boasted to my classmates, "I'm g-g-going to M-M-Madison Square Garden tonight t-to s-see the G-G-Great B-B-Benny Leonard!" Even if they had been able to understand me, I don't think the other kids would have known what I was talking about. When it came to boxing they were illiterates. They simply had no idea that the Rematch between the Great Benny Leonard and the Number One Contender Richie Mitchell was more of an earth-shaker than the election of a new president, the arrival of Prohibition, or the publication of *This Side of Paradise*.

When the moment arrived, Mother helped me dress for my mid-January adventure. I was wearing long white stockings and a blue velvet suit with fur-lined coat and hat. All that was lacking was one of my father's big Cuban cigars. But it didn't matter. I would smoke it vicariously as I sat beside him in the front ringside seats near our idol's corner that B.P. always got from the Great Benny Leonard.

"Well, Buddy," my father said as we got out of the cab near the crowded entrance to the Garden, "I kept my promise. Your mother thought you were still too young. I wanted you to see the Great Benny Leonard in his prime. It's something you'll remember the rest of your life."

There were thousands and thousands of big people, a lot of them wearing derbies, a lot of them puffing on big cigars, a lot of them red-faced from winter wind and the forbidden but ever plentiful alcohol, bellying and elbowing their way toward the entrance to the Garden.

As we reached the turnstile, my father urged me ahead of him and held out a pair of tickets. A giant of a guard in uniform glanced at him, then looked in vain for the holder of the other ticket. When he saw where Father was pointing, his voice came down to me in a terrible pronouncement: "What are ya, nuts or somethin'? You can't take that little kid in here; ya gotta be sixteen years old!"

My father argued. He bargained and bribed. But in a city known for its Jimmy Walker–like corruption, we had come upon that rare bird, an honest guardian of the law.

By this time Father was telling me to For Christ sake, stop crying! He was frantic. The preliminaries had already started, and in those days before television and radio, there were no extra bouts standing by to hold the audience until the preannounced time for the star bout. If there were early knockouts in the prelims, B.P. ran the risk of missing The Great Benny. And we were all the way down on East 23rd Street, miles from home on Riverside Drive near 100th Street. If traffic was heavy he might miss the event of a lifetime. But there was nothing for it but to hail a cab, tell the cabbie to speed across town and up the West Side, wait for him to dispose of his sobbing and expendable baggage, and race back to the Garden. Delivered to my mother, awash with tears, I stammered out my tale of injustice. I would have to wait ten long years to be admitted to the Garden, and by that time our champion would be retired from the ring. Now I would never see him, I cried, never in my whole life!

Mother tried everything in her repertoire of child psychology to console me. But it was too late. For me life simply had come to an end at that turnstile into Madison Square Garden.

To ease the tragedy, I was allowed to wait up until Father came home. And this time, sensitive to the crisis, he did not linger with his cronies over highballs at a friendly speakeasy. He came directly from the Garden, his fine white skin flushed with the excitement of what had happened.

B.P. had given the taxi driver an extra five-spot to disregard the speed limits and get him back to the Garden on a magic carpet. As he rushed through the turnstile and looked for the aisle to his seat, he heard a roar from the crowd that was like the howl of a jungle full of wild beasts. Everybody was standing up and screaming, blocking his view. A frantic glance at the second clock told him it was the middle of round three. When he got closer to his seat and was able to see the ring, the spectacle that presented itself was the Unthinkable. There on the canvas was The Great Benny Leonard. And not only was his hair mussed, his eyes were dimmed as he tried to shake his head back to consciousness. The count went on, "Six... seven...eight..." Thousands of young Jews like my father were shouting "Get up! Get up, Benny! Get up!" And another multitude of Irish and anti-Semitic rooters for Mitchell, "You got 'im, Richie! You got that little mockie sonuvabitch!" But just before the count of 10 The Great Benny Leonard managed to stagger to his feet.

No, I wasn't there, but my father had caught the

lightning in a bottle and had brought it home for me. I sat there watching the fight as clearly as if home television had been installed thirty years ahead of time. Our Benny was on his feet but the quick brain that usually directed the series of rapid jabs and classic right crosses was full of cobwebs. Billy Mitchell was leaning through the ropes and cupping his old fighter's hands to urge his son to "move in, move in Richie, finish 'im!" And Richie was trying, oh how he was trying, only a split second from being Lightweight Champion of the World, one more left hook, one more punishing right hand.... But Benny covered up, rolled with punches, slipped a haymaker by an instinctive fraction of an inch, and managed to survive until the bell brought Leonard's handlers into the ring with smelling salts, ice, and the other traditional restoratives.

In the next round Richie Mitchell sprang from his corner full of fight, running across the ring to keep the pressure on Leonard and land his bruising combinations while he still held the upper hand. Everybody in the Garden was on his feet. Everybody was screaming. There had never been such a fight in all of Father's ringside nights, all the way back to 1912 when he had first started going to the fights with Adolph Zukor and the Famous Players crowd. Benny was retreating, boxing cautiously, gradually beginning to focus on Mitchell's combative eyes. "On his bicycle," they called it, dodging and running and slipping off the ropes, using all the defensive tactics he had learned in his street fights on the Lower East Side and in those 150 battles inside the ropes. And as he retreated he was talking to Mitchell (shades of Ali half a century later!), "Is that the best you can do? I thought you hit harder than that? Look, I'll put my hands down, what do you wanna bet you can't hit me? Come on, if you think you've got me hurt, why don't you fight? You look awful slow to me, Richie, looks like you're getting tired..."

That round had been more of a debate than a boxing match, with Benny winning the verbal battle and Richie swinging wildly and futilely as he tried to chop Benny down. At the end of the round the ferocious Richie Mitchell did look tired and a little discouraged. The drumfire of backtalk from Leonard had disconcerted him. He had let Benny get his goat, exactly what the champion wanted. Some remorseless clock in his head was telling him that he was blowing the chance of a lifetime. In the

next round Benny was The Great Benny again. His head clearing, his body weathering the storm, he was ready to take charge. Back on his toes, he was beginning to move around the slower Mitchell, keeping him off balance with jabs and rocking his head back with that straight right hand. Near the end of the round Mitchell went to his knees.

How many times Father refought Round 6 for me over the years. Benny Leonard's hair was combed straight back again. There was no more talking to distract the near-victorious opponent. Benny was all business. Lefts and rights found Mitchell's now unprotected face. Both eyes were cut and blood dripped from his nose. Caught in a buzzsaw of fast hard punches that seemed to tear his face apart, the brave Irish brawler went down. But he took his count and rose again to face more of the same. Now it was not boxing but slaughterhouse seven and the more humane among the crowd, including the Benny Leonard fans who had bet a bundle it would be over in eight, were imploring the referee to "Stop it! Stop it!" For Mitchell was down again, and he seemed to be looking directly into his own corner, but there was so much blood running down into his eyes that he was unseeing.

"I was watching his father, Billy Mitchell," my father told me. "I could see the whole thing being fought out in Billy Mitchell's face. He was holding a bloody towel, the towel with which he had just wiped the face of his son. His own blood was on that towel. His son Richie got up again. God almighty he was game. He would look at Benny as if to say, You're going to have to kill me to stop me. And Benny, he told us this a lot of times, he loved to win but he doesn't like to punish them once he knows he has them licked. He was hoping the referee would stop the fight. But the ref waved him on. Maybe he was betting on Mitchell. Maybe he figured anyone with the punch of a Richie Mitchell deserved that one extra round to see if he could land a lucky or a desperate punch. Now it seemed as if the entire Garden was chanting together 'Stop it! Stop it! For God's sake, STOP IT!' And then as the slaughter went on, as The Great Benny Leonard went on ripping Richie Mitchell's face to bloody shreds, finally Billy Mitchell, that tough Mick, couldn't stand it any longer. He raised the bloody towel and tossed it over the top rope into the ring. And then, while Richie's kid brother Pinkey and another handler climbed into the ring to revive their battered contender, Pop Mitchell lowered his head into his arms on the apron of the ring and cried like a baby."

In the early twenties, Benny Leonard was enjoying the sweet fruits of summer, his harvest season of success. On the New Year's Eve of bountiful 1925 he had saved enough money to announce his retirement as undefeated lightweight champion of the world. Still only twenty-nine, he could look forward to a life of ease as a coupon clipper who could keep one eye on his investments and the other on his physical fitness as he played golf and handball and traveled south for the winter. He was enjoying the autumn of his life, but winter set in prematurely with the Crash of 1929. Leonard saw his ring savings shrink, dwindle, and finally disappear.

In 1931, at the age of thirty-five, he announced his comeback to the ring. After beating a string of nobodies he was matched with Jimmy McLarnin. Back home in Los Angeles I had watched "Baby Face" Jimmy fight his way to the top of his profession, from bantamweight to welter, against top fighters like Fidel LaBarba, Bud Taylor, and Joey Sangor. He seemed to specialize in destroying illustrious Jewish lightweights: Jackie Fields, Sid Terris, Al Singer, Ruby Goldstein....

From Dartmouth College, where I was then a freshman, I phoned my father in Hollywood for an extra fifty dollars to go to New York to see The Great Benny Leonard, at last, against our hometown sensation, the still baby-faced twenty-four-year-old hailed by Western sportswriters as a coming champion. With excitement building in me as on the day of the Leonard-Mitchell debacle, I promised to phone B.P. at the studio after the fight.

But when I got back to my hotel from that chill October fight night I didn't have the heart to place the call. I felt like getting in my Chevy and driving the long winding miles back to New Hampshire. The Great Benny Leonard, when I finally caught up with him ten years too late, was a rather paunchy over-the-hill lightweight with thinning hair, a tentative jab, and uncertain footwork, no match for the fast, young and lethal Jimmy McLarnin who toyed with him before knocking him out in six of the saddest rounds I ever saw.

Our Great Benny Leonard never should have been in there with a gifted young champion like Jimmy McLarnin. In the fall of '32 old Benny was the Ghost of Chanukah Past. Fifteen years later, after serving as a lieutenant commander supervising boxing in the navy, Benny Leonard would be in the ring refereeing a fight in the wonderfully decrepit St. Nicholas Arena when he received a knockout blow more deadly than anything Richie Mitchell or Jimmy McLarnin could inflict. Felled by a heart attack, he died there in the ring he had dominated throughout my childhood. To this day I can still hear that guardian of the turnstiles who stopped me from seeing The Great Benny Leonard in his glory years.

FROM: CASHEL BYRON'S PROFESSION

This is chapter IX of *Cashel Byron's Profession,* the fourth of Shaw's five unsuccessful novels, and written when he was twenty-six years old. He acquired what knowledge he had of the prize ring by attending a few fights and, as he put it, "wading through *Boxiana* and the files of *Bell's Life* at the British Museum." As is evident in the words of his hero, here pleading his case before his beloved, Shaw was less intrigued by boxing than by the hypocrisy of a society that looked down upon it.

GEORGE BERNARD SHAW

Cashel's pupils sometimes requested him to hit them hard—not to play with them—to accustom them to regular, right-down severe hitting, and no nonsense. He only pretended to comply; for he knew that a black eye or loosened tooth would be immoderately boasted of if received in combat with a famous pugilist, and that the sufferer's friends would make private notes to avoid so rough a professor. But when Miss Carew's note reached him, he made an exception to his practice in this respect. A young guardsman, whose lesson began shortly after the post arrived, remarked that Cashel was unusually distrait, and exhorted him to wake up and pitch in in earnest. Instantly a blow in the epigastrium stretched him almost insensible on the floor. His complexion was considerably whitened when he was set on his legs again; and he presently alleged an urgent appointment and withdrew, declaring in a shaky voice that that was the sort of bout he really enjoyed.

When he was gone, Cashel walked distractedly to and fro, cursing, and occasionally stopping to read the letter. His restlessness only increased his agitation. The arrival of a Frenchman whom he employed to give lessons in fencing made the place unendurable to him. He changed his attire, went out, called a cab, and bade the driver, with an oath, drive to Lydia's house as fast as the horse could go. The man made all the haste he could, and was presently told impatiently that there was no hurry. Accustomed to this sort of inconsistency, he was not surprised when, as they approached the house, he was told not to stop, but to drive slowly past. Then, in obedience to further instructions, he turned and repassed the door.

As he did so, a lady appeared for an instant at a window. Immediately his fare, with a groan of mingled rage and fear, sprang from the moving vehicle, rushed up the steps of the mansion, and rang the bell violently. Bashville, faultlessly dressed and impassibly mannered, opened the door. In reply to Cashel's half-inarticulate inquiry, he said, "Miss Carew is not at home."

"You lie," said Cashel, his eyes suddenly dilating. "I saw her."

Bashville reddened, but replied coolly, "Miss Carew cannot see you today."

"Go and ask her," returned Cashel sternly, advancing.

Bashville, with compressed lips, seized the door to shut him out; but Cashel forced it back against him and went in, shutting the door behind him. He turned from Bashville for a moment to do this; and before he could face him again he was tripped and flung down upon the tessellated pavement of the hall. When Bashville was given the lie, and pushed back behind the door, the excitement he had been suppressing since his visit to Lucian exploded. He had thrown Cashel in Cornish fashion, and now desperately awaited the upshot.

Cashel got up so rapidly that he seemed to rebound from the flags. Bashville, involuntarily cowering before his onslaught, just escaped his right fist, and felt as though his heart had been drawn with it as it whizzed past his ear. He turned and fled frantically upstairs.

Lydia was in her boudoir with Alice when Bashville darted in and locked the door. Alice rose and screamed. Lydia, though startled, and that less by the unusual action than by the change in a familiar face which she had never seen influenced by emotion before, sat still, and quietly asked what was the matter. Bashville checked himself for a moment. Then he spoke unintelligibly, and went to the window, which he opened. Lydia divined that he was about to call for help to the street.

"Bashville," she said authoritatively, "be silent; and close the window. I will go downstairs myself."

Bashville then ran to prevent her from unlocking the door; but she paid no attention to him. He did not dare to oppose her forcibly. He was beginning to recover from his panic, and to feel the first stings of shame for having yielded to it.

"Madam," he said, "Byron is below; and he insists on seeing you. He's dangerous; and he's too strong for me. I have done my best; on my honor I have. Let me call the police. Stop," he added, as she opened the door. "If either of us goes, it must be me."

"I will see him in the library," said Lydia composedly. "Tell him so; and let him wait there for me—if you can speak to him without running any risk."

"Oh pray let him call the police," urged Alice. "Don't attempt to go to that man."

"Nonsense!" said Lydia good-humoredly. "I am not in the least afraid. We must not fail in courage when we have a prize fighter to deal with."

Bashville, white, and with difficulty preventing his knees from knocking together, but not faltering for a second, went devotedly downstairs and found Cashel leaning upon the balustrade, panting, and looking perplexedly about him as he wiped his dabbled brow. Bashville halted on the third stair, and said, "Miss Carew will see you in the library. Come this way, please."

Cashel's lips moved but no sound came from them: he followed Bashville in silence. When they entered the library, Lydia was already there. Bashville withdrew without a word. Then Cashel sat down and, to her consternation, bent his head on his hand and yielded to a hysterical convulsion. Before she could resolve how to act, he looked up at her with his face distorted and discolored, and tried to speak.

"Please don't cry," said Lydia. "I am told that you wish to speak to me."

"I don't wish to speak to you ever again," said Cashel hoarsely. "You told your servant to throw me down the steps. That's enough for me."

Lydia caught from him the tendency to sob which he was struggling with; but she repressed it,

and answered firmly, "If my servant has been guilty of the least incivility to you, Mr. Cashel Byron, he has exceeded his orders."

"It doesn't matter," said Cashel. "He may thank his luck that he has his head on. But *he* doesn't matter. Hold on a bit—I can't talk—I shall get—second wind—and then——" Cashel raised his head with a curiously businesslike expression; threw himself supinely against the back of his chair; and in that position deliberately rested until he could trust himself to speak. At last he pulled himself together, and said, "Why are you going to give me up?"

Lydia ranged her wits in battle array, and replied, "Do you remember our talk at Mrs. Hoskyn's?"

"Yes."

"You admitted then that if the nature of your occupation became known to me, our acquaintance should cease."

"That was all very fine to excuse my not telling you. But I find, like many another man when put to the proof, that I didn't mean it. Who told you I was a fighting man?"

"I had rather not tell you that."

"Aha!" said Cashel, with a triumph that was half choked by the remnant of his hysteria. "Who is trying to make a secret now, I should like to know?"

"I do so in this instance because I am afraid to expose a friend to your resentment."

"And why? He's a man, of course: else you wouldn't be afraid. You think that I'd go straight off and murder him. Perhaps he told you that it would come quite natural to a man like me a ruffian like me—to smash him up. That comes of being a coward. People run my profession down, not because there is a bad one or two in it—there's plenty of bad bishops, if you come to that—but because they're afraid of us. You may make yourself easy about your friend. I am accustomed to get well paid for the beatings I give; and your own common sense ought to tell you that any one who is used to being paid for a job is just the last person in the world to do it for nothing."

"I find the contrary to be the case with first-rate artists," said Lydia.

"Thank you," retorted Cashel sarcastically. "I ought to make you a bow for that."

"But," said Lydia seriously, "it seems to me that your art is wholly antisocial and retrograde. And I fear that you have forced this interview on me to no purpose."

"I don't know whether it's antisocial or not. But I think it hard that I should be put out of decent society when fellows that do far worse than I are let in. Who did I see here last Friday, the most honored of your guests? Why, that Frenchman with the gold spectacles. What do you think I was told when I asked what *his* little game was? Baking dogs in ovens to see how long a dog could live red hot! I'd like to catch him doing it to a dog of mine. Aye; and sticking a rat full of nails to see whether pain makes a rat sweat. Why, it's just sickening. Do you think I'd have shaken hands with that chap? If he hadn't been a friend of yours, I'd have taught him how to make a Frenchman sweat without sticking any nails into him. And *he's* to be received and made much of, while I am kicked out! Look at your relation the general, too! What is he but a fighting man, I should like to know? Isn't it his pride and boast that as long as he is paid so much a day, he'll ask no questions whether a war is fair or unfair, but just walk out and put thousands of men in the best way to kill and be killed—keeping well behind them himself all the time, mind you. Last year he was up to his chin in the blood of a lot of poor blacks that were no more a match for his armed men than a featherweight would be for me. Bad as I am, I wouldn't attack a featherweight, or stand by and see another heavy man do it. Plenty of your friends go pigeon shooting to Hurlingham. *There's* a humane and manly way of spending a Saturday afternoon! Lord Worthington, that comes to see you when he likes, though he's too much of a man or too little of a shot to kill pigeons, thinks nothing of fox hunting. Do you think foxes like to be hunted, or that the people that hunt them have such fine feelings that they can afford to call prize fighters names? Look at the men that get killed or lamed every year at steeplechasing, fox hunting, cricket, and football! Dozens of them! Look at the thousands killed in battle! Did you ever hear of any one being killed in the ring? Why, from first to last, during the whole century that my sort of fighting has been going on, there's not been six fatal accidents at really respectable fights. It's safer than dancing: many a woman has danced her skirt into the fire and been burnt. I once fought a man who had spoiled his constitution with bad living; and he exhausted himself so by going on and on long after he was beaten that he died of it, and nearly finished me, too. If you'd heard the fuss that even the old hands made over it, you'd have thought a blessed baby had died from falling out of its cradle. A good milling does a man more good than harm. And if all these damned dog bakers, and soldiers, and pigeon shooters, fox hunters, and the rest of them, are made welcome here, why am I shut out like a brute beast?"

"Truly I do not know," said Lydia, puzzled, "unless it be that your profession is not usually recruited from our ranks."

"I grant you that boxers aren't gentlemen, as a rule. No more were painters or poets, once upon a time. But what I want to know is this. Supposing a boxer has as good manners as your friends, and is as well born, why shouldn't he mix with them and be considered their equal?"

"The distinction seems arbitrary, I confess. But perhaps the true remedy would be to exclude the vivisectors and soldiers, instead of admitting the prize fighters. Mr. Cashel Byron," added Lydia, changing her manner, "I cannot discuss this with you. Society has a prejudice against you. I share it; and I cannot overcome it. Can you find no nobler occupation than these fierce and horrible encounters by which you condescend to gain a living?"

"No," said Cashel flatly. "I can't. That's just where it is."

Lydia looked grave, and said nothing.

"You don't see it?" said Cashel. "Well, I'll just tell you all about myself, and then leave you to judge. May I sit down while I talk?" He had risen in the course of his remarks on Lydia's scientific and military acquaintances.

She pointed to a chair near her. Something in the action brought color to his cheeks.

"I believe I was the most unfortunate devil of a boy that ever walked," he began. "My mother was—and is—an actress, and a tiptop crack in her profession. One of the first things I remember is sitting on the floor in the corner of a room where there was a big glass, and she flaring away before it, attitudinizing and spouting Shakespeare like mad. I was afraid of her, because she was very particular about my manners and appearance, and would never let me go near a theater. I know nothing about my people or hers; for she boxed my ears one day for asking who my father was, and I took good care not to ask her again. She was quite young when I was a child: at first I thought her a sort of angel. I should have been fond of her, I think, if she had let me. But she didn't, somehow; and I had to keep my affection for the servants. I had plenty of variety in that way; for she gave her whole establishment the sack about once every two months, except a maid that used to bully her and give me nearly all the nursing I ever got. I believe it was my crying about some housemaid or other who went away that first set her abusing me for having low tastes—a sort of thing that used to cut me to the heart, and which she kept up till the very day I left her for good. We were a precious pair: I sulky and obstinate; she changeable and hot-tempered. She used to begin breakfast sometimes by knocking me to the other side of the room with a slap, and finish it by calling me her darling boy and promising me all manner of toys and things. I soon gave up trying to please her or like her, and became as disagreeable a young imp as you'd ask to see. My only thought was to get all I could out of her when she was in a good humor, and to be sullen and stubborn when she was in a tantrum. One day a boy in the street threw some mud at me, and I ran in crying, and complained to her. She told me I was a little coward. I haven't forgiven her for that yet—perhaps because it was one of the few true things she ever said to me. I was in a state of perpetual aggravation; and I often wonder I wasn't soured for life at that time. At last I got to be such a little fiend that when she hit me I used to guard off her blows, and look so wicked that I think she got afraid of me. Then she put me to school, telling me I had no heart, and telling the master I was an ungovernable young brute. So I, like a little fool, cried at leaving her; and she, like a big one, cried back again over me—just after telling the master what a bad one I was, mind you—and off she went, leaving her darling boy and blessed child howling at his good luck in getting rid of her.

"I was a nice boy to let loose in a school. I could speak as well as an actor, as far as pronunciation goes; but I could hardly read words of one syllable; and as to writing, I couldn't make pothooks and hangers respectably. To this day, I can no more spell than old Ned Skene can. What was a worse sort of ignorance was that I had no idea of fair play. I thought that all servants would be afraid of me; and that all grown-up people would tyrannize over me. I was afraid of everybody; afraid that my cowardice would be found out; and as angry and cruel in my ill-tempers as cowards always are. Now you'll hardly believe this; but what saved me from going to the bad altogether was my finding out that I was a good one to fight. The bigger boys were like grown-up people in respect of liking to see other people fight; and they used to set us young ones at it, whether we liked it or not, regularly every Saturday afternoon,

with seconds, bottle-holders, and everything complete, except the ropes. At first, when they made me fight, I shut my eyes and cried; but for all that I managed to catch the other fellow tight round the waist and throw him. After that, it became a regular joke to make me fight; for I always cried. But the end of it was that I learned to keep my eyes open and hit straight. I had no trouble about fighting then. Somehow, I could tell by instinct when the other fellow was going to hit me; and I always hit him first. It's the same with me now in the ring: I know what a man is going to do before he rightly knows himself. The power this gave me, civilized me. In the end it made me cock of the school; and, as cock, I couldn't be mean or childish. There would be nothing like fighting for licking boys into shape if every one could be cock; but every one can't; so I suppose it does more harm than good.

"I should have enjoyed school well enough if I had worked at my books. But I wouldn't study; and the masters were all down on me as an idler, though I shouldn't have been like that if they had known how to teach: I have learned since what teaching is. As to the holidays, they were the worst part of the year to me. When I was left at the school I was savage at not being let go home; and when I went home, my mother did nothing but find fault with my schoolboy manners. I was getting too big to be cuddled as her darling boy, you understand. Her treatment of me was just the old game with the affectionate part left out. It wasn't pleasant, after being cock of the school, to be made to feel like a good-for-nothing little brat tied to her apron strings. When she saw that I was learning nothing, she sent me to another school at a place in the north called Panley. I stayed there until I was seventeen; and then she came one day, and we had a row, as usual. She said she wouldn't let me leave school until I was nineteen; and so I settled that question by running away the same night. I got to Liverpool where I hid in a ship bound for Australia. When I was starved out, they treated me better than I expected; and I worked hard enough to earn my passage and my victuals. But when I was left ashore in Melbourne, I was in a pretty pickle. I knew nobody, and I had no money. Everything that a man could live by was owned by someone or other. I walked through the town looking for a place where they might want a boy to run errands or to clean the windows. But I hadn't the cheek to go into the shops and ask. Two or three times, when I was on the point of trying, I caught sight of some cad of a shopman, and made up my mind that I wouldn't be ordered about by *him*, and that since I had the whole town to choose from I might as well go on to the next place. At last, quite late in the afternoon, I saw an advertisement stuck up on a gymnasium; and while I was reading it I got talking to old Ned Skene, the owner, who was smoking at the door. He took a fancy to me, and offered to have me there as a sort of lad-of-all-work. I was only too glad to get the chance; and I closed with him at once. As time went on, I became so clever with the gloves that Ned matched me against a lightweight named Ducket, and bet a lot of money that I would win. Well, I couldn't disappoint him after his being so kind to me—Mrs. Skene had made as much of me as if I were her own son. What could I do but take my bread as it came to me? I was fit for nothing else. Even if I had been able to write a good hand and keep accounts, I couldn't have brought myself to think that quill-driving and counting other people's money was fit employment for a man. It's not what a man would like to do that he must do in this world: it's what he *can* do; and the only mortal thing I could do properly was to fight. There was plenty of money and plenty of honor and glory to be got among my acquaintance by fighting. So I challenged Ducket, and knocked him all to pieces in ten minutes. I half killed him, because I didn't know my own strength and was afraid of him. I have been at the same work ever since; for I never was offered any other sort of job. I was training for a fight when I was down at Wiltstoken with that old fool Mellish. It came off the day you saw me at Clapham when I had such a bad eye. Wiltstoken did for me. With all my fighting, I'm no better than a baby at heart; and ever since I found out that my mother wasn't an angel, I have always had the notion that a real angel would turn up some day. You see, I never cared much about women. Bad as my mother was as far as being what you might call a parent went, she had something in her looks and manners that gave me a better idea of what a nice woman was like than I had of most things; and the girls I met in Australia and America seemed very small potatoes to me in comparison with her. Besides, of course, they were not ladies. I was fond of Mrs. Skene because she was good to me; and I made myself agreeable, for her sake, to the girls that came to see her; but in reality I couldn't stand them. Mrs. Skene said they were all setting their caps at me—women are death on a crack fighter—but the

more they tried it on the less I liked them. It was no go: I could get on with the men well enough, no matter how common they were; but the snobbishness of my breed came out with regard to the women. When I saw you that day at Wiltstoken walk out of the trees and stand looking so quietly at me and Mellish, and then go back out of sight without a word, I'm blessed if I didn't think you were the angel come at last. Then I met you at the railway station and walked with you. You put the angel out of my head quick enough; for an angel, after all, is only a shadowy, childish notion—I believe it's all gammon about there being any in heaven—but you gave me a better idea than Mamma of what a woman should be, and you came up to that idea and went beyond it. I have been in love with you ever since; and if I can't have you, I don't care what becomes of me. I know I am a bad lot, and have always been one; but when I saw you taking pleasure in the society of fellows just as bad as myself, I didn't see why I should keep away when I was dying to come. I am no worse than the dog baker, anyhow. And hang it, Miss Lydia, I don't want to brag; but there are clean ways and dirty ways in prize fighting the same as in anything else; and I have tried my best to keep in the clean ways. I never fought a cross or struck a foul blow in my life; and I have never been beaten, though I'm only a middleweight, and have stood up with the best fourteen-stone men in the Colonies, the States, or in England."

Cashel ceased. As he sat eyeing her wistfully, Lydia, who had been perfectly still, said bemusedly, "I was more prejudiced than I knew. What will you think of me when I tell you that your profession does not seem half so shocking now that I know you to be the son of an artist, and not a journeyman butcher or a laborer, as my cousin told me."

"What!" exclaimed Cashel. "That lanternjawed fellow told you I was a butcher!"

"I did not mean to betray him; but, as I have already said, I am bad at keeping secrets. Mr. Lucian Webber is my cousin and friend, and has done me many services. May I rest assured that he has nothing to fear from you?"

"He has no right to tell lies about me. He is sweet on you too: I twigged that at Wiltstoken. I have a good mind to let him know whether I am a butcher or not."

"He did not say so. What he told me of you, as far as it went, is exactly confirmed by what you have said yourself. I happened to ask him to what class men of your calling usually belonged; and he said that they were laborers, butchers, and so forth. Do you resent that?"

"I see plainly enough that you won't let me resent it. I should like to know what else he said of me. But he was right enough. There are all sorts of blackguards in the ring: there's no use denying it. Since it's been made illegal, decent men won't go into it. All the same, it's not the fighting men, but the betting men, that bring discredit on it. I wish your cousin had held his confounded tongue."

"I wish you had forestalled him by telling me the truth."

"I wish I had, now. But what's the use of wishing? I didn't dare run the chance of losing you. See how soon you forbade me the house when you did find out."

"It made little difference," said Lydia gravely.

"You were always friendly to me," said Cashel plaintively.

"More so than you were to me. You should not have deceived me. And now I think we had better part. I am glad to know your history; and I admit that you made perhaps the best choice that society offered you. I do not blame you.

"But you give me the sack. Is that it?"

"What do you propose, Mr. Cashel Byron? Is it to visit my house in the intervals of battering and maiming butchers and laborers?"

"No, it's not," retorted Cashel. "You're very aggravating. I won't stay much longer in the ring now: my luck is too good to last. Anyhow, I shall have to retire soon, luck or no luck, because no one can match me. Even now there's nobody except Bill Paradise that pretends to be able for me; and I'll settle him in September if he really means business. After that, I'll retire. I expect to be worth ten thousand pounds then. Ten thousand pounds, I'm told, is the same as five hundred a year. Well, I suppose, judging from the style you keep here, that you're worth as much more, besides your place in the country; so if you will marry me we shall have a thousand a year between us. I don't know much of money matters; but at any rate we can live like fighting cocks on that much. That's a straight and businesslike proposal, isn't it?"

"And if I refuse?" said Lydia, with some sternness.

"Then you may have the ten thousand pounds to do what you like with," said Cashel despairingly. "It won't matter what becomes of me. I won't go to the devil for you or any woman if I can help it; and I— but where's the good of saying if you refuse? I know I don't express myself properly: I'm a bad hand at sentimentality; but if I had as much gab as any of those long-haired fellows on Friday, I couldn't be any fonder of you, or think more highly of you."

"But you are mistaken as to the amount of my income."

"That doesn't matter a bit. If you have more, why, the more the merrier. If you have less, or if you have to give up all your property when you're married, I will soon make another ten thousand to supply the loss. Only give me one good word, and, by George, I'll fight the seven champions of Christendom, one down and t'other come on, for five thousand a side each. Hang the money!"

"I am richer than you suppose," said Lydia, unmoved. "I cannot tell you exactly how much I possess; but my income is about forty thousand pounds."

"Forty thousand pounds!" ejaculated Cashel. "Holy Moses! I didn't think the Queen had as much as that."

For a moment he felt nothing but mere astonishment. Then, comprehending the situation, he became very red. In a voice broken by mortification, he said, "I see I have been making a fool of myself," and took his hat and turned to go.

"It does not follow that you should go at once without a word," said Lydia, betraying nervousness for the first time during the interview.

"Oh, that's all rot," said Cashel. "I may be a fool while my eyes are shut; but I'm sensible enough when they're open. I have no business here. I wish to the Lord I had stayed in Australia."

"Perhaps it would have been better," said Lydia, troubled. "But since we have met, it is useless to deplore it; and—Let me remind you of one thing. You have pointed out to me that I have made friends of men whose pursuits are no better than yours. I do not wholly admit this; but there is one respect in which they are on the same footing with you. They are all, as far as worldly gear is concerned, much poorer than I. Most of them, I fear, are poorer—much, *much* poorer than you are."

Cashel looked up quickly with returning hope; but it lasted only a moment. He shook his head dejectedly.

"I am at least grateful to you," she continued, "because you have sought me for my own sake, knowing nothing of my wealth."

"I should think not," groaned Cashel. "Your wealth may be a very fine thing for the other fellows; and I'm glad you have it, for your own sake. But it's a settler for me. So goodbye."

"Goodbye," said Lydia, almost as pale as he

had now become, "since you will have it so."

"Since the devil will have it so," said Cashel ruefully. "It's no use wishing to have it any other way. The luck is against me. I hope, Miss Carew, that you'll excuse me for making such an ass of myself. It's all my blessed innocence: I never was taught any better."

"I have no quarrel with you except on the old score of hiding the truth from me; and I forgive you that—as far as the evil of it affects *me*. As for your declaration of attachment to me personally, I have received many similar ones that have flattered me less. But there are certain scruples between us. You will not court a woman a hundredfold richer than yourself; and I will not entertain a prize fighter. My wealth frightens every man who is not a knave; and your profession frightens every woman who is not a fury."

"Then you—Just tell me this," said Cashel eagerly. "Suppose I were a rich swell, and were not a—"

"No," said Lydia, peremptorily interrupting him. "I will suppose nothing but what is."

Cashel relapsed into melancholy. "If you only hadn't been kind to me!" he said. "I think the reason I love you so much is that you're the only person that is not afraid of me. Other people are civil because they daren't be otherwise to the cock of the ring. It's a lonely thing to be a champion. You knew nothing about that; and you knew I was afraid of you; and yet you were as good as gold."

"It is also a lonely thing to be a very rich woman. People are afraid of my wealth, and of what they call my learning. We two have at least one experience in common. Now do me a great favor by going. We have nothing further to say."

"I'll go in two seconds. But I don't believe much in you being lonely. That's only fancy."

"Perhaps so. Most feelings of this kind are only fancies."

There was another pause. Then Cashel said, "I don't feel half so downhearted as I did a minute ago. Are you sure that you're not angry with me?"

"Quite sure. Pray let me say goodbye."

"And may I never see you again? Never at all?— world without end, amen?"

"Never as the famous prize fighter. But if a day should come when Mr. Cashel Byron will be something better worthy of his birth and nature, I will not forget an old friend. Are you satisfied now?"

Cashel's face began to glow, and the roots of his hair to tingle. "One thing more," he said. "If you meet me by chance in the street before that, will you give me a look? I don't ask for a regular bow, but just a look to keep me going?"

"I have no intention of cutting you," said Lydia gravely. "But do not place yourself purposely in my way."

"Honor bright, I won't. I'll content myself with walking through that street in Soho occasionally. Now I'm off: I know you're in a hurry to be rid of me. So goodb—Stop a bit, though. Perhaps when that time you spoke of comes, you'll be married."

"It is possible; but I am not likely to marry. How many more things have you to say, that you have no right to say?"

"Not one," said Cashel, with a laugh that rang through the house. "I never was happier in my life, though I'm crying inside all the time. I'll have a try for you yet. Goodbye. No," he added, turning from her proffered hand, "I daren't touch it: I should eat you afterwards." He made for the door, but turned on the threshold to say in a loud whisper: "Mind, I'm engaged to you. I don't say you're engaged to me; but it's an engagement on my side." And he ran out of the room.

In the hall was Bashville, pale and determined, waiting there to rush to the assistance of his mistress at her first summons. He had a poker concealed at hand. Having just heard a great laugh, and seeing Cashel come downstairs in high spirits, he stood stock still, not knowing what to think.

"Well, old chap," said Cashel boisterously, slapping him on the shoulder, "so you're alive yet. Is there anyone in the dining room?"

"No," said Bashville.

"There's a thick carpet there to fall soft on," said Cashel, pulling Bashville into the room. "Come along. Now shew me that little trick of yours again. Come! Don't be afraid: I won't hit you. Down with me. Take care you don't knock my head against the fire irons."

"But—"

"But be hanged. You were spry enough at it before. Come!"

Bashville, after a moment's hesitation, seized Cashel, who immediately became grave and attentive, and remained imperturbably so whilst Bashville expertly threw him. He sat thinking for a moment on the hearthrug before he arose. "I see," he said then, getting up. "Now do it again."

"But it makes such a row," remonstrated Bashville.

"Only once more. There'll be no row this time."

"Well, every man to his taste," said Bashville, complying. But instead of throwing his man, he found himself wedged into a collar formed by Cashel's arms, the least constriction of which would have strangled him. Cashel again roared with laughter as he released him.

"That's the way, ain't it?" he said. "You can't catch an old fox twice in the same trap. Do you know any more falls?"

"I do," said Bashville, "but I really can't show them to you here. I shall get into trouble on account of the noise."

"You come down to me whenever you have an evening out," said Cashel, handing him a card, "to that address, and show me what you know; and I'll see what I can do with you. There's the making of a man in you."

"You're very kind," said Bashville, pocketing the card with a grin.

"And now let me give you a word of advice that will be of use to you as long as you live," said Cashel impressively. "You did a damned silly thing today. You threw a man down—a fighting man—and then stood looking at him like a fool, waiting for him to get up and kill you. If ever you do that again, fall on him as heavily as you can the instant he's off his legs. Double your elbow well under you, and see that it gets into a soft place. If he grabs it and turns you, make play with the back of your hand. If he's altogether too big for you, put your knee on his throat as if by accident. But on no account stand and do nothing. It's flying in the face of Providence."

Cashel emphasized each of these counsels by an impressive tap of his forefinger on one of Bashville's buttons. In conclusion, he nodded, opened the house door, and walked away in buoyant spirits.

Lydia, standing near the library window, saw him go down the long front garden, and observed how his light, alert step, and a certain gamesome assurance of manner, marked him off from a genteelly promenading middle-aged gentleman, a trudging workman, and a vigorously striding youth passing without. The railings that separated him from them reminded her of the admirable and dangerous creatures passing and repassing behind iron bars in the park yonder. But she exulted, in her quiet manner, in the thought that, dangerous as he was, she had no fear of him. When his cabman had found him and taken him off, she went to a private drawer in her desk and took out her father's last letter. She sat for some time looking at it without unfolding it.

"It would be a strange thing, Father," she said, as if he were actually there to hear her, "if your paragon should end as the wife of an illiterate prize fighter. I felt a pang of despair when he replied to my forty thousand pounds a year with an unanswerable goodbye. And now he is engaged to me."

She locked up her father, as it were, in the drawer again, and rang the bell. Bashville appeared, somewhat perturbed.

"If Mr. Byron calls again, admit him if I am at home."

"Yes, madam."

"Thank you."

"Begging your pardon, madam, but may I ask has any complaint been made of me?"

"None." Bashville was reluctantly withdrawing when she added, "Mr. Byron gave me to understand that you tried to prevent his entrance by force. You exposed yourself to needless risk by doing so; and you may make a rule in future that when people are importunate, and will not go away when asked, they had better come in until you get special instructions from me. I am not finding fault: on the contrary, I approve of your determination to carry out your orders; but under exceptional circumstances you may use your own discretion."

"He shoved the door in my face; and I acted on the impulse of the moment, madam. I hope you will forgive the liberty I took in locking the door of the boudoir. He is older and heavier than I am, madam; and he has the advantage of being a professional. Else I should have stood my ground."

"I am quite satisfied," said Lydia a little coldly, as she left the room.

"How long you have been!" cried Alice, almost in hysterics, as Lydia entered. "Is he gone? What were those dreadful noises? *Is* anything the matter?"

"Dancing and late hours are the matter," said Lydia. "The season is proving too much for you, Alice."

"It is not the season; it is the man," said Alice, with a sob.

"Indeed? I have been in conversation with the man for more than half an hour; and Bashville has been in actual combat with him; yet we are not in hysterics. You have been sitting here at your ease, have you not?"

"I am not in hysterics," said Alice indignantly.

"So much the better," said Lydia gravely, placing her hand on the forehead of Alice, who subsided with a sniff.

THE NOSE

Red Smith, who passed away on January 15, 1982, five days after his last column appeared, was the most widely read and quoted sportswriter of all time. He was the Willie Pep of his profession—all solid skill and inventiveness and the master of the unexpected—and, when it had to be done, he could take his man out as cleanly as anyone writing. After all, Pep, not celebrated primarily as a puncher, had sixty-two KOs, and broke Sal Bartolo's jaw in three places.

Fritzie Zivic, handled here, had 232 fights, held the welterweight title and was the master of the unorthodox. Ray Robinson, who beat him twice, once said, "Fritzie Zivic taught me more than anybody. Why, he even taught me how you can make a man butt open his own eye."

RED SMITH

Pittsburgh, February 18, 1947—The most unretired man in North America went all retired again today, this time for beauty's sweet sake. Fritzie (the Nose) Zivic, fresh back from a fist fight in Mexico City—"I run second"—unbuttoned a plaid sports jacket, hooked a thumb into the pocket of a chamois waistcoat as casually as he ever thrust it into an adversary's eye, stretched suede-shod feet out beneath the luncheon table and pensively caressed the beak that looks like a mine cave-in.

"That's all," he said. "I'm through. That last fight was my last."

"How many retirements is this, Fritzie, not counting those suggested by boxing commissions?"

"Two. Yeah, that's right, only two of my own. Of course, the newspapers probably retired me about ten times."

He introduced Justo Fontaine, a stake performer in his expanding fight stable. He handed over a folder of matches labeled: "Send your boy to Fritzie Zivic's new boxing school."

He mentioned the surburban arena where he is proprietor, promoter, manager, second, ticket-taker, and janitor and where he once pleaded vainly for permission to substitute for one of his main-eventers. He displayed the photograph of a lovely child in a boxing pose inscribed: "Janis Zivic, paperweight, aged five, twenty-seven fights, twenty-seven KOs." He brought out a letter from Lew Burston advising that he could "pick up a couple grand" boxing "some local boy" in Puerto Rico.

Then he came through with the convincer. It was a letter from a Philadelphia plastic surgeon, who wrote: "I have often admired your skill at reshaping the noses of your unhappy opponents. You and I have directed our talents along parallel lines." The doctor offered to rebuild Fritzie's sway-backed prow for free, "just for the satisfaction it would give me."

"I talked to him on the phone," the Nose said. "'Doc,' I ast him, 'can you fix up a scar under my left eye?' A cinch, he says. 'One more question, Doc,' I ast him. 'Can you grow hair on my head?' He says, hell, I can be handsome without it. So I'm takin' no more punches on this schnoz. Fella named Perfecto Lopez give it to me in L.A. in 1933. He butt me and busted all the cartilages and I got a doctor out there—a doctor? A horse-doctor—and he took out too much cartilage, so in my next fight it caved in like this. I want a big one, big enough to wear a mustache under it."

"You'll be beautiful with a mustache behind the wheel of that Cadillac of yours."

"You remember that Cadillac? Ever since I was a kid, that's what I always wanted. Figured then I'd be a success. So the day I'm fighting Henry Armstrong for the title in New York, I go and look at the biggest Cadillac I can find.

"That night Henry's givin' it to me pretty good and I can see that Cadillac rollin' farther and farther away from me. Henry's givin' me the elbows and the shoulders and the top of the head, and I can give that stuff back pretty good, but I don't dare to or maybe they'll throw me out of the ring.

"Well, in the seventh round I give him the head

a couple times and choke him a couple times and use the elbow some, and the referee says: 'If you guys want to fight that way, it's okay with me.' 'Hot damn!' I told Luke Carney in my corner. 'Watch me go now.' And from there out I saw that Cadillac turn around and come rollin' back.

"But I sold it when I was in the Army. I'm down in Texas and get a chance to fight in Houston. I ast the lieutenant if I could get a pass and he says: 'We'll ast the Old Man.' I'm in the Army three months and don't know who the Old Man is. Well, he's the colonel and I'm scared. But the lieutenant takes me in and the Old Man puts his arm around my shoulders and says: 'Sit down and have a cigar, son. What'll it be? He gives me a lousy cigar. The lieutenant explains and I sit there kind of groggy because I never smoked a cigar, but I got to make out I enjoy it. The Old Man says sure I can have a pass and I said I'd give part of the purse to the camp athletic fund. Forget it, he says, in the Army I can keep what I get. So I take a couple of guys with me to Houston and I flatten the guy in about four and get a thousand dollars and we have a hell of a party.

"Next time, though, the Old Man says I can have another pass, but he figures I should donate something to the athletic fund. It was me smartened him up, see, and now it's his idea. Well, I promise $500, but my end for the second fight comes to only $850 and with expenses and all I got to write my personal check for about $150.

"Next time it's the same thing but my end is only $300. I can't admit to anybody that I fight that cheap, so I got to write a bigger check. I win about seven or eight fights and it costs me more money all the time. Altogether I give the camp about $7,200 out of $11,000.

"Finally Mike Jacobs calls me up and offers me twenty-five per cent in the Garden with Billy Arnold, that I never heard of. I had a furlough coming to me, so I had Mike wire me a thousand dollars and a bunch of us drove to Pittsburgh; I had the Cadillac then. At home here, we tore into the champagne something terrific before we went to New York. There they tell me this Arnold that I never heard of is four to one to beat me and has twenty-seven knockouts in thirty-three fights. Well, I says, nobody's four to one against Fritzie, and we started betting, the whole crowd of us. I win, all right, and when we collect the bets we got $16,000 wrapped up in a newspaper. I win $4,200 in bets and my end is $11,000. So, I give the Old Man another $500 because he don't know I'm getting $11,000, which if he ever found it out he'd of thrown me in the brig.

"I also send him two boxes of Corona Coronas so the next time I go in his office I'll have a decent cigar to smoke."

FROM: THE THEBAID

Publius Papinfus Statius delivered, in his epic *The Thebaid,* this description of the classic combat—the slugger versus the boxer. In the first century his Alcidamas knew more about pace, footwork, blocking, slipping, hand-feinting and counterpunching than 95 per cent of his twentieth-century counterparts.

STATIUS (TRANSLATED BY J.H. MOZLEY)

"And now is courage needed; wield ye the terrible cestus in close conflict; valor here comes nighest to that of battle and the sword."

Argive Capaneus took his stand—awful his aspect, awful the terror he inspires—and, binding on his arms the raw ox-hide black with lumps of lead, himself no softer, "Send me one," says he, "from all those thousands of warriors; and would rather that my rival were of Aonian stock, whom it were right to slay, and that my valor were not stained with kindred blood." They stood aghast and terror made them silent. At last Alcidamas, unexpected, leaped forth from the naked crowd of Laconians, while the Dorian princes marvel but his comrades knew he relied on his master Pollux, and had grown up in the wrestling school of a god. Pollux himself guided his hands and molded his arms—love of the sport constrained him—and oft he set him against himself, and admiring him as he stood up in like mood caught him up, exultant, and pressed his naked body to his breast. Capaneus thinks scorn of him and mocks at his challenge, as though in pity, and demands another foe; at last perforce he faces him, and now his languid neck swells at anger's prompting. With bodies poised at their full height, they lift their hands, deadly as thunderbolts, safe withdrawn are their faces on their shoulders, ever watching and closed is the approach to wounds. The one is as great in broad expanse of every limb and terrible in size of bone as though Tityos should rise up from the Stygian fields, did the fierce birds allow him; the other was lately but a boy, yet his strength is riper than his years, and his youthful vigor gives promise of a mighty manhood; him would none wish to see defeated nor stained with cruel gore, but each man fears the spectacle with eager prayers.

Scanning each other with their gaze and each awaiting the first opening, they fell not at once to angry blows, but stayed awhile in mutual fear, and mingled caution with their rage; they but incline their arms against each other as they spar, and make trial of their gloves, dulling them by mere rubs. The one, more skillfully trained, puts by his fury, and taking thought for the future delays and husbands up his strength; but the other, prodigal of harm and reckless of his powers, rushes with all his might and in wild blows exhausts both arms, and attacks with fruitless gnashing of teeth, and injures his own cause. But the Laconian, prudent and crafty, and with all his country's vigilance, now parries, now avoids the blow; sometimes by throwing back or rapid bending of his head he shuns all hurt, now with his hands he beats off the aimed assault, and advances with his feet while keeping his head drawn back. Often again, as his foe engages him with superior power—such strength is in his cunning, such skill in his right hand—with bold initiative, he enters his guard and overshadows him, and towering high assails him. Just as a mass of water hurls itself headlong on a threatening rock, and falls back broken, so does he wheel round his angry foe, breaking his defense; look! he lifts his hand and threatens a long time his face or side, and thus by fear of his hard weapons diverts his guard and cunningly plants a sudden blow, and marks the middle of his forehead with a wound; blood flows, and the warm stream stains his temples. Capaneus, yet ignorant,

321

wonders at the sudden murmur of the crowd, but when, as he chanced to draw his weary hand across his face, he saw the stains upon the cowhide, no lion nor tiger feeling the javelin's smart was e'er so mad; hotly he drives the youth before him in headlong retreat over the whole field, and is forcing him on to his back; terribly he grinds his teeth and whirls his fists in countless repeated blows. The strokes are wasted on the winds, some fall on the gloves of his foe; with active movement and aid of nimble feet the Spartan eludes the thousand deaths that shower about his temples, yet not unmindful of his art he flees still fighting, and though fleeing meets blows with blows.

And now both wearied with the toil and their exhausted panting; slower the one pursues, nor is the other so swift to escape; the knees of both fail them and alike they rest. Thus when long wandering o'er the sea has wearied the mariners, the signal is given from the stern and they rest their arms awhile; but scarce have they taken repose, when another cry summons them to the oars again. Lo! a second time he makes a furious dash, but the other tricks him and goes at him with a rush of his own and sinking into his shoulders; forward he pitches his head, and as he rises the merciless boy smote him another blow

and himself grew pale at his success. The Inachidae raise a shout louder than the noise of shore or forest. But when Adrastus saw him struggling from the ground, and lifting his hands, intent on hideous deeds, "Haste, friends, I pray you, he is mad! hasten, prevent him! he is out of his mind—quick! bring the palm and prizes! He will not cease, I see well, till he pounds the brain within the shattered skull. Rescue the doomed Laconian!" At once Tydeus darts forth, and Hippomedon, obedient to command; then scarce do the two with all their might master his two arms and bind them fast, and forcefully urge him: "Leave the field, thou art victorious; 'tis noble to spare the vanquished. He too is one of us, and a comrade in war." But no whit is the hero's fury lessened; he thrusts away the proffered branch and cuirass, and shouts: "Let me free! Shall I not smash in gore and clotted dust those cheeks whereby that eunuch-boy gained favor, and send his unsightly corpse to the tomb, and give cause for mourning to his Oebalian masters?"

So says he, but his friends force him away, swelling with wrath and protesting that he has not conquered, while the Laconians praise the nursling of famed Taygetus, and laugh loud at the other's threats.

[FACT]

OLD MAN BRITT

On September 9, 1905, during the reign of Joe Gans, Battling Nelson and Jimmie Britt fought for "the white lightweight championship of the world" at Colma, California. A celebrated, and overwrought, drama critic reviewed the contest for the *San Francisco Examiner*.

ASHTON STEVENS

Melodrama would be a hollow word—poor old cut-and-dried melodrama! For this duel between Jimmie Britt and Battling Nelson had a nervewrecking shudder for every moment of the

fifty-two minutes of actual fighting. It was a sight such as I hope never to see again; and yet it was the greatest matinee I have ever witnessed. The most colossal audience—and the most expensive, too, that I have ever known—played the horrible mob.

When the right fist of Nelson emerged from a tangle of blows in the eighteenth round and came invincibly against the jaw of Britt, and the champion of his lightweight kind fell numb against the ropes and sank to the canvas floor, his lips geysers of blood, his tongue a protruding, sickening blade of red, the mob went mad.

Referee Graney had declared "all bets off," and it was more merely a matter of passion.

So the crowd opened its throat in unmercenary rapture. The King was dead—curse him!—and long live the Battling One!

A thousand cushions from the hard seats of the Colma arena were thrown into the afternoon air, and picked up and thrown, and thrown again.

Nelson the Great!

Britt the Beaten!

For ten minutes after the determining blow, hell was lidless.

Jubilant arms tossed Nelson again and again in the air as college kids are tossed in blankets. He was the gloat of fifteen thousand throats. The prize ring filled for him, and the policemen detailed to clear it fought to retain their clubs.

In the corner of the vanquished mourned the seconds, and if the truth must be told—for I sat at the ringside in Britt's corner where Britt fell—mourned also the referee, who that afternoon at the last moment had accepted the post in the face of what had appeared to be an implacable grudge 'twixt himself and the Britts.

But more touching still in that near corner was Old Man Britt, pillowing the gore-flecked head of his heretofore undefeated first-born. He bent his body over his broken son and made of his back a shield against the flying cushions.

As well as fake the prize ring has its tragedy, and one sees it with ghastly vividness at the ringside.

Quickly permit me to admit that my small change and my large sympathies had been with Jimmie. I had interviewed him for the Sunday *Examiner* as fistrion and plumber boy. His mind had won me. His neck had appeared to be a bit too long and thin "for the game," yet he had more brains than all of the ringsters I had ever chanced to fall in with. Also he had quickness, muscle and a left arm like a foil. His mentality and fleetness I would have pitted against the brawn of any man of equal weight. And I had seen him defeat Nelson in twenty rounds—where yesterday in a contest of

the practically unlimited number of forty-five, he went down in the eighteenth.

So I motored out to Colma with the rest of the experts and impostors (like myself), wondering just what sort of a foolish dramatic critic's point of view I should be able to bring to bear on Jimmie Britt's victory.

On everything save paper I had my story written before the gong rang. Presently, when I turned and looked two rows behind into the troubled features of Old Man Britt, I felt like a living obituary.

During the fiercest rounds, Mr. Britt was the only man that stood in the great open-air auditorium. Others that attempted to keep their feet were hissed and cussed down.

But the Old Man stood, and even those directly behind him made no murmur. He stood with his black hat in his hand, close against his black coat, like a mourner at a funeral. When big Dean Naughton turned and said, "Nothing but a miracle can save Britt," the foreboding was echoed in the face of the father. When he said, "It's all over now for Jimmie; we have only to wait for the rounds," the Old Man's mouth was working with every blow and his breathing was hopelessness against hopelessness.

Before the finale came, the senior Britt had surrendered. To have taken his game youngster out of that padded square he looked as though he would have given one plumbing shop and some flats.

But Jimmie knew that he was beaten only after he had been lifted to his corner. It's a pity that such grit has to be sold in the market place for purses and percent. It's a crime against what we are pleased to call civilization. If the bloody wage of war must come, and come in response to national pride and protection, then Jimmie Britt should be foremost with the fighters. They deserve a dearer heroism than this cheap one of the glove.

Almost throughout the battle was a fury. Britt seemed bent on throwing fancy boxing to the winds and piercing his opponent by main strength. Vainly the picturesque "Spider" Kelly and the other Britt seconds cautioned him to caution—just as vainly as they urged him to wildness in the fatal eighteenth. He fought his own fight, and the cheers that greeted his defeat were for a stronger but not for a braver man.

I am not depreciating the courage of Battling Nelson. No one can but admire the sand and strength and skill of him. There were times when his expressionless face was a crimson jelly under the thud of Britt's sodden gloves; there were times when his Greek body seemed to be stung through and through by the merciless flogging from Britt's left. But invariably Nelson returned for more, and gradually, cumulatively, he gave rather than took that more. He had rounds to spare, yet, like Britt, he wanted no boxing. The man that called this a "boxing match" was a merry jester. I will leave it to the experience of Otto Floto, Naughton and Hamilton if a harder, bloodier battle has ever been fought in the vision of paying spectators.

Some of these spectators should have been excluded. They were women. A few of them looked like decent women, but the most gave token of being jaded jades in search of some new torment for their sagging nerves. Hoots of mock applause properly met the entrance of each.

Man at a prize fight is not a polite animal. In fact, he has no politeness at all and is much more animal than man.

I saw yesterday professional men, doctors and lawyers high in practice and clubs, writhing rapturously with every blow. Each was "fighting the fight" by himself.

And I saw the eyes of Jack London, who in his novel *The Game* has translated to the stage a prize fight better than Bernard Shaw in either novel or play—I saw the eyes of this great primitive fictionist turn from sympathy with Britt to contempt for the mob that thundered at Britt's fall.

Even London has not written the whole "Game"; and no melodramatist has approached it. Oh, these miserable sublimations of fights that you see in the casual melodrama! They have nothing of the spirit, nothing of the ring; and after all, the ring and those immediately about it are about all you could hope to show within the confines of an ordinary stage.

If we must have the fighter in drama let him be dramatized accurately. Let him have a "Spider" Kelly in his corner screaming:

"That's the candy, Jimmy! Once more where he

bleeds! Draw more of the claret; I like to see it run! Go in, you tiger, you, and finish him before he faints on your shoulder!"

I admit, ladies, that this sounds brutal, but it is only a scented version of what actually is shouted at the ringside.

Then again, if we must have the ring on the stage, give us the real surroundings; the telegraph instruments clicking against shout; the hooded telephone operators; the worried correspondents from all ends of the earth. And if we must have prize fights on the stage, give us an actor to play the part of a Naughton, so that in one of those deadly climaxes where the tension of the crowd is too great for clamor, when what London calls the "blood-cry" is choked in the throats—then I say give us a Naughton on the stage, talking like a phonograph to his telegrapher, the news to be carried from ocean to ocean, from newspaper to newspaper.

"A — couple — of — lefts — to — the — body — brought — Britt's head — forward. As — Britt's — head — came — in — Nelson — showered — rights — and — lefts — on — the — jaw. Nelson — tore — loose — with — a — hard — left — on — the — body. Britt — began — to crumble. Then — Nelson — unloaded — a — right — on — the — head — and — a — left — on — the — stomach. It — was — hard — to — say — which — blow — ended — the — fight — but — Britt — sank — to — the — floor — and — rolled — over — his — tongue — protruding. It — was — blood — red — and — he — was — gasping for — breath. He — grasped — the — ropes — and — tried — to — arise — but—"

If women and children and sedentary gents must see prize fights on the stage, give them to them as they are. This will show the ring for its true worth. Give us everything, I say—save one. Not Old Man Britt erect in the mob and holding his hat like a mourner at his son's funeral. To show "the game" as it is you don't have to go quite that far. I saw a fighter kill a man in the ring; the picture was not half so sad as that of Old Man Britt.

DEATH OF A PRIZE FIGHTER

The venal, callous manager of fighters is the most overworked of characters in sports literature, but Robert Switzer has written him better than anyone else.

ROBERT SWITZER

It was two a.m. Billy Murdoch was at the airport, his small, sharp-chinned face pale with strain. He was catching a plane for Detroit. It was the wise thing to do because a kid named Tony Casino had died here tonight and the way people were acting you would think Billy Murdoch had killed him.

Tony Casino had been a prize fighter. Billy Murdoch had been his manager. And the kid had been hit too hard and had died of cerebral hemorrhage—and it was all Billy Murdoch's fault, of course.

Yes, Billy Murdoch thought sourly. *Oh, hell, yes.*

He slouched low on the bench in the waiting room, the collar of his camel's-hair topcoat turned up and his hat pulled down. He heard somebody say, "Hello, Billy."

He looked up and saw a fair-haired young man. *Another reporter,* he thought. *I haven't seen enough reporters tonight.*

"Hello," Billy Murdoch said.

The young man sat down. "I guess you've had a pretty tough night," he said sympathetically.

Billy Murdoch knew better than to answer that one. Nice traps these sports experts set. If he said yes, he had had a tough night, the paper would say Billy Murdoch felt sorrier for himself than he did for the dead boy. If he said he was all right, the paper would talk about the unfeeling manager. If he said something like, "It was worse for Tony," then he would be making jokes while the boy lay dead. It did not matter what you said; these guys could make you into the worst slob that ever walked.

So he said nothing. He wished he could get aboard the plane.

"Going to New York?" the reporter asked.

"Yes," Billy Murdoch said, and got up and walked across the waiting room to get away from the reporter, hoping the reporter would leave. But as he walked across the room the loud-speaker blared, "Flight 34 for Detroit," and Billy Murdoch knew that the press would be waiting for him in Detroit.

He sat to the rear of the plane. After what seemed a long time, the plane started to roll and then they were in the air. Billy Murdoch closed his eyes and thought of how it had been.

In the last second of the first round, Tony Casino had taken a terrific punch on his left temple, and, as the other boy was about to tear his head off, the bell rang. Tony just stood there, crouching a little, arms hanging straight down from his shoulders. Billy Murdoch and the handler brought him back to his corner. His eyes were glazed. Billy Murdoch and the handler worked on him frantically, with Billy Murdoch thinking: *He was knocked out last week, and now if he quits after one punch I'll have one sweet time matching him again.* Some expression came back into Tony's eyes.

"How you feel?" Billy Murdoch said.

"I'm all right," Tony said blurrily.

"Good. Good. Now listen. Stay away from him. Keep away from him this round."

"Yeah," Tony said.

So the bell rang and Tony went back in and took one more punch. They tried to revive him in the ring, but could not. They carried him to the dressing room and tried to revive him, but could not. Then there was a doctor and a flock of reporters and the other fighters standing around in the dressing room they all shared and the very white body lying completely still on the rubbing table under the light bulb that dangled from the ceiling on the end of a long cord and threw a clear, brittle light on the blue-black smear of Tony's left temple. The doctor bent over the barely breathing body and without looking up said, "Call an ambulance. Quick." There was a scuffling sound on the cement floor as somebody went to telephone, but it was wasted effort because Tony died almost immediately. The doctor looked across the dry, white body at Billy Murdoch and said, "He's dead. Cerebral hemorrhage, probably."

Billy Murdoch kept his eyes on Tony Casino and felt everybody looking at him. There were a lot of men in the room and they were all watching him and waiting for him to say something.

"He was a nice boy," Billy Murdoch said. "It's a lousy thing."

For a moment nobody said anything. It was very hot in the room. Billy Murdoch could feel the sweat running down his sides.

"He was too tall for a welter," one of the fighters said.

"He should have been a middle with that height," a reporter said. "Only his bones weren't big enough."

"You got to have that bone," another fighter said. "Bone soaks it up."

Billy Murdoch wanted to leave, but there were too many people around. Somebody might get mad if he tried to leave too quickly.

"He was knocked out last week," a reporter said. "Just like tonight. He went down like he'd been shot."

The doctor said sharply, "Was he unconscious long? Last week, I mean?"

"No," Billy Murdoch said. "I've seen them out a lot longer. He was all right."

For the first time, Billy Murdoch noticed the man standing next to the doctor. A cop. Not in uniform but one hundred per cent cop. You can tell. The cop was staring at him. Billy Murdoch felt a flash of terror, and then he thought: *They can't do anything to me. I didn't kill the kid. The cop must have been at the fights and heard about this. Cops can't stay away from corpses.*

"How long was he out?" the cop said in a low voice.

"I don't know," Billy Murdoch said. "Not very long."

"About how long?"

"A few minutes, that's all."

The cop's heavy face suddenly looked heavier. "How long is a few minutes?"

"What are you trying to do?" Billy Murdoch said shrilly. "Blame me for this?"

It was very quiet in the room. Billy Murdoch felt his fingers trembling.

"I was here last week," a colored lightweight said. "Tony was out ten minutes anyway. Maybe fifteen."

"So what?" Billy Murdoch said. "I'd like to have a nickel for every boy that's been out ten minutes."

"He looked real bad when he came out of it," the lightweight said. "He was awful pale. I sat here with him for a while after Mr. Murdoch left. He was dizzy. He was sick, too, but he couldn't throw up anything. Just some of that green stuff that burns."

"Dizzy," the cop said. He looked at Billy Murdoch. "Did you ever see him dizzy?"

"No," Billy Murdoch said, thinking of the dizzy spells Tony Casino had had for the past six months. Ever since that night in Cleveland.

"I saw him fight in Cleveland," a reporter said. "About six months ago. He took one of the worst beatings I've ever seen. It was enough to finish any fighter."

"Did he lose all his fights?" the doctor asked in a puzzled voice.

"No," the reporter said. "He had a whole lot of guts. He won his share of fights. Nobody lost money on him."

Billy Murdoch heard grunts from the fighters and saw the angry eyes of the reporters and the flat eyes of the cop, and he thought: *Sure, that's what they're all thinking. I killed the kid for a few crummy bucks.*

He began to edge his way toward the foot of the rubbing table. The door was that way.

"How was he between rounds tonight?" a reporter asked. "When he came out for the second he didn't seem to know where he was going."

"I asked him how he was," Billy Murdoch said. "He said he was all right."

"They're always all right. How did he look?"

"He was hit hard. Maybe he didn't look perfect, but you can't stop a fight every time your boy gets hit."

"Where's the handler?" the cop said.

"Here," the handler said.

"How did he look?"

"He looked bad. I don't think he could see."

"Yeah," the cop said.

"Now, look," Billy Murdoch said, shrilly again. "You're all talking as if I was trying to kill the kid. That's enough of that. I don't have to take that." He started straight for the door and was faintly surprised when nobody tried to stop him.

The cop said viciously, "Murdoch!"

Billy Murdoch stopped.

"I'd like to get you bastards," the cop said in the same vicious voice. "I wish I could figure a way to get you bastards."

Billy Murdoch got out of there. A fat man followed him and caught up with him in the tunnel. He was the man who promoted the fights in this arena.

"Billy," the promoter said, "you better get out of town."

"I was leaving tomorrow, anyway. I got a couple of boys going in Detroit tomorrow night."

"Get out tonight. Don't hang around. Everybody's mad as hell. The papers will have a field day with this. I'm going to have enough trouble. It'll be better if you're not around. You know."

"Sure," Billy Murdoch said. "Tonight."

"About the kid," the promoter said. "Where'll I send him?"

"Somewhere in Brooklyn. I don't know where. The sports writers will find out for you. They'll be looking up his mother."

"I'll take care of it," the promoter said. "So long, Billy."

"So long," Billy Murdoch said, and left the arena, thinking: *Yes, you'll take care of it, you bighearted rat. You'll take care of it out of the purse you didn't pay me. You'd ship the kid C.O.D. if you could get away with it. Keep the money. I'm not stupid enough to argue about that.*

Billy Murdoch went to his hotel, threw his stuff in his bag and went out to the airport, and had to wait two hours for the fog to blow away so the plane could take off.

And now he was in the air for Detroit. The press would be waiting for him. He would have to say something to them. You can't just say, "No comment," when somebody's been killed. He would have to tell them something and it would have to be better than what he had done in the dressing room. He had handled that all wrong. Well, he had been scared. It was foolish, but he had been scared. God, he would hate to have that cop get at him. But what would he say to the reporters?

He thought back again and remembered what he had said about you can't stop a fight every time somebody gets hit. He could work on that. He would have to say it right, though.

The plane came down at Detroit and four reporters jumped him. There was light in the sky now, but the sun was not up and it was chilly.

"We heard about Casino," a reporter said. "What happened?"

Nice and innocent, Billy Murdoch thought. When these guys go innocent, hang on.

"Tony was hit very hard," Billy Murdoch said. "I thought he was all right. But he was hit harder than I thought."

"Did you think of stopping the fight?"

"I thought he was all right," Billy Murdoch said again. "He was hit hard, but you can't stop a fight every time your boy gets hit. What would happen to the fight game if you stopped a fight every time somebody got hit?"

"I know what should happen to it," another reporter said. "They should take it out and bury it."

"Sure," Billy Murdoch said. "Nobody likes the fights. That's why they all go to them."

"What are you doing in Detroit?"

"Just passing through."

"To where?"

"Toronto," Billy Murdoch said. "I'm working on a main go for Danny O'Brien up there."

"How do you feel about this Casino kid?"

"How do you think I feel?"

"He was like a son to you."

"Don't be like that," Billy Murdoch said. "That's not funny."

"Forgive me," the reporter said.

Billy Murdoch got away from them, caught a cab, and checked in under a phony name at a small hotel. He slept until two in the afternoon. Then he got up, bathed, shaved, had something to eat, and felt better. He read what the papers had done about Tony Casino. It was just plain murder, the way they told it. Tony Casino had been having head trouble for months, but his manager, Billy Murdoch, had kept right on making him fight. Tony Casino should never have been a fighter, anyway. He had not been rugged enough to take the punishment. But the fight business was savage and could use kids like Tony Casino, and men like Billy Murdoch were licensed to break these kids, physically or mentally or both. The fight business was rotten from top to bottom and it was high time something was done about it.

Billy Murdoch was glad to read that last sentence. They were spreading their fire. They were shooting at the whole fight game and the target was too big and nobody would get hurt.

Billy Murdoch went to see Max Green. Green was putting on the card tonight that included Billy Murdoch's two boys. Green did not look happy at seeing him.

"I heard you were in town," Green said. "They got the finger on you good."

"I got two boys going for you tonight. Don't you remember?"

"They'll go on all right, but I don't want you out there, Billy. There might be trouble. I don't want to get mixed up in this thing. It's one of those messes and I don't want any part of it."

"All right," Billy Murdoch said. "I'll go to a movie. I'll have a time."

"I wouldn't do that, either. You should go on to New York. Dig in there for a while. A man's better off at home at a time like this."

"I'm getting tired of being run out of towns."

"So stay," Green said. "Stay and get your ears beat in. This is a small town. They'll find you and that'll just keep them all excited. I never saw so much excitement as over this one. But New York is big. You won't stir up anything there. Is that right?"

"Sure," Billy Murdoch said. "I'll see you around."

"Goodbye," Max Green said.

Billy Murdoch caught a plane for New York without being seen, and so there were no reporters waiting for him at LaGuardia Field.

He bought a paper. The Tony Casino death was splashed on page one. Billy Murdoch was surprised. He had not thought it would be played up here like this. They were really going to work on this one. Billy Murdoch could not understand it. Fighters were being killed all the time. Why did they have to knock themselves out over this one?

It was ten p.m. when Billy Murdoch stood on the corner of 58th and Sixth Avenue. There was a hotel down the street. Billy Murdoch and nine other managers kept a room in it. Most nights you could get a poker game there. Billy Murdoch went to the hotel and up to the fourteenth floor.

There were five men in the room, sitting around a table littered with chips and ash trays and glasses. They looked up casually when Billy Murdoch came in and then they all jumped to their feet and gave him a royal welcome.

"Hell," Billy Murdoch said. "I thought you might throw me out. Everybody else has."

"Yeah," Jack Latimer said. "What are you trying to do? Give us a bad name?"

"You got a tough break, Billy," Pete Torelli said. "It was too bad."

"All this hollering," Manny Gold said. "Don't let it get you, Billy. It means nothing. Every so often they got to yell. They'll yell for maybe two more days and then they'll forget it."

From across the room another man called, "What do you take in Scotch, Billy?"

"Water," Billy Murdoch said. "Just plain water."

They all went back to the table and sat down. Billy Murdoch relaxed. It was nice to be back among friends again.

A LAY OF ANCIENT LONDON

George Bernard Shaw once said of Thackeray that he "loved a prize fight as he loved a fool." Thackeray, being dead by then, never denied this, but he did deny, although recognized by friends and journalists at ringside, that he attended the Heenan–Sayers fight, eulogized here in a paraphrase of Macaulay.

Although the Crimean War, which involved England, France, Turkey and Russia, attracted only two special correspondents from the United States, four years later four American newspapers sent reporters across the Atlantic to cover the fight between Tom Sayers, champion of England, and John C. Heenan, champion of America. They met at Farnborough, England, on April 17, 1860, in the first truly international boxing contest, and in the thirty-seventh round, when the 195-pound Heenan seemed about to annihilate his 149-pound opponent, the ropes were cut. The two fought five more rounds until the contest was declared a draw, a decision that ignited the first international post-fight controversy.

WILLIAM MAKEPEACE THACKERAY

(Supposed to be recounted to his great-grand-children, April 17, 1920 A.D., by an Ancient Gladiator.)

Close round my chair, my children,
    And gather at my knee,
The while your mother poureth
    The Old Tom in my tea:
The while your father quaffeth
    His rotgut Bordeaux wine,—
'Twas not on such potations
    Were reared these thews o' mine.
Such drinks come in the very year
    —Methinks I mind it well—
That that great fight of HEENANUS
    With SAYERIUS befell.
These knuckles then were iron;
    This biceps like a cord;
This fist shot from the shoulder
    A bullock would have floored.
Crawleius his Novice,
    They used to call me then,
In the Domus Savilliana,
    Among the sporting men.
There, on benefit occasions,
    The gloves I oft put on,
Walking round to show my muscles
    When the set-to was done;
While ringing in the arena
    The showered denarii fell.
That told Crawleius, Novice

Had used his mauleys well.
'Tis but some sixty years since
    The times whereof I speak,
And yet the words I'm using
    Will sound to you like Greek.
What know ye, race of milksops,
    Untaught of the P. R.,
What stopping, lunging, countering,
    Fibbing, or rallying are?
What boots to use the *lingo*,
    When you have not the *thing?*
How paint to *you* the glories
    Of BELCHER, CRIBB, or SPRING,—
To *you*, whose sire turns up his eyes
    At mention of the Ring?
Yet, in despite of all the jaw
    And gammon of the time,
That brands the art of self-defense
    —Old England's art—as crime,
From off mine ancient memories
    The rust of time I'll shake,
Your youthful bloods to quicken
    And your British pluck to wake.
I know it only slumbers;
    Let cant do what it will,
The British bulldog *will* be
    The British bulldog still.
Then gather to your grandsire's knee,
    The while his tale is told,
How SAYERIUS and HEENANUS
    Milled in the days of old.

The Beaks and Blues were watching,
    Agog to stop the Mill,
As we gathered to the station
    In the April morning chill.
By twos and threes, by fours and tens,
    To London Bridge we drew;
For we had had the office,
    That were good men and true;
And, saving such, the place of fight
    Was ne'er a man that knew.
From east and west, from north and south,
    The London Fancy poured,
Down to the sporting Cabman,
    Up to the sporting Lord.
From the Horse-Shoe in Titchfield Street,
    Sharp OWEN SWIFT was there;
Old PETER left the Rising Sun,
    All in the street of Air;
LANGHAM forsook his beer-taps,
    With nobby ALEC REED;
And towering high above the crowd
    Shone BEN CAUNT'S fragrant weed.
Nor only fighting covies,
    But sporting swells besides,—
Dukes, Lords, M.P.s, and Guardsmen,
    With county beaks for guides;
And tongues that sway our Senators,
    And hands the pen that wield,
Were cheering on the champions
    Upon that morning's field.

At last the bell is ringing,
    The engine puffs amain,
And through the dark towards Brighton
    On shrieks the tearing train;
But turning off when Reigate
    Unites her clustering lines,
By poultry-haunted Dorking
    A devious course it twines;
By Wotton, Shier, and Guilford,
    Across the winding Wey,
Till by heath-girded Famborough
    Our doubling course we stay,
Where Aldershort lay snoring
    All in the morning gray,
Nor dreamed the Camp what combat
    Should be fought here today!
The stakes are pitched, the ropes are tied,
    The men have ta'en their stand;
HEENANUS wins the toss for place,
    And takes the eastward hand.

CUSICCIUS and MACDONALDUS
    Upon the Boy attend;
SAYERIUS owns BRUNTONUS,
    And JIM WELSHIUS for friend.
And each upon the other now
    A curious eye may throw,
As from the seconds' final rub
    In buff at length they show,
And from their corners to the scratch
    Move stalwartly and slow.
Then each his hand stretched forth to grasp,
His foemen's fives in friendly clasp;
Each felt his balance trim and true,—
Each up to square his mauleys threw;
Each tried his best to draw his man—
The feint, the dodge, the opening plan,
Till left and right SAYERIUS tried;
HEENANUS' grin proclaimed him wide;
He shook his nut, a lead essayed,
Nor reached SAYERIUS' watchful head.
At length each left is sudden flung,
    We heard the ponderous thud,
And from each tongue the news was rung,
    SAYERIUS hath "First blood!"
Adown HEENANUS' Roman nose
Freely the telltale claret flows,
While stern SAYERIUS' forehead shows
That in the interchange of blows
    HEENANUS' aim was good!
Again each iron mauley swung,
And loud the counter-hitting rung,
Till breathless all, and wild with blows,
Fiercely they grappled for a close;
A moment in close hug they swing
Hither and thither, round the ring,
Then from HEENANUS' clinch of brass
SAYERIUS, smiling, slips to grass!

I trow mine ancient breath would fail
    To follow through the fight,
Each gallant round's still changing tale,
    Each feat of left and right.
How through two well-spent hours and more,
    Through bruise, and blow, and blood,
Like sturdy bulldogs, as they were,
    Those well-matched heroes stood.
How nine times in that desperate Mill
    HEENANUS, in his strength,
Knocked stout SAYERIUS off his pins,
    And laid him all at length;
But how in each succeeding round

SAYERIUS smiling came,
With head as cool, and wind as sound,
As his first moment on the ground,
Still confident, and game.
How from HEENANUS' sledgelike fist
Striving a smasher to resist,
SAYERIUS' stout right arm gave way,
Yet the maim'd hero still made play,
And when infighting threatened ill,
Was nimble in outfighting still,
   Did still his own maintain—
In mourning put HEENANUS' glims;
Till blinded eyes and helpless limbs,
The chances squared again.
How blind HEENANUS in despite
Of bleeding mug and waning sight
So gallantly kept up the fight,
   That not a man could say
Which of the two 'twere wise to back,
Or on which side some random crack
   Might not decide the day:
And leave us—whoso won the prize,—
Victor and vanquished, in all eyes,
   An equal meed to pay.

Two hours and more the fight had sped,
   Near unto ten it drew,
But still opposed—one-armed to blind,—
   They stood, the dauntless two.
Ah, me, that I have lived to hear
   Such men as ruffians scorned,
Such deeds of valor brutal called,
   Canted, preached down, and mourned!
Ah, that these old eyes ne'er again
   A gallant Mill shall see!
No more behold the ropes and stakes,
   With colors flying free!

But I forget the combat—
   How shall I tell the close,
That left the Champion's Belt in doubt
   Between those well-matched foes?
Fain would I shroud the tale in night,—
The meddling Blues that thrust in sight,—
   The ringkeepers o'erthrown;—
The broken ring,—the cumbered fight,—
HEENANUS' sudden, blinded flight,—
SAYERIUS pausing, as he might,
Just when ten minutes used aright
   Had made the fight his own!

Alas! e'en in those brighter days
   We still had Beaks and Blues,
Still, canting rogues, their mud to fling
On self-defense and on the Ring,
   And fistic arts abuse!
And 'twas such varmint had the power
   The Champion's fight to stay,
And leave unsettled to this hour
   The honors of the day!
But had those honors rested
   Divided as was due,
SAYERIUS and HEENANUS
   Had cut the Belt in two.

And now my fists are feeble,
   And my blood is thin and cold,
But 'tis better than Old Tom to me
   To recall those days of old.
And may you, my great-grandchildren,
   That gather round my knee.
Ne'er see worse men or iller times
   Than I and mine might be,
Though England then had prize fighters—
   Even reprobates like me.

FROM: THE DIOSCURI

Castor and Pollux (Polydeuces) were the twin sons of Zeus and fought their way to seats on Olympus. Theocritus, regarded as the creator of pastoral poetry, lived in the third century B.C., and his is one of several versions of the go between the undefeated Pollux and the muscle-bound Amycus.

THEOCRITUS (TRANSLATED BY ANDREW LANG)

We hymn the children twain of Leda, and of aegis-bearing Zeus—Castor and Pollux, the boxer dread, when he hath harnessed his knuckles in thongs of ox-hide. Twice hymn we, and thrice the stalwart sons of the daughter of Thestias, the two brethren of Lacedaemon. . . .

Even already had Argo fled forth from the Clashing Rocks, and the dread jaws of snowy Pontus, and was come to the land of the Bebryces, with her crew, dear children of the gods. There all the heroes disembarked, down one ladder, from both sides of the ship of Iason. When they had landed on the deep seashore and a sea bank sheltered from the wind, they strewed their beds, and their hands were busy with firewood.

Then Castor of the swift steeds, and swart Polydeuces, these twain went wandering alone, apart from their fellows, and marveling at all the various wildwood on the mountain. Beneath a smooth cliff they found an ever-flowing spring filled with the purest water, and the pebbles below shone like crystal or silver from the deep. Tall fir trees grew thereby, and white poplars, and planes, and cypresses with their lofty tufts of leaves, and there bloomed all fragrant flowers that fill the meadows when early summer is waning—dear worksteads of the hairy bees. But there a monstrous man was sitting in the sun, terrible of aspect; the bruisers' hard fists had crushed his ears, and his mighty breast and his broad back were domed with iron flesh, like some statue of hammered iron. The muscles on his brawny arms, close by the shoulder, stood out like rounded rocks that the winter torrent has rolled and worn smooth in the great swirling stream, but about his back and neck was draped a lion's skin, hung by the claws. Him first accosted the champion, Polydeuces.

P. Good luck to thee, stranger, whosoe'er thou art! What men are they that possess this land?

A. What sort of luck, when I see men that I never saw before?

P. Fear not! Be sure that those thou look'st on are neither evil, nor the children of evil men.

A. No fear have I, and it is not for thee to teach me that lesson.

P. Art thou a savage, resenting all address, or some vainglorious man?

A. I am that thou see'st, and on thy land, at least, I trespass not.

P. Come, and with kindly gifts return homeward again!

A. Give me no gifts, none such have I ready for thee.

P. Nay, wilt thou not even grant us leave to taste this spring?

A. That shalt thou learn when thirst has parched thy shriveled lips.

P. Will silver buy the boon, or with what price, prithee, may we gain thy leave?

A. Put up thy hands and stand in single combat, man to man.

P. A boxing match, or is kicking fair, when we meet eye to eye?

A. Do thy best with thy fists and spare not thy skill!

P. And who is the man on whom I am to lay my hands and gloves?

A. Thou see'st him close enough, the boxer will not prove a maiden!

P. And is the prize ready, for which we two must fight?

A. Thy man shall I be called (should'st thou win), or thou mine, if I be victor.

P. On such terms fight the red-crested birds of the game.

A. Well, be we like birds or lions, we shall fight for no other stake.

So Amycus spoke, and seized and blew his hollow shell, and speedily the long-haired Bebryces gathered beneath the shadowy planes, at the blowing of the shell. And in like wise did Castor, eminent in war, go forth and summon all the heroes from the Magnesian ship. And the champions when they had strengthened their fists with the stout ox-skin gloves, and bound long leathern thongs about their arms, stepped into the ring, breathing slaughter against each other. Then had they much ado, in that assault—which should have the sun's light at his back. But by thy skill, Polydeuces, thou didst outwit the giant, and the sun's rays fell full on the face of Amycus. Then came he eagerly on in great wrath and heat, making play with his fists, but the son of Tyndarus smote him on the chin as he charged, maddening him even more, and the giant confused the fighting, laying on with all his weight, and going in with his head down. The Bebryces cheered their man, and on the other side the heroes still encouraged stout Polydeuces, for they feared lest the giant's weight, a match for Tityus, might crush their champion, in the narrow lists. But the son of Zeus stood to him, shifting his ground again and again, and kept smiting him, right and left, and somewhat checked the rush of the son of Poseidon, for all his monstrous strength. Then he stood reeling like a drunken man under the blows, and spat out the red blood, while all the heroes together raised a cheer, as they marked the woeful bruises about his mouth and jaws, and how, as his face swelled

up, his eyes were half closed. Next the prince teased him, feinting on every side, but seeing now that the giant was all abroad, he planted his fist just above the middle of the nose, beneath the eyebrows, and skinned all the brow to the bone. Thus smitten, Amycus lay stretched on his back, among the flowers and grasses. There was fierce fighting when he arose again, and they bruised each other well, laying on with hard weighted gloves; but the champion of the Bebryces was always playing on the chest, and outside the neck, while unconquered Polydeuces was smashing his foeman's face with ugly blows. The giant's flesh was melting away in his sweat, till from a huge mass he soon became small enough, but the limbs of the other waxed always stronger, and his color better, as he warmed to his work.

How then, at last, did the son of Zeus lay low the glutton? Say goddess, for thou knowest, but I, who am but the interpreter of others, will speak all that thou wilt, and in such wise as pleases thee.

Now behold the giant was keen to do some great feat, so with his left hand he grasped the left of Polydeuces, stooping slantwise from his onset, while with his other hand he made his effort, and drove a huge fist up from his right haunch. Had his blow come home, he would have harmed the King of Amyclae, but he slipped his head out of the way, and then with his strong hand struck Amycus on the left temple, putting his shoulder into the blow. Quick gushed the black blood from the gaping temple, while Polydeuces smote the giant's mouth with his left, and the close-set teeth rattled. And still he punished his face with quick-repeated blows, till the cheeks were fairly pounded. Then Amycus lay stretched all on the ground, fainting, and held out both his hands, to show that he declined the fight, for he was near to death.

There then, despite thy victory, didst thou work him no insensate wrong, O boxer Polydeuces, but to thee he swore a mighty oath, calling his sire Poseidon from the deep, that assuredly never again would he be violent to strangers.

ONE-THIRTY-THREE—RINGSIDE

Few writers of fiction have understood and enjoyed the realm of the fighter as did Charles Emmet Van Loan, who wrote this in 1913 for the *Saturday Evening Post*. He was discovered, ten years earlier, in San Francisco by T. A. Dorgan, who recommended him to the *New York Journal* and started a chain reaction. In Denver, Van Loan discovered Damon Runyon and recommended him to the *New York American*. He also, in Chicago, persuaded Ring Lardner to send some baseball fiction to the *Saturday Evening Post*.

CHARLES E. VAN LOAN

Charles Francis Healy, known to all the world as "Young Sullivan," sat on the edge of his bed and stared incredulously at Billy Avery, his manager, press agent and bosom friend.

"Naw," said Healy, shaking his head, "you don't mean that, Billy. You're only kidding."

"It ain't what I mean, Charles," said Avery, discouragement showing in the dispirited droop of his shoulders and the flat tones of his voice. "It's what Badger means that cuts the ice. I talked to him for four hours—the obstinate mule!—and that's the very best we get, one-thirty-three at the ringside."

"But, man alive," wailed the little fighter, "that's murder in the first degree! He'd be getting me in the ring so weak that a featherweight could lick me!"

"Yes," said Avery, "and he knows that as well as you do. That's what he's playing for—a cinch."

"The public won't stand for it!" stormed Healy.

"The public be damned!" said Billy Avery, unconsciously quoting another and greater public character. "It stands for anything—everything. We're on the wrong side of this weight question, Charles. Badger has got the champion, and it's just our confounded luck that Cline can do one-thirty-three and be strong. Cline won it from Fisher at one-thirty-three ringside, and Badger says that every man who fights Cline for the title must make the same weight—the lightweight limit."

"Huh!" snarled Healy. "There ain't any such thing as a limit! I notice that they called Young Corbett a champion after he licked McGovern, and Corbett couldn't get within a city block of the featherweight limit! They make me sick! It's the champion that makes the weight limit—not the rules!"

"All true," said Avery; "and that's exactly why we're up against it. Cline can do the weight. Badger opened up and talked straight off his chest, Charlie. He says he isn't anxious to fight us because he's got softer matches in sight where Cline won't have to take a chance. He thinks that this weight restriction will stop us bothering him with challenges and chasing him around the country with certified checks and things. I hollered like a wolf for one-thirty-five at three in the afternoon, and he only laughed at me. 'We're not fighting welters, this season,' he says. 'One-thirty-three ringside, or nothing. Take it or leave it.' The Shylock!"

"Well, leave it, then!" said Healy angrily. "If Mike Badger thinks I'm sucker enough to cut off an arm and a leg, just to get a fight with that hunk of cheese that he's managing, he's got another guess coming. I'll go into the welterweight class first!"

"Y-e-e-s," said Avery slowly, "and there isn't a welter in the country today that would draw a two-thousand-dollar house. I suppose we'll have to go back to the six- and ten-round no-decision things, splitting the money even, and agreeing to box easy! Yah! A fine game, that is."

"I suppose you think I ought to grab this fight with Cline?" It was more than a question; it was an accusation.

"Well," said the business manager, looking at the ceiling, for he had no wish to meet Young Sullivan's eyes just then, "the bank roll ain't very fat,

Charlie. We could use a few thousand, you know, and there's more money in losing to Cline—don't get excited, kid; let me talk—than we could get by winning from a flock of pork-and-bean welters. That fight would draw forty thousand if it draws a cent. If you *win*—and it's no cinch that Cline will be as good as he was two years ago—we can clean up a fortune the first year, like shooting fish!"

"If I win!" said Healy bitterly. "I tell you, it'll murder me to get down to one-thirty-three! I'd have to cut the meat right off to the bone to do it. You know I made one-thirty-five for Kelly, and it was all I could do to outpoint him in twenty rounds when I should have stopped him with a punch!"

"The loser's end ought to be eight thousand, at least," said Avery, still looking at the ceiling. "And in case you don't get him, you've got a fine alibi— the weight stopped you. It was your stomach that bothered you in the Kelly fight, remember that."

"See here, Billy," said Charles Francis, "*you* want me to fight Cline, don't you? Even at one-thirty-three?"

"We need the money," said the manager simply.

"I'll gamble you!" said Healy, producing a silver half-dollar. "Heads, I fight him; tails, I don't. Will you stick by it, Billy, if it comes tails?"

"Sure!" said the manager. "Will you go through with it if she comes heads?"

"It's a promise!" said Healy.

The coin spun, flickering, in the air, struck the carpet, and rolled to the fighter's feet.

"Heads!" he groaned. "I lose, Billy!"

Whenever a sporting writer had reason to rake over his vocabulary for the sort of an adjective which should best fit Mike Badger, manager of "Biddy" Cline, the choice usually lay between two words. The scribes who liked Mike selected "astute." The others said he was "obstinate." Both were right.

To be absolutely fair in the matter, Mike was neither better nor worse than any other manager. Only wiser. When he made a business contract, he was prudent enough to demand at least seventy-five percent the best of the bargain, and tenacious enough to hold out until he got it. Mike simply did what the other fellows would have done if they had been given the opportunity, and everyone knows what an unprincipled course that is to pursue. One fight promoter, hoping to secure certain concessions and smarting under Mike's steady refusal to recede from the original proposition, burst out thus:

"Ain't you got any sportsmanship in you at all?"

"Not a stitch," answered Mike. "Sportsmanship and business are two different things. I'm a businessman, and you know my terms. I've got something to sell—buy it or let it slide."

In the "good old days," which some of the scarred bare-knuckle veterans still mourn with sorrowful pride, a fighter needed no business manager for the excellent reason that fighting was not then a business. It was a habit. With the era of large purses and profitable theatrical engagements came the shrewd businessman, and Mike Badger was the shrewdest of them all. He could smell a five-dollar note farther than a bird dog can smell a glue factory.

A champion is the greatest asset a wise manager can have—and vice versa. The very word "champion" is a valuable trade-mark. It means easy money, free advertising, and last and most important, the right to dictate terms. Every ambitious fighter dreams of winning a title some day; the man who has one dreams only of keeping it until the last dollar has been squeezed out and then retiring undefeated.

It is because of the financial value of this trademark that championships are so carefully guarded. It is easier to hale a multimillionaire before an investigating committee than it is to get a champion of the world into the ring with a fighter who has an even chance to defeat him. All sorts of tactics are used in order to sidestep dangerous matches. Managers of heavyweights, lacking poundage restrictions, often bid the ambitious challenger goodbye until such time as he has secured a reputation, fondly hoping that in the process he will be soundly licked and eliminated. Managers of bantams, feathers and lightweights insist that husky aspirants shall "do the weight, ringside." Many a man has saved his title by starving an opponent for a week before a match. The old-time bare-knuckle warriors sneer at this sort of thing. They were used to making matches, "give or take ten pounds," but, as has been pointed out, they were not businessmen. The slogan "May the best man win" has been changed to "May the best-managed man win."

Biddy Cline was a great little fighter—probably the greatest at his weight that the ring had seen during his generation. He was no boxer, but a sturdy, willing, courageous chap, who began fighting when the bell rang and continued to fight as long as the other man could stand in front of him. His record was black with knockouts, though Biddy was not the typical one-punch fighter. His victims succumbed to the cumulative effect of a thousand blows as well as the terrific pace they were compelled to travel. It was a very strong lightweight indeed who could play Cline's game with the champion and hear the gong at the end of the fifteenth round. Biddy's best fighting weight was slightly below one-thirty-three, he had held the championship for three years and, under Mike Badger's careful guidance, expected to hold it for three years more.

Charles Francis Healy had been a large, sharp thorn in the champion's side for some time. He was a dashing, sensational performer, a clever boxer, a hard, clean hitter, and a tremendous finisher—the very ideal of the average fight follower. He had beaten nearly all the men whom Cline had defeated—most of them in shorter fights—but this was only natural, as Healy's best fighting weight was close to one hundred and forty pounds. When he trained below one hundred and thirty-eight he was sacrificing strength and stamina, and one hundred and thirty-five pounds at three in the afternoon was the lowest notch he had been able to make with any degree of safety. In spite of this, Billy Avery challenged the champion once a month with clocklike regularity, and was as frequently informed that the holder of the title had other pressing matters on his hands. The end of Avery's campaign had been the private conference with Badger and the latter's ultimatum:

"One-thirty-three ringside, or no fight."

Then, with the hardihood of a man who gambles when he knows he cannot afford to lose, Healy had risked certain defeat on the flip of a coin.

The match was made with a tremendous thrumming of journalistic tom-toms, and sporting America sat up cheerfully, for this was the one great fight it really wished to see. When the articles of agreement were drawn up—a queer document, half legal, half sporting in its phraseology—Mike Badger dropped a large fly in Billy Avery's ointment. It came with the dictation of the forfeiture clause, Mr. Badger speaking:

"For weight, five thousand dollars; for appearance,—."

"Hold on, there!" yelled Avery. "Who ever heard of a weight forfeit of five thousand dollars?"

"You did—just now," said the imperturbable Mike, with a grin. "I'm going to make it an object for your man to do one-thirty-three. I've had fighters forfeit their weight money on me before this."

Avery argued and Healy glared across the table at Biddy Cline, who glared back, such conduct being customary in the presence of newspapermen; but Mike was firm as Gibraltar.

"Here's the point, gentlemen," said he, ignoring the sputtering Avery. "I don't want this man to come into the ring weighing a ton. This fight is to be for the lightweight championship of the world, at the lightweight limit. If we are overweight, we shall expect to forfeit five thousand dollars. If Avery's man can't do one-thirty-three, I want to know it now. If he can make it, why should he object to a large forfeit? Come on, Avery. Now's your chance to spring some of those certified checks you've been flashing around the country so recklessly!"

In the end Mike Badger won out, as was his habit. Billy Avery had the added worry of knowing that his entire fortune, as well as the sweepings and scrapings of Healy's bank roll, was forfeit unless the challenger reached the lightweight limit.

"We're hooked," said Avery gloomily, when he was alone with his warrior. "If the weight forfeit had been a thousand bucks or so, we could have let it slide and still made money; but now it's one-thirty-three or bust!"

"Bust is good!" said Healy. "We bust if we don't and we bust if we do. You might have known that Badger would slip one over on you somehow. A fine mess you've got us in, Billy!"

"Me?" exclaimed the manager, virtuously indignant. "Say, what's the matter with you? Who offered to toss the coin? Whose idea was that?"

"Shucks!" growled Healy. "I only did that because I knew you intended to make the match anyway."

"You took a chance—"

"Yes; and so did Steve Brodie," interrupted the fighter. "He ought to have had his head examined for doing it, and I'm worse, because Steve had a chance to win and I haven't. I was kind of figuring on forfeiting my weight money if I saw I couldn't get that low without trouble; but now I've got to hang up my hat in a Turkish bath joint for a week before that fight, and I'll be as weak as a kitten! You're one swell manager, you are!"

"And you're a grand squealer," said Avery.

"Your own proposition and now you blame me."

Thus, with mutual reproaches and a general disarticulation of family skeletons, the challenger and his manager set out to secure training quarters for the coming event, the shadow of which loomed dark about them.

II

"Can Healy do the weight and be strong?"

This momentous question agitated every sporting center in the country. It was discussed as far away as London, Paris and Melbourne. Men wrote about it, talked about it, argued about it; and all agreed that the outcome of the match hinged upon the correct answer, and nowhere was there such uncertainty as in Healy's training camp. There were only two men who really knew, and they were not committing themselves. Even the trainer was excluded from the daily weighing process.

The newspapermen argued that the public had a "right to know," spies from the other camp nosed about daily; betting men begged the lowdown and on-the-level; curious ones sought to satisfy their curiosity; close personal friends went away disappointed. Billy Avery would talk about everything but the weight, and when that subject was mentioned, he became an oyster, gripping tight the pearl of information. Healy had but one answer: "See Billy about it."

The best judges had no chance to form an opinion, for they never saw Healy stripped. Whenever he appeared in the gymnasium he was loaded down with sweaters and woolens.

Public opinion was divided. Half the fight followers inclined to the belief that Healy could not make the weight and was therefore secretive; the other half pointed out that Avery might be preparing an unpleasant surprise for the opposition.

"He's keeping Cline guessing," said the optimistic ones. "If he couldn't make the weight, he'd have been a fool to post five thousand bucks."

At the end of three weeks Mike Badger received a telephone message from Billy Avery. He hung up the receiver with a hard little edge of a smile, for he had been expecting something of the sort.

"They're on the run, Biddy," he remarked to his champion. "Avery wants to see me tonight on the strict QT. I knew that big sucker couldn't do the weight, or anywhere near it!"

"Did he say so?" asked the literal Cline.

"Bonehead!" retorted Mike. "He didn't have to

say it. What else could he want to see me about? I'll call the turn now—he wants to rat out on their forfeit. A swell chance he's got!"

"Serves 'em right for going around the country trying to make a bum out of me!" said Cline feelingly. "Hand it to 'em good, Mike!"

"That's the best thing to do," remarked Mr. Badger.

The real heart-to-heart business of the fight game is transacted without witnesses, and it shrinks from publicity. The newspapermen were not invited to attend the moonlight conference of the managers, and the meeting was as secret as if they had been preparing to dynamite a national bank.

"Hello, Mike!" said Avery. "Have a cigar?"

"Thanks! Well, out with it! What's on your mind?"

"I wanted to have a chat with you about this weight proposition," said Avery.

"Haven't you got a copy of the articles of agreement?"

"Yes," said Billy.

"Well, if I remember," said Badger calmly, "it says there that the men are to do one-thirty-three, ringside. Is that correct?"

"Yes."

"That's all there is to it," said Badger. "Have you just found out that Healy can't get down that low?"

"He can get down there, all right," said Avery, "but it'll weaken him pretty bad. Chances are it won't be a very good fight. Can't we get together somehow—and give the people a run for their money? Suppose we should come in a pound or so overweight. You wouldn't grab that forfeit, would you?"

"Why wouldn't I?" asked Badger grimly. "That's business, ain't it? A contract is a contract, and it ain't my fault that you went into this thing without knowing whether your man could do the weight or not. You came to me and asked me for this match. I wasn't anxious to make it, but I turned down some good theatrical offers and signed up. You mustn't expect me to lose money on your mistakes. My dough is posted, and I'm going to carry out my part of the contract. You must do the same thing. I wouldn't let you come in a pound over, or an ounce over. One-thirty-three, ringside, and you'll do it, or I'll claim your five thousand."

"Looking for a cinch, ain't you?" sneered Avery.

"You bet I am; and if you had a champion you'd

be looking for cinches, too! Now, I'm going to tell you something else: Don't pull any of that moth-eaten stuff about breaking a hand or an arm or a leg, and having to call off the match. I won't stand for it. I'll claim your appearance money, and I'll show you up from one end of the country to the other."

"Won't you listen to reason?" begged Avery.

"I haven't heard any yet," said Badger, "and, what's more, I've said all I'm going to. Better have your man down to weight if you want to save that forfeit. I never make any agreements on the side, and when I sign my name to a thing I go through. Good night."

Avery went home, talking to himself. Healy was waiting for him.

"What luck?" asked the fighter anxiously. "Would he do business?"

"Of course, he wouldn't! He's got us, and he knows it. Shylock was a piker beside this guy!"

"I can break my leg," suggested Healy hopefully.

"Yes, and he'll send out a flock of doctors to examine you, and they'll all be from Missouri. It'll take something more than a lot of bandages and a crutch to get by this bird. He'll snatch our appearance money and put us in Dutch all over the country."

"But we've got to do something!" There was a note of desperation in Healy's voice. "Typhoid fever might bring me down to weight; but it's a cinch sweating won't do it. One-thirty-nine tonight, and I've done enough work already to sweat an elephant to a shadow. I simply can't make it, and that's all there is to it. You know what the doctor said—that this excess baggage is due to natural growth. It's in the bone and muscle, and it won't come off! Why the devil didn't we think of that before we got hooked in so strong?"

"Give me a chance to think," said Avery. "I may dig up a way to wriggle out of this match and save the appearance money, anyway. You tear into the hay and leave it to me."

"I wish you'd done your thinking before we made this match!" sighed Healy.

"There you go again!" mumbled Avery. "Always putting it up to me! Didn't you toss a coin, and—"

"I've heard all that before," said Healy. "By the way, there was a man here to see you about eight o'clock. Says he'll be back about ten."

"Another nut!" growled the manager.

"Not this fellow," said Healy. "He looks like class, and he's got a letter for you—from Jim Quinn—"

"Quinn!" said Avery. "Holy cat! I wish Jim was here. He might think of some way to get us out of this jam."

Promptly at ten o'clock the stranger returned. He was small, neatly dressed, of middle age, and wore a close-trimmed beard and nose glasses. He presented Quinn's letter without comment:

DEAR BILLY: I don't know how you're fixed on the weight proposition, but the last time I saw Healy he was falling away to a mere cartload, and I don't think he can do one hundred and thirty-three ringside without the aid of a saw. On the chance that you've got a bad match on your hands, I am sending Mr. George Harden to see you. George is an expert in his line, knows how to keep his mouth shut, and you can bank on anything he tells you being right.

Of course, if Healy can do one hundred and thirty-three without weakening himself, you won't need Harden. If he can't, put Harden on the job. I can't explain here, for obvious reasons, but Harden can make your man a winner, and save you the weight forfeit. Wire me three days before the fight whether I can bet on Healy or not. Yours in haste,

JAS. QUINN

Billy folded the letter and placed it in his pocket.

"This listens well," said he slowly. "What's the idea?"

"The idea is that I can put your man in the ring as strong as he is now and save you the weight forfeit. It'll cost you five hundred dollars."

"It would be worth it," said Avery. "My boy is having trouble getting down to weight. We didn't figure that he has put on several pounds by growth and development, and it's coming off hard."

"I'll take him the way he is," said Harden, "and make him weigh one-thirty-three on any scales they pick out."

"A fake?" demanded Avery suddenly.

"Yes, and a darned good one," said Harden.

Avery shook his head.

"Mike Badger is a pretty wise bird," said he. "He's seen the chewing-gum trick and the little chunk of lead, and all that. I'd hate to try and get by him with a weight-stealing device."

"Has he seen this, do you think?" asked Harden, drawing something from his pocket.

"What is it?" demanded Avery, staring at what

appeared to be a stiff black thread in the palm of Harden's hand.

"Nothing but an innocent little piece of horsehair," said the visitor quietly. "Do you think he's seen that?"

"Horsehair is a new one to me," said Avery. "How does it work?"

"That's *my* business," said Harden. "Leave me alone with your weighing machine for a few minutes and I'll give you a demonstration."

"Fair enough!" said Avery, leading the way.

Three days before the fight Billy Avery presented himself at the office of the promoter of pugilistic events—a wise young man of Hebraic extraction.

"Moe," said Billy, "have you made any arrangements about the scales the men are to weigh in on?"

"Not yet," said Goldstein. "Why?"

"Well, this is a special occasion," said Avery, "and I want a pair of scales that there can't be any question about. I've got a lot of money up and I can't afford to take chances."

"You don't want to use your own, do you?" asked Moe slyly.

"No, and I don't want to use Mike Badger's, either!" snapped Billy angrily. "We're going to be at weight, right enough, but we'll just barely make it and that's all. It'll be so close that there won't be any fun in it, and that darned Shylock says that if we're an ounce over he'll grab the five thousand. Now, I wish you'd write a letter to some reputable hardware concern and ask 'em to send you a brand-new weighing machine to be used at the ringside. They probably have an expert, too, and they might be willing to send him along. I want the scales tested by a government official and balanced by a man who hasn't the slightest interest in the fight either way. I'm not going to monkey with 'em myself, and I want Badger to keep his hands off. There ain't much that fellow wouldn't do for five thousand bucks! Is that a fair proposition?"

"As fair as a June day!" replied Goldstein. "I'll write a letter to Messinore & Jones immediately."

Avery smoked a cigar while the letter was written, and after that he chatted about the coming fight, the advance sale, the probable "cut," and kindred topics. When he rose to go, he picked up the envelope containing the letter.

"I'll drop this in the mail chute when I go out," he said.

The next day the office boy brought Mr. Goldstein a neatly engraved business card, bearing the name of a firm of national reputation as manufacturers of scales. In the lower left-hand corner appeared these words:

"Presented by Mr. Henry C. Darling, Western Representative."

Goldstein tossed the card over to Mike Badger, who happened to be present.

"Let's see what he wants," said Goldstein.

Mr. Henry C. Darling proved to be a dapper little person, with a close-cropped beard and nose glasses. He spoke with the crisp, incisive tones of a businessman, and Mike Badger, surreptitiously running his thumbnail over the pasteboard which he held, was impressed. An engraved card, to ninety-nine men out of one hundred, is a convincing argument; an embossed trade-mark in three colors in the upper corner clinches matters.

"Mr. Darling—Mr. Badger," said Goldstein.

"I beg pardon—I didn't quite catch the name," said the visitor. It had to be repeated, and even then it was evident that it meant nothing to the Western representative, who turned immediately to Goldstein.

"I happened to be calling on Mr. Messmore when your letter arrived," said Darling. He produced Goldstein's letter and laid it upon the desk. "Mr. Messmore suggested that as you needed an expert, it was more in my line than his. I will be very glad to accommodate you. If you will tell me where you wish the scales delivered and when, the details will be attended to."

"I wouldn't want to take up your time—" began Goldstein.

"Oh, that's all right!" chirped Mr. Darling. "It will be a pleasure to do it, I assure you. As a matter of fact, I am—ah—rather interested in the manly art myself. My son is an amateur boxer—you may have heard of him? Peter C. Darling, Chicago Athletic Club? No? Only sixteen years old, but clever as they make 'em! I like to see a good bout when I can."

"Of course!" said Moe. "Why not?" He reached into his desk and brought forth a ticket. "Here's a box seat for the show Friday night."

Mr. Darling fairly gushed thanks as he put the ticket carefully away in his pocketbook.

"Very, very kind of you, I'm sure!" he said. "Now, it is understood that I am to furnish a new weighing machine which shall be tested and certified correct by the Board of Weights and Measures on Friday afternoon. I will then take charge of it myself and deliver it at the fight pavilion that night. Is that satisfactory?"

"Suits me!" said Badger, thumbing the card.

Mr. Darling paused at the door, and there were traces of nervous hesitation in his voice when he spoke.

"May I suggest—ah—that the name of my firm—or my own name—does not appear in the newspapers?" he asked. "This is—ah—rather an unusual service, and—"

"I understand!" said Moe heartily. "You'll be kept under cover, all right. Only three people need to know who you are—the other one is Avery."

Mr. Darling seemed immensely relieved.

"If you are interested in seeing the scales tested," said he, "come to the Bureau of Weights and Measures at four o'clock on Friday afternoon."

"I'll be there," said Mr. Badger. "Moe, you notify Avery."

Mr. Goldstein looked after his visitor with a grin.

"Ain't it funny what some people will do for a free fight ticket?" he remarked. "There's a traveling man whose time is worth money, yet he's willing to go to fifty dollars' worth of trouble to get a twenty-dollar seat! Can you beat it?"

"It saves paying him a fee," said the frugal Badger. "And did you get that about not wanting his name in the paper? I'll bet he's a deacon in a church or something, when he's home!"

III

The official testing of the scales took place on schedule time. The shiny, new weighing machine—of the portable platform variety—balanced to a hair. Mr. Badger almost precipitated a fight by remarking over and over again that an ounce might mean five thousand dollars, and every time he said it Avery snarled.

"Now, gentlemen, if you are satisfied," said Mr. Darling, "we will ask that the scales be placed under lock and key here until I shall call for them this evening. I guarantee that they will not be out of my sight from that time until you are ready to use them. Is that satisfactory?"

"Perfectly!" said Mike Badger, and Billy Avery mumbled something under his breath.

"Well, old top," chuckled Badger to Avery, as they left the room, "my man is under weight. How's yours?"

"We may have to sweat him a bit," answered Avery shortly, "but I'd cut off one of his legs before I'd let you have that five thousand!"

"Cut off his head, instead," suggested Badger pleasantly. "He never uses that when he fights!"

"You make me sick!" growled Avery.

The weight of the contender was still a mystery, but there was an unconfirmed rumor that Moe Goldstein—sworn to secrecy—had been present at the Healy camp on Thursday afternoon and had seen the challenger raise the beam at one hundred and thirty-four pounds. This may have had something to do with the flood of Healy money which appeared as if by magic.

Shortly after the doors of the fight pavilion were opened an express wagon drove up to the main entrance and the weighing machine was carefully unloaded, under the personal supervision of Mr. Henry C. Darling. Moe Goldstein, who was standing in the door, cheerfully contemplating the long line of humanity stretching away from the general-admission window, waved his cigar at Darling and grinned.

"You're here early enough, I see!" remarked the promoter.

"Better early than late!" said Mr. Darling. "Is there a room where we can lock this thing up until it's wanted? I have made myself personally responsible for it."

"Put it in the first dressing room," said Moe. "You can't lock the door, though, except from the inside."

A few minutes later the "Western representative" was alone with the weighing machine, behind a locked door. In two seconds he had the wooden platform unshipped and set aside, exposing the levers underneath. These levers, sensitive to the touch as human ingenuity can make them, are V-shaped and meet in the center, forming an X, the short lever passing underneath the long one.

Mr. Darling whipped a black horsehair from his pocket, tested it carefully for strength, and then bound it about both arms of the short lever, some three inches above the point of contact in the center. Instead of tying the hair in a knot, he fastened it with a dab of beeswax, replaced the floor of the platform, weighed himself carefully, nodded approvingly, and left the room. The entire operation had consumed less than a minute. The next time that Moe Goldstein looked in that direction Mr. Darling was standing in front of the closed door, like a sentinel on guard.

Two tremendous roars announced the entry of the gladiators, naked, save their socks and bathrobes. Behind them came four strong young men carrying the weighing machine, Mr. Darling trotting behind and urging them to handle it as they would a crate of eggs.

Biddy Cline, grinning in his corner, looked up at his manager.

"Here's where we get that five thousand!" he said.

In silence and breathless curiosity the house waited the weighing-in ceremony.

Mr. Henry C. Darling, fussy and important, fluttered about like an old hen, commanding everyone to stand back while he demonstrated that the scales balanced to a hair. At a signal, the fighters rose from their corners and climbed through the ropes, their handlers trooping after them.

"Stand back, everybody!" chirped Mr. Darling. "We must have room here! Stand back! You observe that the scales balance perfectly. I will set the bush poise exactly at one hundred and thirty-three pounds—no more and no less. On the dot. So! Now, then, gentlemen, who goes first?"

Charlie Healy, who had been removing his socks, slipped his bathrobe from his shoulders and stood forth, naked.

"Might as well get it over with!" he said.

Mike Badger, his thin arms folded over his flat chest, flashed a keen, appraising glance at the challenger, as if anticipating the verdict of the scales. Healy's face was lean and leathery, and his cheekbones stood out prominently, but he had not the haggard, drawn appearance of a man who had sapped his vitality by making an unnatural weight, and his muscular armament bulked large under his smooth, pink skin.

"In great shape!" thought Badger. "But he's heavy, good Lord, he's heavy! He ain't anywhere near one-thirty-three!"

Healy stepped gently upon the scales and dropped his hands at his sides. Mike Badger bent forward, his gimlet eyes fixed upon the notched beam. He expected it to rise with a bump, instead of which it trembled slightly, rose half an inch, and remained there, quivering.

"Just exactly!" chirped Mr. Darling. "Next!"

Charlie Healy threw his hands over his head with a wild yell of triumph.

"By golly, I made it! I made it!" he shouted; and then, as if carried away by an excess of feeling, he jumped six inches in the air and alighted upon his heels with a jar that made the weighing beam leap and rattle, and brought a sudden, sharp strain upon the concealed levers—enough of a strain, let us say, to snap a strand of horsehair and allow it to fall to the floor. Healy's action was natural enough, but it was his jump which roused Mike Badger to action and crystallized his suspicion. He had seen that sort of thing before.

"No, you don't!" howled Mike. "You ain't going to put anything like that across on me! I want to look at those scales!"

The "Western representative" bristled with sudden anger, strutting about like an enraged bantam rooster.

"Preposterous!" he said. "Examine them yourself!"

He pushed the weighing machine over toward Badger. Mike removed the wooden platform in a twinkling and bent over the levers. That was the reason he did not see Mr. Darling place the sole of his foot upon a dab of beeswax and the horsehair which clung to it, removing the only bit of evidence.

Sweating and swearing, Mike Badger sought earnestly for wads of chewing gum or other extraneous matter, after which fruitless quest he demanded that Healy weigh again. By this time the challenger was in his corner, calmly partaking of a bowl of beef tea.

"Well, I should say we won't weigh him again!" said Avery. "You've examined the scales, and they're all right. My man has got a pound of beef tea in him by now. He made the weight at the time set, and we won't weigh again. Ain't that right, Goldstein?"

The promoter nodded.

"Go on and weigh your man, Badger," he said. "The crowd is getting restless."

"But I tell you we've been jobbed!" wailed Mike. "Why, look at that fellow! He's as big as a house."

"Forget it!" growled Avery. "My boy has been at weight for the last three days! You saw him weigh yesterday, didn't you, Moe?"

"That's right, Mike," said Goldstein.

"I dare you to put him on the scales again!" raved Badger. "I'll give you a thousand dollars if you'll weigh him now!"

"And him full of beef tea? I should say you would! G'wan and get your champion on there!"

Mr. Henry C. Darling, still bristling in a quiet, gentlemanly manner, stepped forward to adjust the plummet on the notched bar, but Mike swept him aside.

"That'll be about all for you!" he said brusquely. "I'll attend to this myself!"

And Billy Avery was so well pleased with the turn of events that he allowed Mike to weigh his own man. The bar did not rise for Cline. He was safe by a full pound and a half.

He was far from safe after the fight started, however. Biddy Cline, tough little battler that he was, found himself as helpless as a toy in the hands of the challenger. In the clinches, which were Biddy's specialty, Healy worried him and tossed him about like a rag doll.

"This guy is strong as a middleweight!" panted the champion, after the third round. "See the way he hauls me around? It's a job, Mike, as sure as you live!"

"We can't help it now," said Badger. "You've got to lick him if it kills you!"

Let it be placed to Biddy's credit that he did his honest best to follow out instructions. He set a slashing, whirlwind pace, fighting with the desperation of one who feels his laurels slipping away from him; but Healy met him considerably more than halfway, and after the tenth round the most rabid Cline sympathizer in the house was forced to admit that the end was only a matter of time.

The championship of the world passed in a spectacular manner toward the end of the fifteenth round. Cline, knowing that he had been badly beaten thus far, summoned every ounce of his reserve strength and hurled himself upon the challenger in a hurricane rally, hoping to turn the tide with one lucky blow. Healy, cautious, cool, and steady as a boxing master, waited until the opening came, and then shot his right fist to the point of the chin. The little champion reeled, his hands dropped at his sides, and a vicious short left hook to the sagging jaw ended the uneven battle.

Biddy Cline took the long count for the first time in his life, and a dapper gentleman in a box seat smiled through his nose glasses and played with a bit of horsehair in his pocket. Such a trivial thing had changed the pugilistic map.

According to custom, the conqueror offered his hand to the conquered before he left the ring. Biddy would have taken it, but Mike Badger restrained him.

"Don't shake with him!" said Mike. "You've been licked, but by a welterweight."

"You think anybody will believe that?" cackled Healy.

"I'll make 'em before I'm through," said Mike grimly.

IV

The new champion ceased in the midst of the pleasant duty of inscribing his name and title upon photographs. "Badger!" he said. "What does he want, Billy?" "Don't know. He's coming right up."

Mike Badger entered and helped himself to a chair. "You're a nice pair of burglars, ain't you?" he demanded.

"You're a sorehead," said the new champion cheerfully. "Are you still harping on that weight business? Everybody in the country is giving you the laugh!"

"Oh, you think so, do you?" said Mike. "I've been doing a little detective work lately. That fellow—that Darling—I've been on his trail, and I know all—"

"I didn't have a thing to do with him," protested Avery quickly. "Goldstein wrote a letter to a hardware firm and—"

"And you posted it," said Mike. "Remember that? I happened to keep his business card, so yesterday I wired his firm asking for information. Here's the answer." He tossed a telegram across to Avery.

"It says there," remarked Mr. Badger, "that no such man is known to the concern. It was a smooth trick, Billy, but it won't do. I'm going to show you fellows up from one end of the country to the other, and I'll never quit hounding you until you give us another match—at the proper weight. And what's more, we still claim the championship." He picked up one of the new photographs and read the inscription scornfully. "Lightweight champion of the world!" he said. "You ain't a lightweight any more'n I am!"

"Well," said Charlie Healy softly, "they're still pointing me out on the street as the man that licked Biddy Cline—That's good enough for me."

FROM: THE AENEID

Goaded by the fight mob, an old champion comes back.

VIRGIL [TRANSLATED BY H. H. BALLARD]

After the races were run, and all the prizes awarded,
"Now," Aeneas exclaimed, "if any be bold and courageous,
Let him stand forth with his hands and arms enveloped in gauntlets."
Having said this he announced a twofold reward for the contest;
Unto the victor a bull bedecked with gold and with fillets,
And to console the vanquished, a sword and a marvelous helmet.
Instantly, waiting for naught, gigantic and powerful Dares
Lifted his head, and stood mid the loud acclaim of the heroes;
Dares, the only man who used to stand out against Paris:
He, too, it was, by the tomb where Hector the mighty lies buried,
Butes, the giant, smote, the victor who haughtily boasted
Kinship with Amycus' line by descent from Bebrycian princes,
Stretching him hurt to the death on the yellow sand. Such is Dares,
Who is now tossing his head on high for the opening combat,
Vaunting his shoulders' breadth, and his arms, one after the other,
Stretching defiantly forth, and beating the air with a flourish.
Where is his mate to be found? Not one in the whole great assembly
Ventures to meet this man, or to put on the gauntlets against him.
Eagerly, therefore, believing that all have withdrawn from the contest,
Facing Aeneas he stands, and short is his limit of patience,
Then by the left horn seizing the bull; "O son of a goddess,
Since there is none," he cries, "dares trust himself to the battle,
What is the term of delay? How long is it meet to detain me?
Bid me lead off my prize!" The Trojans, all shouting together,
Roar their assent, and demand the promised reward for the hero.
Frowning Acestes, then, with irony lashes Entellus,
Next unto whom he reclines on the verdant couch of the hillside,
"Ah, Entellus! in vain the bravest of heroes aforetime,
Dost thou so meekly allow such prizes, without any contest,
Thus to be won? Where now is that Eryx we worshiped, whom vainly
Thou for thy trainer hast claimed? Where now is thy fame which o'ershadowed
All the Trinacrian isle; and those trophies that hung in thy palace?"
Quickly he answered, "Not quenched by fear is my passion for glory,
Or my desire for praise; but age is retarding the icy

343

Flow of my blood, and the languishing forces congeal in my body.
Had I what once I had, and in which yon braggart confiding,
Vaunteth himself; were mine that youth which has long since departed,
Lured by no thought of a prize, nor hope of a beautiful bullock,
Would I have come! nor now do I tarry for gifts!" and so speaking,
Into the midst he hurled a pair of ponderous gauntlets.
Eyrx the dauntless with these had once been wont to do battle,
Binding on hand and arm these thongs of well-seasoned bull's hide.
Hearts were appalled; seven folds of the hides of bulls so enormous
Stiffened in rigid coils, insewn with lead and with iron.
Dares, himself, was the first to draw back from the sight in confusion;
E'en the brave son of Anchises was moved by the terrible weapons,
While, now this way, now that, he turned the huge links of the cestus.
Then the old hero flung forth from his heart these words of defiance —
"What, then, if one could have seen the arms, and looked on the gauntlets
Hercules owned; and have viewed upon this very shore the grim battle!
Eryx once wore these arms, yes, Eryx, the son of thy mother;
Still canst see how with blood and with brains they are stained and bespattered,
'Gainst the great son of Alcaeus with these did he stand; and I used them
Long as more vigorous blood gave strength; while Age, my dread rival,
Had not yet whitened my locks, not scattered his frost on my temples
But, if your Dares of Troy object to these arms of our choosing,
If good Aeneas approve, and Acestes, my sponsor, be willing,
Make me the light more fair; I spare you the bull's hide of Eyrx;
Banish thy fear; yet thou must relinquish those Ilian gauntlets."
Having thus spoken, he flung from his shoulders the folds of his mantle;
Then the huge joints of his limbs, his powerful frame, and great muscles
Baring, gigantic he stood in the midst of the yellow arena.
Father Aeneas, then, with gauntlets more fairly proportioned
Bound with equal arms the palms of both the contestants.

     Instantly both stand forth, with body erect, and on tiptoe;
High aloft in the air his arms each fearlessly raises;
Back, far away from the stroke, their high-flung heads they are tossing;
Hands intermingle with hands; they challenge each other to combat;
That one, the better of foot, on the quickness of youth is reliant,
This one excels in the bulk of his limbs, but his knees' tardy hinges
Fail, and his giant frame is racked by laborious breathing.
Many blows in vain do the champions thrust at each other;
Many on echoing ribs they rain; and loudly they thunder
Full on the chest, while hands about ears and temples are playing
Heavy and fast, and jaws 'neath terrible buffets are cracking.
Firmly Entellus stands, and, fixed in the same alert posture,
Only with body and vigilant eye is avoiding the gauntlets;
Dares, like one who assails a fortified city with engines,
Or with tented array besieges a hill-crowning fortress,
Craftily tries now these and now the other approaches,
Circling the ring, and attacking in vain with varied maneuvers.
Rising against him, Entellus outstretches his right and uplifts it
High overhead; but his foe, as the blow comes down from above him,
Quickly foresees, and escapes by a sudden swerve of his body.

FROM: THE AENEID

Wasting his strength on the air, Entellus, untouched by his rival,
By his own ponderous bulk overborne, lurching heavily forward,
Falls to the earth; as oft upon Mount Erymanthus or Ida,
Pine trees, hollow and huge, have suddenly fallen uprooted.
Teucrian men and Trinacrian youth spring up in confusion;
Rises a shout to the sky, and Acestes is first to run forward,
And in compassion uplift from the earth the old friend of his boyhood.
But, unhurt by his fall, and wholly undaunted, the hero
Keener returns to the fight, and rouses his strength by his fury;
Shame and conscious worth are also rekindling his vigor;
Fiercely o'er all the plain he drives the fugitive Dares;
Now and again his blows with right and left hand are redoubled.
Neither delay nor rest; with strokes as incessant as hailstones
Rattling from cloud to roof, with blow after blow is the hero
Ceaselessly buffeting Dares and driving him o'er the arena.

     Father Aeneas, now, not brooking so violent passion,
Also restraining Entellus from growing too bitter in temper,
Instantly ends the fight, and rescues discomfited Dares,
Comforts his heart with words, and thus addresses him kindly:
"Ill-fated man! What madness so great hath o'ermastered thy spirit!
Dost thou not recognize here the might and displeasure of Heaven?
Yield to the god." He speaks, and speaking closes the contest.
Faithful young comrades, however, lead Dares away to the galleys,
Dragging his faltering knees, his head all listlessly swaying,
Spitting thick gore from his mouth, and teeth with blood intermingled.
Then they are summoned back and awarded the sword and the helmet,
While they resign to Entellus the bull and the glory of conquest.
Then cries the victor, elated in mind, and proud of his bullock,
"Child of a goddess, and Teucrians all, be taught by this token
Both what strength was mine ere age had enfeebled my body,
And from what death redeemed ye have rescued the life of this Dares."
When he has uttered these words he turns and faces the bullock
Which, as the gift of the fight, is standing beside him; then, backward
Raising his hand on high, he dashes the terrible gauntlet
Midway the horns, through skull, and bursting brain, to the brain pan.
Staggers the bull, and falls, head foremost, trembling and lifeless.
Standing above it, such words as these he pours from his bosom:
"Better than Dares' death, this life do I pay thee, O Eryx!
Here, as a victor, henceforth resigning my art and my gauntlets."

END OF THE LINE FOR LEO

This column appeared, on February 12, 1953, in the *Seattle Post-Intelligencer*. It tells, with great beauty, not only of the end of a fine prospect but of one of the great teacher-trainer-managers.

EMMETT WATSON

It was late afternoon and there were a few people hanging around the gym watching Harry Mathews skip rope. Jack Hurley motioned toward the back room, which was bare of furniture and looked out on First Avenue. Leo Lokovsek propped himself on the window ledge and looked down at the people hurrying about their business.

The side of his face away from the window was shadowed, and you could hardly see the jagged scars around his cheek, ear and temple. It had been three weeks now since the automobile crash outside Everett; three weeks since they had called the priest to the hospital where Leo lay unconscious for twelve hours.

"I got you down here," Hurley said, "to tell you that Leo is through. He isn't going to fight no more."

Lokovsek had come into the gym, feeling well, ready to work out. The Deacon called him into the office, where he told him: "You're all through." Lokovsek argued and pleaded. The X rays had shown no fracture; the doctor had assured him his head was sound.

Hurley tried to explain how it was with Ernie Schaaf, when Primo Carnera killed him with a light left jab. He told him about Lem Franklin, who had a previous head injury that nobody knew about, and how Franklin collapsed and died in the ring without being hit a solid punch.

"Not if all the doctors in the Mayo Clinic told me this boy could fight," Hurley said. "Not even then. He's finished."

"Would you fight for somebody else, Leo?"

Hurley answered the question. "I can't control his life," the Deacon said. "What he does is his own business now. But I think I've convinced him he shouldn't."

Lokovsek nodded.

It was easy then to remember the months of patient training in the gym, the long lean strong body, with the sharp reflexes, the smooth blend of balance and leverage. Experts conceded Lokovsek was a real possibility. It was easy to remember the night in Hoquiam, his first fight, his first knockout, how he drew the deep breath of satisfaction and there was nothing ahead but fight and build-up and fight again—with perhaps a fortune waiting.

Nothing had changed except, possibly, a minute broken blood vessel in his head; something Hurley was afraid of.

"You're young," Hurley said. "You've got a wife and baby to look out for. You got your whole life ahead of you, and if you've got the guts to fight, you should have the guts to start over."

Hurley walked to the door, paused and turned. The steel-rimmed glasses and the tight mouth gave his face a prissy expression.

"They'll come at you," he was saying, in a soft voice. "They'll come at you with money. Parasites. They'll give you money to fight again, because they know you're good and they know they can get it back out of you. Don't go.

"Just remember, I could let you fight. I chase a buck as hard as any man. I could use you for a year in easy fights and then I could back off. I like money real well, but I won't make my money that way."

Hurley went through the door and on out into

the gym. Lokovsek was staring hard at his fists, clenched in his lap, and it was easy to think how things might have been.

The build-up already was well on its way. Even now, in the East, they are waiting the word on Hurley's heavyweight. Lokovsek was a natural for the build-up, with his easy, friendly ways, handsome, photogenic face, and a deep, warm sense of humor.

"When he first told me," the fighter said, "I got all sorts of crazy notions. I went away from him mad and disappointed, and I thought about getting somebody else to manage me. I was going to show him.

"Then I remembered something that happened in that fight in Vancouver. The guy was mussing me up a little. I got a flash of Jack in my corner and I remember thinking: 'Nobody can beat me. I'm Hurley's fighter.' Then I knew that Jack was right, and I would have to quit."

Outside the lights were coming on and traffic thickened in the streets. The faint sound of a bag being punched came through the walls, and Leo again looked down at his hands.

"I was going to do so much," he said. "I was going to be champion of the world. All through my life I'll wonder if I could have made it. Now I'll never know."

[FACT]

ABE ATTELL TAKES THE STAND

Too few writers have availed themselves of the knowledge of Abe Attell. After all, he survived 166 fights, eleven years as featherweight champion, eleven managers and the charge that he did the leg work for Arnold Rothstein in the X (as Pierce Egan would have put it) that was the 1919 World Series. Here he is, in 1950, on the lost science of carrying.

JOE WILLIAMS

It is to be doubted that Abe Attell will ever be canonized in the Cooperstown Monastery due to certain vague peccadilloes dating back to 1919, but in the fight racket the old featherweight champion commands respect.

I do not claim to have been the first white child born on the banks of the Mississippi but I did see Attell fight twice. Down through the years I've seen all the other featherweight champions. Only three or four stand out. Johnny Kilbane, Johnny Dundee, Tony Canzoneri and Willie Pep. But Attell still leads 'em all in my book.

"You gotta put Pep up near the top," Attell said as we sat in Shor's discussing tonight's title fight with Saddler in Yankee Stadium. "He learned his trade good. And he's got it up here, too." Attell tapped his head. Nothing rattled either.... "Still I can't go for him in this one. I'm afraid the old guy's caught up with him." The old guy being, I was amazingly quick to sense, Father Time.

Attell, fighting twenty-rounders at sixteen, had held the featherweight championship eleven years when Kilbane took it from him.

"I think Kilbane had the best one-two punch of all us little fellows," Attell said. "Yet he seldom made a sensational fight. That was because he wouldn't take no chances. Nobody ever hit him when he was good, you know—and he never started a punch until he was sure it was going to land first."

A long time ago Benny Leonard, on the subject of Kilbane, had said to me: "The Mick was just yellow enough to be a great fighter."

Attell blinked. You could see he found it hard to associate the opprobrious adjective with a champion. "Overcautious," he finally compromised.

Attell was twenty-nine when he lost his title. Pep, at twenty-eight, is spotting Saddler four years tonight. Attell got $15,000 against Kilbane. Pep figures to pull down close to $75,000.

"Naturally, we didn't get the dough fighters get today," Attell admitted. "But I used to do all right. Better 'n some of the big guys. If it was a betting fight I always bet on myself, usually my whole end. Like the night I fought Freddie Weeks in 'Frisco. I win $10,000."

Attell had been at the ringside the night Ray Robinson took particular pains not to over-bruise little Charley Fusari in a fight which interested the insiders very keenly. The betting was 2½ to 1 Fusari would be on his feet at the finish. He was. Everybody seemed to agree the welterweight champion had carried Fusari, and not for reasons of mercy. Attell frowned. "It was not a pro job. You could see the rough edges from the back rows."

An old pro was talking. Attell grew hump-backed carrying fighters in his day. But he was a consummate artist. It takes superlative skill to make a bad fighter look good. Attell made 'em look great. And there'd always be a demand for a return bout—which was the main idea from the start. Then if the return was a betting fight Attell would send it in and go to work on the startled young man in front of him.

"The trick was to let the yokel hold you even," Attell said. "In those days the newspapers gave the decisions. I always felt I'd turned in a bad job when they gave me a shade. The line I liked to read was: 'The champion was entitled to no more than a draw.'"

Old-timers still jabber about the fight Attell had with England's Jem Driscoll. Versions differ. I didn't see it. Driscoll was the best boxer John Bull ever developed, fast and smart with it. Some say Attell had a bad night. Others insist the Britisher stabbed him silly.

"I was saving him for 'Frisco," Attell explained. "Jim Coffroth (the promoter out there) and I had it all arranged in advance. Another thing, Charley Harvey had Driscoll, and Harvey was just like this with Little and Big Tim Sullivan, Tammany big shots. They were at ringside that night. I decided it would be wise to make everybody happy."

Years back I had discussed this particular fight with Harvey and what he said supports Attell's disclosure—"For his inches and pounds Attell was the greatest fighter I ever saw."

Incidentally, while Attell may have made the Sullivan boys and others happy that night he wasn't to get another crack at Driscoll. Coffroth had the fight booked but it never took place. Driscoll cabled from London. "I can't make it. I'm sick."

"So was I," Attell grimaced. "I had $20,000 bet on myself."

INDEX